HONDURAS

Guanaja

Guanaja
Town

Punta
Caxinas

Refugio de Vida Silvestre
Laguna de Guaymoreto

Santa Rosa
de Aguán

Sangrelaya

Cabo
Camarón

Palacios

Trujillo

**PN Capiro
y Calentura**

Limón

Río Tinto

Tocoa

Río Negro

Reserva de Vida
Silvestre Montaña
de Malacate

San Esteban

Río Sico

Gualaco

**Parque
Nacional
Sierra de
Agalta**

Catacamas

Juticalpa

El Carbón

Sierra del Río Tinto

COLÓN

Dulce Nombre
de Culmí

Sierra de Agalta

Sierra del Río Plátano

Río Paulaya

Río Plátano

Las
Marías

Brus
Laguna

Reserva de la
Biosfera del Río
Plátano

Río Patuca

Río

GRACIAS A DIOS

La Mosquitia

Laguna
Caratasca

**Puerto
Lempira**

Cabo
Gracias
a Dios

Reserva de la Biosfera
Tawahka Asangni

Ahuahsbila

Río Coco

Sierra de Patuca

**Parque
Nacional
Río Patuca**

Cordillera Entre Ríos

NICARAGUA

Río Segovia

Susun

Siuna

Río

Lago de
Apañas

Estelí

0   25 mi

0   25 km

Gulf of Mexico

CUBA

Caribbean

MEXICO

BELIZE

JAMAICA

Sea

GUATEMALA

HONDURAS

EL
SALVADOR

NICARAGUA

PANAMA

COSTA
RICA

PACIFIC

OCEAN

Contents

HANDBOOKS

HONDURAS
& THE BAY ISLANDS

CHRIS HUMPHREY & AMY E. ROBERTSON

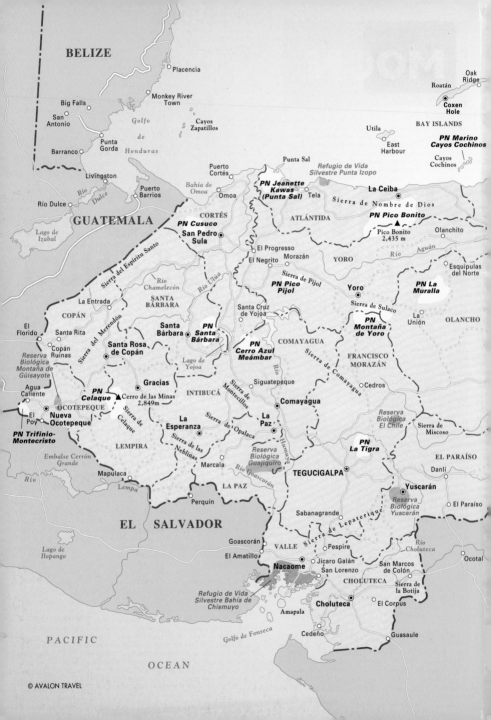

Discover Honduras

Honduras packs several personalities into a country the size of Virginia, boasting fantastic natural beauty, cultural richness, and a relaxing tropical vibe similar to Guatemala, Belize, and Costa Rica, waiting to be discovered along a far less-trodden path.

The Bay Islands are Caribbean jewels of palm trees and sandy beaches lapped by turquoise waves, ringed by some of the finest coral reef in the hemisphere. It's a scuba diver's paradise, but even neophyte snorkelers can easily wade into an underwater world of barracudas and angelfish, coral, and sponge. Back on the mainland, the Mayan ruins of Copán beguile travelers with their profusion of statues and glyphs carved in stone. Art and astronomy flourished in this first-millennium city, a New World Athens. Nearby Copán Ruinas, Santa Rosa de Copán, and Gracias offer glimpses into small-town Honduran life and are launching points for exploring the mountainous countryside.

A different side of Honduras is revealed in the north coast jungles. Search for a shy manatee or quiet crocodile in the shimmering lagoons. Raft down the Río Cangrejal or go for a hike in the verdant Parque Nacional Pico Bonito, then retire to one of the nearby ecolodges. Farther east lies the Mosquitia – Honduras's fabled Mosquito Coast, the country's least accessible region. Intrepid adventurers are rewarded by miles of undisturbed tropical rainforest and opportunities for community-based ecotourism. The

little-visited national parks of neighboring Olancho are home to toucans and parakeets, troops of monkeys, and even the occasional jaguar.

Rhythms speed up in San Pedro Sula and Tegucigalpa, the business and political capitals, respectively. The list of tourist attractions may be short in these bustling cities, but that of eating and entertainment options is long. The two metropolises can also serve as bases for exploring colonial towns and natural attractions in the surrounding regions. Bird-spotting at Honduras's largest lake, Lago de Yojoa, and swimming at its highest waterfall, Pulhapanzak Falls, make for easy day trips from San Pedro. Day-trippers from Tegucigalpa can take their pick of colonial towns like Valle de Ángeles, or head to the Golfo de Fonseca for a swim in the Pacific.

While each region offers unique experiences, the warm, easy-going attitude of the *catrachos,* as Hondurans call themselves, is found everywhere. Come to Honduras prepared to relax. Leave the stress behind when you get off the plane, and let yourself slip into the blissful contentment that has captivated many a visitor.

Planning Your Trip

► WHERE TO GO

Copán and Western Honduras

Tucked into the mountains up against the Guatemalan border, are the ruins of Copán, the Athens of the Mayan world. It's a must-see for anyone with even a passing interest in pre-Hispanic Mesoamerica, together with the adjacent site of Las Sepulturas. Copán has the added attraction of being located next to a friendly small town, full of opportunities for exploration. Farther off the beaten path is Gracias, a colonial town set in the beautiful mountain countryside. Right outside of town is the highest peak in the country, in the cloud-forested Parque Nacional Celaque.

IF YOU HAVE . . .

- **ONE WEEK:** Visit Roatán and the ruins of Copán.

- **TWO WEEKS:** Add Pico Bonito, Chachahuate, and the Reserva de la Biosfera del Río Plátano.

- **THREE WEEKS:** Add Gracias, the Lencan highlands, and Lago de Yojoa.

- **FOUR WEEKS:** Add Comayagua, Yuscarán, Danlí, and Isla del Tigre.

Tiny villages in western Honduras boast centuries-old cathedrals, like this one in the Lenca village of La Campa.

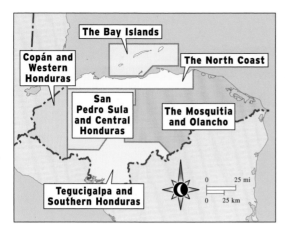

Map labels:
- The Bay Islands
- Copán and Western Honduras
- The North Coast
- San Pedro Sula and Central Honduras
- The Mosquitia and Olancho
- Tegucigalpa and Southern Honduras
- 0   25 mi
- 0   25 km

Beyond Gracias are remote Lenca villages like La Campa, San Manuel Colohete, and Erandique. This is a great and safe trekking destination for the intrepid traveler. The attractive regional capital town of Santa Rosa de Copán makes a good base to explore western Honduras.

The North Coast

The Caribbean north coast has many attractions—first and foremost, its endless beaches. The beaches around Tela and Trujillo are the best known, but the adventurous can find pristine stretches of sand along the entire coast. Garífuna villages are particularly fine places to while away days, swimming, dining on fresh seafood, and drifting into a tropical trance, with Sambo Creek being one of the most popular. More active travelers will find plenty to do, from boat trips through coastal wetland reserves like Punta Sal and Cuero y Salado to world-class white-water rafting on the Río Cangrejal and jungle adventuring in Parque Nacional Pico Bonito. Bird-lovers will not want to miss the tropical garden at Lancetilla, near Tela. And those attracted by the rhythms of Caribbean night-life are obliged to spend at least a night or two checking out the scene in La Ceiba.

The Bay Islands

This collection of three large emerald islands and a couple of dozen smaller cays is ringed with miles of coral reef and sand. The Bay Islands are one of the world's least expensive places to get certified as a scuba diver, attracting visitors from across the globe. Add that to the quirky islander culture, throw in a few mainlander *ladinos,* and you've the fixings for a uniquely entertaining cultural gumbo. Utila is a favorite of the younger crowd, with the focus on diving and meeting other travelers, while on the larger and more varied Roatán, diving is complemented by naturalist trips and exploring many beaches and small towns. Those after a blissed-out deserted island experience can find a number of small cays to camp out on, like Water Cay. Guanaja is much less-frequented than the other two islands, with just a sprinkling of beach hotels

a *palapa* on Tela's Caribbean shore

West Bay Beach on the island of Roatán

and dive resorts but more possibility for exploring remote beaches and pristine reefs.

The Mosquitia and Olancho

The regions of the Mosquitia and Olancho have the most intact primary cloud forest and jungle in Central America. This is where to go if you're after some real adventuring. The Mosquitia's Reserva de la Biosfera del Río Plátano is the largest protected area in Honduras, its pristine tropical jungle alive with wild animals and accessible with the help of local guides. Jungles, lagoons, and coastline stretch farther across the Mosquitia, along the wild Río Patuca and on to Puerto Lempira and the Nicaraguan border. Olancho, populated with cowboys, loggers, and other hardy folk, is blanketed with pine forest and some of the finest high-altitude cloud forests in the country, especially at the national parks at Sierra de Agalta, El Boquerón, and La Muralla. Those who make it out there (with guides) will be staggered by the rich diversity of wildlife and flora. The adventurous can also explore pre-Hispanic ruins still unmapped by archaeologists.

San Pedro Sula and Central Honduras

San Pedro Sula, in the hot lowlands, is Honduras's most dynamic business city and a common point for airplane arrival and bus transfers. Nearby is Lago de Yojoa, the country's largest natural lake and fast becoming a popular destination for the lush tropical forests along the lakeshore and the cloud forests in the two adjacent national parks, Cerro Azul/Meámbar and Santa Bárbara. Stop in at Los Naranjos, a mostly unexcavated pre-Hispanic ruin right next to the lake, and the 43-meter Pulhapanzak Falls along the Río Lindo. Across the mountains from Lago de Yojoa is the picturesque town of Santa Bárbara, set amid green countryside dotted with smaller villages like Colinas and Trinidad, which, together with the far more southern town of Marcala, produce some of the country's finest coffee. Along the highway toward Tegucigalpa is the old colonial capital of Comayagua, where recent renovations have restored several Spanish-era architectural gems.

Tegucigalpa and Southern Honduras

Honduras's least-visited region, southern Honduras harbors attractions for those interested in an out-of-the-ordinary trip. Set in the mountains at 1,000 meters, the capital city of Tegucigalpa, a major air and bus transport hub, is an old mining settlement that grew to take over an entire valley. The downtown area has a number of museums and colonial buildings worth checking out. Numerous colonial villages are within an easy day's trip, including Valle de Ángeles (known for its handicraft shops). Nature lovers can hike around the cloud forest of La Tigra, right above Tegucigalpa. Farther afield, the old mining town of Yuscarán is a fine spot to enjoy the laid-back rhythms of small-town life. Toward the Nicaraguan border is Danlí, the cigar capital of Honduras. On the Pacific side, the Isla del Tigre (Amapala) is a funky, offbeat place to visit, with several tranquil beaches. Hikers should head to Parque Nacional La Botija, a unique dry tropical forest.

the cobblestone streets of Yuscarán

▶ WHEN TO GO

In Honduras, as in many tropical countries, temperature has a lot more to do with altitude and geographic region than with time of year. The Caribbean and Pacific coasts are hot year-round, cooled down somewhat only when it's raining. The Bay Islands, stroked with steady breezes, are a bit cooler, but not much. By contrast, the highland regions across most of the center of the country are usually moderately warm during the day and pleasantly cool at night. The coldest parts of the country are the mountain towns in western Honduras.

Though Honduras is not generally on the hurricane path of the Caribbean or the Pacific, the August–November hurricane season is a time of frequent inclement weather, especially on the Caribbean coast and the Bay Islands, and is best avoided. Less disruptive but sometimes still torrential are the frequent winter storms in January, known as *nortes*. As with most stormy weather, the Caribbean coast is the most affected, but *nortes* can cause rain throughout the country.

The most reliably dry time of year is in March, April, and May, before the spring rainy season starts. The late spring and early summer months are usually dry for most of the day, with a brief early evening thunder shower. By late August and September, the rains return with more intensity. The southern Pacific coast and the border with El Salvador are the most arid parts of the country, while the northern coast (particularly around La Ceiba) and the Mosquitia are the wettest.

Try to avoid Honduras's more popular tourist destinations (the Bay Islands, the ruins of Copán, and the north coast beach towns) during Christmas, Easter Week (Semana Santa), and the first week in August, when they can be overrun by Honduran and Salvadoran vacationers, and the price of accommodations doubles. One of the best parties in the country, the Feria de San Isidro in La Ceiba, held in mid-May, is worth scheduling a trip around.

a wet-season sunset on the island of Guanaja

► BEFORE YOU GO

Visas and Officialdom

Citizens of the United States, western Europe, Canada, Argentina, and Chile are not required to have a visa and are issued a tourist visa on arrival in Honduras. Authorities are currently granting 90-day visas, and any extensions (30 more days are available) must be taken care of at the immigration office in Tegucigalpa. Citizens of all other countries are required to obtain visas before entering Honduras.

Foreigners are required to carry their passport with them at all times, but rarely if ever will it be checked.

Vaccines

No vaccines are required to enter Honduras, but travelers should be up to date on their rabies, typhoid, measles-mumps-rubella (MMR), tetanus, yellow-fever, and hepatitis A and B shots.

Getting There

Honduras has three international airports, in Tegucigalpa, San Pedro Sula, and Roatán. The first two receive daily flights from Atlanta (Delta), Houston (Continental), Miami (American), San Salvador, El Salvador (TACA), and San José, Costa Rica (Copa). Spirit Airlines also services San Pedro Sula. There is weekly service to Roatán from Atlanta, and twice-weekly flights from Houston.

Driving to Honduras from the United States (or elsewhere north of the Panama Canal) is certainly possible, particularly for those with a good command of Spanish. There is also twice-weekly boat service between Placencia, Belize, and Puerto Cortés.

Getting Around

Transiting between the main destinations in Honduras by inexpensive public transport or a private car is not difficult, apart from in the Mosquitia. The main highway system is generally in good shape, although be prepared for a lot of long, bumpy rides (sometimes in the back of a pickup truck) if you head out to more rural areas. The Bay Islands are easily reached by frequent airplanes or ferries from La Ceiba.

Explore Honduras

► THE 10-DAY BEST OF HONDURAS

Day 1

After flying in to San Pedro Sula airport, take a taxi to the first-class bus station for a three-hour drive to Copán Ruinas, near the Guatemalan border. Once there, get a room at the Hacienda San Lucas, an old farm now converted into a fine guesthouse with excellent homemade food.

Days 2-3

Spend the next day in the Mayan city of Copán, taking time to visit the Museo de Escultura Maya (Mayan Sculpture Museum) and to stroll along the nature trail and through the lesser-visited side site of Las Sepulturas. Set aside day 3 for visiting admiring the lush valley and relaxed little town, letting yourself slip into the tranquil rhythms of Honduran life. Take a guided horseback ride to a hidden Mayan ceremonial site in the hills, go visit the Macaw Mountain Bird

Honduras is a place best taken at a leisurely pace, to really enjoy those soporific tropical vibes. But even with only 10 days, it's easily possible to have a vacation combining several different activities and parts of the country, at a relatively relaxed pace. Buy a round-trip airplane ticket to San Pedro Sula, rather than Tegucigalpa, for easier access to Honduras's most popular tourist destinations.

the Great Plaza at the Mayan ruins of Copán, in western Honduras

CARIBBEAN SUN AND SAND

With 735 kilometers of Caribbean coastline, the three main Bay Islands, and a couple of dozen smaller cays, sun worshipers will have no problem finding palm-lined beaches large and small on which to lay their towel or sling their hammock.

BAY ISLANDS AND THE CAYS

If you have to pick just one beach in the country, it's hard to argue with **West Bay, Roatán.** A couple of kilometers of powdery sand fronted by turquoise waters, with a coral reef just a few meters offshore, West Bay is a tropical daydream. Also beautiful, and certainly less crowded, are other beaches and hidden coves in places like **Sandy Bay, Milton Bight,** and **Paya Bay.** Divers may be most drawn to the equally stunning reef and quirky scuba culture of **Utila.** Farther afield, the smallest Bay Island, **Guanaja,** continues to be the least-visited but offers equally extraordinary (or perhaps even better) sea life for divers and snorkelers. Those who prefer to really get away from it all can choose from a stay in **Cayos Cochinos'** single resort, camping on **Water Cay** for a nominal fee and having a fish cookout, or actually renting their very own island, **Sandy Cay** or **Little Cay** near Utila.

Punta Sal, on the north coast

NORTH COAST BEACHES

Probably the nicest beaches on Honduras's north coast are around the bay of **Tela,** lapped by the warm waters of the Caribbean. A short boat ride takes visitors to the unspoiled beaches of the national park at **Punta Sal,** where a powdery beach with turquoise waters is backed with tropical jungle and mangrove wetlands. Right in the town of Tela, in front of the Telamar resort, is a clean and safe beach open to the public. A few kilometers east of La Ceiba, near **Sambo Creek,** are a few modest hotels along a breezy stretch of sand, a good spot to spend a day or three. A couple of hours' drive east along the coast takes you to the sleepy town of **Trujillo,** on a broad bay near the edge of the Mosquitia jungle. The cabins at Tranquility Bay or Casa Kiwi (which also has backpacker dorms) are ideal for soaking up the glorious natural setting and mellow vibe.

GARÍFUNA BEACH TOWNS

This unique group of people, of both African and American indigenous origin, populate numerous towns and villages along the north coast of Honduras. The smaller villages in particular can be magically remote spots, seemingly disconnected from anything but the easy rhythms of the Caribbean. **Tornabé,** just west of Tela, makes a great place to stay for a couple of days, or you can head out to the more isolated **Miami,** a village entirely of thatched huts, at the edge of Punta Sal. Near Trujillo are **Santa Fe** and, farther along, **San Antonio,** both quiet little spots with good seafood and plenty of beach. To really get out there, take a day trip with a tour or an expensive charter boat from La Ceiba, or a less expensive slow boat from Nuevo Armenia to **Chachahuate,** a Garífuna settlement on a tiny island in the Cayos Cochinos, off the north coast. If you come by slow boat, plan on spending a couple of days at least, camping out.

OFF THE BEATEN PATH

The beach west of port town **Puerto Cortés** is surprisingly nice and has a reasonable variety of seaside accommodations, well-located for a visit to the massive Spanish-era fortress in nearby **Omoa.** The **Cayos Zapotillos,** reachable by charter boat from Omoa, are half a dozen blissfully unspoiled islets where it's possible to camp out.

the powdery sands and transparent waters of Roatán

Park, full of parrots, toucans, and other tropical birds, or take a soak in the nearby thermal springs.

Day 4

Take an early bus to San Pedro Sula, and from there on to Lago de Yojoa, the largest lake in Honduras. Stop at the 43-meter-high Pulhapanzak Falls, where you can take

Lago de Yojoa, Honduras's largest lake

a dip in the Río Lindo as well, before heading on to the lakeshore for your room (options range from a backpacker hostel to higher-end hotels).

Day 5

Get up early to spend two or three hours boating on the lake, strolling around the pre-Hispanic ruins of Los Naranjos or bird-watching in the Parque Nacional Santa Bárbara. Then hop a bus back to San Pedro and on to the coast city of La Ceiba (four hours travel time, roughly), staying at one of several ecolodges built at the edge of Parque Nacional Pico Bonito and along the Río Cangrejal.

Day 6

Adventure day. Either go white-water rafting down the jungle-lined Río Cangrejal, or go hiking up to see one of the waterfalls tumbling off the flanks of Pico Bonito. Another option is to tour the mangrove wetlands at Refugio de Vida Silvestre Cuero y Salado. If you've still got some energy after nightfall, hit the disco scene in La Ceiba for some drinks and dancing.

Days 7-10

Fly or take a ferry from La Ceiba out to Roatán, the largest of the Bay Islands. Proceed directly to West Bay, a picture-perfect white-sand beach with coral reef literally right offshore. Beach addicts will want to stay right here, while night owls might opt for a room in one of the low-key hotels of West End. Spend the next three days getting a strong dose of the Caribbean: as much sun, seafood, snorkeling or scuba diving, and general chilling out as you can manage until it comes time to head home, via plane or ferry to La Ceiba and on to the San Pedro airport.

▶ FAMILY AFFAIR

Skip the amusement parks this summer: Honduras has a wealth of activities to keep children from tots to teens active and engaged, and many easy and comfortable enough for grandparents to tag right along.

Copán

Carved skulls, a ball court, even a special stone for making human sacrifices! The Mayan ruins of Copán provide not only a riveting history lesson, but also a great pile of rocks for climbing on, and large fields for running through. Elementary-aged kids can learn about Mayan numbering and pose as a carved stela at the interactive Museo Casa K'inich, a children's museum, while older kids can sign up for a horseback ride, canopy tour or tubing on the Río Copán. A relaxing afternoon at the thermal baths will help everyone to unwind.

The colorful birds and easy paths at nearby Macaw Mountain Bird Park appeal to all ages, and budding entomologists won't want to miss the Butterfly Garden. Teens will likely enjoy staying in a hotel right in town, while those looking for space where small ones can stretch their legs might want to check out the cottages at Hacienda El Jaral, 20 minutes away, with its central grassy field and neighboring water park.

Roatán

Who can resist golden sands, lapping waves, and friendly fish? West Bay combines powdery beach with coral reef so accessible that even the most rudimentary swimmer can easily get a good look, while the glass-bottom boat lets non-swimmers get close to the colorful fish. Plenty of accommodations along the beach have two- to three-bedroom units and kitchens where parents can whip up a plate of pasta for picky or tired eaters.

Older teens are likely to be attracted by the lively vibe of West End, with its shops and beachfront restaurants. Sunset Villas has one- and two-bedroom condos with kitchens, and Georphi's has an entire chalet available.

the interactive Museo Casa K'inich, in Copán Ruinas

The carvings at Copán are considered the most elaborate sculptures of the Mayan empire.

With a rich and varied tradition of indigenous cultures as well as several centuries of Spanish colonial rule, Honduras has numerous historical monuments and ruins worth visiting.

THE MAYAN WORLD

The city of **Copán** was far and away the artistic leader of all the Mayan cities, with ornate sculptures and statues, and the most complete hieroglyphic historical record yet found. The ruins of Copán and smaller surrounding sites, located in a lovely river valley, are worth at least two days, more for the archaeology buff. Don't miss a trip to the sculpture museum, with a full-scale, painted replica of an ancient temple in the center, or **Las Sepulturas,** for a glimpse of how the Mayan daily life.

OTHER PRE-HISPANIC SITES

Long before the Maya, Honduras acted as a meeting point of sorts between groups migrating from North and South America, and the country has a rich and still little-understood history of different indigenous civilizations. Right on the shore of **Lago de Yojoa** is the recently opened **Los Naranjos** ruin. Spend the night in a hotel on the lake, both to enjoy the ambiance and to see the ruins early in the morning, when the surrounding tropical forests are alive with birds. **Petroglyphs** that are a thousand or more years old can be found across the country, near Las Marías in the Mosquitia, and Yuscarán and Ojojona in southern Honduras. In the **Olancho** department are dozens barely explored of ruins, pos-

sibly built by the forebears of the Pech, or by some other group.

COMAYAGUA AND GRACIAS

Comayagua, in central Honduras, was the country's capital during most of the colonial era, meriting a day's stop to see the many architectural monuments and artwork. Gracias is smaller, but the quality of its colonial churches and the overall ambiance make it a much nicer place to spend a couple of days, especially given the proximity to the **Parque Nacional Celaque** and several lovely Lencan villages. Make sure to take at least one day trip to **La Campa** and **San Manuel Colohete,** with elegant and simple colonial churches.

COLONIAL MINING TOWNS

In their lust for gold and silver, the Spanish constructed settlements on any number of mountainsides throughout central Honduras, and these towns are today great places to spend a tranquil afternoon or couple of days, wandering along the cobblestone streets and chatting with locals. In the hills right above Tegucigalpa is **Santa Lucía,** a jumble of white-washed, tile-roofed houses clinging to the hillside, surrounded by flowers and pine trees. Also near the capital is **El Rosario,** a tiny collection of turn of the century 20th mining buildings clinging to a steep cloud-forested hill. A bit farther afield but still easily visited in half a day are **Cedros** and **Ojojona.** A real classic colonial Honduran town is **Yuscarán,** an hour east of Tegucigalpa on the road to Danlí, a good spot to relax for a day or two to check out the town and mountain countryside.

snorkeling off Roatán

Anthony's Key Resort is a great place to spend the day, or the whole vacation, with its dolphin encounters that even toddlers can enjoy, supplied air snorkeling for children as young as five, and scuba training for ages eight and up. Treetop canopy rides provide a thrill for any age, and some have children's harnesses, so little ones as young as four can take the ride (securely hooked to one of the professional guides, of course!).

The North Coast

There are myriad nature and adventure activities in the region surrounding La Ceiba. The Refugio de Vida Silvestre Cuero y Salado is home to 35 mammal species (including jaguars, monkeys, and manatees), as well as countless types of birds and reptiles, accessed by a short ride on a charming antique railcar from the days of the *bananeros* and then by boat. Since early morning and late afternoon are the best times to spot the wildlife, families may want to spend the night in the simple cabins on-site. A variety of trails through the lush foliage of Parque Nacional Pico Bonito means that virtually any level of hiking interest and ability can be

accommodated. The Lodge at Pico Bonito lodge offers luxury in the jungle, or families can consider retiring to the beaches and laid-back hotels of Sambo Creek at the end of the day, from where they can take a short boat ride to the knockout shores of the Cayos Cochinos the following day.

Older kids may be tempted by the rafting trips on the Río Cangrejal; Omega Jungle Lodge runs reliable tours and has a couple of spacious cabins suitable for families as well as a swimming pool on-site. Punta Sal near Tela

flying high on a canopy tour

dolphins at Anthony's Key Resort, on Roatán

The Mosquitia

While the Mosquitia isn't for everyone, it's surprisingly accessible, and an exciting adventure that can easily be managed by kids as young as 10. Skip the grueling arrival by land and fly directly into Brus Laguna, on the edge of the Reserva de la Biosfera del Río Plátano. Kids will be thrilled tubing down the lazy canals, looking for white-faced monkeys on a jungle walk, and crocodile-spotting at nightfall. Downtime can be relaxing on the beach or napping in a swaying hammock.

An easy three-day trip could include two nights in the wood lodge at Raistá and one night in the comfortable cabins at the pine savannah of Yamari. Travel between beach communities is by motorized canoe, which typically takes 1–2 hours and gives plenty of chances for spotting pelicans, terns, and kingfishers.

boasts fine sand and transparent water, which tours combine with a short and sweet jungle walk dotted with hermit crabs and monkeys, all in an easy day trip from town.

▶ FROM CAVES TO CLOUD FORESTS

With its rugged landscape and varied climate, Honduras is an ideal destination for travelers looking to get outdoors and into nature.

Adventure Hiking

There is a fantastic assortment of forested countryside, some with marked trails, and much of it without, but the scenery is spectacular and the friendly locals are always happy to point you the way. The area roughly between Santa Rosa de Copán, Gracias, La Esperanza, and the Salvadoran border is one of the best for backcountry hiking, with endless green mountains dotted with picturesque Lenca villages. The most popular hike in this area is up to the cloud forests at Parque Nacional Celaque, near Gracias, and the circuit from La Campa to Belén Gualcho makes for a fascinating few days.

hiking into El Boquerón canyon in Olancho

DIVING THE REEF

Fish and coral intermingle in the Bay Islands' reef.

Honduras boasts some of the best coral reef in the Americas, as well as rock-bottom prices for diving certification. There are myriad options for shops and sites, making it easy to find the right match for any taste.

ROATÁN

The **largest and most popular of the Bay Islands,** Roatán has **countless dive shops** and perhaps 50 moored dive sites around the island. Many of the best sites are located right off West Bay Beach, West End, and Sandy Bay, with another string of sites on the southern side of the island between French Harbour and Jonesville, and a few others dotting the north coast. People flock here year-round for the diving, and a dozen or more boats leave from West End three times a day for fun dives. Every shop offers certification courses as well. As the **island with the most non-diving activities** (canopy tours, botanical gardens, Garífuna cultural shows, dolphin encounters), it's a perfect fit for those who just want to get in a couple of dives, or who have non-divers along in the group.

UTILA

Diving in Utila is hard-core. With the **cheapest certification classes** around, Utila is **a mecca for the budget diver,** a large number of them youthful backpackers. Expert divers come too, eager to spend time along the island's spectacular reef – many find themselves staying on, working as dive masters and instructors at one of the many shops. Spend a few days in the tiny town and you'll quickly make friends, especially during late nights at the laid-back bars. While the diving is uniformly inexpensive, there are plenty of midrange hotels and even a couple of high-end diving resorts, happily accommodating divers looking for a little more comfort.

GUANAJA

Tourism on Guanaja is limited, making for perhaps the **best preserved sites.** There are 38 moored sites sprinkled around the island, including a 1,800-meter wall that starts less than 9 meters from the surface, labyrinths of caves and tunnels, pinnacles and wrecks. Only a handful of resorts offer diving, ensuring that **sites never get crowded.** While many sites are best for intermediate to experienced divers, novices can explore caves and grottoes teeming with colorful marine life.

The well-organized parks of La Tigra and Cerro Azul/Meámbar have several marked trails that offer easy day-hiking, while the latter also boasts less-visited areas best reached with a guide in multiday trips. The Parque Nacional Sierra de Agalta in Olancho, probably the largest cloud forest reserve in Central America, offers several different hiking options, from the three- or four-day hike to the summit at La Picucha to day trips from Juticalpa or Catacamas to El Boquerón and El Murmullo.

Rafting

With its Class III, IV, and V rapids, the Río Cangrejal on Honduras's north coast boasts some of the premier white-water rafting in Central America. The raging river bordered by lush jungle is easily accessible to the traveler short on time through a day trip from La Ceiba, and more enjoyable still when experienced in conjunction with a night in one of the lodges tucked along the river's winding edge. The nearby Río Zacate is another popular rafting destination. Those with a bit more time can book a trip down the Río Patuca through Olancho and the Mosquitia—all on a balsa-wood raft that you build yourself the first afternoon of the journey.

Bird-Watching

Honduras is a world-class destination for birding aficionados, with over 700 species at last count inhabiting the many different ecosystems in the country. For diversity of species in a relatively small area, Lago de Yojoa is hard to beat, attracting hundreds of species of birds to the varied ecosystems around the lake, easily accessible to go prowling with your binoculars. At the transition between the tropical lowlands and the higher mountain forests, the lake region attracts species from both habitats, as well as a variety of migrants.

Far and away the finest place for spotting bird life is the Reserva de la Biosfera del Río Plátano in the Mosquitia. The coast is home to cormorants, pelicans, white ibis, northern jacanas, vermilion and fork-tailed flycatchers, yellow-winged caciques, kiskadees, and kingfishers, easily seen in the

Honduras is a paradise for birders, with over 700 species, including many hummingbirds.

lagoons and canals near Brus Laguna. Those with more time can hire a local guide and head into the jungle, where harpy eagles are still spotted, and parrots, toucans, antshrikes, macaws, and others are common.

Right outside of Tela are the botanical gardens at Lancetilla, a tropical research station that is one of the premier birding spots in the country, with hundreds of species including motmot, trogon, tanager, antshrike, and many more. Along the coast close to Tela are mangrove wetlands and jungle at Punta Izopo and Punta Sal, with opportunities to spot herons, terns, kingfishers, trogons, pelicans, and gulls. Even more impressive are the extensive coastal jungles of Parque Nacional Pico Bonito, near La Ceiba, with a myriad of species including eagles, hawks, motmots, kites, and trogons.

The most accessible places to scout for cloud forest species like resplendent quetzals, emerald toucanets, tanagers, many hummingbirds, and others are two national parks, La Tigra near Tegucigalpa and Cusuco outside of San Pedro Sula. Each of these can be easily visited in a day trip.

Spelunking

Dedicated cavers can get their fix at one of the more adventurous sets of caves in Honduras, such as the Cuevas de Susmay in Olancho,

the main cave at Olancho's Cuevas de Talgua

requiring headlamps, good shoes, and even a swim to explore the main tunnels. The Cuevas de Taulabé in central Honduras are said to hold hidden treasure within their crevices, while Olancho's Cuevas de Talgua were once a cemetery for glittering human bones. Both have paved walkways for the novice, while experienced guides are happy to take those looking for a challenge into the less-explored depths.

► GOING GREEN AND CONNECTING WITH THE CULTURE

Ecotourism, community tourism, responsible tourism—three different catchwords with overlapping principles. All are about minimizing the negative impacts that tourists can have, and maximizing the benefits their dollars (or euros or pounds) bring. By incorporating these ideas into trip-planning, travelers are often rewarded with more meaningful experiences during their journey and deeper connections with the people and land they visit.

Ecotourism

Parque Nacional Pico Bonito is undoubtedly the country's premier ecotourism destination. The Lodge at Pico Bonito combines luxury rooms with a lush jungle setting and a genuine

a Lencan woman demonstrating her craft of handmade pottery

information and tours in the region. Over in the mountain highlands, Colosuca (www.colosuca.com) proudly combines the living culture of its Lencan villages with regal colonial architecture and the natural beauty of Parque Nacional Celaque—all of which can be enhanced by the knowledge of local guides.

Another well-organized network is Cangrejal Ecoturismo (www.cangrejal .com), which connects visitors with two sets of community-owned cabins, hiking guides and horseback rides led by a local youth group, and local wood-carving artisans near the Río Cangrejal. Travelers willing to go farther off the beaten path can horseback ride or learn how to roast coffee in the mountain town of San Juan, or stay in a locally owned guesthouse on the Pacific island of Amapala.

commitment to its environment (and the lodge supports a local microfinance organization for women to boot). Nearby Omega Jungle Lodge has backpacker dorms, a basic cabin built over a creek, and high-end cabins with luxury touches, all of which benefit from the hotel's gorgeous hillside setting and environmentally friendly waste management system. Both Omega Tours and La Moskitia Eco-Aventuras have good reputations for well-run, low-key but high-adventure trips near La Ceiba, in the Mosquitia, and even exploring the little-visited region of Olancho.

Community Tourism

Community-owned cabins, village walking tours, nighttime crocodile-spotting, and lazy afternoons tubing down the river are all locally organized and owned in the Mosquitia. Whether travelers want the ease of a package or the adventure of organizing their own transportation, La Ruta Moskitia (www .larutamoskitia.com) is the top source for

Responsible Tourism

Not everyone wants to stay in a rustic cabin or a community guesthouse, but that doesn't preclude asking questions about the social and environmental impact of your hotel, restaurant, or dive shop, or supporting locally owned businesses to ensure that they don't get crowded out of tourism-based development.

Environmentally friendly hotels are popping up on Roatán: Cocolobo in West End was designed by a British environmental architect with details such as side windows to capture cross breezes, while Infinity Bay on West Bay beach is being built with soil-preservation principles and has installed solar panels and zero-emission waste treatment. Native-owned businesses on Utila are some of the most committed to their community, such as the Lighthouse Hotel, Utila Water Sports dive shop, and Delany's Island Kitchen.

Just outside of Copán Ruinas, the locally owned Hacienda San Lucas was built entirely without the use of electricity, maintains a low impact through the use of solar power and abundant candles, and shares local

the relaxing setting of locally owned Hacienda San Lucas, outside of Copán Ruinas

culture through meals based on indigenous Maya Chortí recipes. Back in town, Via Via Café, its hotel, and its hostel are all Belgian-owned, but the owners have a deep commitment to working for the betterment of the region, which they enact through their participation in community networks and the payment of fair wages to staff. Their tour agency, Basecamp, offers a "Copán Alternative Hike"—a walking tour that presents the reality of small-town Honduran living, the good and the bad, with half the proceeds donated toward the purchase of schoolbooks for surrounding rural villages.

Even in the urban jungle of San Pedro Sula, environmentally aware travelers now have a good option at the Casa del Arbol, a family-owned boutique hotel that has incorporated solar energy and low-flow toilets as part of its plan to get green-certified.

COPÁN AND WESTERN HONDURAS

Intricately carved Mayan ruins, tiny Lencan villages, impressive cloud forest, and the country's highest mountain are all within this region, but it draws only a fraction of the tourists that flock to similar attractions in neighboring countries. Just a few miles from the Guatemalan border, the ruins of Copán are a must-see for visitors to Honduras. Built by a society of scientists and architects, artists and warriors, the ruins boast stelae (carved statues) and layers of temples, a ball court, and the famed Hieroglyphic Stairway, the longest hieroglyphic inscription found anywhere in the Americas. More than a millennium old, the ruins have been well-preserved, in part thanks to their isolation. In the hills around Copán are villages of Chortí Maya, a people related to their highland cousins to the northwest in Guatemala.

An hour away is Santa Rosa de Copán, with its cobblestone streets, colonial buildings, and renowned cigar factory. Those whose visit coincides with Semana Santa will have the chance to observe the centuries-old traditions of colorful sawdust carpets over which solemn processions march, while visitors in the month of August will be treated to special festivities in honor of the town's patron saint.

Travels farther south are well worth the effort, taking visitors farther off the beaten path. This is Lenca territory, the land of Lempira, a famed Indian chief who battled the conquistadors to a standstill before being tricked and killed, and for whom the national currency is named. This is one of the most naturally beautiful and least-explored areas in all of Central America. Here, the adventurous can lose themselves for weeks,

HIGHLIGHTS

◖ Coffee Plantations: Whether you want to spend half a day or four, the *fincas* near Copán provide a relaxing getaway replete with bird-watching and horseback rides, as well as an education on the world's most popular beverage (page 41).

◖ The Ruins of Copán: The Mayan city of Copán is justifiably the top tourist destination in mainland Honduras, known as the Athens of Mesoamerica for its carved artwork and the detailed city history inscribed on its monuments (page 45).

◖ Museo de Escultura Maya: Journey through the serpent's jaws into the Maya Sculpture Museum, which houses a spectacular replica of the Rosalila temple in all its technicolor glory, along with the originals of many of the finest stelae and carvings from the ruins of Copán (page 53).

◖ Feria Agostina: A quiet colonial town most of the year, Santa Rosa bursts to life during its August *feria*, when *copanecos* celebrate their patron saint with music, food, sporting competitions, and even a Noche de Fumadores, an evening dedicated to fine cigars, and the Tarde con Aroma a Café, an afternoon tasting locally grown coffee (page 60).

◖ Gracias: This was once (briefly) the capital of Spanish Central America, but nowadays it's a sleepy little cowboy town with several beautiful colonial buildings and a newly renovated central park, and it is fast becoming a popular off-beat tourist destination (page 66).

◖ Parque Nacional Celaque: Even a short walk near the base of Celaque mountain can reveal the shy quetzal, while the stiff hike up the trail to the top of the country's highest mountain is well worth it for the fine cloud forest. You can soak your bones in the steaming *aguas termales* (hot springs) near Gracias when you're done (page 73).

◖ Lenca Villages South of Gracias: These villages are set amid some of the most picturesque mountain countryside in Central America, and they boast imposing 18th-century churches. La Campa and San Manuel Colohete are perfect places to hike for an hour, a day, or a week (page 76).

LOOK FOR ◖ TO FIND RECOMMENDED SIGHTS, ACTIVITIES, DINING, AND LODGING.

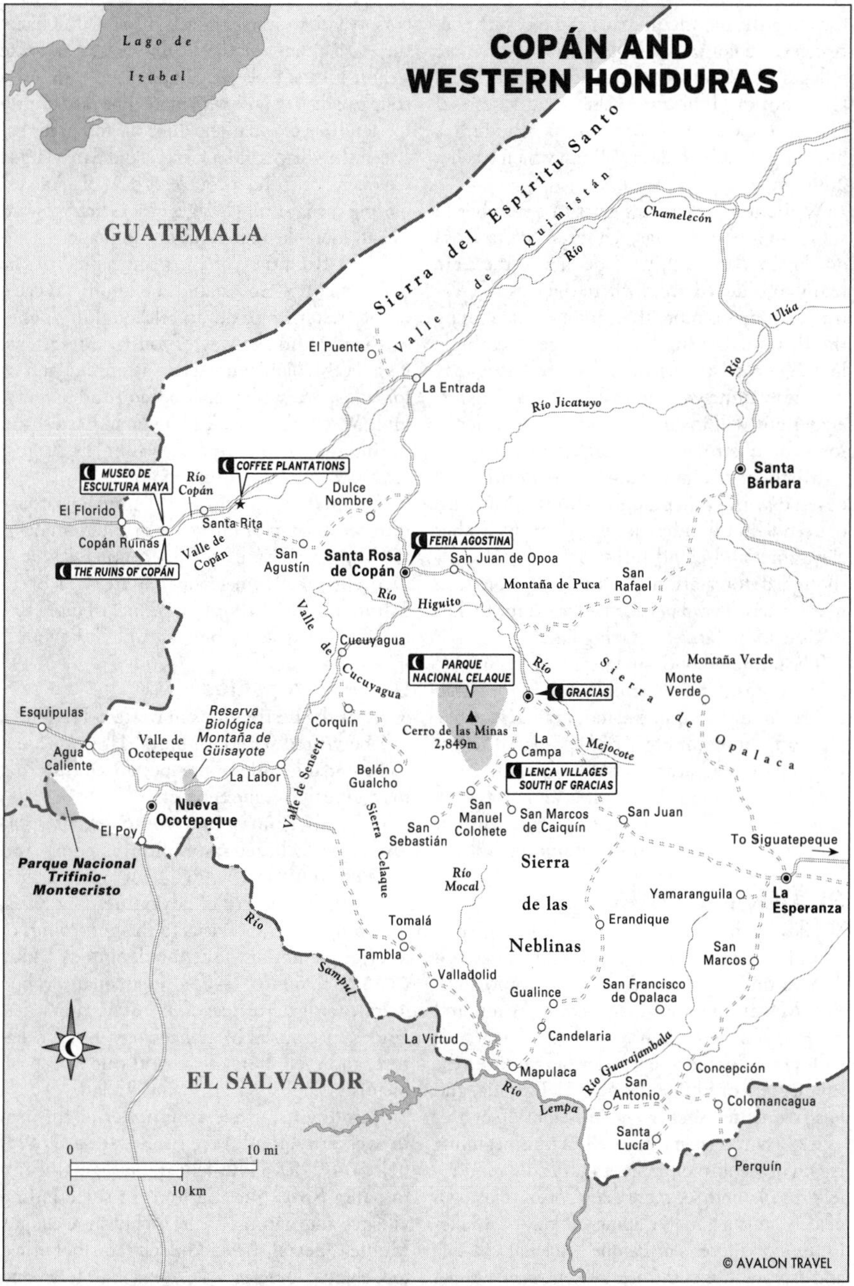

COPÁN AND WESTERN HONDURAS
Lago de Izabal
GUATEMALA
Sierra del Espíritu Santo
Valle de Quimistán
Río Chamelecón
Río Ulúa
El Puente
La Entrada
Río Jicatuyo
Santa Bárbara
MUSEO DE ESCULTURA MAYA
COFFEE PLANTATIONS
Río Copán
El Florido
Copán Ruinas
Santa Rita
Dulce Nombre
Valle de Copán
San Agustín
THE RUINS OF COPÁN
FERIA AGOSTINA
Santa Rosa de Copán
San Juan de Opoa
Montaña de Puca
San Rafael
Río Higuito
Valle de Cucuyagua
Cucuyagua
PARQUE NACIONAL CELAQUE
GRACIAS
Río
Sierra de Opalaca
Montaña Verde
Monte Verde
Esquipulas
Reserva Biológica Montaña de Güisayote
Corquín
Cerro de las Minas 2,849m
Agua Caliente
Valle de Ocotepeque
La Campa
Mejocote
La Labor
Belén Gualcho
LENCA VILLAGES SOUTH OF GRACIAS
Nueva Ocotepeque
Valle de Sensetí
Sierra Celaque
San Sebastián
San Manuel Colohete
San Marcos de Caiquín
San Juan
El Poy
To Siguatepeque
Parque Nacional Trifinio-Montecristo
Sierra de las Neblinas
Río Mocal
La Esperanza
Yamaranguila
Erandique
Río Sampul
Tomalá
Tambla
San Marcos
Valladolid
Gualince
San Francisco de Opalaca
Candelaria
La Virtud
Río Guarajambala
Mapulaca
Concepción
EL SALVADOR
Río Lempa
San Antonio
Colomancagua
Santa Lucía
Perquín
0
10 mi
0
10 km
© AVALON TRAVEL

traveling the mountain roads and footpaths between the colonial town of Gracias and remote villages like Erandique, La Campa, and Belén Gualcho, or climbing to the cloud forests of Sierra de Celaque, which boasts Honduras's highest peak, Cerro de las Minas, which reaches 2,849 meters (9,347 feet).

While tourist services exist in a number of spots—Copán Ruinas, Gracias, Santa Rosa de Copán, San Juan, La Esperanza—there are many untouched areas where the lack of creature comforts is more than compensated for by the thrill of visiting lovely villages seemingly lost in the mists of history, where locals may not know quite what to think of a passing foreigner but will invariably invite him or her in for a cup of strong black coffee and a chat.

Much of the mountainous region is still covered with *ocote* pine forest, mixed in with oak and liquidambar (sweet gum) at higher elevations and cloud forest on the peaks, although deforestation is a serious problem in many areas, as *campesinos* cut wood for fuel or to clear more farm or grazing land.

The rainiest months in western Honduras are June, August, and September, but wet weather can hit at any time in the mountains. If you're planning on camping, come prepared to get wet. The temperature is normally quite comfortable—warm in the daytime and pleasantly cool at night—although it can get downright cold in La Esperanza and surrounding hills.

PLANNING YOUR TIME

While a visit to the primary ruin site at Copán takes just a couple of hours, it takes three full days to do justice to the region, with its multiple Mayan sites, hot baths, coffee farms, and other tourist attractions. The real Mayan buff will want to spend another day or two to see the smaller city of El Puente, near La Entrada, and less-frequented sites in the hills above Copán.

It's easy to become seduced by this beguiling region of scenic mountains and friendly country-folk, and want to see more than Copán. The town of Gracias is a good jumping-off point for hikes in the cloud forests of Parque Nacional Celaque and explorations of the nearby Lencan villages. A

cursory visit to admire Gracias's colonial architecture, visit a couple of the nearby villages, and take a short hike at Celaque can be made with just a couple of days. Those with more time can summit Celaque in a two-day trip, hike the footpaths between the villages of La Campa and San Manuel Colohete, or spend a couple of days or more exploring the far-flung villages past Gracias toward El Salvador, like Erandique or San Juan.

Santa Rosa de Copán is the capital of the department of Copán and the unofficial capital of western Honduras. Although it doesn't boast much in the way of tourist attractions, it's a lovely colonial town and a convenient base for transport, with plenty of food and lodging. Holy Week (the week leading up to Easter) and during the patron saint festival in late August are especially good times to visit.

The main overland travel transport route into western Honduras from Guatemala is via Copán. Those who come in by Nueva Ocotepeque, from either Guatemala or El Salvador, should consider taking an extra day to hike into Reserva Biológica El Güisayote.

Guide Companies

Most of the destinations in western Honduras can be visited without guides. However, several companies offer more specialized trips that may appeal to some travelers.

In Copán Ruinas, **Basecamp** (tel. 504/651-4695, www.basecamphonduras.com) and **Yaragua Tours** (tel. 504/651-4147, www.yaragua .com) offer a variety of adventuresome tours, including hikes and visits to the hot springs or a coffee plantation. The **Asociación de Guías Copán** (tel. 504/651-4018, guiascopan@yahoo .com), with its office right at the ruins, has guides specialized in archaeology, history, nature, and even shamanism, and who can speak Spanish, English, French, and Italian.

Max Elvir, a tireless promoter of tourism in western Honduras, runs **Lenca Travel** (tel. 504/9997-5340, lencatours@gmail.com) in Santa Rosa, offering tours of surrounding villages and natural areas, including Celaque, Monte Quetzal, Belén Gualcho, farther afield to Celaque, Gracias, La Campa, San Juan, and

Erandique, and any other place you might want to visit. Max works exclusively with small groups, and his tours are all customized to the interests of the traveler, and can even include learning about medicinal plants or a culinary class if the visitor is so inclined. A day tour to Belén Gualcho, Corquín, and an organic coffee farm runs US$25 per person for a group of four or more. If you have your own wheels, Max charges US$75 a day for guiding services. There is an association of guides that can be contacted through **Santa Rosa's tourism office** (tel. 504/662-2234 turismosrc@yahoo.com), but these should be booked in advance, as many have other jobs as well.

In Gracias, an excellent **community tourism network** has been developed. Extensive information on the region can be found on the website www.colosuca.com, and the **Asociación de Guías Turísticos Colosuca-Celaque** can do city tours, countryside tours, national park tours, or any combination thereof. The association's coordinator is Marco Aurelio Rodríguez (tel. 504/656-0627, guiamarcolencas@yahoo.com). **Walter Murcia** (tel. 504/656-1113, waltermurcia@hotmail.com), another local guide in the Gracias region, offers one-day or multiday trips to Celaque and to surrounding villages. Day trips for up to four people going to five Lenca villages near Gracias, including going inside the churches (which can be difficult alone), cost US$100. His brother Arnulfo (same number) is knowledgeable about the history of Gracias.

HISTORY

By all accounts, western Honduras was densely populated by different indigenous groups, but archaeologists disagree on exactly which ones. Evidence from the Spanish suggests the people currently known as Lenca were at least a half dozen distinct tribes during colonial times, including the Potón, Guaquí, Cares, Chatos, Dules, Paracas, and Yaras, who lived in an area stretching from Olancho to El Salvador.

At the time of conquest, the Lenca "proper" are thought to have been a relatively small group centered around the mountains near present-day Erandique. They had established villages but were essentially hunters and engaged in little agriculture. Loyalties existed only among those who spoke the same language, and tribes were constantly at war with their immediate neighbors.

Farther west, toward the Guatemalan border in the Copán and Chamelecón valleys and in the department of Ocotepeque, the Chortí Maya dominated. The Chortí were the immediate descendants of the Classic Maya who had built Copán several centuries earlier. Although they were a relatively sedentary agricultural society, their political organization did not extend much beyond a group of neighboring villages at the time of the Spanish conquest.

The first Spanish forays into western Honduras came from Guatemala, when in the mid-1520s an expedition led by Juan Pérez Dardón took control of the Río Copán region under orders from Pedro de Alvarado. By 1530, other expeditions from both the Honduran coast and from Guatemala converged on the mountainous region around Celaque, but they were soon faced with indigenous rebellions led by Lenca leaders Tapica and Etempica, the Chortí Maya leaders Mota and Copán Galel, and later the most famous of all, Lempira. Not until 1539 was the revolt extinguished and Spanish control over the region consolidated.

Part of the Higueras province, western Honduras was extremely poor throughout the colonial period. The small mines of gold and silver found near Gracias were quickly spent, and treasure-seeking conquistadors headed for richer prospects in Peru and Mexico. After a few short years as the administrative center of Central America in the 1540s, western Honduras faded into a sparsely populated region, surviving on the meager income from cattle production and the tobacco industry.

To this day, the mountain highlands region of western Honduras is one of the poorest parts of the country, inhabited mainly by peasants, many of whom survive by subsistence farming supplemented by meager corn or coffee production. The banana plantations and—more recently—*maquila* factories around San Pedro Sula draw a steady stream of job seekers from western Honduras.

Copán Ruinas Town

For many visitors, Copán Ruinas is the first Honduran town they see after crossing over from Guatemala, and it's hard not to be charmed by the relaxed friendliness of the place. Any afternoon and evening in the square, one can watch schoolchildren playing, elders leisurely passing the time of day, and a young man plucking a tune on his guitar under the admiring gaze of his girl.

An attractive town with cobblestone streets, Copán Ruinas has an appealing locale amidst the green hills of the Río Copán valley.

Copán Ruinas was originally a small village, an outlying settlement of the larger Santa Rita, before archaeology and tourism improved its fortunes and made it the largest town in the Valle de Copán. It has become the commercial center for the region, and these days is expanding to annex the neighboring town of Ostuman. Much of the agricultural land in the Valle de Copán was

dedicated to tobacco since colonial times. For many years Copán tobacco was famed through the Americas and well known in Europe. In the 1960s, other strains were introduced to the valley, and pests brought in by the foreign varieties quickly wiped out the Copán plant; tobacco is no longer grown in the region, but coffee plantations have taken up where tobacco left off, with shade-grown varieties becoming an important revenue source for the region.

The annual festival honoring the patron saint of Copán Ruinas, San José, takes place the week running up to March 19. Growing in name is the annual Conference on Honduras, a forum for national and international NGOs working in Honduras, in which a few hundred people descend onto the town and its hotels to exchange ideas and lessons learned. This takes place in early October—check www .projecthonduras.com for the exact date each

© AMY E. ROBERTSON

Tile-roofed adobe homes line the hilly streets of Copán Ruinas.

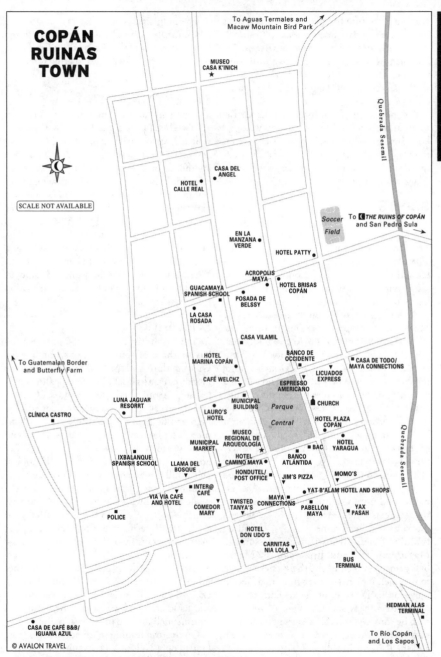

COPÁN RUINAS TOWN

To Aguas Termales and
Macaw Mountain Bird Park

MUSEO
CASA K'INICH
★

Quebrada Sesemil

CASA DEL
ANGEL

HOTEL
CALLE REAL

Soccer
Field

To ◖ THE RUINS OF COPÁN
and San Pedro Sula →

SCALE NOT AVAILABLE

EN LA
MANZANA
VERDE

HOTEL PATTY

ACROPOLIS
MAYA

HOTEL BRISAS
COPÁN

GUACAMAYA
SPANISH SCHOOL

POSADA DE
BELSSY

LA CASA
ROSADA

CASA VILAMIL

To Guatemalan Border
and Butterfly Farm

HOTEL
MARINA COPÁN

BANCO DE
OCCIDENTE

CASA DE TODO/
MAYA CONNECTIONS

CAFÉ WELCHZ

LICUADOS
EXPRESS

ESPRESSO
AMERICANO

CLÍNICA CASTRO

LUNA JAGUAR
RESORRT

MUNICIPAL
BUILDING

Parque
Central

CHURCH

LAURO'S
HOTEL

HOTEL PLAZA
COPÁN

MUSEO
REGIONAL DE
ARQUEOLOGÍA
★

HOTEL
YARAGUA

MUNICIPAL
MARKET

IXBALANQUE
SPANISH SCHOOL

LLAMA DEL
BOSQUE

HOTEL
CAMINO MAYA

BANCO
ATLÁNTIDA

BAC

HONDUTEL/
POST OFFICE

JIM'S PIZZA

MOMO'S

VIA VIA CAFÉ
AND HOTEL

INTER@
CAFÉ

YAT B'ALAM HOTEL AND SHOPS

COMEDOR
MARY

TWISTED
TANYA'S

MAYA
CONNECTIONS

YAX
PASAH

PABELLÓN
MAYA

POLICE

HOTEL
DON UDO'S

CARNITAS
NIA LOLA

BUS
TERMINAL

Quebrada Sesemil

HEDMAN ALAS
TERMINAL

CASA DE CAFÉ B&B/
IGUANA AZUL

To Río Copán
and Los Sapos

© AVALON TRAVEL

year—and be sure to make hotel reservations in advance if your visit coincides.

Copán Ruinas has a few tourist police around town, in their distinctive uniforms, who are always ready to help out with directions, advice, and help in the event of an emergency.

A good website for information about the town and surrounding area is www.copan honduras.org. Most hotels have a webpage on the site, including several of the smaller hotels that don't have their own sites, and they can be contacted via this site.

SIGHTS

The center of town in Copán Ruinas is, of course, the *parque central,* which was redone a few years back with a good dose of concrete. The semicircle of tile roofing across the center and the castle-like wall on one side look rather out of place to many foreigners, but the locals love it.

Although nothing on the level of the Museo de Escultura at the Mayan ruins, the small **Museo Regional de Arqueología** (tel. 504/651-4437, 9 A.M.–5 P.M. daily, US$3 entrance) on the park is worth a visit to admire the complete tomb of a shaman, laid out in a case just as it was found at Las Sepulturas site, or the ceramic incense vessels covered with figures of Copán's rulers. Other items of interest include statuettes, jade sculptures, and a few of the famous obsidian flints with exquisitely carved Mayan faces.

The **Museo Casa K'inich** (8 A.M.–noon and 1–5 P.M. Mon.–Sat.), in the old *cuartel,* a barracks building atop a hill five blocks north of the square, is a small, free interactive children's museum with well-done displays, including traditional musical instruments, lessons on Mayan numbers, and displays of the Mayan ball game. Unfortunately, there doesn't seem to be much money left over from their recent move for maintenance of the exhibits, some of which are already showing signs of wear and tear. Be sure to climb the ladders into the *cuartel* turrets for the expansive views over the town and the Río Copán valley.

The municipal market has just moved into a beautifully restored colonial-style building half a block east of the square; the piles of fresh fruits and vegetables always making for an interesting browse.

ENTERTAINMENT

Two bars in town popular among foreigners are **Twisted Tanya's** and **Nia Lola,** with conveniently consecutive happy hours (4–6 P.M. and 6:30–8 P.M., respectively). **Via Via Café** is another favored spot for the traveler crowd to have drinks in the evening, with salsa night (including an instructor) on Wednesday, '80s–90s party on Thursday, and European dance music on the weekends, starting at 9:30 P.M. Movies are shown at 7 P.M. on Sunday for a buck. The same owners run **Barcito** a few blocks away, a laid-back spot specializing in wine and snacks. **Xibalba** at the Camino Maya hotel is a popular spot, with two-for-one specials and passion fruit margaritas.

SHOPPING

As a major tourist destination, Copán Ruinas has its share of souvenir shops, many with Guatemalan and Salvadoran as well as Honduran crafts, including *junco* palm goods, leather, ceramics, jade and wood sculptures, and the ever-present T-shirts and coffee. The high-end shops at the **Yat B'alam** mini-shopping complex have unique pieces of Lencan pottery and stylish jewelry, as well as other goodies such as hand-carved candle holders and candles made by a women's cooperative. **Algo Maya** also has a good selection of well-made items, including San Rafael eco-sustainable coffee (head to the tiny coffee shop across the street for a brewed cup) and glass plates and trays made by a cooperative near Tegucigalpa.

Across from the Hotel Marina is another mini-shopping center, **Casa Villamil,** housing classy shops selling cigars, jade, silver jewelry, and handicrafts, as well as a coffee shop and gourmet deli (6:30 A.M.–10 P.M. daily).

On the road leading south out of town (past Hotel Popol-Nah) is **Yax Pasah,** selling stone carvings in Mayan designs. If you're looking for something bigger, head out of town toward Ostuman, where the Lara family has a wide variety of stone carvings available for sale right along the highway—and will even carve a full-size stela for you if it's what you want.

An association of Honduran artisans manages a shop called **Pabellón Maya,** one block south of the park, and there is an artisan *mercado* next door, although both have a fairly uninspired selection of crafts.

ACCOMMODATIONS

Because Copán Ruinas is accustomed to tourists of all incomes, from backpackers to luxury travelers, hotels are available in all price and quality ranges. The majority are right in the center of town.

When arriving in town by bus, expect to be surrounded by a horde of young men who offer to help find a room in any price range and will give you a ride there for free. We strongly urge you to avoid dealing with these men and boys, who get a commission for taking you to a less desirable hotel or on an overpriced horseback ride. Spring for a *mototaxi* into town and get the room you really want, and arrange any tours through a reputable agency such as Basecamp or Yaragua.

Under US$10

A few blocks west of the *parque* in a quiet neighborhood is an exceptionally good deal, the ◖ **Iguana Azul** (tel. 504/651-4620, www .iguanaazulcopan.com, US$5 dorm bed, US$11 s, US$13 d), with dormitory beds and small private rooms in a clean, airy lodge. In the back are the communal showers, with hot water, and an area to wash clothes. Lockers are available, as well as free purified water, and reservations are accepted. The lodge is run by the Honduran-American owners of the Casa del Café, next door.

Another excellent dorm-style hostel is ◖ **En La Manzana Verde** (tel. 504/651-4652, http:// lamanzanaverde.com, US$5 pp), with bunks and even a pair of double beds in a dorm-style set-up. There is a *pila* for washing clothes, the

bathrooms are cleaned six times a day (!), and guests have free use of the kitchen until 10 P.M. Reservations are generally only accepted for groups. Both hostels have a wealth of tourist information.

US$10-25

The Belgian-run **Via Via Café** (tel. 504/651-4652, US$12 s, US$16 d) has plain rooms at the back of the restaurant, perfect for crashing after an evening at the restaurant and bar. Another economic option is the **Hotel Calle Real** (tel. 504/651-4230, US$14 s, US$20 d), two and a half blocks up a steep hill from the *parque*. The colonial-style hotel has a leafy sitting area and can fill up with groups, so it's best to call ahead.

Next door to En La Manzana Verde is **Posada Macanudo** (tel. 504/651-4771, US$17 s, US$20 d with fan, US$8–10 more for a/c), a well-located hotel with simple, clean rooms.

A block away, **La Posada de Belssy** (tel. 504/651-4680, US$13–16 s, US$20–25 d) has similar rooms, as well as a rather dilapidated rooftop terrace with wading pool.

Another inexpensive and clean accommodation in town is **Hotel Patty** (tel. 504/651-4021, US$15 s, US$18 d), near the highway bridge leaving town toward the ruins, with sparse rooms with fan and private bath.

US$25-50

A block north of the square is **Hotel Brisas del Copán** (tel. 504/651-4118, US$21 s, US$37 d), with quiet, clean rooms with hot water, fans, and TV. The owners live in the adjacent building, which is separated from the hotel by a small patio with chairs open to guests, and there is another terrace for guests as well—the view is somewhat marred by the electrical wires and neighboring unkempt terraces. The same family also runs the **Acropolis Maya** (tel. 504/651-4634, US$47 d) across the street, a tasteful higher-end hotel with 10 larger rooms with dark wood furnishings and air-conditioning.

Hotel Yaragua (tel. 504/651-4464, www .yaragua.com, US$37 d, US$45 d), on the southeast corner of the square across from the Plaza Copán, has 24 attractive rooms with air-conditioning and TV around a small leafy courtyard. The upstairs rooms are nicer. Check the mattress, as some are mushy. Around the corner is **Hotel Popol-Nah** (tel. 504/651-4645, US$29 s/d, US$52 s/d with a/c), with a nice colonial-style facade but pretty basic rooms— if you are going to spring for air-conditioning, there are better options. **Lauro's Hotel** (tel. 504/651-4068, www.lauroshotel.com, US$23 s, US$29 d, US$16–17 more with a/c) is a comparable quality choice, also close to the park. Ask for a room on the second floor, as those on the ground floor are fairly dark.

US$50-100

A unique setup five blocks southwest of downtown is ◖ **Casa de Café Bed and Breakfast** (tel. 504/651-4620, www.casadecafecopan.com, US$46 s, US$58 d), run by an American-Honduran couple. Behind their very lovely house are several wood-paneled guest rooms, tastefully decorated and featuring elegant wooden writing desks. From the hammocks on the patio, you'll enjoy unmatched views over the Río Copán valley below. This secluded place is perfect for relaxing and soaking in the area's vibes—but if you need further help relaxing, a stop at the tented massage pavilion is highly recommended. Room price includes a hearty, home-cooked breakfast, and coffee and tea all day long. The hotel is about a 10-minute walk from the *parque.*

The same owners are also establishing a boutique hotel closer to the heart of town, scheduled to open to guests in October 2009, called **Casa del Angel** (tel. 504/651-4623, www.casadelangelcopan.com, US$70 s, US$81 d, US$93 suite). Rooms have exposed beam ceilings and hand-crafted wood furniture, plus details like a pillow menu. The massage pavilion here is tucked into the garden.

At the southwest corner of the square is the pleasant **Hotel Camino Maya** (tel. 504/651-4646, www.hotelcaminomaya.com, US$56 s, US$62 d), offering spacious and comfortable rooms with TV, DVD players, air-

© AMY E. ROBERTSON

lush gardens and a mountain view at Casa de Café Bed and Breakfast

conditioning, and wireless Internet throughout the hotel (there are also three computers in the lobby that guests can use). The larger rooms have small sitting areas, and breakfast is included. The hotel also has a "recreation center" for the use of its guests, located at the edge of town, with a swimming pool, children's play equipment, and hammocks.

Plaza Copán (tel. 504/651-4508, www.hotel plazacopan.com, US$52 s, US$58 d), an imposing building on the *parque* next to the church, has 20 attractive rooms, all with tile floors, dark-wood furniture, air-conditioning, and TV, and a few with small balconies. The hotel also has a restaurant and a small pool.

Another elegant boutique hotel to have recently opened in the center of town is **((Yat B'alam** (tel. 504/651-4338, www.yatbalam .com, US$70 s, US$75 d, 10 percent discount for stays of three nights or more), which has just four rooms, in a beautiful colonial-style building that is also home to three high-end gift shops and a café. All rooms have air-conditioning, wireless Internet, TV and DVDs, and sound-proofed windows, and the two rooms that face the street have small balconies as well. There is a small sitting area with views out to the hills, and guests have use of the swimming pool at the Posada Real. The larger rooms can accommodate up to five people.

The 16 guest rooms at **Hotel Don Udo's** (tel. 504/651-4533, www.donudos.com, US$41–87 s, US$46–92 d) are each unique in layout and decor, and the price varies accordingly. The colonial-style building has a central grassy garden with the rooms (and hammocks) situated around it, each with air-conditioning and TV. Hotel facilities include a sauna, whirlpool tub, and a highly regarded restaurant/bar.

Luna Jaguar Spa Resort (tel. 504/651-4746, hlunajaguar@gmail.com, US$70 s/d) has seven small rooms, somewhat overpriced and of varying quality (be sure to take a look before putting down any money), but the best have funky wood canopies on the beds and stylish bathrooms, and the stone Jacuzzi is a real treat.

US$100 and Up

Romantic enough for a honeymoon or anniversary celebration is **((La Casa Rosada** (tel. 504/651-4324, www.lacasarosada.com, US$145 s/d), catering to luxury-lovers with tasteful wood and rattan furnishings, and amenities such as showers that boast a steam function (complete with stools to sit on), as well as music speakers, a pillow menu, and artwork by renowned Honduran artists such as Pito Perez. Rooms 3 and 5 have windows on the doors for peek-a-boo views of the hills when unshuttered. Rates include breakfast (usually served in the small courtyard) and a courtesy drink 6–7 P.M. each day. While there isn't a restaurant, the hotel can arrange for food to be brought in for lunch or dinner. One room on the ground floor has been accommodated for wheelchair access. Room 1 is slightly smaller and has the bathroom outside (although just two steps outside of the room, and behind a wall, so not within view of anyone else); it costs US$87 per night.

The best-known hotel in downtown Copán Ruinas is **Hotel Marina Copán** (tel. 504/651-4070 or 504/651-4071, www.hotelmarina copan.com, US$93 s, US$104 d). The 50 rooms in the attractive, one-level, colonial-style building feature dark-wood furniture and paneling, and a few have terraces and peaceful gardens out back—well worth requesting. Among the hotel amenities are a swimming pool, a sauna and gym, a bar, and a good restaurant. Hotel service is very good, although the rooms themselves are on the simple side given the price.

Apartments

The owners of the Casa de Café B&B also have an apartment and a townhouse available for daily and longer-term rental (www.casa jaguarcopan.com, www.casadedonsantiago copan.com), with two bedrooms, kitchen, a living area complete with library, cable TV, hammock, and maid service included. Both are spotless, tastefully decorated with wood furnishings and Mayan touches, and can sleep up to five guests if you don't mind having one person on the sofabed in the living room. Casa

Jaguar (US$90/night) has air-conditioning, while the Casa de Don Santiago (US$110/ night) has ceiling fans in all rooms. Both rentals have a DVD player and selection of films, CD player, hammock, fully equipped kitchen, and small garden. The prices can be flexible depending on availability, and weekly and monthly rates are available as well (just $900/month for the Casa Jaguar).

Outside of Town

On the far side of the Río Copán from town, on a bluff just about opposite the ruins, is one of Honduras's best ecolodges. **Hacienda San Lucas** (tel. 504/651-4495, www.haciendasan lucas.com, US$120 d) is a picturesque hacienda run by a charismatic owner, Flavia Cueva. Flavia is deeply committed to the nature, archaeology, and people of Copán, and uses the hacienda as a vehicle to preserve and support the community. Electricity came to the nearby village just two years ago, and the painstakingly restored hacienda continues to make minimal use of it, relying instead on candles to light the eight guest rooms and dining area, and solar-generated electricity for the bathrooms. The kitchen, reception, and outdoor dining patio are in the original main house, while the guest rooms are in three bungalows surrounded by lush vegetation. Rooms are simple but elegant, with cedar beds and locally made woven bedspreads. A hearty breakfast is included, but those in the know make sure to have at least one dinner on the property as well. The hacienda's local Maya Chortí staff hand-grind and pat out tortillas, to serve with gourmet versions of traditional chicken and fish dishes in five-course meals. The well-maintained trails in the surrounding hillsides are lovely for walking, and horseback rides can be arranged as well. A small Mayan archaeological site, Los Sapos, is on the hacienda property. Yoga and massages are also available (Hacienda San Lucas also offers a number of yoga retreats). Day use of the property is $2, or come to enjoy a late-afternoon cocktail on the grassy knoll overlooking a corner of the ruins, and stay for the sumptuous dinner (be sure to make a reservation,

preferably at least 24 hours in advance, or they may not be able to accommodate).

An easy walk outside of Copán Ruinas, **Hacienda La Esperanza** (tel. 504/651-4676, U.S. tel. 704/719-3886, www.haciendala esperanza.org, US$75 s, US$87 d) is a homey hacienda-style bed-and-breakfast set up as a nonprofit for the Mayans of the area. All profits are channeled into a small clinic, with any surplus going to the local charity Paramedics for Children, which provides school supplies as well as medical assistance.

Commandingly situated on a hillside above the highway at kilometer marker 164 (about three kilometers from Copán Ruinas) is the large and somewhat nondescript **Posada Real de Copán** (tel. 504/651-4480, www.posadareal decopan.com, US$87s, US$99 d). It is equipped with a sizable patio swimming pool, two bars, a not-so-highly-regarded restaurant (plan on eating in town), and a conference room; travelers in large groups seem to be the hotel's primary clientele. The 80 rooms are spacious and nicely decorated, and each has air-conditioning, cable TV, and purified tap water. The hotel runs a shuttle bus to the ruins several times a day.

FOOD
Snacks, Light Meals, and Coffee

The **Casa de Todo** (tel. 504/651-4185, www .casadetodo.com, 7 A.M.–9 P.M. daily) has a selection of wholesome snacks and light meals like granola with homemade yogurt and fruit (US$3.50), couscous salad, and pesto pasta (US$6).

Café Welchez (7 A.M.–9 P.M. daily), right on the *parque,* has espresso drinks as well as fresh-baked cakes, pies, and light snacks. The *tres leches* and carrot cake are utterly delicious and generously portioned.

There is also a branch of **Espresso Americano** at the northeast corner of the square.

Honduran

The hands-down favorite spot in town is **Comedor & Pupusería Mary** (7 A.M.–9 P.M. daily), half a block from the municipal market, its wooden tables usually crowded with locals. Soups (US$3) are popular with the regulars, and there are also well-prepared fish, beef, and chicken meals, *almuerzos* for US$3, and *licuados* (US$1.50), as well as *pupusas* (US$0.50–0.80).

The real budget-pinchers can eat at the stands located outside the market building in the afternoons and evenings daily.

Carnitas N'ia Lola (7 A.M.–10 P.M. daily), popular with the traveler and expat crowd, has very tasty and filling nachos, quesadillas, huge *baleadas*, and, of course, the namesake carnitas (US$10), as well as other pricier cuts of meat (steaks run about US$15). In the evening, the grill *(fragua)* is cranked up. This place is invariably packed and fun for the 6:30–8 P.M. happy hour.

If you're looking for a steak but hoping to spend a little less, the beef dishes at **Momo's** run US$5–7, although the atmosphere is rather more ordinary.

Right on the square is **Restaurante Yaragua** (7 A.M.–10 P.M. daily), next to the hotel of the same name, with well-prepared Honduran meals like a hearty *plato típico* (US$6), fish fillet (US$6), or the ever-popular *anafre* bean-and-cheese dip (US$3). A block and a half west of the park, **Llama del Bosque** (tel. 504/651-4431) is a similar standby, going strong for over 30 years, with an extensive menu including pastas (US$4–5), beef dishes (US$6), and breakfasts (US$3).

The (**Hacienda San Lucas** (tel. 504/651-4106, www.haciendasanlucas.com), in the hills across the river from town, offers an outstanding set five-course menu for US$20 per person. Made from local produce, the meal might include a fruit, green papaya and fresh cheese appetizer, cream of corn soup, tamales, chicken with the house *adobo* sauce or tilapia fish, and rum cake for dessert. Reservations are required for dinner, although lighter lunches and breakfasts are served for drop-in visitors.

International

A Euro-style café run by Belgians, **Via Via Café** (tel. 504/651-4652, 7 A.M.–10 P.M. daily) is one of several in a network of travelers' cafés around the world. They serve reasonably priced breakfasts and light meals, always with several vegetarian options, like veggie burgers and pasta, and countless daily specials, often based on Asian cuisine. Indonesian *nasi goreng* has been one of the specials. Breakfasts run US$2–3, while most lunch and dinner dishes are US$3–5. There are also a couple of inexpensive rooms for rent in the back, and the bar is frequently full of travelers in the evening.

Run by a British expat named Tanya, (**Twisted Tanya's** (www.twistedtanya.com, 3–10 P.M. Mon.–Sat.) offers creatively prepared courses like curry shrimp, conch soup, or Chinese dumplings with wasabi for US$13 a plate, plus delicacies like cheesecake for dessert (you can order à la carte or pay US$18 for a three-course meal). There are always a few vegetarian choices on the menu, and a three-course backpacker's special is available 4–6 P.M. for just six bucks. The restaurant, a block south of the municipal market, is also a popular spot for happy hour.

Jim's Pizza (11 A.M.–9 P.M. daily), a block south of the *parque*, cooks up an acceptable, shareable pizza (US$7–9) as well as tasty wood-fired rotisserie chicken and burgers.

Pícame, on the road heading out of town toward the ruins, is a great little joint with the best roast chicken in town, rice and veggie options, and renowned burgers, all at fair prices.

INFORMATION AND SERVICES
Information

Two helpful websites are www.copanruinas.com and www.asociacioncopan.org.

MC Tours (tel. 504/651-4453, www.mctours-honduras.com), across from the Hotel Marina Copán, and **Copan Connections** (tel. 504/651-4182, www.copanconnections.com), run by a pair of expats, can help arrange local airline tickets, hotel reservations, and tours elsewhere in Honduras as well as in Copán.

Banks

Banco de Occidente, at the northwest corner

of the square, changes dollars, quetzales, and travelers checks and advances cash on Visa cards. It has an ATM, as do **Banco Atlántida** and **BAC Bamer,** both on the southern side of the square.

Communications and Laundry

Honducor (8 A.M.–noon and 1–5 P.M. Mon.–Fri., 8 A.M.–noon Sat.) is half a block west of the square, next door to **Hondutel** (7 A.M.–9 P.M. Mon.–Fri., 7 A.M.–noon and 2–5 P.M. weekends).

A better place for making calls would be one of the many Internet cafés in town. **Inter@ Café** (8 A.M.–10 P.M. daily) is two doors from Via Via Café, **Maya Connections** (7 A.M.–9 P.M. daily) is a block south of the park, and the **Casa de Todo** is a block east of the park; all charge US$1/hour. The latter two also offer laundry service, charging US$0.80 a pound, with a US$4 minimum. Laundry given early the morning can be returned the same day, while afternoon deliveries are ready the next day.

Spanish School

For those who become hypnotized by the easy lifestyle of Copán Ruinas and want a reason to extend their stay, **Ixbalanque Spanish School** (tel./fax 504/651-4432, www .ixbalanque.com) offers five days of one-on-one classes and a week of housing with a local family for US$235, while five days of classes without lodging costs US$135. Dance classes are also offered.

Another language school in Copán is **Guacamaya** (tel. 504/651-4360, www .guacamaya.com), one block north of the *parque.* Five days of classes, four hours daily, plus a week's room and board with a local family, costs US$225, while five days of classes only costs US$140. Guacamaya also arranges volunteer vacations for US$135/week, providing accommodations, meals, and Internet access.

Spanish classes and family stays in Copán are generally very good—the families tend to be more interested in interacting with foreigners than similar setups in Guatemala.

Spas

New businesses are sprouting in Copán Ruinas as it grows as a tourist destination, including **Spa Ixchel** (www.spaixchelhonduras.com), set in the verdant countryside. Services include massages, steam and mud baths, and even a purification ritual in the igloo-shaped Temascal Maya.

Emergencies and Immigration

The local **police** can be reached at tel. 504/651-4060, although no local seems to have a very high regard for them. Your best bet in a medical emergency is the Red Cross (tel. 504/651-4099), which can arrange **ambulance** service.

Clínica Castro (tel. 504/651-4504, 8 A.M.–noon and 2–4:30 P.M. Mon.–Sat.) is run by a competent doctor who speaks English. His office is at the exit of town toward the butterfly farm.

The local *migración* office has been closed, so you'll have to go out to the border at El Florido to renew your tourist card.

GETTING THERE AND AWAY
To La Entrada, San Pedro Sula, and Santa Rosa de Copán

The best way to get to and from San Pedro is via two express services. The nicer **Hedman Alas** (tel. 504/651-4037, www.hedmanalas .com) has a terminal a few blocks south of the *parque* outside of town. Hedman Alas offers four buses daily (five Sun.–Mon.) between 5:15 A.M. and 2:30 P.M. for US$13.50, as well as connections to Tegucigalpa or La Ceiba for US$21.50. Some buses are "Ejecutivo Plus," with larger seats for a few dollars more.

Casasola Express (tel. 504/651-4078) runs buses to San Pedro at 6 A.M., 7 A.M., and 2 P.M. daily for US$6, with connections to La Ceiba, Trujillo, Omoa, Puerto Cortés, Tela, Tegucigalpa, and the San Pedro Sula Airport. Its terminal is a block down the hill behind the church. You can also get off the bus at La Entrada (one hour, US$3), where you can catch other buses to Santa Rosa de Copán (one hour) or Gracias (two hours), leaving every hour or so between 4 A.M. and 5 P.M. from the bridge at the north end of town. Best to double-check all bus departure times, as they frequently change.

The 72-kilometer road between Copán Ruinas and La Entrada is paved, although it can be rather potted during the rainy season.

To the Guatemalan Border

The Copán Ruinas–El Florido border crossing, between Honduras and Guatemala, is the crossing most frequently used by Central American travelers. The road is paved and has also been significantly cleaned up in terms of security (no more highway robberies), making this a faster way (rather than via Nueva Ocotepeque) to get from Guatemala City to San Pedro.

Minibuses to El Florido, at the border, leave Copán Ruinas from the corner next to the market frequently and charge US$1.60 for the 20-minute, 12-kilometer trip. The last bus to the border leaves around 3 P.M. and returns around 4 P.M.

The border itself is in the middle of a field, with few services: a *pulpería* on the Honduran side, restrooms that cost 3 quetzales, and moneychangers offering bad rates. The border officials here are a fairly relaxed bunch, and crossing is not much of a hassle, although it takes longer now with the increased truck traffic. There is a $3 charge for reentry into Honduras—we don't know why, but since an official receipt is provided, it seems legitimate. There are no charges at all by the Guatemalan office on exit or entry, so don't let them convince you otherwise. The border is supposedly open 6 A.M.–6 P.M. daily, but this seems to fluctuate. The best time to arrive is midmorning, well before lunch.

From El Florido, buses continue on the hour-ride to Chiquimula, Guatemala, for US$2. You can catch buses from Chiquimula to Guatemala City for US$4—which unfortunately do not leave you near the buses that go to Antigua. If Antigua is your final destination, do yourself a favor and take a shuttle bus.

Direct Buses to Guatemala

Hedman Alas (tel. 504/651-4037, www.hedman alas.com), with a terminal on the road south of town heading toward the river, has two direct, expensive, first-class buses daily to Guatemala City for US$35 (four hours) or Antigua Guatemala for US$41 (five hours).

At US$15 the shuttle buses that run from Copán Ruinas to Antigua are a far better deal (you can book one through Basecamp at Via Via Café, among other places). There are plans to also run buses to Cobán, Guatemala City, and Río Dulce/Flores. Service is US$15, and the buses leave daily, at 5:30 A.M., 10:30 A.M., and noon during high season, noon only during low season.

GETTING AROUND

Mototaxis are plentiful in Copán Ruinas, and a ride around town should cost US$0.80 to US$1 max. If you are planning to take the 5:15 A.M. bus to San Pedro with Hedman Alas, you will need to arrange your *mototaxi* the night before; expect to pay US$5.25.

There are plenty of scenic routes for mountain bikers; the chamber of commerce says it can provide itineraries.

Tours

Basecamp (tel. 504/651-4652, www.basecamp honduras.com), with its office at the Via Via Café and restaurant, organizes hiking trips, tours on off-road motocross motorcycles or on horseback, and shuttlebus service to Guatemala. Staff are very knowledgeable on the area and happy to answer questions and point do-it-yourselfers in the right direction. A unique two-hour city walk of the "real" Copán is just US$8 and includes a US$4 donation to an education project; a three-hour horseback tour is US$15, and longer hikes and motocross tours run US$30–40.

Yaragua Tours (tel. 504/651-4147, www .yaragua.com) also can organize a number of different excursions to destinations in the valley and surrounding hillsides, usually charging around US$15–25 per person, with a minimum of four people, for shorter trips to the hot springs, Hacienda San Lucas, or horseback riding, or more for longer trips to see nearby hilltop Mayan stelae or caves. Yaragua can organize an excursions to a Chortí Maya community, where visitors have the chance to pat out tortillas and shape clay pottery (US$25 pp), or trips tubing or kayaking on the Río Copán. Basecamp can also arrange all day or overnight trips to the Finca El Cisne coffee plantation, while Yaragua coordinates half-day visits to other coffee farms.

With its office right at the ruins, the **Asociación de Guías Copán** (tel. 504/651-4018, guiascopan@yahoo.com) has the monopoly on tours at the park, but they also offer many more services, such as horseback rides to the Hacienda San Lucas and La Pintada (US$20 pp for 2–3 hours), guided tours to El Boquerón and El Rubí, and even guiding in places as far flung as La Ceiba and Guatemala. The guides are generally extremely knowledgeable, and many are multilingual (Spanish, English, French, and Italian are spoken). Two of their guides, Yobani Peraza (tel. 504/9992-8792, guiamaya@yahoo.com, speaks Spanish, English, and French) and Tito Ever Serrano (tel. 504/9967-6030, everserrano@yahoo.com, speaks Spanish and French), can also provide transportation service throughout Central America, in SUVs and vans. Another of the guides, **Jorge Barraza** (tel. 504/9873-9620, jorgearnaldo2001@yahoo.es, speaks Spanish and English), is a self-taught birder, and a genius at spotting motmots, toucanets, tanagers, orioles, and blue herons along the Río Copán, and even the occasional quetzal or trogon in remaining forests on nearby hilltops. Trips can be customized to fit energy level and types of birds you'd like to see, costing US$25–75 per person.

An equally renowned Honduran naturalist guide (and former Peace Corps volunteer) is **Robert Gallardo** (tel. 504/651-4133, rgallardo 32@gmail.com), at the Enchanted Wings Butterfly House, who runs specialized trips for visitors on a quest to spot some of the 300 different species of vibrantly colorful **birds** living in the many microclimates and ecosystems in the hills and valleys around Copán.

NEAR COPÁN RUINAS TOWN

In addition to viewing the Mayan ruins, many hikes and excursions can be made in the hills and valleys around Copán Ruinas. The countryside is generally very safe for wandering, and local *campesinos* are helpful to visitors who lose their way. One can also stroll along the Río Copán in any direction from town and enjoy the rural beauty of the valley.

Note: Several tourists have been robbed walking up to El Rubí waterfall near Santa Rita—since then, many tour companies send visitors out with an armed guard, which is hardly relaxing. Ask at your hotel or one of the guide companies for more information if you are considering this hike.

Macaw Mountain Bird Park

A first-class nature-oriented destination in the hills outside of town is Macaw Mountain Bird Park (tel. 504/651-4245, www.macawmountain .com, 9 A.M.–4 P.M. daily), a couple of kilometers outside of Copán on the road to the hot springs (walk or take an inexpensive taxi). The beautifully designed bird park is filled with brilliantly colored macaws, toucans, and parrots from Honduras and elsewhere in Latin America. The owner, American Lloyd Davidson, relocated the park from Roatán to Copán in 2003. The wooden walkways, aviaries, and restaurant, built on four hectares of land in the heavily wooded Quebrada Sesemil valley, are lovely. Most birds are kept in aviaries, but in one area, visitors can hold and feed birds. There's a larger coffee plantation nearby with coffee roasters at work. The reserve costs US$10 (both dollars and lempiras accepted); each ticket is good for three days of visiting. The ticket price also includes a guided tour, which is highly recommended to maximize your visit, as the guides not only explain about the birds, but also take them out of their cages. The restaurant has seafood, chicken, and beef for US$9–12 for a main course.

Enchanted Wings Butterfly House

Just outside of Copán Ruinas on the road to El Florido is the Enchanted Wings Butterfly House (tel. 504/651-4133, 8 A.M.–5 P.M. daily, http://hondurasbutterflyfar.tripod.com/copan .htm, US$6 adults, US$2.60 children), set up by former Peace Corps volunteer Robert Gallardo and his wife, with some 20 species of tropical butterflies in a screened-in, terraced garden at the edge of a small river, and an orchid garden across a small river. Visitors are given a laminated butterfly identification card for self-guided tours, or you can request a guide. The deck and flagstone gardens make a relaxing place to hang out and write letters. Gallardo can arrange birding and butterfly-watching tours in the hills around Copán.

Canopy Tour

Near the entrance to Hacienda San Lucas is **Los Sapos Canopy Tour** (tel. 504/9856-3758), a 14-stage zipline that takes adventurers across the Río Copán and ends at the southwest side of the Acropolis.

Aguas Termales

A trip out to the *aguas termales* (hot springs), 21 kilometers and one hour's drive northwest of town on a rough dirt road leaving town at the corner by Hotel Patty, is a great way to spend the afternoon. The springs bubble out of a hillside just above a small river, out in a lovely area of Honduras countryside dotted with coffee plantations and small farms. If you have your own transportation, it's worth coming out in the late afternoon (to enjoy the scenery) and staying at the springs until after dark. If you don't have wheels, hitching out the dirt road for US$1–2 is not difficult, but make sure you head back toward Copán Ruinas by midafternoon to ensure a ride. Entrance to the public pools is US$3. A small stand at the springs sells soft drinks, beers, and snacks.

There have been very mixed reports about the private installations on the other side of the river run by Luna Jaguar (tel. 504/651-4746, US$10). Some visitors have loved them, others felt they were overpriced, and still others felt they were downright unsafe (particularly for children). Tickets are available in town at the same-named hotel, as well as at other hotels and travel agencies, who can also help arrange transportation, but it may be better to take a look for yourself before deciding between the private baths and the public ones.

Coffee Plantations

Forty-five minutes north of Copán Ruinas is a century-old hacienda and coffee plantation, **Finca El Cisne** (tel. 504/651-4695, www.fincaelcisne.com, US$30 s, US$45 d, breakfast included). The hacienda offers one- to four-day visits, in which travelers explore on horseback, learn about coffee and cardamom production, hike the surrounding primary forest, and relax in thermal baths as an experience in the farming life (tours in English or Spanish). Overnight visitors stay in an adobe guesthouse. Day visits cost US$59 per person; it's US$77 per person when combined with a night in the "Casa Castejón."

About half an hour east of Copán Ruinas, is **Finca Santa Isabel** (tel. 504/651-4204, www.cafehonduras.com), the plantation and processing plant for Welchez coffee. Half-day tours are offered that include transportation from Copán Ruinas and a meal for $30 per person. If you have your own wheels, you can come at anytime, and the staff on-site will arrange the tour and meal for US$25. Numerous birds make their homes in the coffee trees, so keep your eyes peeled as you walk the trails.

Santa Rita and Vicinity

Eight kilometers northeast of Copán Ruinas, on the highway to La Entrada, is the cobblestone village of Santa Rita, which was originally the main Spanish town in the area. Formerly, the village was named Cashapa, which means "sweet tortilla" in Chortí Maya. The last buses back to Copán Ruinas pass at around 5:30 P.M.

On the far side of the Río Copán from Santa Rita, a rough dirt road winds up over the mountains to the southeast, ending up in **San Agustín,** where rides can be found to Dulce Nombre de Copán and on to Santa Rosa de Copán. The hike can be done in one day and passes along sections of the old *camino real* (royal road) and near the cloud forest of Monte Quetzal. You can hitch part of the way with passing pickup trucks.

El Jaral

On the highway toward San Pedro Sula, 15

kilometers from Copán Ruinas, is the venerable **Hacienda El Jaral** (tel. 504/552-4457 or 504/552-5067, US$50 d), founded as a working ranch in 1870. Now run as a hotel by the great-grandson of the original owner, the hacienda is around a large grassy field. Accommodations are in cozy cabins with stucco walls and wood furniture, each with hot water, ceiling fan and air-conditioning, TV, a mini-fridge, and a hammock on a small porch. There is a small swimming pool, a game room, a restaurant, and even a chapel, and weddings are occasionally held here. Activities include horseback riding, hiking, mountain biking, and tubing on the nearby Río Copán.

A water park a few meters down the road is run by the same owners as the hotel. **Aqua Park** (9 A.M.–5 P.M. Tues.–Sun., US$4) has several pools and slides, a couple of snack bars serving burgers and the like, a souvenir shop, and even a "Cow Museum," with someone's personal collection of cow knickknacks along with many more cow items that are for sale. There are basketball and volleyball courts, a soccer field, and balls. Paddleboats on the pond cost US$3, and horses are available for rent. Weekdays you're likely to have the place to yourself, which is a drag since they require 5 paid admissions to turn on a big slide, 20 admissions to turn them all on. On weekends all slides are on all day. While it's a relatively small water park, it's well-maintained and can make for a fun day with the kids.

El Boquerón

Spelunkers shouldn't miss the El Boquerón cave, 20 kilometers northeast of Copán Ruinas on the highway to San Pedro Sula. To get there, follow the highway past Santa Rita up a hill called La Carichosa, then look for a dirt road turning left. Ask for El Boquerón (The Big Mouth), about an hour's walk from the highway turn. The Río Amarillo runs through the cave, so visits are best December–April or you may be forced to go for a swim. Almost two kilometers long, it's filled with stalactites, stalagmites, and bats. Guides to the cave (recommended) can be easily found in Copán Ruinas. The Asociación de Guías Copán offers a day trip to the spectacular caves for about US$60 per person, which includes transportation and a meal.

The Ruins of Copán

Although not the largest Mayan city—at its height, a population of 24,000 lived in the surrounding region, as compared to more than 100,000 at Tikal—Copán was, as famed archaeologist Sylvanus Morley put it, "the Athens of the New World." For reasons that remain mysterious, Copán was the principal Mayan cultural center during the 400 years when the city was at the peak of its development, far ahead of other larger and more powerful Mayan cities in its development of sculpture, astronomy, and hieroglyphic writing.

HISTORY OF THE MAYAN CITY OF COPÁN
The Early Years
The rich bottomland in the Río Copán valley attracted farmers of unknown origin as early as 1000 B.C., but archaeological evidence indicates the Maya did not settle the area until about the time of Christ. Construction on the city is thought to have begun around A.D. 100, and the recorded history of the city does not begin until 426, when Copán's royal dynasty began. Some archaeologists believe the dynasty began when outsiders, probably either from the then-dominant Teotihuacán empire in Mexico or allies of theirs, conquered the city and took over administration of the valley.

Detailed information on Copán's earliest rulers is difficult to obtain, in part due to the ancient Mayan tradition of destroying monuments built by past rulers or building over temples erected in their honor. Not until 1989

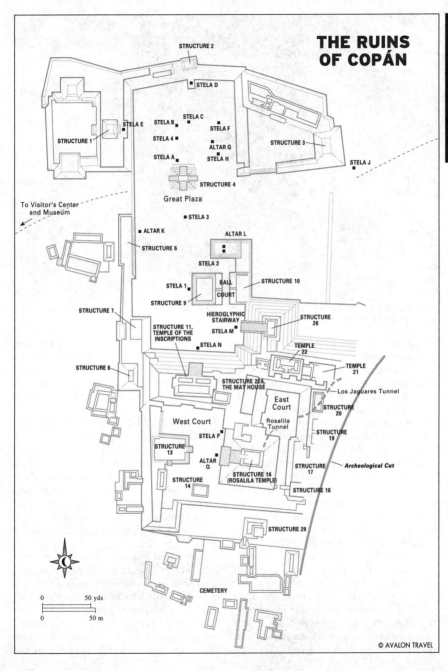

© AMY E. ROBERTSON

Archaeologists rank Copán the culturally most important Mayan site, for the intricate carvings on its temples and stelae.

were references to Copán's first ruler discovered, in a chamber nicknamed the Founder's Room buried deep under the Hieroglyphic Stairway. Apparently built by Copán's second ruler, nicknamed Mat Head for the odd headdress he is always depicted wearing, the room was dedicated in honor of his father, **Yax K'uk' Mo'.** According to a stela found inside, Yax K'uk' Mo', the city's first ruler, took the throne in A.D. 426 and governed until A.D. 435. In an astounding 1993 archaeological find, the tomb of Yax K'uk' Mo' was discovered directly underneath the East Court of the Acropolis. Evidence indicates he was not a conquering warrior, but a powerful shaman who was revered by later rulers as semidivine.

Little solid information is available on the next seven members of the dynasty, apart from a few names and dates. Apparently ruling only a small, provincial settlement at that time, these leaders created few lasting monuments or hieroglyphics telling of their deeds. At that time, Copán's dynasty was thought to be consolidating control over its domain, as well as establishing trade links with other Mayan cities in Guatemala, non-Maya groups farther south and east in Honduras, and even civilizations as far off as Teotihuacán in Mexico, as evidenced by *teotihuacano*-style pottery in Copán tombs.

The Height of the Royal Dynasty

The period of greatest architectural construction, considered to be the height of Copán's dynasty, began on May 26, 553, with the accession of **Moon Jaguar** to the throne. Moon Jaguar, Copán's 10th leader, built the Rosalila Temple, which was discovered in 1989 buried under Structure 10L-16. A replica of the temple can now be seen in its full glory in the Museo de Escultura Maya.

After Moon Jaguar, a series of rulers of unusual longevity governed Copán, providing the stability and continuity necessary for the city to flourish. **Smoke Imix,** the city's 12th ruler, took the throne February 8, 628, and ruled for 68 years, leaving more inscribed monuments and temples than any other ruler. Frequently depicted in full battle regalia and with representations of the jaguar god Tlaloc, Smoke Imix is thought to have been a great warrior. His successor, **18 Rabbit,** was also a prolific builder; he gave final form to the Great Plaza and the Ball Court. He also encouraged the development of sculpture, from low-relief to the nearly full-round style of later years. Despite these achievements, 18 Rabbit's reign ended in tragedy; he was captured in battle by the nearby city of Quirigua, formerly a vassal state of Copán, and beheaded on May 3, 738.

The Decline

Possibly because of the devastating blow of 18 Rabbit's death, the 14th ruler, **Smoke Monkey,** erected no stelae in his own honor and built only one temple during his 11-year rule. He apparently conducted the city's affairs in a council with nobles, demonstrating the weakness of the regime. In what archaeologists consider an attempt to regain the dynasty's former glory, Smoke Monkey's successor, **Smoke Shell,** dedicated the impressive Hieroglyphic Stairway, the longest hieroglyphic inscription known in the Americas. The 2,500 glyphs narrate the glorious past of Copán, but the poor construction of the staircase itself reveals that Smoke Shell could not mimic the impressive work of his predecessors.

The final leader in Copán to complete his reign, **Yax Pac,** governed the city for 58 years. One of the most important monuments left by Yax Pac is the famous Altar Q, a square bench illustrating all 15 prior rulers of the dynasty around its sides, with the first, Yax K'uk' Mo', passing the baton of leadership to Yax Pac. Although he may not have known it when he commissioned it, Yax Pac left on the small stone altar a brief résumé of the city's entire history.

A 17th leader, **U Cit Tok',** assumed the throne on February 10, 822. But for unknown reasons, his rule was never completed. The pathetic, half-completed Altar L, which he ordered built to commemorate his rule, suggests the dynasty ended with a single tragedy or defeat, rather than slowly fading from power.

The debate over the reason for the collapse of the Classic Maya kingdom has raged since serious archaeological work began at the end of the 19th century. The most accepted current explanation for Copán's collapse puts the blame on environmental factors and population growth. By the final decades of the 8th century, the city had grown to cover some of the best alluvial bottomland in the river valley; consequently, farmers were pushed farther up the hillsides, where land was not as productive. Recent investigations indicate that during this time the Río Copán valley experienced droughts, deforestation, massive soil erosion, and sudden floods during the rainy season. In addition, the Mayans followed slash-and-burn agricultural practices, which may have become unsustainable as their population grew. It's likely Copán simply outgrew its environment.

Although the city center was abandoned, evidence suggests the population in the region did not drop drastically until about 1200, when the region reverted to the small village groups found by the Spanish when they entered the valley in 1524.

THE RUINS OF COPÁN

The ruins of Copán are about a kilometer east of Copán Ruinas on the road toward San Pedro Sula, set off the road in a six-hectare wooded archaeological park along the edge of the Río Copán. After buying your US$15 entrance ticket, walk up the path from the visitors center (where there is a small cafeteria and gift shop) through tall trees to the entrance gate, where a guard will take your ticket. If you'd like to enter the **archaeological tunnels,** buy an additional ticket for US$15 (a high price for the experience, recommended for archaeology buffs only). (Tickets for the adjacent Museo de Escultura Maya are also sold at the visitors center, US$7 and highly recommended.)

Much of the original sculpture work at Copán has been removed from the grounds and replaced by exact duplicates. Although this is a bit disappointing for visitors, it is essential if the city's artistic legacy is not to be lost forever, worn away by the elements and thousands of curious hands. Most of the finest stelae and carvings can now be seen in the Museo de Escultura Maya.

REDISCOVERING COPÁN

Working our way through the thick woods, we came upon a square stone column, about fourteen feet high and three feet on each side, sculptured in very bold relief, and on all four of the sides, from the base to the top. The front was the figure of a man curiously and richly dressed, and the face, evidently a portrait, solemn, stern, and well fitted to excite terror. The back was of a different design, unlike anything we had ever seen before, and the sides were covered with hieroglyphics.... The sight of this unexpected monument put at rest at once and forever, in our minds, all uncertainty in regard to the character of American antiquities, and gave us the assurance...that the people who once occupied the Continent of America were not savages.

John Lloyd Stephens, *Incidents of Travel in Central America, Chiapas, and Yucatán,* 1841

Copán became known to the wider world through the work of John Lloyd Stephens and Frederich Catherwood, two talented men who visited the ruins in 1839 – and then, as the story goes, bought them for US$50 from a *campesino.* An American diplomat, adventurer, and author, Stephens had already published the famous travelogue *Incidents of Travel in Arabia Petrea* before he convinced United States president Martin Van Buren to send him on a diplomatic mission to Central America. Stephens was accompanied on the expedition by his friend Catherwood, an English architect and artist.

The pair spent several weeks at the ruins, clearing underbrush, taking measurements, and sketching buildings, sculptures, and hieroglyphics. After many more adventures and explorations in Guatemala and the Yucatán, Stephens and Catherwood returned to the United States and published *Incidents of Travel in Central America, Chiapas, and Yucatán,* which was an immediate success and went on to become one of the most widely read books of the time, going through 10 editions in three months. Stephens's detailed measurements and lively descriptions, accompanied by Catherwood's accurate and elegant drawings, captured the public's imagination.

THE FIRST ARCHAEOLOGISTS

Largely because of *Incidents of Travel,* British archaeologist Alfred P. Maudsley made his way to Copán in 1881. Although he stayed for only three days, Maudsley was entranced by the enigmatic and beautiful Mayan artwork. He returned four years later to begin a full-scale project of mapping, drawing, photography, excavation, and reconstruction that continued off and on until 1902. Maudsley's voluminous work on Copán and several other Mayan sites was compiled in the five-volume *Biología Centrali-Americana,* which was enhanced considerably by the superb drawings of Annie Hunter, still used in research today.

Maudsley was followed by a long line of Mayanist scholars, foremost among them Sylvanus Morley and J. Eric Thompson, who developed what has become known as the

Just before the place where the guards check your ticket is a kilometer-long nature trail with examples of ceiba, strangler fig, and other plants characteristic of the jungle originally covering the Valle de Copán, worth taking a brief stroll along either before or after visiting the ruins.

The Acropolis

Past the gate, where colorful macaws hang out, the trail heading to the right brings visitors to the Acropolis, a massive architectural complex built over the course of the city's history and considered to be the central axis point of Copán, around which the rest of the city was focused. At the highest points the structures stretch 30 meters above the Great Plaza (thus it was dubbed the Acropolis, or "high city," by archaeologists), and the many large trees still standing atop the huge structure only add to its

"traditional" model of Mayan civilization. Completely enamored with Mayan art and astronomical science, Morley and Thompson concluded that the Classic Maya were peace-loving philosophers living in something akin to a New World Athens, minus the warfare.

DIGGING DEEPER

Beginning in the mid-1950s, the view of the Classic Maya as a miraculous, almost flawless society began to fall apart. As archaeologists investigated smaller pre-Classic sites and the residences of ordinary ancient Maya, a more complex, richer picture of Mayan society began to emerge. New theories hold that Mayan society developed like many other ancient civilizations – amidst warfare, trading, agricultural innovation, and exploitation of the lower classes.

Probably the most stunning breakthrough in understanding the Maya came in 1959 and 1960, when archaeologists Heinrich Berlin and Tatiana Proskouriakoff began deciphering Mayan hieroglyphics, a process that continues to this day. Archaeologists had long presumed that hieroglyphics were a form of writing, but they could do little more than guess at the meanings. It is now recognized that the glyphs are nothing less than a history of the cities where they are inscribed, recording in stone events such as battles and dynastic successions.

In 1975, the Peabody Museum of Harvard University, which sponsored Maudsley's initial investigations, began a second major project at Copán, a main component of which was to excavate the many layers of buildings buried underneath the Acropolis, in order to learn about the city's

growth over time. Knowing that when successive Copán rulers erected new buildings, they generally carefully buried the previous structures intact, archaeologists undertook a project of tunneling under the Acropolis and back into Copán's history. One of the first results of this fascinating work was the 1989 discovery of the Rosalila Temple, with much of its brilliant original paint still visible, by Honduran archaeologist Ricardo Agurcia. The tunnel to Rosalila, now open to the public, offers a cramped view of the temple, while a full-scale replica of Rosalila is the centerpiece of the Museo de Escultura Maya. Tunneling farther under the East Court led archaeologists to a massive block of stone covered in glyphs, which appeared to be dedicated to the founder of Copán. Then, in 1993, several meters directly under the East Court, archaeologist Robert Sharer of the University of Pennsylvania and his team opened up what they and many other archaeologists believe is the tomb of Yax K'uk' Mo', the founder of the Copán dynasty. The tomb was built when the rest of the Acropolis did not exist, and it appears to form the axis for the construction of the rest of the city. Confirmation of the identity of the bones was provided by a jade pendant found near the skeleton's neck – identical to the one depicted on Yax K'uk' Mo' in the famed Altar Q. Medical tests determined the skeleton had a disfigured right forearm, which interestingly is hidden from view by a shield on Altar Q's portrait of Yax K'uk' Mo'. The University of Pennsylvania team continues work on the Yax K'uk' Mo' tomb to thoroughly evaluate the new discoveries, while other teams from Tulane and Harvard Universities continue work in other areas of Copán.

imposing grandeur. The current Acropolis—perhaps only two-thirds as big as it was during the city's heyday—is formed by at least two million cubic meters of fill. Some of the most fascinating archaeological finds in recent years have come from digging under buildings in the Acropolis and finding earlier temples, which were carefully buried and built over.

A steep set of stairs leads up to the West Court, a small grassy plaza surrounded by

temples to the underworld. At the base of Structure 16 in the West Court is a square sculpture known as **Altar Q.** Possibly the single most fascinating piece of art at Copán, it depicts 16 seated men, carved around the four sides of a square stone altar. For many years, following the theory of archaeologist Herbert Joseph Spinden, it was believed the altar illustrated a gathering of Mayan astronomers in the 6th century. However, following

© AMY E. ROBERTSON

a sculpture at the Acropolis

generations as semidivine. The tombs were built at a time when none of the rest of the Acropolis existed and are thought to have formed the axis for the rest of Copán's growth. Studies are still underway on the tomb discoveries, which for the moment remain out of public eye.

Underneath Structure 16, in 1989, Honduran archaeologist Ricardo Agurcia found the most complete temple ever uncovered at Copán. It's called **Rosalila** ("rose-lilac") for its original paint, which can still be seen. Rosalila is considered the best-preserved temple anywhere in the Mayan zone. The temple was erected by Copán's 10th ruler, Moon Jaguar, in 571. The short tunnel accessing the front of Rosalila is open to the public for a US$15 fee, paid at the museum entrance. A full-scale replica of Rosalila is in the Museo de Escultura Maya, which gives a much better sense of the grandeur of the temple than what can be glimpsed through the two small windows in the tunnel.

The ticket price of the tunnel allows visitors to go inside a second, longer tunnel, which begins in the East Court and goes underneath Structure 20 to come out on the far northeast corner of the Acropolis. This tunnel has many more windows, which reveal sculptures of the temple beneath the temple. Both tunnels are well lit and have written descriptions in English and Spanish explaining aspects of Copán archaeology.

On the eastern side of the East Court, the Acropolis drops off in an abrupt cliff down to where the Río Copán ran for a time, before it was diverted to its current course in 1935. Since the river ran alongside the Acropolis, it ate away at the structure, leaving a cross section termed by Mayanist Sylvanus Morley, "the world's greatest archaeological cut."

Climbing up the northern side of the East Court brings visitors to **Temple 22,** a "Sacred Mountain," the site of important rituals and sacrifices in which the ruler participated. The skull-like stone carving on the side of the structure is of a macaw, the God of Brilliance.

Next to Temple 22 is a small, not visually arresting building called the **Mat House,**

breakthroughs in deciphering Mayan hieroglyphics, archaeologists now know the altar is a history of the city's rulers. The 16 men are, in fact, all the rulers of the Copán dynasty, with the first ruler, Yax K'uk' Mo', shown passing the ruling baton—and the symbolic right to rule—on to the last, Yax Pac, who ordered the altar built in 776.

Between the West Court and the nearby East Court is **Structure 16,** a temple dedicated to war, death, and the veneration of past rulers. Heading around Structure 16 toward the East Court, one can look out to the right over the Cemetery, so called for the many bones found during excavations. Archaeologists later came to realize that the area was residential, where the royal elite lived. Homes were clustered around courtyards, and as per tradition, the deceased were buried next to their homes.

The **East Court** was Copán's original plaza. Deep underneath the floor of the plaza, found by archaeologists in 1992 and 1993, are the tombs of Copán's founder, Yax K'uk' Mo', and his wife, who were both venerated by later

VISITING THE RUINS: A LITTLE ADVICE

- The ruins are open 8 A.M.-4 P.M. every day. Entrance to the main park plus Las Sepulturas is US$15, and the Museo de Escultura Maya is another US$7 (all highly recommended). It's another US$15 to enter the tunnels – pretty pricey for the experience. It's very nice to get in right when the gates open. In the early morning hours, you'll be able to enjoy the ruins in relative solitude, and you'll have good low-angle light for photographs. This is also the favorite time for a group of white-tailed deer that live in the woods to come out and wander through the ruins.

- When walking around the ruins, refrain from walking on stairways that have been roped off.

- Try not to lean on sculptures, stelae, or buildings – salts from your skin can corrode the stone, especially when multiplied by the 60,000 or so visitors who come to Copán each year.

- It should go without saying, but let it be said: It is illegal to remove any stones from the park.

- Two pamphlet-guides to the ruins are sold at the ticket office: *History Carved in Stone,* by William Fash and Ricardo Agurcia Fasquelle, and *Copán, Legendario y Monumental,* by J. Adan Cueva. The former, written in English, has an excellent interpretation of the growth of the city and advances in archaeology, but does not discuss each monument individually. The latter, in English and Spanish, is weak on recent advances in archaeology, and although it does give descriptions of many major sites, they are often incomplete and not entirely useful.

- Guides can be hired at the site for US$25 for a two-hour tour. Some of these local men have worked at the ruins for many years and have a positively encyclopedic knowledge about the archaeology of Copán – not just the names of buildings, but explanations on how archaeological views changed, when

Guides have near-encyclopedic knowledge of the ruins at Copán.

© AMY E. ROBERTSON

certain discoveries were made and why they were important, and all sorts of other details. In addition to providing information on the ruins themselves, guides often relate interesting local legends and tall tales about the area. Casual tourists may find their brains spinning with the endless stories of temples, rulers, and altars, but if you're really curious to learn more about Copán, you are definitely encouraged to hire a guide. They charge an extra US$10 to accompany you to the Museo de Escultura Maya, and US$15 for Las Sepulturas – both worthwhile expenses.

- Although English-speaking guides are available, their language abilities vary. If your Spanish is nonexistent, check beforehand to make sure you and your guide can communicate well. You may want to consider contacting the **Asociación de Guías Copán** (tel. 504/651-4018, guiascopan@yahoo.com) ahead of your visit to reserve a guide in English, particularly during high season (Holy Week, July, and August). Guides who speak other languages are available as well.

a stela standing guard at the famed Hieroglyphic Stairway, with its more than 2,500 glyphs

occupying a corner of the Acropolis near the top of the Hieroglyphic Stairway. It was erected in 746 by Smoke Monkey, not long after the shocking capture and decapitation of his predecessor, 18 Rabbit. Decorated with carvings of mats all around its walls, the Mat House was evidently some sort of communal government house; the mat has always symbolized a community council in Mayan tradition. Following 18 Rabbit's death, the Copán dynasty weakened so much that Smoke Monkey was forced to govern with a council of lords, who were commemorated on the building according to their neighborhood. The dancing jaguar carved onto the steps leading up to the Mat House is of Smoke Jaguar.

The Great Plaza

After sneaking a peek of the Great Plaza through the trees, visitors head down a stairway that brings them to the extraordinary **Hieroglyphic Stairway,** the longest hieroglyphic inscription found anywhere in the Americas. Rising from the southeast corner of the plaza up the side of Acropolis,

and now unfortunately covered with a roof to protect it from the elements, the 72 steps contain more than 2,500 glyphs. It was built in 753 by Smoke Shell to recount the history of Copán's previous rulers. Since the city was declining in prestige at that point, the stairway was shoddily made compared to other structures and collapsed at some point before archaeologists began working at the ruins. In the 1940s, the stairs were assembled in the current, random order. It is thought that about 15 of the stairs, mainly on the lower section, are in their correct position. A group of archeologists have been using computer analysis of photographs to try to recreate the correct order of the stairway and thus read the long inscription left to us by Smoke Shell 1,250 years ago.

Underneath the Hieroglyphic Stairway, a tomb was discovered in 1989. Laden with painted pottery and jade sculptures, it is thought to have held a scribe, possibly one of the sons of Smoke Imix. In 1993, farther down below the stairway, archaeologists found a subtemple they dubbed **Papagayo,** erected by the

© AMY E. ROBERTSON

the dramatic Great Plaza

second ruler of Copán, Mat Head. Deeper still, under Papagayo, a room was unearthed dedicated to the founder of Copán's ruling dynasty, Yax K'uk' Mo', dubbed the **Founder's Room.** Archaeologists believe the room was used as a place of reverence for Yax K'uk' Mo' for more than 300 years, possibly frequented by players from the adjacent ball court before or after their *pelota* matches.

Just north of the Hieroglyphic Stairway is the **Ball Court,** perhaps the best-recognized and most-often-photographed piece of architecture at Copán. It is the third and final ball court erected on the site and was completed in 738. No exact information is available on how the game was played, but it is thought players bounced a hard rubber ball off the slanted walls of the court, keeping it in the air without using their hands. (A video, made by *National Geographic* of a re-creation of the ball game filmed in Mexico, is on continuous loop at the Casa K'inich.) Atop the slanted walls are three intricate macaw heads on each side, as well as small compartments, which the players may have used as dressing rooms.

The Ball Court leads out to the **Great Plaza.** In this expansive grassy area, which was graded and paved with white stucco during the heyday of the city, are many of Copán's most famous stelae—freestanding sculptures carved on all four sides with pictures of past rulers, gods, and hieroglyphics. Red paint, traces of which can be seen on **Stela C,** built in 730, is thought to have once covered all the stelae. The paint is a mix of mercury sulfate and resins from certain trees found in the valley. Most of the stelae in the Great Plaza were erected during the reign of Smoke Imix (628–695) and 18 Rabbit (695–738), at the zenith of the city's power and wealth.

All of the stelae are fascinating works of art, but one of particular interest is **Stela H** (built in 730), which appears to depict a woman wearing jewelry and a leopard skin under her dress. She may have been 18 Rabbit's wife.

Also worth noting is the round stone next to Stela 4, with a bowl-shaped indent carved into the top, from which curving indentations swirl down the sides. It is believed that human sacrifices were made upon this rock, the blood caught in the bowl-shaped indent, then running down the sides of the stone along the curved indentations, where it was either collected or spilled on the ground.

A wide path leads out of the plaza through a forested area, with many uncovered mounds among the trees, returning visitors to the entrance gate.

Las Sepulturas

Two kilometers up the highway toward San Pedro Sula from the main ruins is the residential area of Las Sepulturas. Ignored by early archaeologists, Las Sepulturas has, in recent years, provided valuable information about the day-to-day lives of Copán's ruling elite. The area received its macabre name ("The Tombs") from local *campesinos,* who farmed in the area and, in the course of their work, uncovered many tombs of nobles who were buried next to their houses, as was the Mayan custom.

Although these ruins are not as visually interesting to the casual tourist as the principal group, they are well worth a visit. The forested trails are always tranquil and uncrowded, and it is interesting to see the residential structures up close, which contain little more than bedrooms and tombs, as cooking was done in separate open-air common kitchens.

Most of the sculpture has been removed, but one remaining piece is the **Hieroglyphic Wall** on Structure 82, a group of 16 glyphs cut in 786, relating events from the reign of Yax Pac, Copán's last ruler. On the same structure is a portrait of **Puah Tun,** the patron of scribes, seated with a seashell ink holder in one hand and a writing tool in the other.

In **Plaza A** of Las Sepulturas, the tomb of a powerful shaman who lived around 450 was discovered; it can be seen in its entirety in the Museo Regional de Arqueología in Copán Ruinas. In this same area, traces of inhabitation dating from 1000 B.C., long predating the Copán dynasty, were found.

Las Sepulturas is connected to the principal group of ruins by an elevated road, called a *sacbé,* which runs through the woods. The road passes through private property, so visitors must go around by the highway. Be sure to bring your ticket from the main ruins, as you must show it to get into Las Sepulturas.

The men hanging out at the entrance offering guide service are highly knowledgeable, some having formerly worked as excavators, and their explanations help bring the ruins to life. Whether you use one of these guides or bring someone from the main site, you can expect to pay US$15 for the service.

Other Sites

In the hills on the far side of the Río Copán, just opposite the ruins, is the small site of **Los Sapos** (The Frogs). Formerly, this rock outcrop carved in the form of a frog must have been quite impressive, but the years have worn down the sculpture considerably. Right near the frog carving, and even harder to make out, is what looks to be the figure of a large woman with her legs spread, as if giving birth. Because of this second carving, archaeologists believe the location was a birthing spot, where Mayan women would come to deliver children. Although the carvings are not dramatic, the hillside setting above the Río Copán valley, across from the main ruins site, is lovely and makes a good two- to three-hour trip on foot or horseback. To get there, leave town heading south and follow the main road over the Río Copán bridge. On the far side, turn left and follow the dirt road along the river's edge. A little farther on, the road forks—follow the right side uphill a couple hundred meters to **Hacienda San Lucas.** The ranch owners have built a small network of trails for visitors to wander along and admire the views, thick vegetation, and noisy bird life. Entrance is U$2. At the ranch is a restaurant serving excellent traditional Honduran countryside food with products made by hand on the farm, like tasty fresh cheese, and a spectacular five-course dinner with revived Mayan recipes (reservations recommended). There are upscale guest rooms here too, if you'd like to stay for a night.

Higher up in the mountains beyond Los Sapos is another site, known as **La Pintada,** a single glyph-covered stela perched on the top of a mountain peak, still showing vestiges of its original red paint. The views out over the Río Copán valley and into the surrounding mountains are fantastic, particularly in the early morning. By foot or horseback, La Pintada is about 2–3 hours from Copán Ruinas. Take the same road to Los Sapos, but stay left along the river instead of turning up to Rancho San Carlos. The road winds steadily up into the mountains, arriving at a gate. From here, it's a 25-minute walk to the hilltop stela. It's best to hire one of the many guides for a negotiable fee in Copán Ruinas to take you there either by foot or on horseback to ensure you don't take a wrong turn. The Asociación de Guías Copán also offers tours to the site.

On the far side of the Río Copán valley is **Stela 10,** another mountaintop stela, which lines up with La Pintada during the spring and fall equinoxes. Covered with glyphs, some of them badly eroded, the stela stands about 2.5 meters high. To get there, drive or walk 4.5 kilometers from Copán Ruinas on the road to Guatemala, and look for a broad, well-beaten trail heading uphill to the right, which leads to the stela in a 10-minute hike. This stela can be easily found without a car. For those without a car, catch a ride to the trail turnoff with one of the frequent pickup trucks to the Guatemalan border.

© AMY E. ROBERTSON

Many of the original carvings from the ruins are now carefully preserved in the sculpture museum.

◖ MUSEO DE ESCULTURA MAYA

As of the summer of 1996, Copán has had a museum befitting the ruins' importance in the world of the ancient Maya. Designed by Honduran architect Angela Stassano, the museum is built into a hillside and illuminated by a massive, open-air skylight. Apart from the full-scale reconstruction of a buried temple, which is the centerpiece of the building, the museum contains some of the finest examples of Mayan sculptures ever found.

The museum's architecture was designed to depict different aspects of Mayan cosmology. The four sides of the building are aligned with the cardinal points of the compass, which were fundamental to the Maya, and also represent the four sides of a cornfield. The two-story design symbolizes the Mayan concept of a lower underworld and the aboveground reality. The first floor contains sculptures of skulls, bats, and other images of death and violence, while the upper floor displays facades from buildings and many of the original stelae commemorating Copán's leaders.

Visitors enter through the gaping jaws of a serpent, used by the Maya to communicate with their deceased ancestors, and a tunnel, similar to those used by archaeologists in uncovering the buried temples, tombs, and buildings at Copán, and meant to evoke a journey to the past. Dominating the center of the museum is a full-scale replica of the Rosalila Temple found under Structure 16 in 1989; the temple was built in 571. The bright colors may be a bit of a shock at first, but all Mayan buildings were once covered with plaster and brightly painted. It will certainly change your attitude toward the Mayan aesthetic—not one of somber elegance but a more exuberant, Technicolor style. With time, exposed to the elements from above, the temple's colors are expected to fade somewhat, replicating the process that must have taken place at the original temple.

A visit to the Museo de Escultura Maya (Mayan Sculpture Museum, 8 A.M.–4 P.M. daily, US$7) is a must to admire the dazzling sculpture of Copán. Apart from displaying the originals of some of the best-known stelae and sculpture in the Mayan world, the museum contains many pieces never before seen by the public. These pieces give a full view of the prodigious abilities of the Mayan craftsmen. The informative signs are in English and Spanish. Take the time to read them all, or hire a guide (US$10) to draw out the highlights—it's a short course in Mayan history and archaeology.

La Entrada and the Ruins of El Puente

LA ENTRADA

Nothing more than a highway junction with a town built around it, La Entrada is worth stopping at only to transfer buses, or to visit the nearby ruins of El Puente, the second-most-developed Mayan site in Honduras after Copán.

Should it be necessary to spend the night in La Entrada, the three-story **Hotel San Carlos** (tel. 504/661-2377, US$26 s, US$37 d), right at the highway junction, has the best rooms and restaurant in town, with air-conditioning and a swimming pool.

While waiting for a bus to Copán (72 kilometers), Santa Rosa de Copán (44 kilometers), or San Pedro Sula (126 kilometers), fill up on *baleadas* and other cheap eats at El Triangulo store and lunch counter, next to the Texaco gas station. Buses to all these destinations frequently pass by, the last usually around 5 or 6 P.M.

EL PUENTE

Located north of the Río Florida valley on the banks of the Río Chinamito, two kilometers north of the Río Chamelecón junction, the modest Mayan ruins at El Puente (8 A.M.–4 P.M. daily, US$3) were first visited by an archaeologist in 1935, when Danish explorer Jens Yde drew a detailed map of the structures. El Puente then received little attention until 1984, when the Japanese Overseas International Cooperation Agency began work on the site in an effort to create a second archaeological attraction in Honduras (thus the

anomalous exhibit on Japan at the visitors center). Of more than 600 sites identified in the La Venta and Florida valleys, only El Puente has been thoroughly excavated and studied. It is thought to have originally been an independent Mayan city-state at the far southeastern periphery of the Mayan zone, trading with the Maya of Guatemala and Copán and also with other Mesoamerican groups farther south and east. By the time of the Classic Maya, A.D. 550–800, El Puente had become a satellite of the opulent, powerful dynasty at Copán.

Because it does not have the incredible artwork of Copán, El Puente does not see even a fraction of the tourists of its more famous neighbor. As a result, it makes for a quiet, relaxing side trip on a journey between Copán and the north coast, if you've got a couple of hours to spare.

The 210 known structures at El Puente cover two square kilometers, but only the main group has been restored. Generally oriented east to west, the main group has five well-defined plazas and is dominated by **Structure 1,** an 11-meter pyramid with six platforms, thought to have been a funerary temple.

Other buildings of note include **Structure 10,** a long pyramid on the south side of Structure 1 that holds an ornate burial chamber, and **Structure 3,** a pyramid complex whose south staircase holds an example of an *alfarda,* an inclined plane of decorative stonework. Tunnels on the top of Structure 10 and

© AMY E. ROBERTSON

The smaller ruins of El Puente are about 90 minutes from Copán Ruinas.

on the side of Structure 3 allow visitors access into both of these buildings.

At the entrance to the site is a small museum with displays on the site itself and on Mayan culture in general, with descriptions in Spanish only.

From the museum, it's about a one-kilometer walk down a shady dirt road to the ruins, which are set amid grassy fields at the edge of a small river. Although the main buildings don't take long to admire, the location is a pleasant place to relax or have a picnic. A nature trail runs through a small wooded area, and you can also take a dip in the river to cool off.

El Puente is in the municipality of La Jigua, six kilometers from the La Entrada–Copán Ruinas highway on a newly paved road. The turnoff is at La Laguna, where you can catch a ride with a passing pickup truck to the ruins for US$1 or so. This road continues past El Puente to a lonesome stretch of the Guatemalan border. Traffic is fairly regular but not always frequent—better in the morning. A return ride can often be found with trucks carrying workers from the site back to La Entrada. A taxi from La Entrada costs US$12–15 round-trip, with a couple of hours at the ruins.

COPÁN

Santa Rosa de Copán

If you liken Tegucigalpa to Washington, D.C., for its politics, San Pedro Sula to New York for its business, and La Ceiba to Miami for the parties, then Santa Rosa de Copán would be the Berkeley of Honduras, a small liberal town that makes a great stopping point for exploring the fascinating and beautiful western highlands and for crossing between Honduras and El Salvador or Guatemala.

Santa Rosa de Copán sits on a hilltop with a commanding view over the surrounding mountainous countryside—including the country's highest peak, Cerro de las Minas in the Sierra de Celaque, to the east. Save for a local cigar factory, Santa Rosa doesn't boast any specific tourist sights in itself, but visitors frequently find themselves staying longer than they planned in this overgrown colonial town of 28,000 people. The climate is pleasantly cool, accommodations and food are inexpensive, and the residents are happy to see outsiders enjoying their town.

Although technically only the capital of the Copán department, Santa Rosa functions as the unofficial capital for all of the western highlands. Almost all commerce in the region passes through Santa Rosa, and *campesinos* from rural areas often wander the city's streets looking for merchandise or selling produce.

Santa Rosa takes pride in its colonial heritage, and the central section of the town is a protected area, with restrictions on building and renovations, to preserve the remaining colonial buildings.

History

During pre-Columbian times, the region around Santa Rosa was a transition zone between the Lenca tribes, centered farther east and south, and the Chortí Maya, who inhabited

view of Santa Rosa de Copán from the city cemetery

© KATE SUCHOMEL

the hill country along the Guatemalan border. The remnants of indigenous villages have been discovered at several sites near Santa Rosa, such as El Pinal, Yarushin, and Zorosca.

Early in the colonial period, the Spaniards established a major settlement nearby at Gracias, but Santa Rosa itself was not founded until 1705. Juan García de la Candelaria, a captain of the Gracias town militia, applied for and was granted an *encomienda* in the name of Santa Rosa de los Llanos, also known as La Sábana. The site was strategically chosen on a hill above a fertile valley, along the royal road between Guatemala City and Gracias; the town quickly prospered as a transport way station and a cattle-ranching area.

A major boost in the nascent town's fortunes came in 1793, when the Spanish crown chose to move the Royal Tobacco Factory from Gracias to Santa Rosa, as the young town was nearer to the producing regions of the Valle de Copán. Santa Rosa grew steadily after this, with migrants coming from Guatemala and directly from Spain to establish their own small farms and businesses. In the late colonial period and well into the 20th century, the tobacco industry based in Santa Rosa was by far the most important economic activity in western Honduras, and as a result the city quickly eclipsed Gracias as the most important urban center in the region.

Santa Rosa, along with Comayagua and Tegucigalpa, was deeply involved in the independence wars and the resulting strife between the different Central American republics. Honduran president José Trinidad Cabañas briefly made Santa Rosa the country's seat of government in 1853, when Honduras was under constant threat from Guatemala. In 1869, when the department of Copán was established, Santa Rosa was designated as its capital.

Orientation and Getting Around

Santa Rosa's downtown is a compact area of several blocks, but the town extends in all directions. The central market is east of the square, near the Ocotepeque highway, which continues down around the edge of town before looping northwest on its way to San Pedro Sula. The bus station is on the highway down the hill about one kilometer north of downtown. Taxis anywhere in Santa Rosa should cost US$0.75.

Addresses frequently refer to quadrants of the city: SO (*suroeste,* or southwest); SE (*sureste,* or southeast), NO (*noroeste,* or northwest), and NE (*noreste,* or northeast).

SIGHTS

In addition to the relaxed ambience, there's one actual attraction in Santa Rosa: the **Flor de Copán cigar factory** (tel. 504/662-0185), formerly in the center of town but now in a larger location next to the bus station, a block off the main highway. Flor de Copán employs 240 workers rolling stogies for export as fast as they can, more than 30,000 cigars a day on average.

Entrance to the factory costs US$2, including tours in Spanish, which are given weekdays at 10 A.M. and 2 P.M. The original Flor de Copán factory (now owned by Altadis USA),

between the park and Hotel Elvir on Avenida Centenario, now serves as the company offices and store—no cigars can be purchased at the factory. Prices are generally about half of U.S. prices. The Santa Rosa mark is considered mild and smooth, while the Don Melo is considerably stronger, made with a Honduran wrapper, a Honduran grown binder, and a blend of Honduran and Nicaraguan filler. The very strong and award-winning Flor de Copán line is actually now produced by Altadis's factory in Danlí. Both the cigar shop and the factory are closed on weekends.

Should you have a passion for coffee, you could also consider stopping by the **Beneficio Maya** (tel. 504/662-1665, www.cafecopan .com), a coffee brokerage where coffee from the surrounding countryside is graded and processed for export. Tours are informal and free. The building is one kilometer west of the bus terminal.

The simple, whitewashed *catedral* on the square was finished in 1803. Under the watch of Bishop Monsignor Ángel María Navarro, it

Santa Rosa's whitewashed cathedral

© KATE SUCHOMEL

HOLY WEEK IN SANTA ROSA DE COPÁN

While Comayagua is famed for its Holy Week celebrations, *Copanecos* put on impressive processions throughout the week to reenact the events of Jesus' final week, his death and resurrection. The town typically posts a schedule of services and processions on the door of the cathedral at the town square.

· **Palm Sunday:** There are several services around town, but the 8 A.M. mass at the **Iglesia de San Martín** is the one to attend, as it's followed by a procession to the cathedral. Evening masses are then held at the cathedral Monday, Tuesday, and Holy Wednesday, at 5 P.M.

· **Maundy Thursday:** At 7 P.M. there is a special Eucharist mass in remembrance of the Last Supper, followed by a washing of feet and a procession. The Procesión de Prendimiento, to remember Jesus' capture by the Romans and incarceration, begins at 10 P.M. at the **Iglesia de las Misericordias** and ends at the cathedral.

· **Good Friday:** Flower and sawdust carpets are laid on the street for the Via Crucis, known in English as the Stations of the Cross, which remembers Jesus' journey to Golgotha with the cross on his shoulders. The procession begins at 8 A.M. at the cathedral and follows a two-kilometer route around town. Arrive early to view the carpets before they are trampled by the processioners. A re-enactment of the crucifixion is held at noon. At 3 P.M. there is another procession, in remembrance of Jesus' burial. At 9 P.M. there is a procession in honor of the "Virgin of Loneliness," an all-woman procession illuminated by candlelight.

· **Holy Saturday:** An Easter Vigil service is held at 10 P.M.

· **Easter Sunday:** Those late to bed or very early to rise have the chance to witness the **Carreritas de San Juan** at 4 A.M., when a statue of Saint John is raced from the cathedral to the **Iglesia de San Antonio,** in representation of John racing to tell the Virgin Mary that Jesus has been resurrected. An hour later the final procession of the week departs from the **Iglesia de San Antonio,** bearing Jesus back to the cathedral, and is followed by Easter Mass. There are several more services during the day for those who can't get out of bed quite that early.

© KATE SUCHOMEL

Residents carefully lay out colored sawdust to create beautiful carpets for Holy Week processions.

was reconstructed in 1948 with a larger altar and other improvements.

In the middle of the square is a two-story kiosk that houses the tourist information booth (tel. 504/662-2234, turismosrc@yahoo.com, 8 A.M.– noon and 1:30–6 P.M. Mon.–Sat.). Limited English is spoken by the staff, but they are happy to supply information on the town, and maps are available for purchase. They also offer Internet access for US$0.75/hour and sell **Copan Dry,** a locally made fruit soft drink. The office can arrange tours of the city center and of a local organic farm, including lunch, with one day's notice (Spanish only). Information about Santa Rosa is also available on its website, www.visitesantarosadecopan .org, including pictures of many of the hotels.

A block south of the square is the **Casa de la Cultura,** which sells books and artwork and has some information on the city and surrounding region.

Several high points near Santa Rosa offer fine views over the town and surrounding countryside on a clear day. One close point is **El Cerrito,** reached by following Avenida Centenario west until the cobblestones end, then following the stairs up to the hilltop. Farther off is the **Hondutel tower,** about a 45-minute walk from town, starting south along 3 Avenida SO.

ENTERTAINMENT AND EVENTS
Festivals and Events

Semana Santa, or Easter Week, is quite a spectacle in Santa Rosa, with elaborate parades throughout the week. Locals create beautiful carpets of colored sawdust and flowers on the streets for the processions to walk on. The culminating parade is the Via Crucis on Friday morning, with "Jesus" carrying his cross through town in a solemn procession.

Another great time to visit is during one of the thrice-annual **Feria de los Llanos.** This artisanal fair with music and cultural performances is held August 25–30, the second week of April, and the second week of December.

◖ FERIA AGOSTINA

A quiet colonial town most of the year, Santa Rosa bursts to life during August, when *copanecos* celebrate their patron saint, the Virgin of Santa Rosa de Lima, with music, food, sporting competitions, and other events. Highlights include the artisanal fair, called **Feria de los Llanos,** held the last week of August, which includes music and cultural performances; the **Noche de Fumadores** (on the third Friday of August), an evening dedicated to fine cigars; and the **Tarde con Aroma a Café,** an afternoon tasting locally grown coffee.

Other events during the month include **Juegos Florales,** a literary competition hosted by the Casa de la Cultura, and the **Feria de Ganaderos,** a cattle expo held in the AGAC field in the Colonia Miraflores. Goods ranging from hand-crafted saddles to handicrafts and cheap toys are sold, and those looking to spice up their visit can try their luck at the mechanical bull or on the dance floor.

Note: The Feria de los Llanos is repeated during Holy Week and in December, should you not be able to make it in August.

Bars

One good option is to go to the bars at **El Rodeo** or **Las Haciendas** restaurants for a few drinks, particularly when they have live music (frequently on weekends). Two other good spots for a drink are **Antigua Hacienda** (from 10 A.M. daily), 1.5 blocks from the *parque,* facing El Rodeo. **Cuates** (from 10 A.M. daily) is another popular spot, serving up Mexican *comida* with its beers. **Zotz,** two blocks from the *parque,* is a slightly yuppified bar with a convivial atmosphere and the best mix drinks in town. Open late.

Movies

Cinema Don Quixote (Plaza Saavedra, 3 Av. NE, across from Hotel Rosario) shows late-release movies from the United States every day at 7 P.M. for US$2. Tuesdays are two-for-one and the movies change weekly on Friday.

ACCOMMODATIONS

There are several budget and midrange options for accommodations in Santa Rosa. Most hotels are within three blocks of the park.

Under US$25

Of the lower-price hotels in town, **Hotel Rosario** (tel. 504/662-0211, US$8 pp shared bath or US$11 pp private bath), half a block north of Hotel Copán, is one of the better, with clean and quiet rooms.

Recently refurnished and much better than previously, **Hotel Santa Eduviges** (tel. 504/662-0380, US$13 s, US$21 d), two blocks from the park, has simple rooms with private bathrooms, TV, fan, and hot water.

An interesting low-cost option, available through the tourist office in the park, is a **homestay** (tel. 504/662-0425, US$10.50 s, US$18–24 d) run by the very sweet Doña Aura de Montalván, who lives on the ground floor. Doña Aura rents out three rooms upstairs that share a sitting area and kitchen—all very clean, comfortable, and spacious. You can also book via email by contacting the tourist office (turismo src@yahoo.com) and see pictures of the rooms at the town's website, www.visitesantarosade copan.org (click on *hoteles,* then *alojamiento con familia*).

US$25-50

Two similar new places almost opposite each other on Avenida 2 SO are **San Jorge** (tel. 504/662-2521, US$21 s, US$32 d, a/c available for US$5 more) and **Alondra** (tel. 504/662-1194, US$17 s, US$29 d), the former with enormous and rather barren rooms (although with parking and free wireless Internet), and the latter cozier and friendlier, and with great showers.

For travelers getting in late or leaving early, **Hotel Grand Mayaland** (tel. 504/662-0233, US$21 s, US$36 d), across from the bus station on the highway below town, has its own restaurant and modern rooms, and breakfast is included with the room. The hotel parking lot has a night watchman, and there's also a pool.

The best hotel in town is **Hotel Elvir** (tel./fax 504/662-0103, www.hotelelvir.com, US$35 s, US$47 d, US$11–13 more for a/c), three blocks west of the park on Calle Centenario, with modern rooms; credit cards accepted. The staff is helpful and the cafeteria serves tasty and reasonably priced food. Room service and Internet

are available, and there's a pool, too. Max Elvir, an enthusiastic promoter of small-scale tourism in the area, runs **Lenca Travel** (tel. 504/9997-5340, lencatours@gmail.com) out of the hotel, offering tours of surrounding villages and natural areas, including Celaque, Monte Quetzal, Belén Gualcho, San Manuel Colohete, and any other place you might want to visit. Rates depend on how many people want to go, and Max—who speaks English—is an excellent and affable guide. If you have your own wheels, Max charges US$75 per day for guiding only.

A new hotel with a charming old colonial style is the **Hotel Antiguo Roble** (tel. 504/662-0472, US$26 s, US$36 d, hotel antiguoroble@hotmail.es), half a block east of BAMER bank. The hotel has clean rooms with air-conditioning, free wireless Internet in the lobby, and a coffee shop. Guests receive a coupon for a free coffee and pastry for breakfast.

A step up in comfort is **Hotel Casa Real** (tel. 504/662-0802, US$42 s, US$57 d), four blocks northwest of the *parque,* with clean rooms with TV and hot water, or a bit more for air-conditioning. Amenities include free wireless Internet throughout the hotel, a nice, clean swimming pool, and a restaurant open until 10 P.M. that even serves tea. **Hotel VIP Copán** (tel. 504/662-1576, US$25 s, US$37 d), two blocks east of the church, has smallish rooms (with the exception of its spacious suites), an attractive swimming pool, and parking.

FOOD
Snacks and Coffee

Ten Napel Café, now on 1 Calle NE, next to Banco Atlántida, has great wooden decor, free wireless Internet, and an outdoor garden, and serves posh coffee and snacks, including bagels.

Honduran

For breakfast, there's a cluster of inexpensive places just west of Hotel Elvir, and also along 1 Calle NE between 2 and 3 Avenidas.

Pollito Dorado, a block west of Hotel Elvir, serves basic Honduran standards and good fried chicken in a relaxed, inexpensive restaurant.

The egg and bean *baleadas,* in a large, crispy flour tortilla, are an excellent light meal for only US$0.50. The restaurant serves a decent breakfast also. Open daily until 10 P.M.

Buffet Baleadas y Más has the best *baleadas* in town (US$0.60 for a *simple,* US$0.75 with egg or avocado), as well as a *plato del día,* usually chicken or beef.

For a wide selection of well-cooked Honduran standards, try **Hemady's Típico** (7:45 A.M.–10 P.M. daily), one and a half blocks west of the park on Centenario, a simple restaurant with good renditions of Honduran classics for US$2–5.

A step up is **Las Haciendas** (US$3–7 per entrée), with two locations in the center of town, both with bars. One good, low-price deal is the large sandwich for US$2. The westernmost location is open until late (midnight-ish) most nights, and even later (3 A.M.) on the second and fourth Saturdays of the month, when they host live music. In the same neighborhood is the similar **El Rodeo,** with a good *plato típico,* nachos, hamburgers, and inexpensive drinks. They have live music frequently throughout the week, especially on weekends. Owned by the mayor, this is one of the places the local intelligentsia like to hang out.

If you're hungry while waiting for the bus, the *comedor* at the terminal serves fried chicken, and the **JM** buffet restaurant right nearby has a hearty all-you-can-eat buffet for US$5 per person.

International

The American-owned **Pizza Pizza** (tel. 504/662-1104, daily except Wednesday until 9 P.M.), on Calle Centenario at 5 Avenida NE, serves up a decent pizza pie, as well as grinders, spaghetti, and garlic bread, all at reasonable prices. It does not serve beer.

Weekend's Pizza (tel. 504/662-4121, 4 Av. and 2 Calle SO, 10:30 A.M.–9 P.M. Wed.–Sun.) is owned by a former Peace Corps volunteer and her Honduran husband. They drive to San Pedro Sula weekly to bring back ingredients you can't find anywhere in Santa Rosa, such as Gouda cheese and sun-dried tomatoes.

INFORMATION AND SERVICES
Banks

Banco de Occidente is the best for exchanging dollars and travelers checks, while **Banco Atlántida** has a cash machine at its branch by the bus terminal, in the new shopping center with the 20 Menos supermarket. Cash advances on a Visa card are available at Banco Atlántida and BGA.

Communications

Hondutel (7 A.M.–9 P.M. daily) and **Honducor** are next to each other on the west side of the park.

For Internet access, several places downtown have computers, including **Zeus Cyber Café** (9 A.M.–10 P.M. daily), one block west of the park, for US$0.80 per hour, and **SIMA Internet,** a block and a half west of the park on Calle Centenario, for the same price.

Laundry

At **Lavandería Wash and Dry,** on 1 Calle NE, half a block from Plaza Saavedra, laundry is a steep US$5 a load.

Spanish Schools

Should the climes and friendly feel of Santa Rosa tempt you to stay a while, you could fill your time taking Spanish classes at the **Santa Rosa de Copán Language School** (tel. 504/662-1378, www.spanish-ili-copan .com). Santa Rosa would certainly be a relaxing place to spend a few weeks or months studying, and unlike in Antigua, Guatemala, you wouldn't speak a whole lot of English in your free time. The school costs US$240 a week for four hours of classes a day in a program of two to four weeks (or $120 per week for two hours a day), and homestays are sometimes available, for $12.50 per day.

Emergencies and Immigration

If you have an emergency, you may find the following numbers helpful: *policía,* tel. 504/662-0091 or 504/662-0308, or dial 199; **fire department,** tel. 504/662-1719, or dial 198; **Red Cross** (for an ambulance), tel. 504/662-0045, or dial 195; and the **hospital,** tel. 504/662-0128 or 504/662-0093.

The *migración* office is one block northwest of the park.

GETTING THERE AND AWAY
Bus

Unless otherwise noted, all buses depart from the main bus terminal on the San Pedro Sula highway about one kilometer north of town. Taxis between the terminal and downtown cost US$0.80, although sometimes you take a scenic tour dropping off other passengers on the way into town.

To **Gracias,** 10 buses depart daily between 6:30 A.M. and 6 P.M. (US$2.15, about 90 minutes).

To **Nueva Ocotepeque, Sultana** (tel. 504/662-0940) runs hourly buses starting at 8:45 A.M., with the last departing at 8 P.M., charging US$4. Most go on to the **Guatemalan border,** while the 8:45 A.M. bus heads to San Salvador (US$16).

To **San Pedro Sula, Toritos y Copanecos** runs three direct buses daily that take only 2.5 hours instead of four (8 A.M., 9:30 A.M., and 2 P.M., US$5.60) and are worth planning on. Regular buses run 4–11 A.M., and cost US$3.70. The express buses continue to **Tegucigalpa** (US$8.80, six hours), or take any bus to San Pedro in the morning and transfer at the San Pedro terminal. Regular buses (*ordinarios* to San Pedro leave every 30 minutes between 4:30 A.M. and 5:30 P.M. from the main terminal for US$2.80.

To **Copán Ruinas,** take a bus to La Entrada and catch another bus or a *rapidito* on to Copán Ruinas.

To **Corquín,** eight buses depart daily between 8 A.M. and midafternoon (US$2.25, one hour).

To **Belén Gualcho,** there are two buses a day at 10:30 A.M. and 11:30 A.M. (US$2.50, about three hours).

To **San Agustín,** one bus departs daily at 3 P.M., returning at 7 P.M. (US$2). From here, hitchhike or walk over the recently graded

camino real down to Santa Rita near Copán Ruinas, an easy day's walk.

Car

The highways to La Entrada (44 kilometers), San Pedro Sula (170 kilometers), Gracias (47 kilometers), and Nueva Ocotepeque (92 kilometers) are all paved and well maintained, although a good rainy season can make a liar out of anyone.

NEAR SANTA ROSA DE COPÁN

A portion of the old *camino real,* now a dirt road, passes near Santa Rosa, beginning in the village of San Agustín, beyond Dulce Nombre de Copán. From here you can walk over the crest of the mountains down to Santa Rita, near Copán Ruinas, in a day. It's also fairly easy to catch a *jalón* on a passing pickup truck along the scenic road, which comes out by Hacienda El Jaral, just north of Santa Rita.

Near the *camino real,* on the south side, close to the highest point in the road, is the privately owned **Monte Quetzal,** a 1,900-meter mountain with dense cedar forest and plenty of its avian namesakes flitting among the trees. On the top of the mountain is a lush fern forest. An old mine, abandoned in 1965, can be explored up to 200 meters into the hillside. Max Elvir of Lenca Travel knows the owner and can arrange trips there for US$25 a day per person for a small group. Although the mountain is rich with its namesake birds, quetzals are notoriously difficult to spot, but with a bit of luck and patience, you just might see the long-tailed bird. Easier to spot are the countless centennial trees, including cedar, liquidambar (American sweet gum), oak, and calabash.

Sixteen kilometers from Santa Rosa on the San Pedro highway is a dirt road turnoff to the east leading to **Quezailica,** a small town centered around the beautiful **Santuario del Milagroso Cristo Negro, El Señor del Buen Fin,** built in 1660 and declared a national monument in 1987. In the church is a carved wooden Cristo Negro (Black Christ), made by an unknown artist who was apparently a student of famed sculptor Quirio Cataño, who made the Cristo Negro of Esquipulas. A major Chortí Mayan community in pre-Columbian times, this area contains many relics of the Chortí Maya, including an odd rock monolith carved in the shape of a face, which was found hidden in the church's atrium and is now sitting outside the church. One bus drives to Quezailica from Santa Rosa at 1 P.M., every day but Sunday. You can also take any bus to La Entrada and get down at the turnoff to San José. From there you can either catch a *rápidito* or walk the seven kilometers to Quezailica.

The town festival, on January 15, is a major event for the entire region. Pilgrims follow an old *camino real* to the church and the Cristo Negro, with some 50,000 people visiting in a period of five days. Max Elvir of Lenca Travel has arranged a tour that costs US$10, providing transportation to the village of Las Sandías, from where visitors walk on an old *camino real* the 1.5–2 hours to Quezailica. Max will drop avid hikers in Belén for a longer walk that meets up with the other visitors in Las Sandías.

Belén Gualcho

Accessible by dirt road from Santa Rosa de Copán via Cucayagua and Corquín, high on the side of the Sierra de Celaque, is the mountain town of Belén Gualcho. The town is dominated by a well-maintained triple-domed colonial-era church, among the most beautiful in the country. Great views of the church are had from the local grade school—the guard will usually let you in if you ask nicely.

The town hosts a large **Sunday market,** which attracts *campesinos* from the mountain villages and is quite a colorful and lively event, well worth scheduling your trip to see. It's pretty much done by 11 A.M., so if you want to see it, you have to get there the night before, and best to be early on Saturday before the hotels fill up.

Belén's annual festival is held on January 17 in honor of San Antonio de Abad. The story goes that in years past, a spirit was so impressed by Belén's festival that every year he arrived on a black mule and took part in the revelry himself,

afterward disappearing into the hills. But one year, a group of young men thought it would be amusing to attach a bunch of firecrackers to the mule's tail. Offended by this evident lack of respect for his otherworldliness, the spirit—known as El Hombre de Belén Gualcho—rode off in a huff and has never returned.

A comfortable hotel in Belén is **Hotelito El Carmen** (no phone, US$2–6), with 20 clean rooms. Bathrooms are communal, and no hot water is available. Some private rooms are available for a bit more. Don't come out here expecting luxury. Similar although less clean is **Hotel Olvin** (US$3–6, the pricier rooms with private bath). Both hotels are often full on Saturday nights, before the Sunday market, but other rooms can often be found by asking around, particularly in the stores.

Of the local eateries in town, **Comedor Raquel** serves good, inexpensive *típico* food in a friendly little dining room.

There's a small Internet shop open daily next to Hotel Olvin.

It's easy to combine a visit to **Corquín** with a trip to Belén Gualcho. Corquín is an attractive colonial village, and there are waterfalls nearby. Both *comida típica* and tourist information are available at **La Casa Grande Restaurante,** located in a colonial house in town.

One bus travels daily between Belén and Santa Rosa de Copán, via Cucayagua and Corquín, leaving Santa Rosa at 1 P.M. There are also buses that go between San Pedro Sula and Belén Gualcho, passing Santa Rosa at 10 A.M. and 2 P.M., reaching Corquín in another 1.5–2 hours and Belén Gualcho another 45 minutes after that. Alternatively, you can catch the more frequent buses to Corquín and try to hitch from there, though pickups are often full already. The schedule for buses back to Santa Rosa from Belén (US$2) varies, but they all leave early in the morning, the exception being Sundays, when the last buses leave at midday. If coming by car, the turn to Corquín and Belén Gualcho is off the Santa Rosa–Nueva Ocotepeque highway, 16 miles from Santa Rosa. Be forewarned that the 24-kilometer stretch between Corquín and

Belén Gualcho can be pretty challenging, best for a four-wheel-drive.

Near Belén Gualcho

Two or three hours of stiff hiking from Belén Gualcho, via the *aldea* (village) of El Paraíso, takes a visitor to the spectacular, 50-meter **Santa María de Gualcho waterfall,** up a narrow canyon on the Río Negro. A guide is necessary to find the trail. COHDEFOR workers José Alonso de Diós and Juan Alberto Martínez, who live in El Paraíso, charge US$5 to guide the five- or six-hour round-trip.

La Mohaga, about a three-hour hike from Belén, is a good day hike, to see both this lovely little village (known for locally made wine) and the spectacular scenery on the walk. To get there from Belén, take the main road out of town, and before the houses stop, turn left uphill. Continue up for an hour, and then the path levels off, with fine views. Pass two junctions, sticking to your left at both. It's usually possible to sleep in the community building across from the *pulpería* in La Mohaga if you get there late in the day.

From La Mohaga you can head back to Belén, or if you want to continue for more than one day, ask locals to point out the trail for Hojalaca, and from there on to Rancho Pericón and then to San Sebastián in a few hours, where you can spend the night and continue on the next day to San Manuel Colohete and Gracias. It's possible to walk from Belén Gualcho to San Sebastián in six hours if you keep up a good pace. Part of this walk is on portions of an old *camino real,* or Spanish royal road.

Adventurous hikers can find guides up into Sierra de Celaque from Belén Gualcho, and from there continue down the far side to Gracias. This is best done with a guide.

Lepaera

Heading south toward Gracias, about 45 minutes from Santa Rosa, is the town of Lepaera. Settled in 1538, Lepaera is one of the oldest settlements in the area, although it wasn't granted the title of city until 1956. Be sure to take note of the town church, which, according the inscription over its entrance, dates from July 28, 1640.

Lepaera is in the foothills of the Puca mountain, and guides in town can take travelers on a visit to the cloud forests of the **Refugio de Vida Silvestre Puca.** The high elevation is perfect for coffee, and plantations in the area are booming.

The **Hotel Murillo** (tel. 504/655-5383, US$10.50 s, US$16 d) offers rooms with air-conditioning and Internet access.

There are several spots in town where tourists can buy homemade ground coffee, known as *café de palo.* Coffee from Gregorio Martinez's farm took first prize at a national "Cup of Excellence" competition in 2004.

The town's holidays are January 25, in honor of the Señor de Esquipulas, and July 25, in honor of Santiago (Saint James).

To get to Lepaera by car from Santa Rosa, take the turnoff a couple of kilometers after Las Flores (in between two tight curves), about 15 kilometers before Gracias.

Gracias and the Lenca Highlands

One of the natural and cultural treasures of Honduras, the mountain country between Gracias, La Esperanza, and the Salvadoran border is a beautiful region of pine forest and infrequently visited colonial villages. Foreign tourists who make it to the town of Gracias and to the nearby Sierra de Celaque, a national park boasting the country's highest peak, are rewarded with thoughtful opportunities for community tourism, constantly improving amenities for accommodations and food, and spectacular scenery.

The dirt roads and trails connecting the highland villages of Belén Gualcho, La Campa, San Manuel Colohete, Erandique, and beyond are lovely places to lose yourself for days at a time, admiring the colonial villages seemingly long-forgotten in their secluded corners of the rugged countryside. The Lenca *campesinos* populating the region are extremely friendly, and although some might wonder what you're doing out there, the worst that will happen is you'll be invited in for so many cups of coffee you'll never get anywhere and end up all jittery on caffeine.

Those who spend time in this region should try to keep a certain sensitivity to the realities and customs of the *campesinos* who inhabit the countryside. One is expected to stop and greet others met on the trail, at least with a gentle handshake (none of those U.S. finger-breaking grips, please) and a friendly hello. You are not, of course, required to stop, have coffee, and talk at every home you pass, but always offer a polite decline. It's worth accepting the invitation once in a while. You never know—a conversation with a *campesino* family out in the mountains of Honduras, asking about their lives and telling them about yours, may end up being one of your most memorable travel experiences. Try to take it with aplomb when you are surrounded and pursued relentlessly by a dozen local kids.

Tours

In Gracias, the **tourist office** (tel. 504/222-2124, turismo-colosuca@yahoo.com) has developed fantastic tourist information for the **Colosuca Tourist Circuit**—the region encompassing Parque Nacional Celaque, the town of Gracias, and the villages of La Campa, San Manuel Colohete, San Marcos de Caiquín, San Sebastián, and Belén (that's Belén, Lempira, not Belén Gualcho, Ocotepeque).

The **Asociación de Guías Turísticos Colosuca-Celaque** has 15 community guides (with limited English) available for tours in Gracias, Celaque, and the surrounding villages. They can also arrange trips on horses. Village day trips cost US$26, and overnight trips to Celaque are US$42. They also offer day trips to La Campa village with pottery-making demonstrations for US$21, a six-hour tour to a waterfall (US$16), and a four-hour tour of Gracias

for US$10.50. Tour prices exclude transportation, but the guides can arrange for service in minivan, by bicycle, or on horseback. The coordinator of the association is Marco Aurelio Rodríguez (tel. 504/656-0627 or 504/9870-8821, guiamarcolencas@yahoo.com). Marco is the owner of El Jarrón restaurant near the entrance to town, so you can also just stop by for information.

With better English, and a bit pricier but also very good, **Walter Murcia** (tel. 504/656-1113, waltermurcia@hotmail.com) can organize transport to Celaque park and guides one-day or multiday trips to the mountain and surrounding villages. He is very knowledgeable about the local area. A day trip for up to four people going to five Lenca villages near Gracias, including going inside the churches, which can be difficult alone, costs US$100. Celaque trips are also available.

Both guide outfits can help arrange camping gear if you don't have any.

◖ GRACIAS

A sleepy colonial town, its days of glory as the capital of Central America more than four centuries in the past, Gracias makes a great base to explore this beautiful region of western Honduras. Formerly just a destination for backpackers, Gracias is these days attracting more tourists of all varieties, drawn by the town's colonial architecture; the cloud forest atop the Celaque mountain range, southwest of town; and nearby Lenca villages, including La Campa and San Manuel Colohete.

Fossil hunters will be interested to learn that in the vicinity of Gracias are Miocene-era **fossil beds.** Though picked over by major foreign expeditions in the 1940s, plenty of fossils remain to be discovered.

Summer in the area is March and April, when it can get quite hot and air-conditioning becomes a good investment. Not even a fan is necessary for a visit October through January.

History

Founded in the earliest phase of the conquest of Honduras, Gracias a Dios was relocated twice

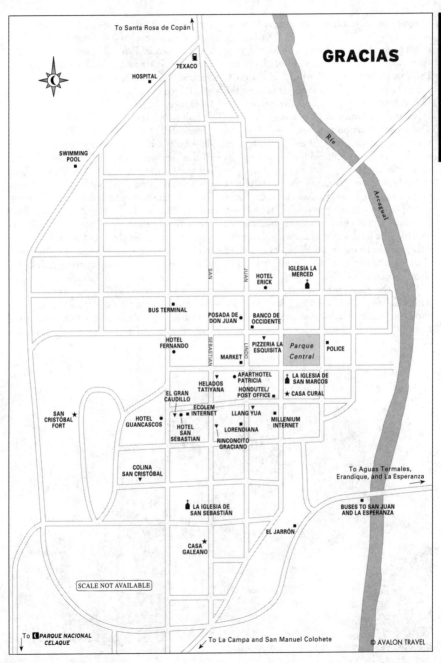

GRACIAS

To Santa Rosa de Copán

TEXACO
HOSPITAL

SWIMMING POOL

Río Arcagual

SAN JUAN

HOTEL ERICK

IGLESIA LA MERCED

BUS TERMINAL

POSADA DE DON JUAN

BANCO DE OCCIDENTE

SEBASTIAN

HOTEL FERNANDO

MARKET

LINDO

PIZZERIA LA ESQUISITA

Parque Central

POLICE

HELADOS TATIYANA

APARTHOTEL PATRICIA

LA IGLESIA DE SAN MARCOS

EL GRAN CAUDILLO

HONDUTEL/ POST OFFICE

CASA CURAL

SAN CRISTÓBAL FORT

ECOLEM INTERNET

LLANG YUA

HOTEL GUANCASCOS

HOTEL SAN SEBASTIAN

LORENDIANA

MILLENIUM INTERNET

RINCONCITO GRACIANO

COLINA SAN CRISTÓBAL

To Aguas Termales, Erandique, and La Esperanza

LA IGLESIA DE SAN SEBASTIÁN

BUSES TO SAN JUAN AND LA ESPERANZA

EL JARRÓN

CASA GALEANO

SCALE NOT AVAILABLE

To **PARQUE NACIONAL CELAQUE**

To La Campa and San Manuel Colohete

© AVALON TRAVEL

before being established at its current location on January 14, 1539, by Bishop Cristóbal de Pedraza and Juan de Montejo under orders of Francisco de Montejo, then ruler of Honduras. In those early years, the would-be colonists were engaged in a fierce struggle against the Lenca leader Lempira, and the settlement was apparently moved for strategic reasons. The second location reportedly served as the main Spanish base for quelling the revolt, after which the town was moved farther south to its present location.

According to legend, the town received its name because one of the conquistadors had a heck of a time finding any land flat enough for a town in the mountainous region. When a suitable spot was located, the Spaniards reportedly gave the heartfelt cry, "Thank God we've finally found flat land!" Hence, Gracias a Dios (later shortened to "Gracias").

With the establishment of the Audiencia de los Confines in Gracias on May 16, 1544, the town became the administrative center of Central America. The *audiencia* was a royal court of sorts with power to impart civil and criminal justice and a jurisdiction ranging from the Yucatán to Panama. Some of the larger towns in Guatemala and El Salvador quickly became jealous of the prestige accorded Gracias and forced the *audiencia* to move to Antigua, Guatemala, in late 1548.

Following the removal of the *audiencia,* Gracias fell into a long, slow slide. When the little gold and silver in the area were quickly worked within a couple of decades after the conquest, local colonists had little to fall back on beyond cattle-ranching and tobacco production. Gracias remained an important administrative center for Honduras throughout the colonial period, but by the early 19th century, nearby Santa Rosa de Copán had taken over the tobacco industry and, not long after, also became the de facto regional capital.

Over the past decade Gracias has worked hard (and successfully) to put itself back on the map through the development of a tourist industry. Capitalizing on the rich human and natural resources in the region, the town has

the 400-year-old Iglesia La Merced in Gracias

© AMY E. ROBERTSON

established itself as a premier base for travelers looking for that elusive travel experience—approachable authenticity.

Sights

Of the four churches in Gracias, **La Merced,** a block north of the *parque* (square) is by far the most attractive. Construction on its ornate sculpted facade began in 1611 and lasted 30 years. It is open on Saturday, when mass is held. The main church on the *parque,* **La Iglesia de San Marcos,** was built in 1715 (open on Sunday). Next door, formerly used as the *casa cural* (priests' house) and now housing a radio station, is the building that once housed the Audiencia de los Confines. A total renovation of the central park is scheduled to be completed in 2009, which will hopefully turn it back into a sight worth seeing.

In the center of a shady square a few blocks southwest of the main square is **La Iglesia de San Sebastián,** also known as La Ermita. Built in 1930, the exterior at least is in good condition—it's hard to know anything about the interior, since the church only opens for a mass once a year, on its namesake day (January 20, commemorating the death of Saint Sebastian). Gracias has four churches but currently only one priest. The surrounding park is basically a dirt lot, but it has some good play equipment.

On the east side of La Ermita is the **Casa Galeano** (9 A.M.–6 P.M. daily, US$1.60), the former colonial residence of a prominent longtime Gracias family. Nicely restored with the help of the Spanish government, the Casa Galeano now houses a simple museum on the region, worth the small admission fee for a quick look. Admission also includes entry to the unimpressive botanical garden behind the house.

The Galeano family now resides in another building, and Eduardo "Mito" Galeano is a respected Honduran painter who will sometimes show visitors samples of his work—ask around to find his nearby workshop. Many of Galeano's paintings take as their subject matter village life in western Honduras.

Perched on a hill just west of downtown, the **San Cristóbal fort** was built in the mid-

19th century as an afterthought to the turbulence raging across Central America in earlier decades. In spite of its impressive construction, the fort never saw any action and now fills with families on outings and lounging teens on a Sunday afternoon. The fort was the idea of Honduran and Salvadoran president Juan Lindo (he served 1847–1852), and the fort was built around his tomb six years after his death. In addition to admiring the two cannons (brought from the fort at Omoa), a good reason to visit is to check out the views across Gracias, the surrounding countryside, and Sierra de Celaque looming up to the southwest. The fort's gates are open 7 A.M.–5 P.M. daily.

Gracias's fourth church is **La Iglesia de Santa Lucía,** two kilometers down the road toward the Celaque visitors center.

Entertainment and Events

Thanks to its four churches, Gracias celebrates four *ferias patronales* a year: January 20 (San Sebastián), April 25 (San Marcos), September 28 (La Merced), and December 13 (Santa Lucía). Of special note are the unique **guancascos** that take place during the January and December festivities. A *guancasco* is a traditional masked dance representing peace and communication between two communities. In Gracias, the neighborhoods of San Sebastián and Mexicapa (by the church of Santa Lucía) reenact this encounter.

On July 20 the town commemorates the death of the Lencan hero Lempira, with hundreds of schoolchildren parading in Indian-style costumes and a reenactment of Lenca's betrayal and death.

If you happen to be in town close to Christmas, be on the lookout for the *posadas,* where children carol around the town (December 16–24, 6–7:15 P.M.). Head to the restaurant Rinconcito Graciano at 5:30 P.M. and talk to the owner, Lizeth Perdomo, if you are interested in either participating or watching.

According to Lizeth, at Christmastime families also set up crèches, or nativity scenes, in their living rooms, and in the afternoons leave their doors open, welcoming passersby to peek in and admire the crèche.

It bears noting that Gracias has virtually no nightlife and is proud of its quiet, small-town nature. Your best bet after dinner is a beer at the terrace of **Hotel Guancascos** for some conversation and a view, or a drink at **Candil,** half a block east from Guancascos.

Shopping

Although small, the gift shop at **El Jarrón** probably offers the best selection of souvenirs in town, ranging from tourist kitsch to well-made Lencan pottery made by women in La Campa. Another possibility is **Artesanías y Más,** a block north and 1.5 blocks east of the central park.

A visit to **Lorendiana** is a must, if only to admire the eye-catching displays of jarred pickles, chilies, pineapple, onions, and salsas. Candies made with *dulce de leche* mixed with vanilla (yum!) or with nance fruit (gag!) are available, or satisfy your sweet tooth with a homemade popsicle from one of the giant freezers. Flavors include mango, milk with cinnamon, and blackberry, to name just a few of the dozen or so varieties.

Recreation

The perfect remedy for limbs aching from all that traveling, especially if you've just slogged up to the top of Sierra de Celaque, is a visit to the *aguas termales.*

The cheapies are about five kilometers east of Gracias, a couple of bumpy kilometers off the road to La Esperanza. The first set, Las Marias, has three stone pools—one at 40°C (104°F), the other two at 37°C (99°F)—are built around the springs, surrounded by large trees and thick vegetation. One of the pools is long enough to take a few swimming strokes across, a very pleasurable experience in the warm water. A small restaurant at the pools serves up soft drinks, beers, and snacks and meals, and a barbecue pit is available for rent.

The second set of four pools, Presidente, is a bit lower down, and pleasant but not quite as warm. There is one shallow pool perfect

for kids, and at the pool off to the right ask the locals to show you the sulfur stone that can be crushed on the spot into a facial mask. The lower pools have a snack bar selling chips, sodas, and beer, as well as changing rooms and restrooms. Bring your own towels. Both sets of pools are open 5 A.M.–11 P.M. or later daily, and cost US$1.50. Reputedly there will soon be massages available here.

To get there without a car, hire a *mototaxi* for US$3 (one way), hitch a ride up the La Esperanza road to the turnoff, or start walking up the road and keep an eye out for a path heading off to the right—a shortcut to the pools, just past the second bridge outside of town. It takes about 90 minutes walking by the road and about an hour by the trail—or just 10 minutes if you have your own wheels.

Alternatively, head seven kilometers toward Santa Rosa de Copán to reach **Termas del Río** (5 A.M.–11 P.M. daily, US$5.25), a complex that offers nature trails, horseback rides, children's play equipment, massages, barbecue pits, and handicapped access, in addition to the pools.

In addition to the fantastic hiking on Sierra de Celaque, there are a number of **trails** in the foothills near Gracias. There is a trail map available at the Hotel Guancascos, indicating paths that lead to the thermal baths, or through the *aldeas* (villages) around Gracias.

Horseback riding can be arranged through Hotel Guancascos, US$42 for one person, US$53 for two, and US$21 per person for three or more, including transportation and a guide.

Accommodations
UNDER US$25

Travelers looking to save their lempiras should head directly to **Hotel Erick** (tel. 504/656-1066, angelcar@yahoo.com, US$10.50 s/d with hot water, US$8 s/d without), one block north of the square, which has spotless if bare-bones rooms.

Another budget option, on the road heading out of town, is **Hotel San Antonio** (US$5.50 pp) for basic rooms with shared baths.

The modern **Hotel San Francisco** (tel.

504/656-1559, www.hotel-sanfrancisco.com, US$20 s, US$24 d, with fan, US$29 s/d with a/c), above a shop a block west of the *parque central,* has spacious, travel lodge–style rooms with cable TV and nice bathrooms. The windows in rooms 1 and 2 face out toward the street and hills, while the windows of all other rooms face the interior hall.

Around the corner from Hotel Guancascos, conveniently sandwiched between a decent restaurant and an Internet café, is **Hotel San Sebastián** (tel. 504/656-0398, hotel-san sebastian@yahoo.com, US$17 s, US$24 d, US$2.50 more for air-conditioning). The eight simple rooms have TVs and clean, good bathrooms.

Hotel Fernando (tel. 504/656-1231, fmg 1insoprosa@yahoo.com, US$16 s, US$21 d), a block north of Hotel Guancascos on the same street, has seven double rooms in a motel layout, the exterior of each one painted in a different color. The rooms have fans, cable TV, and wireless Internet (at least in the rooms closest to the router at the hotel restaurant).

US$25-50

The most popular digs in town are at **Hotel Guancascos** (tel. 504/656-1219, www.guan cascos.com, US$25 s, US$32 d), three blocks west and one block south of the *parque central,* offering 17 rooms tastefully built in a rustic style, with hot water, cable TV, fan, and a large window. Banana trees and other plants grow around the grounds. Rooms 7, 8, and 9, under the restaurant, have beautiful views. The restaurant is a good place to meet other travelers in Gracias and to gather tourist information, and it has a computer with free Internet access for hotel guests to use. Guancascos also rents sleeping bags (US$2) and tents (US$5–10), and can arrange outings on horseback.

A fantastic addition to Gracias's hotel scene is **Finca El Capitán** (tel. 504/656-1659, www.hotelfincaelcapitan.galeon.com, hotel fincaelcapitan@yahoo.com, US$16 s, US$32 d, a few dollars more for a/c), facing the Santa Lucía church on the outskirts of town (on the road that leads to Celaque). The 20 rooms

are spaced through 12 cabins painted in rose, peach, and teal, encircling a large common area with grass and banana trees, a swimming pool, and children's play area. Beds have colonial-style dark-wood headboards, and the cabin porches have hammocks and rocking chairs in which to while away an afternoon. There is a full-service restaurant (breakfast US$2–3, dinner US$4–5), decorated with hollow gourds and animal hides.

The swankiest place in town is **Posada de Don Juan** (tel. 504/656-1020, www.posadade donjuanhotel.com), with luxury linens and flat-screen TVs, as well as a restaurant, swimming pool, parking, and wireless Internet access. The best rooms are around the pool; the others encircle the parking lot motel-style, jarring with the otherwise decidedly-upscale ambience. Singles are US$24–52 and doubles US$34–58, depending on if the room has a fan or air-conditioning, and whether the beds are full-size or queens. There are also rooms available with three double beds (US$46–79).

The much simpler **Aparthotel Patricia** (tel. 504/656-1281, US$32 s/d) is another acceptable option, with five spacious rooms with tiled bathrooms and cable TV. The hotel has one very large apartment for US$53, with two bedrooms and a full kitchen. The furnishings are nothing special, but if space is what you need, Patricia's got it.

By the Presidente thermal baths is **Villas del Agua Caliente** (tel. 504/656-1172, villasdel aguacalientehotel@hotmail.com, US$32 s/d), with 16 rooms in three cabins, plus a restaurant. The cabins have ochre stucco walls and exposed beams, as well as a fan and TV; some rooms can accommodate up to six. The pools are fun to visit at night, and after a few hours in the pools, with a couple of beers, having a bed nearby is not such a bad idea.

Outside of town is the group-friendly **Villa de Ada** (tel. 504/656-0763, www.villadeada .com, US$25 s, US$27 d), with square cabins set near lagoons. There are swimming pools for adults and children, and it's possible to take a boat ride or fish in the lagoon (the restaurant is known for its fried tilapia).

COPÁN

Food

Restaurante Guancascos (tel. 504/656-1219, 7 A.M.–10 P.M. daily) has cornered the market on travelers, and it's easy to see why. The restaurant, with a fine view over Gracias and the surrounding countryside, is run by a friendly and knowledgeable Dutch woman who offers Honduran standards at reasonable prices. Something vegetarian is always available. The food might take a while to arrive, so relax with a couple of beers and talk with other travelers about the many places to see around Gracias. Books and handicrafts are for sale, camping gear for Celaque hikes is rented here, and you can arrange rides to the park and guided trips with Walter Murcia, who can be contacted through the restaurant. You can also look at topographical maps for the area, although they aren't for sale.

◖ **Rinconcito Graciano** (tel. 504/656-1171) serves both creative and traditional Lenca dishes with all-natural ingredients in an atmospheric environment with wood tables and Lencan decor. The chicken in a *loroco*-spinach-mushroom sauce is delicious, as are the fruit juices and *atoles* that come served in cups made of gourds. The *artesanías* adorning the walls are all locally made. The owner, Lizeth Perdomo, is a fervent preservationist of local culture, one of the community guides, and a great source of information on the region. She can be contacted for guiding information at 504/9869-1335 (Spanish only). The restaurant is sometimes closed when Lizeth is running errands, but just give her a call and she'll come cook you a meal.

Around the corner from Guancascos, **El Gran Caudillo,** "the great chief," so named in honor of Chief Lempira, serves tasty tacos (US$3.50 for a plate of four) and dishes not found on most Honduran menus, such as beef "Gordon Blue" (US$10) and chicken lollipops (US$3.50).

El Jarrón, in new digs a few minutes walk from the center along the highway, has low-priced *desayunos* and *cenas* (US$2–3) as well as a special "Jarrón-style soup"—cream of corn with chunks of beef, chicken, or pork, served with rice and tortillas (US$2). There is a small shop with *artesanías* and coffee as well. Owner Marco Aurelio Rodriguez (tel. 504/656-0627 or 504/9870-8821, guiamarcolencas@yahoo.com) is the coordinator of the local guide association, and he has a van available if you need transportation. They are also building guest rooms on the property.

Pizza (US$7–11) with a thick, crispy crust and smothered in cheese is the specialty at **Colina San Cristóbal** (closed Sunday evenings), a tableclothed restaurant near San Sebastián church. The small makes for two generous portions. Burgers, fish, and the standard *comida típica* are available as well. The cheaper and much more basic **Pizzeria y Repostería La Esquisita** is always hopping with locals, and offers cake to go with your pizza.

Mesón de Don Juan at the hotel has all the usual suspects, plus items like French toast and omelets for breakfast (US$3–4), as well as *churrasco* (Argentine-style grilled beef, US$8) and pasta for dinner (US$7–11).

For bargain eats, head to the street corner by the Posada de Don Juan, where ladies set up charcoal barbecues in the evenings. You can stock up on supplies at the mini grocery store **Super El Milagro.**

Information and Services

Excellent tourist information is available through the regional website www.colosuca.com. Tourist information and a sketch map of the Celaque trails can also be found at Restaurante Guancascos.

Banco de Occidente, a block west of the square, changes dollars and travelers checks. There are no ATMs in town—the closest is at Santa Rosa de Copán.

Hondutel (7 A.M.–9 P.M. daily) and **Honducor** are a block south of the square. Lower-priced international calls can be made at **Ecolem Internet** (8 A.M.–10 P.M. daily), along with Internet access for US$1/hour. There are several other Internet places in town.

Getting There and Away

A couple of buses to Santa Rosa de Copán leave every hour between 6 A.M. and 6 P.M.

(90 minutes, US$2.15). Not far up the highway toward Santa Rosa is a dirt-road turnoff north up the mountains to San Rafael, reached by hitchhiking only. From here, you can catch a once-daily bus onward to Santa Bárbara through a little-seen and very beautiful region of central-western Honduras. One bus a day goes to San Rafael at noon, leaving from the turnoff on the Gracias–Santa Rosa highway at noon. It might be quicker and more comfortable to catch a *jalón.*

The 80-kilometer dirt road from Gracias via San Juan to La Esperanza is slowly, very slowly, being paved. Work has gone on for years, and it is only about half done (from Gracias almost to San Juan, then for another few kilometers after San Juan). The unpaved stretch can get pretty rough in the rains, particularly right in the town of San Juan. It is a very beautiful drive through pine-forested country, and the quickest way to Tegucigalpa, instead of returning toward Santa Rosa and San Pedro Sula. There are several points where the road forks and there's no signage, so be sure to ask frequently if you are headed the right way (there is even a point at which one sign points left to La Esperanza and right to Los Dolores, contrary to the actual directions).

One bus leaves Gracias daily from the bridge southeast of town at 5 A.M. for the three-hour ride to La Esperanza (US$4), connecting to the direct bus to Tegucigalpa. (This bus heads back to Gracias at 11 A.M.) The *busitos* (minibuses) to San Juan are more frequent, and from there you can get another bus onward to La Esperanza. One bus a day goes to Erandique at noon (four hours, US$2). Hitchhiking is also usually possible. A couple of buses also go this way to the Salvadoran border.

There are four buses daily to San Pedro Sula, all leaving in the morning (between 5 A.M. and 9 A.M.). From San Pedro, there are three buses: Cooperativa Transportes Lempira (tel. 504/656-1214) at 1 P.M.; Gracianos (tel. 504/656-1403) at 2 P.M.; and Toritos y Copanecos (tel. 504/662-0156, or 504/516-2086 in San Pedro) at 3 P.M., charging US$5.25–5.75.

There are also frequent buses all day to Santa Rosa de Copán (US$2), from where it's easy to catch a bus to San Pedro.

See each town for details on bus service, or the tourist office website at www.colosuca .com/como-llegar. While bus service between the villages is limited, it is easy enough to get a *jalón,* a ride in the bed of a pickup. Many travelers prefer to use Gracias as a base, to take advantage of the city's hotels and restaurants, but each of the villages has at least a *comedor,* and there a few simple, small hotels as well. If you don't mind the limited creature comforts, the villages offer unique opportunities to experience Honduran mountain life.

◖ PARQUE NACIONAL CELAQUE

One of the premier natural protected areas in Honduras, Celaque boasts the country's highest mountain, Cerro de las Minas, at 2,849 meters, as well as an impressive cloud forest on the high plateau. Towering trees are covered with vines, ferns, and moss, forming a dense canopy completely blocking out the sun, with little undergrowth between the trees. Celaque means "box of water" in Lenca; 11 major rivers begin at Celaque, which gives an idea of how wet it can be.

The park covers 266 square kilometers, with 159 square kilometers in the core zone above 1,800 meters. Although treacherously steep on its flanks, Celaque levels off in a plateau at about 2,500 meters, which is where the true cloud forest begins. You can spend hours or days admiring the flora and quietly keeping an eye out for quetzals, trogons, hawks, or any of the other 150 bird species identified in the park, as well as for the rarer mountain mammals, such as armadillos, raccoons, white-tail deer, howler monkeys, wild boar, and gray foxes. Patient watchers might catch a glimpse of a quetzal at Celaque, particularly on the lower trails, and during the months of March and April. (Some of the best bird-watching is closer to the visitors center; be sure to bring your binoculars.)

Added bonuses are two well-maintained trails, one leading to the highest peak, which

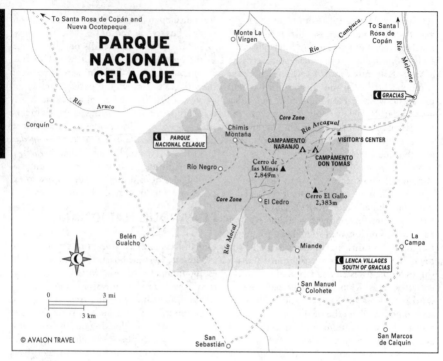

passes a visitors center and two basic encampments on the way, and another to a slightly lower peak, also passing the visitors center and one encampment. This makes Celaque accessible for the casual backpacker who is after a good hike but doesn't want to hire a guide or try to navigate by compass and topographical map.

The more adventuresome hiker should plan for at least one night out, to be sure to have time to spend in the cloud forest, which is only in the highest reaches of the mountain. This would require spending a night at Don Tomas camp, in a very rough, rather nasty hut; better yet, come prepared with your own tent. Trips up into the forest and, if you're really industrious, all the way up to the top and back in one day are possible but exhausting.

Visitors Center

The Celaque visitors center, some nine kilometers from Gracias at the base of the mountain, has just been entirely redone. Located at the edge of the forest next to the Río Arcágual, this is a very peaceful spot to relax, and plenty of easy day hiking is possible nearby, along the river. There are restrooms and cold-water showers, as well as a barbecue pit, if you're inspired to lug food and fuel up the mountainside. There is currently no charge to enter the park, but once a tollbooth gets installed at the entrance, it will be US$2.50 to enter and an additional US$2.50 to stay the night.

To get to the visitors center from Gracias, arrange a ride (US$15) with one of the two guide companies or at Hotel Erick to the last gate blocking vehicles from entering the park, from which point the visitors center is another half-hour walk. Or you can start walking from Gracias and hope a pickup truck comes by. It's about a 2.5-hour walk from Gracias to the center by the road, or a bit less by a trail leaving the road just outside Gracias, which follows along a stone wall and rejoins the dirt road to the visitors center near a school.

On the Trail

From the visitors center it is possible to hike several shorter trails; even a 45-minute walk brings you across creeks and through the forest. A map of the trails from the Hotel Guancascos is not necessary for the main trails, but it's sometimes nice to have along. Otherwise ask the park caretaker for indications.

The trail up Celaque follows the Río Arcágual upstream from the visitors center for a short while, ascends a steep hillside, then parallels the mountain. It continues upward at a less steep grade to **Campamento Don Tomás** at 2,050 meters, about a three-hour walk from the visitors center, where you'll find a tin shack with three rudimentary bunks

---

CELAQUE SUMMIT – THE HARD WAY

For some people, the idea of getting to a cloud forest in Honduras simply by hiking up a well-marked trail is altogether too easy. Never fear – there are more adventurous routes to the peak. Before venturing off into the woods, however, beware: The terrain on Celaque is extremely rugged, confusing, and often blanketed with fog. Even locals who live within the boundaries of the park have been known to get lost. In 1996, one El Cedro resident wandered around the plateau for three days, hungry and half-frozen, before he eventually struck the Gracias Trail and was helped out by a passing group of foreign hikers.

Apart from the well-marked trail up the Gracias side (which locals call *el sendero gringo,* the gringo trail), the most common route begins in **Belén Gualcho,** reached via bus or truck from Santa Rosa de Copán. From Belén Gualcho, it's a several-hour hike up to the lovely village of Chimis Montaña, set on a hilltop at about 2,000 meters on the west side of the plateau. From Chimis, it would take another 2–4 hours to hike up to the Celaque plateau. There, if your guide knows what he's doing, you will meet up with the Gracias Trail near the peak. Juan Alberto Martínez and José Alonso de Diós both guide visitors for US$10-15 a day (guiding services only – you provide their food and drink). Both can sometimes be found in Belén, but more often, at their homes in El Paraíso, an *aldea* about a 20-minute walk from Belén. You could also hike up to the fairly well-beaten path from Belén to Chimis on your own and find a guide there willing to take you up to the Gracias Trail.

Another option is to go by road from Gracias to San Manuel Colohete, and from there, hike up 5-6 hours to the village of **El Cedro,** where Julian Vázquez is one local who definitely knows the route to El Castillo, as Cerro de las Minas is known. From El Cedro, it's a brutal 3-4-hour hike (at Julian's pace) straight up through thick forest to the Gracias Trail, which you reach shortly before the final ascent to the peak.

A third fairly well-established back route up Celaque starts in **El Naranjo,** an *aldea* about a 30-minute walk from San Manuel Colohete up the mountain. Guides Hilario Mateo and Fucio Martínez will happily take hikers up to the top of Celaque and down the far side to Gracias, or via El Cedro to Belén Gualcho, for US$10-15 a day (again plus food and drink). You might be able to find lodging in El Naranjo by asking around, or spend the night in San Manuel.

If you take a trip across the mountain, also expect to cover transportation costs for the guide back to his home. Guides tend to be more expensive from the Gracias side, where they are more accustomed to dealing with tourists. To find a guide on the Gracias side, contact Marco Aurelio Rodríguez (tel. 504/656-0627 or 504/9870-8821, guiamarco lencas@yahoo.com).

The villages around Celaque are desperately poor, so any small gifts of food, pens, flashlights, or other useful items (please, not candy!) are greatly appreciated. Although visitors are rare on this side of the mountain, locals are friendly and hospitable.

inside and an outhouse. It's pretty grim accommodations, best avoided if possible. The shack is sometimes locked, so check with the guard at the visitors center beforehand. You might prefer to pitch a tent rather than use the cabin, though it can be a relief to have a roof overhead if it's raining.

Beyond the first camp, the trail heads straight up a steep hillside. This is the hardest stretch of trail, and climbing it often entails clinging to roots and tree trunks to pull yourself up the invariably muddy path. Descending this stretch of trail is particularly treacherous. After 2–3 hours of difficult hiking, the trail reaches **Campamento Naranjo,** nothing more than a couple of flat tent sites and a fire pit on the plateau's edge, at 2,560 meters. As you wipe the sweat and mud off your face as you climb, take a look around at the plants and trees. By the time the trail reaches the plateau, you will have entered the cloud forest.

From Campamento Naranjo, it's another two hours or so to the peak, but it goes up and down over gentle hills instead of straight up. Keep a close eye out for the plastic tags tied to tree branches—the lack of undergrowth in the tall, spacious forest makes it easy to lose track of the trail. The final ascent to the top of **Cerro de las Minas** (2,849 meters) is a half hour of fairly steep uphill climbing, but go slow and listen for the quetzals and trogons that live there. The peak is marked by a wooden cross, and if the clouds haven't moved in, you'll have superb views over the valleys to the east. From the visitors center to the peak is six kilometers and about 1,500 meters in elevation gain.

You could, theoretically, hike all the way from the visitors center to the peak and back in a day, but it would be a tough day and would leave no time for enjoying the cloud forest. A better plan for a short trip is to spend the night in a tent either at Campamento Don Tomás or higher up at Campamento Naranjo. On your way down be sure to leave the high plateau not long after midday to ensure that you get back to the visitors center before dark, and hopefully catch a ride into Gracias. If you leave the trail in the high part of the cloud forest, take

good care to keep your bearings, as it's very easy to get lost.

Shortly after leaving the visitors center on the way to Campamento Don Tomás, you will see a trail branching off to the left, leading to Cerro El Gallo (2,383 meters), a slightly lower peak. The view from the ridge ranges from incredible to very weird and misty to no view at all, depending on the clouds. After climbing the peak, the trail arrives back down at the main trail just above Campamento Don Tomás. The loop via El Gallo and Don Tomás makes a great, but long, day hike through three different habitats, with occasional clearings from which to admire the view and wildlife. From the visitors center the round-trip takes 6–8 hours.

It's often cold and always wet, so come prepared with proper clothing, including stiff boots, a waterproof jacket, and a warm change of clothes kept in a plastic bag. Both campsites are next to running water. Many visitors drink the water untreated, as there is no human habitation above, but it's better to treat the water first.

The trail map from the Hotel Guancascos is much more useful than the topographical map, which does not show the trails. A map is not really necessary if you're just planning to hike up the main trails, but it does give an idea of the lay of the land and is not bad to have just in case. The topographical maps covering the entire park are *Gracias 2459 I, La Campa 2459 II, San Marcos de Ocotepeque 2459 III,* and *Corquín 2459 IV.* Some camping gear is available for rent at Restaurante Guancascos.

◖ LENCA VILLAGES SOUTH OF GRACIAS

The "Colosuca Community," as defined by Gracias's tourist office, encompasses the hillside villages of La Campa, San Marcos Caiquín, San Manuel Colohete, San Sebastián, and Belén, with the town of Gracias as the hub. All but Belén have beautiful and grandiose colonial churches, vestiges of the influence and religious fervor of Guatemala City in the 1700s. Major efforts have been made to develop

COLOSUCA: THE LEGEND BEHIND THE NAME

Lencan legend has it that a poor widow struck out in the forest in search of food for her 10 children. Finding only a few fruits, she cried out "Lord, help me, I'm alone and cannot feed my children!" her voice shaking and eyes filled with tears.

A breeze began to blow, creating a whirlwind of leaves. A ray of light broke through the trees, and a loving voice spoke. It was God, whispering in the widow's ear what she needed to do in order to provide for her children, and letting her know that she was not alone.

The next morning, the widow awoke to the sound of her children laughing. She observed the innocent joy of her little ones, the glorious blue sky, and thought, "What I heard couldn't be true! Why would God speak to me? It's better I go out again in search of food for my children...."

Hearing her words, God decided to punish this woman of little faith, and as soon as she reached the forest, a breeze began to blow once more, and a ray of light penetrated the trees, illuminating the woman, whose feet were transformed into talons, and whose arms began to sprout white feathers.

"Noooo!" shouted the widow, until her lips could no longer form a word, but only a whistle. According to the legend, this bird is called the colosuca, which flies over the land to watch over her children.

Today, the word Colosuca has been adopted by the region, particularly to refer to the Lenca towns in Lempira – Gracias, Belén, La Campa, San Marcos de Caiquín, San Manuel Colohete, and San Sebastián – and the Parque Nacional Celaque.

community tourism, and there are increasing numbers of activities and amenities for visitors. A trip to La Campa and San Manuel Colohete can easily be made in a day if you have or arrange your own transportation, or adventurous travelers can easily stretch out their time in the region over several days, with plenty of great hiking in the pine-covered hills.

La Campa

Sixteen kilometers from Gracias by a fairly well-maintained dirt road is the Lenca village of La Campa, famed in the region for both its earthenware pottery and its annual festival, celebrated February 22–25. Even if you only have a short time to spend in this region, a day trip from Gracias to La Campa is a must, to get an idea of what village life is like in the rural mountains of western Honduras. With only about 400 residents tucked into a small valley, La Campa is one of those supremely calm, quiet, uncomplicated mountain villages where it seems nothing, not even visits from outlandish foreigners, disturbs the rhythm of everyday life.

The **Iglesia de San Matías** in the center

of town was begun in 1690 and renovated in 1938. It's a fine example of the churches found in many nearby villages, complete with a carved altarpiece and painted saint statues—although only open during Sunday mass (if you ask around, you may be able to find the groundsman to open it for you). The local priest is very knowledgeable on the region and happy to talk with visitors. The smaller **La Ermita** church on a hill above town was built in 1890.

During the week leading up to February 22, La Campa transforms from a sleepy village into the bustling site of one of the best-known annual *ferias* in the region. Pilgrims from all over western Honduras and Guatemala flood the town to pay homage to the town's patron saint, San Matías, and participate in the celebrations, which include the traditional *guancascos* exchange of saints with other villages, music, and ritual costume dancing. Watch for the Baile del Garrobo; a *garrobo* is a type of lizard, and the dance *(baile)* recalls when a man followed a lizard to a hole in a tree where an image of San Matías was found.

The canyon and dramatic hillsides behind town can be reached by trail. Several caves

© AMY E. ROBERTSON

Traditional pottery techniques are demonstrated in La Campa.

reputedly line the riverbank. On the hill behind the church, a trail winds upward, leading to **Cruz Alta** four kilometers away, a good day hike through the forest. This hill has long been venerated by people throughout the region. According to local legend, long ago the valley was struck by a series of earthquakes, which terrified the populace. So strong were the quakes that a new mountain was created. In hopes peace would return, the local priest advised the people to carry crosses and sacred images to the top of the new mountain. When this was accomplished, the quakes ceased, and since then, the hill has been considered sacred. A 30-minute hike takes you up to the **Mirador San Juanera** above town, a great spot taking for panoramic pictures if the day is clear.

La Campa is the renowned center for traditional Lencan pottery, which is brown or red, not black and white like the "Lencan" pottery that is sold in most souvenir shops across the country (that black and white pottery comes from the region surrounding Nacaome, in southern Honduras). The **Centro de Interpretación de Alfarería Lenca** at the top edge of town is a new museum with good displays of pottery. In three homes around town (each marked by a blue sign with a symbol of a pot), you can watch pottery demonstrations and then have a go yourself. Be forewarned; you will have to wait until the following afternoon to take home your masterpiece. Pottery made by locals is available in the homes that offer demonstrations and in a couple of other shops.

At the top of the park is a **tourist information office,** but it's not always open and doesn't always have information. You'll have much better luck getting information at a locally run website, www.visitlacampa.blog spot.com. There is info on horseback tours (US$16 pp for a three-hour ride, four riders maximum), hiking, half-day pottery classes, and more. To book a horseback or hiking excursion, call guide Alan Reyes at 504/9867-1389, or email hiking guide Carlos David Perez at losdape1@yahoo.com.

PRACTICALITIES
The **Hostal J.B.** (tel. 504/625-4737, hostal -jb@yahoo.com, US$10.50 pp, US$2.50 each

additional person, up to three per room), one block north from the bottom of the park, has five simple rooms in a large house, each with private bath. Guests can use the attractive living and dining rooms or hang out in the garden with its spectacular view of the hills. The *hostal* has also just opened a tiny cafeteria with *empanadas, baleadas,* tacos, *ticucos* (a type of tamal), and coffee. The other option in town is the 16-room **Hotel Vista Hermosa** (tel. 504/625-4770, www.visitlacampa.blogspot .com, US$10.50 s, US$16 d, or US$8 pp for shared bath). Rooms are clean and simple with a TV, drinking water is provided for free, and the eponymous beautiful view *(vista hermosa)* is from a small shared balcony where it'd be nice to sit with a beer and relax. There are very basic rooms available on a monthly basis as well, for US$79; you are expected to bring any furniture you want beyond the bed.

To get to the Lencan villages, there is a daily bus leaving Gracias at noon, passing through La Campa about 1 P.M. and onward to San Manuel de Colohete and San Sebastián. A second bus leaves half an hour later. To get back to Gracias from La Campa, your choices are either first thing in the morning (one bus at 5:30 A.M., and a second that comes from San Marcos and stops in La Campa at approximately 7:30 A.M.) or late in the evening (7:30 P.M.). Private transportation can also be arranged by asking around at the tourist office or hotels.

There is a **Centro Comunitario de Conocimiento y Comunicación** (9 A.M.–9 P.M. Mon.–Fri.) across the small square behind the municipal building on the south side of the park.

Public restrooms are next to the tourist office.

San Marcos Caiquín

West of La Campa, the road to San Manuel Colohete deteriorates. Three kilometers from La Campa, a dirt road turns off, leading another five kilometers to Caiquín. A recently restored colonial church stands in the center of the village, again open only for Sunday mass.

Reportedly, the Caiquín church holds some well-preserved paintings on the plaster walls and a fine wooden altar. The folks at **Comedor Daniela** by the church are very friendly, and they can usually help find a bed. Doris who works there can help you find guides nearby also. Grim accommodations are also available at Casa de Angela up the hill. Internet service is available at the municipal **Sala de Computo** next to the *alcaldía* (city hall).

From Caiquín, well-beaten trails head east over spectacular mountain countryside, past one of Lenca warrior Lempira's old fortress at Cerro Caraquín, near the village of Guanajulque. The hike is possible in one day or a more relaxed two days, and guides can be found in Caiquín by asking around. You can also make it to the reputedly fine village of Santa Cruz, passing through unusual colored-earth countryside, in about five hours from Caiquín.

One bus leaves Gracias for San Marcos at 12:30 P.M. (this is the bus that also goes to La Campa). The return is at 6:30 A.M.

San Manuel de Colohete

From the crest of the last hill on the road from La Campa, the view down over San Manuel is exceptionally lovely. The village sits on a rise above the junction of three rivers pouring off the side of Celaque, which soars skyward in a sheer wall that dwarfs the whitewashed village. With clouds almost perpetually wreathing the hills above town, it feels as though San Manuel has been lost in the mists of time, disconnected from anything save the stunning landscape surrounding it.

Similar in design to La Merced church in Gracias, the plaster, tile-roofed **Iglesia de Nuestra Señora de Concepción** features an ornately sculptured facade, and remnants of centuries-old mud paintings are still visible around the beautiful painted gold-leafed wooden altar. Not one nail was used in the ceiling, which bears traces of centuries-old floral designs. Locals proudly claim that it's known as "the Sistine Chapel of Latin America," and only the most insensitive won't be entranced by the church's primitive elegance. Out front is a

© AMY E. ROBERTSON

Many consider the ornately sculptured cathedral in the tiny town of San Manuel de Colohete the most impressive in the Colosuca villages.

colorful flower garden with benches. Built in 1721, it has an air of decaying beauty, although a restoration plan is underway with financial help from the Spanish government.

Comedor Edin, opposite the turnoff to San Sebastián near the entrance to town, has *baleadas* and tacos for a buck apiece, and meals for US$2. **Golosinas Conchita** (6:30 A.M.–9 P.M. daily) has a larger menu, including *licuados,* and soup on Sundays, and Conchita will make anything you want (that she knows how to make) if you order in advance so that she can get the ingredients.

Just down the road is **Hotel Emanuel** (tel. 504/9949-5259), with nine simple rooms. Rooms with shared bath cost US$3.60 per person, while the rooms with private baths cost US$16–18 and can sleep up to five people.

Internet is available at the **Centro Comunitario de Conocimientos y Comunicaciones,** facing the park (closed Sun.).

The town's annual *feria* is December 7–8. The 1st and 15th of each month are market

days, where you can find wicker crafts and chairs as well as standard market goods.

Don't be surprised if San Manuel residents don't know quite what to make of a foreign visitor, especially if not accompanied by a Honduran. But the worst that will happen is everyone will stare wordlessly at you, and the children will pester you relentlessly, often asking for money to buy junk food. Keep a friendly smile on your face and all will be well.

From the grass square, look for the trail with the church on your right heading down to the river, for a place to cool off and admire the scenery. Here you can cross over and hike up the far side along trails as high as you'd like, or walk upriver to the *aldea* of San Antonio, where you can be sure they haven't met too many foreigners.

San Manuel is 14 kilometers by very rough dirt road west of La Campa. One bus to Gracias passes through at 6 A.M., and a second bus departs at 6:30 A.M. From Gracias, the bus to San Manuel departs at 12:45 P.M. (if it's full, you can also take the 12:45 P.M. bus to San

Sebastián and get off in San Manuel). The ride takes a little over two hours.

San Sebastián

The dirt road from San Manuel to San Sebastián, another attractive village farther west around Celaque, is not too bad, although there is a deep river crossing. Simple accommodations are available at a no-name *hospedaje* for US$1.50 a night, and **Comedor Alicia** on the square has meals (and also a couple of basic rooms). If no ride is available, walk the road in 3–4 hours, and from there, you can continue walking several more hours on a remnant of the old *camino real* to Belén Gualcho, where you can spend the night and catch a ride the next day to Santa Rosa de Copán. One bus a day runs between San Sebastián and Gracias, leaving San Sebastián at 5 A.M.

South of San Sebastián, the adventurous can hike down to Tomalá through lovely, little-visited, and safe countryside in southern Lempira, near the border with El Salvador. Locals say the mostly downhill route can be hiked in 10 hours, but more likely it would require camping out one night. From Tomalá, transportation is available to San Marcos and on to Santa Rosa de Copán or Nueva Ocotepeque. Guides can be found in San Sebastián who know the way.

Belén

Twenty-four kilometers south on the Gracias–La Esperanza road, take a left and follow three kilometers to reach the tiny town of Belén. The pavement ends just when you reach the town, whose dirt roads can be severely rutted during the rainy season. Although Belén has joined the Colosuca Tourist Circuit, it is only just beginning to develop any kind of amenities for visitors. There are two churches: 19th-century El Rosario on the main square, and the Ermita de Belén a block away. **Comedor Lourdes** has the standards at cheap prices (US$2.50–3). There are six buses a day between Gracias and Belén.

SAN JUAN

About halfway up the mountain road between Gracias and La Esperanza, where a side road

turns south toward Erandique, is the town of San Juan, set amidst fine countryside. Peace Corps volunteers have worked with the community to develop tourist information and amenities for naturalist and cultural experiences in the region, including local guides, simple but clean accommodations, and good food, all at very reasonable prices.

Sights and Tours

The **tourist office** is run from the shop Docucentro Israel by owner Gladys Nolasco (tel. 504/754-7150 or 504/9885-9635, glaisra7@yahoo.com), who has a folder of information (also available at Guancascos in Gracias) about trips to the nearby "enchanted" canyon, the waterfall "of the guitar playing elves," and the Reserva Biológica Opalaca, among other places, as well as information on the nearby village of Erandique. Well-run day trips, with food and all, run US$25 for one person, US$16 per person for two, and $14 per person for three or more, but they are very happy to tell you how to get to places on your own. Tours by horseback can also be arranged for just a few dollars more. Also nearby are some natural pools (not hot really, more like lukewarm, but still nice, US$1), coffee plantations, and a clay tile–making place (you can make your own tile, but you won't have time to fire it unless you stick around for a few days). Guides can take you pretty much anywhere you fancy, including to the top of Congolón or Piedra Parada of Lempira fame. These tours are best arranged at least a day in advance. Gladys can help arrange horseback rides and even bicycle rentals.

If you just have an hour or two to spend in San Juan, Gladys can arrange for you to watch a toasting and have a tasting of locally grown coffee, or see a demonstration of clay pottery being made, each for US$1.50.

Accommodations and Food

Hotel J. B. Martinez (tel. 504/754-7154, US$9 s, US$12 d) is a new hotel in town, with 12 pretty nice rooms around a small courtyard, all with private bath.

COPÁN

LEMPIRA: THE MAN IN THE MONEY

The name of Honduras's currency, lempira, honors the country's first great hero, a Lenca warrior who led his people in a fierce but little-known war against the Spaniards during the first years of the conquest of Honduras.

Spaniards first penetrated the mountainous region of present-day western Honduras in the early 1530s. From the start, the native Lenca, led initially by a chief named Etempica, fiercely resisted the newcomers. By 1536, the situation in the province had grown so precarious that the Spanish leaders called on the bloodthirsty conqueror of Guatemala, Pedro de Alvarado, to lead an expedition from that country to pacify the region. Alvarado laid siege on a few indigenous villages in the Río Mejocote Valley, then sent Juan de Chavez farther south to found Gracias a Dios. Chavez ran into thousands of Lenca warriors enraged by Alvarado's actions and spoiling for a fight, so he wisely left without founding a town. Later in the same year, three colonists on their way from the Spanish base at Siguatepeque to Guatemala were waylaid and killed by unknown Indians. On hearing of the event, Honduran governor Francisco de Montejo led a strong contingent of soldiers into the region and called a meeting of native chiefs. All but one of the chiefs showed up – and were promptly hanged by the Spaniards.

The only chief who did not attend the meet-ing was Lempira ("Lord of the Mountains" in Lenca), described by the Spaniards as about 35-40 years old, "of medium stature, with strong arms, brave, and intelligent." Rather than being cowed by the Spanish brutality, Lempira gathered a large force of warriors at Peñol de Cerquín – a natural fortress – and at several other mountain redoubts near what is now Erandique, in southwestern Honduras. Through either intimidation or negotiation, Lempira convinced the Cares tribe, traditional enemies of the Lenca, to join the fight against the Spaniards. Legend has it that Lempira swayed wavering Cares by scorning them: "How is it so many brave men in their own land can be subjugated miserably by so few foreigners?"

At that time, the Spaniards did indeed have very few men in Honduras – compared to the treasure-laden regions of Peru and Mexico, it was not a rich province. Just when Montejo thought he had subdued the region with his show of force, Lempira coordinated surprise attacks on several Spanish settlements in Honduras from his mountain fortress. When the conquistadors learned of his role in the attacks, they assembled a force led by Captain Alonso de Cáceres to take the fortress at Peñol de Cerquín.

Lempira had chosen his spot well. The steep,

There is a simple but attractive cabin in the hills available for tourists, run by Jesús Castillo, for a mere US$3.70 per person. Reservations can be made through Gladys at the tourist office, or if you speak Spanish, you can call Jesús directly at 504/9658-9629. Jesús will also prepare meals (US$2) and arrange trips, horseback riding, etcetera, at a charge. Tips are welcome.

There are several *comedores* sprinkled throughout town.

Getting There and Away

San Juan is 83 kilometers, or about 70 minutes, from Gracias, on a road that is well-paved for all but the last 10 minutes. Buses cost US$2.35 and depart San Juan for Gracias a 6, 8:30, and 11:30 A.M. and 12:30 P.M. While the roads of San Juan itself can be rutted messes, there is another small paved section right after town, which turns into a well-maintained dirt road after a few minutes, leading to La Esperanza. Buses from San Juan to La Esperanza also cost US$2.35, and leave at 6, 6:30, 7:30, 8:20, and 9 A.M. (Check with Gladys or other people in town for current bus schedules—it's often just as easy or easier to catch a *jalón* in a pickup.) It takes about an hour from San Juan to La Esperanza.

Erandique

About halfway along the dirt road between

rugged Peñol did not allow the Spaniards to employ their horses, and they were unable to take the fortress by force. After six months of blockading, the Peñol still had not been taken, as Lenca warriors easily snuck past the Spanish soldiers in the forest and had no trouble keeping themselves provisioned. Other Indian groups, seeing Lempira's success in holding out against the Spaniards, began their own uprisings across the province.

History offers us at least three different versions of what happened next. In the classic version, the frustrated Cáceres, unable to take the fortress by direct attack or by siege, decided to trick Lempira. Calling on the Lenca chief to discuss peace terms, Cáceres hid a soldier among the Spanish horses. Just as Lempira was disdainfully rejecting any terms short of Spanish withdrawal, from a rocky bluff several meters from the Spaniards the hidden soldier shot and killed the chief with an arquebus.

Much of this history is derived from *Historia de América*, written by Spanish historian Antonio de Herrera almost 100 years after the event. More recently, Honduran and Canadian historians uncovered a document in Seville, Spain, from the *Audiencia de México*. In the report, dated 1558, Spanish soldier Rodrigo Ruíz states that *he* killed the Lenca leader, whom he called "El Enpira," in single combat (not by ambush) and took his head back to Siguatepeque as proof of his actions.

Yet another version comes from the Lenca town of Gualcinse, not far from the Peñol, and at the time of the revolt one of Lempira's allies. Local tradition has long held that Lempira was indeed shot while listening to a peace proposal by the Spaniards, but that he was only wounded, and that his warriors carried him off to hiding. According to the Gualcinse account, a contingent of Spaniards heard of Lempira's whereabouts, came to the town, and killed him on his sickbed. They then cut off his head and brought it back to Siguatepeque. This sequence of events would explain why, according to Honduran lore, Lempira was killed at Piedra Parada, which, although nearby, is clearly not the same location as Peñol de Cerquín, by all accounts the location of his fortress.

From all the supporting witnesses reported in the Ruíz document, it's clear that the soldier played some essential role in killing Lempira, but whether through treachery or single combat remains a mystery. In some manner, Lempira's uprising and death must have been a last gasp for the Lenca; the formerly fierce warriors never again threatened Spanish rule in the region.

Gracias commemorates its beloved hero every July 20 with parades.

Gracias and La Esperanza is San Juan, where a rough dirt road turns south 24 kilometers to Erandique, an exceptionally beautiful, rural colonial town set amid the Sierra de las Neblinas. The mountains around Erandique were the old stomping grounds of Lenca warrior Lempira when he waged his guerrilla war against the Spanish conquistadors in the 16th century.

Erandique has three *parques* (squares), each fronted by a small but very fine colonial-era church. Formerly, each of the squares had a massive ceiba tree in front, planted more than a century ago, but now only two survive. One of these remaining two ceibas was nearly split in half when struck by lightning. The one intact tree is impressively huge, dwarfing the square and the church behind it. A large statue to Lempira now stands in the center of the main square.

Bemused visitors to Erandique may find themselves surrounded by men, women, and children asking if they would like to buy opals. As it turns out, the surrounding countryside is one of the most famous areas in the Americas for the precious stone. Several different grades of opals are mined nearby, including black, white, river, garden, rainbow, milk, and the valuable aurora opals. Honduran opals are considered particularly valuable because of the frequent presence of scarlet coloring. Local *campesinos* are also always turning up obsidian arrowheads and other objects from pre-Columbian and conquest times and often trying to sell them to visitors for very little money.

Apart from the occasional opal-buyer, Erandique doesn't receive many foreign visitors, so you may be the recipient of a few curious but usually good-natured stares from town residents. Anyone with a modicum of openness and minimal Spanish will quickly find the friendly townsfolk ready to chat about the town or the world at large. The town's annual festival is held on January 20 in honor of San Sebastián, and holidays for San Antonio (June 13), Lempira (July 20), and the Virgen de La Merced (September 8) are also observed. Gladys Nolasco in San Juan also has information on tourist activities in Erandique.

Reportedly, **Hotel Steven** (Barrio Gualmaca, US$5.50 s, US$8 d) has comfortable rooms, hot showers, cable TV, and good prices. Lodging is also available at Hotel Sinai and Hotel Torre Fuerte. There are a couple of basic *comedores* with standard *típico* food. There are also a couple of Internet cafés (domestic and international calls can be made from the one near the central park), a gas station, and a small medical clinic.

One minibus runs between Gracias and Erandique daily, leaving Erandique early in the morning for the 2.5-hour, US$2 trip. Another bus leaves at 5 A.M. for the four-hour trip to La Esperanza, US$2.50. Finding a *jalón* on one of the regularly passing pickup trucks is frequently possible.

Near Erandique

The pine-forested mountains around Erandique are excellent for hiking, with footpaths leading in all directions. For a short afternoon trip, ask the way to **Las Cuatro Chorreras,** a wide waterfall about a half-hour walk south of town down the valley.

Those with an interest in history, or looking for a good long walk, may want to make a pilgrimage to **Peñol de Cerquín,** Lempira's unconquered fortress in his war against the Spanish. Ask a local for directions to the path leaving Erandique up the southeast flank of Montaña Azacualpa to **San Antonio Montaña,**

a collection of huts and a small primary school perched on the side of the mountain. The trail rounds the side of the mountain near the schoolhouse, and from that spot, the rocky spire of the Peñol can be seen in the valley below. From the schoolhouse, a trail continues down the mountain to the Peñol, or you can continue up the trail on the far side of Azacualpa, which eventually connects to the Erandique–Mapulaca road. This round-trip can be done easily in a day, with plenty of time to admire the views, but a trip to the Peñol would probably require one night of camping.

Other nearby mountains, such as **Coyucatena, Congolón,** and **Piedra Parada** (according to local lore, the site of Lempira's assassination), can also be hiked up—generally, trails lead in all directions. Reportedly, a monument to Lempira sits atop Cerro Congolón, and vestiges of indigenous fortresses are found on Coyucatena. From Erandique, you could walk northwest to Celaque and Gracias in a couple of days, if equipped with good maps and a compass or a local guide. Camping is safe, but it's always best to check with a local *campesino* before pitching a tent. Guides for this region can usually also be found in San Juan, and Max Elvir of Lenca Travel in Santa Rosa de Copán also offers tours in the area.

San Francisco de Lempira, 28 kilometers from Erandique (hitchhiking very possible), is a lovely little village, with electric power supplied by solar panels from a UNESCO project. About three kilometers from town is a cave with a number of interesting prehistoric paintings of animals, hands, and one dancing human figure. Ask in San Francisco for someone to show you the way.

South Toward El Salvador

The road leaving Erandique to the south heads up over the mountain behind town and continues on to Mapulaca near the Salvadoran border. Little traffic passes on this road even in the dry season, but hitchhiking is possible if you're patient. It might be quicker to find a guide and walk by trails through the lovely countryside. From Mapulaca, a dirt road winds its way north via Valladolid and Tomalá to La Labor, where it meets the Nueva Ocotepeque–Santa Rosa de Copán highway. This is serious adventure-travel country—pickup trucks and hiking are the only means of transport all the way. Don't plan on getting anywhere quickly. A couple of veteran Honduran travelers report that this is one of their favorite parts of the country, with friendly folk and spectacular scenery, as well as horrifically bad dirt roads. Decent hostels and basic food are available in both Tomalá and Mapulaca, and probably elsewhere too if you ask around.

LA ESPERANZA

The capital of the Intibucá department, La Esperanza lies in the heart of the most traditional Lenca region in the country. Although the town itself only has a population of about 5,000, the market area often swarms with residents from surrounding villages coming in to trade their produce or buy goods. The market is especially lively on weekend mornings, when you can watch Lenca women wearing colorful dresses and head scarves going about their business. Local handicrafts can be found in a few shops, most notably the cooperative **Tienda de Artesanías UMMIL,** with fruit wines, pottery, pine needle baskets, and the like, all made by Lencan women.

Set in a mountain valley surrounded by pine forest in the heart of the Sierra de Opalaca at 1,980 meters, La Esperanza is Honduras's highest city. The climate is cool, with daytime temperatures normally hovering between 10 and 20°C (50–68°F). Originally the Lenca village of Eramaní, which means "Land of Pottery" in Lenca, La Villa de La Esperanza was officially founded on September 23, 1848. The Spanish name derives, according to local legend, from a priest who came to the area with his younger cousin during colonial times to convert the Lenca. The young cousin became enamored with a local girl and fathered a child with her. The priest promptly sent his cousin away in anger, but the girl and her child never gave up hope *(esperanza)* that the young Spaniard would return.

Somewhat confusingly, Intibucá is a city as well as a department—and a twin with La Esperanza, located so close together that they form a single chunk of urbanity. They share the central park, but each has its own Catholic church.

On a hill just above town is **La Gruta,** the cave, with a small chapel inside known as **La Ermita,** which is the site of religious services during Semana Santa and other special occasions. The main street running past the square turns into a stairway, reputedly built in the

LA ESPERANZA

1930s by recruits from the local prison, which leads up to the cave.

The **Festival Gastronómico del Choro y el Vino** celebrates the local wild mushrooms and fruit wines (two regional specialties) at the last weekend in June each year. A potato festival is celebrated at the beginning of August, and a Lencan crafts fair is held in December.

Accommodations

Perhaps the best budget hotel option in town is the centrally located **Hotel Urquía** (two blocks north of the church). The ground floor rooms are quite dismal, but the newer ones on the second floor are quite decent (US$10.50 s/d). The rooms at **Hotel Venezia** (tel. 504/783-1424, US$10.50 s, US$16 d) are rather dingy, encircling a small courtyard. Cramped and depressing single rooms with shared bath go for just US$4, if you're on your last lempira.

The motel-style **Hotel Mina** (tel. 504/783-1071, US$21 s/d) is a good deal, with spacious newer rooms that aspire to elegance and smaller, older rooms for five bucks less. Semi-suites with two double beds and a small sitting area are also available for US$37. On the next block is **Gran Hotel La Esperanza** (tel. 504/783-0068, luispalencia04@yahoo .com, US$16 s, US$26–42 d), with some worn rooms and other new ones. Perhaps most importantly, Gran Hotel La Esperanza is one of the few places in town where city maps and tourist books are available, for US$1.50 each.

Around the corner and rather more drab, although with wireless Internet, is the four-story **Hotel Ipsan Nah** (tel. 504/783-2086, hotelipsan -nah@yahoo.com, US$21 s, US$26 d). The chicken with *choros* (a kind of wild mushroom) is popular at the Ipsan Nah's restaurant. These three hotels can often be full, so be sure to book in advance if you have a preference.

A unique option in town is the **Posada Mi Antigua Casa** (tel. 504/783-0415, may-aguero@yahoo.com, US$21 pp with breakfast, US$18.50 pp without), a bed and breakfast set in a 200-year-old colonial home. The three rooms have large windows, high ceilings, and colonial furniture, and the entire home can be rented (for up to seven people) for US$100 per night. Parking is available.

There are two nice sets of cabins outside of town, popular with weekenders from Tegucigalpa. **Cabañas Los Pinos** (tel. 504/783-2034, lospinosresort@yahoo.com, US$31 s, US$43 d, rooms with cabins US$43 pp) is a quirky, artistic development a couple of kilometers down the road to Siguatepeque, with a good if slow restaurant and some children's play equipment. The rooms have attractive wooden furniture and some have sleeping lofts; there is a bit of forest on the property for wandering in, and hammocks in a gazebo for relaxing. There is also an unheated swimming pool, which, given the cool weather in La Esperanza, doesn't see much use. **[Cabañas Bosque del Llano de la Virgen** (tel. 504/783-0443, US$47 s/d) has attractive cabins in a countryside setting, each with a full kitchen, dining area, and living room—bring what you want to prepare for breakfast, because there isn't any restaurant on-site. Visitors can wander through the pine forest or read a book in one of the Adirondack chairs on the cabin porches, and there is children's play equipment to keep the little ones busy.

Food

Choros, a type of wild mushroom similar to oyster mushrooms, are the local specialty, although they are only seasonally available. When they're in season, many restaurants offer chicken, beef, and pork dishes with *choros*.

One of the best restaurants in town is **[La Hacienda** (9 A.M.–10 P.M. daily), with colorful dining rooms decorated with hides, gourds, and Lencan pottery, and a small garden dining area as well. Grilled meats are the specialties, there are seven varieties of *plato típico* (US$3.50–5), as well as burgers, tacos, *pinchos* (meat on a skewer), and much more. There is also a small selection of used books in English for US$1.50 each. Lighten your bag by dropping off that book you just finished—the proceeds from the book sales go to a scholarship program.

A block north is the popular **Restaurante Opalacas,** specializing in meats served fajitastyle on a sizzling hot plate *(a la plancha)*. *Lomo a la plancha con salsa de hongos,* a thin steak served with a sauce of the famous *choros,* sells for US$6. Portions are generous, and there is some children's play equipment inside the restaurant for anyone who might get restless during the longish wait for the food.

With tequila nights on Fridays and live music and dancing on Saturdays, the restaurant **El Fogón** (9 A.M.–10 P.M. Mon.–Thurs., until 10 P.M. Fri. and midnight Sat.) may be your best bet for entertainment.

Good for a light meal and a cup o' joe, **Friends Café y Más** (11 A.M.–9 P.M. daily), on the southern side of the park, serves sandwiches and Mexican food.

Information and Services

Banco Atlántida will change dollars and travelers checks, and provide an advance on a Visa card.

Hondutel and **Honducor** are next to each other on the western edge of the square. There are Internet shops all over town, many offering domestic and international calls as well; one is **Internet Explored** (7 A.M.–10 P.M. Thurs.–Tues., opening an hour later on Wednesdays), with Internet for US$0.60/hour. An Internet café, also serving inexpensive food, is just off the southwest corner of the park.

Getting There and Away

La Esperanza is connected by a well-maintained, 67-kilometer paved road to Siguatepeque. The road heads down out of the mountains, across the Río Otoro valley, past the town of Jesús de Otoro, and back up into the mountains to the junction with the San Pedro Sula–Tegucigalpa highway.

Buses to Siguatepeque leave roughly every hour from the terminal on the edge of town until 4 P.M., charging US$3 for the 90-minute ride. These buses are legendary for being so slow that, according to one laconic local, they will stop on the side of the road even if a chicken appears to wave its wing in the air.

Buses to Tegucigalpa and to San Pedro Sula with **Carolina** (tel. 504/783-0521) leave the

terminal 11 times daily between 4 A.M. and 3 P.M. Both take about four hours and charge US$6.

An 80-kilometer road connects La Esperanza to Gracias; it is years into the paving process and only halfway done. That said, the dirt portions are usually well-maintained, and the road passes through some lovely high-mountain country. One minibus drives to Gracias each day, leaving at a variable hour in the morning, charging US$3 for the four-hour ride. Finding a ride in the back of a pickup is also easy and safe. Get out to the junction early, and expect to pay a few lempiras for the ride.

Buses to Marcala leave from in front of the Hotel Mina and charge US$3.

South of La Esperanza, dirt roads continue to the villages of Santa Lucía (87 kilometers) and San Antonio (93 kilometers), in the hotter canyon country near the border with El Salvador.

Getting Around

A taxi just about anywhere in town should run US$0.70–0.80, and there is a taxi stand in the *mercado quemado,* the burnt market that is now just a big dirt square.

Near La Esperanza

Seven kilometers from La Esperanza is one of the most traditional Lenca communities in the country, **Yamaranguila.** Although they don't see a lot of tourists, residents are accustomed to outsiders, as a Peace Corps agricultural training center is nearby. On certain holidays, traditional dances like the *guancascos* can be seen, though it's hard to find out when and where the dance will be held. You could try asking the local *alcalde* (mayor) for more information on the festivals. Near Yamaranguila is an impressive waterfall, reached by footpath—just ask for directions to **La Chorrera.** Yamaranguila can easily be reached by frequent buses from La Esperanza (US$0.50).

On the dirt road heading to San Francisco de Opalaca, 11 kilometers from La Esperanza, is **Laguna Chiligatoro,** a picturesque spot to relax and go for a ride in a rowboat, available

GUANCASCOS: PEACE CEREMONIES OF THE WESTERN HIGHLANDS

The language and many of the traditions of the Lenca have been lost over the past four and a half centuries. One Lenca ritual still celebrated on certain days in the southern and western highlands is the *guancascos*, a bilateral ceremony between two towns, often neighboring. The *guancascos* is a sort of peace ritual, marking the friendship between the two communities. Many *guancascos* are thought to commemorate a past agreement over the division of farming land or hunting grounds. In the colonial era, and up to the present day in more remote areas, the *guancascos* is the single most important event of the year, marking the time when new village leaders take office and a day of many weddings and baptisms. Although originally a pre-Columbian ritual, since colonial times the *guancascos* has incorporated elements of Catholicism, particularly the use of saints, in the ritual exchange between the communities.

The specific dances and format of the *guancascos* varies widely from town to town, but the general outlines are usually similar. In the days running up to the principal celebration, the townsfolk hold several preliminary ceremonies, such as the Traída de la Pólvora, the bringing of the gunpowder, when the all-important fireworks bought with communal money are brought into the village and divided up among the *mayordomos* (neighborhood leaders). In certain towns, locals hold the Danza de las Escobas, the Broom Dance, so named because the newly elected village leader hands a flowered broom to the previous leader and in return receives La Vara Alta, the Tall Staff. In colonial times, the staff marked the individual responsible for mediating between the community and the Spanish authorities.

On the "big day" of the *guancascos*, festivities begin with the townsfolk parading their patron saint through the streets and then out of town to a designated spot, where the procession meets a second parade from the partner community. Lengthy greetings ensue, punctuated with much fireworks and music, and the two saint icons are exchanged. The two groups then walk together to the church

---

for rental at the lake. There is a simple restaurant and a nature trail in the surrounding pine forest.

There are four supposedly protected natural areas in Intibucá: Montaña Opalaca, Mixcure, Montecillos, and Montaña Verde. Unfortunately, much of the forests have already been severely logged, leaving little of the original flora and fauna intact. Because of its isolated location, only **Refugio de Vida Silvestre Montaña Verde** is still worth visiting, but getting into the forest is no easy task. Located near the border of the Lempira department, in the San Francisco de Opalaca municipality, Montaña Verde can be reached by first getting a bus or *jalón* from La Esperanza to the village of Monte Verde, where a guide can be hired to explore the mountain. As yet, no trails exist, and facilities are limited, but the forest is reputed to be very beautiful and

intact. Topographical maps covering the reserve are 1:50,000 *La Iguala 2559 IV* and *La Unión 2560 III*.

For those with an exploratory inclination, the high, pine-forested hill country around La Esperanza provides lovely hiking and mountain biking and is generally considered to be quite safe. A nearby "dwarf forest" is touted as a tourist attraction, but worth visiting only for the most devout bonsai nut.

A special market called **Mercado Hijas de Intibucá** is held 7 A.M.–4 P.M. Friday–Sunday, in the village of Maracía, a few kilometers outside of La Esperanza on the highway to Siguatepeque. Homegrown fruits and vegetables, plants, and homemade foods are brought and sold by Lencan women from the surrounding area, to sell in what is surely one of the cleanest markets in all of Honduras.

If the weather is warm and you have kids in

of the main town, which has been decorated with pine branches and filled with copal incense smoke. Representatives of both towns give special speeches in the church, followed by a party of dancing and drinking.

Formerly, the culminating dance of the *guancascos* in many towns was the Danza del Gorrobo, or Dance of the Black Iguana, performed with elaborate costumes, and with musical accompaniment provided by *chirimía*, a type of flute, *caramba*, a stringed bow, and *sacabuche*, a gourd drum. This dance is no longer widespread – these days, the processions and saint exchange continue, but the elaborate dances have devolved into more unstructured parties.

The few anthropologists who have researched the *guancascos* believe that some three dozen communities in southern and western Honduras still hold the ceremony in one form or another. Both **La Campa** and **Belén,** in the department of Lempira, are well known for their festivals, usually held on February 14 and October 10, respectively. In Gracias, the neighborhoods of San Sebastián and Mexicapa (by the church of Santa Lucía)

reenact this encounter, with San Sebastián hosting on January 20 and Santa Lucía hosting on December 13. **Yamaranguila,** in the department of Intibucá, also hosts a celebration on December 8. Other towns include Ojojona in Francisco Morazán, Santa Cruz in Lempira, Lejamani in Comayagua, and Ilama, Chinda, and Gualala in Santa Bárbara.

Although the *guancascos* are meant to be celebrated on certain days, the chosen day seems a bit flexible, and the festival may not be held at all in certain years, depending in large part on whether the townsfolk have enough money for the festivities or not. In a way, it works out perfectly, as the only foreigners who ever get to the festivals are the rare ones who hang out in these villages and get to know the inhabitants, and thus find out. And all in all, those are the sorts of folks who should witness these ceremonies, rather than the video camera-toting package-tour crowd. Almost all *guancascos* are held in January and February, during the dry season, but beyond that, you just have to head to the hills and start asking around.

---

tow, the **Aqua Park El Molino** (tel. 504/783-1411, 8 a.m.–6 p.m. Fri.–Sun.) is at kilometer 37 on the highway La Esperanza–Jesús de Otoro. There are three pools, a restaurant, and swimsuits available for rent if you've forgotten yours.

From La Esperanza to El Salvador

South of La Esperanza, a dirt highway (in good condition only during the January–May dry season) descends an escarpment down into the hotter lowlands near the Salvadoran border. Beginning from around the area of **San Marcos de Sierra,** on a clear day one can see the volcanoes of San Vicente and San Miguel across the border in El Salvador. The road continues down into a small valley, in the middle of which is the town of **Concepción,** and then continues up again briefly. Beyond Concepción, the road forks

three ways, the southeasterly road going through **Colomancagua,** the southern road through **Santa Lucía,** and the southwesterly road through **San Antonio.** All eventually go into El Salvador, but the road through Colomancagua is in the best condition. It first passes through the border crossing of San Fernando, with (at last report) a Honduran border guard who is happy to stamp your passport, but nobody on the Salvadoran side. Continue to the first major Salvadoran town, **Perquín,** where there is an interesting museum about the civil war. From Perquín, the road is paved farther into El Salvador, but be aware that you may have to pay a small fine if you leave El Salvador through a different border, because you don't have an entry stamp. Returning through the same border is no problem. The travelers who've made the trip rate it as well worth it for the adventure of crossing a remote border, with fine views over the countryside.

Ocotepeque

NUEVA OCOTEPEQUE

A scruffy border town, Nueva Ocotepeque is blessed with a fine setting amid the beautiful mountains at the junction of Honduras, Guatemala, and El Salvador. The town's name derives from the words *ocote,* a local pine tree, and *tepec,* meaning hill. Most travelers who enter here get on the first bus heading in whatever direction they're going, but the hiking aficionado may want to dawdle for a couple of days to see the nearby **Reserva Biológica El Güisayote,** on the crest of the mountains rising right behind town, or **Parque Nacional Trifinio-Montecristo,** which forms the border of the three countries. It's also possible and safe to meander up any of the trails winding into the surrounding hills for a short hike (although it's best not to go alone).

Nueva Ocotepeque and Antigua Ocotepeque are divided by a river. There's not much in Antigua beyond the church and a few duty-free stores.

Accommodations

Of the several low-priced hotels in town, **Hotel Turista** (tel. 504/653-3639, US$5.25 s/d with shared bath; US$8 s, US$9.50 d with cold-water private bath; US$10.50 s, US$12 d with hot water private bath) is a good value, with clean and spacious rooms with different prices and amenities.

Two blocks up from the bus station is the remarkably nice **Hotel Maya Chortí** (tel. 504/653-3377, US$21 s, US$31.50 d with fan, including breakfast). All rooms have hot water, cable TV, and fans, and some have small refrigerators and air-conditioning for just US$3 more. The restaurant (7 A.M.–9 P.M.) has very good meals for US$6–10, and the staff speaks some English. A good value all in all. Parking is available.

Also very good is **Hotel Sandoval** (tel. 504/653-3098, US$26–37 s, US$35–44 d, including breakfast). Prices vary according to the size of the room and whether it has air-

conditioning or fan. The hotel has a pool, and its restaurant, open daily 7 A.M.–9 P.M., has good food.

Hotel Internacional (Calle Internacional between 1 and 2 Av., tel. 504/653-2357, US$21 s, US$30.50 d with fan, a few dollars more for a/c) is a large new hotel in the center of town. Breakfast is included in the rate.

Food

A number of cheap *comedores* serve up good *plato típico,* eggs, chicken-and-rice plates, and other dishes. One recommended joint is **Comedor San Marino,** on the main highway that runs through town and across the street from the Congolón bus station. It has great *carne asada* (much better than a lot of the *carne asada* in Honduras), chicken, and chorizo. All meals come with beans, toasted tortillas, fried plantains, cheese, sometimes avocado, and *chismol,* a condiment made of chopped tomato, bell pepper, onion, and cilantro. A dinner plate plus a drink is about $3.80. It's delicious.

There are also plenty of places to get *baleadas.* Local favorite is the kiosk located in the park, which is moving into a restaurant location across the street from the Liberal Party headquarters.

Hondutel is across from the Hotel Sandoval, open daily 7 A.M.–9 P.M., while **Honducor** is near the square. For Internet access, try **CiberCafé,** around the corner from Hotel Internacional, on the same street as the police station (US$1/hour), or head to the library, where you can use Internet for free 2–3 P.M. Monday–Friday.

Information and Services

Banco de Occidente exchanges dollars and travelers checks, but changing Salvadoran colones or Guatemalan quetzales is best done with moneychangers at the border, who are usually reliable. There are also money changers right across the street from the Transporte San José office. Everyone in town knows where they are and they also tend to ask foreign-looking people who are walking by if they want to change money. There also is a new ATM in town right next to Banco Occidente. **Banco Atlántida** can also give a cash advance cash on a Visa card, and will change dollars to lempiras.

There is a bilingual school, **My Little Red House** (www.mylittleredhousebilingualschool.com), that is always looking for **volunteers.** They will accept volunteers for as little as one month, and while teaching experience is always welcome, nothing more than native English-speaking skills is required. Accommodation is provided to volunteers. For more information on volunteering contact Ana Penman at 504/653-3042.

Getting There and Away

From Nueva Ocotepeque, you can catch any of the frequent Toritos y Copánecos, Tranporte San José, or Congolón buses coming from the Guatemalan border at Aguas Calientes onward to San Pedro Sula for US$6. There are also three direct buses daily (at varying times) to San Pedro Sula from Nueva Ocotepeque.

Buses depart every hour or two between Nueva Ocotepeque and Santa Rosa, charging US$4 for the 2.5-hour ride, until 3 P.M. Sultana tends to stop the least, getting to Santa Rosa in a fairly reliable two hours instead of three.

Buses to the border at Agua Caliente cost US$1.50 and run about every half hour until 6 P.M. You can also get to either of the borders, Agua Caliente for Guatemala or El Poy for El Salvador, by taxi. To El Poy by *colectivo* taxi is just US$0.85 or US$5–6 for a private taxi. On the way you will pass El Soldado, a statue on the left side if heading towards the border, commemorating the 1969 war with El Salvador. There are also minibuses, *rapiditos,* that leave for El Poy every 20 minutes from Transportes San Jose, for US$0.65. Although the border at El Poy is safer than Agua Caliente, it's still much better to pass through both during the day.

Agua Caliente/Guatemalan Border

Regular buses depart Nueva Ocotepeque all day to the Guatemalan border at Agua Caliente (22 kilometers, US$1.50). Between the Honduran and Guatemalan border posts is about three kilometers of lonely road—rides are infrequent, so make sure to get to the border by midafternoon at the latest. Travelers arriving from Esquipulas, Guatemala, will find frequent transportation to Nueva Ocotepeque until 6 P.M. daily. The border reportedly closes at 2 A.M., but it's best to get there earlier. Taxis from Nueva Ocotepeque charge US$10 (less if you share) and usually go until about 10 P.M. Moneychangers arrive at 9 A.M.; some offer decent rates, while others are happy to rip you off if you don't know the rates. Beware.

At least six buses daily between 5 A.M. and 6 P.M. drive from the border to San Pedro Sula in six hours (US$7), with stops at Nueva Ocotepeque and Santa Rosa de Copán, with Toritos y Copánecos or Empresa Congolón. Toritos y Copánecos also runs several buses a day directly to Tegucigalpa, nine hours.

El Poy/Salvadoran Border

Buses run frequently between Nueva Ocotepeque and El Poy at the Salvadoran border (seven kilometers, US$0.50) until 7 P.M., but consider taking a collective taxi since it's just US$0.85. Private taxis are about US$6. It's always best to get to the border early to ensure buses onward. The border itself, not much more than a roadside collection of buildings with a lot of semitrucks lined up waiting to cross, is open daily 6 A.M.–7 P.M.

Exit and Entry Fees

There are sometimes exit fees randomly applied at both borders, typically US$3–5. There shouldn't actually be an exit fee, but Honduras does have a US$3 reentry fee for those from outside of Central America.

NEAR NUEVA OCOTEPEQUE
Reserva Biológica El Güisayote

The Güisayote reserve is what you would call a last-ditch effort to save a patch of disappearing cloud forest. The reserve covers a ridge above Nueva Ocotepeque, and the remaining strip of forest looks for the world like a mohawk hair-cut, surrounded by denuded hillsides.

It may not be anything like Celaque or some of Honduras's other mountain reserves, but Güisayote has a number of endangered birds and mammals hanging on in the reserve, including quetzals, blue foxes, wild hogs, monkeys, and maybe even a couple of pumas. The views across three countries on a clear day (admittedly rare) and easy access to a cloud forest are enough to make it worth a day trip from Nueva Ocotepeque if you travel this way, easily accomplished with or without a private vehicle.

One of the reasons the forest is so decimated is that the Honduran Army built a road along the ridge at the time of the 1969 war with El Salvador in order to patrol the frontier, which gave farmers and ranchers easy access into hills. That same road is now being allowed by environmental authorities to deteriorate into a trail, which can be used by hikers in the reserve.

To get to Güisayote, take any Santa Rosa–bound bus from Nueva Ocotepeque 18 kilometers uphill to El Portillo (The Pass)—at 2,000 meters, this is the highest point of any paved road in Honduras. El Portillo is a collection of huts at the pass, from which a dirt road turns south up into the hills, following the ridge to a Hondutel tower five kilometers from the highway, inside the reserve. A 45-minute walk past the Hondutel tower, the road comes to a three-way junction. The left road turns into a path descending the hillside, while the middle and right-hand paths (formerly dirt roads) continue into the forest. The middle road continues around the mountain to the villages of Ocotlán and Plan de Rancho, from which one can catch a truck ride back to Nueva Ocotepeque. The right-hand branch leads to Cerro El Sillón (Big Chair Mountain), the massive wall behind Nueva Ocotepeque. At 2,310 meters, it's the highest peak in the vicinity. Even if you don't go that far, walking along these trails, with forays along animal and hunters' paths deeper into the forest, is an easy way to get a taste of the cloud forest, without

having to camp out. Wildlife is not extensive, but the patient and quiet can spot a variety of cloud-forest birds.

Those visiting the park by car can drive up the entrance road as far as the junction and from there must walk, as the road deteriorates beyond that point.

In the southern section of the reserve is a large mountain lake called Laguna Verde; ask a local *campesino* to guide you there. North of El Portillo, on the other side of the highway, another dirt road follows the ridge through another, smaller patch of forest.

The reserve extends north on from the Ocotepeque–Santa Rosa highway and has a good-sized patch of cloud forest, but it is more difficult to reach than the south side, as no roads or major trails head in this direction.

The topographical map covering Güisayote is *Nueva Ocotepeque 2359 II*. Some limited information on the reserve can be found at the Plan Trifinio office (tel. 504/653-3009) in Nueva Ocotepeque, on the edge of town on the road toward El Salvador. Guides are reportedly available into the reserve from the village of San Marcos.

Parque Nacional Trifinio-Montecristo

This national park, jointly administered by Honduras, Guatemala, and El Salvador, comprises a cloud-forested mountain peak forming the boundary between the three countries. The park is accessible from the Honduran side, but only with difficulty. One local forestry officer's advice for accessing it was, "Take a bus into El Salvador, where buses go up to within a few minutes' walk of the peak." Clearly, the concept of actually walking up the mountain is not big in Montecristo. From the top, you can see the Pacific on a clear day. Pablo Rosas and his brother in Las Hojas are two reliable guides. A small cabin in the forest set up by Plan Trifinio is available for use, and Pablo has the key.

The topographical map covering the Honduran portion of the park is *Montecristo 2359 III*.

THE NORTH COAST

Seemingly endless golden shore. Lush jungles raucous with wildlife. The steaming hot, verdant mountains, banana tree–blanketed plains, and sandy coastline of the Caribbean coast have a whole different style of life than the rest of the country. The north coast is a polyglot melting pot, closer to the Anglo–African Caribbean islands than the more reserved Hispanic culture of the interior. North coasters are more extroverted: They like to dance, to party, to get out and have a good time.

Travelers will likely find themselves spending a lot of time on the north coast, in particular in the unofficial coastal capital of La Ceiba, both because of the many attractions in the region and also as a way station on the way to and from the Bay Islands or the Mosquitia. Settled by the Black Carib Garífuna, North American

banana men, Honduran job seekers, and immigrants from across the globe, the north coast is so diverse one never knows whether to address a stranger in Spanish, English, or Garífuna; chances are they know a bit of all three.

For the traveler, the north coast boasts the perfect trio of sun, sand, and sea. Superb beaches, where you can sling a hammock between two palms and enjoy the gentle offshore breezes in peace, line the entire coast. It's no surprise the north coast is home to a large contingent of expatriates.

Add to that several of the country's most important natural protected areas, including the mangrove wetlands and lowland jungles of Punta Sal, Punta Izopo, and Cuero y Salado, as well as the mountain jungles, cloud forests, and rivers of Parque Nacional Pico Bonito.

HIGHLIGHTS

◖ **La Feria de San Isidro:** Party-lovers won't want to miss La Ceiba's annual festival of music and dance, the most famous revelry in the country (page 103).

◖ **Río Cangrejal:** For a dose of tropical adrenaline, go for a day of white-water rafting down this jungle-clad river right behind La Ceiba, or find a quiet trail or peaceful cabin with one of the area's community tourism projects (page 115).

◖ **Parque Nacional Pico Bonito:** The emerald-green, diamond-shaped mountain behind La Ceiba has the densest primary tropical jungle outside of the Mosquitia (page 118).

◖ **Refugio de Vida Silvestre Cuero y Salado:** At this coastal wetland, a network of waterways through dense mangroves, the quiet is broken only by the chatter of monkeys or squawk of a parrot (page 120).

◖ **Tornabé:** Of the many laid-back Garífuna villages lining the north coast, Tornabé is one of the friendliest to visit, with plenty of beach and a few places to eat seafood (page 135).

◖ **Parque Nacional Jeanette Kawas (Punta Sal):** This coastal reserve west of Tela is a picture-perfect deserted beach with lush forests behind it (page 137).

◖ **Jardín Botánico Lancetilla:** The tropical garden here is a birder's paradise, one of the best places in the country to spot hundreds of species in a small area (page 140).

LOOK FOR ◖ TO FIND RECOMMENDED SIGHTS, ACTIVITIES, DINING, AND LODGING.

Visitors can boat through the many estuaries and lagoons in search of monkeys, parrots, and manatees; hike to waterfalls; or white-water raft on the spectacular Río Cangrejal and Río Zacate.

Plenty of hotels, restaurants, and nightlife can be found on the beaches near Tela, Trujillo, and La Ceiba, while adventurers looking to get away from the crowds may be drawn to the laid-back Garífuna villages set along the coast. There are luxury ecolodges and well-maintained community-run cabins dotting the coast, particularly around Pico Bonito.

Most of the north coast is a narrow plain extending roughly 350 kilometers from the Guatemalan border west of Omoa to Cabo Camarón, east of Trujillo. Backed by the rugged Sierra de Omoa, Nombre de Diós, and Colón mountain ranges, the plain is only a few kilometers wide for most of its length, extending farther inland only along the deltas of Ríos Chamelecón, Ulúa, Lean, and Aguán, which flow north out of the highlands to the sea.

The coastal plain is primarily dedicated to fruit plantations (mainly banana and pineapple), coconut palm groves, and pasture. The most intensive cultivation, due to the rich alluvial soils, is along the river deltas. Coastal mangrove swamps were also once extensive but have been hemmed in to a few protected areas (Punta Sal, Punta Izopo, Cuero y Salado) by the steady growth of plantations and cattle-ranching.

The coast is hot February–August, with average mean annual temperatures around 25–28°C (77–82°F). The prevailing easterlies of the western Caribbean Sea dump 200–300 centimeters of rain annually, with a short (sometimes nonexistent) dry season March–May. Both the amount of rain and its timing vary dramatically from year to year, and wet weather can arrive at any time.

Tropical storms and, less frequently, hurricanes are an annual ritual, most often coming in October and November and frequently causing flooding, especially in the Valle de Sula.

PLANNING YOUR TIME

There are so many choices of ways to spend your time on the Caribbean coast that trips of any time length are possible. If time is short, four or five days is sufficient to get a flavor for both the beach and one or two of the many nature reserves. One itinerary would be to spend a day at the beach in Tela, another day touring one of the nearby natural areas like Punta Sal, Punta Izopo, or Lancetilla Gardens, and a third at the seaside Garífuna village of Tornabé. Then move on to La Ceiba and take a trip (rafting or hiking) along the Río Cangrejal, combined with a night out of food, drink, and music in La Ceiba's party scene. A second day is required to explore the mangrove wetland reserve at Cuero y Salado.

Those really after a lotus-land beach vibe should head out to Trujillo, a sleepy town on a big bay at the end of a long dead-end road, where the days will slip by unnoticed. The beach hotel region around Sambo Creek, east of La Ceiba, is another soporific spot. The more energetic might want to take a multiday guided trek into Pico Bonito National Park, the jungle-covered mountain range right behind La Ceiba.

Many Central America travelers on their way down from Guatemala and Belize enter or depart Honduras via Omoa, west of Puerto Cortés, long a favored spot among the international backpacker crowd, slipping back into sleepiness now that the road to Guatemala has been fully paved.

Guide Companies

A number of guide companies specialize in different aspects of north coast touring, all with a focus on nature and outdoor adventure travel.

Of the several companies offering rafting trips on the Río Cangrejal near La Ceiba, the most professional is **Omega Tours** (tel. 504/440-0334, www.omegatours.info), operating out of a lodge on the river. Half-day rafting trips cost US$49 per person, everything included, and a night in the lodge dorm is included too. Omega Tours is the only operator in La Ceiba with internationally licensed rafting guides. In addition to rafting, Omega offers kayaking, mountain biking, hiking, white-water swimming, horseback riding, and a number of multiday trips around the La Ceiba area and in the Mosquitia.

La Moskitia Eco-Aventuras (Colonia El Toronjal, tel. 504/414-5798, www.honduras.com/moskitia, 8 A.M.–noon and 1–5 P.M. Mon.–Fri., 8 A.M.–noon Sat.), run by veteran Honduras explorer Jorge Salaverri, offers rafting trips on the Cangrejal for US$58 per person. A visit to Cuero y Salado is US$89 per person for two, or US$66 per person for groups of 10 or more. He will also organize multiday tours hiking in Pico Bonito, Olancho, or to the Mosquitia jungles.

Long established in Tela, **Garífuna Tours** (Av. San Isidro and 1 Calle, tel. 504/440-3252, www.garifunatours.com) also has an office in La Ceiba. Rafting trips on the Cangrejal and hikes to the Río Zacate falls in Pico Bonito cost US$39 per person; tours of Cuero y Salado are US$59 per person; hikes in Pico Bonito

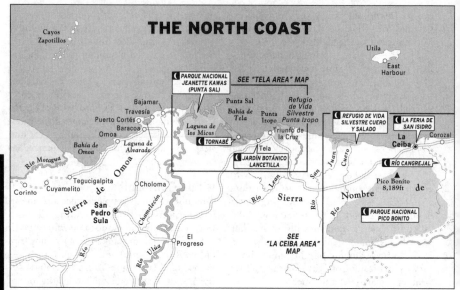

THE NORTH COAST

are US$34 per person; and trips to the Cayos Cochinos are US$49 per person. Multiday trips to the Mosquitia and elsewhere in Honduras can also be arranged.

Based in La Ceiba, **Turtle Tours** (tel. 504/429-2284, www.turtle-tours.com) is a small, highly regarded company run by a pair of Germans who offer highly regarded tours along the north coast, as well as to Copán and the Mosquitia.

A newer and very interesting option is the community network **Cangrejal Ecoturismo** (Colonia El Sauce, 3a Etapa, Bloque D, Casa #20, tel. 504/406-6782, www.cangrejal.com), which can arrange for community-based guides (often the most knowledgeable!) on various trails along the Río Cangrejal, many well off the beaten path.

Tourist Options (www.hondurastourist options.com) is a traditional tour company with mixed reviews, but it has tour options across the north coast, including in Trujillo, a region that none of the other companies cover.

Safety

All the main towns along the north coast—La

Ceiba, Tela, Trujillo, and especially Puerto Cortés—have problems with street crime. The smaller towns along the coast are less of a problem, but care should be taken nonetheless. In particular, it is not recommended to walk along sections of beach away from towns.

HISTORY
Pre-Columbian Residents

Archaeological and historical evidence suggests that at least three indigenous groups lived on the Honduran north coast in pre-Columbian times, but because of the hot climate and lack of easily cultivated land, habitation was sparse.

The Maya are believed to have extended their influence to western Honduras around A.D. 300, and although settlements were located mostly in the highlands around Copán and near the Guatemalan border, they did farm land in the lower Valle de Sula. On the coast itself, the Maya maintained several important trading posts, the farthest east at Punta Caxinas near Trujillo. Similarly, Nahuatl traders from central Mexico had outposts on the Honduran coast as far east as Trujillo.

Although Jicaque, or Tolupán, people

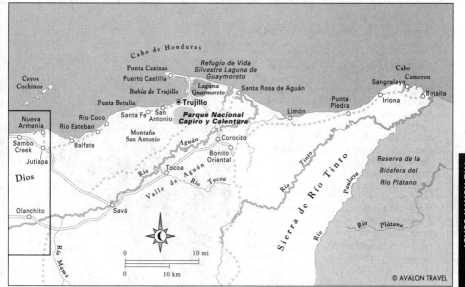

inhabited the entire north coast region from the Guatemalan border to the Mosquitia, their settlements were almost all in the mountains, and they apparently ventured down to the coast only to trade.

1502-1860

Following Columbus's first landing on the Honduran coast near Trujillo in 1502, two decades passed before Spanish explorers returned. But when they did, they converged on the country in three opposing factions led by Gil González Dávila, Cristóbal de Olid, and Francisco de las Casas. In the midst of their power struggle, the three factions' bands of soldiers managed to establish settlements by 1525 at Puerto Caballos, now Puerto Cortés; Triunfo de la Cruz, near present-day Tela; and Trujillo.

The nascent colony was briefly ruled from Trujillo, but by the 1540s the seat of government and most colonists had moved to western Honduras. If the lack of gold and quality agricultural land, uncomfortable heat, and danger of disease didn't scare away most colonists, the pirates who appeared in the western Caribbean by the mid-16th century certainly did. The

pirates sacked the relatively unprotected towns of Trujillo and Puerto Caballos with regularity. By 1643, Trujillo had been abandoned and only a small settlement remained at Omoa, near Puerto Caballos.

The first widespread settlement of the north coast was undertaken by the Black Caribs, or Garífuna, who were forcibly deported to Honduras from the Caribbean island of San Vicente by the British in 1797. The Garífuna first established a community in Trujillo and then migrated up and down the coast, building villages from the edge of the Mosquitia as far north and west as Belize. Apart from a few refugees from 19th-century violence elsewhere in Honduras, the north coast remained sparsely populated until North Americans and Europeans developed a taste for bananas.

The Banana Industry

The development of the modern north coast is essentially the story of the growth of the banana industry. Bananas were introduced to Central America by Spanish missionaries in the first years of colonization but were cultivated only on a small scale for local consumption.

SAM THE BANANA MAN

Of the many fascinating and colorful characters involved in Honduras's banana industry, few, if any, can top Sam Zemurray, better known as Sam the Banana Man. In an industry run mainly by cold-blooded bankers living in the United States, Sam was famed throughout Honduras for traveling his plantations on a mule, speaking bad Russian-accented Spanish, and cultivating the loyalty of his workers by personally bringing Christmas presents and throwing parties.

Born Samuel Zmuri, a Bessabarian Jew, Sam emigrated to the United States in his youth and got his start in the banana business in Mobile, Alabama, in 1895. At the age of 18, Sam offered to buy $150 worth of ripe bananas that needed to be sold quickly. He fast cornered the market on selling "ripes," and within three years he had $100,000 in the bank.

Heeding the call of the tropics, Sam headed to Puerto Cortés in 1905 as the owner of a formerly bankrupt steamship company, with United Fruit Company and a partner named Hubbard as temporary financial backers. By 1910, he made the daring move of buying 5,000 acres of land, all with borrowed money, and set up the first foreign-owned plantation in Honduras, along the Río Cuyamel southwest of Puerto Cortés. All the debt scared off both his partner and United Fruit, but Sam was happy to get rid of them anyway. Naming his new company the Cuyamel Fruit Company, Sam promptly sank even deeper into debt to acquire more land.

His small plantation could not produce enough bananas to pay off the debts quickly enough for his creditors. Sam needed more land. The usual acquisition method was to grease enough palms to ensure a large concession from the government, but conditions within Honduras made this an unlikely proposition. At the time, the U.S. government was considering taking over the country's customs

© AMY E. ROBERTSON

Once a banana republic, Honduras still depends on the banana as a top export item.

receipts to cover bad debt, and it was unlikely the United States would look favorably on granting Sam a concession. Rather than panic, Sam decided a change of government was in order, so he organized his own revolution to install Manuel Bonilla, a personal friend and the former president of Honduras, who had recently been overthrown.

Sam's right-hand man in this adventure was one Lee Christmas, another larger-than-life character in the early years of the banana industry. A New Orleans railroad man who relocated to Honduras in the late 19th century, Christmas never missed a good fight, and when Sam contacted him in 1910, he was itching for a little "revolutin," as he liked to call it. Christmas, Bonilla, and Sam planned the revolt in New Orleans in December 1910, under the watchful eyes of federal agents who knew full well what was brewing and were determined to stop it. But Sam managed to dupe the agents with an unusual sleight of hand. The *Hornet,* a 160-foot ship recently bought by Sam and stuffed full of weaponry and eager mercenaries, sailed out to sea on the 20th, but as Christmas and Bonilla stayed in town, the U.S. agents had no reason to stop it.

Christmas and Bonilla spent the evening in a famed New Orleans bordello, until the agents outside got tired of watching the fun and went home for the night. Whereupon Christmas declared to Bonilla, "Well, compadre, this is the first time I've ever heard of anybody going from a whorehouse to the White House. Let's be on our way!" Sam met the two on the docks with his own private yacht and ferried them out to the *Hornet,* which was waiting offshore. The drunken warriors sailed off to Honduras, which they took after a month of intermittent skirmishes. With Bonilla safely installed in the presidency, the Banana Man received his concession.

The Cuyamel Company grew by leaps and bounds over the next two decades, making Sam a very wealthy man. In 1930, apparently succumbing to pressure from United Fruit, Sam sold Cuyamel to United for US$30 million and returned to the United States. It was assumed Sam had tired of the banana business and was looking to enjoy his wealth, but that was not quite the case. Much of United's payment for Cuyamel was in the form of stock, and, unbeknown to the company, Sam had proxies quietly buy up more shares over the years, ultimately giving him a controlling interest. By 1932, a combination of poor management and the Depression had caused stock prices to fall precipitously. Sam traveled to Boston and attended a board meeting, asking politely for an explanation.

In a condescending reference to Sam's accent, one director said, "Unfortunately, Mr. Zemurray, I can't understand a word you say." Sam reportedly looked at the directors a few seconds, muttered something under his breath, and walked out. He returned a few minutes later with all the papers demonstrating his control of the company, slapped them on the table, and said, very deliberately, "You gentlemen have been f–ing up this business long enough. I'm going to straighten it out."

Thus began Sam's second coming in the banana industry. He was head of United Fruit for two decades. He quickly reorganized the management strategy of the company, handing responsibility to managers actually on the plantations rather than in U.S. boardrooms – a move fought by the Boston-based managers and cheered loudly by United Fruit workers in Central America.

The Banana Man had no compunction about manipulating local governments to suit his purposes – he is reputed to have uttered the famous quote, "In Honduras, a mule is worth more than a congressman" – but, unlike most banana men, he also actually cared for his adopted country and its people. Under his leadership, United began diversifying away from mono-crop agriculture and developed other products, such as pineapple, grapefruit, and African palm. Palm oil in particular has developed into a major industry in Honduras.

To help seek out more nontraditional products for Honduras and all of Central America, and to improve the region's agriculture, Sam funded the Lancetilla Botanical Research Station and the Escuela Agrícola de las Americas at Zamorano, both set up by William Popenoe. Zemurray stepped down as president of United in 1951 but just couldn't stay away from the fray. During the 1954 coup in Guatemala, which was due in large part to the interests of United Fruit, Sam directed the company's media efforts. He removed himself from the board of directors shortly thereafter, and he died in 1961.

Banana exports began in the 1860s, when locally owned plantations on Roatán started to sell their fruit to passing tramp freighters, which in turn sold their loads in the United States and Europe at a tidy profit.

For the first few decades, Hondurans owned and worked the banana fields, meaning local growers could sell to the highest bidder and make significant profits. By the turn of the century, however, North American exporters realized they could boost their earnings by running their own plantations and set about gaining control of as much of the Honduran north coast as possible. The north coast soon became a virtual North American colony, led by three companies: United Fruit (now Chiquita), based first in Tela and now in La Lima; Cuyamel, which controlled lands west of Puerto Cortés; and Standard Fruit (now Dole, but often still referred to as Standard), centered around La Ceiba.

Some land was actually purchased by the companies, but much more was awarded to them by the government in massive concessions, in return for railroad construction and jobs. Although the government was generally in favor of the concessions, wanting to modernize its backward country, the companies took no chances. To help their cause, company officials resorted to bribery and arm-twisting, even fomenting the occasional revolution to ensure a friendly, concession-generous administration.

By the second decade of the 20th century, the banana companies held almost one million acres of the country's most fertile land, were making huge profits, and unabashedly manipulated government officials to maintain the status quo. One historian writes: "If Honduras was dependent on the banana companies before 1912, it was virtually indistinguishable from them after 1912."

In the course of building their fiefdoms, the companies completely transformed the north coast. Puerto Cortés changed from a sleepy seaside village into one of the largest ports in Central America, and Tela and La Ceiba were essentially created out of nothing. The companies drained swamps to create plantations, constructed railroads between the plantations and newly built warehouses and docks, and drew migrants from across Honduras and around the world with the lure of quick money. The country's first modern banks, breweries, hospitals, and myriad other services were built by the companies to suit their own needs.

Coastal development never strayed far from the direct interests of the banana companies, falling far short of what many Hondurans had envisioned when the generous land concessions were awarded. For example, railroads were built only between plantations and docks, and the companies preferred to pay token annual fines rather than fulfill their contractual promises to extend lines inland, connecting the coast to Tegucigalpa. To this day, the north coast has the country's only railway lines, and now that the companies use trucks, the lines have been allowed to fall into disrepair. The supposed original intention of the banana concessions, that the railroads would stimulate the Honduran economy, was forgotten long ago.

The industry has fallen off steeply from the glory days between 1925 and 1939, when Honduras was the world's top producer and bananas constituted 88 percent of the country's exports. Still, Chiquita (the biggest banana company in the world) and Dole remain the top economic forces on the north coast and have diversified into pineapple, African palm oil, and other fruit products. The two companies are still easily the largest landowners in the country, after the Honduran government, and almost all of their holdings are on or near the north coast.

Since the beginning of the 20th century, the north coast has been the most dynamic economic sector of the country, and with the rise of San Pedro Sula as a major center for light industry and commerce, this trend has accelerated. Although San Pedro is not on the coast, its success is due to the short rail and highway connection to Puerto Cortés (the biggest port by volume in Central America), and the city's growth has stimulated the entire north coast. In terms of population and economy, the four coastal departments comprise Honduras's fastest-growing region.

La Ceiba

The largest city on the north coast, with a population of just around 115,000 and growing, La Ceiba is not particularly attractive at first glance, but those who give it a chance may find themselves charmed. The beaches are dirty, there is no architecture of interest, and it's almost always steaming hot, but La Ceiba has a certain carefree Caribbean joie de vivre that has earned it the nickname "Honduras's girlfriend."

The most overt expression of this spirit is the unsurpassed nightlife and dancing scene centered on a strip of discos right along the beach, where you can boogie until all hours every weekend and find a fun spot to hang out any night of the week. There's no doubt about it—*ceibeños* know how to party. As the saying goes, *"Tegucigalpa piensa, San Pedro trabaja, y La Ceiba se divierte"* ("Tegucigalpa thinks, San Pedro works, and La Ceiba has fun"). The town's good times culminate in the annual Feria de San Isidro, or Carnaval, a weeklong bash of dancing and music held in May.

The main reason travelers come to La Ceiba is not to visit the town itself, but rather to use it as a convenient base to explore nearby nature refuges, such as Pico Bonito, the Cuero y Salado wetlands, and the rapid-filled Río Cangrejal, as well as the nearby beach towns of Corozal and Sambo Creek. It's also an inevitable stop-off point for travelers on their way to the Bay Islands, Trujillo, or the Mosquitia, and a good place to take care of any business that needs attending to while on the road.

Following the lead of Tela, La Ceiba now has a squad of about 20 **tourist police** wearing green pants and khaki shirts, who are always ready to help out in case a visitor needs directions, advice, or help in an emergency.

History

The area around La Ceiba was first settled by a few Garífuna families from Trujillo who built a village on the west side of the estuary in 1810. They were followed by Olancho immigrants

fleeing violence in their homeland in the 1820s. One of these *olanchanos,* Manuel Hernández, built his house near a massive ceiba tree, which became the town's informal gathering place. The tree was cut down in 1917 to make way for the customs building, but the name stuck.

In the late 19th century, La Ceiba was in the midst of the booming banana industry. The first banana plantations on the mainland were planted near the mouth of the Río Cangrejal, and others soon followed in the vicinity. But the population of La Ceiba was still only about 2,000 when the Vaccaro brothers of New Orleans arrived in 1899, scouting for banana lands. They were awarded a concession at Porvenir, just west of La Ceiba, and quickly built a railroad track to transport their fruit to La Ceiba, where it could be shipped north. By 1905 the Vaccaros had moved their company headquarters to La Ceiba and began transforming the town.

The company offices and housing for American employees were built in what came to be known as the Mazapan district, unsubtly surrounded by high cyclone fencing. The Vaccaros—who by 1926 had named their operation the Standard Fruit and Steamship Company—built the city dock, managed the town port, supplied the city's electric power, set up the first bank, built the D'Antoni Hospital, and even brewed the first version of Salva Vida, one of Honduras's most popular beers.

Standard's business quickly expanded to the Trujillo region and into the rich Valle del Aguán, in the process attracting workers from across the globe and turning La Ceiba into one of the north coast's great cultural melting pots. Garífuna, Honduran *campesinos* (peasants), Jamaicans, Cayman Islanders, North Americans, Arabs, Italians, Spaniards, French, and Cubans, to name only the most prominent, all lived side by side in La Ceiba, and their mark can still be seen on the city today.

Standard Fruit—now Dole—is still La Ceiba's largest employer, although it has long

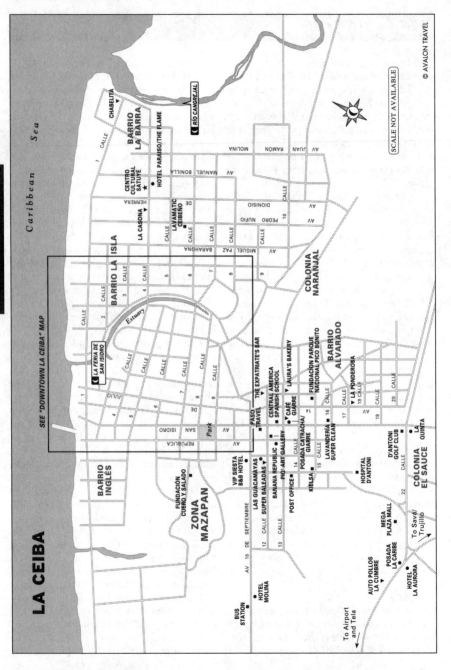

LA CEIBA

Caribbean Sea

SEE "DOWNTOWN LA CEIBA" MAP

BARRIO INGLES

ZONA MAZAPAN

FUNDACIÓN CUERO Y SALADO

BARRIO LA ISLA

Estuary

BARRIO LA BARRA

CHABELITA

CENTRO CULTURAL SATUYE ★

HOTEL PARAISO/THE FLAME

LA CASONA

LAVAMATIC CEIBEÑO

RÍO CANGREJAL

AV HERRERA DE

AV MIGUEL PAZ

AV BARAHONA

AV PEDRO NUFIO

AV DIONISIO

AV MANUEL BONILLA

AV RAMÓN

AV JUAN MOLINA

CALLE 1

CALLE 2

CALLE 3

CALLE 4

CALLE 5

CALLE 6

CALLE 7

CALLE 8

CALLE 9

CALLE 10

COLONIA NARANJAL

BARRIO ALVARADO

LA FERIA DE SAN ISIDRO

THE EXPATRIATE'S BAR

CENTRAL AMERICA SPANISH SCHOOL

LAURA'S BAKERY

FUNDACIÓN PARQUE NACIONAL PICO BONITO

LA PONDEROSA

CAFÉ GIARRE

PASO TRAVEL

AV REPUBLICA

AV SAN ISIDRO

Park

AV 15 DE SEPTIEMBRE

AV JULIO DE

CALLE 1

CALLE 4

CALLE 5

CALLE 6

CALLE 7

CALLE 8

CALLE 9

CALLE 12

CALLE 13

CALLE 14

CALLE 15

CALLE 16

CALLE 17

CALLE 18

CALLE 19

CALLE 20

CALLE 22

VIP SIESTA B&B HOTEL

LAS GUACAMAYAS

SUPER BALEADAS

BANANA REPUBLIC

PICO ART GALLERY

POSADA CATRACHA/ GIARRE

LAVANDERIA SUPER CLEAN

KIELSA

POST OFFICE

HOSPITAL D'ANTONI

D'ANTONI GOLF CLUB

LA QUINTA

COLONIA EL SAUCE

MEGA PLAZA MALL

POSADA LA CARIBE

AUTO POLLOS LA CUMBRE

HOTEL LA AURORA

HOTEL MOLINA

BUS STATION

To Airport and Tela

To Savá/ Trujillo

SCALE NOT AVAILABLE

© AVALON TRAVEL

since diversified its products. Most of its produce is now shipped out of Puerto Castilla, near Trujillo; the dock in La Ceiba is no longer used.

Orientation and Getting Around

Although La Ceiba is the largest city on the north coast, visitors usually spend most of their time in a relatively small area bounded by the square, the sea, and the strip of discos and beach to the east of the estuary, which divides the downtown area from the La Isla and La Barra neighborhoods. Taxis within this area should only cost US$1–1.30 per person (jumping to US$2.60 after 9 P.M.), but expect drivers to stop and pick up other passengers. Taxis to the ferry dock from here typically charge US$2.50–3.50. The main drag in town is Avenida San Isidro, running from the ocean south past the square all the way to the Burger King on 22 Calle.

SIGHTS

La Ceiba is not bursting with tourist sites—most people come either because it's a stop-off point to the Bay Islands or to visit natural attractions in the area near La Ceiba. The town's beaches are downright filthy and not very safe, which is unfortunate since they could be attractive if cleaned up. Swimming in the beaches in town is not advised, as the water is not kept clean.

The downtown *parque* (park) is nothing special, though it does provide a shady place to sit on a hot afternoon. The nearby main commercial district, centered on Avenida Atlántida and Avenida 14 de Julio, between 4 and 6 Calles, is a lively and colorful scene. The central market is a 1931-vintage, weather-beaten wooden building at 6 Calle and Avenida Atlántida.

Anyone with an entomological inclination should be sure to visit the **Museo de Mariposas** (tel. 504/442-2874, www.hondurasbutterfly .com, 8 A.M.–5 P.M. Mon.–Sat., US$3 adults, US$1.50 children), displaying some 9,000 butterflies and 4,000 other insects, in glass cases lining the walls. Those especially interested can take advantage of the free guide service, if one is available. Included are examples of the two largest butterflies in the world. The museum is in Colonia El Sauce just south of the golf course, Segunda Etapa, Casa G-12. Take the main entrance to El Sauce and turn left on the last paved road, and look for the museum two and a half blocks up on the right side.

ENTERTAINMENT AND EVENTS

◖ La Feria de San Isidro

In a town notorious for partying, La Feria de San Isidro is *the* party in La Ceiba—a several-day bash culminating in a blowout Saturday night that attracts some 200,000 revelers from across Honduras and the Caribbean. The country may have other national celebrations, but the Feria—held in mid-May—is Honduras's time to cut loose.

According to La Ceiba legend, three Spanish immigrants started the *feria*. The Spaniards—supposedly named Norquer, Artuche, and Pallares—arrived in the village in 1846, bringing with them the tradition of honoring San Isidro Labrador, a patron saint of *campesinos*. According to custom, they held a party in honor of the saint. The annual fiesta became a popular event with the Garífuna, who, although hardly *campesinos* themselves, are always ready for a reason to get out and dance. It quickly became a local institution. The *feria* was declared La Ceiba's official annual fiesta in 1886, and in 1929, the tradition of parades and floats was added.

On the final Saturday of the Feria de San Isidro, floats bearing scantily clad women proceed down Avenida San Isidro beginning in the late afternoon, headed by the Queen of the Carnaval. After the parade has passed, well-known Honduran and Central American bands on stages lined up and down the length of the avenue crank up, and the music keeps going until morning.

Many visitors, expecting to see crazed dancing in the streets, come away from Carnaval a bit disappointed. The only ones dancing, usually, are the fans at the band stage who have a grand time head-banging and slam dancing,

and the occasional group of gringos in front of one of the salsa or *punta* (traditional Garífuna music) stages.

The secret, for those who really want to dance, is to enjoy the stage music on the avenue until midnight or 1 A.M. and then head out to the discos on 1 Calle. Normally packed anyway on weekends, the discos are bursting at the seams during the *feria* and should not be missed by the serious partyer. When out on the streets during the *feria,* beware of pickpockets in the crowds.

Saturday may be the official biggest party, but many locals insist that the "real" bash is on Friday night in Barrio La Isla, with bands on 4 Calle on the east side of the estuary from downtown. Other mini-*ferias* take place the previous Sunday in Sitramacsa and Miramar *colonias,* Monday in Barrio Bellavista, Tuesday in Barrio Alvarado, Wednesday in Colonia Alhambra, and Thursday in Colonia El Sauce. La Ceiba on the Sunday following Carnaval is usually utterly and completely dead, with most people rousing themselves only if there's a decent soccer match on TV.

Discos

As the party capital of Honduras, La Ceiba boasts a hopping nightlife, mainly centered around the discos on 1 Calle east of the estuary, the so-called *zona viva*, or live zone. Foreigners, mainly men, have been known to get addicted to the scene, spending days or weeks on end drinking, dancing, chasing local women, and consuming the odd illicit substance until all hours night after night.

Monday and Tuesday are slow, but even then the discos are open until at least midnight. Thursday and Saturdays are best, when the strip is an adventure, with large crowds in all the discos and milling around on the street until daybreak.

The odd shooting or stabbing is not unheard of, and fistfights are considered just good fun. Generally, unless you do something stupid like try to pick up someone else's date, none of the violence is directed at foreigners. The crowd is totally mixed—*ladinos* (people of mixed Spanish and indigenous blood), Garífuna, Bay Islanders, Miskito Indians, and gringos all enjoy themselves shoulder to shoulder.

One musical twist sure to amuse visiting foreigners who are expecting to hear only the hot rhythms of salsa, merengue, *reggaeton,* and *punta* (the traditional music of the Garífuna) is the popularity of American country and western music on the north coast. Don't be surprised to walk into a disco and see couples doing a slow two-step to the latest Nashville hit.

Warning: The area on 1 Calle around the discos, and in particular near the poorly lit Parque Bonilla, can be dangerous at night. If you do go out dancing, use caution on your way back to your hotel. Walk in groups and stick to the main avenues. It's simply not a safe idea for women to go solo.

Considered the most upscale (read: expensive but relatively safe) of La Ceiba's clubs is **Hibou,** just east of Hotel Partenon, also on the beach side. The club is open Thursday–Saturday starting at 7 P.M. Come dressed in style. Another popular place is **La Casona** ("the big house"), which, despite its farmhouse appearance, gets packed with 20- and 30-something *ceibeños.* The music is mainly techno and *reggaeton.* Discos open and close with regularity, but generally the better ones are at the far end of 1 Calle, while the close end, near the estuary, is considered a bit of a red-light district by locals.

To check out some *punta* sounds, find out what's happening at **Centro Cultural Satuyé** (4 Calle in Barrio La Isla), a Garífuna cultural center that frequently hosts live bands and dance.

Bars

If the disco scene sounds a bit too energetic, but you'd still like to go out for a few drinks, you could go to the **Expatriate's Bar** on 12 Calle, two blocks east of Avenida San Isidro. The bar TV is invariably showing the sporting event of the moment.

There are many bars open every night of the week in Barrio La Isla (the *zona viva*). A top hot spot, **La Palapa,** next to the Quinta Real, is a bit of a chameleon, changing from low-key restaurant to sports bar to disco, depending on what's happening in town, and hours vary depending on the crowds. There's a deejay on Monday and Thursday and live music on Saturday. This giant *champa* (thatched roof hut with no walls), has a lengthy list of cocktails and frozen drinks, and a full menu is available (most plates US$7–9). It gets even more packed than usual during Semana Santa, when it's best to call ahead to reserve your table and you can expect to pay a cover charge.

Take care at the bars and discos just over the estuary, closest to town—that's the local red-light district.

Movies

Cine Milenium, on the second floor of the mall south of town, has two screens.

For Kids

Parque Bonilla near the waterfront has good children's play equipment, perfect for burning off some of that energy.

The water-slide park **Water Jungle** (9 A.M.– 5 P.M. Fri.–Sun.), 20 kilometers outside of town near the Palma Real hotel, is the largest park of its kind in the country, complete with wave pool, and there are pool games for smaller children.

SPORTS AND RECREATION
Golf
The **D'Antoni Golf Club** (tel. 504/440-2736, 6 A.M.–4 P.M. daily), for the confirmed links addict only, is at the southern end of Avenida San Isidro. Two rounds on the flat, nine-hole course cost US$10.50 for nonmembers; club rental is an additional US$5.25. The tennis courts, pool, restaurant, and bar are for members and their guests only.

Tour Operators
The adventure travel possibilities in the area around La Ceiba are legion, from white-water rafting on the Río Cangrejal to hiking up jungle paths to waterfalls in Parque Nacional Pico Bonito to paddling quiet mangrove canals spotting toucans and howler monkeys at the Cuero y Salado wetland refuge. Travelers can head out to these places on their own or choose from several tour operators based in La Ceiba. The prices quoted are all per person and can vary depending on the number in the group.

Note: Any of the adventure trips offered by these companies, and particularly the rafting trips, have a certain level of danger and should not be taken lightly. They are best done by travelers who are fit and active, and it's essential to pay close attention to your guides at all times.

Omega Tours (tel. 504/440-0334, www.omegatours.info) is an outfit run by expat German and Swiss rafters who work out of a lodge in the Río Cangrejal valley, about 10 kilometers upriver from the bridge at La Ceiba. Half-day rafting trips cost US$49 per person, everything included. Hikes with experienced local guides through the dense jungle surrounding the Río Cangrejal to the El Bejuco waterfall cost US$39, horseback riding on the beach costs US$65, and a day trip to the Cacao Lagoon is US$62. All tours include a night's accommodation in Omega's guesthouse or US$10 off lodging in one of its cabins, and a free lunch. Omega Tours is the only operator in La Ceiba with internationally licensed rafting guides, some with more than 10 years of experience rafting around the world, and the only one that rafts the upper part of the Río Cangrejal, with its Class V rapids. Omega consistently earns positive reviews from those who have gone on its tours.

La Moskitia Eco-Aventuras (Colonia El Toronjal, tel. 504/414-5798, www.honduras.com/moskitia, 8 A.M.–noon and 1–5 P.M. Mon.–Fri., 8 A.M.–noon Sat.) is run by veteran Honduras explorer Jorge Salaverri. Famed for his trips to the Mosquitia jungles, Jorge also offers trips around La Ceiba, such as half-day white-water rafting for US$58, day treks in the jungle-clad flanks of Pico Bonito near the Río Zacate, including a light snack, a guide, and pickup and drop-off, for US$41–58, and tours to Cuero y Salado for US$66–89. La Moskitia Eco-Aventuras also gets high marks from those who have toured with them in the Mosquitia; their excursions around La Ceiba are pricier than those at Garífuna Tours (if you try one, let us know how it is!).

Long established in Tela, **Garífuna Tours** (Av. San Isidro and 1 Calle, tel. 504/440-3252, www.garifunatours.com) also runs an office in La Ceiba. Rafting trips on the Cangrejal cost US$39 per person, and hikes to the Río Zacate falls in Pico Bonito are US$34 per person; tours of Cuero y Salado are US$49 per person; and full-day trips to the Cayos Cochinos are US$39 per person. There have been some mixed reports about their tours—some readers seem to have received more "guiding" (in terms of naturalist explanations) than others, who felt that the tour didn't offer much more than transportation. Be sure to ask specific questions about what is included in your tour, so as not to be disappointed.

Tourist Options (www.hondurastouristoptions.com) also offers a number of hiking and exploring tours with bilingual guides, including a city tour for US$14, hiking in Pico Bonito for US$29, or a visit to the Garífuna beach town Sambo Creek and lunch for US$25. Tours in other parts of Honduras can be arranged as well.

Fútbol

Two local first-division teams are Victoria and Vida, the former generally much more successful than the latter. Vida fans are known for their perennial meager hopes—invariably dashed at the end of the season to the resignation of the long-suffering supporters. *Vida sufrido,* as the saying goes in La Ceiba.

Both teams play at the municipal stadium, on the east side of the *estero*. Tickets, easily acquired the day of the game, cost US$1.75–9, depending on the seat location.

SHOPPING

PiQ' Art Gallery (Av. República, between 12 and 13 Calle) has a great selection of higher-end crafts such as jewelry, cards, soaps, and wood carvings, several of them made by local cooperatives, as well as paintings. Most, but not all, items are locally made, but all are handmade.

Out near the highway is La Ceiba's newest shopping mecca, the huge **Mega Plaza Mall,** with dozens of fancy stores, several Internet cafés, and a movie theater with two screens.

ACCOMMODATIONS

La Ceiba has dozens of hotels in all price ranges. With a little effort, visitors should have no trouble finding a room that suits exactly their taste and budget. During the mid-May Feria de San Isidro, hotel owners raise prices considerably, sometimes as much as double, and rooms fill up fast. Usually, it's possible to get a room as late as Wednesday during the *feria* week, but don't count on it after that. Many of the cheap hotels fill up on regular weekends, with people in town from the islands, the Mosquitia, and elsewhere in Honduras.

Under US$25

Most inexpensive hotels are found between the square and the ocean, on or between Avenidas San Isidro, Atlántida, and 14 de Julio.

The best backpacker digs in town are **☾ Las Guacamayas** (Av. Colon no. 252 between 11 and 12 Calles, tel. 504/406-8198, www.hostal lasguacamayas.com, US$9 pp with fan, US$11

pp with a/c), just around the corner from Super Baleadas. Two co-ed dorm rooms with six beds each share a bath in the hall, while a third room has its bath inside (these beds cost US$1 more). There is a great common sitting area with a TV and board games, and a small terrace for relaxing outside. There is also one private room with two twin beds and a bath (US$16 s, US$21 d with fan, US$8 more with a/c). The kitchen and bathrooms are all very clean. Thirty minutes of free Internet is included with the room.

A popular hostel in town is the **Banana Republic Guesthouse** (Av. República between 12 and 13 Calles, shared baths, cold water), run by the controversial Jungle River tour company but popular with backpackers for its US$6 per person dorm. The dorm is a bit run down, with Formica flooring, but the bathroom is clean, and 30 minutes of free Internet is tossed in. Cheap private rooms are also available: US$13 with shared bath, US$15 with private bath (and hot water!).

With rooms above a rumbling bakery and busy *comedor,* **Hotel San Carlos** (Av. San Isidro between 5 and 6 Calles, tel. 504/443-0330, US$8 s, US$10.50 d, cold water only), in the middle of town is an acceptable choice. Rooms aren't great, with mismatched linens and worn towels, but they're clean, and you can enjoy the scent of freshly baked bread most of the day.

Hotel Álvarez (Av. San Isidro between 4 and 5 Calles, tel. 504/443-0181, US$15 s, US$17 d, cold water only) is a good value, with a pleasant lobby, cheery yellow and orange hallway, decent rooms, and good security. Air-conditioning is available for US$3 more. Down a block toward the market on the opposite side of the street is the **Hotel Granada** (Av. Atlántida, between 5 and 6 Calles, tel. 504/443-2451, US$8–18 s, US$14–19.50 d, all cold water only), with relatively clean rooms with private baths around an interior courtyard. Price varies according to amenities: All have private bath and a fan, some TVs and air-conditioning. The inner rooms are quiet and a bit dark, a plus for late sleepers.

A favorite among backpackers for its location on the beach near the discos is the two-story **Hotel Rotterdam** (tel. 504/440-0321, US$13 d, US$18.50 t, cold water only). We visited during low season, when it had a somewhat depressed feel, compounded by the worn paint and Formica flooring, but it's right next to the beach and a good price. Trips with La Moskitia Eco-Aventuras can be booked here, and there is other tourist information available as well. Next door is **Hotel Amsterdam 2001** (tel. 504/443-2311, US$5.25 in the communal room and US$12 d, cold water only), a ramshackle little hostel run by an old Dutch sailor. The nearby **Dutch Café** is open 7 A.M.–11 P.M. daily.

Another acceptable option downtown at 5 Calle and Avenida 14 de Julio (with bargain private rooms for solo travelers) is **Hotel Florencia** (tel. 504/443-0679, US$8 s with fan and bath; US$13 s/d with fan, TV, and bath; US$18 s, US$21 d with a/c, TV, and bath; all cold water only), with 15 functional, tile-floored rooms on the second floor of a corner building, near the market on Avenida 14 de Julio. Unfortunately, sometimes the smell of rotting veggies wafts in from across the street.

US$25-50

One of the best values in this price range is the **(Gran Hotel Ceiba** (tel. 504/443-2737, hotelceiba@hotmail.com, US$28 s, US$33 d), about halfway between the central square and the waterfront. Rooms are spacious and clean, some have balconies, and all have a desk, a TV, air-conditioning, and a mini-fridge. There is a nice little restaurant in the hotel, open 6 A.M.–10 P.M. Note to families with babies: Cribs are available here.

Another very good option, popular with middle-class Hondurans and tourists alike, is **Hotel Iberia** (Av. San Isidro between 5 and 6 Calles, tel. 504/443-0401, US$30.50 s, US$37 d). Rooms are nice, with decent furniture and some with a balcony, and all with air-conditioning and cable TV. The doubles are spacious.

The **Hotel Olas del Mar** (tel. 504/440-1851, US$27 s, US$36 d) is the only beachfront hotel

west of the estuary, but mysteriously doesn't capitalize on its location, and none of the 17 rooms have views. A few do have wireless Internet or king-sized beds, and they are reasonably clean, unlike the beach they ought to overlook.

In a quieter part of town, four blocks south of the center, is **La Posada Catracha** (Av. San Isidro between 13 and 14 Calles, tel. 504/440-2022, US$18 s, US$32 d), with nice furniture and clean bathrooms, as well as air-conditioning, TV, and wireless Internet. Rooms go for almost half if you don't use the air-conditioning. Don't let the overbearing owner put you off.

Over in Barrio La Isla, a recent addition to the hotel scene is the good value **Hotel Costa Dorada** (Av. La Bastilla, between 1 and 2 Calles, tel. 504/442-2158, www.hotelcosta doradahn.com, US$26 s, US$29 d), which is close to the nighttime action. All rooms have TV and air-conditioning, and laundry service is available. Rooms with four bunks are available for just a few dollars more, a fantastic deal for groups of backpackers.

Also relatively new, and a step up, is the **(Hotel Versalles** (tel. 504/440-2405, US$42 s/d), opposite Mango Tango. All rooms have two double beds, a mini-fridge, air-conditioning, and TV, and the furnishings are nice, if a little baroque-ish. The hotel has a swimming pool; a bar and suites are reputed to be in the works.

A third midrange option in the Barrio La Isla (zona viva) is **Hotel Paraiso** (tel. 504/443-3535, tuhotelparaiso@yahoo.com, US$28 s, US$37 d, cold water only), a bright yellow hotel with sunshine walls, Formica floors, and simple rooms. The hotel is a few blocks from the beach action, but it has a great Asian restaurant on-site. Furnished and unfurnished apartments are also available, for about US$315/month.

Out on the highway near the mall is the new **Posada La Caribe** (US$31 s, US$46 d), with slightly spartan rooms. Suites with either two queen beds or one king are US$55. All rooms have TV and air-conditioning, and some have mini-fridges. The hotel has a decent restaurant open 6 A.M.–9 P.M. daily.

US$50-100

First opened in 1912, the **Hotel Gran París** (8 Calle, between Avenidas República and San Isidro, tel. 504/443-2391, www.granhotelparis .net, US$43 s, US$51 d), on the square, is a La Ceiba landmark. From the outside the hotel looks to have seen better days, but it's been updated inside and is decent if nothing special, with an attractive lobby, restaurant, and interior courtyard with a pool and bar. Rooms are spacious, with white tile floors, desks, and armchairs, and some with king beds, a few with mini-fridge, and all with air-conditioning and cable TV.

The Quinta Real's sister hotel, **La Quinta** (south end of Av. San Isidro facing the D'Antoni Golf Club, tel. 504/443-0223, www.hotel laquinta.net, US$62–124), near the highway, is no longer the plushest spot in town, but its 113 rooms spread out over a large area interspersed with grassy patios, a pool, and even a few slot machines make for a comfortable enough stay. Room price depends on size and location in the hotel. Inside, Maxim's Restaurant serves good seafood and steaks for US$9–12 per plate and sports an extensive wine selection.

Right on the highway by the mall is **Hotel La Aurora** (tel. 504/440-2060, http://laaurora hotel.com, US$46–49 s, US$52–64 d), located on the Ceiba–Tela highway near the turnoff to Trujillo. The hotel is past its heyday (despite the glamorous photos on its website), but the rooms are spacious and comfortable. The hotel has a small outdoor pool, a restaurant (with good breakfasts), conference/banquet facilities, and a computer with Internet in the lobby for guest use. Both this hotel and Posada La Caribe are best suited to travelers with their own cars.

US$100 and Up

A new addition to La Ceiba's shore, the **Quinta Real** (tel. 504/440-3311, www.quinta realhotel.com, US$104–141 s/d, US$141–228 suite) is a sprawling, tile-roofed, beige and white, resort-style hotel with all the amenities, including a pool, restaurant, three bars (one of them poolside), a spa and gym, a beauty salon, tennis courts, and a business center. (The website might leave you thinking there's even scuba diving instruction onsite, but it's not.) The 81 rooms and suites, offering air-conditioning, telephone, TV, and Internet access, range in price depending on whether they look over the sea or back toward town. Those facing town are also just across the street from the very popular La Palapa bar, so unless you plan to be up late as well, it's worth springing for an ocean view. There have been very mixed reports about service. The grounds are beautiful and they keep their portion of the beach clean. Unfortunately, the ocean at La Ceiba is unswimmably filthy from city sewage.

Near the Bus Terminal

The most convenient choice for those arriving late or departing early by bus is the **Hotel Molina** (tel. 504/441-1958, fax 504/441-5175, US$15 s, US$18 d), facing the central terminal. It's a tidy hotel, with some spacious rooms. Air-conditioning is available (US$6–8 more), and oddly enough, free legal and dental consultations are as well.

Near the Airport

There's not much to choose from near the airport, but if you have an early flight, many recommend **Rainbow Village** (tel. 504/408-5696, www.hotel-rainbow-village.com, US$32 s, US$43–54), which is also known for the Sunday buffet at its German restaurant. Five cottages have two bedrooms each (it's possible to rent just one of the bedrooms), a kitchen, and a living/dining area, and there's a swimming pool on the grounds.

FOOD

Eateries in La Ceiba are almost exclusively low-key, but many can keep the discerning palate satisfied.

Cafés and Bakeries

Laura's Bakery (13 Calle and Av. Ramón Rosa, tel. 504/443-1494, 7 A.M.–6 P.M. Mon.–Sat.), serves up delicious freshly baked goods, including cinnamon rolls, muffins, cakes, and breads (get there early for the best selection), as well as good cappuccinos, soup, and sandwiches. A second location, on the second floor of the Mega Plaza Mall, is open 9 A.M.–9 P.M. daily. Although Laura had left when we visited, the new owner Sherry was doing a great job of keeping up quality, and was talking about changing the name.

Ki'bok Café (7 A.M.–8 P.M. Mon.–Sat., 8 A.M.–noon Sun.) is a great new spot serving coffee and desserts, as well as breakfast items (all day) and sandwiches. There is a book exchange and a comfy reading room—perfect for whiling away a rainy day. The café is between La Plancha Restaurant and the Cuquis plant, behind the Esso gas station on the street that runs from downtown to the stadium.

No Honduran city would be complete without multiple branches of **Espresso Americano** (6:15 A.M.–8 P.M. daily); one is located right on the park.

Honduran

◖ Pupusería Universitaria (1 Calle and Av. 14 de Julio, 10 A.M.–11 P.M. daily), with its charming interior of bamboo and woven mats, has particularly good and generously sized *pupusas* (US$0.75 each, two here is a good meal, three should leave you stuffed), a sort of fried tortilla stuffed with cheese and meat, as well as beef *pinchos* and roast chicken (US$4).

Perhaps the best cheap meal in town is at **◖ Super Baleadas** (7 A.M.–noon and 4–11 P.M. daily), conveniently located next door to Guacamayas Hostel and just a short walk from Banana Republic. Price varies according to the number of fillings, which include butter, beans, egg, sausage, and more (US$0.40–1.50).

Very inexpensive and popular with locals is **Baleadas Alma,** a block from the park, with its namesake *baleadas* for US$0.40–0.80, and *burritas,* two flour tortillas served with a piece of meat, refried beans, a sprinkle of cheese, and if you're lucky, a slice of avocado, for US$1.85.

◖ Cafetería Cobel (7 Calle between Av. Atlántida and Av. 14 de Julio, tel. 504/442-2192) is a Ceiba institution, serving good home-cooked Honduran fare, cakes and pastries, and fresh fruit juices. Food is good and the prices are great, keeping the restaurant busy from morning till night.

Cafetería Masapan (7 Calle, between Av. República and Av. San Isidro, 6 A.M.–10 P.M. daily), right behind the Hotel Gran Paris, is an extremely popular, cavernous buffet restaurant. The extensive buffet always has a lot of low-priced choices, including a few vegetarian plates.

Seafood

Located in a white cement building with an air-conditioned dining room and small brick courtyard, **Chabelita** (1 Calle, just short of the Río Cangrejal, tel. 504/440-0027, 10 A.M.–10 P.M. Tues.–Sun., dinner only Mon.), has some of the better seafood in town, though you may die of hunger before the food arrives. Don't go in a hurry and you'll enjoy yourself. Flavorful conch soup, fried snapper, and monster shrimp are served at reasonable prices (US$6–10 per entrée).

Mango Tango (1 Calle in Barrio La Isla, open from 5 P.M. Wed.–Mon.), a large *champa* restaurant near Hotel Versalles, is a popular spot with a good selection of seafood, as well as pork chops and steak and always at least one vegetarian dish for about US$5–12 a plate. Most entrées include a trip to the salad bar.

Just across the street is the **Office Bar and Grill**—although the feel is decidedly more *champa* than office. Dishes include seafood soup, fish, shrimp, and conch, as well as meat kebabs *(pinchos)* and fajitas (US$9–11 a plate).

For eats right on the beach, try **El Guapo** (4–11 P.M. Tues.–Thurs., 11 A.M.–11 P.M. Fri.–Sun.), in a *champa* a few steps west along the beach from the Quinta Real. El Guapo serves a variety of seafood plates, including fish, shrimp, and ceviche for about US$5–10.

Locals heartily recommend the seafood at the Garífuna seafood restaurant **La Kabasa** (5 Calle in Barrio La Isla), especially its ceviche.

International

One of the most popular places to eat in town is (**The Expatriate's Bar** (12 Calle, two blocks east of Av. San Isidro, tel. 504/440-3373, 3:30 P.M. onward Mon.–Sat.), a favorite haunt, as the name suggests, of many foreign residents living in La Ceiba. The menu, including hearty, American-style burritos, barbecued chicken, stuffed baked potatoes, quesadillas with chicken and guacamole, and a generous ribs plate, is of excellent quality and in hearty portions—not cheap but a good value at around US$5–9 a plate. The large thatched-roof bar and patio is on the building's second story. This is also a good place to come for a beer or two. Locals know it as "Expatriados."

In the same corner building (and with the same owner) as La Posada Catracha is the Italian-style **Giarre** (Av. San Isidro and 13 Calle, tel. 504/440-2022, 11 A.M.–2 P.M. and 5–10 P.M. Mon.–Sat.). Diners can sit out on the sidewalk or in interior rooms with their plaster and exposed brick walls. The steaks (US$10.50) are decent though unexceptional, but the different pasta dishes (US$5–9.50) are a better value.

The Flame, at the Hotel Paraíso, has tasty Asian dishes, including Thai chicken satay with peanut sauce and Vietnamese summer rolls, with most dishes in the US$5–10 range.

Steak and Burgers

Anyone with a hankering for a steak should head to the open-air restaurant **La Ponderosa** (Av. 14 de Julio between 17 and 18 Calles), which serves up generously portioned *churrascos* with salad and sliced plantains, as well as grilled chicken and pork, and shrimp 10 ways (US$9.50–12).

(**La Plancha** (tel. 504/443-2304, 11 A.M.–2 P.M. and 5–11 P.M. daily), just off 9 Calle by the Esso gas station, near the stadium, serves arguably the best steaks in town, *pinchos,* and other hearty Honduran standards at US$8–12 per entrée in a two-story converted house, complete with linen tablecloths and napkins.

Cric-Crik Burgers (3 Calle and Av. 14 de Julio, 8 A.M.–11 P.M. daily), opposite Parque Bonilla, cooks up burgers and french fries for US$3 a plate.

Groceries

While the market is a good source of fresh fruits and vegetables, the supermarket **Despensa Familiar** (7 A.M.–7 P.M. Mon.–Sat., 7 A.M.–4 P.M. Sun.), right at the corner, is perfect for picking up the rest of the items on your list.

INFORMATION AND SERVICES
Information

La Ceiba now has three different tourist information booths. The one in the *parque central* has limited information but sells handicrafts, postcards, and tickets for the train tours around town. The booth at the airport works with some 35 hotels in town as a booking service. The best of the lot is the **Unidad Turística Municipal** (8 Calle between Av. 14 de Junio and Av. San Isidro, unidadturisticamunicipal@tevisat.net, 8 A.M.–4:30 P.M. Mon.–Fri.), a block from the central park, with information on local attractions as well as tours. A few interesting handicrafts are available for sale here as well.

Travel Agent

For airline tickets and other travel information, try **Paso Travel Service** (tel. 504/443-1990, 7:30 A.M.–5 P.M. Mon.–Sat.), on Avenida San Isidro between 11 and 12 Calles. Some English is spoken.

Banks

Several banks downtown will change dollars and travelers checks, including **Banco Ficohsa, Banco Atlántida,** and **Banco de Occidente.** Ficohsa and Occidente also receive Western Union wires, while Atlántida receives MoneyGram. **BAC Bamer** (Av. San Isidro, between 5 and 6 Calles, tel. 504/443-3330, 9 A.M.–5 P.M. Mon.–Fri., 9 A.M.–noon Sat.) advances cash on Visa and MasterCard accounts with no commission. The ATMs at Banco Atlántida work only with Visa and Plus accounts. There's a Citibank on the west side of the park, but be forewarned that U.S. accounts are not fully linked here. If you need a bank on a Sunday, try at the Mega Plaza Mall, where at least Banco Atlántida (who isn't requiring an account to change dollars) is open 10 A.M.–4 P.M.

Communications

Honducor (Av. Morazán between 13 and 14 Calles, tel. 504/442-0030, 8 A.M.–4 P.M. Mon.–Fri., 8 A.M.–noon Sat.) is several blocks southwest of the square, and **Express Mail Service** is available. **Hondutel** (one block east of Av. 14 de Julio between 5 and 6 Calles—look for the orange tower) is open 24 hours a day.

Of the many Internet cafés in town, the national chain **MultiNet** (7:30 A.M.–8 P.M. Mon.–Sat., 8 A.M.–4:45 P.M. Sun.) has a branch two blocks north of the park on Avenida San Isidro, and charges US$1 per hour, with webcams, fax service, and phone booths (US$0.05/minute to U.S. and Canada) available too. Next door to the Hotel Paris on the central square, there is a café open 8 A.M.–6 P.M. Monday–Saturday (US$1/hour). **Joe's Internet** (Av. Atlántida between 4 and 5 Calles, 8:30 A.M.–5:30 P.M. Mon.–Sat.) charges US$1 an hour for Internet and US$0.05 per minute for calls to the United States. Near the beach is **Internet Redic** (9 A.M.–8 P.M. Mon.–Sat., US$1/hour).

Laundry

Run by an English-speaking owner who spent some time in the United States, **Lavamatic Ceibeño** (Av. Pedro Nufio between 5 and 6 Calles in Barrio La Isla, tel. 504/443-0246, 7 A.M.–10 P.M. daily), not far from downtown, has American-style, self-service washers and dryers for US$1 per load and drop-off service for US$1.50 for a wash and dry with soap.

Lavandería Tiffany (9 A.M.–7 P.M. daily) is in the middle of town, on Avenida Atlántida between 4 and 5 Calles, while **Lavandería Super Clean** (16 Calle just off Av. San Isidro, 8 A.M.–5:30 P.M. Mon.–Fri., 8 A.M.–noon Sat.) is south of the square toward the highway.

Lavandería Soap Opera (7:30 A.M.–6:30 P.M. Mon.–Sat., 9 A.M.–2 P.M.Sun.) is next door to Super Baleadas.

Spanish School

For anyone looking to take Spanish classes in La Ceiba, there are a couple of choices. **Central America Spanish School** (Av. San Isidro between 12 and 13 Calles, tel./fax 504/440-1707, www.ca-spanish.com) has offices in La Ceiba and the Bay Islands. The bright, motivated, small staff offers 20 hours of individual classes, as well as a homestay with a local family, for US$220, or US$150 without a homestay. At least once a week, classes are held outside of the classroom at a nearby destination like Pico Bonito or Sambo Creek. The school has offices in Utila and Copán and can arrange multiweek Spanish study between the different locations if desired.

Another option is **Centro Internacional de Idiomas** (tel. 504/440-1557, www.honduras spanish.com), offering 20 hours of classes per week for US$140, or with a week's homestay with three meals a day for US$220.

Emergencies

There are pharmacies all over town, including **Kielsa** (Calle Hospital Vicente D'Antoni and 15 Calle, tel. 504/443-2970) and **VaVer** (9 Calle between Avenidas 14 de Julio and San Isidro, tel. 504/443-3545).

If you need to see a doctor, and not just a pharmacist, the biggest clinic in town is the **Hospital D'Antoni,** on the road heading toward the sea and city center by the mall. The hospital was established by Standard Fruit of Honduras (Dole) to service its workers, their families, and the community. Another highly regarded clinic is **Medicentro,** on 13 Calle just east of Avenida 14 de Julio.

For the **police,** dial 504/441-0795, or simply 199. For the **fire department,** dial 504/442-2695 or 198. If you need an **ambulance,** call the Red Cross at 504/433-0707 or 195.

Immigration

The *migración* office (tel. 504/442-0638,

9 A.M.–5 P.M. Mon.–Fri.) has moved to Edificio Los Erezos, at the southern end of Avenida 14 de Julio.

Car Rental
Agencies include **Thrifty Rent a Car** (tel. 504/442-1532) at the airport; **Tropical** (tel./fax 504/443-3071) at the Hotel La Quinta; **Molinari** (tel./fax 504/443-0055) at Hotel Gran París; and **Econo Rent-a-Car** (tel. 504/442-8686 in town, or 504/442-1688 at the airport). Most charge around US$50 a day for the least expensive vehicle with insurance and unlimited mileage.

GETTING THERE AND AWAY
Because of its strategic location in the center of the north coast, La Ceiba is a major transportation hub for the Bay Islands, the Mosquitia, and other towns and villages on Honduras's Caribbean coast.

Air
Golosón International Airport is 12 kilometers from downtown La Ceiba on the highway toward Tela. Airport taxis parked at the terminal usually charge US$8 for a private cab. If you're light on luggage, you can also walk out of the airport to the highway and pay much less—offer US$1 per person. A taxi from downtown should cost US$3.25 and arrive one hour before flight departure. There are a couple of snack stand/gift shops at the airport, and the usual Espresso Americano. There is a BAC Bamer bank (open 9 A.M.–4 P.M. Mon.–Sat.) and an ATM. Thrifty Car Rental (tel. 504/442-1532) and Econo Rent-a-Car (tel. 504/442-1688) both have stands in the airport.

Note: Because of its limited facilities, the La Ceiba airport cannot handle poor weather conditions and shuts down frequently during heavy rains and poor visibility. If you are traveling to or from the Bay Islands or the Mosquitia in bad weather, don't be surprised to get stuck for a couple of days.

Taca/Isleña Airlines (tel. 504/443-0179) has offices in the Mega Plaza Mall (tel. 504/441-3190 or 504/441-3191, 8 A.M.–5 P.M. Mon.–Fri., 8 A.M.–noon Sat.) and at the airport (tel. 504/441-2151). Isleña flies several times daily to Roatán, Tegucigalpa, and San Pedro Sula, and once daily to Utila and Guanaja. Taca has flights every day to Miami via San Pedro Sula.

The **Sosa** office is downtown on the *parque* (tel. 504/443-1399, 7 A.M.–5 P.M. Mon.–Fri., 7 A.M.–noon Sat.), and there's another at the airport (tel. 504/440-0692). Sosa flies to Tegucigalpa, San Pedro Sula, and all three of the Bay Islands every day, except there are no Guanaja flights on Sunday. To the Mosquitia, Sosa flies to Brus Laguna (US$113 one-way) on Monday and Friday, and to Puerto Lempira once daily Monday–Saturday.

Rollins Air has a desk at the airport, offering service to the Cayman Islands.

Central Bus Terminal
The central bus terminal on Boulevard 15 de Septiembre is west of downtown, just across the railroad tracks. Taxis to or from the terminal cost US$1. Basic meals and snacks can be bought at stands and eateries at the terminal. There is a public bathroom (US$0.15), an Internet café, several places from which to place inexpensive international and domestic calls, and a Banco Ficensa (8 A.M.–3:30 P.M. Mon.–Fri., 8 A.M.–noon Sat.), where money can be changed and Western Union transfers retrieved.

Note: Schedules and prices are subject to frequent change, so be sure to double-check the information provided here upon arrival.

To **San Pedro Sula: City Tupsa-Catisa** (tel. 504/441-2539) has hourly buses 6 A.M.–5 P.M. (US$5.50). **Diana Express** (tel. 504/441-6460) has departures 8:30 A.M., 9:30 A.M., and 3:30 P.M. (US$5.50). Diana also has connections to Copán Ruinas for an additional US$5.25. **Mirna** runs buses every hour on the half hour between 4:30 A.M. and 4:30 P.M. **Contraipbal** buses depart 4 A.M.–2 P.M. on the hour. **Rey Express** (tel. 504/441-6460, www.reyexpress.net) has buses to San Pedro Sula with connections to Copán Ruinas, Tegucigalpa, Choluteca, San Marcos de Colon, and Guatemala.

To **Tegucigalpa:** Direct buses take seven

hours with stops in **Tela** (US$3) and **El Progreso** US$5); there are four departures daily (3:10 A.M., 7:30 A.M., 9:10 A.M., and 2:15 P.M.) with **Kamaldy** (tel. 504/441-2028), or nine departures daily (the first at 3:30 A.M. and the last at 4 P.M.) with **Cristina** (tel. 504/441-6741). Both lines charge US$11.50.

To **Tela:** Local buses take two hours and depart every hour between 4:30 A.M. and 6 P.M. (US$2). **City Tupsa-Catisa** (tel. 504/441-2539) has hourly buses 6 A.M.–5 P.M. for US$4.80.

To **Trujillo:** Local buses take 4.5 hours, and there are eight buses between 4 A.M. and 4 P.M. (US$3.75). Direct buses with **Contraipbal** depart 9 A.M.–7 P.M. on the hour (US$4).

To **Tocoa:** Many local buses depart daily between 4:30 A.M. and 5:15 P.M. for the three-hour trip (US$3.40).

To **Olanchito:** Eight local buses depart daily between 6:30 A.M. and 5:30 P.M. for the three-hour trip (US$3.70).

To **Nuevo Armenia** and **Jutiapa:** Twice daily buses take 90 minutes, departing at irregular hours (US$1.50).

To **Corozal** and **Sambo Creek:** Departure times are very vague; there are usually four buses daily with the last at 6 P.M. (US$0.60 to Corozal, US$0.65 to Sambo Creek). To get to these villages you can also hop on any westbound bus to Tocoa, Trujillo, Jutiapa, or Olanchito, get off at the highway turnoff, and walk the short distance into town.

To **La Unión** (for Cuero y Salado): Several buses depart daily with the last at 5 P.M. (US$0.90).

To **El Porvenir:** Several buses depart daily with the last at 5 P.M. (US$0.75).

To **Yaruca** and **Urraco** (for the Río Cangrejal): Five buses depart daily with the last leaving at 4 P.M. (US$1.70 to Yaruca, US$2 to Urraco, 2.5 hours). On Sundays there are only two buses. It's possible to take a taxi out to the Urraco turnoff, just across the Río Cangrejal bridge, and wait for a bus or *jalón* (ride) there, instead of at the bus terminal. The last bus returns from Urraco in the early afternoon.

Other Buses

Hedman Alas (tel. 504/441-5347, www.hedmanalas.com), with its terminal next to the supermarket on the highway exit toward Trujillo, runs three buses daily, stopping at San Pedro Sula (US$14, 2.5 hours) and continuing on to Tegucigalpa (US$23), at 5:15 A.M., 10 A.M., and 2 P.M., and a fourth bus just to San Pedro at 5:45 P.M. From San Pedro Sula, connections can be made directly onward to Copán (US$23) and Guatemala City (US$56).

Cotuc (tel. 504/441-2199) has a small ticket office in Barrio Buenos Aires on the La Ceiba–Tela road, where semidirect buses to and from Trujillo (US$5.25, 3.5 hours, 9 A.M.–7 P.M. on the hour) and San Pedro Sula (US$4.75, three hours, last passing at 5 P.M.) stop frequently throughout the day.

Viana (tel. 504/441-2330) runs two luxury nonstop buses daily to San Pedro Sula (US$15, 2.5 hours), continuing on to Tegucigalpa (US$29), with movies, a meal, and coffee. A third bus goes directly to Tegucigalpa on Sundays, saving an hour, for US$36. The ticket office and bus departure point are at the Esso gas station a few blocks west of the main bus terminal.

Car

The 101-kilometer, two-lane highway west to Tela is in fairly decent condition and takes a bit more than an hour to drive. East of La Ceiba, the highway continues along the coastal plain to Jutiapa, where it cuts through a low point in the Cordillera Nombre de Dios into the Valle del Aguán at Savá, 80 kilometers from La Ceiba, and continues on to Trujillo, another 86 kilometers. The entire stretch is generally well maintained, although that can change quickly during a bad rainy season.

Boat

The municipal dock, called **Cabotaje,** is east of the Río Cangrejal, reached by a road turning off the Trujillo highway two kilometers past the Río Cangrejal bridge on the road toward Sambo Creek, on the left side. The side road is three kilometers out to the dock, making it too far to walk, so it's best to take a taxi from town (US$3).

Note: The schedules listed are all for times of high traffic. When demand is low, trips are sometimes cut back, so it's always a good idea to call ahead and check.

The **MV *Galaxy Wave*** (www.safeway maritime.com) departs Cabotaje to Roatán (US$28 regular, US$33 first-class, 90 minutes) daily: It leaves Roatán for La Ceiba at 7 A.M., returns from La Ceiba to Roatán at 9:30 A.M., makes another trip from Roatán to La Ceiba at 2 P.M., and comes back from La Ceiba to Roatán at 4:30 P.M. The large ferry has comfortable indoor seating in two separate cabins, with videos playing during the ride, as well as plenty of room to stand on deck. For more information, call the office in Roatán (tel. 504/445-1795) or in La Ceiba (tel. 504/442-0780). In rough weather, the ferry may be cancelled—call to check. A private taxi from town costs US$3.50 to Cabotaje, and a shared one coming back into town is US$1.50 per person.

The **Utila Princess II** (www.utilaprincess .com) travels between Cabotaje and Utila (US$22, one hour) daily on the following schedule: Utila to La Ceiba at 6:20 A.M.; La Ceiba to Utila at 9:30 A.M.; Utila to La Ceiba at 2 P.M.; and La Ceiba to Utila at 4 P.M. This is a much smaller ferry, resulting in a rougher ride. For more information, call the office (tel. 504/408-5163). *Note:* There are often extra trips during Semana Santa, except on Good Friday, when the ferry doesn't run at all.

Lagoon Marina (tel. 504/440-0614, cell 504/991-5401, radio channel 69, www.lagoon marinalaceiba.com), just behind Cabotaje, has long been the best-equipped marina in Honduras, but it is up for sale. The adjacent **La Ceiba Shipyard** (tel. 504/441-9426, www .laceibashipyard.com) also has mooring space and repair services.

A bus to the Cabotaje can be caught on Avenida República, half a block from the central park, but it can take an hour to reach the dock, while a taxi gets there in 15 minutes.

SOUTH AND WEST OF LA CEIBA
Río Cangrejal

Forming part of the eastern boundary of Parque Nacional Pico Bonito, the Río Cangrejal tumbles off the flanks of the jungle-covered mountains through a narrow boulder-strewn valley before reaching the Caribbean at La Ceiba. Anyone spending a couple of days in La Ceiba should be sure to visit the middle or upper reaches of the river, at least on a day trip, to enjoy the spectacular scenery, take a dip in one of the innumerable swimming holes, or raft some of the finest white water in Central America.

A very well-maintained dirt road winds upstream along the Río Cangrejal, turning off the La Ceiba–Trujillo highway just past the Saopin bridge outside of La Ceiba. The road follows the Valle de Cangrejal through the villages of Las Mangas, Yaruca, and Toncontín, ending in Urraco.

Not long after the turnoff, on the right-hand side is the **Pico Bonito National Park visitors center** (7 A.M.–4 P.M. daily, US$7),

a trail near the Río Cangrejal

AMY E. ROBERTSON

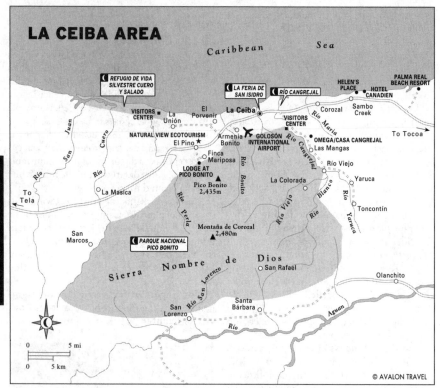

LA CEIBA AREA

Caribbean Sea

REFUGIO DE VIDA SILVESTRE CUERO Y SALADO

LA FERIA DE SAN ISIDRO

RÍO CANGREJAL

HELEN'S PLACE

PALMA REAL BEACH RESORT

HOTEL CANADIEN

VISITORS CENTER

La Unión

El Porvenir

La Ceiba

Corozal

Sambo Creek

NATURAL VIEW ECOTOURISM

El Pino

Armenia Bonito

GOLOSÓN INTERNATIONAL AIRPORT

VISITORS CENTER

To Tocoa

Río María

Río Cangrejal

OMEGA/CASA CANGREJAL

Las Mangas

Finca Mariposa

LODGE AT PICO BONITO

Río Bonito

Río Viejo

La Colorada

Yaruca

Río Blanco

To Tela

La Masica

Pico Bonito 2,435m

Río Perla

Río Viejo

Río

Toncontín

Río Yaruca

San Marcos

Montaña de Corozal 2,480m

PARQUE NACIONAL PICO BONITO

Sierra Nombre de Dios

San Rafael

Olanchito

Río San Lorenzo

San Lorenzo

Santa Bárbara

Río

Aguan

0   5 mi

0   5 km

© AVALON TRAVEL

where visitors can enter to follow one of two fairly moderate and well-marked trails three kilometers to **El Bejuco waterfall.** The river was once crossed exclusively by a basket and pulley system, but a hanging bridge has been added, and the spectacular crossing can be made either way. Camping overnight is possible for US$5.25, and tents can be rented at the visitors center for an additional charge. Although the park officially opens at 7 A.M., the staff arrives by 6 A.M. and is happy to let in birders and other early risers.

Thirteen kilometers from the Saopin bridge on the road along the Río Cangrejal is the community of **El Naranjo,** an interesting stop for its handicraft shop Artesanías Saravia and its 90-minute community tour, which includes a visit to the school church, orchid farm, an agriculture farm, the handicraft

workshop, and a final stop at a swimming hole of the Río Cangrejal, where guests are treated to seasonal fruit. The tour is just US$8 for 1–4 people, or US$16 for a group of five or larger. Other guided walks are available as well—see www.en.picobonito.org and click on "Communities," then "El Naranjo" for more information and contact details, or try calling Antonio Hernández (tel. 504/9957-8920) to make arrangements.

Las Mangas, just below where the road crosses a bridge, is a particularly lovely spot to admire the emerald-green mountainsides and go for a swim.

Beyond Las Mangas, the road follows the river valley upstream on the western bank to the *aldea* (village) of El Pital. Upstream from here, the river passes through a tight gorge, which the road bypasses by crossing over a low

SAFETY IN ADVENTURE TRAVEL

Thousands of travelers a year participate in adventure activities in Honduras, the vast majority of them with no greater mishap than perhaps delayed luggage. Safety, however, should never be taken lightly, and would-be adventure travelers would be smart to thoroughly check out any outfitter they are considering, both in advance and once they reach Honduras.

We are distressed to report that since 2007 two rafters have died while on rafting excursions on the Cangrejal. Both of these tragic incidents occurred on days when the Río Cangrejal was especially high from recent rains; the accident of October 2008 was at a section of the river that included Class V rapids, considered suitable only for experienced rafters even under the best of conditions. (For perspective, Class VI rapids are considered unrunnable.) Guide companies such as **Omega Tours** and **La Moskitia Eco-Aventuras** have strong records for safety, but again it's recommended that you research any companies before signing up, and it's crucial to know your own skill level.

According to the International Scale of River Difficulty, Class V rapids are:

Extremely long, obstructed, or very violent rapids which expose a paddler to added risk. Drops may contain large, unavoidable waves and holes or steep, congested chutes with complex, demanding routes. Rapids may continue for long distances between pools, demanding a high level of fitness. What eddies exist may be small, turbulent, or difficult to reach. At the high end of the scale, several of these factors may be combined. Scouting is recommended but may be difficult. Swims are dangerous, and rescue is often difficult even for experts. A very reliable eskimo roll, proper equipment, extensive experience, and practiced rescue skills are essential.

American Whitewater

The website **www.americanwhitewater.org** has an excellent section on rafting safety, as well as descriptions of the rapid classifications.

---

ridge, coming down the far side to meet the river again at the village of Río Viejo.

At Río Viejo, three smaller rivers join to form the Río Cangrejal: the Río Viejo, the Río Blanco, and the Río Yaruca. The main road continues up to Yaruca and then to the village of **Toncontín**, where four cabins are available for rental with **Cooperative Reyes y Asociados** (www.cangrejal.com). The cabins are simple and rely on solar electricity. There is plenty of hiking, and horseback riding can be arranged, as well as guide service for the hikes. Toncontín is also home to an orchid farm.

The road continues on to Urraco, from where a deteriorated road leads down to Olanchito in the Río Aguán valley, making for great mountain biking. The bike trip from La Ceiba can easily be accomplished in one day, and convincing a bus driver in Olanchito to put your wheels on a La Ceiba–bound bus is not that difficult.

Usually five buses daily make the bouncy and uncomfortable 2.5-hour run between La Ceiba and Urraco (US$2). It is also easy to catch the bus at the Saopin bridge, right where the dirt road up to Urraco begins. Be sure to check when the last bus leaves Urraco back for La Ceiba, as car traffic is scarce in the afternoon. By private car, the road is generally well-maintained as far as Río Viejo, beyond which four-wheel-drive and high-clearance vehicles are recommended. A taxi to Urraco might charge around US$16.

RAFTING THE CANGREJAL

For rafters and kayakers, the Río Cangrejal is one of the premier destinations in Central America. Depending on the water level, the four distinct sections of the river boast dozens of different rapids, ranging from Class II to Class V, offering stretches exciting enough for river-running enthusiasts of any skill level.

Total novices can take a several-hour trip, in which they will be shown the very basics of boating skills and sent down an appropriate stretch of the river with a group of trained guides. More experienced rafters and kayakers can tackle the more daunting rapids. Although it's not common, rafters and kayakers have been injured and even killed on the Cangrejal, so don't take river trips lightly.

Most rafters will go down the lower section of the river, also known as the "commercial" section. Although fairly safe all in all, this section has a couple of long rapids, Class III–IV depending on the water, more than sufficient to get your adrenaline flowing. Above the lower stretch is the middle, starting at the bridge at Las Mangas. This is considered the most complex stretch of the river, littered with boulders of all sizes, a veritable labyrinth of drop-offs, chutes, and all manner of problems. One particular drop-off is not overly difficult, but on the far side is an underwater hazard known as El Submarino, which can suck an unsuspecting boater under. Most boaters wisely portage around El Submarino. Although it is possible to raft the middle, usually only kayakers brave this stretch.

The top, between the gorge and El Pital, and the upper, between El Pital and Las Mangas, both have several Class III–V rapids, plenty of boulders and drop-offs, and stretches shooting through bare rock riverbed. Like the middle, these stretches are more frequented by kayaks than rafts, although Omega regularly rafts the top section. This section is recommended for expert rafters only.

The rapids can be enjoyed year-round but are best run during or just after the fall rains when the river is deep. September–March are considered the best months, with the most water in November and December. That said, tour operators do occasionally cancel their trips during the November rains, because the water gets too high.

With **Omega Tours** (tel. 504/440-0334, www.omegatours.info), half-day rafting trips cost US$49 per person, everything included. Omega Tours is the only operator in La Ceiba

with internationally licensed rafting guides, some with more than 10 years of experience rafting around the world, and the only one that rafts the upper part of the Río Cangrejal, with its Class V rapids.

La Moskitia Eco-Aventuras (tel. 504/414-5798, www.honduras.com/moskitia) is run by veteran Honduras explorer Jorge Salaverri. Half-day white-water rafting trips cost US$58.

With **Garífuna Tours** (tel. 504/440-3252, www.garifunatours.com), rafting trips on the Cangrejal cost US$39 per person.

◖ Parque Nacional Pico Bonito

Chances are the first thing you noticed when you arrived in La Ceiba, especially if you came in by plane, was that massive emerald-green spike of a mountain looming beyond the airport. This is the 2,435-meter-high Pico Bonito, centerpiece of the national park of the same name. Covering 107,300 hectares in the departments of Atlántida and Yoro, of which 49,000 hectares are a buffer zone, Pico Bonito is the largest protected area in Honduras apart from the Río Plátano Biosphere Reserve. It is also one of the least explored, a dense, trackless jungle, ranging from humid tropical broadleaf forest in the lower regions to cloud forest on the peaks.

Some 20 river systems pour off the park's mountains; the rivers display their fullest splendor during the fall-winter rainy season. Because of its rugged, natural isolation, Pico Bonito is a refuge for animal life seen only rarely in other regions of the country. Still, getting in to a place where one might run across a jaguar or ocelot requires some serious effort.

The park can also easily be accessed via the Río Zacate, a river pouring off the southern flanks of the mountains to the west of La Ceiba. Here, one can hike into the **La Ruidosa** waterfall, reached by a well-kept trail through lush jungle alive with birds and sometimes monkeys at the edge of the mountains. Continue upstream to explore additional falls and look for more wildlife. To get to the Río Zacate, take a bus or drive on the highway to

© FRANKLIN RAMIREZ, GUARUMA.ORG

Frogs are just one of the many residents of Pico Bonito National Park.

Tela, and look for a dirt road turnoff in the middle of a pineapple plantation between kilometer markers 174 and 175, past the highway village of El Pino. Walk straight up the dirt road toward the mountain until it hits a junction with another road, by some power lines. Turn right and continue to the end of the road, where there is a watchman, who should take your US$6 payment and give you a receipt in return. Past the ranch, you'll come to the river's edge at a waterfall with a deep pool, good for swimming. Look for a series of stone steps, which lead up the hillside through the jungle to the Ruidosa falls, an impressive sight in the jungle. The walk takes about an hour from the ranch and a little less back down. The trail is generally in good condition but can be muddy. The Pico Bonito foundation in La Ceiba may be able to arrange guides farther into the forest along fainter trails. A better option, though, is to go to the village of El Pino along the La Ceiba–Tela highway and get a guide there (easily reached by frequent local bus from the La Ceiba terminal).

For the adventurer, it would be hard to find more of a challenge in Honduras than a trip to the top of Pico Bonito. It may look like a relatively short jaunt, but in fact it takes a solid 9–10 days of hacking through the jungle while clinging to a steep, muddy hillside, hoping there are no snakes nearby. Jorge Salaverri of La Moskitia Eco-Aventuras (tel. 504/414-5798, www.honduras.com/moskitia) has climbed the summit and can organize a trip (well in advance) for those who want to try their luck.

For more information about the park, stop in at the offices of **Fundación Parque Nacional Pico Bonito** (FUPNAPIB, tel. 504/442-3044, www.en.picobonito.org, 8 A.M.–5 P.M. Mon.–Fri., 8 A.M.–noon Sat.), on 15 Calle half a block east of Avenida 14 de Julio in La Ceiba. Local guides and other activities can be arranged through the tourism committee in El Pino.

The Butterfly Farm

On the northern flanks of the Pico Bonito range, right next to the Lodge at Pico Bonito, is the **Tropical Butterfly Farm and Gardens** (tel. 504/440-0388, http://hondurasbutterfly far.tripod.com/butterfly_house.htm), a private butterfly farm run by former Peace Corps volunteer Robert Gallardo, who both exports butterfly larvae to the United States and organizes tours for interested visitors at US$6 per person. On the grounds is also a **snake vivarium.** Access is via a three-kilometer dirt road south from the village of El Pino, on the La Ceiba–Tela road just a few minutes west of La Ceiba. To get there without a car, take any of the frequent buses from the La Ceiba terminal to Tela, San Francisco, or La Masica, and get off at El Pino. From the highway, it's a relaxed 20-minute walk. The trees around the farm are alive with birds and the occasional white-faced or spider monkey. The farm charges a US$2 entrance fee and is usually open 9 A.M.–4 P.M. daily, but call the Lodge at Pico Bonito (just past the farm, tel. 504/440-1902) to confirm.

El Pino

The tourist committee at El Pino offers a variety of tours going into the park and in the surrounding area. Trips can be arranged to La Ruidosa as well as several other destinations in and around the park, including full-day and overnight hikes. One nice excursion on the lower Río Zacate takes you into the mangrove forest and offers a good chance of seeing howler monkeys. For guided tours contact Efrain Cuellar (tel. 504/3386-9878, turismoelpino@ yahoo.com) or ask at the small tourist information office on the highway at Vivero Natural View, opposite Ferretería Águila. Tour descriptions are on the website www.en.picobonito .org; click on "Communities," then "El Pino." Three-hour hikes are US$9–16 per person, and a demonstration of traditional pottery-making can be arranged for just US$4 per person, minimum two people.

There are two community accommodations in El Pino, the **Posada El Buen Pastor** (tel. 504/9950-3404) and the Natural View Ecotourism Park. El Buen Pastor is a clean, quiet two-story house with four rooms on the top floor. There's a large common area that looks out over the highway and into El Pino. All rooms have private baths with hot water,

and breakfast is included in the room price. Rooms are US$16–21 and can accommodate up to three people. Owner Doña Vita lives on the first floor. El Buen Pastor is on the main highway at the entrance to El Pino's public school; it's a large, two-story yellow house with a small sign.

A budget, nature-oriented option, **Natural View Ecotourism Park** (tel. 504/431-3147, US$13 pp), is within walking distance of Pico Bonito park, about 10 kilometers from La Ceiba going toward Tela along the highway. Catch any Tela-bound bus and get off at El Pino. The rustic adobe and thatch-roof cabins are clean and cool. The grounds, dotted with fruit trees and flowering plants, feature a two-story *champa*-style restaurant, a covered hammock area, a soccer field, and a slightly oldish pool. Staff can organize tours into Pico Bonito and Cuero y Salado refuge with English-speaking guides.

Rapiditos (minibuses) travel from El Pino to La Ceiba from 5:30 A.M. until around 8 P.M. (always double-check for the latest schedule). Minibuses return from La Ceiba to El Pino from 6 A.M. until 11 P.M. Regular buses depart from La Ceiba bus terminal (they park next to the Banco Occidental until 6 P.M., when they start departing from Taquitos Mexicanos Restaurant, Barrio Potreritos (but all buses at least pass by the bus terminal). The bus costs about US$0.50 from the terminal and a couple of lempiras more from the center of town. Buses heading to La Masica, San Francisco, Santa Ana, San Juan Pueblo, Esparta, and even Tela (as long as it's not a direct bus) will also drop you off at El Pino, and they charge about the same.

◀ Refugio de Vida Silvestre Cuero y Salado

Formed by the estuaries of Ríos Cuero, Salado, and San Juan, which flow off the flanks of the Cordillera Nombre de Dios to the south, the Cuero y Salado Wildlife Refuge comprises 13,225 hectares of wetlands and coastline filled with plant and animal life endangered elsewhere in Honduras. Jaguars, howler and white-faced monkeys, manatees (the reserve's mascot), turtles, crocodiles, caymans, fishing eagles, hawks, and several species of parrots are among the 196 bird and 35 mammal species identified within the reserve's boundaries.

The swampy, mangrove-covered wetlands perform several important ecological functions. The dense walls of mangrove roots in the water act as a nursery for marine animals, such as shrimp and several fish species, who make their way out to the open ocean after they've had a chance to grow. The vegetation serves as a way station for many migratory birds and as a buffer zone protecting the surrounding area during ocean storms and floods coming down from the mountains.

Much of the north coast was formerly covered with similar wetlands, but most have since been converted to pasture or plantations—a process all too evident as Cuero y Salado is surrounded by encroaching cattle-grazing land. An estimated 40 percent of the reserve's wetlands have been drained since 1987, when the land was donated by Standard Fruit to become a reserve. Recent efforts to transition cattle-ranchers into the forestry industry (primarily planting palm and mahogany) seem to be working. However, chemicals leaking in from nearby pineapple and African palm plantations also threaten the wetlands.

By far the best way to appreciate Cuero y Salado is on a guided boat tour of the reserve, either on a tour or by just showing up, although finding a boat can be difficult at times. Independent boats charge US$21 per person. The trips, taking about two hours, tour through different waterways, with frequent stops to listen and watch for monkeys, birds, crocodiles, and other wetland denizens. Early morning tours are the best for wildlife-watching. The guides are usually volunteers at the reserve and are very knowledgeable about the ecosystems and wildlife in the area. They can usually help visitors get a good look at a troop of howler monkeys or some of the more colorful bird species in the reserve. Be sure to bring some repellent or wear long sleeves— the mosquitoes aren't too bad on the beach

or the encampment but can be fierce in the swamp. There is a wide-open, deserted stretch of Caribbean beach that can be reached by foot from the visitors center (although it's not a short walk), perfect for a cooling-off swim after your boat tour.

For tourists, the interior section of the reserve is accessible by boat only, but don't be surprised to see a couple of locals standing on the shore farther in the swamps, fishing for their dinner. They know all the paths to get into the reserve and don't mind getting munched by mosquitoes to catch a free meal for their families.

The park is open 6 A.M.–6 P.M. A US$10 (US$5 for students with credential) entrance fee is charged above the price of the boat ride. Visitors who are not with a group can then choose between a canoe (for one or two passengers) with a guide (US$8) or a larger boat (which can accommodate up to six passengers) with a guide (US$20, or US$5.50 pp for 4–6 passengers, plus US$5.50 for the guide). Canoeing is ideal, as it's easier to spot animals when you don't have a buzzing motor to scare them off.

Since the early morning and late afternoon are the best times for wildlife-viewing, some visitors may wish to spend the night. The reserve has a rustic five-bedroom cabin; beds are US$7 per person. Beds can be reserved directly with the visitors center, tel. 504/440-1990. Otherwise, visitors can pitch their own tent for US$3. Locals will cook up a meal for unprepared visitors, but it's best to come with food. The beach is a great spot for a bonfire cookout (but bring mosquito repellent). Accommodations may be simple, but those who have stayed the night rave about the wildlife out for spotting in the early morning.

Cuero y Salado is 30 kilometers from La Ceiba. To get there, take a bus or car from La Ceiba past the airport on the road to Tela, and turn right into pineapple fields shortly after crossing the Río Bonito bridge. This road continues to the village of La Unión, but get off where the railroad tracks cross the road. From here, the Ferrocarril Nacional runs a small car for US$10 for a solo ride round-trip, or US$5 per person with two or more passengers. There are seven departures a day, at 7 A.M., 8:10 A.M., 9:20 A.M., 10:30 A.M., 11:40 A.M., 12:50 P.M., and 2 P.M. The train returns to La Unión immediately after arriving in the park, with the last return at 2:30 P.M. Prices for returning the following day are 50 percent more. For those saving their pennies, it's a hot two-hour walk along the rails to reach the headquarters. Buses from La Ceiba to La Unión leave from the main terminal every hour between 6:30 A.M. and 6 P.M. When returning, keep in mind that the last bus bound for La Ceiba passes at 4 P.M. The Bar El Bambú at the end of the train line makes a fine place to sip a cold beer or soft drink while awaiting the bus.

It's recommended that independent visitors make reservations with **Fundación Cuero y Salado** (FUCSA, tel. 504/443-0329) in La Ceiba for boat tours, as groups often visit the reserve. Staff can also put you in touch with the *ferrocarril* to reserve your train ride. You can also stop in to the **Unidad Turística Municipal** on 8 Calle half a block from La Ceiba's central square for more information.

Ecolodges
ALONG THE RÍO CANGREJAL
Located just off the Río Cangrejal is the ◖ **Omega Jungle Lodge** (tel. 504/440-0334, www.omegatours.info), a relaxed lodge run by a German rafting outfit. Accommodations include a plain guesthouse, with shared bathroom and communal lounge (US$10 s or US$14 d), one simple but attractive cabin (*sans* bathroom) built over a gurgling creek (US$40.50 for 2–3 people), and a couple of two-story luxury cabins that can sleep up to five with high-end amenities and decor (US$116 d). All guests are welcome to use the beautiful outdoor shower in a stone cabana, whose water runs warm by the end of a sunny day. Penny-pinchers can rent a tent for US$5 per person. A very good option for a low-priced day of rafting is their one-day package for US$49, including a room in the guesthouse, lunch, and a day of rafting. Omega offers a wide variety of day trips

and longer expeditions, including white-water swimming, jungle hiking, horseback riding, mountain biking, kayaking, a jungle survival course, and multiday trips near La Ceiba and in the Mosquitia. The grounds are lovely, with a small pool, three easy trails, and a thatch-roof restaurant serving very good international cuisine. There are several vegetarian options, and creative dishes such as *kasspatzle* and ginger chicken, all generously portioned (US$5–10). Omega is highly eco-conscious, with an earth-friendly septic system, among other features. The lodge is roughly 10 kilometers up the well-maintained dirt road from the highway. The lodge offers a shuttle service from La Ceiba, the ferry dock, and the airport (US$15, US$18, and US$25, respectively; price is per car, up to four passengers).

At the same turnoff is ◖ **Casa Cangrejal** (tel. 504/408-2760, www.casacangrejal.com, US$87 s, US$104 d), a new and spectacular four-room bed and breakfast, built out of stone along a mountain brook (and overlooking a natural swimming pool). Beautifully designed by owner Karen Treherne, the stone home is warmed by the woven tapestries on the walls and luxury linens on the beds. There is a large shared patio with a bar, pool table, lounge furniture, and a grill, where barbecues are occasionally prepared for guests. Amenities include wireless Internet and a small fitness room. There's no air-conditioning, but rooms stay cool thanks to the foot-thick stone, and each has a fan as well. Transport can be arranged from either La Ceiba or San Pedro Sula.

The hilltop ◖ **Cabañas del Bosque** (in Las Mangas, tel. 504/406-5782, www.cangrejal .com) offers simple wood cabins (each with two rooms) with private bathrooms, fans, and wide porches with breathtaking views of the mountains and jungle. The *electroducha* hot water showers were getting strained due to the irregular electricity supply, so the goal is to transition to solar-powered water heating, but for now it's cold water. Another building, just below the cabins on the hillside, holds a small lounge area and restaurant, serving breakfast, lunch,

© MARCUS SABINI, CANGREJAL.COM

the restaurant at Cabañas del Bosque, a community-run ecolodge

and dinner (US$3–4); they are happy to attend nonguests, but call first, so that they can be sure to have supplies on hand. This community-run project is tied in with Guaruma, a nonprofit youth organization dedicated to creating environmental awareness that can provide visitors with knowledgeable guides to the area. It's best to book a guide in advance through the office in La Ceiba, especially if you need an English-speaker, but it's also possible to pop into the youth center (usually staffed) to find a guide. Internet is available in the center for US$0.25 for 15 minutes. The group has trails up and down the Río Cangrejal, some longer and more demanding, all quite off the beaten path.

Twenty-three kilometers from the Ceiba–Trujillo highway along the Río Cangrejal is the community-run **Cooperativa Reyes y Asociados** (www.cangrejal.com), with four wooden cabins tucked into the forest around the village of Toncontín. Each cabin has a porch and bathroom and is solar-powered. Hiking and horseback riding and guides are available. There is a kitchen where food can be prepared for you, or you can bring your own and cook.

A unique and relatively new option is the **Casa Verde** (www.wendygreenyoga.com), along the Río Cangrejal, in a lush setting opposite a slender 75-meter waterfall. Owner Wendy Green prepares organic raw food meals and leads daily yoga classes. With no more than five guests at a time, attention is highly personalized, with profound rejuvenation as the goal. Guests stay either in the riverside guest room in the main house or in an attractive cabin, both with tasteful, modern decor. Weekly rates are US$999–1,365 per person and include all meals, hiking, and yoga.

Just half a mile from the eastern entrance to the Parque Nacional Pico Bonito is **Villas Pico Bonito** (tel. 504/449-0045, U.S. tel. 972/535-8450, www.villaspicobonito.com, US$75–290), a collection of cabins and *champas* set along the river. While the villas are a bit hodgepodge in their decor and layout, each has a kitchen and, more importantly, a waterfall and jungle view. A restaurant and swimming pool are on-site.

WESTERN SIDE OF PARQUE NACIONAL PICO BONITO

While there are more lodges on the eastern flank of Parque Nacional Pico Bonito (along the Río Cangrejal), the western side has access to equally stunning hiking and is well-located for rafting on the Río Zacate.

One of the finest hotels in Honduras, **Lodge at Pico Bonito** (tel. 504/440-0388, U.S. tel. 888/428-0221, www.picobonito.com) provides a taste of what tourist development can look like if done really well. Nestled up against the emerald-green flanks of the Pico Bonito range are 22 wood and stone cabins, each with louvered wood windows and an overhead fan, some with air-conditioning. Six rooms are in individual cabins ("superior plus" cabins with a/c, US$319 s/d, US$377 high season), and the others are in eight two-room cabins (with fan US$276 s/d, US$278 high season, US$52 more with a/c). The location is really superlative—hundreds of species of birds as well as occasional troops of monkeys and other animals frequently venture down from Pico Bonito to sample the fruit trees around the lodge, making it a fine location for wildlife-watching. Nearby and reached by trail is the Río Coloradito, a steep, narrow river pouring down a narrow, jungle-clad gorge, with an excellent swimming hole. Just below the lodge is a butterfly farm and serpent vivarium. The lodge is reached from the Ceiba–Tela highway, turning off south at the village of El Pino, eight kilometers west of the airport. Rates include breakfast and transportation to and from the airport, and taxes, but do not include a 10 percent service charge that is tacked on. Meals are pricey, but excellent—reservations are required for day visitors.

A budget, nature-oriented option, **Natural View Ecotourism Park** (tel. 504/431-3147, US$13 pp), is within walking distance of Pico Bonito park, about 10 kilometers from La Ceiba going toward Tela along the highway. Catch any Tela-bound bus and get off at El Pino. The rustic adobe and thatch-roof cabins are clean and cool. The grounds, dotted with fruit trees and flowering plants, feature a two-story *champa*-style restaurant, a covered hammock area, a soccer field, and a slightly oldish pool. Staff can organize tours into Pico Bonito and Cuero y Salado refuge with English-speaking guides.

Finca El Eden (tel. 504/3345-2833, bertiharlos@yahoo.de) is a great budget accommodation run by a German, Berti Harlos, offering backpackers a chance to enjoy the Pico Bonito jungle for not much money. Berti operates a large ranch—with some 40-odd kinds of exotic fruit trees—just off the La Ceiba–Tela road, 32 kilometers from La Ceiba and just before the village of Santa Ana. The main building houses a full-service restaurant downstairs, **Edelweiss** (US$3–10 per plate), while upstairs is an open-air *champa* with floor space for mattresses and mosquito nets (US$8 pp, including purified water). Berti serves the only German beer available in the region, for US$1.50, and fresh juices from the fruit of his own trees. Berti has also built a small cabin on a nearby hilltop called **Mayabell,** which also costs US$8 a night to sleep in, plus US$15 if you want to ride horseback to and from. Berti will happily help arrange a variety of other horseback or hiking tours for groups, such as a trip to Cuero y Salado. All the direct buses between La Ceiba and San Pedro, except Hedman Alas, will pick up and drop off travelers at Berti's front door, or you can catch a Santa Ana bus at La Ceiba's main terminal. From La Ceiba to Santa Ana is US$0.85.

EAST OF LA CEIBA
Playa de Perú

About the best decent beach near La Ceiba, Playa de Perú is reached by a 1.5-kilometer dirt road turning off the Tocoa highway between kilometer markers 205 and 206, about eight kilometers east of the Río Cangrejal bridge. There's nothing on the beach apart from a few *champas* built by fishermen and a couple of apparently abandoned restaurants. The beach itself is windswept and unkempt, and usually deserted. To get there by public transport, catch a bus headed for Sambo Creek, Tocoa, or Olanchito, get off at the turn, and walk down to the beach.

Corozal

Not one of the more attractive Garífuna settlements on the Honduran coast, Corozal is an unremarkable fishing village on the beach about 20 kilometers east of La Ceiba. In town are a couple of basic *comedores,* as well as the **Ocean View** hotel and restaurant (tel. 504/429-1025, www.oceanviewhn.com, restaurant 11 A.M.–11 P.M. daily). The hotel is in an attractive two-story wooden building facing the beach, with four simple but spacious apartments, each with a living/dining area, bedroom, TV, hot water, and fan, renting for around US$65. The adjacent restaurant is in a large open-air *champa,* serving seafood specials for around US$8. Nearby is **Playa de Zambrano,** a decent though unspectacular stretch of beach.

A few hundred meters uphill from the highway, near kilometer marker 209 and marked by a sign before arriving at Corozal from La Ceiba, is **Los Chorros,** another local swimming hole on a small river gushing off the tropical hillside, with many pools, boulders, and falls, similar to Río María.

On the highway just east of the Corozal turnoff is **Villa Rhina** (tel. 504/443-1222, www.honduras.com/villarhina, US$30 s, US$37 d, US$59 for a bungalow, reservations required), a resort hotel set into the hillside with views out over the Caribbean. On the four-hectare grounds are three freshwater pools, a small waterfall, and a trail up into the forest above, where you can catch views of the Cayos Cochinos. The wood-paneled rooms are attractive and the hotel is well run, but the location is above the highway and away from the beach. The owners do their best to make up for that with attentive service, including arrangements for local jungle and beach activities, often with transportation.

It's possible to reach Corozal by *colectivo* at the taxi hub in Barrio Potreritos in La Ceiba, on 6 Calle between 4 and 5 Avenidas, behind Hondutel. Taxis leave every half hour.

Sambo Creek

A few kilometers east of Corozal and more appealing is Sambo Creek, another Garífuna village at the mouth of a small river. Two good seafood restaurants, often filled with Ceibeños out for a meal, are **La Champa Kabasa,** right at the entrance to town, with an excellent, hearty seafood soup, and **Sambo Creek Restaurant,** just to the east on the beach.

Just east of the main entrance to Sambo Creek on the Tocoa highway is another dirt road leading toward the water, with signs for Villa Helen's, Hotel Canadien, and the Diving Pelican, three adjacent hotels on a quiet, clean, and safe stretch of beach—the first two are run by (unrelated) Canadian expats, the latter by Americans. **☾ Villa Helen's** (tel. 504/408-1137, www.villahelens.com, US$24–32 s, US$37 d) has eight spacious rooms in a small house close to the tawny beach, all immaculately clean with tile floors, air-conditioning, hot water, and small refrigerators, as well as six small cabin/apartments with efficiency kitchens around a grassy parking area on the other side of the road (cabins run US$42–53 and sleep 2–6). There is a small swimming pool; day use is US$1.50. No credit cards are accepted.

Right next door is **Hotel Canadien** (tel. 504/440-2099, www.hotelcanadien.com, US$52 d, US$11 each additional person, four maximum), a three-story white building with two floors of hotel-style rooms, each with a small sitting room (whose sofa converts to a bed) and a refrigerator and air-conditioning, set around a small terrace and two large pools right behind the beach. It was probably very nice when it opened, but it has seen better days. Helen's and Hotel Canadien both have good restaurants—Helen's (the tastier and much cheaper of the two—burgers US$3, fish dishes US$6) is on a relaxed open-air terrace, and the Canadien's is on the third floor of the hotel, with great views.

The **Diving Pelican Inn** (tel. 504/3369-2208, www.divingpelicaninn.com, US$60 s/d) has a more intimate feel with just three rooms, two on the beachside property and a third in a tiny cabin just across the road. While there's no restaurant, Texan owner Jim makes a

THE CARIBBEAN ODYSSEY OF THE GARÍFUNA

The Garífuna, who populate the Caribbean coast from Belize to as far south and east as the Mosquitia, are the product of a unique ethnic and historical odyssey. Most of the Garífuna's 50-odd villages are in Honduras, where they first arrived in Central America in 1797. With their own language, customs, dances, and music, the Garífuna have maintained a distinctive lifestyle in the midst of the Honduran north-coast society. Colonial-era English and Spanish called the Garífuna "Black Caribs," an accurate description of the two ethnic strains that combined to create a new race.

For the first two centuries following Columbus, the Caribbean island of San Vicente, in the Lesser Antilles, was left to the Black Caribs, who originated from the coast of South America, where Carib speakers still live today. During this time, the island became something of a refuge for black slaves, who were either shipwrecked in the area or escaped from plantations on nearby islands.

Details on the early encounters between the slaves and the Black Caribs are nonexistent, but it must have been a fascinating experience – two completely different cultures, one from Africa and the other from the rainforests of South America, meeting by chance on an island in the middle of the Caribbean. Not only did they not see any need to fight, but they mixed their blood and their cultures, borrowing from each to develop a new language and new customs. One of many examples of the mixed culture is the *yancunu*, a Garífuna New Year's dance; it's very similar to dances of rainforest

Indians in South America, while the music is clearly of West African origin. Possibly in an effort to distance themselves from their past as slaves, the Black Caribs on San Vicente, and later the Garífuna in Central America, fiercely denied their African blood. In spite of their obviously African physiognomy, both groups insisted they were American Indians. In more recent times, though, the Garífuna have become much prouder of their African heritage.

In the beginning of the 18th century, French settlers from Martinique moved to San Vicente and began cultivating small-scale plantations of cotton, cacao, and indigo. They seem to have gotten along peacefully with the Caribs, both black and "yellow," as the pure-blooded Indians were called. The French were soon followed by the English, who abortively attempted to colonize the island in 1713. San Vicente was officially recognized by both countries as neutral territory until 1763, when it was ceded to England in the Treaty of Paris. The English, intent on establishing large-scale sugar plantations, tried to cajole the Garífuna off their valuable island, with little success. When war broke out again between France and England in 1779, the Garífuna and French took the opportunity to seize control of San Vicente.

The island was formally returned to the English in 1783, at which point the new settlers began pressuring the Garífuna to get off their land. Tensions finally broke out into open war in 1795, pitting the Garífuna and a few remaining Frenchmen against English troops. The

great breakfast (US$6), and he and his wife are happy to arrange trips to the Cayos Cochinos and river rafting, as well as transportation to the airport, bus, or ferry.

All three hotels, on a fine stretch of beach, make great places to have a relaxed few days near La Ceiba. To get there, either catch a Jutiapa or Tocoa local bus and get off at the turn, or take a US$12 private taxi from La Ceiba (a bit more at night). It's possible to reach Sambo Creek by *colectivo* at the taxi hub

in Barrio Potreritos in La Ceiba, on 6 Calle between 4 and 5 Avenidas, behind Hondutel. Taxis leave every half hour.

Day trips to the Cayos Cochinos can be arranged through boatmen in Sambo Creek, either by asking around in town the day before if you already have a group or, if not, by checking in at either Helen's or the Canadien to see if they have any groups going. Prices vary, but usually a boat should do the trip for US$60–100 for up to 10 people, or maybe US$20–30

Garífuna gained a reputation for uncommon ferocity and bravery during the war, which lasted two full years. The Garífuna were led by chief Chatoyer, or Satuyé, who remains a legendary figure among modern Garífuna. The British finally overcame Garífuna resistance by bringing in massive numbers of troops from Jamaica.

Having taken full measure of the Garífuna after years of battle, the British elected to deport the whole troublesome lot. Among the several sites considered were Africa, the Bahamas, and the island of Hispaniola. Eventually, the British decided on Roatán, in the Bay Islands off Honduras, assuming the warlike Garífuna would become a headache for the Spanish.

On March 3, 1797, some 3,000 Garífuna were loaded onto a convoy of 10 boats; the fleet departed San Vicente, stopping briefly in Jamaica before landing near Port Royal, Roatán, on April 12. A small group crossed to the north side of the island and started the village of Punta Gorda, the oldest continually inhabited Garífuna town, but most of the Garífuna apparently did not like the looks of Roatán and moved on to the mainland to Trujillo, probably with the help of the Spanish.

The first communities set up by the Garífuna on the mainland of Central America were at Río Negro and Cristales, on either side of Trujillo. The old port had recently been reconquered by the Spanish after 150 years of abandonment, and the Garífuna were welcomed as workers and mercenary soldiers. Over the next century, groups of Garífuna made their way up and down the Honduran coast, building villages as far north as Belize and as far east and south as the Nicaraguan Mosquito Coast. The Garífuna carved a niche for themselves on the north coast as boatmen, loggers, and superb soldiers. They fought, defending coastal towns from pirates and in the wars of independence.

Although they gave up soldiering long ago, the Garífuna have firmly established themselves as an integral part of the Honduran Caribbean coast. In keeping with their history, the Garífuna are known for their constant travel, either with fishing fleets, the merchant marines, or to Garífuna communities in New York and Los Angeles. In spite of this constant movement, the Garífuna have retained a strong sense of ethnic identity. Unlike other minority groups in Honduras, they show no signs of losing their culture. The Garífuna have a built-in resilience immediately apparent on the proud, strong faces and direct gazes that greet visitors to any Garífuna community.

Garífuna communities are increasingly becoming involved in the debate over development along the north coast. Many of the finest stretches of coastline are owned collectively by Garífuna communities, and they are facing ever-greater pressures to sell to hotel developers. Many Garífuna see a proposed new law attempting to reform collective land rights as a move to take away this weapon, which has allowed them to hold onto their lands so far. How the debate is resolved remains to be seen, but pressures on their land are sure to continue.

THE NORTH COAST

---

per person if you join with a group already going. One boatman based out of Sambo Creek that runs tours to Cayos Cochinos is Omar Acosta (tel. 504/408-1666).

Also just off the highway near Sambo Creek is the **Sambo Creek Canopy Tour** (tel. 504/3355-5481, 7 A.M.–6 P.M. daily, US$45). Prices include a 40-minute horseback ride to the zipline site and a stop in nearby hot springs. It's also possible to do just the hot springs and horseback riding for US$25 per person, which may be something to consider, as the canopy platforms haven't always been sturdy in the past.

Four kilometers past Sambo Creek toward Jutiapa, 22 kilometers from La Ceiba, is an upscale beachfront hotel complex, **Palma Real Beach Resort** (tel. 504/429-0501, www .grupopalmareal.com). The large complex of pastel-colored buildings right on a fine beach houses 161 well-equipped rooms, each with a balcony or terrace. Facilities include a casino, separate pools for children and adults, tennis and basketball courts, a restaurant and snack bar, a bar, a disco, and a theater. Popular with wealthy Hondurans and Salvadorans, the hotel offers package deals with food and drink included for US$55–133 per person per day, varying with the day of the week, season, and number of guests in the room. Children (2–10) are US$28–40. Day passes are available and cost US$37–73 for adults, US$23–35 for children. Prices are higher during Semana Santa and over the year-end holidays.

Near the entrance to Palma Real is **Water Jungle** (9 A.M.–5 P.M. Fri.–Sun.), Honduras's largest water park, with a wave pool and pool games for small children, as well as huge water slides.

Cacao Lagoon

Approximately 24 kilometers east from La Ceiba is the small, oceanside Cacao Lagoon. Mangroves surround the water and provide shelter to tropical birds and howler and white-faced monkeys. The lagoon is named for the nearby tropical cacao plants, once used as money in pre-Columbian times, now used in the manufacturing of chocolate, of course. The neighboring village makes a living from its cacao and sugarcane plantations, and is interesting in and of itself. A tour is the easiest way to see the lagoon (both Moskitia Eco-

Aventuras and Tourist Options run tours, the latter much cheaper), but those who can arrange their own transportation to the town can likely also negotiate a boat tour with a local guide, on a dugout canoe. From the beach it's possible to see the Cayos Cochinos, just 15 kilometers out to sea.

Jutiapa, Nuevo Armenia, and Farther East

Just before the highway turns inland through the hills toward Savá and the Valle del Aguán, 33 kilometers from La Ceiba, is the small town of Jutiapa, where a dirt road (in horrible condition at last report) turns off 10 kilometers down to Nuevo Armenia at the sea's edge. From here, you can arrange a trip on a motorized *lancha* (launch) out to the nearby Cayos Cochinos. Prices continue to go up but should be somewhere around US$100–150 for a boat, depending on negotiating ability and number of people going. Finding boats already going out for a less expensive ride is next to impossible these days. Rene Arzú (tel. 504/9937-1674) is one person in Nuevo Armenia who can help arrange a private boat trip, but there are others. A simple hotel in Nuevo Armenia offers inexpensive, very basic rooms.

East along the coast beyond Jutiapa are the Garífuna villages of Balfate, Río Esteban, and Río Coco, all connected by a rough dirt road.

Tela

Honduras tourism officials, eyeing the wealthy beach resorts in Mexico with envy, tirelessly promote Tela Bay as Honduras's Cancún-to-be. Certainly all the elements appear to be in place: mile upon mile of beaches, sleepy Garífuna villages, and three nearby natural reserves—Punta Sal, Lancetilla, and Punta Izopo—chock-full of exotic plants and wild animals. For the time being, however, the town remains a sleepy beach-front backwater. Long-talked about development just west of Tela near the Laguna de Los Micos may change all that, but it remains to be seen.

Reactions to present-day undeveloped Tela vary wildly. Some visitors are charmed by the town's relaxed vibe, while others take offense at the stray dogs and bit of trash on the main city beach and hastily pack their bags. There's no doubt the downtown beach area is not pristine, but it would be a shame to let this put travelers off from the many attractions around the bay.

Originally, Tela (pop. 28,300) was built as a United Fruit Company town in the early years of the 20th century, but the banana business is now less important to the local economy

THE NORTH COAST

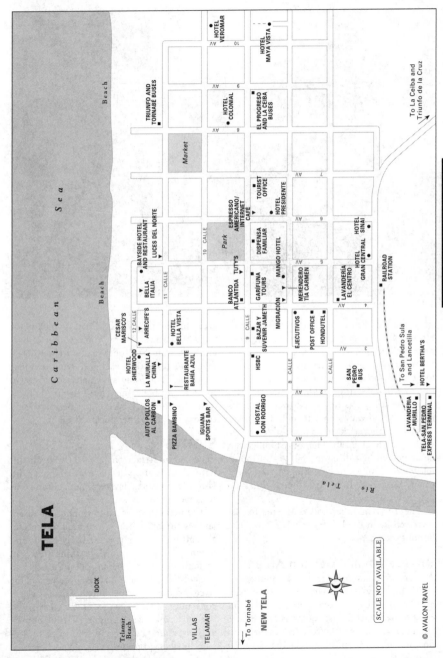

TELA

SCALE NOT AVAILABLE

© AVALON TRAVEL

To La Ceiba and
Triunfo de la Cruz

To San Pedro Sula
and Lancetilla

To Tornabé

NEW TELA

Telamar Beach

VILLAS TELAMAR

DOCK

Caribbean Sea

Beach

Beach

Beach

Río Tela

HOTEL VEROMAR

HOTEL MAYA VISTA

TRIUNFO AND TORNABÉ BUSES

HOTEL COLONIAL

EL PROGRESO AND LA CEIBA BUSES

Market

TOURIST OFFICE

HOTEL PRESIDENTE

ESPRESSO AMERICANO/ INTERNET CAFÉ

Park

DISPENSA FAMILIAR

MANGO HOTEL

HOTEL SINAI

HOTEL GRAN CENTRAL

LAVANDERÍA EL CENTRO

RAILROAD STATION

MERENDERO TÍA CARMEN

GARIFUNA TOURS

BANCO ATLANTIDA

TUTY'S

BELLA ITALIA

BAYSIDE HOTEL AND RESTAURANT

LUCES DEL NORTE

ARRECIFE'S

CESAR MARISCO'S

HOTEL BELLA VISTA

BAZAR Y SUVENIR JAMETH

MIGRACIÓN

EJECUTIVOS

POST OFFICE

HONDUTEL

HSBC

HOTEL SHERWOOD

LA MURALLA CHINA

RESTAURANTE BAHÍA AZUL

AUTO POLLOS AL CARBON

PIZZA BAMBINO

IGUANA SPORTS BAR

HOSTAL DON RODRIGO

SAN PEDRO BUS

HOTEL BERTHA'S

LAVANDERIA MURILLO

TELA-SAN PEDRO EXPRESS TERMINAL

10 CALLE

11 CALLE

12 CALLE

9 CALLE

8 CALLE

7 CALLE

1 AV

2 AV

3 AV

4 AV

5 AV

6 AV

7 AV

8 AV

9 AV

10 AV

Tela's beachfront

© AMY E. ROBERTSON

since the Tela Railroad Company—United's Honduras division, also called Chiquita—moved its headquarters to La Lima, near San Pedro Sula, in 1965. Currently, the town earns most of its money from African palm plantations, cattle-ranching, and tourism.

While safety has improved over the years in Tela, it's always smart to take care after dark, and either stick to the main streets while walking or catch a cab. The tourist police can be contacted by calling tel. 504/448-0150 or tel. 504/448-0253, or by asking at your hotel (many businesses in town chipped in to help pay their salaries).

The Tela Chamber of Commerce has its own website in English for tourists: www.tela honduras.com.

Orientation and Getting Around

A couple of kilometers off the El Progreso–La Ceiba highway, downtown Tela is a compact area bounded by the ocean, the Río Tela, and the railroad tracks. The square is two blocks from the beach. The Río Tela divides the main downtown area from "New Tela," a residential

area built by the Tela Railroad Company for its U.S. officials. Apart from a couple of bars and restaurants, the only reason to go to New Tela is to enjoy the beaches in front of Villas Telamar. Taxis going anywhere around town, including to New Tela or out to the highway, have a fixed rate: US$0.80 per person during the day and US$1 per person at night.

SIGHTS

Tela's main attractions are in the beautiful natural areas and villages nearby. That said, visitors can spend a day keeping themselves entertained around town.

The main town beach in front of the discos and restaurants does not lend itself to peaceful sunbathing—it's not particularly clean, and leaving your possessions while taking a dip is an invitation to theft. A better spot is the beach in front of Villas Telamar (in New Tela, west of the river and the municipal dock), which is clean, constantly patrolled by the resort's guards, and open to anyone who springs for a drink or meal at the restaurant. East and west of town, isolated beaches are lovely but should not be visited without asking one of the tourist police to come with you or going in a large group.

Tour Operators

A couple of doors off the town square, **Garífuna Tours** (tel. 504/448-2904, www.garifuna tours.com) offers popular day trips to Punta Sal for US$29 per person, including a bilingual guide and boat transport, plus an extra US$3 for the park entrance fee. Sign up the day before the trip, and be prepared to get wet while riding in the boat, although the boats do have a screen for shade. Tours to Laguna de los Micos and the Garífuna village of Miami (US$29) and kayak trips to Punta Izopo with a stop at the village of Triunfo de la Cruz for a meal (US$24) are also available. The latest addition to the tour list is a night crocodile watch (3:30–9 P.M., US$34). The company also has an office in La Ceiba (tel. 504/440-3252), with river-rafting and trips to Pico Bonito, Cayos Cochinos, and Cuero y Salado reserve.

It must be noted that while some readers have reported good trips with this tour company, others have said that it fell short of their expectations. (For example, will there be a Garífuna dance presentation at Miami, or will you simply have free time for walking around, and so a tour guide is irrelevant? Readers have reported both.)

An alternative is **Honduras Caribbean Tours** (tel. 504/448-2623, English and Spanish spoken, or tel. 504/3374-9383, German spoken as well, www.honduras-caribbean.com), which offers essentially the same tours, for a few dollars more. Tours to Lancetilla (which include bird-watching, for US$29) or sport-fishing (US$289) can be arranged as well.

ENTERTAINMENT AND EVENTS

Tela is second only to La Ceiba for nightlife on the north coast. A cluster of discos on the beach on the east side of town is the center of the action, with crowds meandering back and forth between the dance halls until daybreak on weekends, although the crowds can be rather unseemly at times. The **Bayside Hotel and Restaurant** (tel. 504/448-1210, www.bayside tela.com) is fashioning itself as the most happening spot on the beach, with men juggling fire and deejayed techno street/beach parties on the weekends. Plans for a rooftop disco at the hotel are also in the works.

A few blocks away, **Iguana's** (tel. 504/984-8671, 8 P.M.–3 A.M. Thurs.–Sun.), two blocks from the beach near Río Tela, with a big-screen TV for sport events and a disco, charges around US$3 cover, depending on the night. **Arrecife's** on the promenade always has people relaxing with a beer. On 10 Calle, just east of Iguana's, is a nameless **pool hall** with relatively well-maintained tables and, of course, beer for sale.

SHOPPING

Casa del Sol (a branch of the renowned crafts store in San Pedro Sula) on the boardwalk has a range of good quality items, and **Bazar y Suvenir Jameth** (9 Calle between 3 and 4 Avenidas) has some decent cigars and leather items.

ACCOMMODATIONS
Under US$25

The best cheapie in town in **Hotel Sinai** (5 Av. and 6 Calle, tel. 504/448-1486, US$8 s, US$16 d, shared bath, cold water only). Don't let the attractive lobby fool you—the rooms are quite basic, but the sheets look clean. Rooms with private baths are also available but cost US$8–10 more, in which case, you could find a better room. One reader reported having credit cards stolen here, which could not be verified, but watch your valuables to be on the safe side.

Hotel Bertha's (2 Av. facing the Tela-San Pedro Express, tel. 504/448-3020, US$12 s or d, US$18 with a/c, cold water only) has rather barren rooms, but those on the second story have plenty of light, they are clean, and the reception is pleasant enough. Too bad the neighbor has a yard full of roosters—consider yourself forewarned.

The backpacker hangout in town is **Mango Hotel** (tel. 504/448-0338, www.mangocafe.net, US$15 s, US$21 d with fan, US$7 more with a/c), on the second floor of a building a block from the park, run by the folks at Garífuna Tours. The rooms are decent but not spotless, and amenities include bike rentals (US$5/day) and a Spanish school.

US$25-50

New to the scene, and one of the best values in town, is **(Hostal Don Rodrigo** (9 Calle and 1 Av., tel. 504/448-0303, www.hostaldon rodrigo.com, US$18 s, US$26 d, or US$31 s and US$43 d with a/c), with the same owner as Hotel Cesar Mariscos. Tasteful rooms have walls of white adobe and exposed brick, attractive furnishings, tile floors, stylish artwork, and some king beds. For those who don't mind the four-block walk to the beach, this is an excellent value, despite the rather unfinished concrete top floor.

Anonymously modern from the outside, but with nice, new rooms is **Hotel Colonial** (8 Av. between 8 and 9 Calle, tel. 504/448-3222, US$31 s, US$45 d, including breakfast). Headboards, nightstands, and chairs are hand-carved wood, and there is a restaurant (open 8 A.M.–5 P.M.). The location is on a noisy street a couple of blocks from the central park, not ideal for solo female travelers. Those seeking peace and quiet can request one of the much quieter inner rooms.

Hotel Bella Vista (tel. 504/448-1064, US$30 s or US$48 d), a block south of Hotel Sherwood (both have the same owner), is nothing fancy, but the decent rooms have air-conditioning and are well-maintained, and it's only a block from the beach.

For self-contained apartments, try **Ejecutivos** (tel. 504/448-1076, www.ejecutivos ah.com, US$32 s/d, US$34 for three adults, US$37 for four), which features spacious studio-style apartments (that is, no separation between the living and sleeping areas) with fully equipped kitchen, air-conditioning, and TV on the first and second floors of a modern, gleaming white building four blocks from the beach; on the third floor are somewhat smaller rooms equipped with air-conditioning, TV, and hot water, but no kitchen, for US$26–32.

A creatively designed place to stay is **Hotel Gran Central** (tel. 504/448-1099, gran central@hotmail.com, US$40 s, US$50 d), in a two-story house near the old railway station, thoroughly renovated and remodeled by the French owners. The spacious rooms are tastefully decorated, with palm trees painted in warm hues on the walls, and all have air-conditioning and TV. Guests also have use of Internet. There is a larger suite with kitchen available as well. The owners serve breakfast (not included) in the downstairs café and have a small bar.

US$50-100

Clearly the realization of a personal vision of paradise is **(Hotel Maya Vista** (tel./fax 504/448-1497, www.mayavista.com, from US$46 s, US$52 d), a multitiered coral structure perched high on a hill just east of the bus station, offering breathtaking views across the bay. Built by French-Canadian owner Pierre Couture, the hotel has a range of rooms, including singles, doubles, triples, a suite, and an apartment (the latter has two bedrooms, three beds, and goes for US$99 per night). The nine rooms are stylishly decorated and feature French doors, terra-cotta floors, and plenty of windows; all have balconies overlooking the sea, and several of the walls and ceilings have been painted by local artists. Pierre and his wife are wonderful hosts, and the hotel restaurant serves excellent food 7 A.M.–9 P.M. daily, later if the hotel is full. Meal packages are available. Be sure to make reservations, as they are frequently booked up.

On the park, the modern **Gran Hotel Presidente** (tel. 504/448-2821, fax 504/448-0019, US$26 s, US$53 d) looks promising at first glance but is dark at night and not terribly clean (beware the roaches!), and the pool is murky.

Beach Hotels

Be forewarned that there is a cacophony of birds chattering in the beach palm trees at sunrise and sunset, which can make for an early start of the day if you're a light sleeper.

A handful of hotels dot the beach

promenade. One favorite is [C] **Hotel Cesar Mariscos** (tel. 504/1934, tel./fax 504/448-2083, reservaciones@hotelcesarmariscos.com, US$55 s, US$70 d), right on the beach above the excellent seafood restaurant of the same name. It has 19 attractive tile-floored rooms featuring cable TV and air-conditioning (in most), and many with balconies and ocean views (for the same price). The hotel has a small infinity-edge pool and Jacuzzi on the second floor, and bikes and kayaks are available for rent. Guests can be picked up directly from the San Pedro Sula airport for US$60 per person.

Next door is the pricier but not quite as nice **Hotel Sherwood** (tel. 504/448-1064, US$54 s, US$74 d, including breakfast), with wood-trimmed rooms; "executive rooms" have private, ocean-facing balconies. The hotel is not as sunny or lively as its neighbor, but is still a decent option. The pool is clean, and there is a restaurant and free Internet for guests.

At the end of the promenade strip is the **Bayside Hotel and Restaurant** (tel. 504/448-1210, www.baysidetela.com), with clean but somewhat drab rooms, with air-conditioning and TV. The hotel hosts parties on the weekend, making the stumble from the disco to your room a short and safe walk.

Located at the eastern end of the beach, far from the action, is pink **Hotel Veromar** (tel. 504/448-1705, US$32 s, US$47 d), with new, nice rooms, a couple of which boast an ocean view. There is a restaurant and a swimming pool, and private access to the beach, although the beach here is better for a stroll than a swim. There are also older, cheaper motel-style rooms that open onto the parking lot.

A sort of tropical suburb, certainly unlike any other resort on the Honduran coast, **Hotel y Villas Telamar** (tel. 504/448-2196, www.hotel telamar.com) was built by the Tela Railroad Company in the 1920s to house its U.S. executives. The freestanding wooden houses, each with hardwood floors, wicker and mahogany furniture, a fully equipped kitchen, and perfectly maintained lawn, are located in a well-patrolled complex along a beautiful beach just west of the Río Tela. Maintenance of the villas can vary widely, but the rooms in the hotel section are consistently nice. Facilities include two pools, four restaurants, a nine-hole golf course, tennis courts, a children's playground, banquet and conference center, horseback riding, boating, and fishing. Double rooms (which can sleep up to four) are available for US$128–168, the priciest with kitchenette, while villas go for US$284–812 a night, the largest of which are four-bedroom and can sleep up to nine. Day visitors are welcome, provided they have a meal at one of the restaurants.

On the western side of Telamar and a block away from the beach is sunny **Hotel Playa Bonita** (tel. 504/448-3450, www.hotelplayabonita tela.com, US$60 s, US$65 d, breakfast included), a good choice for the price-conscious. The building and rooms are not the most inspired, but there is a small swimming pool, and the location is good.

A few kilometers outside of Tela is the beautiful **La Ensenada Beach Resort** (tel. 504/448-0605, www.laensenadaresort.com), with king-bed suites and two-bedroom villas for US$75–190 per person per night for all-inclusive accommodation. If you tire of the sea, there are two swimming pools on-site.

FOOD
Snacks, Breakfasts, and Light Meals
Merendero Tía Carmen (tel. 504/448-2606, 7 A.M.–8 P.M. daily) serves locally famed *baleadas* stuffed with various fixings, as well as tacos, simple meals, and fresh juices in a cafeteria a block south of the square. The first batch of *baleadas* usually sells out by 10:30 A.M. at the latest, but a second batch is made around 4:30 P.M.

Opposite Garífuna Tours next to the park, **Tuty's** (tel. 504/448-0013, 7 A.M.–6 P.M. daily) serves decent *licuados* and juices, as well as an assortment of pastries, flan, breakfasts such as pancakes (US$2), and rotisserie chicken (US$2). Be prepared to wait; service can be slow.

Near the bridge between Tela and Nueva

Tela, **Auto Pollos al Carbon** serves up standard rotisserie chicken.

At the southeast corner of the park, **Espresso Americano** has cappuccinos, *granitas,* and the standard selection of cookies and other pastries.

Honduran and Seafood

With its spectacular view, twinkling white lights, and wafting scent of garlic, the breezy patio restaurant of the **(Hotel Maya Vista** (tel. 504/448-1497, 7 A.M.–9 P.M. daily) is perfect for a sunset cocktail or a romantic evening out, with seafood dishes (the lobster is superb) as well as some pasta, prepared with homemade sauces, for US$5.50–11 per entrée. The hill-climb up is steep, but a taxi is just US$0.75–1 from the beach.

Luces del Norte (tel. 504/448-1044, 7 A.M.–10 P.M. daily, sometimes earlier) on 11 Calle, one block north of the park, is a favorite among foreign visitors. Service can be painfully slow, which is a significant drawback given how hot it can get inside, but it's worth the wait for the flavorful curried conch soup, lobster, grilled snapper (US$6–10), and very good breakfasts (US$2–4). Pasta, chicken and beef dishes are available as well.

Also serving good conch and shrimp, as well as great flauta-style tacos, is **(Cesar Mariscos** (tel. 504/448-1934, tel./fax 504/448-2083, 7 A.M.–10 P.M. daily), with open-air seating facing the beach. Entrées, including many seafood dishes and salads, run about US$10, although the tacos and a sprinkling of other dishes are cheaper.

The **Restaurante Bahía Azul** (tel. 504/448-2381, 7 A.M.–11 P.M. daily), on 11 Calle just past the bridge, is surprisingly nice inside, with polished wood tables and cloth napkins. Seafood is the specialty, with shrimp and snooker *(robalo)* dishes going for around US$10 each.

International

(Bella Italia (4 P.M. onwards Mon.–Thurs., noon onwards Fri. and Sat.) is a good, Italian-owned pizzeria right on the town boardwalk,

with individual pizzas for around US$3.50, or medium (two-person) for about US$7.

Pizza Bambino (tel. 504/448-1086, 9 A.M.–11 P.M. Mon.–Fri., 9 A.M.–midnight Sat.–Sun.) on 11 Calle near the bridge also makes an acceptable pizza, as well as *pupusas* and other Honduran dishes. There is a little bit of children's play equipment.

The Chinese owners at **La Muralla China** (tel. 504/448-2934) on 11 Calle between 2 and 3 Avenidas serve up popular Chinese standards for around US$8.

Groceries

Despensa Familiar (7 A.M.–7 P.M. Mon.–Sat., 7 A.M.–6 P.M. Sun.), on the square, has an array of groceries.

INFORMATION AND SERVICES
Information

There is now a **tourist office,** located on 9 Calle near the corner with 7 Avenida.

Prolansate (tel. 504/448-2042, www .prolansate-ecoturismo.com, 7 A.M.–noon and 1:30–5:30 P.M. Mon.–Fri., 8 A.M.–noon Sat.), opposite Telamar, is a local environmental organization that helps manage nearby natural protected areas—a mission that does not always endear its staff to ranchers, developers, and land-hungry *campesinos.* The staff is happy to help visitors learn more about Punta Sal, Punta Izopo, or Lancetilla, and can provide practical details to visit the reserves.

Banks

BAC Bamer, HSBC, and **Banco Atlántida** (each with an ATM, although Banco Atlántida's is Visa only) change travelers checks and cash Monday–Friday and Saturday mornings.

Communications

Hondutel (7 A.M.–9 P.M. daily) and **Honducor** (8 A.M.–4 P.M. Mon.–Fri., 8 A.M.–noon Sat.) are on the same block, two blocks southwest of the square. Internet telephone calls (much cheaper than Hondutel) can be made cheaper elsewhere.

Sharing space with the Espresso Americano at the southeast corner of the park is a nice **Internet café** (7:30 A.M.–6 P.M. daily), with flat-screen monitors, charging US$0.25 for half an hour. International and domestic calls can also be made here (calls to the United States are US$0.05/minute).

Laundry

Lavandería El Centro (4 Av. between 6 and 7 Calle, tel. 504/448-0568, 7:30 A.M.–5:30 P.M. Mon.–Sat.) charges US$3.75 to wash, dry, and fold 10 pounds of laundry, as does **Lavandería Murillo,** near the Tela Express terminal, and the latter will also deliver your laundry to your hotel.

Spanish School

Hotel Mango runs a Spanish school (tel. 504/448-0338, www.mangocafe.net), which is really a network of private tutors, charging US$114 per week for 20 hours in the mornings for beginners (US$140 per week for advanced students) or 10 hours per week in the afternoons for US$75.

GETTING THERE AND AWAY
Bus

Tela has direct buses to San Pedro Sula, relieving travelers of having to switch buses at El Progreso. Eight buses a day leave from the **Tela Express** terminal near the Río Tela on 1 Avenida heading out of town (Mon.–Sat., first at 6 A.M., last at 5 P.M.; Sun., first at 7 A.M., last at 5:30 P.M.), for US$4. Buses to La Ceiba leave every 25 minutes from the corner of 9 Calle and 10 Avenida (4:10 A.M. until 6 P.M. daily), charging US$2 for the 2–2.5-hour trip (with many stops), from the main bus terminal four blocks east of the park. Faster buses heading from San Pedro Sula to La Ceiba can be flagged down at the DIPPSA gas station on the highway. (US$2.50).

Car

The 68-kilometer, two-lane road to El Progreso through African palm and banana plantations is in good shape, and the additional 28 kilometers to San Pedro Sula is a smooth four-lane highway. To the east, the 101-kilometer, two-lane road to La Ceiba is also well maintained.

WEST OF TELA
San Juan

Heading west from Telamar, the paved road eventually gives way to dirt and after a few bumpy kilometers reaches the Garífuna village of San Juan. Services in town include **El Pescador** restaurant and four **cabins** run by a small women's group, each with two bedrooms (they can sleep up to six), an equipped kitchen, and a porch with two hammocks. The cabins are quite nice, and a very good deal (US$40/night). To reserve, call Benita Diego (tel. 504/3271-4652) or Esmeralda Arzú (tel. 504/3378-2723).

One kilometer before reaching San Juan is the spectacular 14-bedroom private home rental **El Cocal** (tel. 504/545-2660, U.S. tel. 561/212-6924, www.elcocalhouse.com), a wooden beach mansion built along the sea, complete with kayaks and a tennis court. The base rate is US$360 per night for six bedrooms (come with friends!), with a minimum three-night stay.

◖ Tornabé

Seven kilometers west of Tela via a rough dirt road is Tornabé (from its original name, "Turn Bay"), the largest Garífuna village on the north coast. Lined along a dirt road parallel to the beach, it's a quiet place to relax and let the sun and waves lull you into a trance. The beach here is relatively clean. Accommodations and food are limited, so don't come looking for luxury. Local fishermen will take visitors out to Punta Sal for a negotiable fee, either dropping them off for the day or acting as guides. Trips into Laguna de los Micos can also be arranged.

About the best place to stay in town is with **Don Santos,** who rents a few simple cabins on the beach for US$12, with fans and a communal latrine. A couple of other folks around town also have rooms for rent. There's a beach

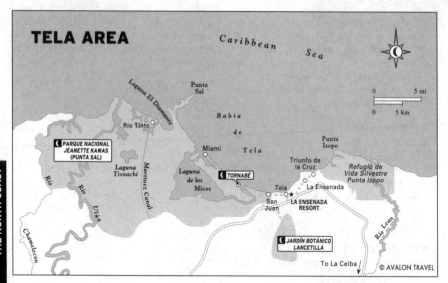

hotel at the east end of town aptly called The Last Resort, but it was in poor shape at last report and is not recommended. Good food can be found, among other places, at **Merendero Naidy,** just near the Baptist church, with inexpensive local food. **Ansela Santos** also sells food out of her house. Fill up on *pan de coco* (coconut bread), as the women here make the best on the coast.

Buses between Tornabé and Tela (US$0.50) depart several times a day, the last in either direction at around 5 P.M. Buses leave Tela from near the market. Two roads reach the village, the shortest via San Juan near the beach, but this is frequently impassable during the rains, as the lagoon opens an outlet to the sea. Another all-weather road departs the Tela–San Pedro Sula highway from the police post three kilometers past Lancetilla Garden. Follow this paved road 5.5 kilometers to a dirt road on the right side leading to Tornabé in 1.5 kilometers. Taxis are also cheap—a driver may try to charge you US$3 if you are going alone, or US$5 for a carload (up to four passengers).

Note: It's not recommended to walk on the beach outside of Tornabé toward either Tela or Miami, as muggings have been reported. Stick to the beach near town and you'll be just fine.

Past Tornabé (if you've come from the main road, and not via San Juan and its bumpy road) is **Honduras Shores Plantation** (tel. 504/448-1887, www.hondshores.com), a private resort development along the beach with great cabins available for rent. The cabins are one- and two-bedroom (US$106 or US$150, respectively), with a fully-equipped kitchen and living room. They are also unfortunately at the far end of the development, a good 10-minute walk to the beach, but there is a swimming pool right next to the cabins, and access to Los Micos lagoon, with kayaks available. While the rack rate is a bit overpriced, there are often specials during the low season, such as three nights for the price of two, or even two for one at times. Monthly rates are available as well, and some owners also rent out their larger three- and four-bedroom properties. The resort has tight 24-hour security, so call before showing up.

Across the road and along the beach is the **Tela Beach Club,** part of the same resort, with a restaurant, a large pool, and a fantastic beach with palms trees swaying in the breeze. Day use of the property is welcome, although if you come on a weekday in the low season, you may be the only one around. A taxi from Tela should be around US$3.

Miami

The idyllic thatch-hut village of Miami rests on a narrow sand spit, backed by Laguna de los Micos and fronted by the Caribbean. Unlike Tornabé or Triunfo, Miami is almost totally undeveloped (so far), with most families still living in the traditional Garífuna thatched huts. Facilities are minimal—if you want to spend more than the day here, ask around for food and a room or a place to sling a hammock. One room with space for a hammock is usually available next to the only store in Miami.

Motorized and paddle canoes can be rented to explore the lagoon. More territory can be covered with the motor, but it scares wildlife away. Locals say camping on the inland side of the lagoon is possible, which would be excellent for early morning bird-watching.

Small boats are also available to take visitors to Punta Sal. For the budget camper, the absolute cheapest way to get out to Punta Sal from Tela is to get to Miami by bus and truck, then walk eight kilometers on the beach out to the point.

Prolansate has helped fund a small visitors center in Miami, in a cabin right at the entrance to town, with displays, maps, and photos of Punta Sal and Laguna de los Micos. The staff person is a good source of information about the village or for arranging visits around the lagoon. The center is usually open daily. Because Miami is part of the national park, visitors are charged US$3 (for foreigners) to enter the village.

Trucks leave Tornabé heading west to Miami a couple of times a day (none on Sunday) at irregular hours, but usually early in the morning, charging US$0.75 for the half-hour drive (expect a tight fit as they pack 'em in). It's possible to walk the road in a couple of hours, but bring a hat and plenty of water, as there's not much shade on the way. Don't try driving this road unless you have a four-wheel-drive vehicle—there's lots of soft sand.

Note: In 2005 the InterAmerican Development Bank approved a US$16 million loan for the development of ecotourism at Los Micos, and in the fall of 2008 the Hilton chain announced plans for a hotel at Los Micos, so many more options may become available over the next few years, for better or for worse.

Laguna de los Micos

A *mico* is a white-faced monkey, and they are easily spotted in the trees around this lagoon, as well as 250 species of birds. Garífuna Tours runs laid-back day trips to the lagoon that focus on bird-watching, for US$34 per person (not including lunch), and nature enthusiasts can keep their eyes peeled for kingfishers and spotted-breasted orioles, among others, as well as the white-faced monkeys and several species of butterflies. It's just as easy to visit the lagoon independently by asking at the restaurant in Miami to arrange a boat tour.

(Parque Nacional Jeanette Kawas (Punta Sal)

One of the most biologically diverse natural reserves in Honduras, the 782 square kilometers of protected territory around Punta Sal include humid tropical forest, mangrove swamp, coastal lagoons, rivers and canals, rocky and sandy coastline, coral reef, and ocean. Almost 500 types of plants have been identified within the park, as well as 232 animal species, including endangered marine turtles, manatees, jaguars, ocelots *(tigrillos)*, caymans, white-faced and howler monkeys, wild pigs, pelicans, and toucans.

Most tours arrive by boat at the base of the point on the east side, offering visitors a chance to enjoy the beautiful **Playa Cocolito** beach before taking a half-hour hike over a low part of the point to the **Playa Puerto Escondido,** a beach-lined cove on the far side. This steep trail is a good opportunity to see the park's abundant and colorful birds and, if you're lucky, troops of howler or white-faced monkeys. A second trail diverges to the north before reaching the far side of the point, leading to another small bay on the west side of the point, **Playa**

© AMY E. ROBERTSON

The idyllic retreat of Punta Sal makes for a great day trip from Tela.

Puerto Caribe. At certain times of year the trails can be impassable due to absolute clouds of mosquitoes.

Apart from the rugged and beautiful 176-meter-high Punta Sal, most of the reserve's territory is flat, encompassing the Los Micos, Diamante, Río Tinto, and Tisnachí lagoons; the Martínez and Chambers canals; and the Río Ulúa. The Río Chamelecón forms the western boundary of the park. Traveling up these waterways by boat provides opportunities for viewing wildlife—have binoculars and mosquito repellent at the ready.

No facilities are available in the park apart from two small *champas* at Playa Cocolito, which sell meals of fried fish to tour groups (about US$6, not included with your tour). Camping on the beach is allowed and would be a superb way to spend a few days; come prepared with food, fresh water, and a tent or hammock. A park ranger maintains a small cabin at Playa Cocolito, where most tour boats stop. Although tour operators like to tout the great snorkeling, there's little in the way of interesting reef, and visibility is limited in the choppy water. Better to just enjoy the wonderful swimming and sunbathing.

The easiest way to visit Punta Sal is via boat tour with Garífuna Tours or Honduras Caribbean Tours in Tela. Their essentially identical day trips cost US$29 and US$34 per person respectively, leaving almost every day, weather permitting. A second option, better for those who want to set their own schedule and go by themselves or in a small group, is to set up a freelance tour, looking for a boat and negotiating a price either in Tela (best place is the outlet of the Río Tela to the sea) or in Tornabé. The really industrious can take the daily truck out past Tornabé to Miami and either hire a boat there or walk along the beach for a few hot hours.

An entrance fee of US$3 is collected by a park *vigilante* (some tours include this in the price), and the money goes to help the activities of Prolansate, a nongovernmental environmental organization working at Punta Sal. The Prolansate office (tel. 504/448-2042, www.prolansate -ecoturismo.com), which has more information on the park, is in Tela opposite Telamar.

JEANETTE KAWAS AND THE STRUGGLE FOR PUNTA SAL

The national park at Punta Sal is named for Jeanette Kawas, former president of Prolansate, an environmental organization dedicated to protecting Punta Sal, Punta Izopo, Lancetilla, and Texiguat. In Honduras, as Kawas discovered, defending the environment is more than signing petitions and sending out leaflets like in the United States or Western Europe. It's a matter of life and death.

Several different groups and individuals – Honduran Colonel Mario "El Tigre" Amaya and an African palm cooperative run by the National Campesino Union, among others – have claimed ownership of Punta Sal land. But Kawas forcefully advocated the creation of a national park at Punta Sal. Although the effort was ultimately successful – national park status was granted in November 1994 – she paid the price for her activism. Kawas was gunned down in April 1995, and her murder remains unsolved.

The environmental battles around Punta Sal continue, with the ongoing disputes over the planned development at Los Micos. Private investors backed by the Honduran government and the Inter-American Development Bank (IADB) are slowly moving ahead with a huge tourist development between Tornabé and Miami, on the strip of land between the Caribbean and the Laguna de los Micos.

With two large hotels, an 18-hole golf course, and private villas, the resort will completely change the sleepy character of the coastline between Tela and Punta Sal, and will certainly have a major impact on the delicate wetland ecosystem of the lagoon and adjacent Punta Sal.

Garífuna leaders have opposed the project, saying it does not respect their community land rights, and they have been threatened and harassed as a result. One Garífuna leader in San Juan had his house burned down in late 2005 for his activism against the project. In 2008, another Garífuna man from San Juan was abducted, beaten, and threatened with death by up to 10 men, just hours after publicly accusing representatives of a local real estate company of pressuring Garífuna people to sell their land.

Concerns of overdevelopment and respect for community land rights have apparently taken a back seat to the desire to boost tourism and bring in more jobs and income to the bay, not to mention a few people (well-connected people, of course) making a killing on real-estate deals. Hopefully the builders will find a way to put in the resort without destroying Miami and the delicate ecosystem around Los Micos, but it does not seem likely.

EAST AND SOUTH OF TELA
La Ensenada

Just east of Tela is the Garífuna village of La Ensenada (not to be confused with the resort of the same name), a tiny beachfront town wildly popular on the weekend with locals for a day on the beach. *Champas* with picnic tables line the waterfront and are available for rent, and boatmen ply the beach, putting together short water tours. While foreigners might attract a few looks, people are friendly, and the town is a great place to get off the well-trodden tourist path.

Triunfo de la Cruz

Another Garífuna town similar to Tornabé, Triunfo is eight kilometers east of Tela. The beach in town, though lined by fishing boats and not kept conspicuously clean, is a quiet place to sunbathe and swim in the warm waters. Locals are not bothered by visitors, and though they may not seem very friendly at first, neither do they hassle the few backpackers who come in search of a little peace and sun.

If you are interested in seeing a group of local dancers perform a traditional *dugu* dance, it can easily be arranged by asking around. The townsfolk often hold dances in different houses for their own purposes, and a polite visitor might be allowed to watch, if he or she asks nicely. Triunfo's annual festival is held on May 3, the Day of the Cross. It's also possible to arrange trips out to Punta Izopo in motorized canoe, usually around US$40 per boatload (up to 10 people) for a day trip.

The best place to stay in town, although overpriced for the services provided, is **Caribbean Coral Inn** (tel. 504/9994-9806, www.globalnet.hn/caribcoralinn, US$46 s, US$58 d, including breakfast), with five small but comfortable cabins, each with fan, TV, and hot water. The cabins can sleep up to four, and children up to 12 stay at no charge. The hotel, run by a non-Garífuna family, is on the beach, two blocks from the main road into town. They run a decent restaurant (reservations only) and will pick you up from your hotel in Tela upon request.

A couple of blocks away, also right on the beach, is **Cabañas Colón** (tel. 504/9982-0966), a cluster of small cabins (US$16 s/d, cold water only). Some are concrete and others bamboo, two have air-conditioning, several have TVs, and most have hammocks. Nearby **Panchi** (tel. 504/9929-0600) also has cabins that rent for US$10–20. A friendly watchman keeps an eye on things, so visitors can relax without fear of theft.

Jorge's Restaurant, just east of the hotels, serves up succulent fried snapper, as well as a hearty, veggie-filled conch stew. Another great place to eat is at **Playa Miramar,** at the far west end of Triunfo, almost two kilometers from where the entrance road comes into town. The owners serve excellent seafood and take care to keep their beach clean for visitors to swim. There is a restaurant on the highway toward La Ceiba that some Hondurans claim serves the best conch soup in the country.

Several buses daily run to and from Tela (US$0.40), usually every hour or so. The buses leave Tela from near the market, the last returning to Tela in midafternoon. A taxi to Triunfo costs about US$5 for a carload (up to four passengers), or US$3 if you are solo. Sometimes one that has just dropped off passengers in Triunfo will offer a ride back to Tela for US$0.50. The two-kilometer dirt road to Triunfo leaves the Tela–La Ceiba road roughly five kilometers from the Tela turnoff. Formerly,

the two- to three-hour walk to Tela via the small village of **La Ensenada** was a pleasant way to return from Triunfo, but several muggings have been reported, so it's best to take the bus or a car. Near La Ensenada is the site of Cristóbal de Olid's first landing on Honduras, marking the beginning of Spanish colonization. Triunfo was originally established as a settlement by Olid, but the colonists soon moved elsewhere and the area was not permanently occupied until the Garífuna moved there from Trujillo in the early 1800s.

(Jardín Botánico Lancetilla

A small miracle of botanical science and one of the finest bird-watching sites in Central America, Lancetilla was first set up in 1925 by plant biologist William Popenoe of the United Fruit Company, who is also responsible for starting the Escuela de Sciencias Agrícolas in the Valle de Zamorano, near Tegucigalpa. Initially Lancetilla was designed as a research station for testing different varieties of bananas, but Popenoe's endless inquisitiveness soon led to experiments with fruits and plants from all over the world. One of Honduras's most profitable agricultural products, the African palm, *Elaeis guineensis,* was first introduced by Popenoe in Lancetilla, and he did further work with coffee, cinchona (the source of quinine, for years the only treatment for malaria), cacao, rubber, mango, and a myriad of other plants.

Although Popenoe left Lancetilla in 1941 to go to Zamorano, United Fruit continued the work he began until 1974, when Lancetilla was turned over to the Honduran government. The garden has since become part of the Escuela de Sciencias Forestales and is still a fully functioning research station.

Lancetilla boasts one of the most preeminent collections of fruit trees, flowering trees, hardwoods, palm trees, bamboo, and other assorted medicinal and poisonous plants in Latin America. Named after the indigenous lancetilla palm, *Astrocaryum standleyanum,* the garden contains 764 varieties of plants in 636 species, 392 genera, and 105 families on a mere 78 hectares in the William Popenoe Arboretum, and another 60 species of fruit and hardwood trees in the experimental research station.

Attracted by this profusion of fruits and plants, all manner of tropical birds throng the trees of Lancetilla, making it a premier bird-watching destination. Honduran birding expert Mark Bonta reports that more than 300 species can be spotted at Lancetilla. First-time tropical birders will be delighted by close views of toucans, trogons, motmots, tanagers, orioles, and parrots. More seasoned birders should investigate the brush and rainforest understory and canopy to find the great antshrike, cinnamon becard, rufous piha, lovely cotinga, keel-billed motmot, purple-crowned fairy, tawny-throated leaftosser, and many others.

The Lancetilla Biological Reserve, in the surrounding hillsides, contains both primary and secondary tropical humid and subtropical humid forest. At least one trail crosses the range of hills to the far side—ask the staff for directions.

Many plants are labeled to help identification. Labels are color-coded as follows: Green indicates hardwood; red indicates fruit; yellow indicates ornamental; and most important, black indicates poisonous. Feel free to sample fallen fruit, but be sure not to try anything from a black-labeled tree! Keep an eye out for the mangosteen trees, *Garcinia mangostana,* a Malaysian native considered by some connoisseurs to produce the finest fruit on the planet. Guided tours are also available for US$5.25 per group, and are a great way to spot trees like the mangosteen and quinine, learn interesting factoids about the plants, and get to try lots of tropical fruits.

Just under two kilometers from the visitors center, past groves of palms and bamboo, are two swimming holes along the Río Lancetilla. Though unspectacular, they're a good way to cool off after a hot walk.

Lancetilla sells tickets (US$6) 7 A.M.–4 P.M. daily, but visitors can stay until 5 P.M. You can arrange guides (US$5.25) and purchase maps of the arboretum for a self-guided tour of one of the trails at the large, wooden visitors center a couple of kilometers from the park entrance.

Mosquitoes are often fierce in the arboretum, so come prepared. There are cabins (three twin beds, US$20) and guest rooms (two twin beds, US$13 s, US$15 d) on-site, ideal for those interested in early-morning bird-watching, although they are sometimes full with the many research and student groups who visit the gardens. Check with the visitors center (tel. 504/448-1740) to make reservations.

Buses to Lancetilla (all the way in to the visitors center) leave from Tela at 6 Avenida and 11 Calle. The highway turnoff to Lancetilla is just south of the power station outside of Tela, five kilometers from town (look for several stands selling lychee fruit near the entrance). You could take an El Progreso bus, get off at the junction, and walk the 45 minutes into the gardens, or take a taxi from town for US$4. Another option is to rent a bike at Garífuna Tours and pedal out at your own pace. The entrance fee is collected at a *caseta* (toll building) at the highway junction.

Refugio de Vida Silvestre Punta Izopo

Visible around the bay to the east of Triunfo is Punta Izopo, Tela Bay's second largest protected area, covering 112 square kilometers, of which about half is a buffer zone and half is a supposedly untouchable nuclear zone. This refuge is much less frequently visited than Punta Sal but has similar ecosystems and wildlife; the swamps and waterways stretching into the jungle south of the point are superb for watching birds and animals.

Inside the reserve's boundaries are the small Río Plátano (not to be confused with the river of same name in the Mosquitia) and Río Hicaque and the larger Río Lean on the point's eastern side, as well as kilometers of swamps, lagoons, and estuaries. Several small settlements are also located inside the boundaries of the reserve, including Hicaque, Las Palmas, Coloradito, and the intimidatingly named Salsipuedes ("get out if you can").

The easiest access to Punta Izopo is by kayak with Garífuna Tours in Tela, which charges US$27 per person for a day trip. Trips normally start by driving in on a dirt road east from Triunfo to the Río Plátano, where you put the boats in. Conversely, it's possible to find boats in Triunfo to take up to 10 people on day trips for US$30. A low-budget option is to hunt around Triunfo for a local willing to rent you a dory (US$7 a day would be a reasonable amount for a two-person wooden boat with oars) and then paddle out to the point with a companion. Don't try it alone,

as it's a lot of work to fight the waves. Once at the point you can hang out on the beach or walk around the point (beware the hordes of sand flies), or cross the low sandbar into the Río Plátano or Hicaque and paddle up the waterways.

Bear in mind that a visit to Punta Izopo is best made approaching by land, as trees and debris can block access to the river mouths that lead into the park from the ocean.

Puerto Cortés and Omoa

Situated on a deep natural harbor on the northwest corner of Honduras, only 60 kilometers from the industrial capital of San Pedro Sula, Puerto Cortés is perfectly located to serve as a transfer point for much of the country's trade. It handles the largest amount of boat traffic—though Puerto Castilla near Trujillo moves more total tonnage—and is considered to have one of the best port facilities in Central America. Since a duty-free zone was created in the port area in 1976, a sizable assembly industry has developed, mostly of clothing exported to the United States. More recently, international cruise ships have begun docking at Puerto Cortés for a day stop, while their tourist clients spend the day visiting the ruins at Copán. City officials have made much talk of cleaning up the docks and downtown area for the new tourists, but they've got a long way to go to make Puerto Cortés look attractive. And beware of downtown during a heavy rain, as the mostly dirt streets flood with regularity. Several hotels just outside of town on the road to Omoa on Playa Cienaguita keep their strip of golden sand clean and inviting, perfect for a day out or an overnighter.

The thriving economy supports a population of 45,000.

History

The Spanish first settled west of present-day Puerto Cortés early in the colonial era, recognizing the value of the fine natural harbor. The first settlement was named Puerto Caballos (Port of Horses), after conquistador Gil González Dávila was caught in a fierce storm nearby in 1524 and was forced to throw several horses overboard.

Puerto Caballos was repeatedly struck by epidemics and marauding pirates, and by the turn of the 17th century the Spanish relocated to the better-protected harbor of Omoa, to the

jícaros (calabash) growing near Puerto Cortés

© AMY E. ROBERTSON

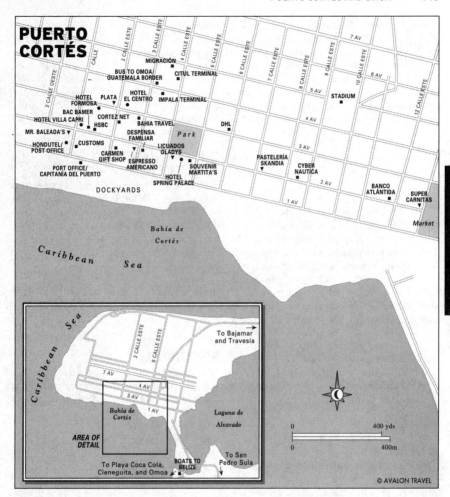

PUERTO CORTÉS

Bahía de Cortés

Caribbean Sea

Area of detail inset: Caribbean Sea, Bahía de Cortés, Laguna de Alvarado, AREA OF DETAIL, To Bajamar and Travesía, To San Pedro Sula, BOATS TO BELIZE, To Playa Coca Cola, Cieneguita, and Omoa

0   400 yds
0   400m

© AVALON TRAVEL

west. Modern Puerto Cortés was established in 1869 on the other side of the bay from the old colonial port, at the terminus of a new railway line connecting San Pedro Sula to the coast.

In the late 19th century, Puerto Cortés was a favorite destination for all manner of shady characters, swindlers, and soldiers-of-fortune from the United States and Europe. Many were on the run from the law, as Honduras had no extradition treaties until 1912. For a time in the 1890s, the Louisiana Lottery, banned in its home state, found refuge in Puerto Cortés and became one of the largest gambling concerns in the world.

Orientation and Getting Around

Although Puerto Cortés is a large city, the downtown area is compact and can easily be navigated on foot. Taxis around downtown should cost US$1.50, US$2 out to the dock where boats depart for Belize, or US$5.25 out to Playa Cienaguita. There is a taxi stand in front of the Hotel Formosa, another facing the park, and taxis constantly circulating throughout town. Buses all leave from within a couple of blocks of the shady *parque.* If you are headed out after dinner, choose your locale carefully, and beware of walking out on 1 Avenida at night, as muggings are common. For car drivers, the north–south *calles* are one-way streets, while the east–west *avenidas* are two-way (except for 1 Avenida, which runs east to west only). While the main roads in Puerto Cortés have been paved, many around town are not, and are best traversed in a vehicle with four-wheel drive.

SIGHTS

The travel writer who once declared Puerto Cortés "the foulest blot on Central America's coastline" was perhaps overly unkind. The tropical seediness can be somewhat appealing, if one appreciates that sort of thing. But there's no doubt that the port city itself offers little draw for tourists. Most foreigners are either there to take care of some shipping business or stopping off on the way between Guatemala and Honduras, either by boat or bus.

The *parque,* punctuated by several towering Caribbean pines and few other trees and plants, is a shady, tranquil place to sit, but otherwise there's little to do in town. The bustling dockyards are off-limits without a special pass, though you can check them out from behind a tall fence.

Beaches

The **Playa Municipal,** also known as Playa Coca Cola, is the closest beach to town, just over the bridge that leads to the road to Omoa—either a US$2 taxi ride or a long hot walk from downtown. Unsurprisingly, it is neither clean nor particularly safe. East of downtown (go to the Texaco refinery, take a right, and go to the end of the road) is **Playa El Faro** (Lighthouse Beach), which is not much better, though it does have a pleasingly windswept feel, and food and accommodation at the Costa Azul hotel.

Much nicer is **Playa Cienaguita,** west of the municipal beach. There are several hotels along this beach, as well as the city's best seafood

restaurant. Taxis to Cienaguita from Puerto Cortés cost US$5.25, or take an Omoa bus and hop off at the sign for Hotel Playa (US$0.30). From the turnoff to Hotel Playa, it's a 10-minute walk up the road to the beach entrance. The hotels and beach at Cienaguita are usually packed on weekends with vacationers from San Pedro Sula and completely deserted during the week.

ENTERTAINMENT AND EVENTS

At 9 Calle and 4 Avenida, a few blocks east of the *parque,* is the local soccer stadium, home to **Platense,** a sometimes competitive first-division team. Tickets are always available for the weekend games, selling for US$4–5. For a game schedule, call the club at 504/665-6242.

Should you have a desire to consort with the local riffraff, there are plenty of pool halls around town. They offer beers and pool until midnight or later daily.

The city's annual festival day is August 15.

SHOPPING

With a surprisingly large selection, the best handicraft shop in town is **Souvenir y Curiosidades Carmen** (2 Av. between 2 and 3 Calles, 8 A.M.–5:30 P.M. Mon.–Sat.), with lots of hand-carved wood and leather items, as well as the standard embroidered blouses and tacky keychains.

Farther down the avenue is the smaller **Souvenir Martita's** (tel. 504/665-2431, 8 A.M.–6 P.M. Mon.–Sat.), jam-packed with carved wooden boxes, hammocks, and paintings.

SPORTS AND RECREATION

Located at the Hotel Playa is the only dive shop in the area, PADI-certified **Honduras Divers** (tel. 504/9991-0778 or 504/665-0453, www.hondurasdivers.com, 8:30 A.M.–5 P.M. Sat and Sun.). The first number is the cell phone of Hotel Playa's manager, Roberto Alvarez, who runs the dive shop. Scuba classes are offered, as well as local diving and outings to the idyllic

Belizean islands **Cayos Zapotillos.** An open-water dive course costs US$315. Local diving can be done year-round at La Picuda site; it's best January–October. Honduras Divers charges just US$24 per person for a single dive (US$18 if you have your own equipment). A scuba tour of the Cayos is $110 per person, or snorkeling tours can be arranged for $100 per person (both including lunch and equipment, as well as the entrance fee to the Cayos). No visa or immigration paperwork is required for a visit to the Cayos Zapotillos.

Mountain-bike enthusiasts should get in touch with Roberto Alvarez (tel. 504/665-0453 or 504/3390-3061), the general manager of the Hotel Playa, who can organize tours and should be able to help find bikes and equipment.

ACCOMMODATIONS
Under US$25
The venerable **Hotel Formosa** (3 Av. between 1 and 2 Calles E, tel. 504/665-0853, US$13 s, US$18.50 d, a few dollars more for a/c and TV, cold water only) has very basic rooms with private baths, and the owners speak English.

The best inexpensive rooms in town are at **Hotel El Centro** (3 Av. between 2 and 3 Calles E, tel. 504/665-1160, US$17 s or US$24 d, US$16 more for a/c), with clean rooms with TV and private baths.

US$25-50
A good midrange choice is the **Hotel Spring Palace** (tel. 504/665-1471, US$27 s, US$30.50 d), facing the park, whose tidy rooms have TV and air-conditioning, and a few have balconies that overlook the park.

US$50-100
Far and away the best place to stay in town is ◖ **Hotel Villa Capri** (tel. 504/665-0860, US$38 s, US$56 d). The converted house right near the entrance to the docks at 2 Avenida and 1 Calle has only nine rooms, but each is spacious, comfortable, and equipped with hot water and air-conditioning, as well as tile floors and carved wood furniture. The price includes a continental breakfast.

On the Beach
At Playa Cienaguita, a couple of kilometers outside of town on the way to Omoa, is the **Hotel Playa** (tel. 504/665-0453, US$65 s, US$99 d), a charming hotel with rooms in upscale cabins, each with a small porch, air-conditioning, and TV. Service is very good and there's an inviting pool area, but the hotel is a bit pricey all in all. There is a large restaurant area around the pool with gazebos in a setup reminiscent of a Jersey boardwalk, and if you buy food or drinks you can hang out all day in the gazebos and sand (the breakfast crepes are very tasty). Use of the pool is US$5 a day.

Right next door is **Hotel Palmeras Beach** (tel. 504/665-3891, US$24 s, US$32 d during the week, US$45 s, US$55 on weekends), with seven somewhat shabby but decent and spacious rooms, all with TV and air-conditioning. The facilities include a pool, a decrepit children's play area, and a restaurant. As at Hotel Playa, the Hotel Palmeras Beach encourages nonguests to use its facilities (and no charge for the pool here) in return for consumption of food and drink.

Just across the road from Palmeras is **Brisas Resort** (tel. 504/665-4164, US$34 s, US$42 d during the week, US$41 s, US$53 d on weekends). Most of the 21 rooms are a bit cramped, but the swimming pool is crystalline, and there are hammocks lining the breezeway, free wireless Internet, and, for those who need to stretch their muscles, a couple of exercise machines. There is also a very spacious triple available with sink and mini-fridge, for US$68 during the week, US$70 on weekends. While it's not beach-front, it's easy enough to use the beach facilities at the other two hotels nearby, or reach the beach without using hotel facilities through the access path just to the right of Hotel Playa's entrance.

With two good restaurants nearby, a stay in one of the Playa-Palmeras-Brisas trifecta is ideal, but there are also a couple of decent hotels at other spots on the Cienaguita beach. The **Casa de Playa** (tel. 504/553-2424, US$66 s, US$78 d) is laid out motel-style, but it's attractive and right on the beach. All the standard amenities (TV, air-conditioning, wireless Internet, Internet in the lobby) and breakfast are included in the rate, but there's no swimming pool. The **Sol y Mar Hotel** (tel. 504/665-3988, www.solymarhotel.hn, US$65 s/d) has 14 guest rooms, some with a view. The hotel has a restaurant and bar, swimming pool, Internet, and two boats (one banana boat, one *lancha*) for taking a spin on the ocean. Rates include breakfast. To get to either hotel just look for the signs along the Puerto Cortés–Omoa highway.

FOOD

The best restaurant in town is 𝐂 **Super Carnitas** (tel. 504/665-4215, 11 A.M.–midnight daily) at 2 Avenida and 13 Calle on a large wooden deck above a dirt lot, highly recommended for its generously portioned grilled meat dishes. This simple but good restaurant offers a tasty *pollo asado,* served with tortillas, beans, cheese, and a salad, for US$3. A second branch has opened on Playa Cienaguita, by the Hotel Palmera Beach.

Another good choice is **Mr. Baleada's** (2 Av. at 1 Calle E), clean and popular with locals, offering *baleadas* for US$0.60–1.25, as well as a few other items like burgers.

The local favorite seems to be **Plata** (3 Av. and 2 Calle E, 6 A.M.–7 P.M. Mon.–Sat., 6 A.M.–noon Sun.), a very clean buffet restaurant and bakery. A plate at the ample buffet runs about US$4.

If you're after a juice or *licuado,* head to **Licuados Gladys** (2 Av. near 6 Calle, tel. 504/665-2777, 7 A.M.–6 P.M. Mon.–Sat.). Blended drinks run about US$1, fresh juices US$0.50, and light snacks (including *baleadas* and sandwiches) US$0.50–1.

San Pedro's tasty **Pastelería Skandia** (corner of 2 Av. and 7 Calle E, 7:30 A.M.–8 P.M. daily) has a branch here, serving up pastries and *licuados* all day long.

Caffeine jolts and refreshing *granitas* are available at **Espresso Americano** (2 Av. and 3 Calle E, 7 A.M.–7 P.M. daily).

For picnic fixings or other supplies, **Despensa Familiar** (7 A.M.–7 P.M. Mon.–Sat.,

7 A.M.–6 P.M. Sun.) just down the street is a full-service supermarket.

On the Beach

Next to the Hotel Playa at the far end of Playa Cienaguita is **Ancla Bar y Restaurante** (tel. 504/665-2331), with a good selection of fresh albeit pricey seafood (US$10–13 per entrée, less for snacks, US$24 for lobster). The main part of the restaurant is built on a pier out over the water, although there is also dining room on the sand for Semana Santa crowds.

If you prefer meat over seafood, there is a branch of local favorite **Super Carnitas** right on Playa Cienaguita as well.

Tasty meals are also available at the Hotel Playa, with tables spread across the property, including several under gazebos right on the beach.

INFORMATION AND SERVICES

A moderately helpful website on Puerto Cortés is www.mipuertocortes.com.

Travel Agents

Bahia Travel Service (3 Av. between 2 and 3 Calles, tel. 504/665-5803, U.S. tel. 954/323-2460, leo-mirrieles@yahoo.com, 8 A.M.–6 P.M. Mon.–Sat. and 8 A.M.–noon Sun.) can arrange airline tickets, rental cars, hotel rooms, and courier service. Bahia has English-speaking staff members. **Yax Pac Tours** (tel. 504/658-9082, www.yaxpactours.com), run by Roland Gassmann of the hostel Roli's Place in Omoa, offers day tours for cruise shippers arriving in Puerto Cortés, as well as customized tours in English, German, Swiss, or Spanish throughout Honduras and Guatemala.

Banks

Banco Atlántida on 2 Avenida near the market exchanges dollars and travelers checks, has an ATM (Visa only), and also offers cash advances on Visa cards. **BAC Bamer** and **HSBC** are next to each other on 2 Avenida between 1 and 2 Calle E, open Monday–Friday and mornings on Saturday. There is a 24-hour

ATM at HSBC. MoneyGrams can be picked up at Banco Atlántida, and Western Union has an office at Banco Ficensa (2 Av. and 3 Calle E).

Communications

Honducor and **Hondutel** are both on 1 Calle next to the main dock entrance. **Express Mail Service** is available at the post office.

There are several Internet cafés with fast connections and charging less than US$1 an hour. The owner speaks English at **Cyber Nautica** (2 Av. between 8 and 9 Calle E, 8 A.M.–8 P.M. daily). **Novedades y Ciber Angel Net** (8 A.M.–5 P.M. Mon.–Fri.), tucked along the *peatonal* between Despensa Familiar and Banco Atlántida, has the cheapest Internet in town, at just US$0.50 per hour, as long as you don't mind that it's also a clothing thrift shop. **Cortez Net Cyber Cafe** (2 Calle between 2 and 3 Av., tel. 504/665-4574, 8:30 A.M.–9 P.M. Mon.–Sat.) charges a bit more but provides 10 flat-screen computers in a clean, air-conditioned space. Calls to the United States from any of the cafés are just US$0.05 per minute.

Emergencies

In case of emergency, the **police** can be reached at 504/665-0133 or 504/665-0420, or simply by dialing 199. The number for the **fire department** is 504/665-0223 or 504/665-0500 (or just dial 198), and the Red Cross has an **ambulance**—dial 195. The phone number for the local **hospital** is 504/665-0562 or 504/665-0787.

Immigration

The *migración* office (tel. 504/665-0582, 8 A.M.–5 P.M. Mon.–Fri., sometimes only until 4 P.M.) is near the port office at 1 Calle and 1 Avenida. This is the place to come if you've entered Honduras by boat from Belize (if you don't, you will run into problems upon exiting the country). An interview is conducted, and charges can be levied for a tourist stamp.

For dealing with any port business, the **Capitanía del Puerto** (7 A.M.–4 P.M. daily) is inside the main port on 1 Avenida.

GETTING THERE AND AWAY

Bus

Impala (4 Av. between 4 and 5 Calle E, tel. 504/665-0606) runs buses every 20 minutes to San Pedro Sula, the first departing at 6 A.M., the last at 8 P.M. Two minivans are usually filling up right next to each other; be sure to get the *directo,* which charges US$2.50 for the hour-long ride (the one that stops takes an extra half-hour and is only pennies cheaper).

Around the corner, **Citul** (4 Calle E between 4 and 5 Avenidas, tel. 504/665-0466) operates frequent buses to San Pedro Sula, the first departing at 4:30 A.M., the last at 6 P.M. Citul also has *directos,* which cost about US$1.80.

Buses to Omoa depart from the lot at the corner of 4 Avenida and 5 Calle E every half hour between 6 A.M. and 7 P.M., charging US$0.80 for the ride, or US$0.30 to get off at Playa Cienaguita.

Buses to the border town of Corinto depart several times a day, the last at 3:45 P.M., and charge US$2.25 for the 75-minute ride.

Buses to Bajamar and Travesía leave from next to the Citul terminal, on 2 Avenida and 5 Calle Este. Three buses depart each day for the 20-minute, US$0.35 ride to Travesía; the last bus leaves at 4 P.M.

Car

The 60-kilometer, four-lane highway between San Pedro Sula and Puerto Cortés is in good condition and takes less than an hour to drive. A toll of US$0.30 is levied leaving San Pedro to Puerto Cortés, but not the other way. The highway on to Omoa and the 51 additional kilometers to the Guatemalan border have now been fully paved. On the other hand, the dirt road from Puerto Cortés east to Bajamar and Travesía continues in rough shape.

Boat

D-Express (tel. 504/9991-0778, info@honduras divers.com), run by Hotel Playa manager Roberto Alvarez, runs boats from Puerto Cortés to Big Creek, Mango, and Placencia, Belize, departing Mondays at 11 A.M. from under the bridge over the mouth of the Laguna

Alvarado. Coming from Belize, the boat departs Fridays from the Placencia Shell Dock at 9:30 A.M. and from Big Creek at 11 A.M. The ride costs US$53 per person.

BAJAMAR AND TRAVESÍA

Bajamar and Travesía are two of a loose string of Garífuna communities spread along the road that follows the coastline east from Puerto Cortés. There are various simple restaurants, *pulperías*, bars, and shady beaches, not to mention the gregarious Garífuna people going about their business. Travesía and Bajamar are relatively safe and relaxed, especially the farther away from Puerto Cortés you go. Locals support themselves by fishing, selling coco-bread, and, increasingly, with money wired from relatives in the states (mostly in New York City), allowing many male townsfolk to sit back and drink copious quantities of *gifiti*, a lethal Garífuna concoction of herbs, roots, spices, and *aguardiente* (the favored Honduran poor-quality booze).

Bajamar is the site of the annual **National Garífuna Festival,** normally held in late July, which draws Garífuna from Belize, Guatemala, and Honduras for a party of dancing and music.

Beyond Bajamar, the road continues, ending five minutes past the village of Brisas de Chamelecón. Curious travelers can continue farther by renting a *lancha* (US$2 per boat) to carry them across the river's mouth to La Barra Chamelecón, where they will reportedly find several eateries serving fresh fish and alcohol on the beach.

Accommodations
Hotel Frontera del Caribe (tel. 504/665-5001), located on its own beach at the northeastern exit of Puerto Cortés, on the road toward Travesía, is a self-contained hotel and restaurant with eight simple rooms with fans and private baths that have seen far better days; US$13 a room sleeps up to three people. The cute seafood restaurant, with seating in individual *champas* overlooking the beach, serves up tasty fish plates for around US$8.50. The beach itself is pretty dirty, but the veranda between the restaurant and beach helps hide the trash from view while you dine.

Getting There and Away
Buses to Bajamar leave five times a day from next to the Citul station in Puerto Cortés, 7 A.M.–5:30 P.M. (US$0.40), with the last two buses of the day remaining in Bajamar. By taxi, expect to pay about US$5.25 to Travesia or US$8 to Bajamar, or hire a cab to take you out for a day trip for about US$6 an hour.

OMOA

The sleepy fishing village of Omoa is built around a small bay 13 kilometers west of Puerto Cortés, where the Sierra de Omoa mountains meet the Caribbean. The town itself was never a major population center, but for strategic purposes the Spanish built the largest colonial-era fort in Central America here. Given the formerly rough road conditions, Omoa was long a popular stop-off point for travelers moving between Guatemala and Honduras—as recently as the mid-1990s, the connection between Corinto and Puerto Barrios in Guatemala was a footpath—but thanks to the recent paving, Omoa is slipping back into slumber.

Omoa's houses and shops are scattered along the two-kilometer road between the Puerto Cortés highway and the sea. The main beach, lined with fishing boats and several small restaurants, is nothing spectacular, but it's a relaxing place to spend a couple of hours after admiring the impressively massive fort, located on the main road running between the highway and the beach. About a 45-minute walk south of the highway junction is a small waterfall in the woods—ask someone to point out the trail. A few robberies have been reported on this trail, so ask at your hotel for the latest situation before venturing this way.

Omoa celebrates its annual carnival on May 30 in honor of San Fernando. The town has a website, www.omoa.net.

Sights
Located on the road into town, the **Fortaleza San Fernando de Omoa,** or El Castillo, as the

© AMY E. ROBERTSON

the beach at Omoa, a quiet fishing town

locals call it, is open for tours daily (tel. 504/658-9167, 8 A.M.–4 P.M. Mon.–Fri., 9 A.M.–5 P.M. Sat.–Sun., US$2). Entrance includes a visit to the adjacent **Museo de Omoa,** which has small but insightful exhibits on the history of the area, an overview of the fort, and displays of antique guns and swords. The fort is undergoing restoration thanks to a loan from the Inter-American Development Bank, and excavated cannons and munitions are on display within its walls. The small souvenir shop stocks good-quality pottery and jewelry made from coconut shells.

Sports and Recreation

For the most part, people come to Omoa for a bit of seaside relaxation. But visitors who want to explore what lies beneath the sea can contact **Omoa Divers** (tel. 504/9909-5592, www .omoadivers.com), the first and only dive school in town. The PADI instructor offers everything from Open Water through Rescue certification in German, English, and Spanish. A 20-minute boat ride carries divers to the southern tip of the famed Belizean Reef, where there are 20 or 30 dive sites, including the remains of some

Spanish galleons. With its strong surface currents, however, this area is only recommended for experienced divers. At the beach head right, to the end of the road, and the dive shop is located in the restaurant Macarela.

Banana boats and covered *lanchas* offer five- to ten-minute rides in the bay for US$1.50 per person.

With its sheltered cove, Omoa offers an excellent harbor for **boaters.** Only during the rare northeast wind are conditions bad. The port captain (tel. 504/658-9274 or 504/991-6110, radio channels 16 and 28), located on the main road, is open 24 hours a day. There are no fees for boats entering the harbor or for docking.

Travelers with kids may be interested in checking out the water park near the entrance to town.

Accommodations

The fanciest place in town (such as it is) is **⟨ Flamingo's** (tel. 504/658-9199, flamingos omoa@yahoo.com.ar, US$47 s, US$57 d), right on the beach, with attractive wood-paneled rooms with tile floors, nice bathrooms, TV, and

FORTALEZA SAN FERNANDO DE OMOA

© AMY E. ROBERTSON

Omoa's fort was built under orders from King Fernando VII of Spain in the 18th century.

The Caribbean coast of Honduras was sparsely populated throughout the colonial era, making it an easy target for attacks by pirates, marauding Miskito Indians, and, later, the British Navy. Although pirate assaults began just a couple of decades after the Spanish started to colonize Central America, it was not until the mid-18th century that colonial authorities made serious efforts to combat the marauders and fortify their positions on the coastline.

As early as 1685, the Spanish recognized Omoa as an ideal location for a fort – strategically situated on a deep, protected harbor between English settlements in Belize, the Bay Islands, and the Mosquitia. But distractions elsewhere, a lack of funding, and bureaucratic inertia combined to delay actual construction until 1752, when royal engineer Luis Diez de Navarro arrived with a plan for a massive triangular bastion.

Work on the fort was painstakingly slow. For a start, there was no adequate stone in the area; it had to be cut and transported from as far as 150 kilometers away. Even more dire was the lack of workers; disease and heat took a brutal toll on the conscripted Indians. Omoa became known as the graveyard of Honduras among the highland Indians, and able-bodied males fled their villages when they heard that colonial officials were coming to look for workers. Eventually, the crown brought in black slaves to finish the fort.

Finally completed in 1773, the fort was an in-

timidating sight. Two of the three sides were 60 meters long, while the ocean-facing base measured 25 meters. The walls were 6 meters tall and 2 meters thick. The complex overflowed with 150 pieces of artillery and was surrounded by a moat. Despite its daunting appearance, the fort was never particularly successful.

A combined British-Miskito force of almost 1,000 men, led by Commodore John Luttrell, took it in 1779, just six years after construction had been completed. After that inauspicious first defeat, the fort at Omoa fell variously to Spanish royalists, Francisco Morazán's forces, and, later, Guatemalan soldiers. Apparently easier to get into than out of, the fort was finally converted into a prison by the Honduran government in 1853.

In spite of its dismal record of defense, the fort is visually impressive, squatting ominously in the tropical heat a kilometer or so from the ocean. The Caribbean has receded in the years since its construction, leaving the fort standing amidst the fields and swamp between the Puerto Cortés highway and the beach. It is undergoing a significant restoration thanks to a loan from the Inter-American Development Bank.

The fort (tel. 504/658-9167) is open 8 A.M.-4 P.M. Monday-Friday, 9 A.M.-5 P.M. Saturday-Sunday; admission is US$2. Next to the fort is a museum with interesting descriptions (Spanish only) of the history of the colony and the construction of the fort. Guides are available for US$5.

air-conditioning. Prices include a *desayuno típico* of eggs, beans, and tortillas. Unlike at many beach-front hotels, the prices do not change during peak times such as Semana Santa. There is a comfortable bar, and the most attractive restaurant on the beach, built up on a platform at the water's edge.

Roli's Place (tel./fax 504/658-9082, www.yaxpactours.com) is a five-minute walk from the beach, with a wide variety of accommodations. True penny-pinchers can camp or sleep in a hammock for US$3, or take a bed in the rather dank dorm room for US$4. There are several shared toilets and showers, one of which has hot water (although it's available only during the cold season). Cramped but tidy private rooms start at US$8 for one person with a shared bath, US$12 with a private (cold water) bath. The rooms surround a shady yard of mango and coconut trees, with an outdoor communal kitchen, *pila* for washing clothes (or pay US$2 to have five pounds washed for you), and a ping-pong table. The dorm patio shelters a large wood table, perfect for writing out postcards while nursing a chilled beer. Note that while beer and wine are allowed on the premises, hard alcohol is not, no parties are allowed, and guests are expected to keep it quiet after 10 P.M. A second yard is lined by three much, much nicer private rooms with their own patio and hammocks. These rooms are spacious and tasteful, with decent linens and tiled floors, private bathrooms, and hot water, and are a steal at US$13 d, US$16 d (US$4 more for a/c). Abundant guest services (free drinking water, bikes, kayaks, games, guitars, etc.) complete the scene. Roli's is on the road toward Omoa center, on your left-hand side, 70 meters before you reach the beach.

Many of the other rooms in town are either overpriced or rather disappointing—be sure to take a look before putting money down, so you know what you're getting. Across the road from Flamingo's is **Hotel Bahia de Omoa** (tel. 504/658-9076, US$26 s/d), with four second-story rooms, two with bathtubs, all with air-conditioning, hot water, private bath, and cable TV—all in all rather basic for the price. The

midrange **Hotel Tatiana** (tel. 504/658-9186, US$21 s or d, US$42 s or d with a/c) is a motel-style setup down by the beach with parking, with overpriced but simple and clean rooms. **Hotel Michelle** (tel. 504/658-9104), down the road, has rooms starting at US$13, along with a murky pool. The **Coco Bay** (tel. 504/658-9001, www.cocobayomoa.com, US$49 s, US$61 d), past Roli's heading away from the beach, looks promising at first glance, but the rooms are pretty basic and cold water only. The one plus is the clean pool.

Those looking for luxury will be happy with **Omoa Bay condominiums** (tel. 504/553-4358, www.vrbo.com/134328), right on a safe, semi-private stretch of beach. There are six three-bedroom apartments, fully equipped with quality linens, plasma TVs, wireless Internet, and the like, along with three shared decks and a swimming pool. The views are fabulous. Rates are US$1,100–1,400 per week depending on the season and number of guests, or higher during Holy Week and New Year's.

Food

The best cheap eats (*baleadas, licuados,* etc.) are at the *comedores* lining the road away between the beach and the fort—look for **Comedor Doña Rafa,** which serves generous portions for just a couple of bucks.

For seafood, and a relatively more upscale setting, try the restaurant at **Flamingo's** (tel. 504/658-9199), built on a terrace overlooking the water, which with its linen tablecloths is far more charming than most of the beachfront shacks. Entrées range US$9–11, which is no longer any more expensive than other places, now that the seafood shacks have inflated their prices to make the most of the tourist trade. There is even a vegetarian pasta on Flamingo's menu for those who have tired of seafood.

If you decide to try one of the other restaurants or *champas* crowding the beach area, ask yourself these questions: How loud do I want my music? How bright do I want my lights? How cheap do I want my fish? Then go out and make some comparisons. **Aquí Pancha** (504/658-9172), right on the intersection where the Omoa road reaches the beach, is a long-time, relaxed favorite run by a friendly local family serving up seafood dishes for US$5–8. **Champa Johnson,** a nice, shady spot that plays mellower music than some of the others, serves up seafood—grilled, fried, ceviche, or soup—in the US$5–9 range.

On the road between the fort and the highway is **Punto Italia** (9 A.M.–9 P.M. Wed.–Sun.), with pizza, pasta, and other Italian specialties for US$6–15, as well as a small grocery store with a small selection of gourmet goodies such as olives and anchovies.

Services

At the highway junction are a few **pulperías** (minimarts), a burger joint, and, opposite the Copena gas station, a **migración** office.

Dollars and travelers checks can be exchanged at Roli's, Pia's, and the Hotel Flamingo, but not at the Banco de Occidente in town. The same hotels can also provide expensive telephone service, or you can go to the also expensive and very slow **Hondutel** office (tel. 504/658-9010). The Omoa **police** can be reached at 504/658-9156.

The hotel Bahía de Omoa offers **laundry service** to nonguests.

Taximotos tootle around town, charging US$0.50 for the ride between the fort and the beach.

Buses return to Puerto Cortés all day long until 6 P.M. Those returning directly to San Pedro Sula from Omoa should ask the driver to stop at the highway junction outside of Puerto Cortés, where the direct San Pedro buses stop to fill up with passengers. Roli of Roli's Place offers shuttle bus service to La Ceiba, with a minimum of eight people.

Crossing into Guatemala

Formerly a long walk through the jungle, the border crossing to Puerto Barrios in Guatemala is now quick and painless. Just about every bus heading west on the highway from Omoa is going to the border, charging US$2 for the hour-long ride. Take a *taximoto* from Omoa to the highway and flag down the next bus you see. There is no charge to exit Honduras, but there's a US$3 fee upon entry (or re-entry).

Cayos Zapotillos

Tucked into the Golfo de Amatique are the Cayos Zapotillos, a collection of beautiful patches of sand, palm trees, and reef whose ownership is unclear. The water around the cays is exceptionally clear, and the reef is in good condition and teeming with marine life. The cays—Hunting Cay, Lime Cay, Nicholas Cay, Raggedy Cay, French Cay, and two others—are claimed by Honduras, Belize, and Guatemala. Belize has erected a police station on Hunting Cay, the largest of the islands, so it seems to have taken charge of the situation for the moment. A tourist official is also usually present. All visitors must register at the police station, show a *zarpe* paper (an international permit for a boat, available at the port captain's office in Omoa or Puerto Cortés), and pay US$10 for each visitor. Everyone must have a passport.

No facilities exist on the cays, so bring camping gear. Roberto Alvarez at the Hotel Playa on Playa Cienaguita, near Puerto Cortés, runs snorkeling and scuba day trips, which include the entry fee. Less expensive trips might also be negotiated with fishermen in Omoa. Keep in mind the *zarpe* paper costs around US$40, and gas is expensive.

Trujillo

Coralio reclined, in the midday heat, like some vacuous beauty lounging in a guarded harem. The town lay at the sea's edge on a strip of alluvial coast. It was set like a little pearl in an emerald band. Behind it, and seeming almost to topple, imminent, above it, rose the sea-following range of the Cordilleras. In front the sea was spread, a smiling jailer, but even more incorruptible than the frowning mountains. The waves swished along the smooth beach; the parrots screamed in the orange and ceiba-trees; the palms waved their limber fronds foolishly like an awkward chorus at the prima donna's cue to enter.

– O. Henry, Cabbages and Kings

One of many foreigners who have been waylaid by Trujillo's lotus-land vibes, American writer O. Henry renamed the town Coralio for his short story, but the description is as good as one could ask for. The country's oldest settlement, Trujillo feels like a forgotten, sleepy corner of Honduras, where no one is in a hurry to do anything. The very idea of being in a hurry in Trujillo seems preposterous.

Even the local tourist industry has failed to take off, despite the obvious attractions of a broad bay lined by a beach and palm trees, a national park close to town comprising jungle-covered mountains and mangrove lagoons, and several quiet Garífuna villages not far away. It doesn't help that no airline currently flies to Trujillo (although Sosa will fly in if a group books the entire plane), and the town is three hours by bus from La Ceiba, and twice that from San Pedro Sula.

Despite the difficult access, Trujillo is a favorite stop-off for the overland backpacker-traveler crowd, and popular with anyone looking to get away from it all, those who appreciate the tranquil vibes. It's an easy place to let a couple of days or weeks slip away, if you can do without luxury.

The capital of the Colón department, Trujillo has about 30,000 residents.

History

Though Trujillo was officially founded on May 18, 1525, by Juan de Medina, acting under orders from Hernán Cortés, the natural bay had long before drawn other settlers. According to colonial testimony and archaeological evidence, Trujillo Bay had been occupied for many hundreds of years before the Spanish arrived. Trujillo was apparently something of a pre-Columbian crossroads, the site of Pech and Tolupán villages as well as settlements of Mayan and Nahuatl traders from Mexico and Guatemala.

The early Spanish colonists established their new town on the site of an Indian village named Guaimura, amid approximately a dozen other villages totaling several thousand inhabitants. Trujillo was named for the Spanish hometown of Medina's superior officer, Fernando de las Casas.

In the first years after conquest, Trujillo was the administrative center of the new colony, housing both the governor of Honduras and the only bishopric, established in 1545. But the lure of gold in the mountains soon drew colonists to the interior towns of Gracias a Dios and Comayagua, which by the middle of the century had superseded Trujillo.

Trujillo faded into a backwater colonial port. The constant threat of pirate assault on the poorly guarded harbor was all the more reason for colonists to relocate. French corsairs first attacked in 1558, and others followed repeatedly from their bases on the Bay Islands and in the Mosquitia. Since colonial authorities were unable to mount an effective defense, even the Spanish merchants who depended on the port took to living inland and came to the coast only when the Spanish fleet arrived.

In 1642, English pirate William Jackson led an assault on Trujillo with 1,500 men, almost entirely destroying the town. While Trujillo

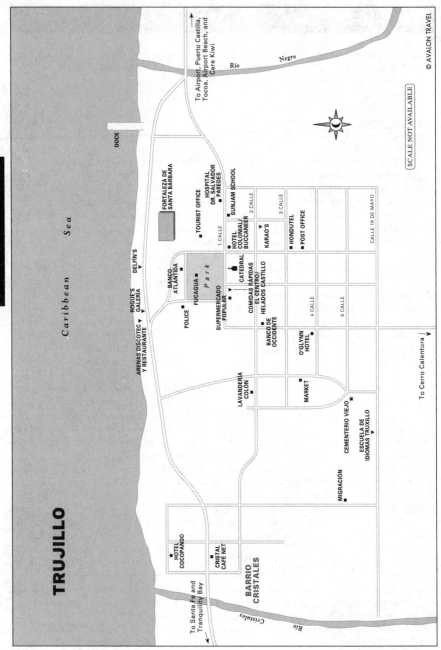

TRUJILLO

Caribbean Sea

To Santa Fe and
Tranquility Bay

Río Cristales

**BARRIO
CRISTALES**

HOTEL
COCOPANDO

CRISTAL
CAFÉ NET

MIGRACIÓN

CEMENTERIO VIEJO

ESCUELA DE
IDIOMAS TRIXILLO

LAVANDERÍA
COLÓN

MARKET

O'GLYNN
HOTEL

BANCO DE
OCCIDENTE

4 CALLE

5 CALLE

POLICE

FUCAGUA

SUPERMERCADO
POPULAR

Park

BANCO
ATLÁNTIDA

COMIDAS RÁPIDAS
EL CENTRO/
HELADOS CASTILLO

CATEDRAL

ARENAS DISCOTEC
Y RESTAURANTE

DELFIN'S

ROGUE'S
GALERÍA

DOCK

FORTALEZA DE
SANTA BÁRBARA

TOURIST OFFICE

HOSPITAL
DR. SALVADOR
PAREDES

SUNJAM SCHOOL

HOTEL
COLONIAL/
BUCCANEER

KARAO'S

1 CALLE

2 CALLE

3 CALLE

HONDUTEL

POST OFFICE

CALLE 18 DE MAYO

To Cerro Calentura

Río Negro

To Airport, Puerto Castilla,
Tocoa, Airport Beach, and
Care Kiwi

SCALE NOT AVAILABLE

© AVALON TRAVEL

THE FALL OF WILLIAM WALKER

Filibuster William Walker – "the gray-eyed man of destiny," as he was called in his years of fame – was possessed by a burning desire to govern parts or all of Central America. He offered varied reasons, including a desire to expand slavery and to establish U.S. control over the fractious republics before England did. But the more important driving force behind his actions seems to have been a slightly crazed messianic fervor.

Walker invaded Nicaragua and ruled it 1855-1857. His presence accomplished the heretofore impossible task of unifying El Salvador, Guatemala, Honduras, and Costa Rica in a common goal – namely, getting rid of the hated gringo. After a series of bloody battles, Walker surrendered in Nicaragua on May 1, 1857, and returned to New Orleans. His hero's welcome there took the sting out of his defeat, and, convinced as ever of his destiny to rule Central America, he soon organized an expedition to conquer Nicaragua once again. It would be his last.

Walker departed New Orleans in June 1860, planning first to take control of the island of Roatán, then join forces with Honduran Liberal Party leader Trinidad Cabañas to overthrow the Honduran government. However, at the time, the British occupied Roatán. They had been about to turn the island over to Honduras, but on hearing of Walker's plan, they postponed their departure. When Walker arrived off Roatán and saw the Union Jack still flying, he changed plans and decided instead to take Trujillo. Landing on the bay a few kilometers from town at night, Walker and his 200 men marched on the fort at dawn and took it in a 15-minute battle.

Walker quickly hoisted the flag of the Central American Republic over the fort and reassured the townspeople of his good intentions. However, he made the fatal mistake of taking over Trujillo's customs house – which, unbeknown to him, was technically managed by the British. This gave British forces in Roatán the pretext they needed to help Honduras attack Walker. The British warship *Icarus*, commanded by Captain Norvell Salmon, soon appeared in the harbor, and word came of a force of 700 Honduran soldiers just outside of town. Rather than give in to the inevitable, Walker chose to lead his men out of town during the night. They made their way east into the Mosquitia in hopes of joining forces with Cabañas.

Walker eventually stopped to regroup on the banks of the Río Sico, where he and his men came under attack from Honduran soldiers. They fought off the attack for five days, but with many of his "immortal" soldiers dead or wounded, and himself ill with a fever and shot in the cheek, Walker knew he was defeated. When the *Icarus* appeared near the scene of the battle, Walker surrendered to Salmon, figuring he and his men would at worst return in shame to the United States.

Walker's men were placed under the protection of the British flag, but Salmon had no sympathy for Walker; he turned him over to the Hondurans in Trujillo. At first Walker protested, but soon he resigned himself to his fate. On September 12, 1860, Walker was led to the outskirts of town – now the site of the town hospital – flanked by two priests and a crowd of heckling Hondurans, clearly relishing the sight of the famed invading gringo's execution. Walker remained calm, received his last sacraments from the priests, and stood straight in the face of a firing squad.

residents were still recovering from the blow, the next year Dutchman Jan Van Horn arrived and finished the work entirely. Those who hadn't been killed gave up the port as a lost cause, and the Spanish deserted Trujillo for almost 150 years, although British traders intermittently used the ruined town as a stop-off point.

In the late 18th century, the Spanish began a major counteroffensive to turn back British settlements along Central America's Caribbean coast. As part of this effort, Trujillo was reoccupied by a contingent of soldiers in 1780. Although the Spanish colony was on its last legs, the new settlement took hold. It received a boost in 1799, when several hundred

Garífuna, deported by the British from the south Caribbean island of San Vicente and unceremoniously dumped on nearby Roatán, built a village just west of Trujillo in what is now Barrio Cristales.

As with the rest of the north coast, Trujillo participated in the banana boom of the early 20th century. Both Standard and United Fruit acquired lands in the area. Standard still controls much land in the nearby Valle del Aguán and ships most of its produce out of nearby Puerto Castilla. Trujillo's economy relies on the port, the departmental government, and the fledgling tourist industry.

Orientation and Getting Around

The center of Trujillo is on a rise above the beach and consists of a small square surrounded by government buildings, the church, and a few stores. The town continues several streets back up the hill, where the bulk of hotels and restaurants are located. To the west of downtown is Barrio Cristales, the first Garífuna settlement on mainland Honduras.

Robberies have been reported in the vicinity of Trujillo, but generally the downtown area, the main town beach, and the stretch between the airport beach and Casa Kiwi and beyond are safe. Less safe are the more deserted stretches of beach between Trujillo and Santa Fe, and the beach around the airport at night.

Most visitors will find themselves easily able to walk between their hotel and the main beach in town. A taxi anywhere in town costs US$1.

For those staying out at the beach hotels, be forewarned that seasonal rains can make getting there—or away—impossible.

SIGHTS

First and foremost among Trujillo's attractions is the **beach** right below town—a wide, clean swath of sand lined with *champa* restaurants and lapped by the protected waters of the bay. Swimming and sunbathing here are safe, but don't tempt fate by leaving possessions lying around unguarded. The bay is not as clear as

waters off the Bay Islands, but still it's warm, fairly clean, and calm. Beware of swimming in front of town, however, during or after rains, as the runoff brings lots of nasty stuff from town into the bay.

The **airport beach,** east of town in front of the airport and dominated by the aging Christopher Columbus Hotel, is an equally fine spot for relaxing, usually a bit quieter as it's farther from town. Sand flies are common enough on Trujillo's beaches, depending on the breeze and season, but not as bad as they are farther out by Puerto Castilla.

East of the airport, beaches continue all the way around the bay to Puerto Castilla. One particularly good place to hang out is the beach by the Casa Kiwi hotel, about seven kilometers from town, easily reached by a Puerto Castilla bus. The entire beach all the way out to Puerto Castilla is generally safe, but if you plan on heading to more isolated areas, it's best not to go alone; don't bring valuables.

For all its storied history, Trujillo retains little in the way of colonial monuments. The most interesting is the **Fortaleza de Santa Bárbara** (9 A.M.–5 P.M. daily, US$3), which was built piecemeal beginning in 1575. As was the fort at Omoa, Trujillo's fort was notably unsuccessful, falling continually to attackers over the course of the colonial era. Invaders were repelled with success only after the arrival of the Garífuna in 1799. The Garífuna were superb soldiers who gained experience from a half century of guerrilla warfare against the British on San Vicente. The last real battle for the fort took place in 1910, when a Honduran general landed here in an unsuccessful attempt to launch a coup. The fort was closed in 1969 when its guard troops were called into action against El Salvador in the "Soccer War." Shortly thereafter, it was converted into a tourist attraction. Several colonial-era cannons are still set up on the fort's ramparts. Known locally as El Castillo, it contains three rooms filled with artifacts such as Lenca pottery and stone carvings, cannonballs and pistols from the colonial era, and informative exhibits. If you're an early riser, it can be possible to

The Santa Bárbara fort is perched at the edge of town.

© AMY E. ROBERTSON

visit the fort even before its regular opening at 9 A.M., since the guard-slash-ticket sellers are already on-site.

Although Trujillo was the site of the first cathedral in Honduras, the original church was destroyed long ago. The unexceptional **Catedral de San Juan Bautista** was built in 1832 and remodeled 1930–1939.

The *cementerio viejo* **(old cemetery),** south of downtown, is worth a visit to see the grave of the "gray-eyed man of destiny," William Walker, whose filibustering days came to a violent end in Trujillo on September 12, 1860. Apart from Walker's grave, the cemetery (8 A.M.–noon and 1–4 P.M. Tues.–Sun.) also offers an interesting, if decrepit, assortment of grave monuments from across 300 years of Trujillo history. At last check, it was completely overgrown with weeds reaching well above the cemetery's walls.

Tourist Options (tel. 504/443-0337, www.hondurastouristoptions.com), based in La Ceiba, has four tours (half or full day) in Trujillo: of the Garífuna communities, Puerto Castillo, Guaymoreto Lagoon, and Capiro and Calentura National Park, for US$37–55 per person based on a group of 3–4.

ENTERTAINMENT AND EVENTS

Discoteca Truxillo is the main disco in town, with a good mix of music and people. Entrance ranges US$1.50–2.50, depending on the night, but a stamp allows guests to leave, barhop, and come back. Thursday is karaoke night. Right on the beach is **Arenas Discotec y Restaurante.** A good local bar is **Henry's Place,** with several pool tables. The restaurant/ bar at the **Casa Kiwi,** outside of town on the road to Puerto Castilla (you'll have to take a taxi at night if you're not staying there), always has a group of young travelers drinking beers, playing pool, and swapping stories.

Trujillo's annual patron festival is held on June 24 in honor of San Juan Bautista. The festival lasts an entire month, with each neighborhood hosting a party on a different day. The hotels can get pretty busy, and drunks are plenty.

SHOPPING

In Barrio Cristales, **Waniehügu,** next to the Hotel Cocopando, sells a variety of Garífuna *artesanías.* Also near the Hotel Cocopando, **Artesma Garífuna** (tel. 504/434-3593, 7 A.M.–10 P.M. daily) is worth seeking out for its drums, carvings, jewelry, paintings, and *punta* cassettes. Unfortunately, it also stocks a number of shells and starfish pilfered from nearby waters.

The handicraft store **Made in Honduras** (tel. 504/9839-2768, www.hondurastreasures .com), at the entrance to town, has an excellent selection of both traditional and creative crafts. The store was initiated by a missionary and is run by a community group; all the goodies inside have been handmade by local Hondurans who have been taught a thing or two about style. Treebark *tuno* pictures have been brought from the Mosquitia, but the rest of the items, such as fabric purses and beaded jewelry, are made by local community members.

ACCOMMODATIONS

With tourism still in first gear, and not much else going on in Trujillo either, good hotel options in town are limited. Visitors can camp out at Casa Kiwi or Casa Alemania.

In Town

Conveniently located in front of the park, although rather dark, is **Hotel Colonial** (tel. 504/434-4011, US$26 s/d), with air-conditioning- and TV-equipped rooms.

The **O'Glynn Hotel** (tel. 504/434-4592, US$20 s, US$26 d), three blocks uphill from the square, rents modern, spacious rooms with air-conditioning in a newly built annex. In the lobby of the hotel is a complete set of framed topographical maps of the region, an interesting collection of pre-Columbian jade figurines, and a copy of the testimony of the founding of Trujillo on May 18, 1525, in the name of Cortés, written by Captain Francisco de las Casas.

For something more upscale, try **Villa Vista Dorada** (tel. 504/434-4465, U.S. tel. 404/872-4111, www.trujillohonduras.com/rental-villa-vista.htm), a three-bedroom private home available for rent (US$120/night for up to four people, US$20 extra for additional people, or US$600/week). Although it's far from the beach, the hillside location grants a fantastic view, and the owners have a private strip of beach available for guest use, complete with guardhouse, *champa,* and shower.

On the Beach

In Barrio Cristales is **Hotel Cocopando** (tel. 504/434-4748, US$8 s/d with fan, US$26 s/d with a/c and TV), a three-story concrete structure on a clean stretch of beach; the cheap rooms are popular with backpackers. The Garífuna restaurant serves decent fish and *chuleta de cerdo* (pork chops).

Three kilometers from town along a very bumpy dirt road leading west to Santa Fe is **◖ Tranquility Bay** (tel. 504/9928-2095, www.tranquilitybayhonduras.com, US$46 s, US$52 d), in a great setting right on the bay. Five small cabins are lined across a grassy yard

that gives way to sand and sea. The pastel cabins are basically large guest rooms, with soft yellow walls, Guatemalan bedspreads, and large Mayan wood carvings on the walls. One of the cabins also has a full kitchen (all have mini-fridges and purified water). There are no TVs or air-conditioning, but porch hammocks provide entertainment, and ceiling fans and shuttered windows generate a great breeze. The two *champas* on the beach shelter stone tables, perfect for a picnic or a beer, or try a wood-fired pizza at the hotel's restaurant. The American-Peruvian hotel managers, Jim and Gloria, will do everything to make sure you have a great stay. Rates are negotiable in the low season.

Right next door is **Campamento Hotel and Restaurant** (tel. 504/9991-3391, US$42 s/d with fan, US$63 with a/c and private porch), where service has reportedly gone downhill. The beach remains great, and there is air-conditioning, so it may be a good option for some, but readers have reported exceptionally slow service at the restaurant (even for Honduras) and mediocre food. Aggressive dogs are often let loose on the beach at nightfall, so don't come here with visions of a evening stroll on the golden sands. There's a swimming pool for the use of guests only.

Five kilometers past the entrance to Trujillo down the road toward Puerto Castilla is **◖ Casa Kiwi** (tel. 504/9967-2052, www.casakiwi.com), an excellent and popular option for backpackers and other low-key travelers run by a friendly New Zealander with plenty of knowledge about the area. The large house just off the beach has two dorm rooms with beds (US$5.25 pp) and three private rooms (US$8.50 s, US$9.50 d), all simple but clean, with hot water and fans. There are also two rooms with fans and shared bath (US$9.50–17 depending on the number of guests—up to four). More recently constructed and closer to the beach, three individual cabanas have high vaulted ceilings, air-conditioning, hot water, and private baths (US$32 s, 37 d). The grounds also make a great place to pitch a tent (only US$3). The owner runs a screened-in bar and restaurant with three meals a day, making it worth a trip out from town for an afternoon to eat, drink some beers, enjoy the beach, and chat with other guests. Outside is a covered shelter with hammocks, encouraging an excellent community vibe. Internet is available to guests. The hotel has a van and they're happy to pick up and drop off guests at the bus station (no matter the hour) for a reasonable rate (around US$5, depending on gas prices). They'll also help travelers get into town, for example, to hit the discos on weekends. Otherwise, to get there, catch a Puerto Castilla–bound bus or, in the evening, a US$10 cab.

Casa Alemania (tel. 504/434-4466) is a relaxed beachfront hotel, with top-notch German cooking by the owner, Gunther. (Nonguests can come for a meal if they call ahead.) No two rooms on the property are alike, but they are all simple, decent, and spacious, as well as very clean. Rooms (US$24–30.50 s, US$30.50–37 d) have tile floors, TV, and hot water; most are spacious. There is a small apartment with eight twin beds that rents for US$10 per person. Budget travelers can camp out for US$5,

or if you're really down to your last lempira, borrow a hammock and sleep out for free. (If the hotel isn't full, you can probably negotiate a cheaper rate for one of the rooms if you don't feel like camping.) Hearty breakfasts are available for US$3.75, as is laundry service (same price). Gunther's Honduran wife is a professional masseuse.

On the far side of the airstrip, at the airport beach is the two-story **La Quinta Bay Hotel** (tel. 504/434-4398, US$26–42 s/d). The well-maintained rooms each have two double beds, air-conditioning, TV, and porch, and the pricier rooms have nicer decor and better views.

FOOD
In Town
Comidas Rápidas El Centro (tel. 504/434-4567, 7 A.M.–10 P.M. daily), opposite the park, is a buffet restaurant where a heaping plate of fried chicken, plantains, and cole slaw will set you back about US$4. The patio seating faces the town square. Adjoining is **Helados Castillo,** serving ice cream and pastries, including tasty cinnamon rolls.

THE NORTH COAST

© AMY E. ROBERTSON

Small restaurants line Trujillo's beachfront.

Buccaneer in the Hotel Colonial (in front of the park, tel. 504/434-4011) is a decent place to grab a hamburger, reported to be the best in town.

An interesting recent arrival to the Trujillo restaurant scene, **Karao's,** two blocks southeast of the park, offers a spacious, clean, air-conditioned (but windowless) dining room and bar, and is a good place for Honduran standards.

Reputed to be the best place for Garífuna cuisine is **Don Benny's,** in Barrio Cristales.

On the Beach

Rogue's Galería is a laid-back hangout popular on the weekends with travelers and a local expats, serving up fried chicken and fish, conch, lobster, burgers, and shrimp. The food is great-tasting and well-priced (US$4–9), and the restaurant keeps the nearby beach clean. Open for lunch and dinner, Rogue's closes at 9 P.M.

A little farther down the beach, **Delfín's** serves up a decent meal, but customers can suffer long waits for their food, and groups rarely get served all at once, but as the food is ready.

Groceries

The **Supermercado Popular** (7:30 A.M.–7:30 P.M. Mon.–Sat., 8 A.M.–noon Sun.), on the square, has a large selection of groceries. The public **market,** a couple of blocks south of the square, does not offer much variety but has a basic selection of staple fruits and vegetables at inexpensive prices.

INFORMATION AND SERVICES

Information

Fundación para la Protección de Capiro, Calentura y Guaymoreto, a.k.a. **Fucagua,** staffs (occasionally) an office in the second story of the kiosk in the park. The office can provide you with a simple map and descriptive pamphlet of the surrounding natural areas, and may be able to put you in touch with a guide.

There is a **tourist information office** next to the fort, which opens at 9:30 A.M.

Banks

Right on the park, **Banco Atlántida** has an ATM (sometimes broken or out of cash), and the bank can exchange dollars and travelers checks, as well as receive MoneyGrams. While only Visa works in the ATM, cash advances can be made on MasterCard inside. Western Union wires are received at **Banco de Occidente,** a block and a half from the park. In general, though, it's best to take care of money matters before getting to Trujillo; things have a way of happening slowly or not at all here.

Communications

Hondutel, a couple of blocks south of the square, is open 7 A.M.–9 P.M. daily. Faxes are received at 504/434-4200. **Honducor** is right next to Hondutel.

There are several Internet cafés in town, including **Cristal Café Net** (8 A.M.–10 P.M.), where international calls can be made as well.

Laundry

Lavandería Colón, almost opposite Hotel Mar de Plata, charges US$2.50 per load to wash and dry clothes and is closed on Sunday.

Spanish Schools

Those interested in learning Spanish can try out the **Escuela de Idiomas Truxillo** (tel. 504/434-4135, www.globalnet.hn/escuela), offering 20 hours of instruction per week for US$150, or private instruction for US$7 an hour. Homestays are possible for just an additional US$70. Another possibility is the **Sunjam School,** near the fort.

Massages

Swedish massages are available from Paula De Wassmus at **Casa Alemania** (tel. 504/434-4466) for just US$18, as well as acupuncture and reflexology services.

Emergencies

In case of emergency, head to the **Hospital Dr. Salvado Paredes** (tel. 504/434-4093) at the entrance to town. For the **police,** call 504/434-

4038 or 504/434-4039, or dial 199. Trujillo has no Red Cross or fire department.

Immigration

Migración (tel. 504/434-4451) is in Barrio Cristales, a 15-minute walk from the park, but no longer renews visas—that now requires going to Tegucigalpa. The office can provide the requisite paperwork for anyone arriving by boat from Nicaragua or elsewhere.

GETTING THERE AND AWAY
Air

There is no regular air service to and from Trujillo. Sosa, however, will fly charter groups in and out of Trujillo if they book the entire plane (which may require as few as seven in the group).

Bus

Contraipbal (tel. 504/434-4932) runs eight buses to San Pedro Sula with plenty of stops (US$9.60, six hours) between 1 A.M. and 12:20 P.M. The buses leave from the terminal a kilometer from the park, adjacent to the Texaco gas station on the highway out of town. **Cotuc,** with a terminal in Barrio Cristales, has similar service (with even more stops), but the buses pass along the beach road in front of town, meaning you don't have to take a taxi out to the highway if you can find out when they go. Cotuc buses always stop at the Texaco terminal also.

Regular buses to La Ceiba (US$3.75, three hours) leave from the Texaco terminal every 45 minutes between 1 A.M. and 1:45 P.M. (just buy a ticket for La Ceiba on one of the buses to San Pedro Sula), as do buses for Tocoa (US$2, 90 minutes). For either destination, you'll be taking a bus to San Pedro Sula but getting off early. Contraipbal also runs buses to La Ceiba for US$4.

Avoid arriving to Trujillo on any of the late-night buses, as not even the taxis are out late at night.

To Limón, take a Tocoa-bound bus to Corocito in the morning and catch one of the frequently passing buses on to Limón from there.

Buses run Monday–Saturday between Trujillo and Puerto Castilla for US$0.75 (7:15 A.M., 9:30 A.M., 11 A.M., 12:15 P.M., 2 P.M., 4 P.M., and 5:45 P.M.), and three run on Sun. (6 A.M., noon, and 4 P.M.), from the Texaco gas station or the old station just downhill from the park.

Buses to Santa Fe, San Antonio, and Guadalupe leave from the old cemetery, from 9:30 A.M. until around 5 P.M. Monday–Saturday. Usually three buses daily run to Santa Fe for US$1. An *especial* (private) taxi to Santa Fe would cost US$15, while a ride in a *colectivo* is about US$5. Note that the last bus leaves Santa Fe at 2 P.M.

Car

Rains in late 2008 washed out two bridges on the main road between Tocoa and Trujillo. Since it's impossible to know when the bridges might be fixed, directions for the alternative route, on a well-maintained gravel road, are as follows: Just past Tocoa, take a left at a little sign that indicates "Margen Isquierda," a right when you get to the T, and a left when you get to the end of the gravel road. Just a few meters onto the paved road, there is a turnoff to the left for Trujillo. The regular route takes about an hour from Tocoa, while the alternative route takes only an extra 30 minutes or so. To return to Tocoa, look for the right-hand turn toward Río Claro just after the gas station about 15 minutes outside of town, and take it. You'll then need to take a left-hand turn after maybe half an hour to get back to Margen Izquierda, or keep going and exit the back roads through Sonaguera. From Tocoa (or Sonaguera) to La Ceiba the highway is in quite decent shape and takes two hours to drive.

If you're driving to Tegucigalpa from Trujillo, the dirt road turning off from Corocito and heading through the mountains of Olancho is much more scenic than the route via La Ceiba and San Pedro Sula, but it's notorious for highway robbery, even during the day (a bus had been held up just 10 days before our visit to Trujillo).

A much-improved dirt road from Corocito

branches off to the east along the coast, with turnoffs to Limón, and continues as far as Iriona and Sangrelaya, at the edge of the Mosquitia. It's possible to drive as far into the Mosquitia as Belén, if you don't mind driving along the beach in parts.

Boat

Ferry service between Guanaja and Trujillo has been revived (US$30). Departures from Trujillo are Tuesday at 3 P.M. and Saturday at 9 A.M. Departures from Guanaja back to the mainland are Wednesday at 9 A.M. and Sunday at 3 P.M. The ferry is operated by Team Marin Travel (Guanaja tel. 504/3371-0373, Trujillo tel. 504/434-3421, and La Ceiba tel. 504/441-2091, www.teammarintravel.com). The ride takes about three hours and can be fairly rough.

NEAR TRUJILLO
Santa Fe and San Antonio

A large Garífuna town 10 kilometers west of Trujillo, Santa Fe is strung along a sandy road parallel to a fairly cluttered beach. Cleaner patches of sand can be found nearby to the east and west of Santa Fe. At the western end of town are two very elemental concrete hotels, **Hotel Tres Orquídeas** and, just across the way, **Hotel Mar Atlántico,** each charging US$7 s or d with a fan and private bathroom.

C Comedor Caballero, better known as **Pete's Place,** is worth making a trip to Santa Fe. The one-room restaurant, with the kitchen right next to the five tables, serves up superb conch stew, lobster tail, shrimp in wine sauce, snapper, pork chops, and other dishes daily for lunch or an early dinner (Pete's closes at 6 P.M.). Meals cost US$4–12, and portions are generous. The chicken tacos and the seafood soup are particularly delicious. The amiable owner, Pete, presides over the cooking with an eagle eye and is very knowledgeable about the Trujillo area. Come with time to spare; the food is all cooked fresh to order and arrives very, very slowly—but is definitely worth the wait. The setting is simple, but Pete used to be a chef on a cruise ship, and the meals are certainly high-class.

There is a small patch of reef with decent snorkeling known as **Cayo Blanco** lying off-shore in front of Santa Fe; it can be reached with the help of a local fisherman, around US$35 for the trip.

Beyond Santa Fe, the dirt road continues to the smaller villages of San Antonio and Guadalupe. Rooms can be found in San Antonio by asking around, and there is reportedly a small hotel in Guadalupe.

Thrice-daily buses ply the dirt road between San Antonio, Santa Fe, and Trujillo, leaving at irregular hours. The last bus normally returns to Trujillo around noon. It would also be easy to arrange a boat ride out this way for a nominal fee with the fishermen who pull up daily near the dock in Trujillo.

Parque Nacional Capiro y Calentura

Comprising 4,537 hectares between 667 and 1,235 meters above sea level, Parque Nacional Capiro y Calentura is centered on the two jungle-clad peaks right behind Trujillo. The park has few trails or tourist facilities, as tourism was a secondary reason for establishing the reserve, the primary reason being to protect Trujillo's water supply. The easiest and most common access is via the dirt road past Villa Brinkley, which winds up the mountain to the radio towers just below the peak of Cerro Calentura. Formerly, the U.S. Drug Enforcement Agency (DEA) maintained a radar station here, but now the caretakers of a Hondutel tower and the Catholic radio station antenna are the only occupants. From the radio towers, you can see out over the Valle del Aguán, and a trail goes east a short distance to a lookout point with great views out over the bay and Laguna Guaymoreto. The peak of Cerro Calentura is a bit farther east, but there are essentially no trails. To get out there would require a machete.

The two- to three-hour walk up to the towers from town is best done in the early morning, when it's cool and the birds are most active. Muggings have been reported on the road, so it might be wise to go in a group. A small wooden cabin at the bottom of the road is where the park *vigilante* stays—he will collect your US$3.50 entrance fee between 8 A.M. and 4 P.M. daily.

Another popular hike in the park is up the Río Negro, in a valley between Cerro Capiro and Cerro Calentura. The trail follows a water pipe along the river to a dam, above which are two small waterfalls.

Just outside the western edge of the park, a colonial-era stone road cuts over the mountains to the village of Higuerito on the south side of the mountains. The trail begins east of the village of Campamento, on the road to Santa Fe. Somewhere in the sides of the mountains—good luck finding them—are the **Cuevas de Cuyamel,** which archaeologists say have been used as a ritual site since pre-Columbian times.

Because the trails are not well maintained and the route steep, a guide is highly recommended for hiking in the park. The **Fundación Capiro Calentura Guaimoreto** (Fucagua, tel. 504/434-4294) oversees the park and may be able to help identify an able guide. Its office is on the second floor of the kiosk in Trujillo's central park. It is also possible to arrange a tour with Tourist Options (www.hondurastourist options.com) if you are a group of three or more.

Puerto Castilla

The largest container port in Honduras in terms of total tonnage transferred (Puerto Cortés handles more ships), Puerto Castilla is 28 kilometers from Trujillo, just inside Punta Caxinas. Most of the freight shipped out of Puerto Castilla is agricultural products and raw materials, much of it produced by Standard Fruit. There is little reason for tourists to visit Puerto Castilla, except perhaps for its fishing, reputed to be excellent. Waters drop straight down to 20 meters, allowing deep-water fish to be caught right off the docks.

Frequent buses run between Trujillo and Puerto Castilla.

Refugio de Vida Silvestre Guaymoreto

The Guaymoreto Wildlife Refuge, covering more than 7,000 hectares, surrounds a broad

lagoon formed by the Cabo de Honduras, east of Trujillo. The lagoon, canals, mangrove swamps, and a small island are excellent bird- and monkey-viewing areas. Local fishermen reputedly have organized an ad-hoc organization to take visitors on tours of the lagoon in *cayucos* (canoes), charging US$20 for up to four people for a three-hour tour, while more formal tours can be arranged through Tourist Options.

Limón

Another seaside Garífuna settlement, east of Santa Rosa and reached by a 34-kilometer dirt road, Limón is infrequently visited by outsiders and has a very remote, isolated feel, lost between the Mosquitia and the rest of Honduras.

Beyond Limón, the road goes via Plan de Flores and Planes to Punta Piedra, where it hits the beach, and then continues on to Sangrelaya, at the edge of the Mosquitia. From here, usually one truck a day continues on the beach to Batalla, near Palacios, or it is usually possible to get a ride by boat. Five buses a day run between Tocoa and Sangrelaya, the last leaving from Tocoa at 1 P.M. for the five-hour drive. Buses between Tocoa and Limón pass more frequently, the last in the early afternoon. If you're in Trujillo, get off at Corocito and wait for a Limón bus there.

SAVÁ

A hot agricultural town on the south side of the Río Aguán where the La Ceiba highway meets the Olanchito–Tocoa–Trujillo road, Savá is a common transit point for bus travelers. The town holds a couple of nondescript *comedores* and a gas station. Should you for some odd reason need or want to spend the night in Savá, rooms are available at **Hospedaje Carmen,** half a block from the main highway junction, among several other hotels. Buses to La Ceiba and Trujillo stop at the Contraipbal/Cotuc office, half a kilometer from the main junction on the road toward La Ceiba.

On the road to Olanchito, on the west side of the Río Mamé 28 kilometers from Savá, a dirt road turns off south, up toward the mountains.

This road leads to La Unión in Olancho—86 kilometers away and the closest town to Parque Nacional La Muralla—and eventually on to Juticalpa and Tegucigalpa. This road has in the past had a rather grim reputation (known as "El Corridor de la Muerte," or "The Corridor of Death") because of repeated holdups, particularly between La Unión and Salamá. The situation has improved considerably in recent years, but it's always best to stop at the police post and ask about the current situation. As well, the road can be in very poor condition in the rain. It's best to at least have high clearance, if not four-wheel-drive, to drive this road, even in the dry season.

OLANCHITO

The second-largest community in the Valle del Aguán after Tocoa, Olanchito sits in the heart of Standard Fruit Company (Dole) lands. The town was founded in the 17th century by migrants from San Jorge de Olancho, a colonial town near Catacamas that was destroyed by a natural disaster. The town church, set on a palm-lined square, holds a small statue of San Jorge, the town's patron saint. The statue was reputedly carried here from San Jorge de Olancho by the original migrants. The April 23 festival in the saint's honor is quite a bash, with some 20,000 people dancing in the streets.

Most of the year, though, Olanchito is hot, dusty, and altogether uninteresting to the casual traveler. For anyone curious to see what a classic company town looks like, take a taxi or bus to nearby **Coyoles,** where practically all the buildings were built and are still owned by Standard Fruit. Almost all Olanchito residents, apart from a few small-scale ranchers and farmers, derive their income either directly or indirectly from Standard. In the wake of Hurricane Mitch, Standard was planning on closing several fields around Coyoles but had held off due to protests by workers afraid of losing their livelihoods.

Just outside of Coyoles is the largest intact **thorn forest** in Honduras, a rare dry tropical ecosystem fast disappearing in the country. Several species of rare birds are found here, including an endemic green-backed sparrow, green jays, elegant trogons, and white-lored gnatcatchers. The forest is the only known habitat for the white-bellied wren and endemic Honduran emerald in Honduras. Adventurers can also access the south side of Parque Nacional Pico Bonito from near Olanchito.

It's possible, but not easy, to continue west from Olanchito to Yoro. The road deteriorates beyond Olanchito; swollen rivers can flood the route, cutting it off entirely. Twice-daily buses cross the mountains to Yoro when the road is in good condition, the last at noon (4.5 hours). A bus to La Unión in Olancho, near La Muralla park, departs once a day at 11 A.M., road conditions permitting.

The last bus from Olanchito to La Ceiba leaves at 3 P.M., but it's sometimes possible to catch a bus to Savá and there change to another bus continuing to La Ceiba or Trujillo.

TOCOA

A bustling agricultural town 29 kilometers east of Savá, Tocoa has nothing whatsoever to attract a tourist, except as the place to catch long, bumpy bus rides into the Mosquitia. Even the downtown square is ugly, although the bizarrely designed church, reportedly the work of a Peace Corps volunteer, is an unusual sight.

Though lacking in tourist attractions, Tocoa is a magnet for land-hungry migrants who use the rapidly growing city as a base to invade the Río Sico and Río Paulaya valleys on the western edge of the Río Plátano rainforest. Many of these homesteaders are moving in on protected land, but little can be done to stop them, even if the government wanted to, which it doesn't always—it's easier to sacrifice a remote stretch of jungle than deal with the thorny problem of land redistribution and rural poverty in the rest of the country.

Accommodations

Because of all the agricultural and business activity in Tocoa, several hotels offer rooms, of varying quality. **Hotel Victoria** (tel. 504/444-3031, US$18.50 s, US$24 d), near Supermercado Celia, is a good deal with air-conditioning, TV, and private bath. Just opposite Celia's is **Executivo Hotel** (tel. 504/333-3333, US$24 s, US$32 d), popular with missionary groups. Another option is the **Gran Hotel Europa**. Two cheap, acceptable places near the market and buses are **Hotelito Rosgil** and **Hotelito Yendy**.

Food and Drink
The classiest restaurant in town, such as it is, is **La Gran Villa** (tel. 504/444-3943, 7:30 A.M.–9 P.M. Mon.–Sat.), on Boulevard Colón near the park. The restaurant offers shrimp, conch, and steak dishes at US$4–7 per entrée, as well as sandwiches, breakfasts, and a full bar.

Restaurante Aquarium (tel. 504/444-3761, 7 A.M.–10 P.M. Mon.–Sat., 10 A.M.–9 P.M. Sun.) serves seafood and meat dishes (US$5–8) in an air-conditioned dining room with a full bar. Next to Banco Atlántida on the main street is the ever-popular **Cafeteria Damir** (tel. 504/444-3863, 7 A.M.–6 P.M. Mon.–Sat.), with snacks, breakfasts, and inexpensive *típico* food, like heaping bowls of steaming beef soup.

For a drink out, try **Karibu Bar**, right on the main road through Tocoa.

Services
BAC Bamer, Banco Atlántida, and **Bancahorro** in the center of town all change dollars and usually travelers checks.

Getting There and Away
In the fall of 2008, two bridges on the Tocoa–Trujillo were washed out—one completely, the other so that it formed a V across the river (we actually saw a car drive over that bridge, but it didn't seem like a great idea). There is an alternative route between the two cities—it's slightly more direct but slower since it's not paved. This alternative route was soon graded at least, but it gets ruts during every rain. Hopefully there will be a commitment to its maintenance, because no one is talking about repairing the bridges yet.

To get to Trujillo from Tocoa by car, take a left at the sign for Margen Izquierda shortly outside of town (be alert!). There are a few turns on the road (mainly one to the right when you get to a T), but the best thing to do is follow the other traffic and stop once in a while when you see pedestrians, to check with them that you're headed the right direction.

Cotuc buses (tel. 504/444-2181) follow this same alternative route. The **Contraipbal** buses (tel. 504/444-3823) follow the main highway toward Trujillo, miraculously crossing the first bridge and then sending passengers across the second river in boats. Either route costs US$2. Cotuc's terminal is opposite the DIPPSA station on the main highway, while Contraipbal's is in the main bus terminal near the market. Cotuc and Contraipbal also have buses to La Ceiba (two hours) and San Pedro Sula (five hours).

The main bus station is four blocks north of the square, next to the market. Local buses to La Ceiba depart frequently all day, charging US$3.40 for the three-hour ride. The last bus to Trujillo leaves at 6 P.M., and the last bus to La Ceiba leaves at 4 P.M.

Travel from Tocoa to Batalla in the Mosquitia, not far from Palacios, is by *paila,* or pickup truck (US$31, eight hours). The trucks leave at 9 A.M., to allow travelers to make it all the way from La Ceiba to Batalla in one day if they catch the first bus out of town from La Ceiba in the morning. The *pailas* depart from near the central market.

THE BAY ISLANDS

The white powdery sand, transparent waters, and abundant sea life of these emerald islands and their coral cays form Honduras's most popular attraction. As one of the world's cheapest places for scuba certification, the Bay Islands (Islas de la Bahía) are a paradise for novice and experienced divers alike, while snorkelers can simply wade out a few feet to immerse themselves in the rich undersea world boasting hundreds of multihued species of fish and coral.

For novice scuba divers, finding a more convenient place to get an Open Water certification or advanced training would be difficult. Eager instructors by the dozen are just waiting around for their next client, ready to take potential divers through the paces in calm, clear, 28°C (82°F) waters, all at remarkably low prices.

Diving and snorkeling may be the activities of choice for many Bay Island visitors, but life above the waves has its own appeal. The islands have a tangled history of pirate raids, immigration, deportation, and conquest, including more than 200 years of British ownership of Roatán, Utila, and Guanaja. English is the first language of most native islanders, some settlers from the British Cayman Islands, others Black Caribs that claim runaway slaves as ancestors—although recent influxes of mainlanders ("the Spanish," as the islanders like to say) are spreading the use of the Spanish language. Resident expatriates have opened restaurants that span global cuisine, but seafood is naturally the traditional culinary choice, and grilled lobster dinners can be found for as little as 10 dollars.

© AMY E. ROBERTSON

HIGHLIGHTS

◖ Diving Roatán's Reef: Diving around all three Bay Islands is spectacular, and there are 100 dive sites surrounding Roatán alone, including walls and channels, sunken shipwrecks, and caverns. Hawksbill turtles, moray eels, spotted eagle rays, and yellowtail damselfish are just a few of the species easily spotted among the colorful coral gardens (page 182).

◖ Fishing: The waters off Roatán, with shallow, sandy waters on the south side and a 3,000-meter-deep channel on the north, are perfectly situated for fishing excursions in pursuit of marlin, wahoo, tarpon, barracuda, kingfish, and more (page 183).

◖ West Bay: Roatán's West Bay is a vision of Caribbean bliss, a powdery ribbon of white sand in front of sparkling clear turquoise water with coral reef just steps offshore (page 195).

◖ Utila's Nightlife: Those after the international traveler party life will not want to miss a few days frequenting the many bars making up the nightlife on Utila (page 225).

◖ Utila Cays: With their crystal waters and powdery, isolated beaches, the tiny cays off the island of Utila make for getaways that are fantasies come true. What might seem like the realm of millionaires – the rental of an entire island – is available on Sandy Cay or Little Cay for just US$100-115 a night, while budget travelers can pop over to islets like Water Cay for a secluded picnic or campout (page 237).

◖ Guanaja's North-Side Beaches: These rarely visited beaches, like Dina Beach and West End, are home to nothing but kilometers of sand and palm trees, where you can camp or stay in one of the low-key and reasonably priced hotels (page 241).

◖ Chachahuate: Long popular as a day trip from either Roatán or the mainland's north coast, newly developed cabin rentals and even a small hotel now make the Garífuna village of Chachahuate in the Cayos Cochinos a fantastic place to spend a few days snorkeling and sunning, at a fraction of the cost of the other Bay Islands (page 247).

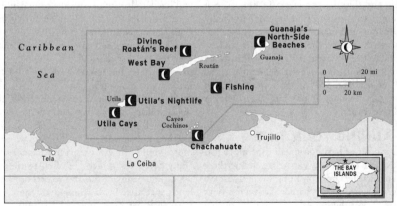

LOOK FOR ◖ TO FIND RECOMMENDED SIGHTS, ACTIVITIES, DINING, AND LODGING.

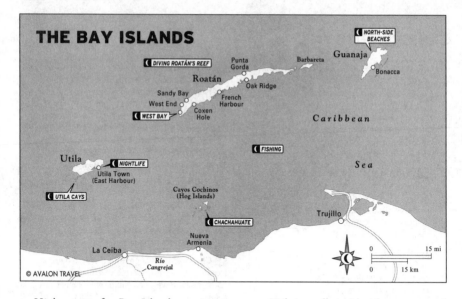

THE BAY ISLANDS

NORTH-SIDE BEACHES

Guanaja

Barbareta

DIVING ROATÁN'S REEF

Punta Gorda

Bonacca

Roatán

Oak Ridge

Sandy Bay

French Harbour

West End

Coxen Hole

WEST BAY

Caribbean

FISHING

Sea

Utila

NIGHTLIFE

Utila Town (East Harbour)

Cayos Cochinos (Hog Islands)

UTILA CAYS

CHACHAHUATE

Trujillo

Nueva Armenia

La Ceiba

Río Cangrejal

© AVALON TRAVEL

0   15 mi

0   15 km

High season for Bay Islands tourism is most of the year apart from the September–November hurricane season. Vacation times in Central America, such as Christmas, Easter week, and the first two weeks in August, can be very hard times to find lodging, especially on Roatán, and many establishments take advantage to jack up their prices. Mid-January to mid-February is a great time to come to the islands, as tourists are fewer. September is the best month to take advantage of the low season prices, as it tends to be less rainy than October and November.

PLANNING YOUR TIME

You can never have too much time on the islands, a fact the many expatriates living there will cheerfully confirm. But most of us are on a tighter schedule. If you have only a few days or a week on the Bay Islands, you'll probably end up choosing between the three. Which island to visit is really a question of personal taste. All are surrounded by coral reef. Roatán is by far the most popular, with plenty of great beaches, towns, services like hotels, restaurants and dive shops, and places to explore to keep divers and nondivers alike happy for a week or

more. Utila is smaller, with only one town and a couple of beaches, and is generally more popular with those focused on diving and the low-budget international traveler crowd. Nondivers will likely only want to spend a couple of days here. Guanaja is much less frequently visited than the other two, but it has equally good reef, a few hotels and dive resorts, and many deserted beaches to wander. Divers may want to stay a week, but nondivers again will likely feel content with a few days for R&R.

Those planning on doing some serious diving or taking a four-day scuba certification course will plan on five days or a week, with all the amazing diving on offer. A week or more would allow for trips out to more far-flung dive sites, which are often in the best condition. Many of the dive resorts on the islands specialize in weeklong dive, room, and meal packages, often around US$1,000–1,800 per person.

All three of the main Bay Islands are serviced by air flights Monday–Saturday, and Roatán has flights on Sunday as well. Utila and Roatán also have daily ferries to and from La Ceiba, and ferry service from Trujillo to Guanaja is available twice a week. There are a few charter air and boat services as well. Both air and ferry service can be suspended in the event of bad weather. October and November are the rainiest months, while high season is mid-December through May (although there can still be frequent rain in December and early January). September can be a great time to visit, taking advantage of low-season rates, but typically enjoying good weather.

THE LAND

The Bay Islands, arrayed in an arc between 29 and 56 kilometers off the Caribbean coast of Honduras, are the above-water expression of the Bonacca Ridge, an extension of the mainland Sierra de Omoa mountain range that disappears into the ocean near Puerto Cortés. The Bonacca Ridge forms the edge of the Honduran continental shelf in the Caribbean. Thus, on the northern, ocean-facing side of the three main islands, shallow waters extend only just beyond the shore before disappearing over sheer underwater cliffs to the deep waters, while on the south side the waters fronting the Honduran mainland are much shallower. The height of the islands generally increases west to east, from the lowland swamps of Utila to the modest mid-island ridges of Roatán to two noteworthy peaks on Guanaja, the highest being 412 meters.

Flora and Fauna

Ecological zones in the Bay Islands include pine and oak savannah, arid tropical forest, beach vegetation, mangrove swamp, and iron shore, or fossilized, uplifted coral. Much of the once-dense native pine and oak forests has not survived centuries of sailors seeking masts, immigrants looking for building material, and hunters setting fires to scare game. The only forests left are on the privately owned island of Barbareta and in a few remote sections of Roatán, like by Brick Bay or around Port Royal. What was left of the famed forests of Guanaja was utterly flattened by Hurricane Mitch's 290-kph winds—the island's vegetation has only recently begun to recover.

Many of the once-abundant animal species endemic to the Bay Islands have been hunted to extinction or to the brink of it: Manatees, seals, fresh- and saltwater turtles, white-tailed deer, green iguanas, basilisk lizards, boa constrictors, yellow-crowned and red-lored Amazon parrots, frigate birds, brown pelicans, and roseate terns have all vanished or are now seen only rarely. Crocodiles were once frequently seen crossing streets in Utila, but when one was spotted (and promptly killed) in December 1995, the event was a major local news item.

In spite of the depredations of hunters, 15 species of lizard still survive on the islands, along with 13 species of snake (including the poisonous but rarely seen coral), wild pigs, the small rat-like agouti, two species of opossum, and 13 species of bat. More than 120 bird species, most of which are migratory, have been spotted on the islands. Once at least 27 species of macaws, parrots, and parakeets lived on the islands; now the only macaws found are pets, and only about half the parrot species still survive in the wild.

The Bay Islands Conservation Association (BICA, www.bicautila.org), with offices on all three islands, coordinates efforts to protect different endangered species as well as the islands' remaining forests by overseeing reserves at Port Royal and Carambola in Roatán, Turtle Harbour in Utila, and, supposedly, the entire island of Guanaja. BICA now also oversees the entire reef around Utila with a marine patrol, except for the shallow waters around the cays, from which only the fishermen of the cays can fish. They've also been active in Utila distributing environmentally friendly bug spray, doing bird surveys, and conducting ecotours.

Climate

The Bay Islands have a superbly comfortable climate, with year-round air temperatures ranging 25–29°C (77–84°F) and east–southeast trade winds blowing steadily most of the year. Temperatures average 27°C (81°F) in the daytime, 21°C (70°F) at night—hot but not stifling during the day, and pleasant for sleeping at night.

Annual rainfall averages 220 centimeters,

COPING WITH THE INSECTS

Sand flies and mosquitoes can be voracious on the Bay Islands, so come prepared. Sand flies (also called jejenes and "no-see-ums") can be a nightmare on the beach, turning the arms and legs of an unsuspecting sunbather into pincushions of little red welts. Avon Skin-So-Soft and coconut oil are good repellents, as, of course, are long, loose-fitting clothes. DEET works great, but kills the coral, so be sure to rinse off before heading into the water. A good stiff breeze will get rid of the sand flies entirely, so with luck, the trade winds will be blowing during your trip. Some beaches, including Roatán's famed West Bay Beach, are sprayed with eco-friendly insecticides, which has been highly effective in eliminating the problem.

more than half of this coming in October and November, the height of the hurricane season. Water visibility is best when there is the least rain, usually March–September. Water temperature ranges from 26°C (79°F) midwinter to 30°C (86°F) in summer. The rains usually start in summer, often in June, and continue until December or January. February and March are usually the driest months. However, weather patterns vary widely from year to year, and rain can hit at any time.

HISTORY
Pre-Columbian Residents

In spite of almost 50 identified archaeological sites, little is known of the early inhabitants of the Bay Islands. Most archaeologists now agree, after years of dispute, that pre-Columbian islanders were related to the mainland Pech, who, prior to conquest, lived close to the coast near Trujillo. These island Amerindians are sometimes referred to as "Paya," but that is a term that has been rejected by the Pech, as it was a demeaning word used by the Spanish conquerors to mean wild or savage.

The first full-time residents are thought to have arrived no earlier than A.D. 600. After A.D. 1000, several major residential areas sprang up, such as Plan Grande in eastern Guanaja and the "80-Acre" site in eastern Utila. Because all the sites are located inland 10–20 meters above sea level, one theory has it that the first islanders hated sand flies even more than the current residents and fled the shoreline to escape the pests.

The island Pech grew manioc (cassava) and corn, hunted for deer and other game, fished from dugout canoes for reef fish and shark, and carried on a lively trade with the mainland Maya and Pech, as evidenced by discoveries of obsidian, flint, and ceramics with mainland designs.

Most pre-Columbian sites have long since been thoroughly sacked by fortune hunters both foreign and local. The best place to see examples of pottery and jade is in the museum at Anthony's Key Resort in Sandy Bay, Roatán. Locals may still try to sell visitors "yaba-ding-dings," as they call the artifacts, but after years of looting there aren't many pieces left to sell.

Conquest and Colonization

Believed to be the first European to visit the Bay Islands, Columbus landed near Soldado Beach on Guanaja in late July 1502 on his fourth voyage. After anchoring and sending his brother Bartholomew ashore for a look around, the admiral named the island "Isla de los Pinos" (Island of the Pines) in honor of the impressive forests. He then commandeered a passing merchant canoe laden with goods from the mainland and forced its owner to accompany him to the Mosquitia coast to serve as an interpreter. He remarked in his journal on a "very robust people who adore idols and live mostly from a certain white grain with which they make fine bread and the most perfect beer."

When the Spaniards returned on a slaving expedition in 1516, they made off with 300 Indians after a brief skirmish, only to have the would-be slaves take over the ship near Cuba and promptly set sail back to their home. But other ships looking for slaves soon followed, and not long after that, in 1530, the first *encomienda* was awarded on the Bay Islands. *Encomiendas* granted a conquistador rights to demand labor and tribute from the local inhabitants, theoretically in return for good governance and religious education.

This new economy had barely been established when European freebooters began appearing on the horizon, drooling at the thought of all the gold mined in the interior of Honduras passing through relatively isolated and unprotected Trujillo. French raiding boats appeared in 1536, followed by the English, who used the Bay Islands as a hideout for the first confirmed time in 1564, after capturing four Spanish frigates.

By the early 17th century, the persistent use of the Bay Islands as a base for pirate assaults and, briefly, as a settlement area for the British Providence Company had become a serious threat to the Spanish, so colonial authorities decided to depopulate the islands. By 1650 all the native islanders had been removed, most with the sorry fate of ending up in the malarial lowlands on Guatemala's Caribbean coast. The now-uninhabited islands were even more appealing to the pirates, who pursued their ventures unabated.

The many pirates who found shelter on the islands before the British military occupation in 1742—including Henry Morgan, John Coxen, John Morris, Edward Mansfield, and a host of others—spent most of their time hunting, fishing, or fixing up their boats, never bothering to set up any buildings beyond temporary camps. Smaller groups preferred to anchor in the bay on the south side of Guanaja, with at least seven escape routes through the cays and reef, while larger fleets stayed at Port Royal, Roatán, with just one narrow, easily defensible entrance.

Following the declaration of war between England and Spain in 1739, British troops occupied Port Royal for several years, building two small forts and granting homesteads in Port Royal and Sandy Bay. The Spanish were awarded the islands as part of the Treaty of Aix-la-Chapelle in 1748, and the last settlers were finally removed in 1751. The British returned in 1779 following another outbreak of war. In 1782 Spaniards attacked Port Royal with 12 ships and took the forts after two days of fierce fighting. The forts and surrounding town were destroyed, and Roatán was left uninhabited.

Development of the Modern Bay Islands

The earliest immigrant settlement in the Bay Islands that has survived to the present day is the Garífuna village at Punta Gorda, Roatán. Some 4,000 Garífuna were unceremoniously dumped on the deserted island on April 12, 1797, by the British near Port Royal. Most of the Garífuna moved on to the mainland shortly thereafter, settling first at Trujillo and then elsewhere up and down the coast, but one group decided they liked the looks of Roatán and settled at Punta Gorda.

The Garífuna were followed in the 1830s by a wave of immigrants, both white and black, leaving the Cayman Islands in the wake of the abolition of slavery there. Although some isolated settlers lived on the islands when the Cayman Islanders arrived, the newcomers laid the foundations for the present-day towns. They moved first to Suc-Suc (Pigeon) Cay off Utila in 1831, and shortly thereafter to Coxen Hole, Flowers Bay, and West End in Roatán and Sheen and Hog Cays off Guanaja, which would eventually become Bonacca Town.

The British government, seeing the Bay Islands as a useful geopolitical tool in its struggle with the United States for control over Central America, initially claimed ownership of the islands. In 1859, the British were forced to recognize Honduran sovereignty over the Bay Islands, but many islanders continued to think they were part of the British empire until the early 20th century, when the Honduran government first began asserting its authority over the islands.

Current Society

The economy of the Bay Islands has long relied almost entirely on the ocean, despite brief forays into the banana and pineapple exportation business in the late 19th century. Fishing has always been and continues to be the mainstay of the economy, with a fleet of some 400 commercial boats on all three islands, fishing mainly for shrimp, lobster, and conch. Overfishing has led to bans *(vedas)* during certain months of the year, but with only two inspectors, the several plants on Roatán pretty much buy whatever comes their way, whatever time of year it is. A modest boat-building industry, based particularly in Oak Ridge, has declined in recent years. Islander men frequently join on with the merchant marine or work on international cruise ships for several months of the year.

This low-key existence began to change starting in the late 1960s, when tourists discovered the islands' reefs, beaches, and funky culture. Since the late 1980s, the pace has picked up dramatically. In 1990, an estimated 15,000 tourists came to the islands; by 1996 it was 60,000. The accelerating development of Bay Island tourism took a blow from Hurricane Mitch in 1998 and the ensuing bad publicity. But as memories of the hurricane have faded (at least outside Honduras), tourists are returning to the islands in skyrocketing numbers, and further growth and development is underway. The cruise ship trade is also accelerating, with anywhere from one to eight ships a week docking at Roatán, depending on the season, unloading 250,000–300,000 cruise shippers a year. (That's roughly one-third of all tourists to Honduras.) Carnival Cruise Lines is building a second ship terminal to accommodate the dramatic growth, scheduled to open in the fall of 2009.

The changes wrought by tourism have benefited many islanders immensely, and most now live off the trade in one way or another. Even before the tourist boom, islanders had always maintained a better standard of living than their mainland countrymen. Consequently, a steadily growing number of Latino immigrants have come over to get a piece of the good life, and foreigners (particularly Canadians and Americans) continue to come in increasing numbers to run a business or to retire—trends some islanders are not too happy about. The last census put the population of all three islands at about 38,000, with an annual growth rate of 9 percent (compared to just under 3 percent for the country as a whole).

Scuba Diving

Upon arrival in the Bay Islands, divers can be overwhelmed by the number of dive shops and courses. Here's some basic information to get you started, whether you're a first-time diver in need of certification or an old hand looking for the right shop.

GETTING CERTIFIED

First, try to realistically decide if you are ready to go diving. Bay Islands dive instructors have many stories of would-be students who, believe it or not, could barely swim or were actually scared of the water. Although it's relatively cheap and other people seem to like it, if you just can't get rid of that lurking panic after a couple of shallow dives, accept the fact that diving is not for you. One of the best ways to find out how you will react to scuba diving is to try snorkeling a few times to see how you feel in the underwater world. Some people find they prefer the more relaxed shallow-water experience of snorkeling, which does not require all the gear, training, and expense of scuba diving.

Most divers getting certified in the Bay Islands follow a course created by the Professional Association of Dive Instructors (PADI), the best-known scuba certification organization. Almost all dive shops on the islands work with PADI, but a couple of shops have other certifications instead or as well, such as Scuba Schools International (SSI) and National

COURSE AND DIVE PRICES

Below are the standard course and dive prices, but naturally they are subject to change. While Utila used to be significantly less expensive than Roatán, that's no longer such a big factor, especially for dive courses. When budgeting, remember that courses on Utila include hostel-style accommodations if desired, and that the required accompanying dive book can run US$30 and up, depending on the course. Prices outside of West End in Roatán can be a bit higher.

- **Open Water:** US$250-325 (Roatán), US$270 (Utila)

- **Advanced Open Water:** US$250-300 (Roatán), US$270 (Utila)

- **Rescue:** US$250 (Roatán), US$270 (Utila)

- **Dive Master:** US$670-770 (Roatán), US$750-835 (Utila) – these prices include the US$70 PADI fee

- **Single Dive:** US$35 (Roatán), US$35 or two for US$55 (Utila)

- **Ten-Dive Package:** US$250-300 (Roatán), US$220-250 (Utila)

The Open Water certificate at Coral Bay Resort on Guanaja costs US$375.

Association of Underwater Instructors (NAUI). While PADI is by far the most popular, all three organizations have good reputations, and almost all scuba shops around the world accept certifications from any of them.

Novices ready to take the plunge into the world of scuba have a choice of either a Discover Scuba Diving or Open Water certification. A **Discover Scuba Diving** course, normally costing US$70–125 (with the cheaper rates at Utila dive shops), is an introductory dive for those who aren't sure if they'll like diving or not. It involves a half day of instruction followed by a shallow, controlled dive.

The **Open Water certification** is typically 3.5–4 days, starting with half a day of videos, then a couple of days combining classroom work, shallow water dives, and open-water dives. The last day is two open-water dives. You are then allowed to dive without an instructor—but never without another diver, invariably a dive master. It's standard practice in the Bay Islands for all divers to go out with a dive master or instructor, as guides and to ensure the protection of the reef.

Dive shops will sometimes take referrals, wherein a person completes the academic and shallow-water training at home and finishes the open-water dives with the shop. Considering that the shallow-water training could be accomplished for less money in balmy, clear Caribbean waters instead of the local YMCA pool, there's not much attraction in using a referral unless your time on the islands is extremely limited.

Many newly certified divers come out of their Open Water course feeling slightly uneasy about the idea of diving without that reassuring veteran instructor at their shoulder; they may want to immediately continue their controlled training with the **Advanced Open Water course.** The advanced course offers five different advanced dive options, with two required: instruction in undersea navigation and multilevel diving—essential for planning your own dives—and a deep dive (to 30 meters). Other dive choices include multilevel, night, wrecks, naturalist, photography, search and recover, and peak performance buoyancy. Some shops will combine two of these in one dive (for example, photography and naturalist).

Recreational divers are allowed to descend to a maximum depth of 30 meters. Going deeper puts divers in serious danger of both nitrogen narcosis and severe decompression problems when ascending. With a different mix of gases in the air tanks, however, it is possible with training to descend deeper and stay down longer than with a regular air tank. Nitrox, a mix of nitrogen and oxygen, allows divers to (depending on the mix) extend their time at depth by 20 or 30 minutes or minimize the surface

THE BAY ISLANDS REEF SYSTEM

Coral reefs are one of the most complex ecosystems on the planet, comparable in diversity to tropical rainforests. The Bay Islands reef is particularly varied because of its location on the edge of the continental shelf, at the transition between shallow-water and deep-water habitats. Some 96 percent of all species of marine life known to inhabit the Caribbean – from tiny specks of glowing bioluminescence to the whale shark, the largest fish in the world – have been identified in the waters surrounding the Bay Islands. Divers and snorkelers flock here in droves to experience a dizzying assortment of fishes, sponges, anemones, worms, shellfish, rays, sea turtles, sharks, dolphins, and hard and soft corals.

WHAT IS CORAL?

Contrary to what many people understandably assume, coral is a stationary animal, not a plant. Each "branch" of coral is made up of hundreds or thousands of tiny flowerlike polyps. Polyps, thin-membraned invertebrates, compensate for their flimsy bodies by extracting calcium carbonate from the seawater and converting it into a brittle limestone skeleton. Through this continual, tireless construction process, the bizarre and beautiful undersea forests seen by divers and snorkelers are created, at a rate of about a centimeter per year.

Tiny, extended tentacles bring in food drifting by in the water, but the anchored coral polyps must supplement their intake by housing minuscule algae cells; these cells in turn produce nutrients for the polyps through photosynthesis. Because of this symbiotic relationship, coral always grows in relatively shallow waters, where the sun can penetrate. Reduced water clarity due to pollution or erosion from construction, agriculture, or deforestation can be fatal for coral, robbing the algae of the light needed to photosynthesize.

The main reef-building coral in shallow areas is leafy lettuce coral (*Agaricia tenuifolia*). This species virtually excludes other corals from many spur tops, growing in some areas to within 10 centimeters of the surface. In areas with greater wave energy, such as along the north sides of the islands, forests of treelike elkhorn coral (*Acropora palmata*) are common. Star coral (*Montastrea annularis*), brain coral (*Diploria spp.*), boulder brain coral (*Colpophylia natans*), and elegant columns of pillar coral (*Dendrogyra cylindrus*) are often seen on the fore reef, at a depth of 10-15 meters. Black coral is still found around the Bay Islands, usually in deeper waters on reef walls. Many shallower patches have been destroyed by jewelry-makers. In the water, black coral appears silver, only turning black when exposed to the air.

Fire coral, or hydrocoral, is not a true coral but a "battery of stinging nematocysts on tentacles of coral polyps," as Paul Humann, author of a good three-volume reference on reef systems, describes it. Learn what fire coral looks like right away, and keep well clear of it – even a light brush can be painful. Should you accidentally bump into it, remember never to rub the affected area or wash it with fresh water or soap, as this can cause untriggered nematocysts to release their barbs. Two recommended treatments are vinegar or meat tenderizer, both of which immobilize the nematocysts.

THE REEF

It's often claimed that the Bay Islands reef and the Belize reef system to the north together make up the second-longest reef in the world – after Australia's Great Barrier Reef. Technically, the Bay Islands reef is distinct from the Belize reef – not only does a 3,000-meter-deep undersea trench separate the two, but they are different kinds of reef. The Belize system is a barrier reef, with the coral wall separated from shore by a lagoon at least a mile wide, while the Bay Islands system is a fringing reef, essentially beginning right from the shore. Sections of the north-side reef on the Bay Islands show characteristics of developing into a barrier reef in time but are still considered fringing reef.

Reef geography is generally the same on all three of the main islands. The north-side reef forms almost a complete wall, with only a few narrow passages allowing access to the shallow lagoon between the reef and the shore. The

Guanaja north-side reef is much farther offshore (about a mile, or 1.5 kilometers, in places) than on Utila and Roatán. From the reef crest, which sometimes almost breaks the surface, the reef slopes to a plateau at around 10 meters, then falls off the wall. The south-side reef frequently starts literally at the water's edge and slopes down at a more gentle grade to a depth of around 10-12 meters, when it hits the sheer reef wall bottoming on sand at around 30-40 meters. The southern reef is generally more broken up than the north, with channels, chutes, headlands, and cays. Sea mounts – hills of coral rising up off the ocean floor – and spur-and-groove coral ridges are common and are often the best places to see diverse sea life.

The Cayos Cochinos reef system shares similar characteristics with the other islands, except it lacks steep drop-offs and lagoons on the north side.

THE HEALTH OF THE REEF

Generally speaking, the Bay Islands reef is in pretty good shape, although certain high-impact areas are showing signs of damage from overdiving and decreasing water quality. According to a recent study, the Roatán reef has 25-30 percent live coral cover (the rest covered by sand, sea grass, sponges, rubble, algae, dead coral, fire coral, etc.), a relatively healthy percentage compared to other Caribbean reefs.

Tourism development poses the most direct threat to the reef, since coastal and hillside construction generates runoff and other forms of water pollution. Degraded water quality leads to algae blooms, which steal sunlight, oxygen, and other nutrients from the coral, literally choking the reef to death. This threat is particularly severe on Roatán, where the island's long central ridge is being carved up on all sides for roads and houses, while coastal wetlands, which filter runoff, are being filled in for construction. The reef off West Bay in Roatán is particularly threatened, due to all the construction and tourist activity in the hills backing the beach. While Guanaja is quite hilly, construction on the main island is still limited, making runoff less serious. However, water

pollution around Bonacca, Mangrove Bight, and Savanna Bight has damaged most of the reef surrounding those towns. Utila, mostly flat and still retaining much of its wetlands, does not face much erosion at the moment, but water pollution is a problem around East Harbour and Pigeon Cay.

Coral bleaching occurs on the Bay Islands reef, as it does on reefs all over the world. During these usually temporary events, higher water temperatures than normal cause the coral to expel the zooxanthellae (algae cells) that give coral its color pigments. The cells return when the sea temperature returns to its normal level, ideally 23-30°C (73-86°F). In 1998-1999, there was a global bleaching event, in part as a result of the warming of the world's seas after the 1997-1998 El Niño phenomenon. Hurricane Mitch – so devastating above the water – helped spur the recovery of the Bay Islands reef from the prolonged bleaching episode by bringing up colder water from deeper in the ocean and cooling off the waters near the surface by as much as 3°C.

The proliferation of divers is beginning to take a toll on the reef; some oversaturated dive sites are closed off to allow for the coral to recover. These days, dive boats more regularly tie off on buoys instead of anchoring on the reef, but divers continue to bump and grab coral in spite of frequent warnings. Each brush with a piece of coral wipes off a defensive film covering the polyps, allowing bacteria to penetrate. Just one small gap can compromise the defenses of an entire coral colony. Think about that when you see the reef in front of West Bay Beach, Roatán, swarmed with thousands of cruise-ship visitors.

Black coral, formerly common around the Bay Islands, has been depleted in recent years by jewelry-makers, whose work can be seen in several local gift shops. For those tempted to buy a piece, remember it is illegal to take black coral into the United States.

Two websites with detailed research information on the Bay Island reef system are www .yale.edu/roatan/index.htm and www.wfu .edu/~dkevans.

DIVING SAFETY

Fortunately, safety standards are high throughout the Bay Islands. But when choosing your shop, it is a good idea to personally verify minimal safety standards. Below is a set of questions to ask (and be sure to verify the answers with your own eyes; don't just take the staff's word for it).

- Do you carry oxygen on the boat?

- Do you carry a VHF radio? (A cell phone is not nearly as reliable.)

- Does the boat stay at the dive site after dropping off divers?

- Is the boat manned by a captain at all times? (Some shops expect dive masters or instructors to also serve as the captain.)

- When was your air last analyzed? (The analysis certificate should be dated within the past three months.)

interval and allow more dives in a single day. As well, divers seem to be slightly less tired at the end of the day. Nitrox is very popular with live-aboard dive boats, which try to squeeze in as many dives as possible in a week. Nitrox diving requires certification and special equipment, which not every dive shop has. Extreme depth freaks will be pleased to hear that another, even more specialized gas mix known as Trimix (Nitrox plus helium) allows divers to go as deep as 150 meters, a truly spooky deep-sea world.

Nitrox has become pretty widely available, but Trimix is less common, and easier to find on Utila. The Bay Islands College of Diving and Utila Dive Center offer full tech courses, Trimix, and rebreathers. Ocean Connections in West End has one complete Trimix set.

CHOOSING A SHOP

So, you've decided you're ready to take a course or go on a series of dives. How to choose between all the different dive shops? Both Utila and Roatán have set minimum prices among nearly all of their shops to avoid price wars—that price is currently at US$250 for an Open Water course in Utila and US$280 for an Open Water course in West End, Roatán. A few shops charge more, but typically include course materials and other fees (Utila has a US$4 daily reef tax, and Roatán a once-annually US$10 Marine Park fee). Dive shops do get together throughout the year, though, to change prices based on the cost of fuel and the level of activity on the islands, so these prices may fluctuate. Guanaja has fewer dive shops, and they are more expensive.

Perhaps the most important criteria for choosing a shop, especially for novice divers taking their first course, is the quality of the instructors. A good instructor can mean the difference between a fun, safe, and informative course, and one that just follows the book—or worse. Certified divers will also want to ensure their dive leader is competent, as they will be, in part, relying on that person's judgment and safety skills. Ask how many dives a dive master has completed—100 is very few; 500 is a decent amount; 1,000 or more is a lot. Also, a dive master with 100 or so dives is likely to have gone through all or most of his or her courses on the Bay Islands, where conditions are excellent much of the time. Consequently, that dive master will have less experience dealing with emergency situations than a diver trained in, for instance, the North Sea or the northern Pacific off California. At the same time, experience on Bay Island reefs is essential to understanding local conditions. If you can find an instructor who has worked on the islands for several years but also has experience in other parts of the world, that's best of all. Dive masters trained in commercial diving, mixed-gas diving, cave diving, or military diving can be very good because of their experience, but they are also sometimes extremely cavalier with safety precautions.

After talking to the dive masters, look closely at the gear you would be using. The newer, the better. Especially crucial is having a well-maintained air compressor to ensure clean air in your tank. Cast an eye over the hoses, regulator, and BCD air vest, which should all look new and be without signs of wear and tear. Most shops should and do replace their gear on a regular basis. Ensure fins and mask fit snugly and comfortably—this may seem like a trivial detail in the dive shop, but a tight fin or a leaky mask can be very distracting in the water and ruin a dive if annoying enough. A large dive boat is also a great bonus, much more stable and easier to get in and out of than the smaller launches used by many shops, and provides a less choppy and wet ride to and from the dive sites—but it usually also means more divers at each site. Those prone to seasickness should bring motion sickness pills, which are sold by many dive shops. Waters around the Bay Islands are usually a fairly balmy 28°C (82°F) or so, but if the water temperatures get down to the low 20s, as they sometimes do, you will want to make sure your shop has good wetsuits, full-length if you get cold easily.

Another factor to consider is the setup and schedule of dives at the different shops. Utila shops usually send out two dive boats a day for a total of four dives, two on the morning boat (around 7 A.M.) and another two on the afternoon boat (around 1 P.M.). Roatán shops usually send out three dive boats a day with one dive each, at 9 A.M., 11 A.M., and 2 P.M., although some have dives half an hour earlier or later. While the shop chooses the sites, clients should not be shy in requesting certain dives. Most dive shops are happy to accommodate, although some may put up resistance in going to a far-off site. And be sure the group you are going with will not be too large. An ideal group size is 4–6 divers, dive master included. Certainly, you don't want to go with more than eight divers, or it starts to feel a bit like an underwater procession. Be aware that many shops advertise low instructor-to-student or dive master-to-diver ratios, but fail to mention that their groups number 12 or 15 divers, with three or four dive masters/instructors to herd everybody along.

Roatán

Rattan-Island is about 30 miles long and 13 broad, about eight leagues distant from the coast of Honduras.... The south side is very convenient for shipping, having many fine harbours. The north side is defended by a reef of rocks that extend from one end of the island to the other, having but few passages through, and those of but small note, being mostly made use of by the turtlers.... It is likewise very healthy, the inhabitants hereabouts generally living to a great age.

– Thomas Jefferys, *Geographer to the King of England, 1762*

Jefferys may have been a bit off on the measurements—Roatán is actually about 40 miles (64 kilometers) long and only a little over 2 miles (3.2 kilometers) wide—but he did accurately describe the natural features that have long made Roatán the choice of Bay Island immigrants, from the first pirates 400 years ago to the resort builders, vacationers, and expatriates of today.

Tourists and retirees began arriving on Roatán in the 1960s, and in recent years the influx has increased dramatically. Roatán has been deemed respectable—enjoying fawning write-ups in travel publications and the limelight of frequent celebrity sightings—and is now home to a large expatriate community consisting mainly of Americans but also many Canadians and a sprinkling of Europeans.

After years of raging real-estate speculation and building fever, few nooks and crannies have escaped the scrutiny of developers. Remote sections of coastline on all sides of the island have been divided up in lots for development as private homes or resorts. Nevertheless, towns like

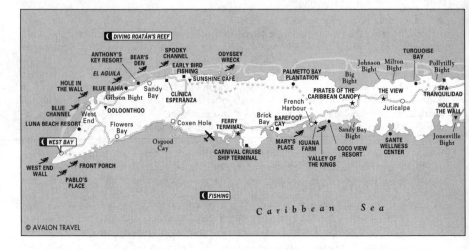

West End and Sandy Bay remain relatively slow-paced and not outrageously expensive when compared to other Caribbean islands.

One facet of the tourist profile that sets Roatán apart from the other Bay Islands is the international cruise ships. The monstrous crafts come in several days a week, especially in high season, and disgorge hundreds of tourists for the day. West Bay can get rather crowded those days, particularly at the southern end of the beach. While the crowds can be a bit disconcerting for other foreign visitors, the islanders are all for the new business, especially since the tourists spend well and only stay for the day, thus offering high income and limited stress on local infrastructure.

Theories on the source of the island's name vary wildly. The most popular explanation, supported by Jefferys and many other colonial-era chroniclers, is that Roatán is a derivation of rattan, the English word for a common vine found in the Caribbean. Another possibility is that it's a severe corruption of the Nahuatl expression *coatl-tlan,* "place of women." A third, far-fetched hypothesis is that the name comes from the English expression "Rat-land," referring to the island's pirate inhabitants.

Just less than two-thirds of the Bay Islands' population, or around 22,000 people, live on Roatán. Coxen Hole, the island's largest town,

is the department capital. Thanks to highly effective spraying, sand flies are no longer the plague they once were on Roatán, although it's always wise to pack repellent.

GETTING THERE
Air

As the most frequently visited of the three Bay Islands, Roatán has plenty of air service, although much of it comes via La Ceiba. There are also a few direct flights per week to the United States, and for those staying at one of the Henry Morgan resorts, weekly charter flights from Milan, Rome, and Toronto. Those flying out of Roatán to an international destination must pay a US$34 departure tax in the Roatán airport; for a domestic flight the departure tax is US$2.

Sosa (tel. 504/445-1154) offers flights twice daily to and from La Ceiba (US$56), with connections to San Pedro Sula, Tegucigalpa, and the Mosquitia. **Taca/Isleña** (tel. 504/445-1918, www.taca.com, www.flyislena.com) offers twice-daily flights to San Pedro Sula and thrice-daily flights to La Ceiba with connections onward to Tegucigalpa and elsewhere, including Miami, New York, and Houston.

At the time of writing, **Continental** (no office in Roatán, www.continental.com) was running two flights on Saturday and one each

HOUSTAN - 12TB Connected
Atlanta - 12TB - Delta Sat

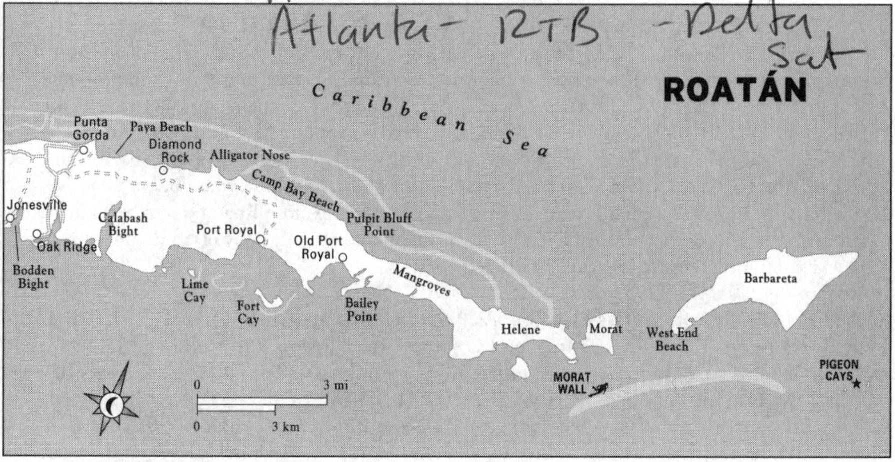
ROATÁN
Caribbean Sea
Punta Gorda
Paya Beach
Diamond Rock
Alligator Nose
Camp Bay Beach
Jonesville
Calabash Bight
Port Royal
Pulpit Bluff Point
Old Port Royal
Oak Ridge
Bodden Bight
Mangroves
Lime Cay
Fort Cay
Bailey Point
Barbareta
Helene
Morat
West End Beach
MORAT WALL
PIGEON CAYS
0
3 mi
0
3 km

on Sunday and Wednesday direct between Roatán and Houston, Texas, a less than three-hour trip.

Delta (www.delta.com) also has two direct flights to Roatán from Atlanta on Saturdays, with service to San Pedro Sula (3–4 flights per week) and Tegucigalpa (4–5 flights per week).

There are a couple of charter services available for local flights. **Bay Island Airways** (tel. 504/9858-8819, U.S. tel. 303/242-8004, www.bayislandairways.com) can pick passengers up from La Ceiba, Utila, or Guanaja. Prices are US$250–360 for two people. Island tours are available as well. **Roatan Air Services** (tel. 504/445-1417, Gill García, www.roatanair.com) is another charter service that is said to be a bit flaky at times, but will usually show up if you call to remind them. Prices depend on the size of the plane as well as the route; it's US$185 for Roatán–Utila on a three-passenger (plus pilot) Cessna 172, while the newer Aero Commander costs US$470 but can take up to six passengers.

Apart from rental car stands and a couple of uninspired gift shops, there's not much to hold a traveler's attention at the airport. There is a cigar shop (9 A.M.–5 P.M. Mon.–Fri., 8 A.M.–6 P.M. Sat.–Sun.), which also rents cell phones (US$25/week), although you have to buy the prepaid phone cards elsewhere, due to mysterious airport regulations. There's a small café and an **Espresso Americano** if you need a food or caffeine fix before heading on your way, as well as an ATM and a branch of the travel agency **MC Tours** (tel. 504/445-1930, www.mctours-honduras.com).

The airport is three kilometers from downtown Coxen Hole, on the highway toward French Harbour. Taxis to West End cost US$25, US$5 to Coxen Hole (there is a price sheet posted on one of the columns near the exit). Prices are applicable 6 A.M.–6 P.M.; at other times it's up to your bargaining skills. If you haven't got a whole lot of luggage or cash, it's possible to walk the short distance out to the highway and catch a bus to Coxen Hole, and from there on to West End (US$2). Buses run until about 4 P.M. You can also catch cheaper taxis out here, which charge about US$5 (more or less, depending on your negotiation skills) to West End.

Note: When visibility is poor on the north coast due to bad weather (not uncommon for much of the year), the airport at La Ceiba closes with regularity. Don't be surprised to find yourself stranded if the weather turns bad.

Boat

The **MV *Galaxy Wave*** (www.safewaymaritime.com) runs daily between La Ceiba and the new Transporte Marítimo Charles McNab dock just east of the Roatán airport; the 90-minute ride costs US$28 (or US$33 for first class). Some snacks are available on the boat, and a movie is shown in the cabin. There is a small coffee shop and gift shop at the ferry dock. The *Galaxy Wave* normally leaves Roatán at 7 A.M. for La Ceiba, then departs from La Ceiba at 9:30 A.M.; it then leaves Roatán again at 2 P.M. and departs from La Ceiba at 4:30 P.M. For more information, call the office in Roatán (tel. 504/445-1795), or in La Ceiba at the Cabotaje dock (tel. 504/443-4633). As with air transport, though not as frequently, the boat is sometimes cancelled due to bad weather. Because the boat is quite large, the ride is pretty smooth, but if the wind has been blowing and the boat goes anyhow, be prepared for some stomach-turning swells. You can get a free antiseasickness pill (à la Dramamine) at the security checkpoint.

If coming from (or heading to) Utila, it might be possible to sail by **catamaran** with Captain Verne Fine (tel. 504/3346-2600). He charges US$50 for the ride and travels back and forth a couple of times per week.

GETTING AROUND

Roatán has the Bay Islands' only major highway; it runs east–west connecting various island settlements. While the majority of visitors are likely to stay put in West End, West Bay, or the confines of their resort, the more adventurous, and in particular those who don't scuba dive, may wish to explore Roatán's less frequented corners, and this highway offers easy access.

Bus and Taxi

Most of the island can be covered on Tica minibuses, which leave Coxen Hole frequently from 7 A.M. until 6 P.M. The buses run to Sandy Bay (US$0.75), West End (US$1), French Harbour (US$1), Punta Gorda (US$1.50), and Oak Ridge (US$1.50). All buses leave from the main street in Coxen Hole near the post office, but they will stop anywhere they are hailed (both in town and on the main Roatán road). Be sure to verify the rate *before* stepping onto the bus. Fares must be paid in lempiras.

Colectivos (collective taxis) run the same routes for a bit more money—just make sure you clarify that you want a *colectivo,* not a

THE BAY ISLANDS

© AMY E. ROBERTSON

Roatán's comfortable ferry to La Ceiba, the *Galaxy Wave*

private taxi, which will cost considerably more. *Colectivos* stop along the way and pick up whoever flags them down. It's about US$1.50 from the airport to Coxen Hole by *colectivo,* and another US$2 from Coxen Hole to West End. It is virtually impossible to get *colectivo* rates in Coxen Hole on the days the cruise ships are in. After 6 P.M. all rates go up and are negotiable. *Note:* Most taxi drivers are mainlanders who do not speak much English.

Hotels can call for private taxi service when needed, but if you prefer to call directly, a couple of services are: **English Speaking Taxi Drivers** (tel. 504/455-7478), based in French Harbour, and **Roatan Island Cab Service** (tel. 504/445-1882), based in Coxen Hole. The 10-minute ride from West Bay to West End typically costs about US$10.

When negotiating taxi rates, be sure to specify the currency (lempiras or dollars), as the occasional unscrupulous driver may try to take advantage of the obvious tourist.

Car, Motorcycle, and Bicycle Rental

Several companies rent compact cars and small four-wheel-drive vehicles at rates ranging US$45–75 per day. Many have stands in the airport (sometimes staffed only if they are expecting someone with a reservation), as well as central offices elsewhere on the island, and many will bring the car to your hotel or resort. **Budget** (tel. 504/668-4421, www.budget.com) and **Avis** (tel. 504/445-1568), both at the airport, have a couple of automatic cars—be sure to book in advance if this is what you need—as well as plenty of stick shifts. The best rates can be had by booking through the U.S. website, but be sure to bring a printout of your reservation with you. **Ramirez Rent-A-Car** (tel. 504/445-2228 or 504/9903-9616) has a representative in Coxen Hole at the ferry dock. Two other companies are **Sandy Bay Rent-A-Car** (tel. 504/445-1710 or 504/445-1871, fax 504/445-1711), with offices in Sandy Bay and the airport; and **Caribbean Rent A Car** (tel. 504/445-6950), with an office at the airport (cars start at US$50/day or US$147/week

plus tax). **Roatan Rentals** (tel. 504/445-4171, www.roatansalesandrentals.com), in West End, has a variety of Nissans, Toyotas, Suzukis, Jeep Wranglers, and Trackers for US$50–85 a day. Airport pickups are available only with a rental of a week or more, but West End, West Bay, and Sandy Bay pickups can be easily arranged. Not all cars have air-conditioning.

Note: Sign a contract only for the number of days you are absolutely sure you want, as it can be very difficult to get any money back if you end up turning the car in early. You may also want to take a look at the car before signing the contract if you are with a lesser-known company. While most are reputable, there have been some reports of cars being in less than tip-top condition, and it's good to know what you're getting into.

Captain Van's (www.captainvans.com, 9 A.M.–4 P.M. daily), in West End (tel. 504/445-4076) and at the West Bay Mall (tel. 504/445-5040), rents motorcycles for US$45–55 a day, scooters for US$39 a day, and mountain bikes for US$9 a day. Weekly rates are available, and they provide maps, helmets, and information on the best spots on the island. Cell phones, DVD players, and DVDs are available for rent as well at the West Bay location.

Tour Operators

TransTours (tel. 504/9928-6579, www.transtoursroatan.com) offers tours around the islands for US$25 per person (for a group of four; discount of $5 pp for larger groups), as well as day trips to the mainland to hike in Pico Bonito or river raft on the Río Cangrejal, and overnight trips to the ruins of Copán.

ACCOMMODATIONS

There is something to suit absolutely every budget and taste on Roatán, from US$10 dorms to the extravagant US$22,500 six-bedroom Mayoka Lodge. Many house vacation rentals are available across the island. A few are listed here, or try Roatan Life Vacation Rentals (tel. 504/445-3130, U.S. tel. 970/300-4078, www.roatanlifevacationrentals.com) for a larger selection, of both short-term rentals and

◖ DIVING ROATÁN'S REEF

© JOZEF MAERIEN

an underwater jungle of coral

The reef topography in Roatán, as with Utila and Guanaja, is divided into a north side and a south side. On the north side of the island, the reef is separated from shore by a shallow lagoon, sometimes a kilometer wide but usually less. From the crest, which sometimes almost breaks the water's surface, the reef slopes down to a plateau or moat, followed by the reef wall. On the north side, sponges, sea fans, and elkhorn coral are common. The south-side reef slopes out gently until reaching the edge of the wall, normally dropping from 10 meters down to 30 meters, with a sandy bottom. Here grow a bewildering assortment of colorful soft corals. On the western end of the island, where the north- and south-side reefs meet, the reef shows characteristics of both formations.

The most popular dive sites in Roatán are in the Sandy Bay Marine Reserve, a protected water reserve between Sandy Bay and West Bay on the western end of the island, conveniently near the dive shops in West End. The reefs on the northern, eastern, and southern sides of Roatán have many spectacular, infrequently visited sites – the best bet is stay at one of the resorts out that way, or ask around in West End for shops diving more remote sites. While dive shops often have a site in mind, some are open to requests by divers.

NEAR WEST END

Hole in the Wall, a crack in the reef just around the bend from Half Moon Bay on the way to Sandy Bay, is justifiably one of the favorite dives near West End. Cruise down a steep sand chute from the upper reef, which leads downward through a cleft and pops out on the reef wall at around 40 meters. Below is very dark water – here is one of the places the Cayman Trench comes in closest to Roatán, and water depths just below Hole in the Wall are around 800 meters. Keep a close eye on that depth gauge. While the wall is the obvious highlight of the dive, leave time to explore around the labyrinth of sand chutes on the

long-term leases. There are also listings on the website for Subway Watersports (www.subway watersports.com).

BOATING

The clear, clean waters surrounding Roatán, stroked by steady trade winds most of the year and stocked with most of the known fish species in the Caribbean, are superb for sailing and

fishing trips. The Bay Islands are a growing destination among the yacht crowd, although docking services are limited to Barefoot Cay on Roatán, and in La Ceiba.

Many boat owners offer fishing trips, either deep-sea or flats fishing, or both. Day trips, cocktail cruises, and other customized boat trips can be arranged. One of the easiest ways to get what you are looking for is simply

upper reef, where you might spot a barracuda or eagle ray.

Right out front of West End is **Blue Channel,** a canyon with a narrow opening that gradually widens and deepens as you swim away from shore. A mellow dive, good for the afternoon, the channel has swim-throughs, interesting rock and coral formations, and plenty of fish to watch. Look for a green moray that hangs out near the entrance to the channel.

Off the southwest point of Roatán is **West End Wall.** Because of its location, strong currents flow past the site, meaning divers need to plan a drift dive. While the wall is worth seeing, it's also fun just to let the current zip you across the reef fields above the wall, which are invariably filled with hawksbill turtles, spotted eagle rays, and a dazzling array of colorful fish.

NEAR SANDY BAY

Near Anthony's Key Resort is the wreck of *El Aguila,* a 71-meter freighter the resort bought and sank in sand flats at 34 meters, near the base of the reef wall, to create a dive site. Take good care not to catch yourself on any metal parts as you swim around the deck – and look for the green moray and large grouper that live at the site.

Just east of Anthony's Key, right in front of Sandy Bay, is **Bear's Den,** a cave system lit from above. The cave entrance, on the upper part of a steep reef wall decorated with much boulder and lettuce coral, is tight to get in but widens out into a spacious cavern inside. Beautiful, shifting light from above illuminates schools of glassy-eyed sweepers that patrol the cave. The cave system continues farther,

but only experienced cave divers should continue beyond the main cavern.

Spooky Channel, at the eastern end of Sandy Bay, is exactly what it sounds like, a channel through the reef almost completely closed over, and a bit unnerving to swim through for the dark water. The dive starts at 12 meters or so and deepens as you go in to a maximum of about 38 meters. While rock and fossilized coral predominate in the lower reaches of the channel, up higher on the reef barrel sponges, sea fans, and hard corals are common.

ELSEWHERE ON THE ISLAND

Considered one of the most dramatic dives on Roatán, **Mary's Place,** just west of French Harbour on the south side, is a narrow cleft in the reef wall. Enter at around 25 meters, then zigzag into the cleft, where you'll see plenty of large sponges and also lots of seahorses. Because of the tight channels, Mary's Place is for experienced divers only.

Right in front of Coco View Resort, east of French Harbour, is **Valley of the Kings,** an exceptionally lovely wall dive noted for the tall stands of pillar coral, several different types of sponge, and a profusion of marine life tucked into crevasses and overhangs on the wall.

OTHER RECOMMENDED DIVES

Other sites around the island that are highly recommended by divers who know the Roatán reef well include: Mandy's Eel Garden, Lighthouse Reef, Half Moon Bay Wall, Fish Den, Canyon Reef, Odyssey Wreck, Peter's Place, Pablo's Place, and Front Porch.

to ask around, or keep an eye out for posted fliers offering cruises. **Roatan Sailboat and Catamaran Charters** (tel. 504/3336-5597 or U.S. tel. 813/435-6337, www.sailroatan.com) has various options available, from a three-hour sail for US$65 per person to seven-day sail and dive packages. **Captain Dusty** also runs daily five-hour snorkel and sail trips for US$49 per person, beer and gear included.

◖ Fishing

Situated at the division between the shallow waters toward the mainland on one side and the 3,000-meter-deep Cayman Channel on the other, Roatán and the other Bay Islands are ideally located to go after a variety of different shallow- and deep-water species. Favorite game fish around Roatán are marlin, wahoo, tarpon, barracuda, kingfish, and jack, to name just a few. Waters around most major settlements are usually heavily fished by the locals, so more isolated spots, particularly on the north and east sides of the island, offer the best luck.

Captain Loren Monterrosa of **Early Bird Fishing Charter** (tel. 504/445-3019, or 504/9955-0001, www.earlybirdfishingcharters .com), in Sandy Bay, offers deep-sea and flats fishing as well as island tours and trips to Utila. Half-day deep-sea fishing trips cost US$350–400 (up to four people, including drinks, snacks, and fruit), and full-day trips cost US$600 (up to four people, including drinks, snacks, fruit, and lunch). Fishing trips can also be arranged with **Hook 'Em Up** (tel. 504/9919-7603, www. westendroatan.com/hookup.htm), run by top-notch local fisherman Captain "O" Miller, who can also be found by asking at Diddily's gift shop near the church in West End. He charges US$65–75 per hour for fishing trips, and also does snorkeling outings (US$20 pp per hour) and island tours (from US$300). **Eddie and Donna's Fishing Charters** (tel. 504/9653-1293 or 504/9553-3302), in West End, charges US$150 (up to six people) for six-hour trips on their small boat (a *lancha*) and US$350 (up to 10 people) on their larger boat, including snorkeling and drinks. On the smaller boat, a tour through the mangroves can be included as well. Other fishermen in West End, West Bay, Sandy Bay, or elsewhere will also happily set up fishing trips for a negotiable fee.

Marina and Boat Services

Yachties can tie up in Roatán at **Barefoot Cay** (tel. 504/455-6235, VHF Channel 18A, www .barefootcay.com), between French Harbour and Brick Bay, charging US$1.25 per foot per day, or US$18 per foot per month. Boats up to 165 feet can be accommodated; water and electricity are extra.

WEST END

Although it is the main tourist town of Roatán and lined with cabañas, restaurants, and dive shops, West End remains a slow-paced seaside village and an undeniably superb location to lose yourself in the relaxing rhythms of Caribbean life. Even during the high season (mid-December–April), people and events move at a languid pace up and down the sandy, seaside road that constitutes "town." It's a telling sign that the road has been left rutted and unpaved—cars and bicycles must slow to a snail's pace, bouncing along, while pedestrians are free to wander at leisure, stopping to browse for T-shirts or to admire yet another spectacular sunset.

Construction of new houses and cabañas continues, but in a relatively unobtrusive way—new developments are tucked away among the palms and don't dominate the visual landscape. West End is not overwhelmed by wealthy tourists, as it has no luxury resorts, but there are a few higher-end options for those who prefer a few more comforts. The roughly 500 local residents have not lost their easy friendliness and, fortunately, seem to be influencing the newcomers more than the newcomers are influencing them.

Sights

West End's main attractions are in plain view: beaches, 28°C (82°F) bright-blue water, and, a couple hundred meters offshore, the coral reef, marked by a chain of buoys. The waters around West End are kept very clean, and visitors can jump in pretty much wherever it's convenient. The best beach in town is **Half Moon Bay,** a swath of palm-lined sand right at the entrance to West End, bordered by points of iron shore (fossilized, raised coral) on either side forming the namesake shape. A good spot to lay down a towel is in the stretch in front of the Posada Arco Iris hotel. Another good place to swim and sunbathe is off the docks at the far south end of town, just after the road ends. Both of these spots happen to be near two good snorkeling sites off West End. The reef passes right across the mouth of Half Moon Bay, an easy swim from shore, with better reef near the more southern of the two points. Sea turtles and rays are often seen in the sand flats and shallower sections of reef here.

One of the buoys in front of the south end of the town beach marks the entrance to **Blue**

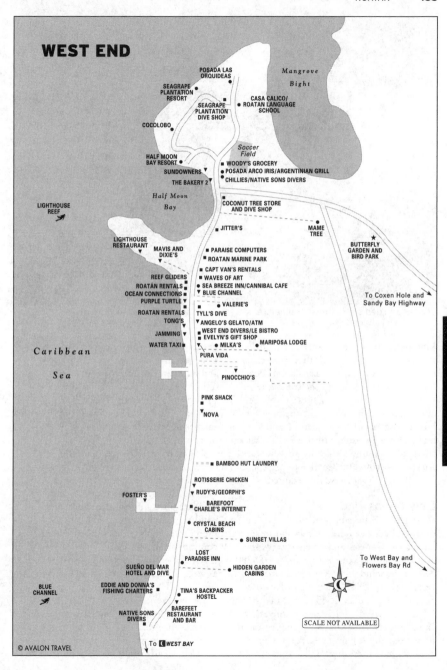

WEST END

POSADA LAS ORQUIDEAS

Mangrove Bight

SEAGRAPE PLANTATION RESORT

CASA CALICO/ ROATAN LANGUAGE SCHOOL

SEAGRAPE PLANTATION DIVE SHOP

COCOLOBO

Soccer Field

HALF MOON BAY RESORT

WOODY'S GROCERY

POSADA ARCO IRIS/ARGENTINIAN GRILL

SUNDOWNERS

CHILLIES/NATIVE SONS DIVERS

THE BAKERY 2

Half Moon Bay

COCONUT TREE STORE AND DIVE SHOP

LIGHTHOUSE REEF

JITTER'S

MAME TREE

LIGHTHOUSE RESTAURANT

BUTTERFLY GARDEN AND BIRD PARK

MAVIS AND DIXIE'S

PARAISE COMPUTERS

ROATAN MARINE PARK

CAPT VAN'S RENTALS

REEF GLIDERS

WAVES OF ART

ROATÁN RENTALS

SEA BREEZE INN/CANNIBAL CAFE

OCEAN CONNECTIONS

BLUE CHANNEL

PURPLE TURTLE

To Coxen Hole and Sandy Bay Highway

VALERIE'S

ROATAN RENTALS

TYLL'S DIVE

TONG'S

ANGELO'S GELATO/ATM

JAMMING

WEST END DIVERS/LE BISTRO

EVELYN'S GIFT SHOP

WATER TAXI

MILKA'S

MARIPOSA LODGE

Caribbean

PURA VIDA

Sea

PINOCCHIO'S

PINK SHACK

NOVA

BAMBOO HUT LAUNDRY

ROTISSERIE CHICKEN

RUDY'S/GEORPHI'S

FOSTER'S

BAREFOOT CHARLIE'S INTERNET

CRYSTAL BEACH CABINS

SUNSET VILLAS

LOST PARADISE INN

To West Bay and Flowers Bay Rd

SUEÑO DEL MAR HOTEL AND DIVE

HIDDEN GARDEN CABINS

BLUE CHANNEL

EDDIE AND DONNA'S FISHING CHARTERS

TINA'S BACKPACKER HOSTEL

NATIVE SONS DIVERS

BAREFEET RESTAURANT AND BAR

SCALE NOT AVAILABLE

To **€** WEST BAY

© AVALON TRAVEL

THE BAY ISLANDS

Docks sprinkled along the shoreline are perfect spots for taking in the view.

Channel, a dramatic channel cutting through the reef. It's a bit of a swim for snorkelers, so take your time heading out to conserve energy for exploring the reef and the trip back.

There are several other sites on the reef off West End, but in looking for them beware of boat traffic. Snorkel gear can be rented from many of the dive shops for US$7, or a bit less from stores in town, like the gift shop at the **Roatan Marine Park** office. A passport or US$10–15 deposit is usually required.

Dive Shops

West End's fully equipped dive shops offer dives and courses for all levels and in several languages. Courses and dive packages should cost close to the same everywhere: US$280–325 for the standard or Advanced Open Water certifications, US$100 for a half-day Discover Scuba Diving course, US$35 for a fun dive, and US$25–30 per dive for 10 or more dives. Prices can fluctuate somewhat with the season and have risen slightly over the years. Generally, all shops have three dives daily—one at 9 A.M.,

one at 11 A.M., and one at 2 P.M. (although some run dives half an hour earlier or later)— and start new certification courses every couple of days. Apart from the shops listed, there are a few outfits based out of West Bay, for people who prefer to stay there. Fun dive prices typically do not include equipment, which can tack on another US$5–15.

Coconut Tree Divers (tel. 504/403-8782, www.coconuttreedivers.com), in the same building as the Coconut Tree Store in front of Half Moon Bay, has plenty of good gear, a well-equipped 40-foot dive boat, and an air-conditioned classroom. The PADI-certified shop can pick up guests in their West Bay accommodations for morning and afternoon dives. They offer Nitrox and instructor courses as well. Equipment rental is included in their fun dives (US$35 each).

Native Sons Divers (tel. 504/445-4003, www.nativesonsroatan.com) has offices on the beach at the south end of town and at Chillies Hotel. Native Sons is a frequently recommended, locally run shop certified with PADI and providing experienced instructors. The shop can also arrange fishing trips.

Ocean Connections (tel. 504/403-8221, www.ocean-connections.com), a well-respected dive shop, has equipment for Nitrox and other technical dive training, as well as the standard courses and dive tours. PADI classifies it as a Gold Palm dive center, in recognition of the shop's quality and volume of business.

Pura Vida (tel. 504/445-4130, U.S. tel. 786/319-4571, www.puravidaresort.com), another PADI five-star Gold Palm resort-rated shop, has three boats, an air-conditioned classroom, and a spacious wooden porch for hanging out.

Reef Gliders (tel. 504/403-8243, www.reefgliders.com) is run by an English couple who rebuilt the two dive boats, bought new gear, and refurbished the shop. The reputable Reef Gliders offers all of the courses through Dive Master, as well as numerous specialties. Penny-pinchers will be happy to find that free dorm-style accommodation is offered to dive students—but at the rather run-down Valerie's hotel in town.

Seagrape Plantation (tel. 504/445-4297, www.seagraperoatan.com) is well-located for visitors staying at any of the hotels on the point, such as Posada las Orquideas, Cocolobo, and Casa Calico.

Sueño del Mar (tel. 504/445-4343, www.suenodelmar.com), housed in a large building out on its own private dock in the West End harbor, has a dive shop on the "ground" floor and a popular restaurant/bar above. The shop has two skiffs and a boat kept at Brick Bay to dive on the south side. Sueño has about the best dive gear shop on the island. They offer lodging and dive packages, with rooms both at what they call the Roatan West End Hotel (a.k.a. the Sea Breeze Inn), in the middle of town for a bargain basement US$411 per week, and in their relatively new, white-washed resort lodge on the south end of town right on the water, with breezy tile-floored rooms, a very good value at US$550 per person per week.

Tyll's Dive (tel. 504/403-8852, www.tylls-dive.com) is one of the oldest shops in West

End. It offers a full range of courses in a variety of languages, and prices are on the lower end of the scale.

West End Divers (tel. 504/445-4289, www.westenddivers.com) is known for diving a larger variety of sites and venturing farther out than some of the other shops. The fun dives at West End cost a bit more (US$40 each, or US$30 when purchased in a package of 10 or more), but the course prices are competitive.

Snorkeling

Snorkel equipment is available for rent at the offices of the Roatan Marine Park (US$5 for 24 hours), as well as at the Sea Breeze Inn (US$5 for 4 hours) and at many of the dive shops.

Other Recreation

While diving and snorkeling are justifiably premier attractions on Roatán, there are plenty of other excellent water and land-based activities, many based in West End.

Sea kayaks are available for rent at the Sea Breeze Inn (tel. 504/445-4026), for US$7 an hour for a double. Half-day rentals cost US$18, and full-day rentals cost US$21. *Note:* Visitors should take good care when paddling out into the open water on sea kayaks. Choppy waters and ocean winds can quickly get the better of inexperienced kayakers. If in any doubt at all, stick close to shore and be absolutely sure you have enough energy not only to get out, but to get back, too.

Glass-bottomed boat tours (US$30 for an hour) leave from a dock on the southern half of town—look for the sign, and double-check on the schedule, as it varies with the seasons. Trips are also available from West Bay Beach, a quick water taxi ride away.

Half Moon Bay has a pretty beach, perfect for a relaxing afternoon. Those looking for a spectacular Caribbean beach should catch a **water taxi** over to West Bay for its seemingly endless stretch of powdery white sand (US$2.50 for the 10-minute ride).

Fishing trips can be arranged with a number of local fishermen; one to try is **Eddie and Donna's Fishing Charters** (tel. 504/9653-1293) on the beach just after the road ends at the southern end of town. Six-hour trips on a boat that can take 6–10 guests run US$350, while a trip on a fiberglass *lancha* is US$150 and can include a tour through the mangroves. Be sure to bring lots of sunscreen for either excursion, as well as your snorkel gear. They also provide water taxi service to West Bay.

Just east of West End on the road to Coxen Hole, walkable if you watch out for traffic, is the **Butterfly Garden and Bird Park** (tel. 504/445-4481, www.roatanbutterfly.com, 9 A.M.–5 P.M. Sun.–Fri., US$7), with a collection of 18 or so butterfly species as well as a few toucans, parrots, and macaws. It's a modest little collection, but a break from all the water-oriented recreations if you're in the mood for something different.

There are a couple of canopy tours available just outside of town, on the road to West Bay.

Entertainment

Perhaps the most popular spot in town for a sunset drink, ⟨ **Sundowners Bar and Restaurant** (10 A.M.–10 P.M. daily), on the beach across the road from Chillies Hotel, draws a mellow crowd of tourists looking for good vibes and a good variety of drinks.

Another favored spot for a drink, the **Purple Turtle** (tel. 504/445-4483, 7 P.M.–midnight Mon.–Thurs., 7 P.M.–2 A.M. Fri.–Sat., 7–10 P.M. Sun.) is a tiny bar featuring a small porch area in back with hammock chairs overlooking the sea, popular with long-haired, laid-back types.

Nova's is a new lounge-style bar (read: low-slung couches) with '80s night on Wednesdays, techno/electronic music on Fridays, and Latin music on Saturdays. Happy hour is 7–8 P.M., when well drinks are just a buck. Another newcomer to West End's nightlife scene is **Jamming,** a small bar built out over the water's edge, with reggae music and a relaxed vibe day and night (the relaxation aided, no doubt, by drink specials such as US$1.80 tequila shots).

Foster's (tel. 504/377-6304, noon–midnight Mon.–Thurs., noon–2 A.M. Fri.–Sat., and noon–10 P.M. Sun.) is an unpretentious hangout that draws a jovial crowd of locals and expats as well as tourists on Friday and Saturday nights. The restaurant/bar is a two-story wooden contraption built on a dock over the water, with a couple of hammocks swinging between the wood beams. It's a shame the place is empty the rest of the week. Happy hour is 4–6 P.M.

The restaurant **Blue Channel** (tel. 504/445-4133) has live music Wednesday–Saturday and frequently shows movies; details are posted on the board out front. **Le Bistro** also has live music on Fridays and Saturdays.

The second-floor bar at **Sueño del Mar** dive shop, a large white building at the southern end of town, is a fine place to nurse a drink and watch the sun take its invariably sublime daily plunge into the Caribbean. There's also a large-screen TV to watch sports.

If you have the energy to keep going when everything closes down, try to track down a cab to take you to **Hip Hop** in Flowers Bay, near Coxen Hole—just don't arrive before 2 A.M. or you'll be the only one there.

Shopping

Pink Shack, in the southern half of town, sells T-shirts with their own quite clever designs, as well as a few other items such as flip-flops and Crocs.

Waves of Art (tel. 504/403-8819, 9 A.M.–6 P.M. Mon., Tues., and Sat., 9 A.M.–8 P.M. Wed.–Fri., www.waves-of-art .com), located in a Victorian-style building across from the church, offers art and handicrafts that promote sustainable living among low-income Hondurans, including candles, carvings, note cards, and jewelry made by co-ops from across the country. The upstairs gallery features art in numerous media, including paintings, photos, sculptures, and metal works, and hosts new gallery showings every six weeks. Credit cards are accepted.

A number of Guatemalan artisans have made their way to the Bay Islands to sell their fine handicrafts; **Evelyn Gift Shop,** next door to the Pura Vida Dive Shop, has a good selection of both Guatemalan and Honduran crafts.

Accommodations

Hotels in West End mostly fall into the moderate range, US$25–50 for a double, generally in a cabin with ceiling fan, screened windows, and private bathroom. The budget traveler will be glad to hear, however, that less expensive digs are still available—although groups of two or three can often find better quality rooms for the same price in the midrange accommodations. There are a couple of higher end spots, too, for those who prefer the buzz of West End over the quiet nights on West Bay beach or at the resorts. Keep in mind that the lower-end prices are available September–November. The 16 percent Honduran tax on hotel rooms has been added here for those hotels that do not include it in their rates. It's worth keeping in mind that hotels that normally charge separately for the tax are often willing to include it in their rates for guests who pay with cash.

For those who become transfixed with diving and the mellow lifestyle in West End, locals rent many apartments and cabins of differing quality for about US$350–800 a month, more in the high season. Rents in nearby locations like Gibson Bight and Sandy Bay are lower.

UNDER US$25

The best low-budget room in town is at 🄲 **Georphi's** (tel. 504/445-4205, www.roatan georphis.com), where one cabin has been converted into a tidy, attractive dorm (US$10 pp) with (gasp!) hot water in the shared bath.

A good alternative for backpackers is **Tina's Backpacker Hostel** (tel. 504/445-4144, moy-1978@yahoo.com, cold water only) at the southern end of town just where the road becomes beach. Dorm beds go for US$10 per person, and the place is clean and cheery. There are two rooms with four beds each, plus another two pairs of beds in the shared living room with a TV, so better nab your bed as soon as possible if you're early to bed. There is a kitchen available for use by guests. The hostel is run by the owners of the adjacent Barefeet Restaurant and Bar.

Chillies Hotel (tel. 504/445-4003, US$20–24 s/d, US$27–30 t, shared bath, cold water), facing Half Moon Bay, is very popular with the low-budget crowd, for its doubles with shared bathroom and kitchen facilities as well as a sociable front porch. There are also a few rooms with private baths and hot water for a few dollars more, available only to those diving with their dive shop, Native Sons.

Milka's (tel. 504/445-4241, milkasrooms@yahoo.com, US$12 pp shared bath, US$25 d with bath and TV, cold water only), located behind Pura Vida, is a bit ramshackle but offers 11 very basic rooms with fans and shared bathrooms, as well as three much better rooms with TV and private bathrooms.

One of the cheapest places in town is **Valerie's** (tel. 504/3290-6055), a run-down hotel in the center of town with dorms for US$8, doubles with bath for US$16, and apartments with refrigerator, cooktop, and bath for US$25. It's all cold-water only and rather grubby.

Many local residents rent rooms out of their houses for US$10–25 d—ask around.

US$25-50

Half a block north from the entrance to town is the highly recommended 🄲 **Posada Arco Iris** (tel./fax 504/445-4264, www.roatanposada.com, US$36–48 s, US$42–54 d), run by an Argentinian couple. The spacious and clean rooms in the wooden house are each decorated with colorful artistic touches. The top-floor ocean-view rooms facing Half Moon Bay are the more expensive rooms, and some have kitchens. The individual wooden cabins, with ample front porches, rent for US$66 (one bedroom) and US$78 (two bedroom) for two people during high season. All accommodations cost US$15 more per day with air-conditioning. Out front is a very good Argentine-style restaurant.

The Sea Breeze Inn (tel. 504/445-4026, www.seabreezeroatan.com, US$25–70 d), at the entrance to town, has a variety of room layouts including studios and suites that can accommodate larger parties with a little bit of privacy. The standard rooms are fairly charmless, and the grounds are rather cramped, but there are a few rooms with porches, hammocks, and kitchenettes. Kayaks and snorkel equipment are available for rent.

In a rambling three-story wooden house built atop a small hill a couple of hundred meters back off the main road, behind Pura Vida, is **Mariposa Lodge** (tel. 504/445-4450, www.mariposa-lodge.com, US$40 s/d, US$55 t, two-night minimum for all rooms), with four simple but spacious apartments with a homey feel, all with private kitchens, TV, fans, and hot water, as well as a breezy porch to relax on. In addition, there's a small house with three rooms that rent for US$26 d, with fan, hot water, and shared bathroom and kitchen facilities—a bit worn, but decent. The Canadian couple who own the place also offer professional shiatsu, therapeutic, and reiki massage service (very popular with the diving crowd) for US$40 an hour.

Located on the second floor, above the restaurant of the same name, the rooms at **Pinocchio's** (tel. 504/445-4466, or 504/9837-7287, US$35 s/d, US$10 each additional person) are a good value. Each has wood floors and walls, two double beds, and hot water. Breakfast at the restaurant downstairs is included, and the dinners there are top-notch. Don't worry about noise from the restaurant, as it closes by 10 P.M. at the latest.

⟨ Georphi's (tel. 504/445-4205, www.roatangeorphis.com), located next to Rudy's restaurant, is named for owners George and Phyllis. The rambling grounds, dotted with tropical plants, feature a number of individual wooden cabins with spacious porches. Prices start at US$25 for one room in a two-bedroom cabin with fan, and go up to US$50 for cabins with more space and air-conditioning; most have kitchenettes. There is even a small chalet available, with a king bed in a bedroom and a twin bed in the loft, and extra beds can be added for more kids (US$75/night, or US$850/month). One cabin has been converted into a dorm, the best low-budget digs in town, for US$10 per person. Internet is available in the lobby (US$3/day or US$10/week), there is free wireless Internet

on the grounds, and laundry service is available too.

Another good choice for cabins is **Hidden Garden Cabins** (tel. 504/445-4131, www.hiddengardencabins.com, US$45 s/d, US$250/week), also set back from the road in lush vegetation, each with hot water, a kitchen, and a porch. Ceiling fans help keep the island breezes moving through the slat windows.

At the edge of town along Mangrove Bight is **Posada Las Orquideas** (tel. 504/445-4387, www.posadalasorquideas.com, US$36–60 d, plus an extra US$15 for a/c), with absolutely lovely rooms in a large wooden building set along the iron shore, an excellent deal if you are looking to get away at the end of the day (although it's only about a 10-minute walk, it's can feel like a bit of a hike, particularly late at night). The PADI-certified Seagrape Dive Shop (tel. 504/445-4297) is just steps away (and charges a few bucks less for its fun dives than its competitors in town).

US$50-100

Half Moon Resort (tel. 504/445-4242, www.roatanhalfmoonresort.com, US$67 s/d), on the quiet northern point of Half Moon Bay, offers somewhat spartan wooden waterfront cabins with air-conditioning and hot water. The cabins closest to the water are the best—enjoy views of Half Moon Bay from your porch hammock. Guests can use free kayaks and snorkel gear in the small bay and reef right out front, the seafood at the porch restaurant is reliable, and the staff is an amiable bunch. The hotel's access to the beach is via iron shore (calcified coral reef).

On the same land outcropping as Half Moon Resort, but facing Mangrove Bight rather than Half Moon Bay, is the surprisingly woodsy **Hotel Casa Calico** (tel. 504/445-4231, US$70–90 for rooms that sleep up to five). The spacious rooms have kitchenettes, tables, and TVs, while smaller rooms that start at US$50 still boast balconies and deck chairs. Two-bedroom condos with full kitchens are also available for US$125–150. The lack of beach at this waterfront property may be a disappointment for some, but kayaks are available for getting into the water right at the shoreline, among the mangroves. Pleasant and roomy one-bedroom apartments with daily and monthly rates are available, especially convenient for those taking Spanish classes through the hotel's **Roatan Language School.** It's a 10-minute walk to the restaurants in the heart of town.

Right in the center of town is **Pura Vida** (tel. 504/445-4110, U.S. tel. 786/319-4571, www .puravidaresort.com, US$74 s, US$90 d), with clean, airy, tile-floored rooms with hot water, air-conditioning, and TV. The hotel has 26 rooms and a rather ordinary restaurant. Three-day and seven-day packages, including diving and breakfast, are also available.

A long-time resident of West End, **Lost Paradise Inn** (tel. 504/445-4210 or 504/445-4306, www.lost-paradise.com, US$79 s/d) rents rooms in well-made wooden cabins on stilts in a nice layout right on the beach in the south end of town. Rooms are equipped with air-conditioning, small refrigerators, and hot water, and some have small porches. Many have two double beds and can sleep up to four. A restaurant operates in the high season only.

US$100 AND UP

Mame Tree Bungalows (tel. 504/403-8245, U.S. tel. 718/710-4392, www.mametree bungalows.com) is set on a bluff above town, just a minute or two's walk along a hillside path from West End's main drag and beach, a perfect place for being close to the hub-bub of town without being in the middle of it. The two main bungalows have two bedrooms and can sleep up to five each (US$157 with a view, or US$133 without), while new smaller rooms are perfect for romantic couples (US$68–80). The young American owners have decorated with a lot of character (mosaic tiling in the Caribbean room, lush fabrics in the Moroccan), as well as with luxury touches such as flat-screen TVs, wireless Internet, and soundproofed walls.

Although only a short path separates

Half Moon Resort from █ **Cocolobo** (tel. 504/9898-4510, www.cocolobo.com, US$122 d, including breakfast), this new hotel feels far removed from the hustle and bustle of West End. Rooms have a sweeping view of the iron shore and ocean. Conceived by a British environmental architect, the wood structures are designed with windows that create cooling cross-breezes—but the air-conditioning is there for those who can't live without it. Luxury touches include an infinity-edged pool, flat-screen TVs, and iPod docks, but the vibe is relaxed, perfect for grown-up beach bums. Small apartments are also available on a weekly basis, with peek-a-boo ocean views.

A big whitewashed development set back a few steps from the main road is the well-appointed **Sunset Villas** (tel. 504/445-4100, U.S. tel. 603/782-4470, www.roatanhotels .com, US$75–98 s/d). Hotel rooms are in a building above the large pool, and are outfitted with either a king bed or two doubles, as well as attractively tiled bathrooms, flat-screen TVs, and a mini-fridge (suites with kitchens cost US$30 more). Spacious and fairly deluxe one- and two-bedroom condos with Tommy Bahama furniture and full kitchens are available for US$153–276 (if you know what Tommy Bahama is, then this is the place for you).

Food

BREAKFAST

One choice breakfast spot in town is **Rudy's** (6 A.M.–5 P.M. Sun.–Fri.), next to Georphi's hotel, where the owner, if he's there, will serve you up a steaming cup of coffee and invariably reply heartily, "Still alive!" when you ask how he's doing. The response is so famous it appears on a specially made T-shirt. The omelets are excellent (you pick the fixings), US$2–4. The smoothies (US$4) are outrageously priced if you're used to mainland *licuados,* but good nonetheless.

Conveniently located in the center of town, **Jitters** (8 A.M.–2:30 P.M. Mon.–Fri., 8 A.M.– noon Sun.) serves up a nice latte, as well as refreshing iced coffees and smoothies, and a few snacks such as heavenly peanut-butter brownies (US$2–3.50 each).

The Bakery #2 (7 A.M.–3 P.M. Mon.–Fri., 7 A.M.–2 P.M. Sat.) is famous for its filling breakfasts, including French toast with house-made bread, and sandwiches, salads, and burgers are available at midday (US$5–8). The best seats in the house are on its small waterfront veranda.

SNACKS AND LIGHT MEALS

At the entrance to Georphi's Hotel is **Creole's Rotisserie Chicken,** serving up quarter-chickens for US$3.70, whole chickens for US$9.50, and sides for two bucks apiece.

Along the beach by Posada Arco Iris is an authentic British **fish and chip truck,** where a plate goes for US$7–8.

The *baleadas* sold next to Ocean Connections dive shop are especially good, and always a cheap way to fill up.

Looking to cool off, or to satisfy a sweet tooth? **Angelo's Gelato** has a small selection of good ice cream, US$1.50 for one scoop, US$2.50 for two.

SEAFOOD

A locally run restaurant specializing in fresh islander food is **(The Lighthouse Restaurant** (7:30 A.M.–10 P.M. daily, no credit cards accepted), located on the south side of the point dividing the main part of West End from Half Moon Bay. A sign on the main road points the way to the classy patio restaurant, right on the water. Fresh fish and shrimp are served in a variety of ways, including with the fiery *escabey* sauce made with lots of hot island peppers, US$8–13. The more extravagant "surf and turf" and seafood platters are US$20–30. The menu is extensive, and it's all good. Lunch is a particularly good deal, with specials such as grouper burgers and lobster avocado salad. A champagne brunch is served on Sundays for US$15.

The waterfront porch at **Half Moon Resort** (tel. 504/445-4242) is a fine location to enjoy mouthwatering fish fillets, lobster, shrimp, and other seafood. Dinners run US$8–14 and are worth every penny. Large chicken or fish

sandwiches with fries cost US$6. The kitchen is open daily until 10 P.M.

Pleasantly set along the beach in the center of town, **Mavis and Dixie's** has excellent shrimp, fish, and lobster for reasonable prices, and a US$6 plate of the day.

Located at the southern end of town right on the beach is **Barefeet Restaurant and Bar,** a casual joint with sandwiches (US$5–8) as well as seafood, meat and pasta (US$10–16), and even king crab (US$19). There is a Sunday barbecue with live music, and happy hour every day 3–7 P.M.

INTERNATIONAL

If all this fish has got you hankering after a steak for a change, stop in at **Argentinian Grill** (tel. 504/445-4264, 3–10 P.M. Thurs.–Tues.), at the Posada Arco Iris, and try the beef tenderloin or the filet mignon for around US$16, or a *chorizo* sausage. Even the half portion of meat, served with a twice-baked potato and veggies for US$13, is a generous plate. Don't worry if your companion isn't a meat-eater, as there's vegetarian lasagna and a daily vegetarian plate. Good seafood is, of course, also available, served with Argentine *chimichurri* sauce for variety.

(Pinocchio's (tel. 504/445-4466 or 504/9837-7287, 6–9 P.M. Tues.–Fri.) is tucked a hundred meters or so off the main road in West End, but well worth seeking out for the excellent, unusual dishes, such as beef tenderloin with sesame and merlot reduction, and its intriguing selection of *tapas*. Prices are not cheap (US$11–20 per plate), but it's great for a splurge. The new European owners include a pastry chef from the Netherlands, who makes desserts to die for, such as a plum tart with earl grey mascarpone.

The **Blue Channel** (tel. 504/445-4133) offers movie screenings and frequent live music along with its Italian-style pastas. The breakfasts are good too.

Featuring Tex-Mex dishes such as tacos, quesadillas, fajitas, and chimichangas, for about US$3.50–5, **Cannibal Café** (tel. 504/445-4026, 9 A.M.–10 P.M. Mon.–Sat.) is in front of the Sea Breeze Inn—you can't miss the life-like "cannibal" sitting out front. The "big Kahuna burrito" is famously large; if you can stuff down three within an hour, they'll give them to you for free.

ASIAN

Opposite Jamming, **Le Bistro** (3–10 P.M. daily, also open for lunch during high season) is a Thai-Vietnamese restaurant with dishes you won't find anywhere else in Honduras, such as *blau blau,* Vietnamese hotpot, as well as plenty of more familiar dishes such as spring rolls and pad thai. The restaurant is on a second-story wood deck, and rather atmospheric, although the thumping music from Jamming tends to drown out the crooning French music in the background. Appetizers are US$2–6, and most mains are in the range of US$8–16.

Tong's Thai Cuisine (5:30–9:30 P.M. daily, plus open for lunch Fri.–Sun.) is a relatively new restaurant set out over the water, wildly popular for its excellent Thai food. The curries and basil chicken are authentically spicy, while those looking for something milder will be happy with the fried rice. Entrées run US$12–18. The staffing has yet to catch up with the restaurant's popularity, so if the restaurant is busy you can expect your food to take a good long while (or consider coming when the crowds are gone).

GROCERIES

The best, and really only, grocery store in West End is **Woody's** (tel. 504/445-4269, 7 A.M.–6 P.M. Sun.–Thurs., 6 A.M.–8:30 P.M. Fri., and 7 A.M.–5 P.M. Sat.), with a decent selection of packaged goods and the occasional, slightly limp-looking vegetable. Eldon's in French Harbour and Coxen Hole are far superior grocery stores, and a Megafoods is opening in the island's new mall. Plaza Mar, on a hill above Coxen Hill (turn up off the main Roatán road by the Bojangles), is another decent grocery store, with an Internet café as well. The **Coconut Tree Store** (tel. 504/403-8782, 7 A.M.–9:30 P.M. daily), at the entrance to town, has a good selection of packaged food and supplies. You can find fresh produce sold from pickup trucks parked throughout West End every day except Sunday.

OUTSIDE OF TOWN

The fanciest place in the West End, **Ooloonthoo** (tel. 504/9936-5223, 6–9 P.M. daily, reservations required), has moved just outside of town, in an elegant hilltop home off Roatán's main drag. Run by a top Canadian chef (who lived in India for three years studying the regional cuisines) and his Indian wife, the restaurant features a different chutney daily and a menu that varies with the season and the available produce. Main courses run the gamut, from coconut-citrus fish to lamb or oxtail curry. Three-course meals will set you back US$40–47.

Services

BANKS

Several stores and dive shops will change dollars, and most businesses accept payment in either dollars or lempiras. Take care of exchanging money in Coxen Hole if you're carrying travelers checks or another currency (like euros). There is a 24-hour **ATM** at Angelo's Gelato, but don't wait until you're down to the last dollar, as it's been known to run out of cash. There is also an ATM inside the Coconut Tree Store at the entrance to town.

COMMUNICATIONS

The small office of **Barefoot Charlies Internet** (9 A.M.–9 P.M. daily), opposite Foster's dock, has a quick satellite connection for US$0.10 a minute, US$6 an hour, or US$10 for a two-week, unlimited time account. Headsets and mikes are also available for semiprivate Skyping. The staff is very helpful on island information; T-shirts, guidebooks, and a selection of used books in many languages are also available.

Somewhat more centrally located, **Paradise Computers** (8 A.M.–10 P.M. daily) also offers Internet for US$0.10 per minute and headsets,

ROATAN MARINE PARK RECOMMENDATIONS

The Roatan Marine Park was formed in 2005 by concerned dive operators and other local citizens, in an effort to help protect Roatán's surrounding reef. A voluntary fee of US$10 is charged to divers to help fund their protection efforts – money well spent. All visitors can also help the efforts by adhering to the following RMP suggestions:

- Use only biodegradable and nontoxic sunscreens.

- Use only eco-friendly insect repellents, especially when swimming. (DEET is highly toxic for the coral. Many stores in Roatán sell a fairly effective product called Cactus Juice, or look for Nuvy's Repelente de Insectos sold in grocery stores and pharmacies on the mainland.)

- Do not consume lobster, conch, iguana, deer, or turtle. (All are currently endangered. We admit to eating lobster; one board member of the RMP told us the problem is the sale of lobsters whose tails are less than 5.5 inches long. Order only in reputable restaurants.)

- Recycle plastic bottles, glass, paper, and aluminum cans. Keep your use of water bottles to a minimum by refilling.

- Do not purchase marine life souvenirs. (And remember that it is illegal to leave the country with them.)

- Turn off the lights, fans, and air-conditioning when you leave your hotel room.

And for those planning to stick around Roatán for a while:

- Volunteer with the Roatan Marine Park (www.roatanmarinepark.com).

as well as international calls (US$0.50/minute to the United States).

LAUNDRY

Bamboo Hut Laundry (8 A.M.–4 P.M. daily), just north of Georphi's hotel on the bottom floor of the owners' house, efficiently washes and dries five pounds of dirty duds for US$4, US$0.80 for each additional pound. Or, drop off your clothes at Woody's supermarket next to Posada Arco Iris Sunday–Friday, and **Hummingbird Laundry** (tel. 504/445-3154, ask for Teri or Walter) will wash it for US$0.80/pound, with a US$6.30 minimum.

SPANISH SCHOOLS

Those interested in picking up a bit of Spanish can study at the **Roatan Language School** (tel. 504/445-4231) at the Hotel Casa Calico for US$9/hour.

MASSAGE

If your muscles need a break from all that snorkeling, diving or beach lounging, try a massage at **Chez Breezy** (tel. 504/3313-3400, US$50/75-minute massage) next door to Hotel Casa Calico or at **Healing Hands** (tel. 504/403-8728, US$40/60-minute massage) located at the Mariposa Lodge.

CONSERVATION GROUPS

The offices of the **Roatan Marine Park** (tel. 504/445-4206, www.roatanmarinepark.com, 8 A.M.–6 P.M. daily) are located in the center of West End, for those interested in finding out more about where their US$10 fee is going. The office also runs the **Marine Park Green Store** on the premises, which sells T-shirts and knickknacks and rents snorkel equipment (just US$5 for 24 hours, with a US$15 deposit).

Getting There and Around

Minibuses to and from Coxen Hole (14 kilometers) leave frequently between 7 A.M. and 7 or 8 P.M., US$1 each way. Collective taxis cost US$2. The ride to and from Sandy Bay is US$0.50 in a minibus or US$1 in a collective taxi. After dark, rides can get progressively scarcer, with the last taxis leaving toward Coxen Hole at around 10 P.M., or later on weekends.

Most taxis hang out by the highway exit by the Coconut Tree Store. After dark, hitching a lift in a passing pickup is often possible.

Water taxis to West Bay leave frequently during the day; they fill up from Foster's dock and cost US$2.50. Arrangements can be made with the captain to get picked up for the return trip later on, even after dark if you like. You can walk to West Bay along the beach in about 25 minutes, although it involves a little scamper around some wet rocks about halfway, and then crossing a tall footbridge over a canal. It can be a little treacherous at night if you don't know the way.

It's possible to buy airline tickets in Coxen Hole, or by calling the airline offices at the airport to make reservations. For the ferry, you have to go buy tickets at the dock, as they do not accept reservations. But apart from unusual circumstances (like the first boat after several days of rough seas), it's not a problem to get a seat if you show up an hour before departure. A few taxis are available early in West End to catch the ferry, but you can also speak to a taxi driver the previous day to arrange for a pickup—the drivers are usually very much in need of business and happy to get up early for the work.

◖ WEST BAY

Around a couple of rocky points about two kilometers south of West End is one of Roatán's greatest natural treasures—West Bay Beach, 1.5 kilometers of powdery, palm-lined sand lapped by exquisite turquoise-blue water. At the south end of the beach, where a wall of iron shore juts out into the water, the coral reef meets the shore. For anyone who wants a low-key encounter with an exceptionally fine reef without a long swim or any scuba gear, this is *the* place. It's almost too beautiful—more like an aquarium than a section of live reef, with brilliantly colored fish dodging about, the odd barracuda lurking, and sponges and sea fans gently waving—all just a few feet from the beach.

The reef comes closest to shore at the beach's south end, but for anyone willing to swim out a

bit, the entire bay is lined by excellent reef, although it's been showing the ill-effects of heavy traffic in recent years. Keep an eye out for boats when in the water. The cruise ship day-trippers frequently descend in numbers on West Bay, so it's worth checking what days the ships are coming in. Even on those days, though, the beach is generally quiet in the early morning or late afternoon, and always quieter at the northern end. Many cruise shippers end up at a section of the beach near the south end referred to as "Tabayana Beach," where beach chairs and snorkel equipment are available for rent.

Until the early 1990s, West Bay was totally deserted, save for a few bonfire-building partyers. After a sudden flurry of real-estate transactions and building, West Bay is now lined with houses and hotels, most thankfully built out of wood in a reserved, unobtrusive style.

The construction boom on West Bay and in the hills behind has brought unfortunate consequences for the nearby reef. A large wetland area a few hundred meters behind the beach, at the base of the hills, formerly served

dock at West Bay

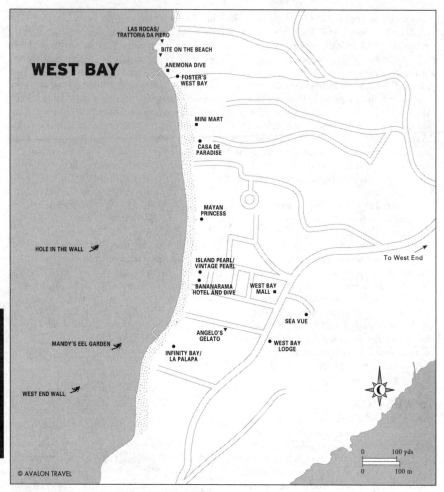

WEST BAY

LAS ROCAS/
TRATTORIA DA PIERO
BITE ON THE BEACH
ANEMONA DIVE
FOSTER'S
WEST BAY
MINI MART
CASA DE
PARADISE
MAYAN
PRINCESS
HOLE IN THE WALL
ISLAND PEARL/
VINTAGE PEARL
BANANARAMA
HOTEL AND DIVE
WEST BAY
MALL
SEA VUE
ANGELO'S
GELATO
WEST BAY
LODGE
MANDY'S EEL GARDEN
INFINITY BAY/
LA PALAPA
WEST END WALL
To West End
© AVALON TRAVEL

0   100 yds
0   100 m

as a buffer, to catch rain runoff and either filter it or let it evaporate in the sun. Developers promptly filled in the wetlands (annoying little swamp!) when construction began in West Bay. As a result, and coupled with the hillside construction and road building, the West Bay reef is coated with waves of silty water after every strong rain. Reefs do not take well to such sudden drops in water quality, nor to the huge increase of inexperienced snorkelers and divers who bump, grab, or step on the reef, causing damage every time. The reef will still be lovely for several years to come, but it remains to be seen whether island authorities will take action to protect perhaps the single most important tourist attraction in Roatán for the future.

Dive Shops

There are several dive shops operating out of West Bay. **Bananarama** (tel. 504/445-5005, U.S. tel. 727/564-9058, www.bananaramadive .com, fun dive US$35, beginner's Open Water certification US$325), toward the southern end of the beach, has a good reputation. **TGI** (tel. 504/403-8049, www.tgidiving.com, fun dive US$35, beginner's Open Water certification US$350) has a PADI five-star dive shop that works with the Henry Morgan and Paradise Beach Club resorts, and is scheduled to open another at Infinity Bay in September 2009. They sell equipment as well as rent. The **Mayan Princess** has its own dive shop (tel. 504/445-5050, U.S. tel. 786/299-5929, www.mayan princess.com), to which the Casa de Paradise hotel also sends its guests. At the northern end of the beach, **Las Rocas** (tel. 504/403-8046, U.S. tel. 877/379-8645, www.lasrocasresort .com) has a dive shop, and **Anemona** (tel. 504/3266-6719, www.anemonadivers.com) is run out of Foster's hotel. All of the shops have package deals available with their affiliated hotel.

Snorkeling

One of the main attractions of West Bay is the reef located right offshore, easily accessible to even the most novice snorkeler. At the southern end of the beach, the reef is just a few meters offshore, while reaching the reef from the northern end of the beach requires a long swim, which should be done with a companion for safety. Tropical fish and colorful coral abound. Stay attuned to the buzzing sound of the occasional water taxi.

Note: Snorkelers must take care to avoid touching the reef at all. The thousands of visitors every month who descend upon West Bay's reef are taking a heavy toll. It may be easy for novice snorkelers to enjoy the reef, but it's also easy for them to bump into or actually step on the coral.

Other Recreation

If you came to Roatán with family and your child is too little to snorkel, or someone isn't able, a trip on the **glass-bottom boat** (US$30 adults, US$15 kids) that moors at the dock near Foster's is a good, albeit pricey, way to see a few of those fish that everyone else is talking about.

SNORKELING

Many of us land-based creatures feel slightly ill at ease strapping on all that scuba gear and descending to the watery depths. We would much prefer to admire the undersea world wearing nothing more complicated than a mask, a snorkel, and fins. Snorkel gear is easily rented at any dive shop on the islands. When renting gear, be very careful to check that your mask fits snugly. Hold the mask against your face and suck in with your nose – it should stay held against your face without the help of your hand. Also, see that the snorkel has no obvious leaks (some shops are more conscientious than others) and fits in your mouth comfortably, and that your fins are neither too tight nor too loose. A constantly dripping mask or a painfully tight fin can ruin a good snorkel trip. Bringing your own mask is one way to avoid this problem. A good fit for the fins is important also.

On all the Bay Islands, snorkelers will find several good locations to paddle out to from shore. But more adventurous snorkelers, who are also confident swimmers, can often go out with scuba boats and snorkel the same site as the divers, but from above. Ask around at different shops for appropriate dive sites, preferably shallow ones.

Somewhat corny, but fun nevertheless, is **Gumbalimba Park** (tel./fax 504/9914-9196 or 504/9946-5559, www.gumbalimbapark .com, 7 A.M.–5 P.M. daily, US$20), a little natural oasis in West Bay complete with a waterfall, cactus garden, 100-plus species of orchids, 25 species of heliconia, and—the part that makes it worth a trip—a parrot, macaw, and monkey park where the trained animals roam and fly free. The animals are best viewed between 8 A.M. and 3 P.M. Be prepared to have any or all of the three tropical critters take perch on your shoulder. Guides are included in the price, as is transportation—be sure to take advantage of both (the guides will make sure you go home

THE BAY ISLANDS

building sand castles on West Bay Beach

with that shot of a parrot or monkey on your shoulder). The park also runs canopy tours.

The park, on the land of the owner of Anthony's Key Resort, has an assortment of attractions catering generally to the cruise-ship crowd, but available to others also, including a beach with snorkeling, clear kayaks for rent (to see the reef below), horseback riding in the park (US$35 for 1.5 hours). Snacks and meals are served at an outdoor restaurant. It can be pretty busy when the cruise ships are in town, or extremely quiet when they are not.

Also located along the road between West Bay and West End is **South Shore Canopy** (tel. 504/9967-1381, US$45).

For a different way to see the beach, or a bit of the jungle if desired, contact **Barrio Dorcas Ranch** (tel. 504/9555-4880, www .barriodorcasranch.com), for a tour by horseback (US$35–40).

If all these activities have left your muscles aching, look for one of the impromptu massage shops that spring up on the beach when the cruise ships are in town, typically charging US$20 for a 30-minute massage.

One of the best places to arrange any activity is at the two **Roatan Tourist Info Centers** (www.roatantouristinfo.com, tel. 504/3336-5597) located near Foster's and Bananarama. They offer tickets to Gumbalimba and for the glass-bottom boat, book catamaran sail and snorkel tours of Roatán (US$35), and can arrange activities around the island, such as a visit to the pirate canopy tour and iguana farm near French Harbour, Jet-Skiing in Flowers Bay, kayak rentals at West Bay, car rentals, and so forth. Surprisingly, prices are usually the same as you pay if you purchase services directly, or slightly more but transportation is included (a big perk).

Accommodations

Hotels in West Bay are a decided step up in price from West End, although there are still many reasonable options by international standards. Those who are really after some peace and quiet, and some serious beach time, may enjoy staying in West Bay. And while the restaurant selection can't compete with West End, there are several spots worth seeking out. Some rooms in West Bay also have kitchens, or at least mini-fridges and microwaves, which can be useful for breakfasts and snacks.

Rates skyrocket from those listed here during

Easter and Christmas weeks, when rooms should be booked well in advance. Remember, all room rates are subject to a 16 percent tax, which has been included here but may or may not be included in the price quoted to you by the establishment itself.

Foster's West Bay (tel. 504/445-1124, U.S. tel. 877/245-5907, www.fostersroatan.com, US$64–81 d, US$87–162 for suites, cabins, and duplexes that sleep 2–5) owns several cabins near the north end of West Bay beach. In addition, a small room built into the branches of a mango tree, complete with electricity and running water, rents for US$64–104 d, depending on the season. One-, two-, and three-bedroom units are also available.

One of the giants in West Bay is **Hotel Mayan Princess** (tel. 504/445-5050, U.S. tel. 786/299-5929, www.mayanprincess.com, US$211–277, with discounts during the low season and weekly rates available), a collection of plaster-and-tile units along the beach equipped with comfortable wicker furniture, satellite TV, telephones, master bedrooms, sofa beds, and kitchens. "Suites" have two bedrooms and rent for US$319–520. The units are all privately owned, and then rented out by hotel management when the owners are not using them. Price includes transportation to and from the airport. The hotel's restaurant/bar is open 7:30 A.M.–10 P.M. daily, although there are better places to eat on the beach.

The newest addition to West Bay's collection of large and luxurious hotels is **❰ Infinity Bay** (tel. 504/445-5016, U.S. tel. 866/369-1977, www.infinitybay.com), located at the southern end of West Bay, close to where the reef reaches the shore. Although construction was still going on at the time of writing, the first-phase units have been completed and were available for rent (US$162–197 studio, US$231–307 one bedroom, US$242–423 two bedroom, US$481–539 3 bedroom). The massive complex will have 145 rooms upon completion, the largest hotel on West Bay. Rooms have beautiful furnishings, patios or balconies, and amenities such as large flat-screen TVs. All but the studios have full kitchens, and many

have sofa-beds for additional capacity. A long swimming pool runs down the center of the complex, leading to the bar on the beach. What's noteworthy about this resort is its significant efforts to have zero negative impacts on Roatán's beach and reef. Environmentally friendly aspects include state-of-the-art water treatment and septic facilities, solar water heating, the use of biodegradable soaps in housekeeping, and an awareness of erosion control in the construction process. The only drawback we found (besides, perhaps, its behemoth size), was that the windows for ground-floor units open onto walkways, limiting privacy for those who like to keep the curtains drawn.

A relatively budget choice on West Bay is **Bananarama** (tel. 504/445-5005, U.S. tel. 727/564-9058, www.bananaramadive.com, US$94–123 d, with specials available in the low season). A variety of simple but decent garden and beach-front rooms can sleep up to five, although there is a US$10 per person charge for more than two guests. There is also a two-bedroom house that can sleep up to 12, priced at US$350 for double occupancy. Cruise ship excursions are offered through Bananarama, so it can get fairly chaotic some days, but the on-site dive shop has a good reputation and fair prices.

Bananarama recently purchased the neighboring property, **❰ Island Pearl** (tel. 504/445-5005, U.S. tel. 727/564-9058, www.roatanpearl.com), but seems to be maintaining it as a quieter, more upscale accommodation, although the unique artwork left with the previous owners. The attractive apartments in four separate houses set among shady trees rent for US$232–290, and a studio with queen bed is available for US$116. Accommodations for 3–5 guests are available for an additional US$10 per person. The on-site restaurant, Vintage Pearl, is very highly regarded.

An Italian conglomerate (tel. 504/445-5009, www.hmresorts.com) is the owner of several all-inclusive hotels on West Bay, including **Henry Morgan Resort, Paradise Beach Club,** and **Las Sirenas.** The first is especially renowned for its throngs of Italian package tourists. Paradise Beach Club has lovely grounds, with winding paths and lush tropical foliage leading between the buildings and around the swimming pool. Guests have reported being disappointed by the somewhat simple rooms given the price. For rates and information, call tel. 504/445-5009 or check www.hmresorts.com.

Casa de Paradise (tel. 504/9961-5311, U.S. tel. 740/251-4123, www.casadeparadise.com) is actually two *casas* (houses), with five different accommodations ranging from a one-bedroom efficiency suite to a deluxe four-bedroom home. Amenities vary by room but may include a king bed, TV, hammock, balcony, or full kitchen. All rooms come with coffee from owners Ron and Myra Cummin's plantation in Olancho. Prices range US$92–327; monthly rates are also available. Unusual in this price range, air-conditioning is charged separately (US$12 per unit used per day). Thankfully the hotel's small size hasn't kept it from getting a generator to keep the air-conditioning running during the occasional power outage. Casa de Paradise works with the well-regarded dive shop at the nearby Hotel Mayan Princess.

Las Rocas (tel. 504/403-8046, U.S. tel. 877/379-8645, www.lasrocasresort.com) has several two-story wood cabins tucked along its own private beach, two minutes along a wooden boardwalk from West Bay proper. Rooms are named after Italian islands such as Capri and Stromboli, thanks to its Italian-expat owner, Piero. The best rooms are the "superior" (US$103–151), which are spacious and tasteful, with wood furniture and floors, and peaked ceilings. Standard rooms (US$80–127) lack water views but are just as spacious and have porches with hammocks, while the "value" rooms (US$75–110) are smaller and in cabins built claustrophobically close together. The resort has its own dive shop, and dive packages are available, a good deal at US$532–730 per week, based on double occupancy.

Set back from the beach a few hundred meters (opposite the West Bay Mall) is **Sea Vue** (tel. 504/445-5002, www.seavueroatan .com, US$75–133 for up to four people), with four very attractive condos, each with a full kitchen, and two bedrooms that can sleep up to six. High ceilings, white walls, and a sleek design give the place an airy, bright feel, and all units have an ocean view. There is an outdoor swimming pool and Jacuzzi, and an ecologically friendly water collection and disposal system for the hotel. A path next to the West Bay Mall leads to the beach, a four- or five-minute walk away. This is a great deal for anyone who doesn't mind the walk. Cars are available for rent from the owners as well.

Another option nearby (that is, also a four-minute walk from the beach) is **West Bay Lodge** (tel. 504/445-5069, U.S. tel. 503/761-7172, www.westbaylodge.com, US$93–145 d), with cute little bungalows tucked into tropical gardens, each with its own porch and hammock. "Supreme" units with kitchens and two double beds are available for US$25–30 more. There is a pool on-site, perfect for cooling off after the beach, and guests rave about the breakfasts.

Note: In December 2008 there were two evening muggings on this path that leads between the beach and West Bay Mall—highly unusual according to local police, but be attentive to your surroundings after dark.

Food and Entertainment

Located on the wooden walkway between Foster's and Las Rocas is **Bite on the Beach** (noon–9 P.M. Tues.–Sat., with extended hours for the bar), a superb spot to enjoy a snack, beer, or full meal on a large, breezy deck right on the edge of the glorious Caribbean. The standard fish, shrimp, lobster, and chicken are available in various preparations, as well as more unusual dishes such as *caprese* salad and Thai curries, for US$5.50–15 per plate. If you've been fishing, they'll even cook up your own catch of the day.

Foster's West Bay (8 A.M.–9 P.M. daily), at the north end of West Bay shortly before Bite on the Beach, serves tasty breakfasts, seafood entrées (US$8–15), and sandwiches (US$5–8) prepared at an open-air *champa,* or thatched hut. The coconut bread French toast and the grilled lobster (just US$12 on Thursdays) are especially recommended. The bar/restaurant is a popular hangout spot with locals and foreigners alike during the lazy afternoons at West Bay.

❲ **Vintage Pearl** is an excellent, upscale restaurant. While the menu selection is limited, every plate is good. The prix-fixe menu changes daily and runs US$25–50 for the three courses. The restaurant has the largest wine cellar on the island. A great place for a romantic splurge.

Trattoria da Piero, at Las Rocas Resort, has good Caribbean food with an Italian twist, thanks to hotel owner Piero. Fresh seafood is of course the specialty, and the shrimp in pesto sauce and seafood risotto are great ways to shake off the monotony of beach cuisine. There is even pasta in meat sauce for those really looking for something different (mains US$16–23).

Set under the palm trees on the sand, Infinity Bay's restaurant **La Palapa** serves up good breakfasts, burgers, and fish sandwiches (US$4–9), as well as fancier dishes like Thai curry, grilled lobster, and filet mignon (US$12–23).

Mangiamo Market and Deli (8:30 A.M.–5 P.M. Mon.–Sat.), in the West Bay Mall, makes excellent sandwiches, including prosciutto with mozzarella, a spicy chipotle chicken, and good ole turkey for US$7–9, perfect for a picnic on the beach. Breakfasts are available too, for take-away or to munch at one of the deli's small tables.

Services

The **Mini-Mart** (8 A.M.–9 P.M. daily, on the beach between Foster's and Henry Morgan) has basic supplies such as Panadol (a good substitute for Tylenol) and pasta, as well as Internet access for US$0.10 per minute.

The petite **West Bay Mall** has a number of handy shops—to get there, follow the path that's between Bananarama and Paradise Beach Club out to the road, and the mall is just to the left. Those looking to stock up on their own supplies can find a nice variety of high-quality goods at

Impromptu massage parlors look out toward the water from West Bay Beach.

© AMY E. ROBERTSON

Mangiamo Market and Deli (8:30 A.M.–5 P.M. Mon.–Sat.), such as gourmet chocolate, granola bars, beer, and ingredients for pasta. There is a branch of **Captain Van's Rentals** (tel. 504/445-5040, 9 A.M.–7 P.M. daily) here, renting scooters, motorcycles, mountain bikes, cell phones, and DVDs. Stock up on wine, cigars, and rum at **De la Viña** (10 A.M.–7 P.M. Mon.–Thurs., 11 A.M.–7 P.M. Fri.). Lastly, the mall also houses **Cool Beans** (tel. 504/445-5048, 7:30 A.M.–5 P.M. Mon.–Fri., 8 A.M.–noon Sat.–Sun.), a nice coffee house with bagels and tasty cakes.

There is an **Internet** shop just across the road from the mall.

Getting There

From West End, you can walk to West Bay (45 minutes along the beach, past the rickety wooden dock on the point—do not carry valuables as there has been the occasional mugging along this route), or take a water taxi (US$2.50 from Foster's) or car (a four-kilometer paved road turns off the main highway near the entrance to West End, while another paved road connects Coxen Hole to West Bay via Flowers

Bay). Water-taxi captains are happy to arrange a return trip to pick up weary but content sun-fried beach bums at the end of the day.

Near West Bay

Along the road from West Bay to West End, just before reaching the latter, is **Luna Beach Resort** (tel. 504/403-8778, U.S. tel. 866/710-5862, www.lunabeachresort.com, US$89–246 s/d, US$25 each extra person), an expanse of wooden buildings and decks spread across the beach and up a hillside between West End and West Bay. It has a fine dock out over the water, perfect for swimming, sunbathing, and watching the sunset, as well as a pool and beachfront bar. A hotel-style portion has spacious rooms along the waterfront, while upscale cabins with kitchens and generous living areas are nestled into the tropical hillside. The furniture is made with local wood, the beach is very well-maintained, including a daily spraying with a natural *jején* repellent, and the amenities (showers, TVs, appliances) are all first-class—pluses that make up for a lack of character in the decor. Enormous four-bedroom houses are available for $408/night. There is a dive shop on-site with competitive prices (fun dive US$35, Open Water certification US$325 for beginners, US$260 for advanced), and the confined sessions can be completed in the hotel pool, a luxury if the sea is choppy.

SANDY BAY

With a full-time population of about 1,200, Sandy Bay is considerably larger than West End, but somehow it doesn't feel like it. The town is a collection of weather-beaten wooden houses, most built on stilts among patches of shady trees a hundred meters or so from the edge of the sea, strung out over three or more kilometers of shoreline. Development has arrived in Sandy Bay, but it's mostly limited to private houses and a couple of low-key resorts tucked away in the corners of town. Anthony's Key Resort (AKR), which literally divides Sandy Bay in two, is a large complex, but most guests don't venture off the grounds into town, so it doesn't much disturb the placid lifestyle of the local islanders. Sandy Bay is a popular place for foreigners living in Roatán to rent inexpensive houses or apartments.

Sights

In one of the few programs of its kind in the Caribbean, **The Institute for Marine Sciences** based at AKR studies the local dolphin population and runs a variety of highly regarded interactions with them. Spectators are welcome to stop by daily at 4 P.M. for the informal dolphin show (call first to confirm the time, as it can vary), where trainers work with the dolphins and perform health checks. Certified scuba divers can enjoy 45 minutes of controlled but unstructured swimming with dolphins over open-water sand flats (US$112, extra to rent equipment). You can also snorkel for 30 minutes with the dolphins for US$84, or have a beachside "dolphin encounter" for US$60, complete with a dolphin kiss. An institute trainer accompanies all diving and snorkeling expeditions. Those interested in more detailed information on the dolphins can take a specialty course, with one day of lessons and activities (US$160 pp for AKR guests, or US$202 for nonguests). Information about the institute and the dolphin activities is available on AKR's website, www.anthonyskey.com.

The IMS has several exhibits on invertebrates, reptiles, birds, fish, coral-reef life, and the geology of the Bay Islands, as well as a small but worthwhile bilingual museum on local archaeology and history. Admission to the institute's museum is US$2; the facility is open 8 A.M.–5 P.M. daily.

Carambola Botanical Gardens (tel. 504/445-3117, www.carambolagardens.com, 8 A.M.–5 P.M. daily, US$5, age seven and under free), located off the highway opposite the entrance to AKR, is the only developed inland reserve on the Bay Islands. Well-built trails wind through forests of ferns, spices, orchids, flowering plants, fruit trees, and even a few mahogany trees. A decidedly steep trail leads to the top of Carambola Mountain. Along the way is a turnoff to the fascinating Iguana Wall, a section of sheer cliff that serves as a protected breeding ground for iguanas and parrots. There are great views from the peak over the surrounding reef and, in the distance, Utila. The staff at the visitors center has some information on the reserves, and if manager Irma Brady is around, she is particularly knowledgeable about the reserve's flora and fauna. Guides can be hired for an extra charge.

Recreation

As its name would suggest, Sandy Bay has plenty of beach right in front of town, but the water is somewhat muddy and not totally clean, making it not as nice for sunbathing as West End or West Bay. The waters around Sandy Bay and AKR were the first established section of the Roatan Marine Park, created in 1989, and the snorkeling and diving are superb. Snorkelers can paddle out anywhere that's convenient across a couple hundred meters of shallow water, much of it blanketed in sea grass, to the edge of the reef. Finding a passage out across the shallow reef can be tricky—the best plan is to ask locals to point out the channels used by boats, marked by buoys. The steep coral and rock cliffs and formations on the ocean side of the reef are dramatic and great fun to explore with a snorkel and fins. When swimming, keep a sharp eye out for boat traffic.

The dive shops at AKR and Blue Bahia will take nonguest divers, for slightly higher rates than at West End. Most West End shops will set up trips out to Sandy Bay dive sites on request.

Accommodations

Sandy Bay's hotel selection tends to the middle and upper price categories. It's often possible to find a local in the many wooden houses lining the beach happy to rent out a room or an entire cabin for a negotiable fee.

Run by Bill and Cathy Service, **Sunnyside Condominiums** (tel./fax 504/445-3006, www.sunnysideroatan.com, US$50–200/night, US$500–1,400/week), on the beach at the eastern end of Sandy Bay, has rental options including two studio apartments, a condo, and two large houses, and priced for a couple on up to a group or family of six or more.

The **Roatan Beachcomber** (tel. 504/9929-4720, www.roatanbeachcomber.com) also has a variety of accommodations, right on the beach. Two apartments are available for those who want their own kitchen (US$58–75 one bedroom, US$116–145 two bedroom), adjacent to the restaurant. There is a large wooden building on stilts that looks out over the water, and its simple cabin-style rooms have peek-a-boo ocean views; they are a great value at US$35–58 (the high end of the range for a/c). Each has a double bed, and mattresses can be brought in for kids. If a group rents several rooms, they can also request use of the common kitchen (off-limits to individual travelers). Lastly, there is a four-bedroom beach house available for US$992–1,334 per week. While none of the digs are particularly fancy, the managers take exceptional care of the beach (our visit was post-storm when no one else was managing to keep the driftwood and seaweed off the shore, yet here the sand had been fastidiously raked), and the reef is a very short swim from the hotel's private dock. Snorkeling equipment is provided, kayaks are available for rent on-site, and fishing charters and diving trips can be arranged. There is a restaurant on-site.

Still a bit up-and-coming is **Tranquil Seas** (tel. 504/445-3351, www.tranquilseas.co.uk, US$122 s/d), with a handful of lovely cabins in a lush tropical setting. The rooms are tastefully decorated, and a few have kitchenettes. An attractive thatch-roof restaurant and bar overlooks the small but nice swimming pool. New cabins are still under construction, however, so until those are finished, the place might not be quite as peaceful as you hoped. Customer service is normally reputed to be stellar, but it seems to fall apart when the owner heads back to his native U.K. for summer vacation. There are plans to put a dive shop on-site, but for now guests can head a few steps down the beach to the Octopus dive shop at the Blue Bahia Resort. This will be a great place to stay when the kinks are worked out.

Roatán's most extravagant option, **Mayoka Lodge** (tel. 504/445-3043, www.mayokalodge.com), is on two hectares of tropical gardens near town. The six-suite lodge has a swimming pool, tennis court, and two holes of golf, as well as luxuries such as a wine cellar, chef, car and driver, and, of course, your own private beach and dock. It's all yours for a mere US$22,500 per week.

Just off the southern side of the highway, the **Oasis Lounge** restaurant (www.roatan-guava-grove.com, US$41/day or US$580/month) also rents efficiency suites, suitable for those with their own wheels to get to the beach. There is also a three-bedroom house for rent with a water view over the treetops (US$174/night or US$986/week). The lounge/restaurant is closed on Wednesdays.

Dive Resorts

One of the premier vacation resorts on Roatán and, for that matter, in all of Honduras, **Anthony's Key Resort** (AKR, tel. 504/445-3003, U.S. tel. 800/227-3483, www.anthonyskey.com, US$973–1,832 pp for one-week dive packages) manages 56 cabins on both the small and serene Anthony's Key and on a tree-covered hillside on the mainland of Roatán. "Leisure" packages are room-only and run US$683–1,460 per person for a week, or US$108–230 per person per night. There's fantastic swimming and snorkeling on all sides and a small sunbathing beach as well as a new pool and poolside bar on the cay. Dive shop facilities are top-notch, with several large boats, new equipment, and everything needed for a variety of PADI courses. The resort is renowned for its dolphin encounter and educational programs. AKR has its own underwater photo/video shop, offering dive light rentals, film and batteries for sale, underwater videos, and pictures from the dolphin encounter and dolphin dives.

A few minutes down the road, but just steps away via the beach, is the **Blue Bahia Resort** (tel. 504/445-3385, www.bluebahiaresort.com, US$115–215 depending on room size, and a 50 percent discount Sept.–Nov.), with nine lovely rooms set around an infinity-edged pool that looks out toward the water. Each has a sitting area and porch with deck chairs, and several have full kitchens as well, although given the quality of the resort's restaurant, the only meal you may find yourself

dolphins performing at Anthony's Key Resort, in Sandy Bay

© AMY E. ROBERTSON

making is breakfast (when the resort restaurant is closed). The beach is not bad, but doesn't compare to West Bay or some of the others; the hotel is best suited to those who have come to Roatán to dive. The **Octopus Dive School** (tel. 504/9737-9120, www.roatan-octopus diveschool.com) is on-site, offering the standard PADI Open Water course for US$325, specialty courses such as Nitrox (US$220), and half-day introductions to scuba for adults (US$60) and children (US$75, ages eight and up). Fun dives are US$25–35).

Located at Gibson Bight, the **Inn of Last Resort** (tel. 504/445-4113, U.S. tel. 888/319-3255, www.innoflastresort.com) offers week-long dive packages for US$806–1,270 per person per week and has rates available for shorter stays and non-divers as well. The resort is located on a small lagoon that opens out to the ocean, and its dive boats and equipment were all new in early 2009.

Food and Entertainment

Those staying in Sandy Bay will likely be eating in their resort restaurant, but a couple of other places serve good meals at midrange prices.

Even if you're not staying at the Blue Bahia Resort, its restaurant is well worth a visit. The **Beach Grill** (open for lunch and dinner every day but Tuesday) smokes its own meats and is renowned for its Louisiana-style barbecue, including brisket, chicken and ribs, as well as pulled-pork sandwiches, the latter served on house-baked bread (US$8–13).

The **Blue Parrot Bar and Restaurant** (tel. 504/992-2807, 11:30 A.M.–10 P.M. Mon.–Sat.) is a nice little street-front joint with a colorful parrot mural on the wall. The owner has recently changed, but locals say it's as good as ever, with sandwiches for around US$5 and entrées like lobster, shrimp kebabs, and surf 'n' turf for US$7–12 a meal.

The **Sunshine Café** at the Roatan Beachcomber is open noon–9 P.M. daily; its specialty is a Friday night all-you-can-eat fish fry with shrimp, conch, and fish for US$15.

The Bay Island Beach Resort hosts crab races at **Deep Ted's Grille** on Thursday evenings,

complete with a pig roast and plenty of tequila. It's a popular event with the local expat community, and proceeds are donated to the Sandy Bay public schools.

The multi-service **Oasis Lounge** (just off the southern side of the highway) has American-friendly snacks such as wings and burgers, as well as more upscale *tapas* and salads, all served in a lounge tented by billowy fabrics. There are nightly activities popular with Roatán expats, such as a pub quiz (Tuesdays) and movies (Thursdays), as well as a swimming pool (with a kids' swim Fridays noon–5 P.M.). There are also efficiency suites and a house for rent (www.roatan-guavagrove.com). The lounge/restaurant is closed on Wednesdays.

Spas

Undoubtedly the finest spa on the island, **Baan Suerte** (tel. 504/445-3059, www.spa baansuerte.com) is tucked into lush vegetation on a hill above the sea, offering five types of massage, seven body treatments (such honey and papaya, or green tea-mint-algae), and other spa standards like facials, manicures, and yoga. Services are expensive (massages and body treatments run US$70–150), but quality is top-notch, and guests are welcome to stay as long as they like on the property, taking advantage of the swimming pool, beach access, kayaks, and snorkel equipment.

Services

On the grounds of AKR is the **Cornerstone Medical Center** (tel. 504/445-3003 or 504/445-3049, VHF channel 16, 8 A.M.–5 P.M. daily, 24 hours for diving emergencies), home to one of the two recompression tanks on Roatán (the other is at Fantasy Island Resort). It has X-ray facilities, and the doctors can treat ailments resulting from diving and other illnesses as well.

For non-diving injuries and illnesses, head to the **Clínica Esperanza** (tel. 504/445-3234), just off the highway, for perhaps the best health care on the island. The drawback? Would-be patients must arrive between 7 and 9 A.M. to take a number, then wait around until called.

Sandy Bay is just off the West End–Coxen Hole highway; minibuses and taxis pass frequently in both directions. Shared taxis to Coxen Hole cost US$1.50; it's US$1 to West End.

COXEN HOLE

A dusty, unremarkable town of weather-beaten wooden houses and shops, Coxen Hole is visited most frequently to change money, buy groceries, or take care of other business. All buses across the island are based out of Coxen Hole, and the airport is three kilometers east of town, on the road to French Harbour.

Named for pirate captain John Coxen, who lived on Roatán from 1687 to 1697, the town was founded in 1835, when several families arrived from the Cayman Islands and settled on the harbor.

Shopping

Yaba Ding Ding (tel. 504/445-1683, 9 A.M.–5 P.M. Mon.–Sat.)—which is the islanders' nickname for pre-Columbian artifacts—carries paintings by well-known Honduran painters like Virginia Castillo, carvings, batik, woven *junco* baskets from Santa Bárbara, Honduran and Cuban cigars, T-shirts, and more. It's one of the best handicraft stores on the island, and well worth a visit if you happen to be wandering through Coxen Hole. The store is on the ground floor of a two-story building next to H.B. Warren's supermarket.

In the center of town (to the left, or east, when arriving into town along the main road from the highway) is **H.B. Warren's** (7 A.M.–6 P.M. Mon.–Sat.), one of the best supermarkets on the island (along with Eldon's in French Harbour, and a Megafoods in the new mall will soon give everyone a run for their money).

Accommodations

Though most sun- and sand-seekers proceed directly from the docks and airport to West End, Sandy Bay, or elsewhere, there are a handful of hotels in Coxen Hole should you need to spend the night there for some reason.

The **Hotel Cay View** (tel. 504/445-1202, US$31 s, US$38 d), on the eastern side of town on Main Street, has some quite decent rooms that have recently been remodeled, a couple of which even have water views, with air-conditioning, TV, and hot water. The older rooms are pretty dingy.

If the Cay View is full, an alternative is the **Hotel Bella Vista** (tel. 504/445-3611, US$35 d).

Food and Entertainment

While there aren't any standout restaurants in Coxen Hole proper, there are plenty of places to try Honduran staples such as *baleadas,* fluffy flour tortillas stuffed with refried beans and a dash of sour cream, and roast chicken; just walk along Coxen Hole's main drag and pop into one that appeals to you.

Banks

Most of the banks in town are on Main Street (the road that runs along the water) and are open Monday–Friday from 8:30 A.M. until 3:30 or 4 P.M., Saturday from 8:30 A.M. until 11 or 11:30 A.M.

Banco Atlántida (tel. 504/445-1225) has a cash machine, linked only to the Visa network. It will advance lempiras on a Visa card, though at a poor exchange rate, and exchange a maximum of US$300 travelers checks. **HSBC** exchanges unlimited amounts of dollars and travelers checks and offers Visa cash advances at a reasonable exchange rate. It also has an ATM, linked to the Plus, Unibanc, and Visa networks. MoneyGrams can be picked up here. **BAC Bamer** (tel. 504/445-1703) offers cash advances on Visa, American Express, and MasterCard, but the exchange rate is not the best. Its cash machine is linked to the Cirrus, Unibanc, and Plus networks.

Be forewarned that the lines to exchange travelers checks can be horrendously long.

Communications

Honducor is in the small square in the center of town. Across the street from Wood Medical Center is **Hondutel** (fax 504/445-1206, 8 A.M.–noon and 12:30–4 P.M. Mon.–Fri.).

Paradise Computers (tel. 504/445-1394,

www.paradise-computers.com), in the Mango Tree Center on the highway headed to Sandy Bay, has Internet access for US$0.10 per minute, and international calls can be made from here (US$0.50/minute for calls to the United States). It has a small Internet and call center on the cruise ship dock as well.

Martinez Cyber Center (tel. 504/445-1432, 8 A.M.–10 P.M. Mon.–Sat.), in the center of town, has Internet connections for US$0.10 a minute or US$2 per hour. It also offers great rates on international calls (US$0.05 a minute to the United States). The shop is along Main Street, not far from H.B. Warren, but on the opposite side of the street.

Emergencies

In case of emergency, call the **police** (tel. 504/445-3438); the main police station on the island is outside of Coxen Hole on the highway toward West End, on the left-hand side about a kilometer outside of town.

For the **fire department** the number is 504/445-0430.

Pharmacy Roatan (tel. 504/445-1260, 9 A.M.–6 P.M. Mon.–Fri., 9 A.M.–2 P.M. Sat.) is on the road leading to the West End highway from downtown.

Wood Medical Center (tel. 504/445-1080) opposite Cay View is not the finest operation in existence, but it does have one of the few X-ray machines on the island.

Immigration

On the small square in the center of town are the *migración* office (tel. 504/445-1326) and the **port captain** (8 A.M.–noon and 2–5 P.M. Mon.–Fri., 8 A.M.–noon Sat.).

Getting There and Away

Office Mart (tel. 504/445-1843), at Welcome's Plaza (at the juncture of Main Street and Thickett Road), can book airline tickets with **Sosa** airlines.

For most visitors, collective taxis or minibuses are the best way to move between Coxen Hole and other parts of the island. Collective taxis gather in front of H.B. Warren's to pick up passengers to West End (US$1.50), Sandy Bay (US$1), Brick Bay (US$1.50), French Harbour (US$1.50), and Oak Ridge (US$2.25). Minibuses cost less than half what taxis charge. Private taxi rides are negotiable (always negotiate before getting in) and usually expensive, especially for foreign tourists.

FLOWERS BAY

The main ocean road heading north from Coxen Hole leads to the small town of Flowers Bay, home to the island's most popular late-night spot, **Hip Hop.** Despite the name, country-western music is the number one rhythm of choice, and the place gets going promptly at 2:15 A.M., when everything else on the island has closed and those in the know start to show up here.

FRENCH HARBOUR AND VICINITY

A large south-coast town set about one kilometer off the highway on a wide peninsula 10 kilometers east of Coxen Hole, French Harbour is home to one of the island's two major fishing fleets (the other is based in Oak Ridge). This is a working town, and while watching the activity on the docks is interesting, French Harbour is not particularly visually attractive. Nevertheless, the town has a cheerful character that Coxen Hole lacks. There isn't much of a beach or dive-worthy reef around French Harbour—it's better to go farther east or west up the coast.

French Harbour is thought to be named for a Frenchman who had one of the first homesteads in the area during the British military occupation in the 1740s.

Accommodations

The best option in town is **Casa Romeo's** (tel. 504/455-5854, www.casaromeos.com, US$65 s, US$87 d, with discounts available in the low season), a large, stylish wooden house built on the dock, with a cool and quiet restaurant downstairs serving excellent seafood (the prices reflect the quality). The seven rooms are a tiny bit worn, but bright, whitewashed, and breezy with wood floors, air-conditioning, fans, and harbor views. Dive and meal packages are available, and rates come down for weeklong stays.

Upstairs from Gio's restaurant and run by the same owners is **The Faro Inn** (tel. 504/445-5214, US$52 s, US$58 d), with seven decent rooms each with cable TV, air-conditioning, and hot water but, at the time of our visit, decidedly unfriendly staff.

A few kilometers outside of town toward Coxen Hole is the lavish **Barefoot Cay** (tel. 504/455-6235, U.S. tel. 866/246-3706, www.barefootcay.com), located on its own private 1.6-hectare cay (island) 100 meters off Roatán's mainland. Rooms are modern and elegant, with tile floors, Balinese showers, wood furnishings, and white linens set off by colorful pillows. Rooms, suites, and villas rent for US$155–395 per person; weekly rates and all-inclusive packages (with or without diving) are also available. There is yacht moorage and a dive shop on site, as well as a beautiful outdoor pool. The dive shop (www.barefootdiversroatan.com) is pricier than those in West End or West Bay, charging US$40 for a fun dive and US$450 for the beginner's Open Water certification.

Five kilometers from town the other direction (toward Oak Ridge) is **(Santé Wellness Center** (tel. 504/408-5156, U.S. tel. 510/455-4232, www.santewellnesscenter.com, US$168–191 d), a quiet hotel on its own cay in front of the large Parrot Tree Plantation. With just three guest rooms and owners that live on-site, everything at Santé benefits from a personal touch. Great snorkeling is available right from the beach, and there is a swimming pool for anyone who tires of the saltwater. Meals are fresh and spa-healthy, complementing the extensive list of spa services.

Food and Entertainment

Famed for its legendary king crab *al ajillo* (cooked in garlic), **Gio's** (tel. 504/455-5214, 9 A.M.–2 P.M. and 5–10 P.M. Mon.–Sat.), set out over the water, also serves fish, shrimp, several kinds of pasta, and a decent cut of beef at US$8–26 an entrée.

Owned by Italian-Honduran Romeo Silvestri, **(Casa Romeo's** (tel. 504/455-5854, www.casaromeos.com, 10 A.M.–2:30 P.M. and 5–10 P.M. Mon.–Sat.), just up the street, has plenty of pastas as well as superb seafood, such as conch chowder, king crab, and the "AKR Special" (squid, shrimp, lobster, and snapper), at US$7–23 per entrée, served in a classy dining room on the edge of the harbor. To reach the restaurant, enter French Harbour from the main road, pass the police station and take the right fork, go over a little bridge, and you will see Romeo's a little farther on the right of the road (Gio's is just a little bit farther down the road).

Eldon's, at the French Harbour turnoff, is considered by some to be the best supermarket on the island and certainly has the best fresh vegetables (7 A.M.–7 P.M. Mon.–Fri., 7 A.M.–8 P.M. Sat., 8 A.M.–1 P.M. Sun.).

People come from all over the island to **H2O** (tel. 504/455-7552, open Thurs.–Sun.), a dance club outside of town.

Services

BAC Bamer just past Casa Romeo's on the left, will exchange U.S. dollars and travelers checks, as well as advance cash on a Visa card. Farther down the road, near Gio's, is **Banffaa,** exchanging dollars and travelers checks.

If you're looking to get online, head to the **Gone Bananas Kafe** in the McNab Plaza at the main road at the eastern end of town.

The Coxen Hole–Oak Ridge buses, which run until late afternoon, pull all the way into town, so there's no need to slog out to the highway. The fare to Coxen Hole is US$0.80. A collective taxi to Coxen Hole costs US$1.50.

The French Harbour **police station** is on the main road, up from the harbor near the bus station (tel. 504/455-5099).

Palmetto Bay

A magnificently isolated beach resort on the north side of Roatán, **(Palmetto Bay Plantation** (tel. 504/445-5702 or 504/991-0811, www.palmettobayplantation.com, US$174–342, depending on cabin size, season, and location, sleeps 2–6, a/c an additional

US$25/day) is three kilometers up and back down a steep dirt road turning north off the highway just west of the entrance to French Harbour. The resort consists of a dozen or so freestanding bungalow houses set amid a shady grove of palms at the edge of a broad, beautiful beach and backed by lush tropical forest. Each of the 19 bungalow houses has 2–3 bedrooms.

The hotel offers dive packages through an on-site branch of the highly regarded dive shop **Subway Watersports** (tel. 504/3387-0579 or 504/445-5707, www.subwaywatersports.com), as well as kayaking and horseback riding to its guests, and has an international restaurant serving three meals a day. All-inclusive packages and weekly rates are available. Provided

CANOPY TOURS

Short of chartering a private plane for an island tour, taking a canopy ride is one of the best ways to enjoy fantastic views of the island, with an adrenaline rush tossed in for free. Children (as young as four!) are welcome on the canopies – for those that require hand-braking, the child is strapped to a guide. There are several rides on the island from which to choose.

Gumbalimba (tel. 504/9914-9196, 8 A.M.-4 P.M. daily, US$45, or US$35 with a ticket to the animal park) has the corner on the West End/West Bay market simply thanks to its location between the two. There are 18 lines that start in the hills and lead down to the beach. The canopy tour takes about an hour, sometimes a bit less, and transportation is included in the price.

Equally convenient, however, is **South Shore Canopy Tour** (tel. 504/9904-7855, south-shorecanopy@yahoo.com, 8 A.M.-4 P.M. daily, US$45), a 12-line tour covering three kilometers. The starting point is on the road between West Bay and West End, closest to the West End side. Transportation is included.

Close to Palmetto Bay is the **Jungle Canopy Tour** (tel. 504/445-4151, U.S. tel. 877/540-9692, US$45), with 12 lines, two suspension bridges, and a climbing wall. Speed here is controlled by design rather than your hand-brake, which makes it a bit easier. Children should be at least four feet tall. There is an animal park next door (not as fancy as Gumbalimba, but only a couple of dollars entrance fee).

Surely the most unique of the lot, but rather far-flung for those staying in West End or West Bay, is **Pirates of the Caribbean Canopy** (tel. 504/455-7576, www.roatancanopy-pi-rates-of-the-caribbean.com, 8 A.M.-5 P.M.

© LUCA RENDA

Thrillseekers can explore the treetops of Roatán.

Mon.-Fri.). There are two different rides: The easier version has nine lines, five bridges, and a rock wall (US$45), while the "extreme" has eight long lines totaling 2,683 meters, including one 1,837-meter line, reputed to be the longest in the Americas (US$65). Speed here is controlled by design rather than with hand-brakes. Night tours are available by appointment. There is a free short trial zipline at the entrance for those who want to test the experience before putting their money down. The canopy is east of French Harbour; there are signs right on the highway.

they can get there, the public is welcome to enjoy the beach at Palmetto Bay, as long as they have at least one meal at the restaurant.

The **Jungle Canopy Tour** (tel. 504/445-4151) is nearby.

East of French Harbour

The narrow, two-lane highway (bicyclists beware) running east of French Harbour to Oak Ridge winds for most of its length along the ridge in the center of the island, affording superb views of both coasts and the reef, visible under the clear water. Between French Harbour and the Punta Gorda turnoff, the highway passes Juticalpa, a small Latino community and the only sizable inland settlement anywhere on the Bay Islands. Once heavily forested, these central island mountain slopes have been almost entirely denuded of their original cover and now support secondary scrub growth, pasture, or farmland.

About a kilometer east of French Harbour, keep an eye out on the right-hand side for a long white fence, at the end of which is a road

turning in, with a sign to the **Arch's Iguana Farm** (tel. 504/455-7482, 8 A.M.–5 P.M. daily, US$5), located just over a kilometer (0.8 mile) from the main highway down a paved road. When you come to a fork, make a left onto the dirt road and follow the signs to the end. Here you can check out some amazingly huge (some more than one meter long) iguanas, frequently unnervingly interested in their human visitors, especially if you have banana leaves to share. There is also a large, enclosed deck area for viewing fish (including barracudas and tarpons), turtles (including hawksbill, green back, and loggerhead), and lobsters (which are in a separate section so they can lay eggs and re-populate the surrounding area, decimated by overfishing).

A bit farther east on the highway is the entrance to **The Coco View Resort** (tel. 504/9911-7371, U.S. tel. 800/510-8164, www.cocoviewresort.com, US$1,100–1,390 for weeklong dive packages) which is, along with Anthony's Key Resort, one of the oldest and most popular dive resorts in the Bay Islands.

At Arch's Iguana Farm, feeding the iguanas is a popular activity for kids and adults alike.

© AMY E. ROBERTSON

The hotel offers several room options, including homey, wooden ocean bungalows and larger apartments, built right over the water with lovely porches facing the water and sunset, and another 10 rooms in an oceanfront building, all with air-conditioning. Those looking for a few more amenities can consider renting one of the eight privately owned beach houses nearby, not used by their owners most of the year (U.S. tel. 800/282-8932, www.playmiguel.com). Rates are US$326–627 per person for a week's stay, depending on the property reserved and the number of guests (up to six can be accommodated). Diving is excellent right offshore—the reef wall starts 30 meters from the hotel and the wreck of the 42-meter *Prince Albert* is entombed in 20 meters of water nearby. Close by is the famed diving site *Mary's Place,* usually the culmination of the weeklong schedule of dives. The dive crew is professional and friendly, and Coco View has a fleet of large, well-equipped dive boats, even with a hatch to come up from underneath directly into the boat in rough weather. *Note:* Children under the age of 10 are not allowed at Coco View.

A few kilometers farther east is Milton Bight, home to the dive shop **Subway Watersports** (tel. 504/3387-0579 or 504/413-2229, ask for dive shop, www.subwaywatersports .com), which takes walk-in clients on dives to the many great reef locations near there for US$35 per dive, and trips to the revered site *Mary's Place* are made daily. Kayaking, Jet-Skiing, water-skiing, water-boarding, shark dives, day trips to farther-flung sites (such as Morat, Barbaretta, Utila, the Sea Mounts, and Cayos Cochinos), and fishing trips can all be arranged as well. Subway is a PADI five-star Instructor Development Center, and the first National Geographic dive center in Roatán (the National Geographic courses teach the same diving, with a heavier emphasis on environmental awareness and marine science).

Subway also can arrange accommodation in a number of nearby **vacation homes,** listed on their website, ranging from nice to luxury, and priced accordingly (US$700–5,000/night, some with nightly rates also available). Subway

is adjacent to the resort **Turquoise Bay** (tel. 504/413-2229, U.S. tel. 786/623-6121, www .turquoisebayresort.com), whose 26 modern, attractive rooms sprinkled along the hill all offer views of the spectacular bay below. The staff is rather uninspired, and the resort hosts day visits by cruise-shippers, but the breathtaking setting and top-notch dive center make up for the shortcomings. There is a pool and restaurant on-site, and in addition to the water-sport center activities, guests can snorkel, play beach volleyball, or arrange for a horseback ride on the beach. Three-night stays are the minimum, and a week-long package runs US$1,194 per person for divers, US$749 per person for non-divers, both based on double occupancy and costing a bit more during high season.

While plenty of places on the island have water views, the best spot for a view of the island itself is the appropriately named **The View** restaurant, right on the highway not far from the turnoff to the Parrot Tree Plantation. From the peak of a steep hill, the view is of lush emerald vegetation leading down to the golden sand and turquoise water. Vendors sell handicrafts and souvenirs in the small grassy area in front of the restaurant.

While there are plenty of ziplines that for most visitors will be closer to their hotel, parents with pirate-crazy kids might want to check out the **Pirates of the Caribbean Canopy Tour** (tel. 504/455-7576, www.roatan canopy-pirates-of-the-caribbean.com), where buccaneers as young as four can try out the ziplines.

Continuing east toward Jonesville, keep your eyes peeled for a spa sign along the highway that leads to **Spa Tranquilidad** (tel. 504/9797-0042 or 504/3260-7173, www.fuegodelmar .com/spa, by appointment only), a bit out of the way, but with some of the best-value spa services on the island. Professional masseuse Blanca Bodden offers hour-long massages for just US$30, and other treatments like facials, wraps, and stone therapy are available as well. The spa is at Politilly Bight—if you pass the Garífuna center Yubu heading east, then you've gone too far.

A bit out of the way, but worth the trip for an unusual dining experience, is ◖ **Hole in the Wall Restaurant** (tel. 504/3270-3577, www .roatanholeinthewall.com, open for lunch and dinner daily) in Jonesville. To get there, either drive or take a taxi to Jonesville, and get one of the boaters on the dock to take you across to the restaurant, built on a dock right over the water on the far side of the lagoon. The seafood is top-notch, and it's a great place to while away a few hours sipping drinks and chatting with whoever happens to be around the popular restaurant (burgers and sandwiches US$3.70–9, entrées US$9–15). On Sundays at 2:30 P.M. (and usually Fridays too, but call first to confirm), the restaurant offers an all-you-can-eat-until-it's-gone dinner with lobster and/or shrimp, barbecued filet mignon, cole slaw, mashed potatoes, beans, bread, and dessert for US$25. Mangrove tours can be arranged too; Clyde is a local old-timer who gladly takes visitors around and regales them with stories, charging US$7.50 per person for a 40-minute tour. If you're coming in a rented car, take the gravel road from the highway down to Jonesville, then the paved road in Jonesville until you reach a fork in the road—take the left branch. The road ends about 100 meters ahead, where there is a large empty area with some houses bordering the sea. Park your car here, and if it's still light out, knock on the turquoise house on the left, whose residents will radio the restaurant to pick you up. After sundown, you'll need to call the restaurant for a pickup (if you don't have a cell phone, ask your hotel to make this call before you hit the road).

PUNTA GORDA

The oldest permanent settlement in Roatán, Punta Gorda ("Fat Point") was founded shortly after April 12, 1797, when some 3,000 Garífuna deportees from the Caribbean island of San Vicente were stranded on Roatán by the British. After settling in Punta Gorda, many Garífuna continued on, migrating to Trujillo and from there up and down the Caribbean coasts of Honduras, Nicaragua, Guatemala, and Belize, but their first Honduran home remained. The anniversary marking their arrival is cause for great celebration in Punta Gorda. Garífuna from all over the coast attend the event. For most of the year, though, Punta Gorda is simply a sleepy seaside town—dozens of *cayucos* pulled up on the beach, a steady breeze blowing in the palms, and Garífuna residents moving at a very deliberate pace, usually happy to spend a few minutes or hours chatting with a visitor. The only visible evidence of the town's history is a modest statue of Satuyé, the revered Garífuna warrior on San Vicente, located at the entrance to town from the highway.

The beaches in town are not very clean, but not far up the coast you'll find fine patches of open sand, like Camp Bay Beach to the east. Local boat owners will take you there for a negotiable fee. There's snorkeling and diving on the reef near Punta Gorda, but it's for strong swimmers only. Watch out for boat traffic if you swim across the bay to the reef, and remember that the north side of Roatán is choppier than the south and west.

Practicalities

On the main road looping through town (both ends connect to the highway) are a few *pulperías* and *comedores,* a pool hall, and a couple of hotels. It's hard to imagine a reason why anyone would stay here over another place with better beaches and services, but if fate brings you here, the best rooms in town are at **North Side Garden** (tel. 504/435-1848, US$16 s/d, cold water only), in a reasonably attractive two-story wooden house with five tidy rooms, each with a TV, fan and one double bed.

Toward the eastern end of town is **Dayia Internet Café** (8 A.M.–9 P.M. Mon.–Sat., sometimes open Sundays), charging US$2 an hour for Internet.

Although not as frequently patronized as the Oak Ridge boaters, locals will gladly help arrange a **boat tour** of the mangrove tunnels and waterways—teeming with wildlife—costing maybe US$15–20 for an hour's trip, depending on negotiating skills and fuel prices.

Back up at the highway is Satuye Park, which, on days that cruise ships are in, has a handful of **handicraft and souvenir** vendors.

OAK RIDGE

From the highway coming downhill to the water's edge, it seems Oak Ridge is scattered all over the place, clinging to hillsides, cays, and peninsulas all around a large harbor, which is literally the center of town. The harbor has always been the town's entire reason for existence, first serving as a refuge for pirates fleeing Spanish warships, then as the center of a major boat-building industry, and now as home to a fishing fleet and processing plant. Oak Ridge is the capital of the José Santos Guardiola municipality, which covers eastern Roatán.

Perhaps because of its relative remoteness (it's about a 40-minute drive from Coxen Hole to Oak Ridge), more of Oak Ridge's 5,000 residents are obviously of English descent than elsewhere in Roatán. But Spanish-speaking immigrants are beginning to settle in Oak Ridge, particularly along the highway coming into town. Though not a major tourist destination, Oak Ridge is near plenty of pristine, little-known dive sites on the southern and eastern Roatán reef. Two local dive resorts welcome walk-in divers. There are extensive mangrove swamps near town, which can be visited by hiring local boats.

Practicalities

Buses stop at the mainland dock next to a **BGA** (which changes cash and travelers checks and advances money on Visa cards) and the fish-processing plant. From there, a visitor can walk along the shore, past the fish plant all the way around the western end of the harbor, over a small bridge, and out to a narrow point facing the ocean.

Apart from a couple of stores and a weather-beaten wooden church, there's not much on the point, though it's interesting to check out the town and docks. The ocean-facing side of the point has no beach, only exposed, rocky coral, which makes it difficult to get out to snorkel on the reef.

At last check, no budget hotels were open in Oak Ridge, though you might find a room by asking around. For food, however, **BJ's Backyard** (www.roatanonline.com/bj-backyard), on the waterfront, is a local institution. B. J. herself is quite a character, and she turns out great

fish sandwiches, served on homemade bread. To get there, take the road from the highway toward Oak Ridge, bear right, then look for the sign on the left. If you reach the Hondutel office, you've gone too far. Mangrove tours can be arranged at BJ's as well.

From the dock by the bus stop, **water taxis** will take a visitor over to the cay ("cayside") for US$1 or so, though some drivers may try to charge you more. Cayside is much the same as the point; several houses sit among the trees behind the rocky, coral-covered shoreline.

Most cayside tourist visitors are coming to the ◖ **Reef House Resort** (tel. 504/435-1482, U.S. tel. 866/478-4888, www.reefhouseresort .com, weeklong dive and meal packages for US$1,038 pp for a couple), one of the oldest dive resorts on the island—but a well-maintained one, having seen recent renovations. Technically, it's not on Roatán, but on Oakridge Cay, a tiny island a five-minute boat-ride away. The owners dive many little-known south-side sites nearby, including an excellent wall right in front of the hotel. The dive packages include three boat dives daily and unlimited shore diving. Daily rates (which still include all meals) are US$157 nondiver and US$168 diver; and packages can be arranged for any length of stay. Come prepared with your own entertainment (a couple of good books? a deck of cards? a watercolor set to paint the landscape?) for when you're not diving or snorkeling.

Near Oak Ridge

Not far from town in both directions, but especially east, are several beaches. Dory captains on the main dock near the bus stop will transport you there for US$10 return. Longer trips to Barbareta, Pigeon Cay (off Barbareta), Helene, Port Royal, or through the mangrove canals are also possible, for negotiable fees. The mangrove tunnels, formerly used by pirates to hide from their pursuers and now filled with all sorts of wildlife, are frequently recommended as a great trip, usually costing around US$15 an hour. Make sure you agree on the amount of time beforehand, as there have been reports of boatmen giving only 15-minute tours.

EASTERN ROATÁN
Paya Bay
Between Oak Ridge and Punta Gorda, a dirt road turns off the highway to the east, marked by a sign for the **Paya Bay Beach and Dive Resort** (tel. 504/435-1037, U.S. tel. 866/323-5414, www.payabay.com, US$1,479 pp for weeklong dive packages, US$1,247 for nondivers). Far, far off the beaten path, this small hotel is set on a bluff above the ocean, at the point of two lovely, secluded beach-fronted bays. While the decor is a bit dated, who's looking at the furniture when every room has a water view and balcony? The steady breezes keep the rooms cool day and night, although all rooms also have air-conditioning. Daily rates are available, and the nightly rate for room-only is US$150, with dives US$35 each. The dive shop has gear for 30 people and offers Open Water certification; guests can dive many infrequently visited sites on the north side and around Barbareta. Flats-fishing and hiking are available as well as the usual snorkel and scuba. The resort claims to be at its most stunning leading up to and during the full moon and, conveniently, lists those dates on its website, as well as the dates of its "naturist" (clothing-optional) weeks.

Port Royal
The dirt road continues past Camp Bay over the hills to Port Royal, once the site of English pirate camps, now the site of luxury homes for wealthy Hondurans and retired expatriates. Named for the famous port in Jamaica, Port Royal was long the favorite anchorage for marauding pirates because of its protected, defensible harbor. It was chosen by the British military as its base in the 1740s for the same reasons. The British built two small forts to guard the harbor: Fort Frederick on the mainland, with one rampart and six cannons, and Fort George on the cay, with one rampart and 17 cannons. In spite of their heavy armaments, the forts didn't see much service before their destruction in 1782 by a Spanish expedition. The remains of Fort George can still be seen, while the foundations for Fort Frederick now hold a private home.

Currently, no lodgings or restaurants exist in Port Royal, but the mega-resort **Princesa de Roatan** is under construction.

Old Port Royal, farther east, is thought to be the site of the ill-fated Providence Company settlement, dating from the 1630s and 1640s. This is the deepest harbor on the island, though it's no longer used for commerce.

The hills above Port Royal were declared the **Port Royal Park and Wildlife Refuge** in 1978 in an effort to protect the principal watershed for eastern Roatán and several species of endangered wildlife. The refuge has no developed trails for hikers.

East End Islands
East of Port Royal, Roatán peters out into a lowland mangrove swamp, impassable by foot or car, which connects to the island of **Helene,** sometimes called Santa Helena. Just east of Helene is the smaller island of **Morat,** and farther east is **Barbareta,** a two- by five-kilometer island, home to pristine virgin island forest and several lovely beaches. All three islands are surrounded by spectacular reef. A resort once operated on Barbareta, but in recent years the island has become known as a way station for drug runners, and the resort owner wisely decamped.

Southeast of Barbareta are the **Pigeon Cays,** a perfect spot for a relaxed day of picnicking and snorkeling with no one around. Boats to Barbareta, Morat, Helene, and the Pigeon Cays can be hired at the main dock in Oak Ridge.

Utila

Utila feels lost in a tropical time warp. Listening to the broad, almost incomprehensible Caribbean English coming out of islanders with names like Morgan and Bodden, it seems pirates ran amok here just a few years back instead of three centuries ago. Life on Utila still moves at a sedate pace; local conversation is dominated by the weather, the state of the fishing industry, and spicy gossip about the affairs of the 2,000 or so inhabitants.

In the past couple of decades, Utila has gradually come face to face with the modern day. A steadily growing stream of budget travelers flow in from across the globe, all eager to get scuba certification for as little money as possible (about US$270 in early 209, including dorm-style accommodation) and to enjoy the balmy Caribbean waters and famed reef. With its semiofficial designation as the low-budget Bay Island, Utila has become one of those backpacker hot spots like Zipolite or Lake Atitlán—packed with young Europeans and Americans out for a good time in the sun.

Utila is also well known among sea life enthusiasts as one of the best places in the world to see the **whale shark,** the largest fish in the world. These monstrous creatures, getting as big as 15 meters, frequent the Cayman Channel right off Utila and can be spotted (with much patience and a good captain) frequently throughout the year, and particularly in April, May, August, and September.

Timing can be hugely important in making sure that you have the vacation you were looking for in Utila. The rainy season stretches from mid-September to mid-December. Visibility is lower when diving during this season, but reasonable, while snorkeling can be flat-out unappetizing due to the colder weather. The hottest months tend to be April and May. If you do visit during the rainy season, bring a pair of Crocs or other rubber clogs; regular shoes will get muddy and wet, while flip-flops fling droplets of sandy mud up the backs of your calves while you walk.

The opportunity to snorkel with whale

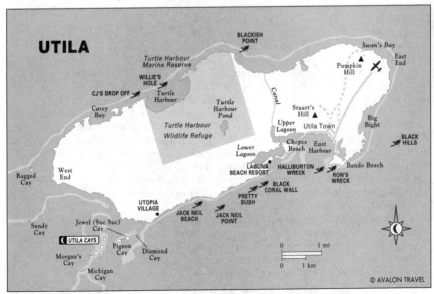

sharks is one of those once-in-a-lifetime travel experiences and, for many, the reason they choose Utila over any other Caribbean island—whale sharks are frequent visitors on the island's north coast. That said, no matter what any hotel or dive shop claims, there is never a guarantee about spotting one, even during the April–May whale shark high season.

Many businesses cater to low-budget travelers, and many of those offer excellent values for their services, be it a dive course, US$10 hotel room, or luscious fish dinner. More recently, slightly more upscale visitors have started arriving, and local hotels and restaurants are beginning to increase their services to this market as a result. But the international backpacker party scene is as strong as ever and will undoubtedly continue for years to come. The majority of backpackers are European, although there are large American and Canadian contingencies as well.

The smallest of the three main Bay Islands, Utila is 11 kilometers long and 5 kilometers wide, with two-thirds of its area covered by swamp. Two small hills on the eastern part of the island, Pumpkin Hill and Stuart's Hill, are volcanic in origin. Sand flies can be voracious on Utila, so come prepared (some swear by Avon's Skin So Soft mixed with a light—10 percent or less—DEET repellent). Just remember that the DEET damages coral; rinse off before you head into the water.

As in Roatán, the Utila reef is under threat from fishermen and careless divers, to say nothing of water pollution. But without the steep hillsides of Roatán and still plenty of undrained wetlands, Utila is not likely to face as serious a water quality problem, at least in the near future. The Bay Islands Conservation Association (BICA) in Utila patrols the entire reef around the island, with the exception of the shallow waters around the cays, where only local residents are allowed to fish. BICA also pays for environmental education in schools and sets up mooring buoys for diver boats.

Utila's name reputedly derives from a contraction of *ocotillo,* which in Nahuatl refers to a place with a lot of black smoke. The smoke is thought to have come from burning the resinous *ocote* pine, supposedly used by pre-Columbian islanders in a type of distilling process.

A good general source of information about Utila can be found at www.aboututila.com, which includes descriptions of dive sites and current average dive prices, as well as information about hotels, restaurants, and other businesses. The website www.utilaeastwind.com is the online home of Utila's monthly local newspaper, and is a good source of info on the island (from local news to restaurant reviews, movie showings, hotel prices, and a directory of phone numbers). The BICA website, www.bicautila.org, also has information on the environment of the island and the reef.

Utila hosts its annual **Carnival** the last full week of July. There are cultural and sporting events, a community bonfire at Chepes beach, and various street parties held in local neighborhoods. Restaurants stay open later, and a few bars even stay open 24 hours a day. If you have a particular accommodation in mind, it's best to reserve well in advance, but the smallest hotels do not typically take reservations, and there's always a room to be found.

UTILA TOWN (EAST HARBOUR)

Almost all Utilians live in East Harbour, on the south side of the island. Universally known simply as Utila, the town wraps around a large harbor that's protected from the open ocean by an arm of reef. The town is divided into four parts: the Point, between the old airport and downtown; Sandy Bay, between the center and the Chepes Beach; the Center, near the main intersection and the municipal dock; and Cola de Mico (meaning Monkey Tail) Road, which cuts inland perpendicular to the shore and leads to the current airstrip. Connecting the old airport, downtown, and Sandy Bay is Main Street. Mamey Lane Road, leaving Main Street in Sandy Bay, also heads inland to the north, roughly parallel to Cola de Mico Road.

Although not a large town in total population, Utila's collection of wooden houses, dive shops, hotels, and restaurants is spread across

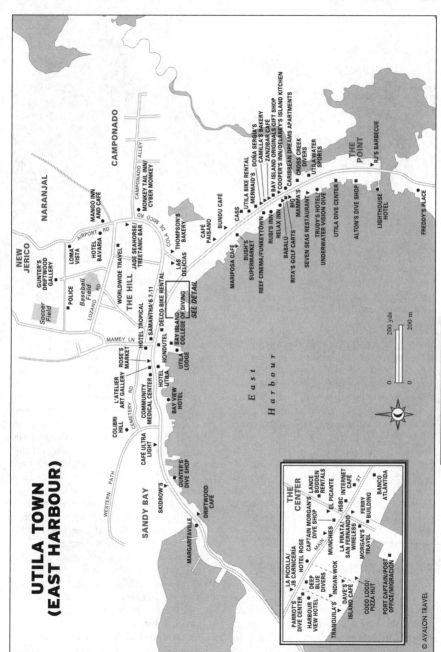

UTILA TOWN
(EAST HARBOUR)

NEW JERICO

NARANJAL

CAMPONADO

THE HILL

SANDY BAY

THE POINT

East Harbour

THE CENTER

SEE DETAIL

0   200 yds
0   200 m

THE BAY ISLANDS

© AVALON TRAVEL

GUNTER'S DRIFTWOOD GALLERY
POLICE
LOMA VISTA
HOTEL BAVARIA
MANGO INN AND CAFÉ
Soccer Field
Baseball Field
AIRPORT RD
LOZANO RD
MAMEY LN
DE MICO RD
COLA RD
WORLDWIDE TRAVEL
JADE SEAHORSE/TREETANIC BAR
MONKEY TAIL INN/CYBER MONKEY
CAMPONADO ALLEY
LAS DELICIAS
THOMPSON'S BAKERY
CAFÉ PAISANO
BUNDU CAFÉ
CASS
CAMILLA'S BAKERY
DOÑA SERGIA'S
ZANZIBAR CAFÉ
UTILA BIKE RENTAL
MERMAID'S
BAY ISLAND ORIGINALS GIFT SHOP
COOPER'S INN/DELANEY'S ISLAND KITCHEN
CARIBBEAN DREAMS APARTMENTS
CROSS CREEK DIVERS
UTILA WATER SPORTS
RJ'S BARBECUE
LIGHTHOUSE HOTEL
FREDDY'S PLACE
ALTON'S DIVE SHOP
UTILA DIVE CENTER
UNDERWATER VISION DIVE
SEVEN SEAS RESTAURANT
TRUDY'S HOTEL
BIG MAMMA'S
BABALÚ
RITA'S GOLF CARTS
RELAX INN
RUBI'S INN
REEF CINEMA/FUNKEYTOWN
BUSH'S SUPERMARKET
MARIPOSA CAFÉ
HOTEL TROPICAL
SAMANTHA'S 7-11
DELCO BIKE RENTAL
BAY ISLAND COLLEGE OF DIVING
UTILA LODGE
HONDUTEL
HOTEL UTILA
BAY VIEW HOTEL
COMMUNITY MEDICAL CENTER
ROSE'S MARKET
L'ATELIER ART GALLERY
COLIBRI HILL
CEMETERY RD
CAFE ULTRA LIGHT
WESTERN PATH
SKIDROW'S
GUNTER'S DIVE SHOP
DRIFTWOOD CAFÉ
MARGARITAVILLE

PARROT'S DIVE CENTER
HARBOUR VIEW HOTEL
DEEP BLUE DIVERS
TRANQUILA'S
INDIAN WOK
DAVE'S ISLAND CAFÉ
COCO LOCO/PIZZA HUT
PORT CAPTAIN/POST OFFICE/MIGRACION
LA PICOLLA/JB CARNICERIA
HOTEL ROSE
CAPTAIN MORGAN'S DIVE SHOP
MUNCHES
SAN FERNANDO WIRELESS
LA PIRATA
MORGAN'S TRAVEL
BODDEN RENTALS
LANCE ST
EL PICANTE
HSBC
INTERNET CAFÉ
FERRY BUILDING
BANCO ATLÁNTIDA
MAIN ST

the town of East Harbour, universally known simply as Utila

© PETER SVANBERG

a largish area. While it's easy enough to walk, renting a bike, golf cart, or scooter can be a fun way to cover the ground between your hotel, dive shop, and favorite restaurants and bars.

While the booming dive industry has brought a lot of money to Utila, native Utilians continue to struggle, especially as all-inclusive dive shops crowd out family-owned hotels and restaurants. Travelers can be sensitive to this situation by making sure to frequent some locally owned businesses during their visit.

Visitors may notice that, unlike everywhere else in Honduras, baseball, not soccer, is the sport of choice on Utila. If you want one of those bonding sports conversations, a pertinent comment on the major leagues will help kick things off.

RECREATION
Dive Shops

If there's any complaint to be leveled against Utila, it's that all anyone ever talks about is diving. All things considered, that's no surprise. Word has gotten out that Utila offers one of the least expensive Open Water scuba certifications in the world, and business has been booming ever since. Competition between shops is fierce, with employees sometimes pursuing potential clients at the docks and on the streets. A whopping 14 shops were in business in Utila at last count. All the competition is wonderful news to the discerning would-be diver, who would be wise to ignore the touts that meet the ferries at the dock and instead spend a bit of time wandering through town, asking around among other travelers and checking out several dive shops before deciding where to go and what courses to take.

Note: Although they are extremely rare, especially considering the very high number of divers passing through the Bay Islands, accidents—including fatal accidents—have occurred on both islands. One advantage of making sure your dive shop is certified by PADI, SSI, or NAUI is that all accidents must be reported and investigated, while noncertified shops can simply fire the dive master/instructor and hire another.

It is certainly true that some shops are more diligent than others, particularly regarding

DIVING UTILA'S REEF

Utila's south-side fringing reef starts relatively close to shore, with tongue-and-groove formations of hard corals in a few meters of water sloping down to the bottom of the reef wall at around 20 meters. Farther south from Utila are numerous sea mounts ringed with reef, known for some of the finest soft corals found in the Bay Islands. Similar to Roatán and Guanaja, Utila's north-side reef is separated from the shore by a lagoon of varying size. The sandy bottom gradually begins to fill in with coral until the reef wall is reached, almost breaking the water surface in places. On the north side, with particularly good dive sites around Turtle Harbour, the wall plunges hundreds of meters over the edge of the continental shelf. Giant sponges and pillar coral are common. Off the east side of Utila are long ridges of elkhorn coral.

Most of Utila's divers frequent sites on the south side of the island, simply because they are quicker and easier to get to from East Harbour than the north side, and also the waters are more protected and tend to be calmer. Ask around for dive shops going to north-side sites, as well as to sea mounts south of the island. Captain Morgan's Dive Shop on Jewel Cay tends to get to the north side more often, by virtue of its location.

SOUTH SIDE

Jack Neil Point and **Jack Neil Beach** are both great long, shallow dives along the tongue-and-groove formations of hard and soft corals. At the western end of the reef here, sightings of hawksbill and green turtles are common.

Among the many similar dives along the southern wall, each starting in around 4 meters of water and dropping to about 30 meters at the base of the reef, **Pretty Bush** and **Black Coral Wall** are two good ones. Despite the name of the latter dive, young black coral is found all along the wall here, as are elkhorn and pillar coral, sea fans, and frequent spotted eagle rays cruising at the deeper sections along the reef wall.

NEAR THE OLD AIRPORT

Right off the point by the old Airport, **Ron's Wreck** isn't all that impressive as wrecks go, but the real attraction is the thriving sea life in the vicinity. A few hundred meters west is another, larger wreck, the *Halliburton*, sunk in 1998 by the local dive association, where careful divers can explore the pilot house and some of the decks.

Farther offshore from the airport, in fact not always easily found by the dive-boat captains, is one of Utila's most popular sites, **Black Hills,** a luscious and varied patch of coral crowning a sea mount. Sharks are common, attracted by the schools of fish that frequent the sea mount.

NORTH SIDE

CJ's Drop Off, at the western end of the reef in front of Turtle Harbour, is famed among divers for the vertigo-inducing coral cliffs plunging straight down into the blue depths. As you descend along the wall, watch for sting rays, moray eels, and hawksbill turtles, and the profusion of giant sponges and hard corals. Be sure to also keep a close eye on that depth gauge as it's easy to lose track with no bottom in sight.

Another popular dive a bit farther east along the same stretch of reef is **Willie's Hole,** a dramatic open cave in the coral wall at around 25 meters, with plenty of pillar and star corals to admire, along with sponges. Don't be surprised to see schools of snapper, jack, and spade fish cruising right past you.

Near the entrance to the old cross-island canal, at the western end of Rock Harbour, is **Blackish Point,** a system of caverns and passages in the reef wall at around 20 meters, with encrusted overhangs to check out. The gentle current makes this a good drift dive.

quality of instructors and upkeep of equipment. Don't make your decision based on price, or at least not exclusively, as most courses and dives cost about the same in the good shops—instead, focus on the background of the instructors (most important), the quality of equipment and boat, your rapport with the dive shop staff, and the quality of the accommodations.

Those who worry about decompression sickness will be glad to hear that Utila has its own **hyperbaric chamber** at the Bay Islands College of Diving (tel. 504/425-3378, VHF channel 71).

Most shops are PADI-certified, and a few have other certifications (SSI and NAUI) as well. Prices currently stand at US$270 for an Open Water or Advanced Open Water course, including accommodations. Those whose prices are slightly higher typically include more things—such as the required PADI notebook (US$7), the daily reef tax (US$4), and drinking water—or have better accommodations. Most classrooms have air-conditioning, which is key if you are on Utila in April or May. If

you're penny-pinching and plan to take advantage of the free accommodation offers, note that a few shops charge US$3 for the first night's stay, some of the dorms are cleaner and more pleasant than others, and a few have hot water. If you are looking for a little more comfort (and a bathroom in your room), consider springing for a private hotel room, either at your shop's affiliated hotel (many shops can get their students a discount) or at a hotel elsewhere in town.

Fun dives currently run US$55 for two (plus the reef tax), and 10-dive packages run US$220–250. Most shops have Open Water courses starting every day, available in English, Spanish, French, Italian, Dutch, and a surprising number of other languages as well—take time to check it out if you are looking for a particular language. (Japanese? Check. Swiss German? Check.)

All of the shops here are PADI-certified and have close to the same prices for all services.

Alton's Dive Center (tel. 504/425-3704, www.diveinutila.com) was named by its former

Sea turtles are easily spotted in the waters around the Bay Islands.

© JOZEF MAERIEN

owner but is now run by a friendly German-Canadian couple who are especially committed to sound environmental practices. PADI certifications are of course available (US$249, including manuals and accommodations but not reef tax), but most notably, Alton's is the only shop on the island offering certifications with NAUI, an organization considered by many to have the highest standards for diving safety (see www.naui.org for more information). Instructors typically have dive counts in the thousands, and readers have reported very positive experiences with the staff. There are kayaks and snorkel equipment available, but for an extra charge. The dorms are not the best in town, nor the cleanest, but acceptable.

Dive masters at **Bay Islands College of Diving** (tel. 504/425-3291, www.dive-utila.com) are pros, and classes are kept small. At the time of our visit, the equipment was very new, and in 2005 the shop won an award for its environmental practices. Like Utila Dive Centre, the college can certify divers all the way up to instructor level. The confined-water dives are done in the shop's indoor pool—a plus for those studying to be instructors, but perhaps less appealing for those in the Open Water certification courses. There is also a Jacuzzi, ideal for relaxing at the end of a long dive day, especially during the cooler rainy season. The only hyperbaric chamber and trauma center on Utila is located at this dive shop (in case you are unlucky enough to get the bends), although it is open to use for any diver in case of emergency. The free accommodation is in the slightly depressing motel-style Hotel Utila, which has fairly steep rates (US$17 s, US$20 d) for those staying on additional nights—but BICD is building its own dorm. This is also the dive shop that forms part of the very nice, but much pricier, Utila Lodge Dive Resort. Boats are spacious and well-maintained.

Captain Morgan's Dive Shop (office near the municipal dock in East Harbour, tel. 504/425-3349, www.divingutila.com) is a bit farther afield than most, run out of the Hotel Kayla on Jewel Cay, a small, tranquil island (with a bit fewer sand fleas) a half-hour boat

© PETER SVANBERG

A dive boat awaits its morning passengers.

THE BAY ISLANDS

ride from East Harbour. All rooms at the hotel have a private bath with cold water, and there is a shared fridge, microwave, and toaster oven. The shop, which has two dive boats, is a great

DIVING RULES AND ETIQUETTE

· Don't dive alone.

· Know your limitations, and only dive if you're in good physical condition.

· Always follow the dive tables.

· Don't anchor anywhere in or near coral – use the buoys.

· Don't litter or discharge foreign substances into the water.

· When diving, always fly a diver-down flag and lower the flag when all divers are back on board. When passing moored boats, or boats flying a diving flag, always pass on the seaward side at least 50 meters (150 feet) away, even in a small boat.

· Avoid contact with any living part of the reef.

· Always observe proper buoyancy techniques and secure dangling equipment.

· Never sit or stand on coral formations, or grab coral to steady yourself.

· Don't grab, poke, ride, or chase reef inhabitants.

· Don't feed the fish.

· Don't fish on the reef.

· Don't remove any marine organisms, alive or dead.

· If you find garbage on the reef, gently remove it and bring it back to shore.

· Take only photographs; leave only bubbles.

place for those who prefer a quieter scene, and trips into town are easily arranged. Its location makes it a lot easier to reach some of the north coast dive sites, considered by many to be the island's best.

Cross Creek (tel. 504/425-3397, www.cross creekutila.com) has the same owner as the Utila Dive Center, but a different vibe, with an entire complex built over the lagoon stretching out behind the shop office. Equipment looks well-maintained, as do the boats, the largest of which is 39 feet and can accommodate 20 divers. They have prescription masks for contact lens wearers. Accommodations are on-site, the free dorm rooms in a long cabin with hammocks hanging in the breezeway. Rooms are acceptable, although not spotless, and a few have their own bathroom (although both the shared and private bath are cold-water only). There's a separate dive master cabin with hot water and—a big step up—four "deluxe" rooms (US$30), in separate cabins built on decks over the mangroves and lagoon, with TVs, hot water, air-conditioning, and minifridges.

Deep Blue Divers (tel. 504/425-3211, www.DeepBlueUtila.com) is a five-star Gold Palm IDC Center, meaning that certification all the way through dive instructor is offered here. The office location is near-perfect for the party crowd: wedged between the island's two most popular bars, Coco Loco and Tranquilo. Class size is limited to just four (although an exception can be made if a group of five friends wants to have the class together). The beginning Open Water certification course is US$249. The shop offers accommodations at a variety of hotels, some with an additional charge (for better rooms).

Ecomarine Gunter's Dive Shop (in Sandy Bay, tel. 504/425-3350, ecomar@gmail.com) offers the beginner's Open Water course for US$259 including two free fun dives as well as accommodation (but not including the reef tax). Kayaks and snorkel equipment are available for rent, and nondivers can ride out on dive boats for a snorkel trip for US$10 (plus equipment rental). Students are put up in the

Backpacker Lodge across the street, which is clean and decent, although cold-water only. Dorm rooms here are US$4 for nondivers, while private rooms are US$10 for nondivers. **Parrots Dive Centre** (tel. 504/425-3772, TatianaLuna22@yahoo.com) is a locally owned dive shop, with a few of those rarest of breeds—Utilian dive instructors. Their accommodations are all private rooms, although always with a shared bath. They have laundry service, as well as a shared kitchen (with two stoves, but never enough forks). Additional nights beyond a course are just US$2, and nondivers can stay for the same rock-bottom price (a room doesn't get any cheaper than this!). There is a doctor on the premises 24/7, and the instructors are highly experienced, most of them having worked at the center for years, in contrast with the high turnover of staff at many other shops. Prices are a touch cheaper than at other centers: US$259 for Open Water certification, night dives for US$40, and 10-dive packages for US$220. Kayaks and snorkeling are free. Parrots is also appealingly located on the same pier as Tranquila's Bar and the Indian Wok.

Underwater Vision (tel. 504/425-3103, www.underwatervision.net) is also locally owned, set on the East Harbour beach front, around a large patch of sand (volleyball net included). The one-day Discover Scuba Diving class is US$80, and the beginner's Open Water course is US$248. The boats are a bit older than at other shops. Free accommodations are at the adjacent Trudy's Hotel, which offers hot showers to guests in the dorms; priceless at the end of a diving day during the rainy season. Private rooms are also available, US$25 for dive students, US$35 otherwise, with funky fish murals, ceiling fans, polished wood floors, and hot water. The breezeway shelters Adirondack chairs and hammocks perfect for relaxing at the end of a challenging day. There are also private rooms with rather grimy, cold-water showers, which can be had as part of the free accommodation in lieu of the dorm.

Utila Dive Centre (on the Point, tel. 504/425-3326, www.utiladivecentre.com)

was the first dive shop opened on the island, in 1991, and is a highly respected shop. In addition to the standard offerings, the shop offers Trimix (a nitrogen-oxygen mix that allows divers to go deeper) and is one of two shops to certify instructors (Bay Islands College of Diving also offers instructor certification). Frequent north-side trips on two 12-meter cabin cruisers are offered; dorm accommodation is at the Mango Inn, including a simple fruit and toast breakfast. While the beginner's Open Water certification (US$279) is a 3.5-day course at most shops, UDC likes to provide a more relaxed pace, taking 4.5 days, and four nights' accommodation are included rather than three.

Utila Water Sports (on the Point, tel. 504/425-3264, www.utilawatersports.com) is one of the few locally owned dive shops, and it has safety-conscious, friendly instructors and several large, very well-maintained dive boats (which they share with the Laguna Beach Resort, under the same ownership). The PADI course is US$249, with four free fun dives, while the SSI course is US$224 (cheaper because it doesn't require the purchase of any books or manuals). The maximum student-teacher ratio is five to one. New accommodations are nearing completion, although hot water was still just an idea rather than a reality. An extra night in the dorm accommodation is US$6, while private rooms are US$12 (US$25 if you're not taking a dive course). The shop also rents out sea kayaks and offers dive trips to the Cayos Cochinos.

Shops selling dive gear include Utila Water Sports, Cross Creek, Utila Dive Centre, and Bay Islands College of Diving. For more information on dive shops and diving in Utila, check out the website www.aboututila.com.

Beaches and Snorkeling

If you take the road east from the center of town, you'll eventually get to **Bando Beach** on the southeastern corner of the island, a groomed, golden beach with several shady *champas* dotting the sand and a large bar *champa* at the entrance. They have public showers and bathrooms and rent snorkel equipment (US$5/

day), kayaks (US$3–5/hour), and paddleboats. Entrance to the beach is US$3 per person. This is the place to be on New Year's Eve.

White-sand **Chepes Beach,** past Sandy Bay on the way out toward Blue Bayou, has a couple of thatch-roof, open-air restaurants, as well as **Patrick's Water Sports** (tel. 504/425-3244), renting Jet-Skis (US$63/hour, US$37/half-hour for two-person; US$79/hour, US$47/half-hour for three-person) and water bananas (US$5.25 pp for a 20-minute ride, with five people max).

Visitors can snorkel at Blue Bayou, a 20-minute walk west of town along the shore, near the mouth of the canal, and at Bando Beach, on the southeastern corner of the island. It's also possible to get in the water at Big Bight, a half-hour walk north of the old airport on the east side of the island, along an unpaved dirt road. You won't see as much colorful coral as on the south-side reef, but rather long ridges of rock and coral, with forests of elkhorn and staghorn coral. Snorkeling and swimming at the airport and Big Bight can be tricky, as the dead coral comes right up to the shore.

All the dive shops rent out snorkel gear for around US$5–7 a day, and many offer it for free if you are diving with them and just want to take a break from scuba. Many will also allow snorkelers to come out on appropriate dives to snorkel while the others scuba.

Kayaking, Boating, and Fishing

Light sea kayaks make a fine way to explore the canals in the center of the island or to tie off at dive buoys and snorkel. Make sure to get detailed directions to find the southern mouth of the cross-island canal, as it can be tricky to locate.

Besides the kayaks at Bando Beach, **Ecomarine Gunter's** (tel. 504/425-3350) and **Cross Creek** (tel. 504/425-3134) both rent sea kayaks for US$7 half-day, US$10 full-day, slightly more for a double kayak.

Note: Visitors should take good care when paddling out into the open water on sea kayaks. Choppy waters and ocean winds can quickly get the better of inexperienced kayakers. If in any doubt at all, stick close to shore and be

© SARAH STEINBERG

A tourist shows off her catch, a giant red snapper.

absolutely sure you have enough energy not only to get out, but to get back, too.

Yacht skippers should call VHF channel 16 to request check-in and clearance-procedure information with Utila Harbour Authority (in Spanish), or go visit the port captain's office next to the police station. Anchoring is permitted in East Harbour and in the Utila Cays Channel for a US$10 monthly fee; always use anchor lights, and do not empty bilges in the harbor or near land. Larger boats may dock at the municipal wharf for a daily docking fee, or get in touch with Troy Bodden at the fuel dock (tel. 504/425-3264), who has water and power hookups for free, but only to take on fuel and water and shop in town. The owners of Utila Lodge (tel. 504/425-3143) can also help find a place to dock.

Fishing trips can be arranged through local fishermen, and lots of signs are up around town. Tarpon, bone fish, mullet, white pompano, and flying fish are all common to the waters around Utila. Fishermen are also happy to arrange trips to the Utila Cays.

Walks and Exploration

The point at Blue Bayou, a 20-minute walk west of town, marks the southern entrance to the cross-island canal, which is fast closing up because it was man-made and now mangrove cutting is illegal. With considerable effort and a local guide, it may still be possible to get up the canal and across a trail to the west to **Turtle Harbour Pond,** in the center of the island. On the north side of the island west of where the canal lets out are a couple of small, deserted beaches accessible by boat only.

From the end of Cola de Mico Road, a paved road continues four kilometers out to the airport, where it is possible to walk across the airstrip to the beach on the north coast and continue west to **Pumpkin Hill Beach.** Much of the coast here is covered with fossilized coral and rocks, but a few patches of sand provide good spots to put down a towel and relax in splendid isolation. Negotiating a safe passage into the water to swim and snorkel is no easy task, but in calm weather the determined will make it. Near the beach is **Pumpkin Hill,** 82 meters high and riddled with caves, one of which is the sizable **Brandon Hill Cave,** reputedly containing pirate treasure. When the weather is dry, a dirt road continues back toward Utila Town, a shorter return than via the airport, but a complete mud bog when it has been raining.

Closer to town is **Stuart's Hill,** like Pumpkin Hill a former volcano. From the top are good views over town and the south side of the island.

Horseback Riding

Red Ridge Horse Stables (tel. 504/425-3143 or 504/3390-4817, kisty@utilalodge.com) offers two-hour rides that explore the beach and some local caves, for US$25–35. Riders can sign up at any dive shop. Same day rides can often be arranged, if you haven't reserved in advance.

ENTERTAINMENT
(Nightlife

With such an eclectic assortment of young travelers from around the globe, as well as a sizable population of fun-loving locals, it's no surprise that Utila has a flourishing nightlife. While the favored location varies depending on one's mood during the week, Friday night invariably sees a large crowd at the **Bar in the Bush,** literally in the bush at the outskirts of town on Cola de Mico Road, a 15-minute walk from the waterfront. The sprawling cabaña complex, with an attached volleyball court, has an unusually loose, festive ambiance, with an odd mix of people wandering about with drinks in hand, enjoying the grooving music. It's open Wednesdays and Fridays only ("9 P.M. till late"). The bar is a few minutes walk on a dark road heading out of town; walking alone back to your hotel is not recommended.

About the favorite bar in town with foreign visitors is **Tranquila Bar** (3 P.M.–midnight Sun.–Thurs., 3 P.M.–3 A.M. Fri.–Sat.), offering one of the few full bars on the island, with a variety of premium liquors, 25 creatively named shooters (Swamp Water, Chameleon, Scooby

THE BODDENS

Spend any time on Utila, and you'll soon notice that Bodden is a well-distributed last name. Boddens on Roatán as well. And wait, again in the Mosquitia.

The original Boddens came from the Cayman Islands – the first as a deserter of Oliver Cromwell's army, when it took Jamaica in 1655. His grandson Isaac Bodden was born on Grand Cayman around 1700, and was the first recorded permanent inhabitant of the Cayman Islands.

Settlers came from the Caymans to Utila and Roatán around 1835, bringing their Bodden surname with them (the surname Cooper arrived at the same time, thanks to the immigration of Joseph Cooper, his wife, and their nine children, Brits who arrived to Utila via the Cayman Islands).

Far away on the Mosquitia, in the tiny community of Raistá, there are Miskitos that also bear the last name Bodden. Nearly a century ago, a young Miskito from Nicaragua crossed into Honduras and made his way to Roatán, where he was adopted by an English-speaking family with the surname Bodden (one of the English-blooded Caymanians, no doubt). He took their name and brought it back to the mainland when he left the islands to work for the United Fruit Company in Puerto Castilla (near Trujillo). In the late 1950s he returned to his native land, the Mosquitia, met his wife and stayed, founding the community of Raistá, whose 180 residents today are nearly all descendants. During our 2009 visit to Raistá, community founder William Bodden was still alive, and estimated to be 106 or 107 years old.

Snack, Sex with the Captain), and a number of cocktails. The large, multicolored bar, driftwood lounge, and dockside tables always host a crowd of tourists and locals and the music is a quality mix of rock, reggae, and nostalgic '70s and '80s tunes.

Another popular spot, with a bit more of a party, electronica vibe, is **Coco Loco Bar** (4 P.M.–midnight Sun.–Thurs., 4 P.M.–1 A.M. Fri.–Sat.), two doors away—another laid-back oceanfront place to chill out with some tunes and a drink. Happy hour, at sunset, features two-for-one drinks.

One unusually located drinking establishment is **Treetanic Bar** (4 P.M.–midnight daily), literally a treehouse bar in the shape of a boat, very creatively designed and decorated in the canopy of a mango tree to the side of the Jade Seahorse restaurant. The cocktails are a bit more expensive than at other bars but are exceptional, and the surroundings are unbeatable—an elevated walkway leads off the bar, meandering above the creatively landscaped grounds, to a couple of semiprivate seating areas, all like something out of a Dr. Seuss book.

Not quite as unusual, but still very charming is **Babalú** (4 P.M. onwards daily), Utila's oldest dock bar newly revamped. Run by Italian expat Dado, the bar is smaller than Tranquila or Coco Loco, with weathered wood, oars hanging from the ceiling, and oil lamps. Only two kinds of beer (US$1.20) are offered, along with well drinks (US$1.50), but at these rock-bottom prices, who's complaining? A simple and inexpensive menu is available as well, if you are looking for some munchies with your drink.

Over in Sandy Point, **Driftwood Café** has a relaxed bar scene with a mix of expats and locals (some of whom are known to play raucous dice games). The house specialty is Monkey Balls shooters, of vodka and house-made kahlua.

Farther along, **La Champa** (tel. 504/425-3893, noon–midnight Wed. and Sat. nights only, and Sun. during the day) is a huge bamboo and thatch-roof restaurant and bar decorated with wild orchids right on Chepes Beach. They play mellow music, sometimes live, and attract a laid-back, mostly expat crowd. Besides the full bar, they have an extensive menu of fajitas, quesadillas, burgers, and the like for US$3–6 a plate. Their "shuttle service," a multicolored golf cart, will transport customers to and from town (about a 10-minute walk).

The billiard aficionado can find two small **pool halls,** on Cola de Mico across from the Jade Seahorse, although they are usually the exclusive domain of Honduran mainlanders. Both are best visited early as the crowd can get a little rough later on. Beer is served.

Late-night incidents walking home after a night at the bars were once a problem, but locals have pretty much stopped it entirely by instituting "tourist police" who patrol at night, with radios to call regular police. Nonetheless, it's not a bad idea to walk home in groups.

Reef Cinema shows several movies a week in a well-designed theater, at 7:30 P.M.

Shopping

Bay Island Originals (tel. 504/425-3372, 9 A.M.–noon and 2–6 P.M. Mon.–Fri., 9 A.M.–noon Sat.) sells locally designed T-shirts, Honduran coffee and cigars, and a variety of better quality tourist collectibles as well as the usual junk. Swimsuits and sunglasses are also available here, if yours have been forgotten at home.

Local character of note Gunter, a German who has lived on the island for many years and who started (but since retired from) the dive shop bearing his name, now dedicates much of his time to sculpture and painting, many works created with natural materials like driftwood found on the beach. Gunter's latest thing is "resin" art, using resin to make different pieces (like shells) appear to float, in an attempt to capture the feel of the underwater world. He also makes jewelry. He shows (and sells) his works at **Gunter's Driftwood Gallery** (tel. 504/425-3113), in his house just off Cola de Mico Road. The best time to visit is in the afternoon, or better yet, call first to make sure he's home.

Another great place to buy art is at **L'Atelier** (tel. 504/3254-6808, 11 A.M.–6 P.M. Mon.–Sat.), the workshop of Argentinian transplant Patricia Suarez. Prices of her abstract paintings

are based on size, and a steal considering the quality, starting at just US$10 for a postcard-sized painting and going up to US$500 for a large canvas.

One place in town with a very good selection of used books for sale or exchange is **Funkytown,** on the ground floor of the Reef Cinema (9 A.M.–7:30 P.M. Mon.–Sat.), from classics to beach trash to foreign language.

ACCOMMODATIONS

In keeping with its status as the least expensive Bay Island, Utila has a plethora of budget rooms for the backpacker crowd, most about US$6–15 d. In recent years the range of rooms has broadened, with several new midrange places and a few higher-end (though still decidedly low-key) resorts. Most of the hotels are in small, wooden buildings, often converted houses, so their proliferation is not visually overwhelming.

One tip for divers: All the dive shops have either lodges or affiliations with hotels and offer free accommodation with a beginner's Open Water certification course, or discounted with other courses or fun dives, typically US$3–5. Although many local families who own small hotels have been put into a difficult situation because of this, it suits budget travelers just fine. All rent out rooms to nondivers as well.

When inquiring at hotels, one important question is whether the establishment has hot water or not. While hot showers may not normally be a question of great importance to some travelers, they can be awfully pleasurable after a day of scuba diving, especially in the rainy season when it's cooler.

Note that while check-out time on the mainland is typically noon, on Utila it's usually 10 A.M.

Under US$10

In addition to the hotels listed, some pricier hotels (such as Mango Inn and Trudy's Hotel) also have dorm rooms for US$10 or under.

The price that can't be beat is at **Harbour View Hotel** (tel. 504/425-3772, tatiana luna22@yahoo.com), where rooms rent for the bargain basement price of US$2 per person. While the bathrooms are shared, and the water is cold, the place is clean enough, and conveniently shares the pier with a couple of the most popular establishments in town, Tranquila bar and Indian Wok restaurant. Harbour View is affiliated with Parrots Dive Center and gives priority to divers and nondiving friends who are accompanying them.

Another good deal is **Loma Vista** (tel. 504/425-3243, US$7 pp), with clean, sunny rooms with communal kitchen facilities (sink and burners, but no fridge) and a porch with a picnic table and hammock.

The simple rooms at **Monkey Tail Inn** (tel. 504/425-3155, US$5.25 pp) are in need of a paint job, but there's a small porch and wireless Internet throughout the hotel, and it's also home to Cyber Monkey Internet café. It's acceptably clean, although flip-flops are recommended for the concrete cold-water showers.

US$10-25

Cooper's Inn (tel. 504/425-3184, www.coopers-inn.com, US$10 s, US$13 d), past Rubi's on the other side of the road, has clean, well-maintained rooms with fans and mosquito nets, shared bathroom (cold-water only), and access to a shared kitchen, though guests are likely to be tempted by the excellent dinners served in front at Delany's Island Kitchen. The inn is conveniently close to several of the dive shops, for those out-of-bed-into-the-dive-boat mornings. Owner Carissa Cooper is a native Utilian, and a good source of information about the island.

Freddy's Place (tel. 504/425-3819, FreddysPlace@gmail.com, US$16 s/d, US$35 with a/c), just over the bridge going toward Bando Beach from downtown, rents the rooms in four two-bedroom apartments with fans. If you rent only one bedroom, you may share the rest of the apartment with another guest; a group that rents both bedrooms will obviously have the whole apartment for themselves. The owner, Fred, a retired fisherman who lived for years in Alaska, is a genial character. Low-season and long-term rates are available. The

building is in a quiet part of town, with a wrap-around deck facing the canal.

Located above the owner's home, the rooms at **Hotel Bavaria** (tel. 504/425-3809, petra whitefield3@hotmail.com, US$13 s, US$16 d) are simple and clean, and just a short walk up Cola de Mico Road. Each has a fan and private bath (cold water only), and they share a porch.

If you want to stay closer to the beach, consider **Margaritaville** (tel. 504/425-3366, US$20 s/d with fan, or US$40 with a/c), opposite Driftwood Café. The 16 breezy, spacious rooms are fairly basic, but each has a clean, tile-floor bathroom, and some have a kitchenette. The hotel's deck affords views of both the harbor and lagoon.

Next to the Utila Lodge, near the Bay Island College of Diving, is the motel-style **Hotel Utila** (tel. 504/425-3340, US$17–58), with rooms varying in price depending on the room size and whether it has air-conditioning or a fan. The whole place is a bit dreary. If you're considering springing for air-conditioning, you can get better value rooms elsewhere.

US$25-50

◖ **Rubi's Inn** (tel. 504/425-3240, US$18 s, US$25 d) on the main road not far from the center of town heading toward the old airport, on the ocean side of the road, offers spotless rooms with private baths and hot water. The pretty garden and cute white house with blue trim hide a much newer property behind: a two-story wooden lodge next to the water. Air-conditioning is available for significantly more, and there is a communal kitchen available, as well as picnic tables for eating your meal or relaxing with a beer. There is one "honeymoon suite" on the second floor with refrigerator, microwave, and private balcony over the water for US$38 d. Laundry service is available to guests and nonguests.

Relax Inn (tel. 504/425-3879, US$35 d, US$40 with a/c), across from Camilla's Bakery and close to several dive shops, has four clean, basic rooms in an attractive wood building, each with refrigerator and hot water. There's a small private dock leading off the hotel's porch.

The owners live on the property and are known to invite guests for an excellent home-cooked meal from time to time.

The family-owned **Trudy's Hotel** (tel. 504/425-3103, US$35 s/d with a/c, US$65 suites with TV, mini-fridge, microwave, and a/c) is a fairly new two-story wood building set along the water's edge, although rooms face a patch of sand rather than the water. Funky fish murals are painted on the walls, and Adirondack chairs grace the breezeway, perfect for relaxing after a day of diving. Nondiving hotel guests can ride out with divers for a snorkel at no charge.

Conveniently located right in the center of town is **Hotel Rose** (tel. 504/425-3127, US$16 s, US$26 d with fan, US$5 more with a/c), a decent deal with hot water, fan, and TV, more for air-conditioning. The upstairs terrace has a fine view of the harbor and is a great place to relax in the afternoon and evening.

US$50-100

The newly renovated **C Lighthouse Hotel** (tel. 504/425-3164 www.utilalighthouse.com, US$50 s, US$65 d) is a great addition to Utila's hotel scene. Built on a pier over the water, the rooms are classy, with ivory wood-paneled walls, blonde wood furniture, and sliding glass doors that maximize light. A couple of rooms command spectacular views of the harbor. Amenities include TV, air-conditioning, a sink and microwave, and a wireless Internet hotspot by the hotel office. There are also two smaller rooms in the building that houses the hotel office with four bunks each, for US$40 a night. Native Utilian Owen O'Niel and his Louisiana wife, Thelma Bodden, go out of their way to ensure that each guest has a wonderful visit to the island.

Colibri Hill Resort (tel. 504/425-3329, www.colibri-hotel.com, US$45 s, US$50 d, US$10 off during low season) is a bit of a mixed bag. Really simply a hotel rather than a resort, the property does have a small swimming pool, and a three-story building with attractive rooms for reasonable prices. Details, however, are often overlooked; at our visit the shower curtain was moldy, and a window

shade was missing from one of the guest rooms. Although it's only 10 minutes from the center of town, the last stretch of road can be deserted at night, with the final block down a street without lighting (bring a flashlight!).

Two blocks along Cola de Mico Road, the cabins, buildings, and swimming pool of the **Mango Inn** (tel. 504/425-3335, www.mango-inn.com, US$55–150 depending on the size and furnishings of room, US$5–20 off during low season) are set in a lush garden, with palm trees and flowers lining brick paths. The cabins are very nice, with tasteful decorations and details like purified water and a coffee maker in the room. The deluxe and standard rooms are a little older, but still pleasant. A few rooms have been converted into dorms, which can fill with divers from Utila Dive Centre, but if there's a space free, it goes for US$10 a night. The shared bathrooms have cold water only, at least for now, but they're clean, as are the dorms, and it's the only dorm with access to a pool. The restaurant, Mango Café, is run by an Italian expat and serves pizza and pasta, among other things.

A most exceptional array of accommodations, certainly out of the ordinary, is found at **C Nightland Cabins at Jade Seahorse** (tel. 504/425-3270, www.jadeseahorse.com, US$100 s/d, US$25 off during low season), located behind the Jade Seahorse restaurant on Cola de Mico Road. Six fantastical cabins with twisted roofs, multicolored windows, carved wood accents, and mosaics in every nook and cranny are tucked into a tropical garden with various octagonal wooden decks, mosaic archways, brick and wood bridges, and gazebos with seating areas. All the rooms have a different color scheme and theme (Shangrila, Mona Lisa, Cama Sutra, Dalai Lama). One of the cabins even has a rooftop porch with views out to the sea. All come with air-conditioning, hot water, refrigerator, and (essential in the rainy season) umbrella.

Dive Resorts

The best-established dive resort in Utila is **The Utila Lodge** (tel. 504/425-3143, U.S.

tel. 800/282-8932, www.utilalodge.com, dive packages are US$1,100–1,275 per week depending on the season, double occupancy, or US$87/night, room only). The lodge, run by Americans Jim and Kisty Engel, occupies the dark-wood building next to the Bay Islands College of Diving, which is its partner dive shop. It has its own dock for fishing boats and dive boats, as well as eight slightly dated but nice rooms with TV, air-conditioning, and private balconies. Rates include three good cafeteria-style meals and three boat dives daily. Nondivers pay US$985–1,159 a week. Jim is an avid fisherman and will arrange flats or deep-sea fishing trips for guests. The hotel has use of the BICD's small swimming pool and hot tub, free Internet for guests, a bar over the water, a sundeck, and a pool table. The max number of guests is 16, with a full-time staff of 10. The restaurant is open to nonguests as well, and the bar and dock are great spots to watch the sunset.

On the south side of the island and the west side of the canal is **(Laguna Beach Resort** (tel./fax 504/425-3264, U.S. tel. 800/668-8452, www.lagunabeachresort.info, US$1,465–1,495 pp double occupancy for a seven-night package, or US$225–230 pp/night, with discounts for nondivers and low-season, and surcharges for single occupancy). Packages include dives, meals, snorkeling, horseback riding, and use of kayaks and bicycles. The locally owned resort (same owners as Utila Water Sports) offers 13 bungalows with air-conditioning and a two-bedroom beach house, all set on a private sandy peninsula accessible only by boat. Rooms are not luxurious, but attractive with polished wood floors, and each bungalow has a small dock that leads out into the water. It's a wonderful spot if you're looking for a secluded place to forget about the world for a while. Swimming and snorkeling are fantastic right off the beach out front, and there is a large swimming pool for those who prefer fresh water. Flats and deep-sea fishing on one of their three fishing boats, windsurfing, and sea-kayaking trips are available, and shore diving is unlimited. Trips to town are regularly

available. Equipment is top-notch, and the dive boats are very well-maintained.

(Utopia Village (tel. 504/3344-9387, www.utopiadivevillage.com) is without a doubt the fanciest digs on the island. Owned by a group of partners from the U.S., U.K., and Canada, Utopia is another secluded, all-inclusive resort, with its own private beach. High season rates range US$1,717–1,972 for seven-night dive packages, and fishing and spa/romance packages are available as well, with special rates available for shorter stays. Rooms are elegant, with polished wood floors, good quality linens, and accents in woven rattan and stone. Facilities include a gourmet restaurant on-site, a full-service spa, and of course, a dive center. Basic packages do not include as many services as at Laguna Beach, but can be customized. No children under the age of 15 are allowed. The PADI Open Water certification course is a whopping US$450, but Advanced Open Water is a more standard US$275.

Deep Blue Resort (tel. 504/9834-4399, www.deepblueutila.com) is run by a British family, also located on a lagoon accessible only by boat. The rooms are nothing fancy, nor is the food, and admittedly the aging dive boat is a bit slow when heading around the island to dive sites on the revered northern coast. That said, overall it's a pleasant place to stay, and guests rave about the dive masters, and diving is what you came for, isn't it? Rates range US$1,014–1,878 for a seven-night dive package, double occupancy.

There are a couple of much cheaper places that describe themselves as dive resorts, but there's some truth to the maxim "you get what you pay for." Accommodations are basic, and service can be a mixed bag. Better midrange options can be had by arranging your own accommodations at a place like Lighthouse, Trudy's Hotel, or Mango Inn, and choosing your dive shop separately.

Certainly Utila's most unique opportunity, the *Utila Aggressor* (www.aggressor.com) is a live-aboard yacht that can accommodate up to 14 guests. One of a worldwide chain of live-aboard dive yachts, it is (as of the time of writing) the least expensive *Aggressor* in the world, offering five-star accommodation on board for a "mere" US$2,200 per person for a week. It is also perhaps the smallest *Aggressor*—be prepared for tight quarters.

Apartments

With so many travelers finding themselves transfixed by Utila's reefs and low-key lifestyle, plenty of apartments are up for rent. Prices can range anywhere from US$200–600, depending on what kind of place you're looking for, but average places go for US$400–500 a month for a one-bedroom. Among the **hotels offering long-term rentals** are Cooper's Inn (US$400/month for a one-bedroom, US$550/month for a two-bedroom) as well as Freddy's Place and Countryside Inn.

Bananaville Apartments (tel. 504/3369-2298, rm.paradisecove@gmail.com) is one recommended lodging, in a residential area roughly 15 minutes walk from the municipal dock. The one-bedroom apartments rent for US$500 per month, and two single beds can be added to squeeze in four people if needed. Monthly renters are preferred, but weekly renters are considered based on availability, at the rate of US$150 per week. **Sandstone Apartments** (tel. 504/425-3692), out on the point, offers rentals for US$450–800 per month, while a one-bedroom at the newly constructed **Caribbean Dreams** is US$450 a month. Many other places can be found by asking around, particularly through dive masters and instructors, or on www.aboututila.com.

FOOD

Travelers will be pleased to hear that they can feed themselves on some excellent food in Utila, and for reasonable prices, due to the high competition and also large number of creative cooks, both islander and expat. You'll find everything from tasty *baleada* snacks to great pizza and fried chicken to superlative seafood prepared in all sorts of inventive ways, generally in large, diver-friendly portions.

Restaurants in Utila are all fairly casual, in keeping with the diver/backpacker clientele, and don't take reservations. You may also find yourself spending a lot of time at restaurants, because service on the island tends to be rather relaxed. Those in a hurry might consider buying ready-made sandwiches and snacks at the several bakeries in town, or going to Mermaid's buffet.

Breakfasts and Baked Goods

❰ Thompson's Café and Bakery (6 A.M.–8 P.M. Mon.–Sat., 6 A.M.–2 P.M. Sun.), on Cola de Mico Road not far from the main intersection, sells utterly fantastic and inexpensive breakfasts. It's always packed with divers stuffing themselves with pancakes, omelets, and the famous johnnycake (biscuits served plain or like a McDonald's Egg McMuffin) and washing it all down with a mug of surprisingly good coffee before running out to their 7:30 A.M. dive. Delectable coconut bread and cinnamon rolls are sold to go, and lunch and dinner are available as well. Burgers, biscuits, *baleadas,* and *burritas* are US$0.65–2, while breakfast and dinner plates (*comida típica* as well as items like pork chops) are about US$3.75.

Munchies (tel. 504/425-3168, 7 A.M.–5 P.M. Mon.–Sat.), on the first floor of a rambling wooden house just west of the dock on Main Street, serves up a solid breakfast with eggs, bacon, hash browns, juice, and strong coffee for US$4 (available all day). It also has sandwiches and salads. The front porch is a fine spot to greet the day and watch the town amble by.

Next to Bush's Supermarket, **GB's** (6:30 A.M.–2 P.M. daily) has a small selection of English tea, scones, meat pies, and toast with toppings like Nutella and Marmite. The iced coffee is tasty, and a light breakfast will only set you back US$2–3.

A bit farther east is **Camilla's Bakery** (8:30 A.M.–2 P.M. Mon.–Fri.), set back from the road in the pink building just before Zanzibar, serving freshly baked croissants, bagels, and baguettes as well as cakes, muffins, and cinnamon rolls. For a quick lunch, stop in for a ready-made ham-and-cheese croissant.

Zanzibar's is a good spot for breakfast, with fluffy pancakes and great smoothies (about US$4), and is open at lunch as well, serving subs and the like.

Honduran

A few steps beyond Rubi's Inn, on the opposite side of the street, is a white shack run by **Doña Sergia,** serving up fresh juices, snacks, and meals such as *baleadas,* tamales, tacos, pork chops, pasta, and even a vegetarian plate. There's nowhere to sit, but at these prices (US$1–4), who's complaining? You can even book a massage with Doña Sergia for the rock-bottom price of US$10 (for 30 minutes).

If you're not in the mood to sit around waiting for your meal, try the buffet at locally owned **Mermaid's** (tel. 504/425-3395, 11 A.M.–10 P.M. Sun.–Thurs., 11 A.M.–3 P.M. Fri. and 6–10 P.M. Sat.), on the Point, east of the municipal dock. Offerings include creamy mashed potatoes, fried rice, baked potatoes, fried chicken, BBQ chicken, meatballs, and fried fish balls. Combo plates, including drinks, cost US$4–5. There's an open-air seating area, plus a room with air-conditioning— perhaps the only air-conditioned dining on the island. There's also an attached Internet café.

Big Mamma's (6 A.M.–3 P.M. Mon.–Sat.), opposite Cross Creek, serves popular inexpensive (US$3.50) daily specials in a bright green restaurant with a nautical theme, but unfortunately the quality is inconsistent.

Seafood and Meats

Locally owned **(** **RJ's Barbecue** (6–9:30 P.M. Wed., Fri., and Sun.), just before the bridge toward the old airport, serves up enormous portions of fresh fish, frequently snapper and tuna, thick steaks, and chicken. Go early as the small restaurant fills up fast and has been known to run out of food.

Also locally owned, **Seven Seas Restaurant** (tel. 504/425-7377, 8 A.M.–10 P.M., closed Sun. and Tues.), on the point across from Utila Water Sports, serves fresh seafood, good fried chicken, inexpensive *baleadas,* burgers, and delicious pork specials. A *baleada* will set you back US$0.60–1.30, while burgers and other meals run US$3–8.50.

On the third floor of the corner building at the municipal dock is locally owned **La Pirata** (tel. 504/425-3988, noon–10 P.M.

daily), serving snacks and light meals (US$3– 10) such as ceviche, chicken wings, and burgers, as well as bigger indulgences such as lobster and T-bone steaks (most meals US$6–13, except the lobster, which goes for US$26). There is a nice outdoor deck with nice views across the town and harbor.

Over in Sandy Bay, Texas transplants Bruce and Sharon specialize in smoked meats and crispy beer-battered seafood at their **(** **Driftwood Café** (11 A.M.–10 P.M. daily). Sandwiches and burgers run US$4–7, while seafood dishes and meats from the grill are US$7– 10. The restaurant is built out over the water and offers a spectacular view with its meals. Alternatively, come here for a sunset drink— which after a couple shooters of Monkey Balls (vodka and housemade kahlua) may turn into a long and lovely evening at the bar.

International

One of the best restaurants on the island just got better: San Francisco chef and long-time Utila resident Dave Ayarra took over The Island Café. **(** **Dave's Island Café** (6:30– 9:30 P.M. Tues.–Sat.) is next to Coco Loco Bar. The menu changes daily, and might include barracuda fillet in mango-chili sauce or masala chicken curry, and there is always a creative vegetarian option (a relief if you've been eating nothing but rice and beans during your Honduras visit). Main dishes run about US$5–7.

Utilian-owned **El Picante** (noon–2 P.M. and 4–10 P.M. Sun.–Thurs., 6–10 P.M. Sat.) serves up tasty fajitas and other Mexican standards.

Perhaps the best addition to Utila's dining scene is **(** **Indian Wok** (tel. 504/3325-1934, 6 P.M. onwards Sun.–Thurs., although possibly changing to Mon.–Sat. in the future), located on the same pier as Tranquila Bar and Parrots Dive Center. It's run by Canadians Shawn Thompson and Christine Peach, and the daily-changing menu has dishes from around Asia. There are usually both Indian and Thai curries, sushi rolls, and often the very popular Vietnamese spring rolls. Lighting is low, and the ambiance features soft music, candles, and cloth tablecloths. Prices range US$8–11 for oversized portions, and half portions are available for as little as US$4.

Popular with travelers is **Bundu Café** (tel. 504/425-3557, 8 A.M.–2:30 P.M. and 5–9:30 P.M. Fri.–Tues.) on Main Street just east of the center of town, serving crepe and waffle breakfasts, panini and salad lunches, and uncommon dinner dishes such as "beer con chicken" and deep-dish pizza (breakfasts US$3.50–5, lunch and dinner US$5–12).

Built out over the water, **Mariposa Café** (tel. 504/9754-9957, 11 A.M.–10 P.M.) is one of the prettiest places in Utila for a meal. The chef focuses on sourcing local meats, seafood, poultry, and seafood, and they have a wood-burning oven for making their own breads (not to mention pizzas). While the café was temporarily closed during our low-season visit (everyone deserves a vacation sometime, we suppose), it's reader-recommended. Main dishes average US$5–10.

An unusual find on Utila, started by a transplanted Israeli and now run by an Utila woman who worked with him, is **Ultra Light Café** (tel. 504/425-3201, 7 A.M.–10 P.M. Sun.–Fri.) in Sandy Bay, with low-priced and healthy Middle Eastern–style food, such as falafel, hummus, and *zlabia*.

The burritos (US$4) at funky and fun **Skidrow's** (6–9 P.M.) in Sandy Bay (opposite EcoMarine Dive Shop) are huge and filling. Come by on Mondays for a raucous Pub Quiz, popular with the expats.

Italian

La Piccola – Kate's Italian Cuisine (tel. 504/425-3746, 5–10 P.M. Wed.–Sun.), on Main Street west of the dock, is managed by Kate, an Italian expat who makes her own ravioli and gnocchi, and several types of very good sauces, such as the *vesuviana,* of olives, capers, and tomatoes. She also offers imported beef and fresh fish entrées. Much of the seating is on an outdoor terrace, surrounded by a pretty wood trellis with winding flower vines, while indoors is painted in warm cream and rust tones with a cute wine bar (with a decent

selection of wines) in the center. It's a bit more upscale than most in Utila, with cloth tablecloths and candles, not to mention good service, but still relaxed. Spaghetti "backpacker specials" are about US$5, while the other dishes are in the US$7–16 range.

Mango Café (tel. 504/425-3326, 6:30 A.M.–9:30 P.M. daily), located at the Mango Inn, serves a variety of entrées, including fresh fish and lasagna, as well as well-loved brick-oven pizzas. Although expensive for their size (US$7.50–11 for a pie that feeds one hungry person or two not-so-hungry people), the pizzas have tasty toppings and crispy crusts.

Delany's Island Kitchen (tel. 504/425-3184, 5:30–10 P.M., closed Wed. and Sun.) is managed by Delany's daughter Carissa, offering generously portioned lasagna and superb pizza, as well as delicious fish in a creamy garlic-lemon sauce. Locals love to pick up a pie for take-out—not a bad idea if your hotel has a deck with a sunset view, although the hanging rice paper lanterns and strands of colored lights lend the seating area some nighttime charm. A meal here will set you back US$6–9.

Pizza Nut at Coco Loco Bar is another popular place to grab a pie.

Groceries

Several stores in town sell fresh produce, cheese, milk, and other perishables, stocked by thrice-weekly shipments from the mainland. Most are open Monday–Saturday only. **Bush's Supermarket** (tel. 504/425-3147, 6:30 A.M.–6 P.M. Mon.–Sat., 6:30 A.M.–noon Sun.) offers the biggest variety of food and the cleanest facilities on the island, and is also one of the few stores open on Sunday. **Samantha's 7-11,** across from the fire station on the way to Sandy Bay, is useful because it stays open until 11 P.M., but selection is limited and prices are on the high side.

A good meat market, though on the small side, is **JB Carnicería** (tel. 504/425-3671, 7 A.M.–noon and 2–6 P.M. Mon.–Sat., 7 A.M.–noon Sun.), with fresh seafood and meat (including beef, pork, chicken) daily.

INFORMATION AND SERVICES
Research Centers and Volunteering

There is a surprising number of volunteer opportunities on Utila with local research centers dedicated to the local flora and fauna. All are flexible with schedules to enable you to take diving courses or Spanish lessons during your stay as well.

One- to three-month stays as research assistants or environmental educators are available with the **Bay Island Conservation Society** (tel. 504/425-3260, www.bicautila.org, 8 A.M.–noon and 2–5 P.M. Mon.–Fri.). The visitors center, a 15-minute walk out of town, up Cola de Mico Road heading toward the airport, has pamphlets, maps, and books on Utila and the Bay Islands. The center is also the office of the Turtle Harbour Wildlife Refuge and Marine Reserve. A one-month program is $350, including accommodation, electricity, Internet, water, and laundry.

The **Whale Shark & Oceanic Research Centre** (tel. 504/425-3760, www.wsorc.com) conducts whale shark monitoring and research year-round, and works to raise public awareness about marine conservation. They offer four-hour whale shark encounter trips for US$44 that include the snorkel equipment, reef tax, and a short lecture on whale shark ecology. There are also a number of one-day PADI specialty courses such as Whale Shark Awareness and Underwater Naturalist available. For those interested in getting more involved, research volunteers are welcome, as are those interested in fundraising or public education.

The **Iguana Research and Breeding Station** (www.utila-iguana.de, 2–5 P.M. Mon., Wed., and Fri., US$2) makes for an interesting expedition to watch the prehistoric-looking and surprisingly large iguanas feed and wander around. The station has several species of swamp iguana, *Ctemosaura baberi,* found only in the mangrove swamps of Utila and in danger of extinction due to overhunting and the cutting of the mangroves. The volunteers are extremely knowledgeable. They offer a few guided tours on the island, such as an "iron-bound tour" through tropical forest to volcanic-rock formations on north shore, US$8 per person. Call or email in advance to arrange a tour.

The **Utila Centre for Marine Ecology** (tel. 504/425-3026, www.utilaecology.org) has six principle areas of research: megafauna (dolphins, orcas, and whale sharks), reef fisheries, coral reef ecology, mangrove systems, seagrass ecology, and island ecology. UCME frequently works with students completing research for undergraduate and post-grad theses. Volunteer stays start at US$1,025 for two weeks and go up to US$3,250 for eight weeks. Volunteers must have PADI Advanced Open Water certification, but specialty research diver training is included in the volunteer program.

Travel Agencies

One very good travel agency on the island is **Worldwide Travel** (tel. 504/425-3394, aliceww travel@yahoo.com, 9 A.M.–4:30 P.M. Mon.–Sat.), located on Losano Road (which is the road that turns left at the Mango Inn) and run by extremely efficient and accommodating Utilian Alice Gabourel. She can book domestic and international flights as well as hotel rooms and car rentals.

Banks

Both **HSBC** and **Banco Atlántida** (8–11:30 A.M. and 1:30–4 P.M. Mon.–Fri., 8–11:30 A.M. Sat.) change travelers checks and dollars, and both have ATMs (although Banco Atlántida's only works with Visa cards). There is also an ATM at Mermaid's restaurant. Several spots in town will give cash advances on MasterCard, Visa, and AmEx, typically charging a 7 percent commission, including at **Rivera's Supermarket** (7 A.M.–8 P.M. Mon.–Sat., 7 A.M.–6 P.M. Sun.).

Communications

Hondutel is in Sandy Bay, next to the police station. Also, there's the **Utila Telephone Co.** (8 A.M.–8 P.M. daily), across the street from Hondutel. **Honducor** (tel. 504/425-3167,

8 A.M.–3:55 P.M. Mon.–Fri., 9 A.M.–11:55 A.M. Sat.) is right on the dock.

Internet service is easily available in Utila, usually by the minute. On the main road in the large building at the corner with the dock is **San Fernando Wireless** (8 A.M.–9 P.M. Mon.– Sat., 8 A.M.–6 P.M. Sun.), charging US$2 an hour. Opposite Banco Atlántida is a little joint that charges only US$1.50 per hour.

The Internet café at **Mermaid's** restaurant (9 A.M.–10 P.M. Sun.–Thurs., 9 A.M.–5 P.M. Fri., 6–10 P.M. Sat.) has good air-conditioning and charges US$2.40 per hour for the Internet and US$0.11 per minute for calls to the United States.

Cyber Monkey, a small Internet café located at the Monkey Tail Inn on Cola de Mico Road, offers Internet and Skype for US$0.80 per 15 minutes or US$2.40 per hour.

Many of the Internet cafés can make wallet-size photos, required for each PADI course, US$0.50 each.

Laundry

There seem to be a million and one places offering laundry service on Utila. Prices are around US$4 for a large bag of dirty clothes. One option is **Alice's Laundry** (7 A.M.–8 P.M. daily), which also has an Internet café on the premises (8:30 A.M.–8 P.M. daily), charging US$2.60 to wash a large grocery bag of clothes.

Spanish School

Although English is more widely spoken on Utila than Spanish, the **Central American Spanish School** (tel. 504/425-3788, www .ca-spanish.com) offers popular and recommended Spanish classes on Utila for US$150 a week for 20 hours of private classes or US$100 for 20 hours of group classes (discounts are often available for the private classes). CASS has its main office in La Ceiba, with offices in Roatán, and Copán Ruinas as well, and can arrange monthlong programs combining a week on Utila with a dive course, two weeks of classes, and a homestay in La Ceiba, and a week of classes and homestay in Copán. It is east of the municipal dock opposite the water.

Emergencies

In an emergency, contact the **police** (tel. 504/425-3145 or after hours at 504/425-3187). The **Utila Medical Store** (tel. 504/425-3400, 8 A.M.–8 P.M. Mon.–Sat.), east of the dock on the water side, sells medications and also does laboratory analysis (urine, blood tests, etc.). For a doctor's advice, visit the **Utila Community Clinic** (8 A.M.–noon Mon.–Fri.), opposite the Mizpah Methodist church, which charges just a few dollars. It's best to get there at 7 A.M., since the wait can be incredibly long and the earlier you arrive, the closer you are to the front of the line.

In the unlikely event of a decompression problem during a dive, your dive shop should take you post-haste to the **hyperbaric chamber** at the Bay Islands College of Diving (tel. 504/425-3378, VHF channel 71, 8:30 A.M.–3:30 P.M. Mon.–Sat., and 24 hours in an emergency).

Immigration

The *migración* office is on the main dock in town. At the time of writing immigration officials had been instructed to automatically give tourists 90-day visas, and renewal of any oddly shorter visas had to be taken care of in Tegucigalpa.

GETTING THERE AND AWAY
Air

Sosa has flights to Utila from La Ceiba Monday–Saturday, and might also have Sunday flights during the March–August high season. Sosa tickets are sold by the dock, at **Morgan's Travel** (tel. 504/425-3161, U.S. tel. 786/623-4167, utilamorganstravel@yahoo .com, 8 A.M.–noon and 2–5 P.M. Mon.–Sat.), in the blue wooden building across from the ferry office. Morgan's can also book international flights.

If you are arriving on an international flight from the United States that connects in San Pedro Sula and La Ceiba, it is highly recommended to check your luggage only as far as San Pedro. Hoteliers in Utila report many cases of luggage that doesn't make the connection—better to retrieve it in San Pedro and get it onto the next flight yourself.

Utila's airstrip on the north side of the island is four kilometers from downtown, following Cola de Mico Road. You *must* reconfirm your flight at the Sosa office the day before your flight. They have a shuttle bus driver who will pick you up and take you to the airport for US$2 per person. Be waiting outside of your hotel promptly at the appointed time—the driver has been known to simply drive on by if the guest is not outside. Taxis meet regularly scheduled flights, charging the same price back into town.

Sosa sometimes offers charter service (particularly during high season, or anytime if you traveling in a group of seven or more), and Morgan's Travel might have information about other charter services. If Utilian native Troy Bodden isn't using his personal plane, he also allows it to be chartered (tel. 504/425-3264 or 504/9869-8972, ask for Claudia). Trips from Utila to Roatán or La Ceiba cost US$300 for 3–5 passengers, depending on the quantity of luggage. If you are arriving by charter flight, be sure to arrange a pickup with your hotel or with Paisano's Taxis, or there won't be anyone around to take you into town. Likewise, if you are departing by charter, you might want to tip your taxi driver to stick around until after your flight has actually taken off.

Note: When visibility is poor on the north coast due to bad weather (not uncommon for much of the year), the airport at La Ceiba closes with regularity. Don't be surprised to find yourself stranded if the weather turns bad.

Boat

The **Utila Princess II** (www.utilaprincess .com) departs Utila for La Ceiba at 6:20 A.M., returns from La Ceiba to Utila daily at 9:30 A.M., departs Utila again at 2 P.M., and departs La Ceiba again at 4 P.M. Departures can vary during the slow season, so check first, especially in La Ceiba where you don't want to take a taxi out to the dock and have to wait around. Travelers can spend the hourlong ride inside or on deck enjoying the breeze. Cost is

US$22 per person, and tickets are sold in the cement building at the entrance to the dock (tel. 504/425-3390). As with air transport, though not as frequently, the boat is sometimes cancelled due to bad weather. This boat is considerably smaller than the one that travels between La Ceiba and Roatán; if the wind has been blowing and the boat goes anyhow, be prepared for some stomach-turning swells. *Note:* There are often extra trips during Semana Santa, except on Good Friday, when the ferry doesn't run at all.

Captain Rusty (tel. 504/3553-7187) does three-day **charter sailboat trips** from Utila to the Cayos Cochinos, for US$250 per person (minimum two people). Bear in mind that if you do an overnight trip with him, it can be fairly tight quarters on his 40-foot boat. He also does Utila–Roatán trips on his boat for US$50 per person. Captain Hank (tel. 504/3379-1049, sunyata84@hotmail.com) has a 55-foot sloop with three private staterooms, air-conditioning, hot showers, kayaks, and snorkeling (diving, of course, can be arranged), charging US$100 per person for an overnighter to Cayos Cochinos and US$200 per person for two nights/three days. He also offers service between Utila and Roatán, charging US$75 per person for three meals and one night on the boat (four-person minimum). Trips to Belize can also be arranged.

Carissa Cooper and her husband, at Cooper's Inn (tel. 504/425-3184), have a boat, and when the whale sharks are around, they will do two-hour trips with the chance to snorkel (US$50 pp, 2–4 people). They can also help put you in touch with reliable local fishermen for trips to Water Cay (US$37 for up to four people).

For more information on local boating, contact the port captain's office (tel. 504/425-3116) by the dock.

GETTING AROUND

Lance Bodden Rentals (tel. 504/425-3245, boddenlance@yahoo.com) rents scooters, ATVs, and motorcycles for US$40–70 a day, including gas. Bicycles are available for US$5 a day.

Rita's Boutique (tel. 504/425-3692) also rents golf carts: US$40 for six hours, US$50 for eight hours, and US$280/week.

Delco Bike Rentals, just west of the dock on Main Street, rents out fairly sturdy mountain bikes at US$5 a day. Slightly more abused bikes are available for a bit less, and rates drop for multiday rentals. Another rental shop is **Utila Bike Rentals,** also on Main Street, past Bush's supermarket on the left, charging US$3 a day, less per week and month.

If you should need a taxi for any reason, call **Paisano's Taxi Service** (tel. 504/425-3311) 24 hours a day. It's based out of a little grocery of the same name.

◖ UTILA CAYS

The Utila Cays are a collection of 12 tiny islets off the southwest corner of the main island.

Jewel and Pigeon Cays

Some 400 people live on Jewel (or Suc-Suc) Cay and Pigeon Cay, which are connected by a narrow causeway and generally referred to jointly as Pigeon Cay. These islanders are descended from the first residents, who came to Utila from the Cayman Islands in the 1830s. Originally, the migrants settled on the main island but soon moved out to the cays, reputedly to avoid the sand flies, which are much less common than on the main island, especially when the easterly breeze is up. If you found Utila residents to be an odd Caribbean subculture, the Pigeon Cay population is odder still—a small, isolated group who tend to keep to themselves, but nevertheless welcome the occasional visitor with friendly smiles.

At the east end of the causeway on Jewel Cay is the small **Hotel Kayla** (no phone), with simple rooms with private baths (cold water only, US$10 s/d). Check at Captain Morgan's Dive Shop (tel. 504/425-3349, www.diving utila.com) to find out if rooms are available—all the divers from the shop stay there. Another hotel next door (Kayla 2) has similar rooms.

For food, **Susan's Restaurant** is famed for excellent fish burgers and conch stew. It also sells *bando* (an Utilian fish stew) to go, for those on their way to Water Cay. At **Bessie's Fish Factory,** visitors heading out to Water Cay and looking to make a cookout can buy a couple of fresh fish—and if you ask nicely, the proprietors will fillet and season the fish for you. They also sell conch, lobster, and (in season) crab. Food (restaurants and groceries) is cheaper here than on Utila proper, and there are far fewer sand fleas.

Sandy and Little Cays

Normally an extravagance few can afford, a stay on a **private island** is also possible in the Utila Cays. George Jackson (tel. 504/425-2005 or 504/408-3100, CayosUtila@hotmail .com) rents out **Little Cay** (US$115/night, up to six people) and **Sandy Cay** (US$100/night for a two-bedroom house, up to six people). Each small cay has one house—perfect for a weekend getaway or lounging in the sand and snorkeling the clear, turquoise waters. If some guests don't mind sleeping on mattresses on the living room floor, an additional eight people can be squeezed into the house on Sandy Cay, and countless more can camp out on the beach, while the house and cabin on Little Cay can accommodate up to 12 (US$15 for each additional person). Little Cay is about 5 minutes by boat from Pigeon Cay or 20 minutes from Utila's municipal dock, while Sandy Cay is a bit farther afield. Reservations can also be made through Captain Morgan's Dive Shop (tel./fax 504/425-3349, www.divingutila.com). The cays are heavily booked, so be sure to plan in advance and make a reservation. More information and some photos can be found on the website www.aboututila.com.

Water Cay

If you were to conjure up the ideal tropical beach paradise, your picture might be something very close to Water Cay. Almost within shouting distance of Pigeon Cay, Water Cay is a patch of sand several hundred meters long, wide at one end and tapering to a point on the other; the only occupants are coconut palms and one small caretaker's shack. Piercingly blue, warm water and a coral reef just a few meters out ring the cay. There are no permanent residents on the island. The caretaker (who shows up most days but doesn't live on the island) collects a US$1.25 entrance fee and also rents hammocks for another US$1 a night, though they're not the finest quality—better to bring your own, or bring a tent. It's also possible to catch a ride on frequent water taxis over to nearby Pigeon Cay for a nominal fee. The best snorkeling is off the south side, though it can be a bit tricky finding an opening in the wall. Water Cay is a popular impromptu party spot for locals and travelers, especially on weekends and on the full moon, which has unfortunately resulted in a bit of trash. Consider taking a plastic bag with you, to carry out a small portion if you can.

To get to Water Cay, check at the Bundu Café, look for any of the brightly painted "charter boat trips" signs around town, ask for Captain Hank next door to Utila Water Sports, or talk to any of the old fishermen hanging out, chatting, or playing dominoes on the stretch of road between Cross Creek and Utila Water Sports. Every August, Water Cay hosts the **Sun Jam** festival, bringing DJs and party-goers out for a wild night of dancing fun (www.sunjamutila.com).

Guanaja

Guanaja has somehow ended up as the forgotten Bay Island, overlooked in the rush of travelers and migrants to Utila and Roatán. This oversight is surprising considering Guanaja's fantastic reef, wide-open north-side beaches, and quirky fishing towns. News reports have frequently heralded big hotel investments for Guanaja by the wealthy and famous, but tourism on the island continues to be low-key and small-scale dive.

It is possible to survive on the island on a budget, though not as easily as on Utila. This is definitely a more unusual destination, not the mainstream feel of Roatán or the backpacker vibe of Utila, but something else altogether, funky and remote. Big-time tourist development may well hit Guanaja soon, but it hasn't yet.

Christopher Columbus landed here in 1502, on his fourth and final voyage to the Americas. Columbus named it Isla de los Pinos—pines long covered the terrain, but were wiped out in 1998 by the 290-kph winds of Hurricane Mitch. The fishing town of Mangrove Bight was also demolished (miraculously with no deaths), and Savanna Bight and Bonacca were heavily damaged as well. Reforestation projects got underway shortly after the storm passed, and the island cover is coming back. The vast majority of Guanaja's population lives in Bonacca, but there are also sprinklings of people at Mangrove Bight, Savanna Bight, and the post-hurricane town of Mitch, for a total of some 10,000 people.

The sand flies can be thick on Guanaja, so be sure to bring your repellent. The north side has many more than the south—but also the best beaches. Remember that DEET damages the coral, and either rinse off before getting in the water or look for a repellent with natural ingredients.

Guanaja is a diver's paradise. Many divers find the wildlife more varied here than at Roatán, with some very dramatic tunnels and caverns ("better than Mary's Place" claims one diver who has been to both Roatán and Guanaja). Sea life includes black, wire, and gorgonian coral, spotted eagle rays, moray eels, turtles, nurse sharks, lobsters, crabs, and much more.

Many hotels do not have hot water, but showers in the afternoon are typically pleasant, the water having been warmed by the sun.

BONACCA (GUANAJA TOWN)

Bonacca—officially Guanaja Town, and often just called the Cay—is not actually on the main island, but on one of the cays, and is home to some 6,000 people. It is an architectural

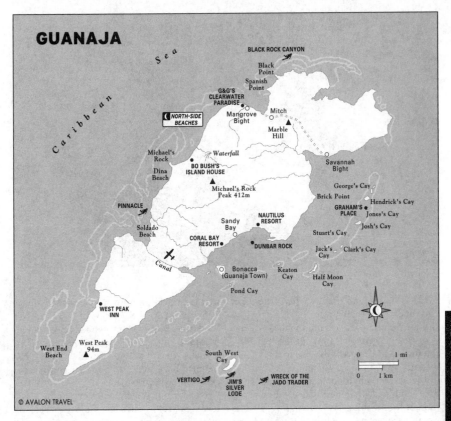

GUANAJA

BLACK ROCK CANYON

Black Point

Spanish Point

G&G'S CLEARWATER PARADISE

Mitch

NORTH-SIDE BEACHES

Mangrove Bight

Marble Hill

Michael's Rock

Waterfall

Savannah Bight

Dina Beach

BO BUSH'S ISLAND HOUSE

Michael's Rock Peak 412m

George's Cay

Brick Point

Hendrick's Cay

PINNACLE

GRAHAM'S PLACE

Jones's Cay

NAUTILUS RESORT

Josh's Cay

Soldado Beach

Sandy Bay

Stuart's Cay

CORAL BAY RESORT

DUNBAR ROCK

Jack's Cay

Clark's Cay

Canal

Bonacca (Guanaja Town)

Keaton Cay

Half Moon Cay

Pond Cay

WEST PEAK INN

West End Beach

West Peak 94m

South West Cay

0   1 mi

0   1 km

VERTIGO

JIM'S SILVER LODE

WRECK OF THE JADO TRADER

© AVALON TRAVEL

THE BAY ISLANDS

oddity, built on rickety wooden causeways over a maze of canals, founded in the 1830s by immigrants from the Cayman Islands. They constructed their homes on what were then Hog and Sheen Cays. These two tiny little islets, with a total of one kilometer of land space connected by a shoal, have since been built to cover 18 square kilometers by generations tossing their garbage out the window and eventually covering it over with sand, shells, and coral. With waterways instead of streets, the town is sometimes described as the Venice of the Caribbean (although the similarities begin and end with the canals).

With no beaches or other obvious attractions, Bonacca is worth a visit only to meet the islander townsfolk and take care of any

business you might have. Anyone who spends a couple of days wandering the maze of causeways that make up the island will soon make a few acquaintances and start to hear the endlessly entertaining local gossip and tall tales.

Water taxis ply the canals of Bonacca, although within town it's easy to get everywhere by foot.

ELSEWHERE ON THE ISLAND
Mangrove Bight

This small fishing village on the northeast corner of Guanaja, formerly perched over the shallow waters of a small bay, had the dubious distinction of being the first inhabited place to come in contact with Hurricane Mitch, at 10 A.M. on October 26, 1998. Luckily, the

© MIKE JONES

Guanaja's main town, Bonacca

storm hit in the morning, so the entire town had time to flee their houses and head up into the surrounding hills, watching as 10-meter waves swept their town away entirely. By 2000, the town had been rebuilt, now located a safe distance away from the shoreline.

Mangrove Bight is populated by a mix of *ladino* and islander families, all dependent on the modest local fishing fleet. Mangrove Bight is usually stroked by a steady breeze, which keeps the sand flies and mosquitoes to a minimum. A couple of *comedores* in town serve up inexpensive eggs, burgers, and other basic meals.

A few points of rock sticking up out in the bay in front of Mangrove Bight indicate the location of the reef. It's a fair swim out but doable for strong snorkelers who keep their eyes peeled for boat traffic. Once to the reef, poke around to find a sufficiently deep opening to pass through, and get ready for a heart-stopping drop-off into the blue depths below on the far side. Visibility is not fantastic and the water is a bit choppy, but the drop-off is a pretty dramatic sight.

Inland from Mangrove Bight

From Mangrove Bight, a dirt road heads southeast past an unused airstrip and across a low point in the interior of the island to **Savannah Bight,** about an hour away through mosquito-filled pasture land. Rooms are often available for rent in Savannah Bight, which has frequent boat service to Bonacca Town, especially in the mornings.

Not far outside of Mangrove Bight is the town of **Mitch,** a small community that sprang up where some of Mangrove Bight's homeless pitched tents after the 1998 hurricane of the same name.

About halfway between Mangrove Bight and Savannah Bight, you'll pass **Marble Hill,** an anomalous, tree-covered outcrop on the west side of the road. On the far side of the hill is the largest known pre-Columbian ceremonial site on the Bay Islands, **Plan Grande.** The site was mapped in the 1930s before being completely pillaged of its pottery and jade artifacts and destroyed. Little remains of either the ceremonial site or a large residential complex nearby, but locals will take a visitor to poke around for a fee. The Instituto Hondureño de Antropologia e Historia (IHAH) is planning a serious excavation at the site, but moving slowly. The road between Mangrove Bight and Savannah Bight offers good views of the mountains in the center of the island.

For the industrious, a trail leads from the western end of Mangrove Bight up a small valley, over a peak, and down the other side to Sandy Bay, on the south side of the island. The summit of the 412-meter peak is flat and reportedly a good spot for camping. Needless to say, the views from the top are stunning. Fresh water can sometimes be found, but it's best to bring enough for the whole trip, which could be done in a long day. The walk is longer than it may look, due to several high valleys not visible from below that must be crossed.

◖ North-Side Beaches

Between Mangrove Bight in the east and West End Beach are a series of very fine white-sand beaches, populated only by low-key resort hotels tucked into the edge of the forest. For maximum enjoyment, stay a couple of days out here, either in one of the hotels or camping (bring everything needed, including water). Day trips while staying in either Mangrove

Bight or Bonacca are also feasible. Don't forget to come prepared for sand flies and mosquitoes; they can be fierce on the north side.

About a 45-minute walk west of Mangrove Bight by trail begins a stretch of beautiful beach winding around to **Michael's Rock,** a rocky headland jutting into the ocean. The entire beach is lovely, but the best sections—two stretches of powdery sand and brilliant pale blue water separated by a grove of coconut palms—are right on either side of the headland. Small patches of reef around Michael's Rock offer snorkeling possibilities, but the main reef is over a kilometer offshore.

On the way to Michael's Rock is **Bo Bush's Island House.** Not far from Bo's place, a small creek comes out of the hills, and a trail follows it a half-hour walk uphill to a small waterfall surrounded by lush vegetation.

From Michael's Rock, **Dina Beach** is visible farther southwest, but walking is difficult as the trail passes through thick underbrush in order to bypass rocky coastline. It's better to get dropped off by boat and picked up

© MIKE JONES

Michael's Rock, on the north side of Guanaja

© MIKE JONES

one of Guanaja's waterfalls

later instead of trying to walk from Mangrove Bight. This is a great beach for camping, but there's no fresh water anywhere nearby, so be sure to bring enough.

Southwest of Dina Beach, near the mouth of the canal, is **Soldado Beach,** the reputed site of Columbus's landing in 1502. Nearby is a half-built monument marking the event—Spain donated money for a small museum, but somehow the money didn't go as far as expected. The snorkeling is great here.

West End Beach, west past the canal on the north side of the island, is a long stretch of beautiful, virtually unoccupied beach. The only facility in West End is the **West Peak Inn.** A nearby trail ascends to the top of West Peak (94 meters) for views across Guanaja and over to Barbareta and Roatán.

RECREATION

Guanaja's dive shops are attached to hotels, but they're often willing to take out day divers. Bo Bush, owner of the Island House on Guanaja's north side, will take out day divers at reasonable prices.

Snorkeling right off Bonacca is an unpleasant adventure, as the surrounding coral is dead and litter content in the water is high. It's better to hire a boat and go to the northwest sides of either Southwest Cay or Half Moon Cay, where vibrant corals are found in shallow water.

The enterprising can ask around in Bonacca to set up fishing trips in local waters. Wahoo, king mackerel, and barracuda are frequent catches.

ENTERTAINMENT

The bars and discos of Guanaja are not for the meek, filled as they are with rough characters who are always ready for a brawl, but they can be a good time if you know how to look after yourself. There are discos in Bonacca, Savanna Bight, and Mangrove Bight. The bars at Bo's and the other resorts can be fun places to spend the evening, and rather more relaxed. The **Pirate's Den Bar** (tel. 504/453-4308, 8 A.M.–2 P.M. and 5:30–9:30 P.M. daily) in Bonacca is a decent place to stop by for a beer in the afternoon.

ACCOMMODATIONS

The favored lodgings for vacationers on Guanaja are several self-contained beach and dive hotels scattered around the island. On the north side, set on deserted stretches of Caribbean beach, are two great low-key resorts—West Peak Inn and Bo Bush's Island House—the small-scale kind of places that are easy on the environment and perfect for those looking to get away from it all.

Budget travelers can seek out less expensive rooms in Mangrove Bight or Savannah Bight, or camp on the mostly undeveloped north-side beaches.

Beach Hotels

Situated on a picture-perfect stretch of north-side beach is ◖ **West Peak Inn** (tel. 504/408-3072, U.S. tel. 831/786-0406, www.westpeakinn.com, US$620 pp/week double occupancy, or US$95 pp/night), a collection of rustic but well-equipped cabins (screened-in porches, mosquito nets, fans, private bath) in a low-key and very relaxed setting. Snorkeling,

TOP DIVE SITES IN GUANAJA

Guanaja may be small, but it boasts 38 moored dive sites – plenty to keep divers busy over a week's time. Novice divers can explore caves and grottoes teeming with colorful marine life, but many of the dives are best suited for more experienced divers. A few of the highlights are:

- **Black Rock Canyon:** This maze of caves and tunnels was created long ago by volcanic activity. There are plenty of silverside sardines, glassy sweepers, groupers, and barracudas. Sharks and moray eels are known to sleep in its nooks and crannies – be sure to bring a dive light.

- *Don Enrique* **Wreck:** The wall here drops 24 meters to a sandy bottom, which slopes down to a sunken shrimp boat, its mast stabbing 15 meters up through the water. Both the wreck and the wall are teeming with sealife, often including spotted eagle rays.

- *Jado Trader:* This is a renowned sunken 60-meter freighter lying on a sandy shelf next to the barrier wall. The maximum depth here is 33 meters. The fish are fed here, and so plenty of grouper and yellowtail hang around, as well as moray eels, horse-eye jacks, and amberjack. Hammerhead sharks have been spotted at the site. This site is not for novices, and Wreck Certification is recommended for those who want to penetrate where the light does not.

- **Jim's Silverlode:** A tunnel along the wall at a depth of 21 meters brings divers into a sandy-bottomed amphitheater-like area populated by huge groupers, yellowtails, and moray eels. Swarms of silverside sardines keep divers company along the way. This is an intermediate-level dive.

- **The Pinnacle:** Located in a channel, the pinnacle stands on a sandy bottom at 135 feet, rising to a point about 55 feet below the surface. The pinnacle is covered with gorgonian, wire, and black coral, while seahorses, groupers, and spotted drums swim nearby. Divers typically sink to 24 meters and then spiral up and around. The wall of the channel also has beautiful coral at only 3-9 meters deep.

- **Vertigo:** This site along the barrier reef wall has spectacular drop-offs. The top of the wall is at about 11 meters, drops to 49 meters where there is a sandy shelf, then drops off again beyond sight. Black and white sea lilies (crinoids) can be found here.

sea kayaking, and hiking are all available at the lodge, and the restaurant serves up tasty seafood and other plates. (Rates include all meals, unlimited use of sit-on-top kayaks and snorkeling gear, hiking, beachcombing, casual fishing from the dock and shore, and boat transport to and from the Guanaja airstrip.) Some diving is available, but limited to experienced divers—they themselves suggest booking with a dive resort (such as Coral Bay or Bo's) if you're looking for a full week of diving. Rates include three meals a day and free transportation to and from the airport. The owners also can organize multiday sea-kayak and camping trips. The showers lack hot water, but the water is warm in the afternoon if it's been sunny. The entire place runs on energy from solar panels.

The beach hotel **Graham's Place** (tel. 504/3368-5495, U.S. tel. 305/407-1568, www .grahamsplacehonduras.com) charges US$100 per person, which includes breakfast, lunch, and airport transportation, and is a great place to relax on a spectacular beach. There's great snorkeling, including a "natural aquarium"— a large penned-off area in the water where guests can snorkel with fish, turtles, lobsters, and conchs. (Some love it, some hate to see the animals penned.) On land you might spot rabbits, iguanas, and birds. There's bone-fishing right off the cay, and bottom-fishing and trolling can also be arranged. Graham's is located on one of the cays off the southern side of Guanaja; water taxis can easily be arranged for those who are coming just for a meal.

THE BAY ISLANDS

Dive Resorts

One of the more relaxed, friendly, and less expensive dive hotels in the Bay Islands is **(Bo Bush's Island House** (tel. 504/9963-8551, www.bosislandhouse.com, US$812 pp per diver, US$696 nondiver, daily rates available), built and managed by Bo, who can trace his ancestry back to the time of the English pirates on the island, and his wife. Bo is a bilingual, experienced island diver with more than 6,000 dives under his belt and a fast boat, and he knows a whole world of north-side dive sites, including caverns, walls, reef gardens, wrecks, and more. The comfortable stone-and-wood house set into the hillside can sleep 18, and two small guesthouse another four, but Bo's boat can only handle six divers, which keeps dive size manageable. Rates include all meals, airport transfer, and (for divers) two daily dives. Sea kayaks are available to guests. The isolated hotel on Guanaja's north shore has a positively tranquilizing atmosphere, with wide stretches of deserted beach all around. Bo, a very friendly and laid-back host, will happily take guests on hiking trips and island tours.

At Sandy Bay, on the southern shores of the island, with a narrow 300-meter beach of its own, is **Nautilus Resort,** a 19th-century country house with seven guest rooms. Its sister property, **Dunbar Villa,** is a five-bedroom house dramatically perched atop Dunbar Rock, right in the middle of the bay. Guest rooms are not fancy, but clean and comfortable, and the views are unbeatable. U.S. Dive Travel will arrange San Pedro–Guanaja flights for all guests (U.S. tel. 952/953-4124, www.usdivetravel.com, US$1,505 pp low season, US$1,621 pp high season for a weeklong package, including all meals and dives; flights and tariffs are extra).

At Pelican Reef, not far from Sandy Bay, is the **Coral Bay Dive Resort** (tel. 504/9695-9557, www.coralbay.ca, US$1,169 pp diver, US$1,056 pp nondiver, with discounts available during the low season), also highly recommended. The resort offers a number of classes in addition to regular dives, including Open Water referral for PADI, SSI, NAUI, and ACUC for US$210, or the full Open Water

course for US$375. Nondivers should bear in mind that the resort pool is occasionally in use for dive instruction in the mornings. Nightly rates are US$140–186. They can arrange to pick you up by boat from Roatán, a 90-minute ride, and have plans to work with Rollins Air for transfers from Roatán by air in the future.

Construction was nearing completion at the time of writing at **G&G's Clearwater Paradise** (tel. 504/3303-7444, U.S. tel. 512/452-6990, www.clearwaterparadise.com), a small resort with eight guest rooms near Mangrove Bight. G&G stands for owners George and Ginger—both divers themselves, and Ginger reputedly a fine cook. The hotel restaurant, **Paradise Bar and Grill,** is built out over the water.

Accommodations in Bonacca and Other Towns

In the middle of Bonacca on the main street is **Hotel Miller** (tel. 504/453-4327, US$19 s, US$22 d with fan and hot water), a large two-story house with rooms on the second floor. There are nicer rooms with air-conditioning and TV for a few dollars more. Rooms are often available for rent in Mangrove Bight or Savannah Bight at around US$10 a night; just ask around.

FOOD

The resorts include meals, but for those looking to strike out, **(Manati** in Sandy Bay is the place to go, run by a German couple who prepare authentic dishes like weiner schnitzel, as well as delicious island fare, German beer, and a variety of European schnapps. Locals love to while away a Saturday afternoon here, and there is often live music.

The restaurants at Graham's, West Peak Inn, and Bo's are all open to the public, and are great places to visit for a meal if you're not already a guest. The Sunday barbecue at Bo's is another popular gathering spot for resident expats.

One of the better restaurants in Bonacca is **Mexitreats** (8 A.M.–1:30 P.M. and 6–9:30 P.M. Mon.–Fri., 6 A.M.–10 P.M. Sat.–Sun.), owned by a Honduran and his Mexican wife, with inexpensive snacks and light meals like *chila-quiles*, *baleadas*, nachos, and burgers. **Commercial Woods** and **Sikaffy's**, both in Bonacca, are the two major grocery stores on the island, although there are plenty of smaller shops and vegetable stands. Friday is the best day for shopping, since the boat comes in with new produce either Thursday afternoon or Friday morning.

SERVICES
Banks and Communications
Banco Atlántida (tel. 504/453-4262) in Bonacca changes both dollars and travelers checks, and can give a cash advance on a Visa credit card. **Hondutel** (7 A.M.–9 P.M. Mon.–Fri., 7 A.M.–4 P.M. Sat.) is at the south end of the main street.

Coral Bay Dive Resort (tel. 504/9695-9557, www.coralbay.ca) near Sandy Bay has an Internet café, with very steep prices: US$7.50 for 15 minutes, US$12 for 30, and US$18 for an hour.

Boat Mooring
Graham of **Graham's Place** (tel. 504/3368-5495, U.S. tel 305/407-1568, www.grahams placehonduras.com) offers free mooring (up to 45 feet) for **yachts**, fresh water (to fill tank and wash down boat), ice, and laundry service.

Emergencies
In an emergency, contact the **police** (tel. 504/453-4310); don't light fires because there is no fire department on Guanaja.

GETTING THERE AND AWAY
Sosa (tel. 504/453-4359) flies once daily except Sunday to Guanaja from La Ceiba; **Isleña** (tel. 504/453-4801, www.flyislena.com) flies daily, charging US$52 one-way. The airstrip is on the main island, with no terminal except a simple shelter. Boats always come out to meet the flights and charge a few dollars (depending on current fuel prices) for the 10-minute ride to town. A water taxi out to one of the farther-flung resorts will cost more, perhaps US$25, although transportation can also usually be arranged directly with the hotel. Both airlines have offices in Guanaja where tickets can be purchased.

There has been intermittent ferry service between Guanaja and Trujillo in the past, but in early 2009 it was suspended. There has also been talk of establishing ferry service between La Ceiba and Guanaja, but for the time being that also remains just talk.

GETTING AROUND
Private boats arrive and depart frequently each day, heading between Bonacca Town and various parts of the main island. Usually islanders arrive in town in the morning, shop or sell goods, and leave again at midday. The only way to find out about them is to just start asking around in Bonacca. A ride to Mangrove Bight, an hour or so away, depending on the size of the outboard, normally costs about US$7 if the boat is already going your way. Boats heading to Mangrove Bight can easily drop visitors off at Dina Beach or Michael's Rock, both superb beaches. Regular boats to Savannah Bight leave Guanaja Town daily at 7 A.M., returning immediately, for US$5. An express boat trip to Michael's Rock or elsewhere on the north side costs about US$35–40 each way, depending on gas prices and your negotiating skills.

It's possible to walk the main island's one road from Mangrove Bight, past Mitch, to Savannah Bight, in about an hour.

Cayos Cochinos (Hog Islands)

The Hog Islands, called the Masaqueras by the early colonists, consist of two main islands and 13 small cays surrounded by pristine reef, 19 kilometers off the Honduran coast. The two larger islands are covered with thick tropical forest and ringed by excellent white-sand beaches. All in all, the Cayos are one of the most spectacular collections of islands, beach, and reef in the western Caribbean, yet they are infrequently visited by most tourists, who instead fly or boat right past on their way to Roatán and Utila.

The Cayos were declared a marine reserve in 1994. All marine and terrestrial flora and fauna within a 460-square-kilometer area is protected from fishing, development, or any other harmful activity. From any point of land in the islands, the reserve extends eight kilometers in all directions. The cays are managed by the **Honduras Coral Reef Fund** (www.cayoscochinos.org), which has a research center on Cayo Menor. Volunteers are welcome—those interested should send a résumé and cover letter to the HCRF director, Adrian Oviedo, at aeoviedo@cayoscochinos.org. Visitors are charged a US$10 fee for a day visit to the islands, or US$5 if arriving with a tour operator (which may or may not be included in your tour price).

The islands are all privately owned, except for Chachahuate, which holds a small community of a couple of dozen Garífuna families who survive by fishing.

Rides to Cayos Cochinos are available with Javier Arzú in Nueva Armenia, who goes back and forth daily, charging US$13 per person each direction. Call him at 504/9790-9838 the night before to confirm what time to show up, or talk to his sister Alba at 504/9950-5214. Day trips to the Cayos Cochinos can also be arranged from Roatán and Utila, and sailboats can be chartered from Utila for trips of 2–3 days.

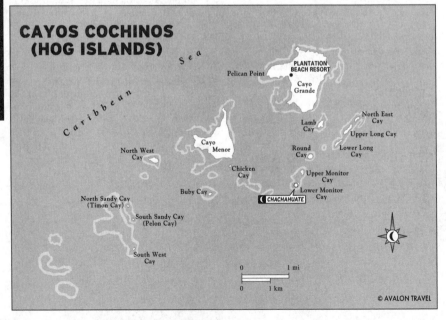

© PETER SVANBERG

Snorkeling is a popular activity on the tiny islands of the Cayos Cochinos.

THE BAY ISLANDS

◖ CHACHAHUATE

Those who wish to appreciate a different side of the Cayos for considerably less money can take a boat from Nuevo Armenia, near Jutiapa on the mainland coast, or from Sambo Creek near La Ceiba, to the Garífuna village of Chachahuate on Lower Monitor Cay. This is the sort of place, as one visitor commented, where you should go with an open mind and heart. Because of its isolation, Chachahuate is one of the more traditional and friendly Garífuna villages in Honduras, so keep that in mind and try to be a relaxed and amiable guest.

An effort is being made to develop ecotourism on the island, and there are now rooms and organized meal service available through the group **Ruta Garinagu Cayos Cochinos.** The mainland coordinator, Chichi, can arrange transportation from Nueva Armenia to Chachahuate (US$130 for round-trip in one day, US$160 for round-trip with a stay of 2–3 days—per boat, not per person), as well as make sure that there are meals and rooms available during your stay. Chichi can be reached at tel. 504/9840-8617 or 504/9937-1702, or

you can stop into **Hotel Chichi** in Nueva Armenia and ask for her. A room in the basic Hotel Chichi is US$5.25 per person, as are the rooms in the simple cabins on Chachahuate (no hot water, and the bathrooms are public baths outside the cabins). In addition to the cabins, there is one hotel, **El Pescador,** which Chichi can also reserve, for US$8 per person. Meals typically consist of a plate of fried fish with rice, beans, and plantain, or *machuca,* a fish soup with plantain. Those who have stayed gave glowing reports about the experience.

Large groups can ask Chichi about the privately owned cay with a guesthouse. Each room in the guesthouse sleeps up to 10.

OTHER CAYS

Plantation Beach Resort (tel. 504/442-0974, U.S. tel. 800/346-6116, www.plantation beachresort.com, US$957 pp/week for divers, US$806 pp/week for nondivers) is located on the privately owned Cayo Grande. The hotel's mahogany and stone cottages with decks and hammocks are tucked into a small valley on the site of a former pineapple plantation. PADI

SWAN ISLANDS

Three days by boat from Guanaja or Puerto Lempira are the tiny Islas del Cisne, the northernmost possession of Honduras in the Caribbean and an extension of the same geological formation that forms the Bay Islands. The Swan Islands lie some 160 kilometers from the Honduran coast. It is said that Columbus landed on the islands in 1502, four days before arriving at Guanaja, and named them the Santa Anas as it was her feast day. The islands are a good source of fresh water, and were frequently used as a way station by Caribbean voyagers over the centuries, and as a result, their ownership has long been disputed. In 1863 the United States decided to take possession under the Guano Islands Act of August 18, 1856, an act that claimed the right to uninhabited and un-owned islands that had plenty of guano – bird dung – for processing as fertilizer. Honduras's claim was made in the 1960s, based on Columbus's stopover on the island, which in their eyes made the islands part of the Spanish colonial empire to which Honduras was the rightful heir. The United States ceded ownership of the Swan Islands to Honduras in 1972 but continued to maintain a radio station there until 1961, reputedly run by the CIA for broadcasting anti-Castro messages in Cuba. The CIA is also rumored to have used the islands as a base for training Nicaraguan Contras.

The Swan Islands – Great Swan, Little Swan, and Booby Cay – can be reached by private boat, helicopter, or plane (there is a small landing strip).

certification courses are available. Those looking for some hiking to complement their diving will find numerous trails over the 140-meter peak or around the shore to the north side, where there is a lighthouse and a small village. Rates include all meals, the use of kayaks and snorkel equipment, and, for divers, three boat dives a day, unlimited shore diving, tanks, weights, and belts. Nightly rates are US$116 per person, US$20 more for divers, and the resort accepts cash, travelers checks, or Visa.

The dive shop **Dive in Caribik,** based at the Hotel Palma Real, has also opened up business on one of the smaller cays, "Isla Paradiso," and built the **Eurohonduras Guest House** (tel. 504/3373-8620, www.dive-in-caribik.com, US$80 pp/night, including breakfast, lunch, and dinner). The hotel can also arrange transportation to the tiny island from La Ceiba for another US$60–80, making it logical to spend

at least a couple of nights on your own piece of paradise.

SNORKELING

There's great snorkeling all around, but visitors should bring their own gear, as well as fresh drinking water and a few other supplies like fruit or crackers. Prices vary, but usually a boat from Nuevo Armenia or Sambo Creek should do the trip for US$150–200 (per boat, not per person), or less, depending on your negotiating skills and perceived financial status.

A variety of one-day cruises to the Cayos Cochinos, normally visiting Chachahuate with stops for snorkeling, can be arranged in Roatán and Utila, often for around US$50–70 per person, depending on how many people go; it's extra to bring scuba gear along. It's also possible to arrange trips with one of the tour companies in La Ceiba.

THE MOSQUITIA AND OLANCHO

With virtually impenetrable jungle and cloud forest thick with wild animals, birds, and bugs, the Mosquitia and Olancho are not for the faint of heart. But those who venture east to this tropical Wild West will be rewarded. The Reserva de la Biosfera del Río Plátano (Río Plátano Biosphere Reserve) is part of the largest surviving area of undisturbed tropical rainforest in Central America, home to several rare or endangered species, including giant anteaters, jaguars, ocelots, margays, manatees, and tapirs. The internationally heralded network of six community tourism projects called La Ruta Moskitia offers simple accommodations in spectacular settings, along with adventure activities such as kayaking, fishing, tubing, and crocodile spotting.

Olancho's national parks, Sierra de Agalta and La Muralla, are equally untamed. Trails are unmarked, but guides can lead visitors through some of the finest high altitude cloud forests in the country. A visit to the Cuevas de Talgua is an easier outing, although no less intriguing, with their stalagmite and stalactite formations, and stories of a cemetery of 3,000-year-old glittering bones.

Gracias a Dios and Olancho are the two largest departments in the country, combining to cover 36 percent of Honduras's territory. Their very remoteness means that few call the place home: Olancho has the second-lowest population density (by far) in Honduras, with 21 people per square kilometer. In the Mosquitia the density drops to just 5 per square kilometer. This is frontier country, populated by Honduran cowboys; Miskito, Pech, and

© JAVIER MARADIAGA MELARA

HIGHLIGHTS

◖ **Reserva de la Biosfera del Río Plátano:** This reserve is an immense and spectacular protected tropical rainforest along a river valley in the heart of the Mosquitia, the Amazon of Central America, accessed only by boat or on foot (page 265).

◖ **Villages on Laguna Ibans:** The wooden ecolodges in tiny coastal communities dotting the edge of Laguna Ibans make perfect bases from which to explore the surrounding creeks by *pipante*, kayak, or inner tube, and get an introduction to Miskito culture (page 267).

◖ **Hiking and Boating from Las Marías:** A challenging three-day hike to summit Pico Dama is one of the most popular outings from this tiny town deep within the Mosquitia, but other interesting options include a visit by *pipante* to ancient petroglyphs and an easy trek near town (page 271).

◖ **Río Patuca:** Farther east in the Mosquitia is this broad, serpentine river cutting through some of the most remote jungle country in Central America, the homeland of the Tawahka indigenous people (page 276).

◖ **Around Laguna Caratasca:** In the far northeast of Honduras, completely disconnected from the rest of the country and the world, is a land of Miskito villages, lagoons, jungle, and endless, deserted beach (page 280).

◖ **Monumento Natural El Boquerón:** One place to get an easy taste of the mountain forests of Olancho is to hike up the lush canyon at El Boquerón, a day trip from Juticalpa (page 288).

◖ **Cuevas de Talgua:** Spelunking novices will be content with a stroll through the main cave at Talgua with its ghostly stories of glowing bones, while more adventurous explorers will enjoy scrambling through the less-visited Cueva Grande or one of the two other nearby cave systems (page 292).

◖ **Parque Nacional Sierra de Agalta:** Aficionados of cloud forests will not want to miss the tough but rewarding hike up to the top of Sierra de Agalta, with truly spectacular natural diversity, including a rare elfin forest on the summit (page 293).

LOOK FOR ◖ TO FIND RECOMMENDED SIGHTS, ACTIVITIES, DINING, AND LODGING.

Tawahka indigenous groups; lobster fishermen; loggers; hunters; smugglers; gold miners—people accustomed to fending for themselves without anybody's help.

If you came to Honduras tired of traveling the same well-beaten gringo trail through Latin America and in search of adventure, don't fail to leave time for the Mosquitia and Olancho. It's not the sort of region where you can expect to find a luxury hotel or haute cuisine, but even a few days can allow for wild explorations.

PLANNING YOUR TIME

Let's face it: Being in a hurry, or on a tight schedule, is not an option. In Mosquitia, a boat might leave one day, or it might leave the next, or maybe the one after that. Air service is limited. Olancho actually has roads (unlike Mosquitia), but few of them are paved, and bus service is often only once a day at early morning hours. And wherever you go, experiencing the amazing nature that is this region's prime attraction requires getting out and walking.

To get the full Mosquitia experience, complete with a river trip up the Reserva de la Biosfera del Río Plátano and a hike into the rainforest from Las Marías, you'll need at least a week, but shorter visits can also be made to get a taste of the region. The less expensive and much slower route is by bus from La Ceiba via Tocoa to Batalla, and in the back of a pickup across the beach to Palacios and on as far as the mouth of the Río Plátano—from there it's all by boat. The quicker but pricier route is to fly in. Sosa offers twice-weekly flights from La Ceiba to Brus Laguna and Puerto Lempira, and Sami flies three times a week during low season, daily during high season, to seven different airstrips across the region.

Visitors can fly into Brus Laguna or Belén and spend three or four nights bumming around on the beaches, exploring the coastal communities, and scouting wildlife or fishing in the lagoons and coastal jungles. Those with more time can take a six-hour boat ride upriver to Las Marías, and then another two or three days for a jungle trip, followed by another day back to "Brus." The plane trip saves you at least

two days of hard traveling. With more than a week, adventurous trips upriver deeper into the biosphere, or up the Río Patuca or Río Coco, are feasible.

You may find yourself spending more days than planned—time starts to take on a different meaning once you get into the Mosquitia. Brus Laguna and Belén are both within the biosphere reserve, making either one an ideal starting point for explorations of the reserve's flora and fauna. Note that those traveling in a large group (seven or more) can charter their own flights with Sosa from La Ceiba, San Pedro Sula, or Tegucigalpa, and fly into Palacios, Ahuas, and Belén as well as Brus Laguna and Puerto Lempira.

The driest (and hottest) months are February–May. The rainiest months of the year are June and November (with plenty of rain in the months in between, somewhat less in September), although rains can fall at any time. The lagoons can get a bit rough in bad weather—not stomach-churning, but certainly resulting in a very wet ride.

There's more flexibility for choosing shorter or longer trips in Olancho, with an extensive road network (mostly dirt) and regular bus service. Juticalpa is just over a two-hour drive by paved road from Tegucigalpa, and from there it's an easy day trip to hike up the nearby El Boquerón canyon, or a longer day trip or campout to hike up to the cloud forest of Cerro Agua Buena. The caves at Talgua, famous for the "glowing skulls" discovered inside some years back, can be visited in a half-day trip from Catacamas, itself a 45-minute drive (again by paved road) from Juticalpa.

Hiking and wildlife-viewing trips up into the cloud forests of Sierra de Agalta National Park can range from a day (around El Murmullo, from Catacamas) to three or four days up to the elfin forest on the summit, La Picucha, from either Catacamas or Gualaco. The trails at Parque Nacional La Muralla are more accessible, but it takes a couple of extra days to get out to the park, which is located in far western Olancho.

A scenic road connects from Juticalpa–Catacamas highway to the Trujillo–Tocoa

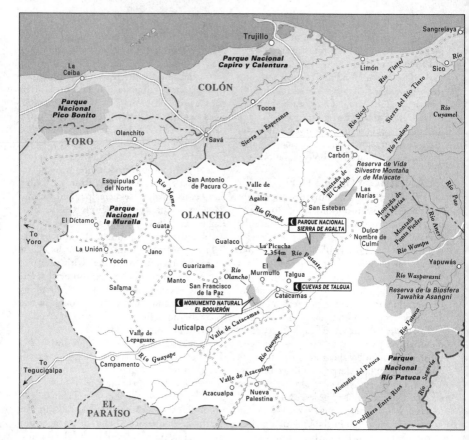

highway, winding through Gualaco, San Esteban, and El Carbón in eight hours or so. Safety, however, is a very serious concern on this isolated road (holdups of private cars and buses are not infrequent), so check for the latest information on safety, be alert, and stick to traveling during daylight hours. Better yet, travel only as far as Gualaco for a hike in the Sierra de Agalta, and then head back toward Juticalpa and find an alternative route north.

Guide Companies

All of the trips described in this chapter can be accomplished by hiring local guides as you go, as long as your Spanish is up to it, you are fully prepared to take care of yourself, and you've

got lots of time. The most popular trip in the region, to the Río Plátano, is not hard to arrange on your own. However, many travelers prefer the convenience of a guide company, to ensure minimal hassles and a reliable trip. And for some of the more extreme trips, like from Olancho into the Mosquitia, along the Río Patuca or in farther-flung jungle regions, a reliable guide who really knows the region is essential.

Of particular note for the Mosquitia is the community tourism project **La Ruta Moskitia** (tel. 504/406-6782, www.larutamoskitia.com), whose website has extensive information on independent travel in the Mosquitia (including helpful tips such as whom to contact in each

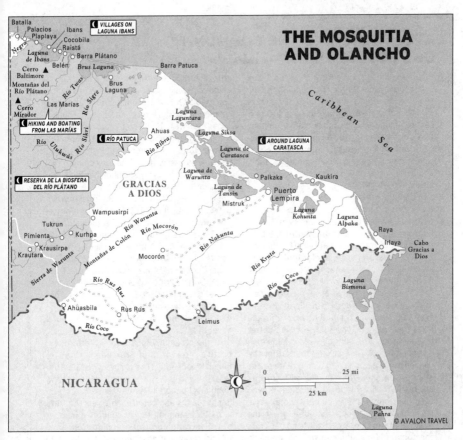

community for a boat ride), as well as excellent package trips, all 100 percent community-owned and -operated. Package trips take a low-key pace, but still include an activity or two in each community; when comparing tours with other companies, be sure to note what you're getting for the price.

A good privately owned guiding company that has tours in both the Mosquitia and Olancho is **La Moskitia Eco-Aventuras** (tel. 504/442-0104, owned by Mosquitia native Jorge Salaverri and based out of La Ceiba). Trips include a five-day visit to the Reserva de la Biosfera del Río Plátano for US$545 per person; a five-day hiking expedition in the Parque Nacional Sierra de Agalta (US$642 pp for a

group of two, down to US$383 pp for a group of 7–10); and a 10–14-day trip from Olancho down the Río Plátano (US$894–1,790 pp, depending on the length of trip and number of participants). Trips to the Mosquitia include a free night in their guesthouse in La Ceiba prior to departure.

Turtle Tours (tel. 504/429-2284, www .turtle-tours.com, referred to by locals as Tortuga Tours) is a small German outfit based in La Ceiba that is also well-regarded and committed to sustainable tourism. It offers four-day tours of the Mosquitia coast for as little as US$510 and weeklong camping, boating, and hiking journeys through Olancho and down the Río Patuca for US$1,285.

STRENGTHENING THE COMMUNITY, ONE ECOLODGE AT A TIME

Established in 2006, **La Ruta Moskitia** defies conventional definitions. Tour company? Well, yes, they do offer a number of package tours throughout the Mosquitia. But it's a 100 percent community-owned and operated company that's also happy to provide independent travelers with all the requisite information about sights, transportation, accommodations, food, and activities in the six participating communities: Batalla, Plaplaya, Raistá, Belén, Brus Laguna, and Las Marías. While the package tours have predetermined activities and destinations, all can be customized, and the activities – nighttime crocodile spotting, tubing and kayaking, traditional dance performances, walking tours, and even jungle survival training – can also be arranged on a one-off basis. All activities are led by local residents.

That said, the Mosquitia is a place where a package tour is well worth considering. Guides are indispensable for activities like jungle hikes and crocodile-spotting, and who better to lead through the wilds of the Mosquitia than a trained local? The package tours offer the convenience of not having to negotiate prices at every step along the way, since all payments are made to a single local coordinator, who then distributes the funds between all local participants in the tour (the hotel owner, the boatman, the guide, etc.). Profits go back into the community: a small portion of the package tour price goes to a community fund that provides for a bonus to the project members at the end of each year, while 10 percent of all

gross tour revenue is held by the office in La Ceiba as reserves that can be accessed by the community for new projects, such as beach cleanup or the building of additional cabins.

La Ruta Moskitia was started by the environmental conservation group RARE and the United Nations Development Program, and has now passed entirely into the community's hands. The well-run organization has been recognized for its quality efforts with a number of awards, including the 2008 World Tourism & Travel Council (WTTC) Tourism for Tomorrow award in the Investor in People category, the 2007 Virgin Holidays Responsible Tourism award, and an honorable mention on the *Condé Nast Traveler* Green List in 2006. *National Geographic Adventure* included La Ruta Moskitia in its 2009 list of the Best Adventure Travel Companies on Earth. It's not perfect (the cabins were out of soap on our visit), and it's certainly not luxury, but it's a darn good adventure.

At the ceremony for the WTTC award, executive director (and Brus Laguna native) Elmor Wood said, "The longevity of La Ruta Moskitia and the jobs it has created depend upon local people taking a stance in protecting our lands and culture. This year, La Ruta Moskitia communities will support a number of conservation projects ranging from environmental education to reforestation to waste management. We are developing an army of environmental activists here in La Moskitia." Sounds good to us.

a simple cabin in one of the ecolodges of La Ruta Moskitia

© AMY E. ROBERTSON

THE MOSQUITIA AND OLANCHO

Another reputable tour operator is **Omega Tours** (tel. 504/440-0334, www.omegatours.info), based in La Ceiba, offering tours lasting anywhere from three to 13 days. The longest trip starts in Olancho and journeys through the Mosquitia on balsawood rafts that you build one afternoon for rafting through small rapids the following day. You're in good hands— Omega is the most highly regarded rafting company in the country.

Fishermen will be interested to learn that the lagoons, waterways, and ocean around the Mosquitia offer some of the finest **sport fishing** in the Americas, with world-class snook, tarpon, snapper, barracuda, and shark fishing. One outfit running fishing tours from Brus Laguna is **Team Marin Honduras** (www.teammarinhondurasfishing.com), offering fishing tours of 2–4 nights (US$689–889 pp based on double occupancy), with flights from La Ceiba, accommodations (very basic), and transport included. Four weeklong set-date tours are offered per year that anyone can sign up for (US$1,950 pp); price includes everything including internal flights from San Pedro Sula. Private trips can be arranged for other trips throughout the year. Team Marin also runs a unique five-day tour of the Mosquitia along the Río Tuas to the **Lalla Sanni ruins** for US$517 per person, minimum group of six.

Safety

Mosquitia and Olancho are frontier territories. There's a lot of illegal logging, drug running, and general lawlessness in some areas, particularly along the border between Olancho and Mosquitia. Foreign travelers need not fear if they stick to the main places worth visiting and use guides when on back roads and trails. The Río Plátano, Brus Laguna, Puerto Lempira, Juticalpa, Catacamas, Sierra de Agalta, La Muralla, El Boquerón, and the paved highway through Olancho to Catacamas are all quite safe.

The places where it's best to take care (or to avoid) are Dulce Nombre de Culmí and beyond, from Olancho north toward the Mosquitia in the upper reaches of the Patuca (especially along Ríos Wampú and Aner),

and the Valle de Paulaya and Sico area farther west. The remote mountain roads in both far-eastern and far-western Olancho have a reputation for highway banditry. The road from Yoro to the Tegucigalpa–Juticalpa highway that passes through La Unión in Olancho has been nicknamed the "Corridor of Death," thanks to frequent highway robberies and the not-infrequent shootout. According to locals, that's a thing of the past on this stretch of road. (It's always possible to double-check with the small police stations at either end of this road for the latest information.) On the other hand, the lonely stretch of road near San Esteban is now considered a no-go zone by locals, due to frequent highway banditry. The paved highway leads first to San Francisco de la Paz before becoming a dirt road that is considered perfectly safe as far as Gualaco. It is strongly recommended to turn back from there, and travelers interested in visiting the Pech village of El Carbón should consider approaching it from the northern side, perhaps before or after a visit to Trujillo. There was interest in 2008 in paving this segment, thanks in particular to President Zelaya's support (Zelaya is an *olanchano*); he may yet be able to push through the project before he finishes his term, which would improve security on this road.

Malaria is rampant in the coastal and savanna areas of the Mosquitia, but is less prevalent in the jungle and in Olancho. Fortunately, the strain is not resistant to chloroquine, a cheap and relatively safer antimalarial that is available in all but the smallest communities. Those who come down with malaria will be prescribed a combination of chloroquine and primaquine; the latter ensures that malaria doesn't remain dormant in the liver. Be sure to take all the medicine prescribed. Natural hazards like poisonous snakes and the like are common, and reliable medical care is not. The best places for medical help in Mosquitia are at the Palacios and Puerto Lempira clinics, and in Olancho at the Hospital San Francisco in Juticalpa or the Predisan clinic in Catacamas.

The Mosquitia

La Mosquitia, the fabled Mosquito Coast, is a huge swath of Caribbean coastline, lagoons, pine savannah, and the largest remaining expanse of virgin tropical jungle in Central America, all covering the northeastern corner of Honduras and continuing across the border into Nicaragua. While the edges of the Mosquitia can be reached by pickups driving along the beach, the vast majority of the region is accessible only by plane, boat, or foot, lending it the feel of a separate country, cut off from the rest of Honduras and the world.

For the nature-lover, a river or hiking trip into the dense jungles of the Reserva de la Biosfera del Río Plátano is one of the most impressive trips available in Central America, a chance to see untamed rainforest teeming with wildlife. Expeditions organized by tour companies or independent trips using local guides are easily arranged; they can be as strenuous as days of hiking and camping or as comfortable as short hikes and R&R and simple ecolodges. Adventurers can seek out boats along the Río

Patuca or the Río Coco, either up from the coast or downriver from Olancho, and also spend days or weeks exploring the Miskito villages lined along the region's endless, wind-swept beaches and inland waterways.

The Gracias a Dios department, which covers all of Honduran Mosquitia, is the second largest in the country, but it had a population of only 67,384 people according to the 2001 census (the only national survey that even bothers to get out to this region). These inhabitants live in isolated villages and towns connected to each other mainly by boat or, less frequently, plane. Much of the Mosquitia is a low-lying plain, by far the largest expanse of flat terrain in Honduras. The land holds practically no agricultural potential, though, as the region is covered either by coastal mangrove swamp, tropical jungle, or marshy savanna dotted with Caribbean pine.

The only road connection to Mosquitia (despite what you might see on a few rather fanciful Honduras road maps) is via the

THE LAND OF MOSQUITOES?

One might understandably assume that the Mosquitia got its name from the voracious mosquitoes that thrive in some parts of the region. But as anyone who has been to the Mosquitia knows, mosquitoes are called *zancudos* there. So a couple of more creative explanations have been offered as to the name's origin. One suggests that the name is derived from the word "musket," or rifle, with which the Miskito were well supplied by the British. Supposedly, the Spaniards took to calling the attacking Indians *mosqueteros* because of their weaponry, which none of the other Indian groups in Central America used. From this developed the name Mosquetos, which over the years became Miskito.

Another possible derivation, favored by Miskito nationalists, is from the name Miskut, a

tribal chief of the Tawakha. Miskut's people lived near Cabo Gracias a Dios and are thought to have been the original Tawakha group that evolved into the Miskito.

But hard-headed realists like to point out that, although modern Hondurans generally call them *jejenes*, the Spaniards called sand flies *mosquitos* (little flies). Early in the conquest, Spanish explorers named several small islands just south of Cabo Gracias a Dios the Los Cayos Mosquitos, or the Mosquito Cays, for the clouds of pesky sand flies still found there today. Because the Miskitos frequented these and other cays in their oceangoing canoes, the Spaniards may have transferred the name to the raiders who, perhaps in the eyes of some metaphorically inclined colonist, plagued their settlements like sand flies.

town of Tocoa (near Trujillo) to Batalla (near Palacios). Pickup trucks travel along the beach from Batalla to Palacios and onward as far as Cocobila. From there onward, apart from a self-contained circuit of dirt tracks across the savanna connecting Puerto Lempira, Rus Rus, and the Río Coco and Nicaraguan border at Leimus, all travel is by boat, plane, or foot.

Unlike in the rest of Honduras, most of the inhabitants of the Mosquitia belong to an indigenous group, either Miskito, Tawahka, Pech, or Garífuna (and many are of mixed descent but identify with one group or another based on language or location). Indigenous is a relative term, though, since the ethnogenesis of both the Miskito and Garífuna people is a fairly recent historical event.

Across the Río Coco and into eastern Nicaragua, the Mosquitia continues down to the banks of the Río San Juan and contains a similar mix of ethnic groups, lush jungle, and coastal wetlands, and a disconnectedness from the rest of Nicaragua. Many Miskitos cross back and forth regularly to visit family and work in both countries with little regard for border formalities. It is possible for foreigners to cross into Nicaragua here.

The Mosquitia is the wettest part of the country, receiving an average of 300–340 centimeters of rain annually. Rains usually hit in May, June, July, and August, followed (again, usually) by a brief dry spell in September, then heavy rains again in October and November, including the occasional hurricane. February–May are the most reliably dry months of the year, but wet weather can arrive at any time. Temperatures are usually hot during the day, reaching 35°C (95°F) during the driest months, but it can be surprisingly cool at night—at a minimum, a lightweight jacket is in order. The coast is usually stroked with ocean breezes, which keep the heat down.

GETTING AROUND THE MOSQUITIA

Considering how remote and undeveloped the Mosquitia is, it's no surprise that traveling there has its challenges. Visiting the most popular destination in the Mosquitia, the Río Plátano Biosphere Reserve, requires taking a twice-weekly flight with **Sosa** from La Ceiba to Brus Laguna, a flight with **Sami** (a.k.a. Honduras Air, tel. 504/433-8032) to one of the region's seven airstrips (Ahuas, Belén, Brus Laguna, Palacios, Patuca, Puerto Lempira, and Wampusirpi), or a full-day, US$31 truck ride from Tocoa, near Trujillo, to Batalla, near Palacios. Many tour companies work only with Sosa, considering it more reliable and safer. La Moskitia Eco-Aventuras works with Sami, which offers a lot more flexibility, noting only that the return flights back to La Ceiba aren't always punctual (worth remembering if you have an onward flight). From there it's another US$8 by *colectivo* boat to Raistá, or US$16 to Brus Laguna. A trip to Las Marías can begin the next day and takes 5–7 hours depending on conditions. It costs US$150–200 for an express boat (for up to four people) or US$21 for a very slow and uncomfortable *colectivo* upriver to Las Marías, where you can organize tours farther into the jungle.

Puerto Lempira, in the farthest corner of Honduras near the Nicaraguan border, is serviced by regular air service from La Ceiba with Sosa. Groups of seven or more can charter a plane with Sosa, for service on a different day, direct service from San Pedro Sula or Tegucigalpa, or to land at the airstrip in Palacios, Ahuas, or Belén. Alas de Socorro, a medical plane based in Ahuas, also flies intermittently.

Boat trips within Mosquitia are either expensive (if you take an express boat) or slow and cramped (on a collective motorized or manually propelled canoe, and still not cheap). Prices are usually relatively standard, fluctuating with the price of fuel. Boats navigate waterways (frequently man-made, or at least widened, and dependent on the seasonal water levels) that connect rivers and lagoons in the Mosquitia. The canal system has been expanded in the past few years, minimizing the formerly frequent heart-stopping voyages in the open ocean.

Sami does also have a few internal flights

BOAT TRAVEL IN THE MOSQUITIA

Prices fluctuate along with the price of fuel, which is much more expensive in the Mosquitia than the rest of the country, but this chart should help in planning a trip budget.

PRICES FOR *EXPRESO* (PRIVATE) BOAT SERVICE

To/From	To/From	Round-Trip Boat Price (per group/per boat)	Trip Duration
Palacios	Raistá/Belén	US$42	1.5 hours
Raistá/Belén	Las Marías*	US$160	5 hours
Raistá/Belén	Brus Laguna	US$80	2 hours
Brus Laguna	Las Marías*	US$185	6 hours

* For the trips to Las Marías, these prices include the cost of the boat driver spending two nights with you in Las Marías, which will give you at least one full day to explore the hiking and other natural attractions of the area. Expect to pay another US$13 per day to the boat driver if you want to spend more nights.

PRICES FOR *COLECTIVO* BOAT SERVICE

To/From	To/From	Price
Ahuas	Wampusirpi**	US$26
Batalla	Raistá	US$8
Batalla	Brus Laguna	US$16
Brus Laguna	Ahuas	US$17
Palacios	Batalla	US$2
Palacios	Plaplaya	US$4
Palacios	Belén	US$13
Palacios	Las Marías	US$26
Puerto Lempira	Ahuas	US$21
Raistá	Las Marías**	US$21

** Your best chance to find a shared boat ride to Las Marías may be to head to Raistá and try to join another group that's going – which may take a couple of days in low season. It may also take a few days to find a boat going from Ahuas to Wampusirpi.

Pipante (a type of canoe) is a common method of travel in the Mosquitia.

within the Mosquitia, and charters can be arranged for groups as small as six.

If you have nothing but time and the requisite equipment and supplies, it's perfectly possible to walk along the beach to different parts of the Mosquitia. At most major river mouths (called *barras*) you'll find local ferries, but expect to get wet.

The only bank in the Mosquitia that changes dollars is in Puerto Lempira, so be sure to bring plenty of lempiras, preferably a bunch of small change (bills of 100 lempiras or less). Locals will usually accept or change dollars in a pinch, but always at bad rates.

HISTORY

In pre-Columbian times, the Pech populated much of western Mosquitia, living across a wide area delimited by present-day Trujillo, the Valle de Olancho and Valle de Agalta, and the Río Patuca. Farther east, several Sumu-Tawahka tribes inhabited the region from the Río Patuca to the Río Coco, and across into what is now Nicaragua. Little is known about the origin of these two groups or their society in preconquest times, other than that they are part of the Chibchan linguistic group and are thought to have migrated from the rainforests of Colombia to Central America. Joining the Pech and Tawahka in around A.D. 1000 were groups of Nahuatl-speaking Pipiles who migrated down from Mexico. The ruins of what are believed to be either Pech or Pipil ceremonial centers have been located along both the Caribbean coast and farther inland as far as Olancho, but intensive archaeological work has yet to be undertaken.

Christopher Columbus was the first European to visit the Mosquitia. On his fourth voyage, after stopping at Guanaja and Trujillo Bay, Columbus sailed east along the coast until he came to the mouth of a major river, where he landed and spoke to the people living there through an interpreter he had brought from Guanaja. The river, which he named Río de la Posesión, could have been the Aguán, the Sico, or the Patuca. Because some of the indigenous people apparently had large earlobes, Columbus named the region La Costa de las Orejas (The Coast of the Ears).

© AMY E. ROBERTSON

THE BIRTH OF A KINGDOM

When Europeans first came to the Mosquitia, the region was inhabited by the Pech and several coastal and jungle subtribes of the Sumu (known as Tawakha). The Spaniards, intent on finding gold and quick riches, made few efforts to colonize the Mosquitia, and in the early 1600s, the British began eyeing the region with interest.

Coastal Tawakha – possibly a group known as the Bawihkas – had always had a different physiognomy from their inland cousins, and in a few decades, the differences became more dramatic. In part, the Miskitos evolved from mixing with the English, but more so from several groups of slaves shipwrecked on the shores of eastern Honduras, the first in 1641. Unlike many other indigenous groups, the coastal Tawakha tribes had an extremely open culture that allowed them to mix freely with outsiders, a trait that sped up the process of racial evolution.

The first written mention of the Miskitos appeared in 1672, when the pirate John Exquemelin said they numbered about 1,600 people. In 1699, an anonymous English traveler wrote, "the Mosqueto-men inhabit the sea-shore, pretty close to the sea-side, or on the sides of some lakes and lagunes hardby," between Cabo Camarón and Cabo Gracias a Dios.

It remains a mystery what process was under way in the latter part of the 17th century, which, from the mixing of African, English, and Indian blood, created a new race with a distinct language and culture – but by the turn of the century, the Miskitos had been born. The English quickly saw the value of cultivating the Miskitos as allies against the Spanish, and in 1687, they invited the tribe's chief to Jamaica and crowned him Jeremy I, the first of the Miskito kings. In time, the British also created governors, generals, and admirals at other Miskito settlements, who sometimes acted more like independent warlords than servants of the king. The chiefs were not recognized as legitimate by their subjects until they had made a ritual trip to Jamaica, or later Belize, to receive the British blessing. Reportedly, the crowning ceremonies were amusing spectacles of bountiful speeches and much drunkenness.

The Miskitos needed little encouragement to fight the Spaniards, whom they detested. With a little training, they became feared raiders with an insatiable thirst for attacking Spanish settlements. At first, they joined pirate expeditions against Trujillo and Puerto Caballos,

---

After Columbus, in the 16th century the Spanish made a couple of abortive efforts to colonize the Mosquitia, but soon they gave up and chased their dreams of gold and riches elsewhere. This left the coast open for the pirates, who flocked over from Europe beginning in the late 16th century to prey on the Spanish treasure fleets in the Caribbean. The pirates used the Bay Islands and the protected, isolated lagoons of the Mosquitia as their bases.

In 1633, the first English settlement was established at Gracias a Dios, and by 1700 the English had cemented a firm alliance with the coastal tribes of the Tawahka—some of whom had metamorphosed over the years into the Miskito—against their common enemy, the Spaniards.

William Pitt settled Black River (now Palacios) in 1699, and shortly afterward migrants moved into Brewer's Lagoon (now Brus Laguna). The Shoremen, as the new English settlers called themselves, frequently joined Miskito raiding parties against the Spaniards. In 1782 the Spanish launched an offensive against the Mosquitia, and by 1786 a deal between the British and the Spanish resulted in the Shoremen moving en masse to British Honduras (Belize).

Would-be Spanish and later Honduran settlers, faced with an unfamiliar and unforgiving natural environment and implacably hostile and well-armed Miskitos, didn't fare so well in the Mosquitia. Honduras gained undisputed control over the Mosquitia in 1860, but the region

but soon they took to launching their own attacks against León and Granada in Nicaragua, Juticalpa, and San Pedro Sula, and any other poorly defended Spanish settlement they ran across in their forays.

During the course of the 18th century, the Miskitos gained complete ascendancy over the Tawahka and the Pech, demanding tribute and often raiding the communities for slaves to sell to the English. Unable to compete with the fierce and well-armed Miskitos, the Tawahka and the Pech abandoned their former territories and fled into the jungle to escape attack, leaving the Miskitos as sole rulers of the shore. In fact, the Miskitos invented the derogatory term "Sumu" to designate their former brethren, the Tawahka.

With the Anglo-Hispanic Convention of 1786, the British agreed to evacuate the Mosquito Coast in return for Belize. The Miskitos, however, were not inclined to submit themselves to their erstwhile enemies, the Spanish. Some 1,300 immigrants from Spain arrived at Black River in 1788, but Miskitos attacked them repeatedly and settlers were forced to flee to Trujillo, which became the eastern limit of Spanish control.

The kingdom state ceased to exist in 1894, when it was occupied by Nicaragua, but a Miskito Nation exists still today, and extends from Cape Cameron, Honduras, to Río Grande, Nicaragua. Since 1978, Norton Cuthbert Clarence has been the hereditary chief of the Miskito Nation, and Pretender to the Miskito Kingdom (that is, the king of an abolished throne).

To this day, many Miskitos hold a special affection for the British, and for that matter, any English-speaking white person, and fondly cherish the thought that they will return and kick out the *indios*, as they derisively call the Spanish. Only a few Miskitos speak English, but many still have Anglo names. The Miskitos were left alone by the Honduran government until the 1950s, when the government began building schools in the Mosquitia to spread the use of Spanish.

Since that time, Spanish has slowly replaced English as the *lingua franca* of the Mosquitia, and the government has gradually begun to assert its authority in the region. But, as with the English and the African slaves who ended up on the Mosquitia shores, the Miskitos seem to be incorporating the Spanish immigrants rather than vice versa. Their open culture, unafraid of change, has proved to be the Miskito's strongest tool in facing the brave new world.

continued to be populated solely by Miskitos, Tawahkas, Garífuna, Pech, and the occasional North American logger or gold miner until the 1930s. Around this time, Moravian missionaries from the United States began arriving in the area, setting up schools and eventually creating the first Miskito dictionary. Because of its years of work in the Mosquitia, the Moravian church remains very strong in the Mosquitia (although most people in the region still consider themselves Catholic).

The Honduran government finally got around to setting up offices, building schools, and promoting the use of Spanish in the early 1950s. The department of Gracias a Dios was created in 1957, and since that time, the government has promoted migration into the region, with limited success.

In the 1980s, the Miskitos again found themselves being used as proxies in a foreign war, armed and encouraged by the U.S. CIA to fight the Sandinista government in Nicaragua. Honduras's Puerto Lempira was the main base for the northern front of the so-called Contra War. The violence led to major immigration from Nicaragua into Honduras, a trend that only recently began reversing.

Most residents of the Mosquitia make a living by fishing or as small-scale farmers. The fishing season is technically only between September and February, but as locals have little other means of income, many fish illicitly all year. The lucrative lobster diving trade, which exports to distributors and restaurants in the United States, is particularly tempting to young Miskito men looking for cash. While dive instructors are often brought in, there is widespread use of alcohol and sometimes illicit drugs by the lobster divers, leading to noncompliance with basic decompression rules and frequent, often crippling diving accidents.

In the last couple of decades, cocaine has begun passing through the Mosquitia on its way north to the United States. Taking advantage of the huge stretches of unpatrolled coastline in this remote corner of Honduras, drug-runners drop off major shipments of coke on the beaches and lagoons of the Mosquitia, where it's taken north overland through Olancho or northward by boat. Every once in a while a kilo or two will wash up on shore, and an entire village will be wired to the gills for a week or so. This all takes place well away from the places frequented by foreign visitors, and the only place you are likely to come in any contact with this trade is in Puerto Lempira or Palacios, where many of the nouveau-riche Miskitos and *ladinos* like to flaunt their wealth. In early 2009 the Honduran government laid the first stone for a military base in the Laguna Catarasca, in an effort to stem the tide.

PALACIOS

Situated on a spit of land near the mouth of the Río Sico, protected from the open ocean by a narrow sandbar, Palacios is a town of about 2,000, scattered across grassy pastures cut out of the jungle. The town was founded as Black River in 1699 by William Pitt, a distant relative of the British prime minister of the same name, on the site of a Miskito village. It was populated mainly by loggers and smugglers until turned over to the Spanish in 1739, when it slid into decline. The town was not repopulated until the early part of the 20th century, when one of the U.S. banana companies made an abortive attempt to start a plantation in the vicinity. The remains of the company's railroad can still be seen, mostly covered over by jungle.

Smugglers are back at it in Palacios, these days moving shipments of white powder up from Colombia to remote lagoons and beaches in Mosquitia, and on up Central America to its

destination market, the United States. One of the several unfortunate results of this growing industry is that Palacios has a slightly spooky vibe, with lots of shifty-looking men hanging around, many with gold chains and odd-shaped bulges under their shirts.

Palacios is the main town in western Mosquitia, and it has a medical center, satellite phones, and several lodgings with more amenities than elsewhere in the region. However, most travelers will not find much need to come here, but will instead go by bus and boat from Tocoa to Batalla, and stay in Batalla, Raistá, or Belén, taking boats from there onward up the Río Plátano.

Sights

Although the jungle has long since claimed most of the old English settlement, some traces can still be seen. A few hundred meters east of Hotel Río Tinto, along the waterfront road, is a large field on the right, where four old cannons from the British fort lie half-buried in the weeds. The owner of the land, who proudly claimed British heritage though he spoke no English, said he understood that the mouth of the river, now farther to the east, was once right in front of his property. This would explain the location of the cannons, on a small rise in the land in front of the water.

On the west side of town, between the airstrip and the lagoon, just about opposite the hospital, lives a Garífuna family, and in the front yard of their humble house is the grave of William Pitt, the town's founder. The worn stone is sometimes covered with dirt, but the amiable family will help you clear it off to see the still-legible inscription.

Practicalities

Options for eating and sleeping in Palacios are limited, and frankly, staying the night here isn't altogether safe. In the center of "town" is the two-story **Hotel Río Tinto** (US$13 s/d) run by Ana Marmol, renting 10 simple rooms with private bathrooms and fans. The *pulpería* next door, in a ramshackle, two-story wooden building, is also the Isleña office and the town's informal gathering place. Between the store and the hotel is a small *comedor* with unexceptional meals for US$2.

About the best lodgings in town are at **Hotel Moskitia** (US$21 d), located right on the water, with five large rooms, each with two big beds and a balcony. Meals are good and cost US$4 for a main course.

The **Hospital Bayan** on the airstrip was first started by Bahai doctors in 1986, but it is now managed by visiting Cuban doctors. It is the largest clinic in western Mosquitia.

Getting There and Away

Sami (tel. 504/433-8032) has a flight from La Ceiba to Palacios three times a week during the low season, daily during high season, for US$98 one-way. Apart from flying, visitors will likely come from Tocoa, where buses leave the central market about 9 A.M. daily to Batalla (eight hours, US$31), where you can catch a boat to Palacios. The 9 A.M. departure is intended to allow early risers from La Ceiba to arrive in time to catch this onward bus and make the entire journey from La Ceiba in one day.

Colectivo boat prices (canoes with small outboard motors) from Palacios to Belén, Cocobila, Raistá, Batalla, and elsewhere in the vicinity of Palacios cost about US$3–8, depending on distance and how wealthy you look. Private trips are more expensive.

Boats to the Río Plátano and Brus Laguna

It is possible to get up to Las Marías from Palacios and nearby villages in *colectivos,* although you have to ask around with determination (locals expect and want tourists to take more expensive special trips), and definitely don't be in a hurry. *Colectivos* to Las Marías cost around US$26 from Palacios. *Colectivos* from Palacios to Brus Laguna run about US$22. Keep in mind that while you will save money, the long, crowded boat trips can be very uncomfortable indeed. Private trips to Raistá should cost about US$42, and round-trips to Brus Laguna go for about US$150.

Batalla

Just west of Palacios, across the Laguna Bacalar, is the large Garífuna village of Batalla. Trips can be arranged through the mangroves of the

© AMY E. ROBERTSON

Dirt airstrips and small planes are the standard in the Mosquitia.

lagoon, home to white-faced and howler monkeys, colorful parrots, and the shy manatee. Interested fishermen can also learn about traditional Garífuna fishing techniques.

Several locals offer spartan rooms and basic meals. Get here either by boat from Palacios (US$2 *colectivo*) or by bus/truck from Sangrelaya, to the west around Cabo Camarón, and Tocoa, near Trujillo.

Plaplaya

Several kilometers east of the mouth of the Río Sico, on the waterways about halfway to Laguna Ibans from Palacios, is Plaplaya, the easternmost Garífuna settlement in Honduras, a large collection of thatched and concrete huts on a sand bar facing the Caribbean. Plaplaya is home to the **Giant Leatherback Turtle Project,** run with the help of the Mopawi, a Mosquitia development organization, and a local Peace Corps volunteer. The project manages a protected nesting area for the turtles, which can grow to be 680 kilograms and are the largest living turtle species. The turtles are most commonly seen between February and May, when they come in to the local beaches to lay their eggs. Being there to watch the mother turtles waddle in, laboriously dig a nest and lay their eggs, and struggle back out sea, is quite an experience. Another good time to visit is between June and September, when the eggs are hatching and the newborn turtles make their journey back to the sea.

Two local women's groups are more than happy to put on an entertaining and lively Garífuna dance performance for visitors, for a negotiable fee (expect to pay at least US$50 for a few performers, more if you are with a large group, if they organize a larger group of performers, or if you look wealthy). Spectators are merrily encouraged to join in the dancing toward the later part of the show, if they would like. At the end, a baby doll, wrapped in a blanket, is passed around to exchange payment, a pleasingly elegant way of dispensing with financial formalities.

Sedy Zenon runs a very simple *hospedaje* (cement walls, zinc roof, US$8 pp), and a couple

© LAURA HELENA BERMUDEZ

artisanal fishing in Plaplaya, the easternmost Garífuna settlement in Honduras

of other places offer similar rooms. A couple of other places offer rooms at the far end of town. Local ladies will gladly whip up a few simple Garífuna dishes, such as coconut-fish soup and cassava bread, for US$3 or so a meal. Be on the lookout for *"guifiti"* (locally brewed spiced liquor), which you may find around town.

Colectivo boat trips between Palacios and Batalla or Plaplaya should cost around US$4 each way (leaving Palacios early in the morning, around 7:30 A.M.).

◖ RESERVA DE LA BIOSFERA DEL RÍO PLÁTANO

Created in 1980 and declared a UNESCO World Heritage site in 1982, the Río Plátano Biosphere Reserve encompasses a huge expanse of broadleaf tropical rainforest, mangrove swamp, sedge prairie, and gallery forest stretching across northeastern Honduras. This is one of the great jungles of the Americas, an untamed, emerald-green wilderness filled with an incalculable treasure of biological diversity in its plant and animal residents. Though much of the reserve is extremely difficult to get to and travel around, guided trips through the coastal lagoons, savannah, jungle, and deeper into the reserve along the Río Plátano from the Caribbean coast are easily accomplished, and are as incredible a travel experience as you could hope for.

By far the largest protected area in Honduras, the reserve covers 815,000 hectares, or about 7 percent of the national territory, in the Gracias a Dios, Colón, and Olancho departments. Of this area, 215,000 hectares are delimited as an untouchable core zone. While the core zone can hardly be said to be "untouched," it remains almost entirely virgin rainforest.

The reserve is bordered on the northwest by the Río Paulaya, on the north by the Caribbean Sea, on the east and south by the Río Patuca, and to the south and west by the Río Patuca

LA CIUDAD BLANCA

- **1526:** Hernán Cortés arrives in Trujillo. He is in search of Xucutaco-Hueitapalan – a great trading Mayan/Nahua city, reputed to be comparable in population and in wealth with Tenochtitlán in Mexico, a city of over 200,000.

- **1544:** Bishop Cristóbal de Pedraza, the bishop of Honduras, writes to the king of Spain and describes a grueling trip to the Mosquito Coast jungles, where from a mountaintop he spied a large city in a distant river valley, where his guides claimed the nobles ate from plates of gold.

- **1939:** Theodore Morde and Lawrence Brown spend five months in the Mosquitia, an expedition sponsored by the Museum of the American Indian in New York. They charted rivers, catalogued animals and insects, and brought back art of the Chorotegans, an agricultural people believed to be contemporary with the Mayans. It is said that Morde

claimed to have found the Ciudad Blanca, the White City, but jealously guarded its whereabouts to protect it from looters – only to be suspiciously run over by an automobile in London shortly thereafter.

The legend of this lost city of Honduras has only grown over the centuries. Hunters, pilots, and other explorers have claimed to have seen a large city deep in the jungle. Some reports mention golden idols; others describe elaborately carved white stones that give the city its name. Some of the Mosquitia's natives claim that the city is not lost, but hidden, providing refuge to indigenous gods.

The line between myth and reality is hazy, as archaeological research has revealed significant sites in the Mosquitia, but the challenges in establishing project sites keep the research slow. The village Las Crucitas del Río Aner is established over a large and impressive archaeological site, and many believe that the fabled Ciudad Blanca is simply awaiting discovery.

MAMMALS IN THE RESERVA DE LA BIOSFERA DEL RÍO PLÁTANO

ENGLISH	SPANISH	MISKITO	PECH
opossum	*tacuacín*	*sikiski*	*maishí*
three-toed sloth	*perezoso de tres dedos*	*siwaiko*	*siwuá*
two-toed sloth	*perezoso de dos dedos*	*siwaiko*	*siwuá*
pygmy anteater	*perico ligero*	*likor*	*kuráhuwuista*
giant anteater	*oso caballo*	*wingkutara*	*kurah ujáh*
tamandu anteater	*oso hormiguero*	*winkusirpi*	*kuráh*
white-faced monkey	*mono cara blanca*	*waklin*	*guayá*
howler monkey	*mono aullador (or olingo)*	*kong kong*	*huquí*
spider monkey	*mono araña*	*urus hurus*	
white-nosed coati	*pizote*	*wistan*	*tuská*
kinkajou	*mico de noche*	*uyuk*	*wuachác*
northern raccoon	*mapachin (or oso lavador)*	*skusku*	
striped skunk	*zorrillo*	*piskrauat*	*wuahá*
river otter	*nutria (or perro de agua)*	*mamo taoó*	
jaguarundi	*jaguarundi*	*limi siksa*	*misto sonwá*
ocelot	*tigrillo*	*krujuba*	*huc brú*
mountain lion	*león (or puma)*	*limi pauni*	*huc pawá*
jaguar	*jaguar (or tigre)*	*limi bulni*	*huc cewáh*
red brocket deer	*tilopo*	*snapuka*	*ichaá pawua*
white-tailed deer	*venado cola blanca*	*sula waika pijini*	*ichaá kamazá*
white-lipped peccary	*jaguilla wari*	*quitán*	
collared peccary	*kekeo*	*buksa*	*wuareká*
Baird's tapir	*danto*	*tilba*	*chajú*
squirrel	*ardilla*	*buston*	*torenah*
porcupine	*eriso*	*haksuk*	
paca	*tepiscuinte*	*ibijina*	*huaquí*
agouti	*guatuza*	*kiajki*	*barka*
rabbit	*conejo*	*bang bang*	*mi nih*
nine-banded armadillo	*cusuco*	*tayra*	*patuhá*
naked-tailed armadillo	*tumbo armadillo*	*takan-takan*	*yucrú*
bat	*murciélago*	*sankanki*	*tiquimi*
vampire bat	*murciélago vampiro*	*sankanki tara*	*tiquimi*

and one of its tributaries, the Río Wampú. Other rivers within the reserve include the Río Sigre (Sikre) and the Río Twas, both of which empty into Laguna de Brus, and of course the Río Plátano itself. Notable mountains include Cerro Baltimore (1,083 meters), Pico Dama (840 meters), Cerro Mirador (1,200 meters), Cerro Antilope (1,075 meters), and Montaña Punta Piedra (1,326 meters).

Most foreigners come to the Río Plátano to admire the plants and animals of the largest remaining tropical forest in Central America, but several pre-Columbian ruins near Las Marías and in the southern section of the park in Olancho are well worth exploring. The ancestors of the Pech, or of Pipil immigrants from Mexico, are the two likeliest candidates to have built the many ruins. Persistent rumor holds that a full-scale city called **Ciudad Blanca** lies in the middle of the jungle, waiting to be discovered.

Visiting the Reserve

While there are numerous ways to get into the huge biosphere, the route used by the majority of independent travelers is to either fly to Brus Laguna or take a bus to the vicinity of Palacios, and continue from there by boat to the coastal communities on Laguna Ibans, then up the Río Plátano to Las Marías, where trained local guides can lead trips of varying length by boat farther upstream or hiking in the jungle.

◖ VILLAGES ON LAGUNA IBANS

Surrounding the Laguna de Ibans are a string of Miskito villages. Most travelers prefer to stay out in these villages or in Brus Laguna instead of Palacios as their stop-off point on their way to or back from the biosphere, or as destinations in and of themselves. They are fine places to relax for a few days, chatting with the friendly locals and strolling deserted, windswept beaches.

About a two-hour walk east on the coast of Plaplaya, or a half hour by boat, is the Miskito village of Ibans, and beyond, in quick succession, Cocobila, Raistá, Belén, and Nuevo Jerusalén. Walking between these settlements, it's difficult to tell where one stops and the next begins—they all blend together, with houses and the occasional store and church scattered along grassy footpaths in the couple hundred meters of land between the ocean and Laguna de Ibans. The beach along this entire stretch is windswept and deserted (and unfortunately, with some trash). The swimming is great, but beware the sharks and strong shore currents.

Cold drinks and basic supplies are sold at *pulperías* in Ibans, Cocobila, and Belén. Camping is possible just about anywhere on the peninsula, but it's always best to ask first.

Lanchas (with outboard motors) and *tuk-tuks* (with inboard motors) up the Río Plátano can be negotiated in any of these villages for usually slightly lower prices than in Palacios. From the northeast corner of Laguna de Ibans, near Nuevo Jerusalén, locals have hacked out a canal to the Río Plátano, meaning boats don't have to go out to the open ocean to cut over to the river.

Three hours' walk east of Nuevo Jerusalén along the beach is the tiny community of Río Plátano, a village at the mouth of the river of the same name. A couple of pickup trucks also drive this route for US$1. To get to the village, be prepared to take a very rickety canoe ride across the calm river mouth for US$0.25, "captained" by a local kid.

A new ecolodge has been built along the shore of the lagoon and should soon be open for business—check with La Ruta Moskitia.

Belén

Belén is a midsized beach community, population 840. It's home to a couple of large, nice schools funded by international aid, as well as an airstrip. The beach is dramatic and undeveloped, but criminally littered with trash, particularly plastic bottles. Community members are working on developing a cleanup and trash removal project—no small feat given that the government does not provide trash removal services anywhere in the Mosquitia. It's an interesting place to visit; if the beach gets cleaned up, it will be spectacular.

THE MOSQUITIA AND OLANCHO

© AMY E. ROBERTSON

a walk on the beach at Belén

Members of La Ruta Moskitia have built a simple but attractive ecolodge, the **Pawanka Beach Cabanas** (US$10 pp). Three thatch-roof cabins high on stilts have four twin beds each, with mosquito nets, towels, candles, and a hammock on the porch. There is a clean outhouse and shower with running water (cold only), and a common open-air kitchen/dining area where tasty starch-heavy meals are served up for US$3–4. A tiny patch of beach right in front of the cabins is kept clean. A solar panel provides light to the dining area at night, where there is also an electrical outlet if you need to charge a phone or batteries.

Packages with La Ruta Moskitia often include a Moskita women's dance performance in the evening here, set on the beach next to a bonfire. Locals may join in on the singing and dancing, which gives the experience an authentic feel. Performances aren't polished, but with locals singing along in the background, they come across as very genuine. The community also offers crocodile-spotting, horseback riding, and a day hike to see howler monkeys, petroglyphs, and a waterfall. If you are

traveling independently, you can arrange for these tours on-site, or in advance through La Ruta Moskitia; prices vary US$10–25 per person depending on the activity and the number in your group. While anyone in town could point you in the right direction, the local coordinator for the cabins and activities is Mario Miller (tel. 504/433-8220).

Lodging (US$5 pp) and meals can also be found at **Hospedaje y Comedor Diana** (US$4), easiest found by asking for the *hospedaje* of Doña Tunisia (Diana's mom). There's a *pulpería,* a *cantina* where you can buy a coke or a beer, a couple of churches, and scattered wooden houses built up on stilts, a safeguard against the rainy season.

Colectivos back to Palacios usually cost US$13, and many leave very early in the morning (as early as 3:30 A.M. to ensure connections with the pickups back to Tocoa and onward connections back to La Ceiba), so it's best to arrange a ride a day ahead of time.

Raistá

A 10-minute walk west of Belén, Raistá is a

tiny community of 140, home to some of the pioneers of ecotourism in the Mosquitia, the Bodden family. (Okay, almost everyone in town is a Bodden, but that's another story.) A recently built community-owned **ecolodge** (tel. 504/449-0198 or 504/8927-1928, US$10 pp) is part of La Ruta Moskitia's network, perhaps the best in the region. The eight rooms each have a double and a single bed, mosquito nets, towels, candles, and a small balcony (many with hammocks). There is electricity in the evening at the very clean shared bathroom, which is a plus, but no hot water, so try to shower in the late afternoon or early evening, when the water has been warmed by the sun. It's a great place to spend a day or two before or after a trip to Las Marías or elsewhere in the Mosquitia.

Doña Elma Bodden privately owns a second four-room lodge on the property, fully rented out to an NGO at the time of our visit. She also has a tiny restaurant, **Elma's Kitchen,** where she cooks up tasty meals for US$3–4. Breakfasts are abundant and sometimes include pancakes as well as eggs, beans, and ham—what a treat. Ask about *wabul,* a delicious traditional Miskito drink made from bananas and coconut milk.

Raistá is just minutes walk from the larger community of Cocobila, interesting to walk to via the little road, by beach, or lagoon-side. While the beach and lagoon are both fine places for a swim, be aware that crocodiles live in the lagoon and lots of sharks live in the nearby ocean, so ask the locals for a good spot before you take a dip!

Besides swimming, activities including crocodile-spotting, hiking, tubing in the canals, a traditional Miskito dance performance, and even a four-hour jungle survival training session can be arranged here (again, tours runs US$10–25 pp), through the local coordinator of La Ruta Moskita, Melissa Bodden (tel. 504/433-8216). Her husband, Jorge Rivera (tel. 504/8926-5635), can also take guests on a community walking tour through Raistá and neighboring Cocobila (with a stop, if you're lucky, to knock fresh coconuts out of a tree

to drink the coconut water), for US$10.50, any size group. He can also take visitors for nighttime turtle-spotting walks on the beach March–June for the same price.

Boats from Raistá up to Las Marías cost about US$200 round-trip, including a couple of days at the village, for a jungle trip in a motorized canoe capable of carrying four travelers. The trip can take anywhere from four to six hours, depending on the water level and the condition of the river. Bring something soft to sit on (those wooden benches are a killer) and protection from the sun. Jorge can take visitors to Plaplaya for US$42.

Cocobila

Cocobila doesn't offer many amenities for travelers (and who needs 'em when you can stay in the great lodge in Raistá?), but it's interesting to walk through this larger community, complete with schools, church, and medical clinic.

Cerro Baltimore

Named by a U.S. missionary (from Maryland, one suspects), Cerro Baltimore rises 1,083 meters from the south side of Laguna de Ibans. The jungle-clad peak is on the inside edge of the biosphere reserve, but in spite of its protected status, the forest on the southwest side is being cut down by invading cattle-ranchers and loggers. The jungles across most of the mountain remain spectacular and stocked with all manner of birds and mammals. A guided, three-day trip to the peak makes a viable and less-expensive alternative to taking a boat up to Las Marías. Ask around at Raistá to contact guides for this area. On the eastern flank of Cerro Baltimore, a trail cuts from the lagoon through the forest to Las Marías, on the Río Plátano—a full day's hike, reputed to be superb for bird-watching. It can be difficult to find a boat ride back from Las Marías, unless you're willing to wait a few days.

There are basic cabins at the top of the *cerro* for US$5 per person. Locals gather here to avoid the floods when hurricane watches are issued.

WHAT TO BRING TO THE MOSQUITIA

- comfortable walking shoes and walking sandals (your feet will get wet on the boats)

- lightweight, long-sleeved clothes, with shorts or a bathing suit for swimming

- rubberized poncho or a lightweight waterproof windbreaker

- insect repellent and sunblock

- wide-brimmed hat, preferably one with a string that ties under the chin (so it doesn't get blown off when the *pipante* picks up speed to cross the lagoons)

- headlamp and/or flashlight

- camera

- malaria pills

- water bottle

- binoculars for bird- and animal-watching

- large, sturdy garbage bag for your pack (it can get wet on the *pipante*)

- Ziploc bags for wallet and camera

- first-aid kit with antiseptic, bandages, antibiotic, and snakebite kit

- fiber pills – despite all the vegetation, fresh fruits and vegetables aren't easy to come by in the Mosquitia, and most meals are heavy on system-slowing starches. If your visit is more than a couple of days, do yourself a favor and come prepared.

Those planning intensive jungle hikes can also add the following to their list:

- hiking boots – lightweight but waterproof is best

- kerosene or gas stove

- tent or hammock with built-in mosquito net

- survival knife

- compass

- sheet or light sleeping bag

- towel, preferably a microfiber hiking/camping one

- water filter or purification tablets

- waterproof matches and/or lighter

- candles

Las Marías

A mixed Miskito and Pech village of about 500 people, Las Marías is a collection of thatched huts spread over a large area on a rise above the Río Plátano, with no electricity and few amenities. Located just downriver from the edge of the primary forest, Las Marías is the base for hiking and river trips into the jungle.

Coming upstream from the coast to Las Marías, the Río Plátano is lined mostly with secondary forest and small riverside *ranchos,* hardly virgin jungle to be sure, but still teeming with birds and small wild mammals visible to the sharp-eyed or, better yet, those equipped with binoculars. On the way, you're sure to see Miskito families cruising down or energetically poling their way up the river in their narrow dugout *pipantes.*

Amazingly, Las Marías is just 18 miles from the coast the way the crow flies. The boat ride, however, take about six hours. Most boats have a thin cushion now for the wooden seats, but wise travelers will consider bringing a good stadium seat cushion from home. Leave it there when you're done if you don't want to haul it around, but trust us, you'll be glad you brought it.

Once you've arrived in Las Marías and extricated your stiff limbs from the boat, get a bed in one of the several *hospedajes* in town, renting beds with mosquito nets for US$4–6 a night per person. Each hostel serves three basic meals a day, with plenty of rice and beans. Locals

Navigating the Río Plátano takes skill and experience.

recommend the rooms at **Hospedaje Diana** (on the riverbank) and **Hospedaje Rutilia,** and the food at **Hospedaje Justa Herrera** (near the health center). As you will be bringing food for camping anyhow, it's worth bringing a bit extra to supplement your diet in Las Marías, too. However, you may be expected to pay for three meals daily. Locals don't appreciate campers, unless you offer to pay to pitch a tent in someone's yard.

The local water hole is a stream behind the medical center (four regular nurses and one doctor who visits irregularly), away from the river. If you are purifying your own water and don't have purification tablets or a purifier, a couple of drops of bleach per quart will kill bacteria (although it doesn't kill parasites). Don't drink the water from the river, as there are houses just upstream. Swimming in the river is considered safe; alligators and crocodiles are rare in the fast-moving water.

An unusual feature of the two churches in town is that their bells are made of old divers' tanks.

The small airstrip is used only by the Alas de Socorro mission plane, which comes for medical emergencies. If you really hate boats and have the money, it may be possible to charter a plane with Sosa or Sami into Las Marías.

It's easy to hire a private boat from the coastal communities to reach Las Marías, but it's critical to make sure you find a qualified boater, as navigating the river (especially after a heavy rain) takes a lot of skill and experience. Qualified boat drivers include the Bodden family in Raistá, Mario Miller in Belén, and Juan Membreño and "El Chele" in Brus Laguna. In Palacios, Doña Ana Marmol can help arrange a qualified boat driver to Las Marías if necessary. There is not regular *colectivo* service between the coast and Las Marías, but if you're lucky you might find a boat.

◖ Hiking and Boating from Las Marías

The Las Marías guides work on a strict rotation among all 100 households in the village, as it's the only way to keep everyone reasonably happy. When you get to town, ask for either Ricardo Torres or Mariano Davis, who can arrange the guides. Don't try to mess with the system, or you will create problems. Quality varies dramatically from one guide to the next—some are quite shy and, although possibly knowledgeable, don't know what gringos want to hear. For best results, keep asking questions. No English is spoken. The prices and number of guides required for different trips is well defined and not up to negotiation, and a US$5 coordination fee is charged, which goes to the local guide committee. Prices quoted do not include tips for guides, which are expected (the equivalent of US$2–4 dollars per day is appropriate for good service on a multiday hike).

Note: Be sure to come prepared. There are very basic cabins on Cerro Baltimore and Pico Dama, but elsewhere a jungle hammock equipped with mosquito netting is convenient, as there's not always enough open space to pitch a tent. You can expect to get very wet and muddy, year-round. Come prepared with

LAS MARÍAS: A BICULTURAL RARITY

Las Marías is one of the few settlements in the Mosquitia where two ethnic groups – Miskito and Pech – live side by side. The locals have a story about how the two groups met. Supposedly, in the early part of the last century, a group of Miskitos went up the Río Plátano from the coast in search of *cuyamel* fish. Above the present site of Las Marías, at a place where there is a small beach on the banks of the river, the fishermen surprised a group of Pech bathing in the river. These Pech were, at that time, still very much jungle people, and the Miskitos didn't know what to make of them.

The Pech fled immediately, and the Miskitos returned to the coast to tell the tale to their compatriots. Eventually, another Miskito group went upriver, this time with clothes, which they left on the beach. Hiding in the jungle nearby, the Miskitos watched the Pech return to the beach, find the clothes, and start putting them

on all wrong – shorts over their heads, shoes on their hands.

The Miskitos jumped out of their hiding spot and ran after the Pech, who fled into the jungle. One girl was too slow to escape, and the Miskitos captured her and brought her back to the coast, where they taught her Miskito and learned Pech. They returned upriver, and gradually the two groups began interacting and trading. Las Marías was founded about two generations ago, according to residents.

Whether the story is legend or fact, it says a lot about the two cultures. The coastal Miskitos have always been more worldly and domineering than the quieter, reserved Pech; these traits continue to the present day. The two still do not always get along with each other and live in separate parts of the village – the Pech upstream and the Miskitos downstream.

proper clothing and plastic bags to keep things dry in your pack. If you're coming during one of the cooler months, be sure to bring something warm to sleep in, as cabins everywhere have sheets only, not any kind of blanket.

For those wanting just a taste of jungle-hiking, the easiest is a **two-hour trail around Las Marías** (perfect if you arrive in the early afternoon). It's easy to follow on your own, or hire a guide to learn about local plants and trees used for medicine, crafts, and construction. Somewhat harder is a five-hour walk to and from **Cerro Zapote,** a viewpoint that offers vistas toward Cerro Baltimore and Laguna de Ibans. From Cerro Zapote you can see what a serpentine course the Río Plátano follows below Las Marías on the way to the coast, and guides claim an abundance of wildlife, including howler and white-faced monkeys, wild turkey, sloths, snakes, and frogs.

But what draws most visitors is the chance to hike **Pico Dama** (840 meters), the jagged peak looming up out of the jungle not far from Las Marías, which offers stunning views over western Mosquitia, as well as the chance to

see local wildlife if you're quiet enough while you hike. A ruler-flat ridge near the summit, clearly visible from below, makes a spectacular high camp (bring water). The excursion starts with a two-hour boat trip, topped with a four-hour hike to the refuge, which is a small wood house with three beds and a bunk. Bring your own candles, matches, toiletries, a towel, and any medications you might need such as aspirin, Imodium, and Band-Aids—but remember that all you bring you'll have to carry on your back on the hike. There is a latrine, and baths can be taken in the stream (keep this in mind if you are a woman, as your guides will be men—a swimsuit could come very much in handy). From here it is another four hours to the summit, of strenuous hiking, scrambling over rocks, holding onto tree roots, etc., with the spectacular views as your reward. The three-day trip, with two boatmen and a guide, costs US$45 per day for two people, plus provisions.

Another interesting trip is to the **Cerro Mico,** or Monkey Hill, a three-day trip that involves one day's travel along the Sulawala creek by boat and hiking, camping out, a day to climb Cerro Mico and return to camp, and a third day to get back to Las Marías.

For trips upriver by *cayuco,* narrow dugouts propelled by poles, travelers must pay for three guides per *cayuco* (two polers for US$5 each and one guide for US$14) plus US$26 per boat each day as rental. Each *pipante* can only fit two visitors, so if you have a group of three, two boats and six guides are required. Although the *pipante* trips are pricier than hiking, it's hard to beat a silent, nonmotorized boat ride on the river, which acts as a sort of cross section of the virgin jungle. Above Las Marías, the river broadens out, at times as wide as 300 meters, with a 150–200-meter-high canopy of tropical forest foliage. Brilliantly colored parrots, toucans, and other birds cruise unmolested overhead from one side of the river to another, troops of noisy monkeys swing about in the trees, meter-long iguanas dive-bomb into the river, and mammals like tapirs, anteaters, or jaguarundi frequent the river banks, looking for a drink of water or hunting other animals.

It's possible to take a day trip as far as **Walpaulban Sirpi,** to admire its prehistoric rock carving. On a large rock in the river, the petroglyph is considered by archaeologists to represent a crocodile with two heads—perhaps in reference to a Pan-American creation myth that says that the world floats on the back of a two-headed alligator. A night camping by the river allows you to press on the next day to see **Walp'ulban'tara,** a set of petroglyphs depicting several different figures, including monkeys, birds, and human figures. Between the two carvings is the Class II–III Brokwell Rapids, so named for an American gold miner who lost all his gear here in the 1950s. To avoid Brokwell's fate, the guides will portage around the rapids if the river is high. This two day-trip costs about US$100 total for two people, plus food.

If you've come as far as Walp'ulban'tara, consider going one more day upstream to the junction of the **Río Cuyamel,** deep in the jungle. Here, you'll have a better chance of seeing the jungle wildlife, more plentiful here away from the hunters in Las Marías. A five-day trip to the Río Cuyamel area for two people would run about US$225, plus sufficient provisions. At the mouth of the Cuyamel, a trail leads to **Cerro Mirador** (1,200 meters), at least a week round-trip from Las Marías, but an excellent opportunity to fully appreciate both a river trip and a several-day hike. Beyond Río Cuyamel are the wild headwaters of the **Río Plátano,** the very heart of the biosphere reserve. From Las Marías, it takes a week to 10 days of boating and hiking to reach the region. All times upriver change dramatically depending on how fast the river is running.

Río Sico and Río Paulaya

Until just 20 years ago, the section of the Río Sico valley (also called the Río Tinto or the Río Negro) above Palacios and all of the Río Paulaya valley were untouched jungle. Unfortunately, they've been invaded in the past decade by a flood of land-hungry cattle-ranchers from other parts of Honduras. In a move of questionable wisdom, the border of the reserve was set at the Río Paulaya itself, rather than the mountains on the western edge of the valley. So instead of encompassing the entire river valley, the reserve supposedly protects one side of the river but not the other. As no authorities patrol anywhere nearby, it's no surprise cattle-ranchers have been hard at work hacking down the forest on both sides of the river.

BRUS LAGUNA

Originally established as the English outpost named Brewer's Lagoon, Brus Laguna is now a mainly Miskito settlement of about 3,000 inhabitants on the southern edge of the lagoon of the same name. Apart from experiencing this quirky little town of wooden shacks spread over the grassy savannah, there's not a great deal to do. Brus Laguna's main attractions are the surreal, end-of-the-world vibe of town itself and as a departure point for trips to the savannah, Río Sigre, and Las Marías. Because Brus has the only regular air service in this part of the Mosquitia, trips from here up the Río Plátano have become common. Ask

© AMY E. ROBERTSON

the landing at Brus Laguna

around for Dorcas Wood, the local coordinator for La Ruta Moskitia, or Reyes Wood, an English-speaking boatman and guide, for assistance in planning trips.

Considering the high population of crocodiles and caimans, swimming in the lagoon is not recommended. Locals do it anyway, but everyone's got a story about someone they know who lost an appendage, so it hardly seems worth the chance. The mosquitoes and sand flies can be a plague, particularly in the rainy season.

The one cannon on the grassy field in the middle of town originally came from Cannon Cay, an island in the middle of Brus Laguna once used by Miskito Indians and British settlers in conflicts against the Spanish. There are still four cannons on the island, one pointing each direction of the compass. If you are crossing the lagoon with a private boat, you can easily stop off for a short walk around the island (La Ruta Moskitia offers half-hour tours to interested travelers on its packages).

The lagoons, waterways, and ocean around this part of the Mosquitia are renowned for their world-class snook, tarpon, red snapper,

mackerel, and barracuda **fishing.** There used to be shark-fishing as well, but numbers have declined significantly since the introduction of large-scale net-fishing in the lagoon. Brus-based **Team Marin Honduras** (www .teammarinhondurasfishing.com) offers fishing tours of 2–4 nights (as well as a five-day tour to the ruins of Lalla Sanni). The company uses the quite basic Laguna Paradise hotel in Brus, so come for the fishing, not the accommodations (and maybe see about negotiating a stay in one of the nicer hotels). Setting up freelance trips with local fishermen is also perfectly feasible.

Accommodations and Food

Brus has several places to stay in town, none fancy, but perfectly adequate.

The newest digs in town are at **Tawan Pihni** (US$18 s, US$29 d, US$40 t), which means White City (Ciudad Blanca), named after the legendary lost city of the Mosquitia. Twelve rooms are ready and eight more are under construction, all with white tile floors, private baths, desks, TV, and air-conditioning (!),

© AMY E. ROBERTSON

the kitchen/dining area and one of the cabins at the ecolodge Yamari, outside Brus Laguna

although no hot water. From the landing head away from the water one block (toward the airport), then take a right, and the hotel is a little over a block away on the left-hand side of the road.

Not quite as fancy but appealingly located is **Hotel Villa Biosfera** (tel. 504/9919-9925), a seven-room building built on stilts out over the water not far from the landing. Rooms are of polished wood, and there are hammocks in the breezeway. Six of the rooms have one double bed and rent for US$10.50, while the one room with two double beds rents for US$21. All are shared bath (cold water) but have fans and desks (TV is coming too, for those who want it). The reception for the hotel is at **Pulpería Hector.**

Close to the docks is **Hotel Estancia** (US$8–13 shared bath, US$13–18 private bath), a simple cement affair with 12 rooms and cold water. On the main road into town is **Hotel Laguna Paradise** (tel. 504/433-8039, US$16), with concrete floors and naked light bulbs. It's not spotless, but it's acceptable, and the price is per room (each with two double

beds), no matter how many people want to cram in.

There are a couple of *comedores* in town, but don't expect much more than *plátano*, rice, beans, shrimp, iguana, or whatever else the latest boat brought in. An actual restaurant has opened as well, **Masap-Almuk Bar and Restaurant,** but we were in town on a Sunday, and it was closed. The open-air wood structure looked nice, and locals thought it was decent.

Practicalities

Domestic and international calls can be placed at **Pulpería Hector,** on the main road leading to the landing, and basic supplies (Cokes, cake mix, a few random but original-copy DVDs) can be purchased.

There is an **Internet café** at the Tawan Pihni hotel (9 A.M.–noon and 6–9 P.M. Mon.–Sat., 6–9 P.M. Sun.), charging a reasonable US$2.60 an hour.

Sosa (tel. 504/433-8043) flies to and from La Ceiba twice a week (Monday and Friday in midmorning), charging US$226 round-trip. The office is in the one-stop-shop **Pulpería**

Hector. There's one rattletrap taxi (it's one of the two or three cars in town) that usually drives out to the airstrip to meet each flight—ask when you get a ticket. It should be US$2.60 for your ride to town.

Sami (tel. 504/433-8032) flies three times a week between Brus Laguna and La Ceiba during the low season, daily during high season, for US$119 each way.

Yamari

An hour outside of town by motorized *pipante* is Yamari (US$10 pp), another community-run **ecolodge** established by La Ruta Moskita. The lodge design is the same as its sister lodge in Belén: three cabins on stilts with four twin beds each (each with mosquito net), a separate open-air kitchen/dining area, and a shared outhouse with shower (no hot water). The setting, however, is quite different, with the cabins placed in a dramatic, flat savannah along the smooth canal. *Yamari* is the Miskito word for the laurel trees found nearby, most notably covering a small hill in the distance. Peaceful and quiet, it is a true getaway—which should be remembered before you leave Brus Laguna, as anything you might want during your stay here beyond the standard meals (a beer with dinner, a candy bar, some Band-Aids) should be brought with you. There's a solar panel to provide light to the dining area at night, although it's not always reliable.

Although the setting is serene, there are plenty of activities: horseback riding on the savannah; fishing, swimming, lazy tubing, and easy kayaking in the crystal-clear waters of the canal; and nighttime crocodile-spotting tours. (A fantastic activity, but get your swimming in first, as it might be hard to get back in the water the following day once you've seen the crocs at night.) Tours run US$10–25 per person.

While there is always a caretaker on-site at Yamari, it's best to make arrangements for a visit in Brus Laguna, and preferably with a day or two's advance notice. A cook will be sent with you to prepare meals (US$3–4). It's possible to walk to Yamari from Brus Laguna in 2–3 hours (best with a guide), or a boat can be arranged for the hour-long ride. To make arrangements, contact La Ruta Moskita's local coordinator in Brus Laguna, Dorcas Wood, or her husband, Macoy (tel. 504/433-8009).

The savannah can be virtually bug-free during the day, but voracious mosquitoes come out in droves at sunset. Bring effective bug repellent, and keep it handy at nightfall.

◖ RÍO PATUCA

The Río Patuca is the longest river that runs completely inside Honduras and the second largest in Central America after the nearby Río Coco, shared between Honduras and Nicaragua. The Patuca's convoluted 500-kilometer course winds from its headwaters in the mountains of the Olancho, El Paraíso, and Francisco Morazán departments, emptying out through the Mosquitia into the Caribbean. From the coast as far up as Wampusirpi, the broad Patuca is lined with a narrow gallery forest, interspersed with many Miskito villages and farms, and backed by grassy savannah extending east to Puerto Lempira and west to Brus Laguna. Farther south, toward the border of the department of Olancho, the river enters the rainforest and the homeland of the Tawahka Indians. Numbering only about 2,650 souls living in villages on the banks of the Patuca, and struggling to hold out against encroaching loggers and settlers from Olancho, the Tawahka celebrated a small victory with the creation of the **Reserva de la Biosfera Tawahka Asangni,** encompassing 233,000 hectares of supposedly protected jungle. The best place to go for guided river or hiking trips into the jungle is Krausirpe, the unofficial Tawahka capital. Although Wampusirpi is downstream of the jungle, surrounded by savanna and secondary forest, it's possible to hire boats there to take you up nearby tributaries of the Patuca into the rainforest.

South of the Tawahka reserve and created on the same day is the **Parque Nacional Río Patuca,** covering 376,000 hectares of jungle and mountains between the Río Patuca and the Río Coco. Beyond the park, the Río Patuca enters inhabited areas of Olancho, where immigrants have turned jungle into pastureland and small farms.

Barra Patuca

At the mouth of the Río Patuca is the large Miskito town of Barra Patuca, with several stores and a couple of basic *hospedajes*. Several families will cook travelers a meal for a fee. Narrow, uncomfortable cargo boats run every day or two upstream 7–10 hours to Ahuas, or through the waterways to Brus Laguna in an hour or two. Likely as not, you'll have to wait around a couple of days to find a boat with an open seat; expect to pay around US$25 to Ahuas or US$7–10 to Brus. Finding boats east along the coast to Puerto Lempira or west to Palacios is more difficult.

Sami (tel. 504/433-8032) has flights to Patuca from La Ceiba three times a week during low season, daily during the high season, for US$143.

Ahuas

The largest town on the Río Patuca, Ahuas has a population of about 1,500, almost all Miskito, spread out over the savanna and pine groves a couple of kilometers from the river. Missionaries have been hard at work at Ahuas, as evidenced by the several churches in town. There's not a lot of reason to come here, except as a stopover on the way upstream to Wampusirpi or into the Tawahka reserve.

An exploratory oil well was sunk near Ahuas in the 1970s, and the remnants of the derrick are still nearby. The rather incongruous big-rig truck in the middle of town was floated up the river by the oil crews and left when the well was abandoned. A local got the semi cranked up again not long back, but there's nowhere to drive it except out to the oil rig and back again.

Usually one or two families in town will offer very basic rooms to travelers who wander through. Basic meals (heavy on rice and beans) are frequently found with families, but bringing some extra food is not a bad idea. A couple of *pulperías* in town sell basic supplies. The mission hospital near the airstrip usually has a western doctor in residence and offers good emergency care.

Ahuas is the base for Alas de Socorro, and you may be able to contact them to catch a ride. Sami (tel. 504/433-8032) flies to and from Ahuas three times a week in low season and daily during high season (US$130 one-way).

At Ahuas, the Patuca is a wide and impressive river, bordered by a narrow strip of jungle. Boats frequently head downriver from here to Barra Patuca (3.5 hours) or upriver to Wampusirpi (7–8 hours). These narrow cargo/passenger boats are often packed and uncomfortable, so be prepared. *Viajes especiales* cost a great deal more.

Wampusirpi

Upriver from Ahuas is Wampusirpi, a former Tawahka town whose population has been joined by Miskitos in recent decades, many having fled the violence of the Contra war in the 1980s. It is now a handicraft center, where most of the *tuno* (beaten tree bark) crafts sold in gift shops across the country are made, as well as pictures made of leaves, and seed necklaces. Wampusirpi is surrounded by savanna and stands of Caribbean pine, with patches of gallery forest lining the nearby rivers. There are three basic *hospedajes*, which charge US$4–6, the best of which belongs to Santiago Rivas. Basic meals can be arranged without too much difficulty, although there are no restaurants per se. It's best to come out this way prepared with a tent and food. The jungle-clad Río Uhra, a tributary of the Patuca on the west side not far downstream from Wampusirpi, makes for great 1–3-day explorations with a hired boatman. Upstream from Wampusirpi on the Patuca are the Miskito villages of, in order, Kurpa, Tukrun, and Pimienta. Sami flies to and from Wampusirpi three times a week in low season and daily during high season (US$143 one-way).

Tawahka Region

Beyond Pimienta is Krausirpe, a riverside village that serves as the unofficial capital of the Tawahka. This is the center of the **Reserva de la Biosfera Tawahka Asangni,** 233,000

THE CANOE-BUILDERS OF THE RÍO PATUCA

On the banks of the Río Patuca, near its confluence with the Río Wampú in the heart of the Mosquitia jungle, are the ancestral lands of the Tawahka, one of the smallest ethnic groups in Honduras. A rainforest tribe thought to have migrated up from South America in the distant past, the Tawahka now number only about 1,000 souls in several riverside villages, the largest of which is Krausirpe.

Originally one of many related subtribes in the Mosquitia, the Tawahka fell under the sway of the newly born Miskito tribe in the 17th century. Well-armed and aggressive, the Miskitos came to control the Mosquitia region during the colonial era, demanding tribute from the Tawahka and even inventing a derogatory term for them that is still used by Miskito and ladinos today: the Sumu.

Although they originally roamed over a much larger territory, centuries of pressure from the Miskito and, especially in the last two decades, ladino colonos (migrant farmers) have whittled down Tawahka territory to a fraction of its former size. The tribe now has access to barely enough land to maintain its traditional lifestyle of small-scale agriculture along the riverbanks, combined with hunting and plant-gathering in the rainforest.

Among their many talents, the Tawahka are renowned as superb builders of large canoes, and in the past, they frequently supplemented their income by selling 10-meter crafts, hollowed out of a single mahogany, to Miskitos on the coast or to ladino farmers upriver. In fact, it is thought the Tawahka first began making the large canoes at the behest of the Miskitos in the 19th century, as part of the tribute the tribe was forced to pay. These days, however, canoe-builders are having an increasingly hard time finding suitable trees, as the valuable wood is coveted by the colonos busy hacking down what was the Tawahka's "canoe forest" near the Río Wampú. Tawahka are leery of venturing up the Wampú, or the nearby Cuyamel, for fear of running into gun-toting colonos.

Poor and uneducated as they are – many speak only faltering Spanish – the Tawahka have found it difficult to halt the steady invasion of aggressive ladinos, who cut down their forest and start homestead farms and cattle ranches. In 1987, the tribe created the Federación Indígena Tawahka de Honduras (FITH), which now works to protect Tawahka land and rights with other indigenous groups in Honduras and with international organizations. One victory for the newly organized Tawahka and their allies was the eventual cancellation of a proposed hydroelectric dam on the Río Patuca, which would have covered part of their lands in a reservoir.

After much pressure by the Tawahka, a new biosphere reserve was decreed by the Honduran government around their homelands. Created on December 21, 1999, the Reserva de la Biosfera Tawahka Asangni covers 233,000 hectares – much less than the Tawahka had hoped for, but at least a reprieve in their constant struggle to hold on to their lands.

hectares of protected lands connecting the Río Plátano Biosphere Reserve to the Bosawas reserve in Nicaragua. The Tawahka, with some international help, pushed strongly for the reserve as a means to combat the constant incursions of *ladino* immigrants from Olancho.

With Tawahka guides, visitors can hike from Krausirpe to preconquest caves, petroglyphs, or into the jungle in any direction. The well-beaten Wankibila Trail cuts from near Krausirpe along the Río Sutawala valley, through a gap in the hills, and over to the Río Coco valley and the town of Ahuasbila, where trucks to Puerto Lempira can be found. The trail takes a full day to hike (leave at dawn) and requires a guide.

Beyond Krausirpe is the village of Krautara, and farther up the Patuca into Olancho are the Tawahka settlements of Yapuwás, Kamakasna, and Wasparasní.

The easiest way into the Tawahka region is by plane to Wampusirpi along the Río Patuca, or by flying directly in to Krausirpe by special flight.

Another route into the Tawahka region available to independent travelers (probably the least expensive all in all) is from Nueva Palestina, a cowboy town in Olancho on the upper part of the Río Patuca, reached by bus from Danlí. Boats and pilots can be hired in Nueva Palestina or on the river at Arenas Blancas, down one or two days to Krausirpe.

PUERTO LEMPIRA

The capital of the Gracias a Dios department, and the largest population center in the Mosquitia with around 6,000 people, Puerto Lempira is laid out in a grid of dirt roads running back from the southern shore of Laguna Caratasca. From the long dock right in front of Puerto Lempira, *lanchas* venture out to Miskito villages around the lagoon or along the connected waterways. While the region around Puerto Lempira is relatively expensive to get to (about US$260 round-trip to La Ceiba) and not known for tourism, the more adventurous and unrushed traveler will find huge expanses of lagoon, savanna, riverside jungle, and windswept, deserted Caribbean beach to explore.

For most of its history an isolated little port in the farthest corner of the Mosquitia, Puerto Lempira experienced a boom in the 1980s, when it became the center of operations for the CIA-directed insurgency against the Sandinista government in Nicaragua. The U.S. spooks are long gone, and now this part of the Mosquitia makes its living mainly from fishing, particularly lobster diving, a relatively lucrative profession, but one that has left several hundred Miskito men crippled with the bends. (One ex-diver attributed a large number of the injuries to men who dive after drinking or doing drugs, rather than a lack of training.) Apart from fishing, most of the area's people eke out a living as small-scale farmers. Puerto Lempira also has a large population of *ladinos* (*indios,* as the Miskitos disparagingly call them), working in the many government offices in town.

A new entrant to the local economy, which makes use of the region's deserted beaches and coastline, is cocaine, smuggled in large quantities from Colombia north to the United States and elsewhere. It's easy to spot the young men driving new pickup trucks, which were expensively shipped in and use gasoline twice as costly as in the rest of Honduras. The smuggling goes on at hidden airstrips and beaches very far from any settlement, so visitors run no risk in the trips around Puerto Lempira mentioned below and are only likely to run into suspicious characters if they go to the local disco.

Few tourists make it to Puerto Lempira, except those stopping in on their way to Nicaragua. It makes a good base, however, for a world-class fishing trip to Laguna Caratasca, and there is plenty of good birding.

Practicalities

The nicest hotel in town is **Hotel Los Pinares** (tel. 504/433-6679, US$42 s, US$47 d, cold water only), with air-conditioning, fan, and TV in the rooms, and a swimming pool, restaurant, and generator on the property. The only thing missing is hot water, but take a shower in the late afternoon, when the water's been warmed by the sun all day, and you won't miss it. Being the fanciest hotel in town, it's almost always full, so call a few days or a week in advance to reserve a room.

Down by the dock is the good value **Yu Baiwan View Hotel** (US$24 s, US$26 d, cold water only), offering 18 clean and spacious rooms with private baths and decent air-conditioning.

A less expensive option is **Hospedaje Santa Teresita** (tel. 504/433-6008, US$13 d), with 18 simple but functional rooms.

Several simple *comedores* offer basic meals in town, but don't expect anything special.

The **Hondutel** office (7 A.M.–9 P.M. Mon.–Fri.) is a couple of blocks north of the *parque.* If it's not open, try the **Centro Comunitario** (7 A.M.–10 P.M. daily), which has phone service at the same prices, plus a few magazines and newspapers for sale. The owner, Chepe, is a friendly sort, happy to answer the questions of a foreign visitor.

Banco Atlántida (tel. 504/433-6086, 8–11:30 A.M. and 1:30–4 P.M. Mon.–Fri.,

8–11:30 A.M. Sat.), in the same building as Hotel Flores, will exchange U.S. dollars for lempiras, as well as advance money on a Visa card. Nicaraguan money is not accepted—you have to get rid of your córdobas at Leimus. Remember this is the only bank in all of the Mosquitia, so be sure you have enough to last during your time in the Mosquitia, and be sure to ask for plenty of 100-lempira notes, since the 500-lempira bill can be difficult to break at times.

Migración (8 A.M.–noon and 2–5 P.M. Mon.–Fri., 8 A.M.–noon Sat.) is next to Hondutel, although all offices seem to be redirecting tourists to Tegucigalpa for any kind of visa renewal.

The **Mopawi headquarters** (Puerto Lempira tel. 504/433-6022, Catacamas tel. 504/799-4127, Tegucigalpa tel. 504/235-8659, www.mopawi.org) is on the edge of the lagoon, a few blocks south of the main dock. Formed in 1985 with the help of World Relief, the name derives from "Mosquitia Pawisa Apiska," which means Mosquitia Development Agency in Miskito. The organization coordinates a variety of social and environmental projects in the region, and its workers are often excellent sources of information on the Mosquitia and its peoples. They also accept volunteers (there is an application form right on their website). Mopawi operates a well-stocked store at its headquarters.

Getting There and Away

Sosa (tel. 504/433-6558), with an office in town, flies to La Ceiba every morning except Sunday. **Sami** (tel. 504/433-6170), otherwise known as Honduras Air, flies an aircraft of questionable safety between Puerto Lempira and La Ceiba every day except Sunday during the high season, three times a week during the low season (US$130 one way).

Small *lanchas* are constantly zigging and zagging across the lagoon to various villages and usually charge US$1–2 a ride if you're going their way.

◀ Around Laguna Caratasca

The expansive Laguna Caratasca, so big it develops good-sized waves, measures 66 kilometers long and 14 kilometers wide. Linked by waterways with the adjacent Tansin and Warunta lagoons, Caratasca is the center of a gigantic freshwater lagoon system across northeastern Mosquitia, fed by the Ríos Mocorón, Warunta, and Nakunta, among others. The wide lagoon entrance, Barra Caratasca, is directly opposite the lagoon from Puerto Lempira, visible on a clear day. Along the edges of this watery world live several thousand Miskito in lakefront communities varying in size from a couple of houses to towns of 2,000. Many of these picturesque villages are well worth visiting to experience the long-lost feel of these isolated places and meet the local Miskitos, as well as to enjoy deserted Caribbean beaches and boat along the inland waterways looking for birds, manatees, monkeys, and other wildlife living in the mangroves and coastal jungles. If you were somehow able to get a sea kayak or light canoe out to Puerto Lempira, it would be the perfect vehicle for exploring these waterways, although beware the waves, wind, and treacherous currents. Heavier wooden *cayucos* might be found for rent in Puerto Lempira or a lakeside village, and you can certainly find boatmen willing to take you on trips of varying length in their motorized *lanchas* for negotiable prices. As always, knowing how many gallons the trip takes, and how much the cost of fuel is, helps negotiating.

The lagoon is a paradise for **fishing,** stocked with world-class tarpon, snook, jack, grouper, and other fish; you'll need to bring your own tackle and hire a boat to take you out, as there are no tourist fishing facilities in Puerto Lempira. The best fishing season is between May and July. Favored places to fish are at the outlets of lagoons into the open ocean, at either high or low tide, or where rivers flow into the south side of the lagoon. Ask around in Puerto Lempira for Eduardo Chow, Delmar Brown, or Delmar Haylock, for help arranging a fishing trip.

One of the more attractive Miskito communities near Puerto Lempira is **Kaukira,** worth visiting if only for the seemingly endless Caribbean beach. A large town spread over a couple of kilometers on a narrow peninsula, with the ocean on one side and the lagoon on the other, Kaukira is easily reached by the frequent daily (except Sunday) *lanchas* cruising back and forth to Puerto Lempira. Boats usually leave Kaukira at 7 or 8 A.M. and depart Puerto Lempira for the return trip midmorning, charging US$6 for a fast boat or US$5 for a slower one. Getting a ride out in the afternoon is difficult—better plan on staying the night, unless you want to pay US$50 or so for a *viaje especial* back to Puerto Lempira. Rooms and food are easy to come by in Kaukira by asking around.

On the north shore of Tansin Island (actually a peninsula), on the shore of Laguna Caratasca, **Palkaka** is a relaxed Miskito village with a small freshwater beach. Fishing in the lagoon nearby is plentiful, and the waterways to the west are full of different kinds of waterfowl, manatees, and other lagoon wildlife. As at Kaukira, boats leave most every day to Palkaka from the main dock in Puerto Lempira.

On the southeastern shore of the Laguna Tansin, and linked to Puerto Lempira by a 17-kilometer dirt road leaving past the airstrip, is the Miskito village of **Mistruk,** with a clean freshwater beach on a corner of the lagoon. The beach sees a few visitors from Puerto Lempira on weekends, and quite a crowd during Holy Week, but is otherwise pretty quiet. Locals will happily arrange boat trips along the lagoons and waterways to watch for birds, crocodiles, manatees, and other critters at a negotiable fee. There are a few wooden cabins along the beach with two beds each and private bathrooms, renting for around US$20 a night. At last report they lacked mosquito nets, so it would be wise to bring your own here. Taxis can be hired to take visitors to the beach, charging around US$34 for a round-trip ride, including waiting time. Hitching rides is possible, particularly in the morning, but finding a ride back in the afternoon might be problematic.

By Road to the Nicaraguan Border

A dirt road winds southwest from Puerto Lempira past Mistruk through savanna and stands of pine to the villages of **Mocorón,** on the banks of the Río Mocorón about three hours from Puerto Lempira by pickup truck.

The dirt road continues southwest past Mocorón another two hours to **Rus Rus** and an hour beyond to **Ahuasbila,** on the Río Coco. Between Mocorón and Rus Rus, a road turns south to the Nicaraguan border at **Leimus,** where travelers can cross into Nicaragua. There are Honduran and Nicaraguan immigration officials at the border. Nicaragua charges US$7 to enter (Honduras charges US$3). There are no official exit fees for either country.

Río Coco and Far Northeastern Mosquitia

A dozen or so Miskito villages line the Río Coco, mostly on the Nicaraguan side, between Leimus and the ocean. One large town is **Sawa,** known colloquially as *yul aikraa,* "dog-killer," in requiem for a local victim of the ferocious mosquitoes. The closest village to Cabo Gracias a Dios itself is **Planghikira,** but nobody lives out on the blustery point itself. Canals head west from the Río Coco to the villages of **Irlaya** and **Raya,** and from there back to Laguna Caratasca.

Regarding **Laguna Apalka,** an apparently landlocked lagoon between the Río Coco and Laguna Caratasca, the locals have an interesting legend. Word has it that a British pirate ship was caught up in a fierce storm trying unsuccessfully to round the cape and ended up getting blown into the lagoon, where it sank. Some say the treasure was removed and buried nearby before the ship sank, while others maintain it remains with the ship, which they claim can be seen from above through the clear waters. But malevolent spirits are said to guard the wreck, and all the divers who have swum down to investigate have never returned. . . .

Off the Caribbean coast from Raya are several small coral cays, including **Bogas Cay,** the closest in, and **Savannah Cay,** farther out and larger. The reef and water quality are reported to be excellent, but they are accessible only with fishermen who come in from the islands to Raya from time to time.

Olancho

It is a broad valley, beautiful and amenable, but ringed on all sides by very high mountains, cut by deep rivers and dangerous canyons. The first explorers who came this way were surely bored of their existence.

— Padre José Antonio Goicoechea, missionary in Agalta in 1802

The far-flung valleys, rugged mountains, and thick forests of Olancho are a sort of Honduran "Wild East," as it were, a wide open territory with immense expanses of wild country to explore.

For the intrepid and self-reliant, Olancho is a superb place to travel. Much of Olancho—the largest of Honduras's 18 departments, covering one-fifth of the national territory—is blanketed with seemingly endless pine-forested mountains. On the higher reaches of these mountains, most particularly Sierra de Agalta and La

Muralla, are some of the densest, most extensive cloud forests in Central America, thriving with wildlife. The rivers and tropical rainforests that continue down into the Mosquitia begin in northern Olancho. The opportunities for wilderness adventuring are endless.

Just as appealing as the natural beauty is the old-school cowboy feel of the local people. Known by its residents, only half in jest, as "La República Libre de Olancho" (The Free Republic of Olancho), this department has long maintained a Texas-style disdain for the central government and a firm belief in taking care of things themselves, thank you very much. The self-reliant attitude arose during the colonial era, when *olanchanos,* isolated from the rest of Central America, developed self-sufficient haciendas where everything needed was made with the materials at hand. Wandering the back roads and trails across Olancho, travelers can still find plenty of old-style *ranchos* filled with

The Río Olancho snakes its way from the canyon of El Boquerón.

handmade wooden furniture carved from *juglans olanchana* (an endemic walnut tree), worked leather clothes, and other antiques. Honduran bargain-hunters took to visiting Olancho *ranchos* to buy up the antiques and resell them in shops in Valle de Ángeles or Tegucigalpa.

Another trait developed during the colonial era is the propensity of *olanchanos* to take justice into their own hands, in a style not unlike the U.S. cowboys of a century ago. As one resident commented dryly to a newspaper reporter, "The *olanchano* isn't violent by nature, but you have to respect him." The family feuds and crimes of passion are not directed at foreigners, and, in fact, *olanchanos* tend to be courtly and hospitable with outsiders in an old-school way, proud to show off the land they love so much.

Travelers who do make it out to Olancho often find the department to be their favorite part of Honduras, offering unparalleled hiking opportunities at El Boquerón, the bird-watching paradise of La Muralla, or the magnificent Sierra de Agalta National Park, ranked by many as the greatest natural area in the country outside of the Mosquitia. Intrepid visitors can also explore many ruin sites in Olancho, such as Dos Quebradas, near El Boquerón, or take it easy with a day trip to the Cuevas de Talgua, dating from the region's dynamic but little-understood pre-Columbian cultures.

Because of the amount of land it covers, Olancho's climate is not easy to categorize. Rainfall in the department ranges between 80 and 260 centimeters per year on average, depending on the region. The southern valleys tend to be driest, while the wettest areas are the mountain forests to the north. The dry season is usually February–April. Temperatures in Olancho also vary wildly, mostly depending on altitude, but it's usually comfortable in most populated areas—warm in the day and cool at night. Bring warm, dry clothes if you plan to camp in the mountains.

The 192-kilometer, two-lane highway to Tegucigalpa from Juticalpa is in good shape and can be driven in two hours. Much of it is lined with graceful gliricidia trees that bloom with tiny pink flowers once a year. Catacamas is 41 kilometers from Juticalpa, while the turn-off to San Francisco de la Paz and Gualaco (for visits to Parque Nacional Sierra de Agalta) is 10 kilometers northeast of Juticalpa on the Catacamas road.

HISTORY

Discoveries at the Cuevas de Talgua near Catacamas have led archaeologists to believe that a sedentary village culture lived in the plains of Olancho 1,000 years before Christ. Little is known about these early *olanchanos,* but evidence suggests the culture evolved on its own, rather than as an offshoot of the parallel cultures developing at that time in the Valle de Ulúa. The region drew indigenous groups from both the north and the south, making it a unique transition zone between Mesoamerican and South American pre-Hispanic cultures. A great deal of investigation remains to be done in the countless archaeological sites in Olancho, which include Dos Quebradas, Talgua, Guayape, Agua Amarilla near El Carbón, Los Encuentros, Las Crucitas, Marañones, Saguasón, and many others. Several of these ruins are extremely impressive in size and complexity, but they remain unexcavated and as yet little is known about their builders.

One fact that may have accounted for the development of an organized society in early Olancho is the extraordinarily rich deposits of gold in the mountains and rivers of the region, much of which has yet to be worked to its full potential. It is said that the Aztecs of Mexico indicated to the gold-hungry Spanish conquistadors that this region was where they received much of their supply.

In search of this gold, the conquistadors came directly to Olancho when they first arrived in this part of Central America. Many different indigenous tribes inhabited Olancho when the Spaniards arrived, including Pech, Lenca, Tawahka, Tolupán, and perhaps descendants of Nahuatl immigrants from Mexico, who later lost their original language and blended in with other groups. According to local legend, the Nahuatl arrived after a long journey from the north, fleeing a great drought. The name Olancho is thought to be a derivation of a Nahuatl word meaning "land of tule trees," which are plentiful in Olancho's forests.

The Spanish era in Olancho began in 1524, when Gil González Dávila, coming from the north coast, and Hernando de Soto, marching overland from Nicaragua, met in the Valle de Catacamas and promptly started a fight over who had the right to conquer Honduras. Fighting continued among Spaniards and with rebellious Pech, Tolupán, and Tawahka until 1540, when the town of San Jorge de Olancho had been established in the Valle de Olancho, near El Boquerón. Its inhabitants forced black slaves and Indians to work the surrounding rivers for gold, especially the Río Guayape. Not long after, colonists established Juticalpa and Catacamas, now the two major towns in Olancho.

Either due to cruel treatment by the Spanish or a generally independent spirit, the indigenous peoples of the colonial province were in constant rebellion. The security of the region was further weakened as the English gained power on the north coast. Their allies, the Miskitos, invaded Olancho by boat from the Río Patuca, Paulaya, or Sico in search of gold or Indian slaves to sell to the English.

When the Spanish regained the north coast and expelled the British at the end of the 18th century, Olancho enjoyed a couple of decades of relative peace. The advent of Honduran independence brought renewed violence, with the prolonged and bloody civil wars in Olancho, first in the late 1820s and then again in 1863. By the late 19th century, Olancho settled into a relatively self-contained rural existence.

The 1980s saw a renewed surge of violence in Olancho, this time from the CIA-directed Contra War, part of which occurred along the long, wild border between Olancho and Nicaragua. The department still maintains a deserved reputation for highway banditry on remote roads and trafficking of illicit goods (particularly Colombian cocaine on its way north) through the jungles from Moskitia or Nicaragua.

Olancho makes its living through cattle-raising, coffee-growing, logging (some legal, much not), and, infrequently, panning for gold. The occasional wild-eyed miner still wanders off to the far-flung reaches of the department hoping for a lucky strike.

JUTICALPA

The capital of Olancho, Juticalpa was first established as a small settlement by the Spaniards, probably around 1530, on the site of an Indian village near the then-capital of San Jorge de Olancho. Stone axes and arrowheads are still occasionally found in town, particularly in the Belén neighborhood.

At the southern end of the Valle de Catacamas 400 meters above sea level, Juticalpa's 34,000 residents make their living either working with the departmental government, ranching, or as merchants for the surrounding area. Juticalpa is often a stop-off point on the way to Olancho from Tegucigalpa. It's a convenient place to take care of business and is a base for hiking trips to the nearby Monumento Natural El Boquerón and Sierra de Agalta, or farther afield to La Muralla and the Mosquitia.

The town's annual *feria* begins the night of December 7 and lasts for a week.

Sights

The **Casa de Cultura** (tel. 504/785-1085), a large yellow colonial building on the south side of the *parque,* makes a quiet place to relax, read a book, or write a postcard. There are some displays on history and archaeology in Olancho, as well as a small library and a collection of pottery made by indigenous women near Guata, Olancho. Anyone with an interest in local history should ask for information here.

The central park is a pleasant place to loll about, flanked by the *alcaldía* (city hall) on one side and a beautiful, relatively modern cathedral on the other.

Entertainment

Juticalpa has a lively disco scene located out along the highway toward Tegucigalpa. Things are usually *tranquilo,* but beware the occasional

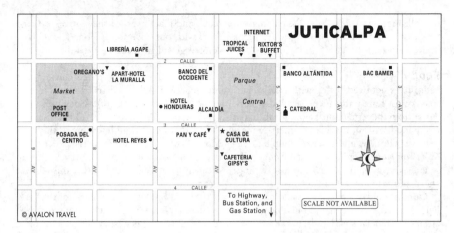

inebriated (and/or wired) brawl or shooting between cowboys over someone looking the wrong way at the wrong girl.

Shopping

The **Saturday market,** set up behind the Aurora bus terminal near the highway, is a great place to wander around and check out local handicrafts and produce.

Accommodations

The best hotel in downtown is ◖ **Posada del Centro** (tel. 504/785-3414, US$29 s, US$40.50 d), two blocks west of the square next to the market. The 26 rooms have high ceilings with wooden beams, TV, and air-conditioning, and are kept very clean by the efficient and friendly staff. The 10 rooms on the third floor are the ones to get, opening onto an atrium with hammocks and clay wind chimes. The hotel has a cafeteria (breakfast is included) and a meeting room. Parking is outside, but the watchman keeps a close eye on things.

Hotel Boquerón (tel. 504/785-1147, US$35.50 s, US$58 d), a few blocks farther west and outside the city center, has the fanciest spread in town, with an imposing facade, a large parking area, and a swimming pool. The 38 rooms (each with air-conditioning and TV) are not quite as nice as at Posada del Centro, but much more spacious. Unfortunately, the

hot water is unreliable, and the staff indifferent. There is karaoke available every night of the week, so if anyone has come in to sing, don't expect to go to sleep early.

The family-owned **Hotel Honduras** (tel. 504/885-1331, US$16 s, US$23 d with fan, US$21 s, US$32 d with a/c), one block west of the square, has perfectly nice little rooms, clean and well-maintained, with wood furniture and a small desk. A few rooms even have tiny balconies overlooking the street. The rooms do smell a little musty though.

Similar, but with cold water and worn towels, is **Apart-Hotel La Muralla** (tel. 504/785-1270, US$13 s, US$18.50 d with fan, around US$10 more for a/c, cold water only). There's parking available.

Dirt-cheap digs can be found at **Hotel Reyes** (tel. 504/785-2232, US$4 s, US$5 d with shared bath, US$7 d with private bath, cold water only), a small family-run hotel one block southwest of the square with very basic rooms and a 9:30 P.M. curfew.

Another higher-end spot outside of town, on the old exit to Catacamas, is **Villa San Andrés** (tel. 504/785-2405, US$30 s/d), with eight spacious, clean rooms with air-conditioning and telephones, in what looks like (and was originally) a large house, rather than a hotel. This is a peaceful and comfortable spot to stay, but only if you have your own car, as it's too far to walk into town. It's along the old road to Catacamas, near the main highway. Taxis know the way.

Food

Juticalpa is not overflowing with creative cuisine—most restaurants focus heavily on beef. Apart from the restaurants below, meals in the many food stalls in the local market are inexpensive, sanitary, and tasty. A couple of *baleada* and *pastelito* ladies are usually out on the square every night until 9 P.M. or so, offering a cheap and tasty light dinner.

Cafeteria Gipsy's (7 A.M.–9 P.M. Mon.–Sat.), half a block from the park in a building with an attractive, colonial-style facade, has an inexpensive buffet all day long, with several different entrées to choose from. Price depends on what you order, but a meal typically runs US$3.50–5.

❰ **Oregano's** (until 8 P.M. Mon.–Sat.), a

COYOL WINE

A traditional Olancho drink, seen more rarely these days as imported *aguardiente* and rum take over, coyol wine can be thought of as a cross between hard cider and champagne. Local Indians once made the wine by climbing up a coyol palm, hollowing out a hole under the bud, and sucking the sap out with a reed. The sap, which is strongest in March and April, in the middle of the dry season, ferments over the course of a few days or a week.

Nowadays, *olanchanos* can't be bothered climbing trees, so they generally just cut the whole thing down. A single tree can yield up to three gallons of wine. Olancho historian José Sarmiento, commenting on the early history of the wine, writes: "It is not known how the drink coming from the coyol palm was discovered, but the first who tried it can be called, with complete confidence, the first *olanchano*."

La Concepción, a short ride from Juticalpa, is renowned for its coyol wine – just make sure it's in season before hopping on the bus.

---

block and a half west of the *parque*, is a tiny spot, with only five stools along a stone and colored glass bar. It has perhaps the only creative cuisine in all of Olancho, with dishes like *curry caribeño*, coconut-breaded chicken in a rum sauce, as well as Italian standards like lasagna and pizza (US$6–10). A medium pizza comfortably serves two.

Tropical Juices (midmorning until 9 P.M. Mon.–Sat.), with locations on the park and on the main road out to the highway, whips up excellent fruit shakes and juices, and sells ice cream too.

Rixtor's Buffet, on the corner of the park, is a decent place for a buffet breakfast or lunch (8 A.M.–2 P.M.). The restaurant remains open into the evening, serving mostly ice cream, and small snacks upon request.

Kitty-corner from the park near the Casa de Cultura is **Pan y Café,** with coffee, baked goods, and a small buffet at breakfast and lunch.

One of the better upscale eateries in town, frequently recommended by locals, is ❰ **Restaurante La Fonda** (8 A.M.–9 P.M. daily), on the highway toward Tegucigalpa just past the DIPPSA gas station on the right-hand side, coming from town. The menu is nothing outrageous—steaks, chicken, *pinchos*, etc.— but the food (US$3.50–7 per plate) is well prepared and the portions are heaping. *Pinchos* are served with an appetizer, called an *anafre,* of hot beans, cream, and chips served in an ingenious clay fondue pot. If you don't have your own wheels, take a taxi out from town and arrange to be picked up later, or hoof it for a half-hour's walk back to town.

Services

Both **Banco Atlántida** and **BAC Bamer** will change dollars and advance money on a Visa card. Banco Atlántida has an ATM (Visa only), and MoneyGrams can be picked up here. **Banco del Occidente** at the corner of the park can receive Western Union transfers and change dollars.

Hondutel is one block east and three blocks south of the *parque,* and the post office is a half block west of the park.

Juticalpa has a couple dozen **Internet** cafés, usually for US$1 or less an hour, many also with inexpensive international Internet phone calls. One convenient choice is the no-name café next door to Rixtor's (8 A.M.–7:30 P.M. daily), with calls to the United States for US$0.08 per minute.

The **Librería Agape** sells school supplies and books—many self-help, religious, or both, but also a decent selection of Honduran authors (in Spanish) if you are looking to replenish your reading supplies.

Emergencies

To contact the **police,** call 504/785-2110 or 504/785-2028, or dial 199. For the **fire department,** dial 504/785-2910 or 198.

For medical care, head to the **Hospital San Francisco** (tel. 504/785-2655). If you need an **ambulance,** call the Red Cross at 504/785-2221.

Getting There and Away

Juticalpa has three **bus stations** a block away from one another on either side of the entrance road from the Tegucigalpa highway. Closest to the highway (across the boulevard from Bomba's) is the terminal for **Discovery** (tel. 504/785-6864), which runs "luxury" buses to Tegucigalpa at 8 A.M., 12:45 P.M., and 4:15 P.M., charging US$8.50 for the 2.5-hour ride.

On the same side of the boulevard but across the street (behind Hotel Santa Fe) is the terminal for **Aurora** (tel. 504/799-4154), with "direct" (no stops, but no frills on the bus) and "normal" (stopping every five minutes) service. The direct buses depart at 6:15 A.M., 6:40 A.M., 7 A.M., 8:30 A.M., 9:15 A.M., 10 A.M., noon, 1 P.M., 2 P.M., and 5 P.M., and charge US$4.50 for the 3-hour ride. There are often two more direct buses in the afternoon on the weekends. Normal buses depart frequently all day and are US$3 for the 3.5-hour ride.

Across the street and one block back toward town is the departmental bus terminal, with buses to basically anywhere in Olancho. It's always best to go the afternoon before to confirm departure times, and then get there at least 15 minutes early. Buses to Catacamas and San Francisco de la Paz both leave frequently 8 A.M.–4 P.M. (US$1.25, one hour); to Gualaco there are two daily at 10:30 A.M. and 3 P.M.

© AMY E. ROBERTSON

The ride from Tegucigalpa to Olancho takes a winding route.

(US$2.75, 1.5 hours); and to La Concepción, two buses leave every hour (US$0.30).

One bus makes the daily run to La Unión, for Parque Nacional La Muralla, at 11 A.M. (2.5 hours, US$4).

◖ MONUMENTO NATURAL EL BOQUERÓN

Between Juticalpa and Catacamas is Monumento Natural El Boquerón, a 4,000-hectare natural area covering two canyons and a mountain peak in the foothills of Sierra de Agalta, on the north side of the highway. The canyon is a fine place to take a day trip, but if you've got a couple of days, consider camping and bird-watching up on the mountain in a small patch of cloud forest, or visiting the little-known pre-Columbian ruins site of Dos Quebradas. Three-toed anteaters, three species of toucans, and endlessly chattering flocks of parakeets are just a few of the easily-spotted animals in the forest.

There are **three trails** into the El Boquerón reserve, one leading along the Río Olancho into the canyon and two others, Tenpiscapita and Agua Buena, which lead to the eastern summit, **Cerro Agua Buena.**

These trails all initiate at the village of El Boquerón, a blink-and-you'll-miss-it town roughly halfway between Juticalpa and Catacamas along the highway. The largest landmark is the Di Express gas station. A bus here from Catacamas is US$0.75.

An excellent source of information on the park is village resident Don José Mendoza (tel. 504/996-1798), also known to locals as "Joche Boquerón," who lives on the northern side of the highway, not far down a little dirt road (ask anyone in town). He is employed by COHDEFOR as the park caretaker, and gladly guides visitors along any of the trails for no charge (but a tip of around US$5 for a day hike is very much appropriate). His son is following in his footsteps and is another good guide. If neither is available, locals can help find an alternative guide, recommended for the two hikes to the summit.

For those who think hiking the summit might be too strenuous, Don José could likely arrange for horses with a couple of days

---

THE DESTRUCTION OF SAN JORGE DE OLANCHO

Not far from the Catacamas-Juticalpa highway near the Río Olancho is the site of San Jorge de Olancho, the region's early capital, which was wiped out by a natural disaster of mysterious character in 1611. William Wells, a North American traveler who passed through Olancho in the 1850s, reports the following local legend of the town's destruction in his book, *Explorations and Adventures in Honduras:*

> *The great wealth of Olancho in olden times had centered at the ancient town.... The inhabitants, however, were niggardly; and, although they had such quantities of gold that the women wore nuggets of it in their hair, they withheld their hordes even from the Church, and were consequently stricken with Divine Wrath.... While the population was collected in the church, the mountain broke forth with terrific violence, and in an hour the whole town was destroyed with showers of rocks, stones, and ashes.*

Locals claim the town was destroyed by a volcano, but since volcanic mountains do not exist in this part of Honduras, that seems unlikely. A massive landslide is a more logical explanation, especially considering the sheer cliff faces of El Boquerón, just behind the town's former location.

The survivors moved on to Olanchito in Yoro, bringing their patron saint, San Jorge, with them. The last vestiges of the old mining town have disappeared, but locals continue to turn up all sorts of early colonial artifacts in the fields between the highway and the mountain.

notice. Check with Manual Vilchez in the Unidad Ambiental (environmental office) at Juticalpa's city hall for how to get in touch with Don José.

While COHDEFOR has long protected this area, a petition was submitted in 2005 to make the area a national park. Several studies on the area's flora and fauna were conducted as part of this petition, which in 2009 is before the Honduran Congress for their approval.

Hiking into the Canyon

The main canyon of El Boquerón, on the Río Olancho, has a very pleasing stretch of quiet forest with several swimming holes and plenty of opportunities for bird-watching. To get to the canyon, get off the bus (or out of your car—it's possible to park at the Pulpería Albita if you buy some water and supplies there) where the Juticalpa–Catacamas highway crosses the Río Olancho (this is also a great photo-op), then follow the dirt road upstream along the edge of the river, which angles roughly north-northwest. Paths follow the river on both sides into the canyon, but the west side is more frequently used, although heavy fall rains often wash away part of the trail (just keep following the river).

The patch of river right by the bridge is a popular swimming hole with locals on the weekends. Hike in just a short distance and you'll be ensconced in forest and have the river to yourself for a dip. Note the water pipe on the western side of the river—it brings water to the community of El Boquerón, and swimming is not allowed above where it is sourced (it's all aboveground, so if you can't see the pipe, you're too high up for a swim).

The forest within the canyon is generally intact, although some small patches have been cut down, especially farther up the canyon. From the highway, the canyon at first seems to support a dry forest, with dense stands of middle-sized trees. But in the serene central section of the canyon, one can feel the humidity increase, and the trees are much taller—up to 30 meters—and covered with bromeliads and other epiphytes. Begonias, bougainvillea,

and a plethora of other flowering plants decorate the banks of the river.

It takes about three hours along this trail to reach the *aldea* (village) of **La Avispa** from the highway, going at an easy pace, with stops to look around. It's not possible to go all the way up the canyon, although venturing farther up along the water past where the trail goes up the hillside is a great exploration.

If you see *campesinos* nearby, you could ask them to show you (it would be nice offer a tip of US$1 or so if they do take you) the entrance to **Cueva de Tepescuintle,** with some impressive stalactites and stalagmites. In the 1940s, an archaeologist found some evidence of pre-conquest habitation at the cave.

Cerro Agua Buena

Summiting Cerro Agua Buena (1,433 meters), the mountain separating La Avispa from the Valle de Catacamas and forming the eastern side of El Boquerón, is a strenuous but rewarding day trip, or a more relaxed and even more rewarding overnight campout. All in all it's a great choice for someone out for a taste of adventure and encounters with friendly locals and lovely forests. The summit can be reached via two trails, Tenpiscapita and Agua Buena.

The views from the ridgetop across the valleys, both to the north and south, and up the Sierra de Agalta to the east, are magnificent. The many wild fruit trees at the upper edges of the coffee plantations attract hordes of different birds, as well as a great variety of small mammals, like *pizote, tepesquintle,* troops of monkeys, and even the occasional jaguar wandering down from Agalta. Bring your binoculars and be prepared to sit quietly for a while before you see anything. Quetzals have even been spotted here, making it one of the lowest-elevation habitats for the bird.

It's possible (with some difficulty) to find a flat spot to camp around the pass, or with less difficulty somewhere in Agua Buena. Try not to block the trail with a tent. Those with jungle hammocks will have an easier time of it. Camping out around the pass and getting up really early is well worth it for the chance to spot wildlife.

For those not prepared for overnight trips, a hike to the top and back is easily doable in seven or eight hours, with plenty of time for stopping to chat with *campesinos* you meet on the trail, admiring the views, and taking a dip in the river on the way back. Come dressed for mud and mosquitoes. A good stick is useful for balance in the higher, muddier parts of the trail. Harvest season (roughly November–February) is an interesting (though often wet) time to go. Be sure to get back to the Juticalpa highway at the village of El Boquerón by 5 P.M. to catch the last bus to Juticalpa. Hitching is feasible, but best before dark.

Dos Quebradas Ruins

In the Valle de Guacoca, west of La Avispa toward the highway between Juticalpa and San Francisco de la Paz, is an extensive pre-Columbian ruins site, rarely visited by anyone besides the *campesinos* who live practically on top of the site. Dos Quebradas was only surveyed by archaeologists once, in the 1930s, and little is known about its builders, other than that they made lots of attractive pottery, which is continually found all over the surrounding valley.

While it's quite possible to get to Dos Quebradas on your own, it's a bit adventurous and not for everyone. Visitors can also arrange a guided visit by asking at the Casa de la Cultura in Juticalpa, which will in turn contact a gentleman named Gustavo Rivera in San Francisco de la Paz. Gustavo is also familiar with several other ruins in the area, including nearby **Chichicaste,** known for its lovely pottery.

Santa María de Real

Thirty-four kilometers beyond Juticalpa, about 15 minutes before reaching Catacamas, is the small town of Santa María. The town has several restaurants catering to city folk who come out for a countryside lunch on the weekend, especially for a plate of fried fish or *comida típica*. **El Puente** is considered the best of the bunch, and has a small artificial lagoon with boats that the kids can take out for a spin, as well as a swimming pool.

CATACAMAS

A dusty town set against the base of the Sierra de Agalta, Catacamas is much like Juticalpa, only smaller, and noteworthy mainly as a stop-off point for visiting the Cuevas de Talgua or take longer hiking and/or rafting trips to Sierra de Agalta or the Mosquitia.

The *parque,* a few hundred meters up from the highway, is dominated by a massive ceiba tree, which spreads generous shade across the park, and has a small ice cream stand on the corner. Three blocks toward the mountains from the park is the Catholic church and the municipal office, as well as the **Galería de Arte,** with a selection of paintings and crafts by local artists. A few blocks farther toward the mountains is a stairway leading up to **Cerrito de la Cruz,** a small hill with a cross on top affording good views over Catacamas and the valley.

Besides visiting the **Cuevas de Talgua,** it is possible to embark on longer hikes here, including up to the summit of La Picucha in the Sierra de Agalta National Park.

Taxis anywhere in town cost US$1.

Accommodations

Close to the road that leads to the Cuevas is the modern and clean **Hotel Juan Carlos** (tel. 504/799-4212, hoteljuanc@yahoo.com, US$22 s, US$29 d). Rooms are painted a sunny yellow, and are clean and attractive, with flowered bedspreads, high ceilings, and tile floors. The best face a small flowery courtyard. Each room has a desk, air-conditioning, and TV, and there is a good restaurant on-site. Popular with mission groups, the hotel can often be full, so it's good to book ahead.

With a rather bizarrely imposing facade, looking a bit out of place in Catacamas, is the **Hotel Papabeto** (tel. 504/799-5006, US$34 s, US$46 d), with 10 tastefully decorated rooms around a small pool and lawn area, each with air-conditioning, TV, telephones, and even a window seat in the bay window. There are another four rooms in an annex across the street. It's a block east and two blocks north from the park.

© AMY E. ROBERTSON

Graceful arches adorn Catacamas's central park.

Half a block from the square, around the corner from the bus station, is the lower-priced **Hotel La Colina** (tel. 504/799-4488, US$9.50 s, US$10.50 d), offering clean rooms with fans and TV. There is a *pila* in the courtyard where you could probably wash your clothes if you ask nicely. It's a perfectly good choice for this price.

A few bucks more and a little bit of a step up is the modern **Hotel Mayling** (tel. 504/799-4523, US$14 s, US$18.50 d with fan; US$16 s, US$21 d with a/c), two blocks south of the park, has tiled rooms with cable TV and telephones. The place is a little worn, but clean (you can smell the bleach). Ask for a room on the second floor, and preferably street side, for a little more light.

Food

The nicest restaurant in town is certainly the **Casa Real** at the Hotel Juan Carlos. The setting is pleasant, and it has an extensive menu in English and Spanish serving all the Honduran standards, as well as *anafres* (a delicious hot bean dip served in a clay pot), conch soup, and Rocky Mountain oysters on a stick *(pincho de criadillas de toro)*. Breakfasts and sandwiches are US$2.75–5, and entrées run US$5.50–9.50.

On the main road into town, Boulevard Las Acacias, is the popular **King Palace** (10 A.M.–10 P.M. daily), with chop suey, fried rice, and kung pao chicken. Most plates are in the US$5–8 range. The owners run a disco on the second floor, so come here for a late-night dinner on the weekend and you won't even have to change venues to keep the evening going.

There are plenty of *comedores* around town serving the standard egg, tortilla, and beans. Groceries can be picked up at the **Despensa Familiar** (7 A.M.–7 P.M. Mon.–Sat., until 6 P.M. Sun.).

Entertainment

The open-air bar **Bohio's** at the corner of the park is a nice place to have a beer, and there's a short food menu as well for anyone with the munchies. Just up the street is **Vaquero's,** a bar with a small dance floor that fills up on the weekends. Make like Cinderella and head home by 12, though, because there is the not-so-infrequent stabbing or shooting as the night wears on and the crowd gets wilder.

Services

The **BAC Bamer** bank around the corner from Hotel Papabeto has an ATM and also advances cash on a Visa and exchanges dollars. There is the ubiquitous **Banco del Occidente,** where Western Union transfers can be picked up, as well as a **Citibank** (U.S.-based accounts are not linked to the Citibank in Honduras).

Hondutel (7 A.M.–8:30 P.M. daily) is a block north and half a block east from the *parque,* and **Honducor** is also a block from the park.

Ciber As.Com (9 A.M.–7 P.M. Mon.–Sat.), facing the park, is one of several Internet places in town; it charges US$0.75 an hour.

The best medical care in Olancho can be found at the new **Predisan** clinic in Catacamas (www.predisan.org), on the highway near the police station.

Getting There and Away

Aurora (tel. 504/799-4154) has a terminal at the highway, a 15-minute walk or US$1 cab to town. Direct buses (US$5.75, four hours) depart at 5 A.M., 6 A.M., 7 A.M., 9:30 A.M., 10:30 A.M., noon, and 5 P.M., with buses also at 3 P.M. and 4 P.M. on weekends. "Normal" (i.e., frequently stopping) buses charge US$4 for the 4.5-hour ride.

Local buses to Juticalpa (US$1, one hour) leave from in front of the terminal all day until 5 P.M.

Tegucigalpa is 232 kilometers from Catacamas and can be driven in 3–4 hours on the well-maintained paved highway. Juticalpa is 41 kilometers from Catacamas.

◖ CUEVAS DE TALGUA

Four kilometers from Catacamas, near the village of Guanaja by the banks of the Río Talgua, are the Cuevas de Talgua, one extensive cavern long known and explored by adventurous locals and the odd spelunker, and a second and less-explored cave. In April 1994, two spelunkers clambering through the cave made an incredible discovery that has rewritten the history of pre-Columbian Honduras.

Explorations of the main cave at the Cuevas de Talgua are aided by a pathway and handrail.

Hondurans Jorge Yánez and Desiderio Reyes were about 600 meters inside the cave when they noticed an opening in a limestone wall 4 meters off the cave floor. Yánez and Reyes scaled the wall, peered into the opening, and saw a scene out of a science-fiction movie: hundreds of skulls and bones apparently made of crystal, glowing in the light of their headlamps.

Three weeks later Yánez and Reyes, together with a group of friends that included Americans Tim Berg and Greg Cabe, returned to the cave with a ladder and carefully documented all that they had found, reporting it to the Honduran Institute of Anthropology and History. Once word of the discovery got out, a team of archaeologists led by Dr. James Brady of George Washington University examined the cave and determined that the bones had been placed on the ledge some 3,000 years ago by a hitherto unknown Mesoamerican civilization. Over the millennia since their burial, the bones had become coated with calcite dripping from the cave roof, which both preserved the remains and lent them their unearthly appearance.

In an apparent ritual burial, the bones of some 200 people were carefully stripped of flesh, painted with a red ochre, and stacked in neat bundles along with pieces of ceramic and jade. As in many other Mesoamerican societies, caves were seen as entrances to the underworld, and the dead were evidently placed there to speed them on their journey to the next world. Additional exploration revealed a second cave nearby, called the Cave of the Spiders, holding more bones and with several pictographs on its walls. A third cave has since been found on a nearby mountainside, the Cueva Grande.

Mounds above ground near the caves are believed to have been the villages of those buried in the caves. Little is known about these first *olanchanos,* other than they were relatively tall and healthy, and they seemed to have traded with other societies in the region, judging from the pottery found. The earliest positive date of the bones is from 1400 B.C.

The visitors center has some information and a few pieces of pottery found at local archaeological sites. The burial chamber itself is off-limits to visitors, and many of the remains are in Tegucigalpa anyhow, so don't expect to see any bones, but checking out the caves is fun nonetheless.

There is a US$5 entry fee to the park, and another US$0.50 per person charge for the use of a guide (obligatory) into the main cave. There are explanation sheets in English available for those who do not speak Spanish. The walk into the cave is on a concrete path with a handrail, and the caves are lit by electricity within, so it's really an excursion for anyone. Some guides are willing to take their group down a short branch off the main trail to see a formation called El Arbol del Niño—don't hesitate to ask about this if your guide doesn't offer.

Those looking for something a little more adventurous can ask their guide to take them up to the **Cueva Grande,** a second, larger cave a 45-minute walk (part of it steeply uphill) from the visitors center. A headlamp is handy for this cave, but not required, as the guides have flashlights. The whole outing takes about 2.5 hours, and the guides charge US$10 (for the group, not per person). Two other cave systems nearby offer further exploration possibilities for those so inclined.

Desiderio Reyes (tel. 504/9730-9957) is still spelunking in Catacamas and will happily lead visitors on caving expeditions. He can guide other hikes, including up to La Picucha in Sierra de Agalta, or find another guide through the local guide association. The association charges US$18 a day for hikes to La Pichucha. Calixto Ordoñez is another recommended guide.

Taxis from Catacamas out to the caves (near the village of Guanaja, well sign-posted) should cost around US$8 one way, while buses from Catacamas cost only US$0.85, departing from a stop near Comercial Palmira at 6 A.M., 11 A.M., and 3 P.M., departing back from the cave to Catacamas an hour later. It's also possible to hitch a ride to the caves. Ask for vehicles going to the villages of Guanaja, La Colonia Agrícola, or La Unión. Rides can be scarce coming back to Catacamas in the afternoon.

SIERRA DE AGALTA
Parque Nacional Sierra de Agalta

More than 60,000 hectares of mountain forest are protected in the spectacular Sierra de Agalta, and in its core zone the park contains the most extensive cloud forest remaining in Honduras, and probably all of Central America. Because of its remote location, Agalta's forest does not get many visitors, but the few people who have seen it rate it as one of the country's most incredible natural areas.

The range's isolation has been its savior—loggers and coffee growers have started chopping away inside the reserve, but the daunting topography slows the destruction somewhat. Around its perimeter, Sierra de Agalta is blanketed by pine forest. Above the pines, moist tropical forests with liquidambar (sweet gum) trees dominate, gradually giving way to the epiphyte- and vine-covered cloud forest, at elevations between 1,700 and 2,000 meters. At the highest elevations grows a rare elfin or dwarf forest, created by high winds and heavy precipitation. Here, stunted, gnarled pine and oak trees 1.5–5 meters high, buffeted by continual high winds, are cloaked in mosses and lichen.

The forests of Sierra de Agalta are considered a sort of transitional ecosystem, similar to the mountain forests of Costa Rica, while Celaque and other cloud forests in western Honduras are more like those of Guatemala and southern Mexico. More than 400 species of birds have been identified in Sierra de Agalta, as well as myriad mammals rarely seen elsewhere in the country. Tapirs, sloths, ocelots, jaguars, and troops of howler, spider, and white-faced monkeys all reside in the park. And in contrast to the wildlife on other mountains, the animals here are not shy about showing themselves. Apart from its natural beauty and the rare flora and fauna it sustains, the Sierra de Agalta is a critical source of water for northeastern Honduras, forming the headwaters for the Ríos Patuca, Sico, and Paulaya.

The best access to the top of Agalta is from Gualaco, in the Valle de Agalta, where a reasonably well-developed trail climbs **La Picucha,** the highest point in the range at 2,354 meters. A more recent trail now reaches La Picucha from the Catacamas side also, starting near the Talgua caves. Both climbs take two to four days round-trip, depending on how fast you go. Hikers can also take day trips in from Catacamas, either starting at the Talgua caves or near El Murmullo, or take a longer trail across a mountain pass between San Esteban and Catacamas.

Many visitors will want to hire a guide in Gualaco. The amiable Ramón Velíz, a.k.a. Monchito (tel. 504/9741-0026), is an excellent guide who knows the trail well and charges US$12 a day plus food. Another good contact is Francisco Urbina (tel. 504/9901-3400), the coordinator of a local association of guides. He is often traveling, but he can help you find someone in town to guide if he and Ramón are not available. The guide association usually charges US$16–26 a day (depending on the size of the group) for trips to La Picucha, a four-day trip.

The topographical maps covering the park are 1:50,000 *San Francisco de la Paz 2960 I, Catacamas 3060 IV, Dulce Nombre de Culmí 3061 II,* and *Valle de Agalta La Venta 3061 III.*

Hiking Up La Picucha

Hiking up to the highest peak in the Sierra, La Picucha (2,354 meters), ranks high on the list of the most rewarding outdoor adventures in Honduras, along with the Río Plátano rainforest. Sierra de Agalta is a thriving forest, fairly bursting with animal and plant life of dizzying variety. And the Picucha climb takes you through all the different ecosystems of the park, from the lower pine forests up through different stages of cloud forest, and out onto the dwarf forest across the summit. If you've got the time and energy (it's a steep, hard climb), the Picucha trail is not to be missed.

The most common way to the top of Sierra de Agalta is via Gualaco, a drive of a couple of hours from Juticalpa on the road to Tocoa, although a newer route has recently opened from the Catacamas side of the mountains also.

To get to the trailhead, drive north from Gualaco on the highway for 10 kilometers and look for a faded signpost on the east side of the road, marking the entrance to a four-wheel-drive track heading into the pine forest. This dirt road continues about five kilometers steadily uphill, the last two kilometers progressively more steep and rough.

At the summit of La Picucha, all the trees around suddenly are remarkably short—this is the famous dwarf forest of Agalta, with its stunted pines and oaks, gnarled and twisted by the wind and soaking wet from the near-permanent clouds. Everything is covered with lichens, moss, and ferns. Apart from being an odd and beautiful sight on their own, the short trees of the dwarf forest also allow visitors to admire truly stupendous views from La Picucha, across both the Catacamas and Agalta valleys and over the mountains extending northward into the jungles of the Mosquitia. From La Picucha, a trail continues over to a nearby peak with a radio tower on it, a good area to hike around and explore the dwarf

The trusty steed is an Olanchan cowboy's best friend.

forest. With the new trail from Catacamas, it is possible to cross from one side of the range to the other, although most guides know only one of the two sides.

It is possible to hike to the peak and back spending only two nights out, but it's quite a slog. It's better to spend a third night at either one of the camps and allow more time to explore the higher reaches of the mountain.

La Picucha from Catacamas

In recent years, locals and a couple of motivated Peace Corps volunteers have opened a route from the Catacamas side to the top. The trail leaves from near the Cuevas de Talgua.

One recommended local guide for trips into the Sierra from Catacamas is Calixto Ordoñez, who lives in the village of Talgua, a ten-minute walk from the caves. He can take visitors on hikes all over the region, including all the way up to La Picucha in 2–4 days, or to local waterfalls, his coffee plantation in the hills, or on bird-watching trips, for US$10 a day or less for half-day trips. Calixto has worked with a number of environmental groups and is trustworthy

and knowledgeable on local flora and fauna. Ask around in Catacamas or at the caves to find him.

Another excellent contact is Desiderio Reyes (tel. 504/9730-9957), one of the Hondurans who originally discovered the glowing bones of Catacamas. He is a hiking and spelunking fanatic who is happy to guide or to make arrangements for another guide from the local association if he is not available. The association charges US$18 per day for hikes to La Pichucha.

It's also possible to simply ask the guide(s) on duty at the Cuevas de Talgua for assistance in locating a guide for hikes farther afield.

El Murmullo Area

It's possible for the adventurous to trek into the Sierra de Agalta on their own from Catacamas. One place to do so is on a trail that starts past the village of El Murmullo. Catch an early morning *jalón* (hitch) to El Murmullo from Catacamas, take an expensive taxi (US$15), or walk in a couple of hot, tiring hours. The dirt road deteriorates past El

Murmullo, continuing mostly downhill in an easy half-hour walk to the smaller village of Las Delicias, at the edge of a river. Beyond Las Delicias, the road becomes a trail—make sure (ask anyone) that you take the correct fork to take you across the river and toward Linares. Upon reaching the river, the trail crosses over immediately to the far side, then upstream crosses back again, then a bit farther crosses over a third time. After the third crossing, on the far side from Las Delicias, the trail begins winding steeply up the hillside, past a lone coffee farm (soon to be more, no doubt) and into the forest. An hour or two of hiking will bring you to the high point on the ridge, deep in primary cloud forest. Day-trippers could content themselves to enjoying half a day exploring the cloud forest looking for plentiful birds or monkeys and walking back to Catacamas in the afternoon—easily doable, especially if you arrange a ride up to El Murmullo early in the morning. Walking all the way, round-trip from Catacamas to the high point of the trail and back in a day, would be a long and hard day. To avoid any route-finding difficulties, and to learn more about the forest and the region, consider asking around in El Murmullo or Las Delicias for someone to guide you up the trail for around US$5 for half a day, or more for a full day.

Make sure to look around when in the coffee plantations between El Murmullo and Las Delicias; these are great places to spot all sorts of beautiful tropical birds, especially in the early morning or late afternoon. Even a totally inexperienced birder can easily spot a toucan or other tropical birds along the walk.

FROM OLANCHO INTO THE MOSQUITIA AND COLÓN
Dulce Nombre de Culmí

A rough frontier town 50 kilometers northeast of Catacamas in rolling pine-forested hills, Culmí lies near the southern boundary of the Reserva de la Biosfera del Río Plátano. This is the southern entry into the Mosquitia for the hard-core adventurer (or suicidal fool, might say some) who wants to cross from Olancho through the jungle north to the Caribbean coast.

Formerly Culmí was a Pech mission settlement founded, along with Santa María del Carbón, by the Franciscan José Manuel Subirana in the mid-19th century. The icon of the Dulce Nombre given to the town by Subirana still rests in the more modern church in town and is widely revered throughout Olancho. Don't come by for the *feria* in early January, though, as you'd be sure to see one or two shootings a day between the drunken cowboys.

The Pech have long since departed Culmí to outlying villages like Agua Zarca, Vallecito, and Pisijire, driven away by ranchers, loggers, and not a few *banditos* flooding in from other parts of Honduras, particularly the south. People in Culmí like to say that just about no one over age 20 in the area was actually born there, apart from the Pech.

The illegal logging under way north of Culmí, in both the buffer and core zones of the biosphere reserve, is prodigious. Another growing problem is smuggling cocaine dropped off from Colombia to the remote Mosquitia coastline and taken upriver through the jungle to Culmí, and from there on up Central America to the United States. Much of the drug-running is reputedly done by the very same crowd in charge of all the illegal logging.

Facilities in Culmí are minimal, which is fine, because it's not a safe place to hang around in anyway.

North from Culmí

Rough dirt roads head north from Culmí, leading to frontier villages and *ranchos* in the southernmost section of the Reserva de la Biosfera del Río Plátano and eventually leading to the headwaters of the Paulaya, Plátano, Aner, and Wampú rivers, which empty out into the Mosquitia. Although this immense, unexplored region offers unbeatable opportunities for venturing into pristine rainforest and seeking out the numerous pre-Hispanic ruins, it is a totally lawless area. Shootings are common. While foreigners are generally not targets, it's always possible to run across someone in particular need of money or just get caught in the crossfire. It's definitely an "at your own risk" sort of place, not to be taken lightly. The Río Wampú region is particularly known to be unsafe. Which doesn't mean you can't go, but the best option for those interested in visiting this dangerous but truly incredible region is to pay for a guided trip. Both Omega Tours and La Moskitia Eco-Aventuras have multiday expeditions that begin in Olancho and end on the Pacific Coast, and those companies have stellar reputations.

Juticalpa-San Esteban Highway

Ten kilometers from Juticalpa on the road to Catacamas, a paved highway turns northwest through a gap in the hills, leading to the town of San Francisco de la Paz, 20 kilometers away. From there, the highway becomes a dirt road that in another 30 kilometers reaches the town of Gualaco, the jumping off point for explorations of the Sierra de Agalta. That's as far as anyone should go down that road. While it's scenic, security along this road is extremely poor, and assaults on both buses and private vehicles are frequent. Check with locals (especially police, who might have a better sense of really how many holdups there are) before considering this route to the north coast.

Gualaco

Settled in the early years of Olancho colonization, the logging and ranching town of

---

LAS VUELTAS DE OCOTE

Always protective of their right to manage their own affairs, *olanchanos* resented efforts by the government of the newly created Honduras to assert control through taxation. In October 1828, beginning in the town of Gualaco, tensions broke out into open rebellion against the central government.

In 1829, war raged throughout Olancho, except in Juticalpa, which remained loyal to the government. General Francisco Morazán himself came to Olancho in late 1829 to lead the government troops, and he managed to put an end to the rebellion with a feat of brave diplomacy. Between Juticalpa and San Francisco de la Paz, at that time a bastion of the rebels, is a stretch of windy road called Las Vueltas de Ocote ("The Turns of Pine"). Knowing the general was on his way, the rebels arrayed their forces at Las Vueltas and waited in ambush. Morazán, aware the rebels were there, ordered his troops to halt just outside Las Vueltas, took off his sword, and walked into the hills alone and unarmed.

The general clearly knew what sort of men he was facing. Deeply impressed with this display of personal bravery, the rebels allowed Morazán into their camp unharmed. The general asked them to explain why they were re-

belling. Over the course of the hot afternoon of January 21, 1830, he hammered out an agreement to end the rebellion, conceding to Olancho a certain degree of self-government. Today, a bust of Morazán, growing moldy in the elements, commemorates the event at the site.

Despite the settlement, many *olanchanos* continued to be unhappy with their new government, and for reasons still not entirely clear, a new, more widespread rebellion broke out in 1863. Conflicts this time had a markedly social character, pitting the lower class, small-scale *mestizo* ranchers and laborers against the wealthy *criollo* cattlemen.

The rebellion continued for two years, spreading into Yoro and threatening Trujillo, before it was put down with extreme brutality by President-General José María Medina, in a campaign known to this day in Olancho as La Ahorcancina ("The Hanging"). The heads of two rebel leaders, Bernabé Antúnez and Francisco Zavala, were stuck on pikes and left on a hillside overlooking Juticalpa for several years afterward, as a warning to any would-be rebels. Apparently the message got through, and Olancho settled into relative peace, resigned to remain part of Honduras.

Gualaco is a good base for anyone wanting to climb up the Picucha trail into the Sierra de Agalta from this side of the mountains. The small, dusty highway town has a couple of decent hotels and *comedores,* as well as places to buy basic packaged food for camping.

The 17th-century **Iglesia de San Jerónimo** on one end of the wide, green *parque* is fronted by a whitewashed facade with sculpted pillars. The two church towers were rebuilt in 1994 in an unfortunately less than subtle style, but the building is worth a look nonetheless.

Hotel Mi Palacio (US$8 s, US$10 d) is probably the best room in town, if only because it's the most recently built, and hey, it has hot water. The hotel is near the entrance to town, in a peach-colored building.

Several *comedores* in town serve up a palatable meal. **Comedor Sharon** on the highway is better than most, and the owners are friendly and glad to talk to visitors. It also has posters on the walls with photos and descriptions in English and Spanish about Sierra de Agalta and the Cuevas de Susmay, written by local Peace Corps volunteers.

Next to the gas station on the highway are the offices of **Grupo Ecológico de Olancho** (GEO) and **COHDEFOR,** where you can get information on the current state of the Picucha trail. Currently, no maps are available, but GEO has a large, detailed topographical map on the wall, which has the Picucha trail marked.

The Trujillo–Tegucigalpa bus passes Gualaco each day in both directions, to Tegucigalpa (US$6) at around 9 or 9:30 A.M. (but you may want to consider paying only as far as to Juticalpa, and catching a direct bus from there). The Juticalpa–Tocoa bus passes going to Tocoa in the early morning and to Juticalpa at around noon. Two buses a day run between Gualaco and Juticalpa (US$2.75).

Near Gualaco

Foremost among the destinations of visitors to Gualaco will be the Picucha trail or the Río Babilonia waterfalls in Sierra de Agalta. But a couple of closer destinations make good day trips.

About an hour's walk from Gualaco are the **Cuevas de Susmay.** The four caves are a 15-minute walk beyond the *aldea* of Jicalapa, at the base of the mountains. At the household of Las Joyas del Zacate you cross a gully and then walk through a pasture, until you reach a patch of trees, where the trail to the caves begins—ask anyone to point the way if you're not sure. The bottom-most cave, which has a bone-chillingly cold river running through it, has interesting stalactites and other formations. You have to wade and swim to get into the cave, ideally with snorkel equipment and a waterproof headlamp, but it's not required. A guide is recommended if you plan to go in very far, as the cave has many branches. About a half hour in, you'll run into a large rock fall, which must be swum under to continue. Most sane folk, by now already numb from the cold water, will turn around here and return to the entrance. An expedition of Italian spelunkers reputedly went in 23 kilometers and still didn't find the end, making this one of the largest water caves in the Americas.

Uphill from the first cave are two more, which have been roughly treated by local youth with spray paint. Farther up is one more cave, with intact formations. The caves are connected inside, with just a narrow tunnel between the second and the third, where you have to rock-climb in order to enter the fourth.

Ramón Velíz, a.k.a. Monchito (tel. 504/9741-0026), is a local caving and hiking fanatic who charges US$10 (or a little more for larger groups) for an expedition into the caves.

An hour's walk from Gualaco toward the mountains on a dirt road is the *aldea* of **Magua,** an area teeming with all sorts of birds, including parrots and toucans. Come with binoculars; the best birding is early in the morning or late in the afternoon.

San Esteban

At the northeastern end of the Valle de Agalta lies the cattle town of San Esteban, founded in 1805 and named in honor of Padre Esteban Verdelete, martyred by the Pech in the early

1600s. Because of its reputation for violence (dating from colonial times, apparently), most people don't spend much time in San Esteban. There's a gas station, a few *comedores* on the highway, and a decent hotel, should you need to spend the night.

Los Encuentros

West of San Esteban is Los Encuentros, a large pre-Columbian ruin of unclear origin. Extensive and solid stone, Los Encuentros, located in what is now a cow pasture near the confluence of Ríos Tayaco and Naranjal, is merely the largest of literally dozens of ruins scattered throughout this wild region near the border of the Colón and Olancho departments. Thought to have been built by the ancestors of the Pech, the ruins of Los Encuentros were used as a refuge and ritual site for the Indians at least until the early 1800s, and possibly later, according to the reports of Spanish missionaries.

El Carbón

On the highway between San Esteban and the coast, in the transition area from the pine and cloud forests of central Olancho to the jungle lowlands, is the village of Santa María del Carbón, usually just called El Carbón. It's one of the most traditional Pech communities left in Honduras. With the Peace Corps' help, a couple of small, humble huts were built for visitors, and a few local men can serve as guides into the nearby mountains. There has also been an effort to revive local handicrafts, and the Pech weave bags, baskets, placemats, and other handicrafts.

Although it's certainly possible to arrive to El Carbón from the Olancho side, given the state of affairs on the road around San Esteban, travelers may want to consider adding a stop here to their itinerary on the way to or from Trujillo.

After arriving in El Carbón, ask around for Linton Escobar, who is most accustomed to dealing with visitors, and who can arrange a hiking guide for US$10 a day. One good hike is to an unexcavated ruin about an hour away, where the outlines of walls and stairs can be made out under the jungle growth. Longer hikes can be made into the Sierra de Agalta.

A few of the other young guides are fairly friendly too, if you speak Spanish and make an effort to talk to them. One, Natividad García, is also a *curandero* (healer); he knows more than most about the plants of the forest and can take visitors on a botany hike. The local Peace Corps volunteer *(voluntario/voluntaria del Cuerpo de Paz)*, if there is one currently, usually lives next to the visitors' huts and is invariably more than happy to help arrange guides and talk about the town and region. The simple but clean huts, built with mud walls in the traditional Pech style, rent for US$6 per person a night. Meals can be arranged, but it's best to come with your own food as well, particularly if you plan to go on a multiday hike.

Don't be surprised if the vibe in town is a little weird. The Pech can be reserved with strangers, much more than the average gregarious Honduran.

Any buses passing between Juticalpa and Tocoa can drop visitors at El Carbón. At last check, three or four a day drove in each direction, but this seems to change frequently. The last bus in either direction usually passes El Carbón around 2 P.M. It's possible to get the bus in Tocoa, or at Corocito, a turnoff on the Tocoa–Trujillo highway, and flag down the next bus heading to Olancho. The last passes around noon. Corocito is 50 kilometers from El Carbón on a rough dirt road.

PARQUE NACIONAL LA MURALLA AND VICINITY

In far western Olancho, near the border with Yoro, is the broad mountain range of La Muralla (The Wall), containing the most extensive untouched swath of cloud forest in the country outside of Sierra de Agalta. La Muralla National Park is particularly famous for birdwatching. It's a very unlucky or impatient visitor who doesn't get a glimpse of the renowned quetzal while at the park.

Apart from the remote location, the reputation of the highways around La Unión for *bandidos* has been a major factor in preventing more visitors from coming to the park (the stretch of highway close to La Unión actually earned itself the moniker "the Corridor of Death." While folks in Tegucigalpa and San Pedro will do nothing but warn you away, locals assure us that the situation has improved dramatically and highway assaults are a thing of the past. If you have any doubts, check with the police posts on either end of the road, at Limones near Juticalpa or Mamé near Olanchito. One bus a day serviced La Unión from both Tegucigalpa and Olanchito at last report, and there is a daily bus from Juticalpa.

La Unión

A small logging town about 200 kilometers each from Tegucigalpa and La Ceiba, set a couple of kilometers off the highway at an elevation of 800 meters, La Unión is the first stop for anyone going to visit La Muralla.

There are several hotels in town, the best of which is **Hotel La Muralla,** which charges about US$15 for a private room with bath. There are also several *comedores,* charging US$3–4 for a meal.

A local guide association serves the park; the coordinator is Rosel Argueta (tel. 504/9672-0218), and a guide costs US$10 per day. If you don't have a phone, stop by the **COHDEFOR** office to get help in contacting Rosel. It's hard to hitch to the park, but Rosel can help arrange for round-trip car service, for US$21.

There is a daily bus from Juticalpa to La Unión, departing at 11 A.M. and arriving about 2.5 hours later (US$4).

Parque Nacional La Muralla

Covering 17,243 hectares between 900 and 2,064 meters, the park hosts forests ranging from pine on the lower fringes to pine mixed with liquidambar (sweet gum) at the middle elevations to broadleaf cloud forest on the peaks. Thirty-seven mammal species have been spotted in the park, including jaguars, ocelots, white-faced and howler monkeys, and tapirs, as well as at least 150 bird species. Little

biological investigation has taken place in the reserve, especially in the more remote reaches away from the visitors center; it's likely other species will be identified.

La Muralla has a visitors center at 1,430 meters, with displays on flora and fauna and several detailed maps on the walls. The park has been in a state of abandonment, but now that the highway is better and visitors are coming through again, the guide association is working on rehabilitating it. Beds are no longer available in the visitors center, but it's possible to camp out in or near the center, to use the restrooms and fireplace. The trees in front of the visitors center are great for bird-watching, especially in the early morning.

In the southwestern corner of the reserve, a system of trails allows visitors to explore a section of the forest without a guide. The shortest hike is a well-marked half-hour jaunt, easy enough for really anyone. More rewarding is the 2.4-kilometer trail. The 3.7-kilometer Pizote Trail makes a loop around a low peak, with several benches at strategic points to watch for birds. For the more ambitious, the 10-kilometer Monte Escondido Trail descends into the Río Escondido valley and up the other side into the higher reaches of the park. Getting to the lookout on Monte Escondido and back is a two-day trip, and a guide would be a good idea. For more information, ask at the COHDEFOR office in La Unión. Hikes deeper into the park, to the peaks of La Muralla (1,981 meters), Los Higuerales (1,985 meters), and Las Parras (2,064 meters), require guides and several days in the woods.

The visitors center is 14 kilometers from La Unión, reached by a rough dirt road connecting La Unión to the village of El Díctamo farther west. Those without a car can walk from town three hours uphill through pine forest and coffee plantations, or try to hitch, although traffic is not frequent. You might be able to catch a ride with one of the COHDEFOR trucks, which usually go to the park every day during the week, or else it's possible to hire a car to drive you to and from the park, for US$21 (arrange through the guide service).

© AMY E. ROBERTSON

Creeks and rivers wind through the verdant mountains of Olancho.

The topographical map covering the park is 1:50,000 *La Unión 2861 II.*

North and Northwestern Olancho

This broad swath of extremely rugged, scenic mountain country is blessed with an extraordinary natural diversity as well as isolated villages of both traditional *ladino* Olancho culture, more akin to the 19th century than the 21st, and recently "discovered" indigenous communities of unclear origin.

Mark Bonta, professor of geography and confirmed Olancho-phile, has visited this area, and this is his write-up on the region:

One of the most intriguingly archaic regions of Honduras is northern Olancho. Owing to a reputation for ferocity among the inhabitants (even in terms of Olancho!), northern Olancho has been avoided by all but loggers and a few migrant farmers. However, recent expeditions in search of palms and cycads (primitive plants), birds, and reptiles and amphibians have been pleasantly surprised by the ruggedly beautiful landscapes reminiscent of highland Guatemala, the remnant indigenous Indios de Guata and Indios de Jano, the traditional *mestizo* culture, and the lingering forests of old-growth pine. Indeed, some of the most traditional villages in Central America can be found here, bearing more similarity to those found in 19th-century travelers' accounts than to the modern day.

The presence of a little-known indigenous group, now recognized as the Nahoa, adds particular interest. Vibrant folkloric traditions survive, and completely unmodified ceramic traditions have also recently been uncovered. Split-rail fences are still lashed together by vines, fields are farmed communally, and houses often have roofs of sugarcane stalks, expertly woven, that reach almost to the ground. Ancient Iberian breeds of pigs, chickens, and cattle have not yet been genetically "improved." *Ladino* towns, particularly in northwestern Gualaco (Chindona and San Antonio) also maintain many traditional customs, including of courtship and in agriculture, hunting, and use of the endemic Honduras treasure, the tree cycad *Dioon mejiae,* the cones of which are processed into several starch-bearing foods that

THE MOSQUITIA AND OLANCHO

form a staple. Other local staple foods are also not found elsewhere in Central America.

Access to this region by road is limited. The only public transportation is to the town of Guata, from which numerous treks or horseback rides can be made throughout the region, south to the historic town of Manto, west to Jano, and east to Gualaco. From the Gualaco side, some roads in decent shape are traveled by a few vehicles a day, north from the town of Gualaco to Saguay (with an enormous cycad population) and east across the northern end of the Valle de Agalta, or north through San Antonio to Cuaca. Also, the route from Pacura can be followed westward, on foot, along the south side of the Botaderos range, to Cuaca. Trails across Botaderos to Colon include the Abisinia and Tayaco routes (the latter is the best) to the east and the Cuaca and Armenia Trails to the west.

One intriguing route involves getting a ride from Gualaco to Los Planes, Chindona, and from there hiking downstream to the confluence of the Río Alao and Río de Oro. From there, the best route is downstream to Pueblo Viejo, Guata, at the confluence of the Alao and Mamé. From there, multiple possibilities include hiking up to Mocanquire and Tezapa, Guata, and on to the town of Guata; downstream along the Mamé canyon and on to Esquipulas del Norte; or up and out to Carrizal. The latter two routes access the main highway. Numerous side trips to fauna-rich habitat are possible on this trip, which is at least four days. Archaeological ruins, some of considerable size, are common along the Alao. The ranch of Carlos Padilla at Pueblo Viejo is a traditional stopping point, and lodging may be found there. It's best to find lodging in villages, either pitching a tent on a porch or in a patio; custom dictates that visitors not camp in "remote" spots. Since few outsiders ever come this way (or likely ever will), extreme hospitality is common, though in indigenous villages

there may be suspicion and even fright (villages may appear abandoned at first sight).

In the town of Guata, the best contact is the Cáceres family, who live right on the square. They have contacts all over Guata and are well respected locally. In addition to the indigenous villages, local attractions include the colonial church in Guata, the site of Old Jano (burned by government troops in the 1800s) on the old *camino real* (royal road) between the two towns, miles of mango forests along the rivers, numerous "enchanted" caves (including the most famous, the Cueva de la Vaca Chinga, or Cave of the Tailless Cow), and the archaeological ruins on the Cáceres's property near Azacualpa.

West of the Telica–Mamé road, extremely rugged mountainous areas and traditional villages are particularly fascinating in El Rosario (where one can hike directly into the Tolupán indigenous area of northern Francisco Morazán) and Mangulile. One of the most spectacular hikes in interior Honduras is a trek down the Río Yaguala canyon, which divides Olancho and Yoro (west of Parque Nacional La Muralla) and is accessible from Mangulile. The canyon is in places 900 meters deep; the river can be rafted.

Finally, the municipality of Esquipulas del Norte, in the northwestern corner of Olancho, appears to contain all the extra landscape that didn't fit in the rest of the department. Apart from the charming Valle de Esquipulas along the raging river of the same name, the region contains sheer slopes, numerous waterfalls, rugged treks into Yoro and the backside of La Muralla, and a few remote indigenous villages. Extensive archaeological ruins are found immediately west of Esquipulas del Norte town. It is here that the traveler has the best chance of tasting cycad tamales (with *cuajada,* fresh cheese, and *mantequilla,* a thick cream), a specialty available during the dry season in spring, of which the townspeople are justifiably proud.

SAN PEDRO SULA AND CENTRAL HONDURAS

Steamy San Pedro Sula is the business capital of Honduras, and a common point of arrival for international visitors, who can avail themselves of the high-quality food, nightlife, and accommodations before heading into the Honduran countryside. Lago de Yojoa, the country's largest natural lake, the 43-meter-high Pulhapanzak Falls, and Parque Nacional Cusuco are popular natural attractions just a short distance from San Pedro (locals often drop the "Sula" when referring to the city). Birders won't want to miss Parque Nacional Santa Bárbara, on the western edge of the lake, with its unique eco-system and hundreds of species of birds. Parque Nacional Cerro Azul/Meámbar borders the eastern edge and has well-marked trails and comfortable cabins for an easy weekend of hiking. The paved highway between San Pedro and Tegucigalpa brings travelers to the colonial gem of Comayagua, while back roads lead through the coffee towns of Marcala and Trinidad.

PLANNING YOUR TIME

The great majority of travelers will see San Pedro Sula either arriving or leaving by plane or making bus connections, with at most a night's stay. A handicrafts market and a regional history museum merit an afternoon, and there are plenty of high-quality restaurants and nightlife for a great evening out. One worthwhile naturalist day trip or campout near San Pedro for those with time to spare here is at the cloud forest of Parque Nacional Cusuco.

The vicinity of Lago de Yojoa is an excellent place to spend a few days in a lush, tropical setting, with plenty of opportunities for

HIGHLIGHTS

◖ Birding and Boating on Lago de Yojoa: With some 400-plus species spotted around Lago de Yojoa, Honduras' biggest lake is a birder's paradise. Getting out onto the water is one of the best ways to spy marsh residents, while fishing fans will enjoy trying their luck for one of the lake's most famous inhabitants, the tilapia (page 331).

◖ Pulhapanzak Falls: The 43-meter Pulhapanzak Falls on the Río Lindo will take your breath away, and the sure-footed and adventurous can follow local boys into a cave behind the falls (page 332).

◖ Parque Nacional Cerro Azul/ Meámbar: For easy access to a lush tropical and cloud forest, hike this park's well-maintained trails, stopping to scout for colorful birds or to take a dip in one of the many waterfalls (page 336).

◖ Villages near Santa Bárbara: Villages like San Luis, Trinidad, or San Rafael, set in brilliantly green mountain countryside, are scenic and friendly places to visit, well off the tourist trail (page 342).

◖ Comayagua's Colonial Center: After more than three centuries as the capital of Spanish Honduras, the city of Comayagua has a number of beautifully restored buildings from the colonial era, including the ornate cathedral on the central square and, half a block away, the Museo Colonial, stocked with religious art (page 349).

◖ Marcala: Located in a little-visited corner of Honduras but still accessible by a smoothly paved road, the town of Marcala serves as a good base for visits to small-scale organic coffee farms and countryside hikes to several nearby waterfalls (page 357).

LOOK FOR ◖ TO FIND RECOMMENDED SIGHTS, ACTIVITIES, DINING, AND LODGING.

naturalist expeditions like boating and fishing on the lake, world-class bird-watching, hiking in nearby cloud forests, visiting pre-Hispanic ruins, and checking out a roaring waterfall. Accommodations are not fancy, but comfortable enough to suit most tastes.

Santa Bárbara and several attractive towns and villages nearby, tucked among the green hills on the other side of a mountain from Lago de Yojoa, are worth spending a couple of days exploring, for a more off-beat experience.

For highway travelers heading toward Tegucigalpa, Siguatepeque makes a good place to spend the night for highway travelers, with lots of low-priced hotels and restaurants, as well as a pleasantly cool climate. Comayagua, just an hour from Tegucigalpa, was Honduras's colonial capital city, and it deserves an afternoon to admire the art and architecture, or a day to do some nearby hiking as well.

The area around Pico Pijol and Yoro, in central Honduras, is far from the beaten path,

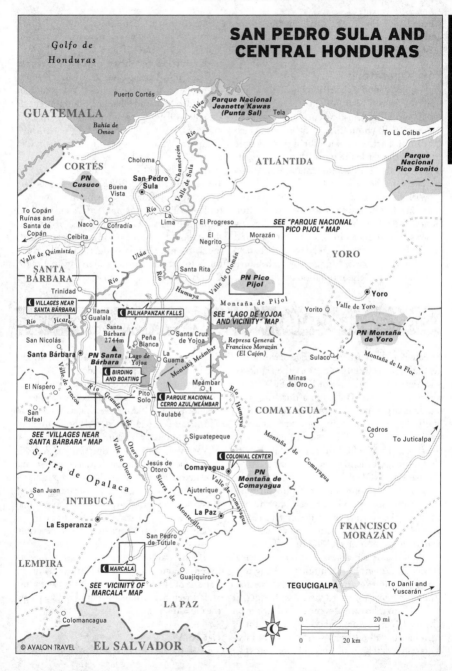

where exploration of the small cowboy towns and mountain country requires several days at least to explore.

Tour Operators

Although **Cusuco Expeditions** (tel. 504/9907-4605 or 504/9771-9049, cusucoexp@yahoo.com) formalized just recently, the group of more than 40 community guides for Cusuco National Park has been bringing people through the park for more than five years. They can also provide information on transportation to the park.

With its office in the lobby of San Pedro's Copantl hotel, **Maya Temple Tours** (tel. 504/509-0555, U.S. tel. 877/467-1692, www.mayatempletours.com) has day trips around San Pedro Sula, as well as full days farther afield (Comayagua, Copán, Lago de Yojoa, the north coast) and overnight and multiday trips.

MesoAmerica Travel (tel. 504/557-8447 or 504/557-3258, www.mesoamerica-travel.com), based out of San Pedro Sula, has trips similar to those of Maya Temple Tours. MesoAmerica has a top-notch reputation, with prices to match. A day tour of San Pedro Sula and a banana plantation costs US$60–89 per person, depending on how many are going. A similar trip with Maya Temple is US$79 per person, minimum two people.

In the Puerto Cortés-Omoa area, **Yax Pac Tours** (tel. 504/658-9082, www.yaxpactours.com), run by Roland Gassmann of the hostel Roli's Place in Omoa, offers customized tours in English, German, Swiss, or Spanish throughout Honduras and Guatemala, including "adventure" and "budget," as well as day tours for cruise shippers arriving in Puerto Cortés, and shuttle bus services.

San Pedro Sula

Situated on the southwestern edge of the broad, fertile Valle de Sula, up against the flanks of the Sierra Merendón, San Pedro Sula (often shortened to San Pedro) is a bustling, hot, modern city. If Honduras's governmental capital is Tegucigalpa, its business and financial capital is San Pedro Sula. According to recent statistics, the 800,000 inhabitants of the city and immediate vicinity produce 40 percent of the national GDP.

Unless they come to San Pedro on business, most foreign visitors stop in the city only briefly. In spite of its nearly five centuries of existence, San Pedro has virtually no remaining colonial architecture. There are two good crafts markets and one historical museum, numerous restaurants offering top-notch Honduran and international cuisine, and nightspots for every taste and budget. If you need to take care of some errands while on the road, San Pedro is a good place to do them, as it has just about every sort of store or business you could hope to find in Honduras. The

city has a grid layout with numbered streets and is very easy to get around.

A large number of expatriates make their home in the city. Those who can afford to live in the wealthier, suburb-like neighborhoods, on the west side of San Pedro at the edge of the mountains, find it a reasonably pleasant place to live.

A word of warning: Crime in San Pedro is fairly widespread. Although much of the crime is related to gang activity that the typical traveler will never come across, tourist muggings are not unheard of, so pay attention to who's around you and where you are, especially after dark.

San Pedro is at about 40 meters elevation, and the climate is steaming hot most of the year, with daytime temperatures varying between 25 and 38°C (77–100°F). Rains in the Valle de Sula, which normally hit between July and November, can be torrential but help cool the city down.

History

The Valle de Sula is one of the longest-

SAN PEDRO SULA

To Choloma and
Puerto Cortés

CERVECERÍA
HONDUREÑA

Río Piedras

0   0.25 mi

0   0.25 km

TEATRO   DHL
SAYBÉ

SEE "WESTERN
SAN PEDRO SULA" MAP

BALEADA ▼▼ BOC-GA
EXPRESS

TACA   SUITES DEL
▼   VALLE

DERIVA

TAMARINDO'S
HOSTEL

DON UDO'S   MERCADO
GUAMILITO

TRATTORIA BEL PAESE ▼

ESTADIO
GENERAL
FRANCISCO
MORAZÁN

MUSEO DE LA
NATURALEZA

SUPERMERCADO
EL CENTRO

Parque
Central

SEE "DOWNTOWN
SAN PEDRO SULA" MAP

SEE
"ZONA VIVA"
MAP

Mercado Medina
Concepción

Mercado
Dandy

MULTIPLAZA MALL

HOTEL
INTERCONTINENTAL

CASA
GUACAMAYA

HOTEL LA   HOTEL COPANTL
CORDILLERA

To Tegucigalpa and
Santa Rosa de Copán

To El Progreso
and Airport

AV CIRCUNVALACIÓN

AV CIRCUNVALACIÓN

© AVALON TRAVEL

14 CALLE
13 CALLE
12 CALLE
11 CALLE
10 CALLE
9 CALLE
7 CALLE
6 CALLE
5 CALLE
4 CALLE
3 CALLE
2 CALLE
1 CALLE
2 CALLE
3 CALLE
4 CALLE
5 CALLE
6 CALLE
7 CALLE
8 CALLE
9 CALLE
10 CALLE
11 CALLE
12 CALLE
13 CALLE
14 CALLE
15 CALLE
16 CALLE

25 AV 24 AV 23 AV 22 AV 21 AV 20 AV B 20 AV A 19 AV 18 AV 16 AV 15 AV 14 AV 13 AV 12 AV 11 AV 10 AV 9 AV 8 AV 7 AV 6 AV 5 AV 4 AV 3 AV 2 AV 1 AV 2 AV 3 AV 4 AV 5 AV 6 AV 7 AV 8 AV 9 AV

inhabited regions of Honduras. A village site excavated in the early 1990s along the Río Ulúa was dated to 1100–900 B.C. Little is known about the site's builders, other than they had some apparent contact with the Olmecs of central Mexico, suggesting a fairly high degree of development.

The Maya are believed to have maintained settlements along the Valle de Sula, but their presence in what is modern-day Honduras was mainly limited to the region farther west and south, near the present Guatemalan border.

The largest Indian settlement in the region, which the Spanish saw when they first penetrated the interior of Honduras, was at Naco, in a small valley on the south side of the Sierra Merendón from San Pedro.

La Villa de San Pedro was founded on June 27, 1536, by Pedro de Alvarado, conqueror of Guatemala, on the flat area of the Valle de Sula, far enough from the edges of the Ríos Chamelecón and Ulúa to protect the settlement from flooding. An early base of operations for the Spanish in their conquest of Honduras, San

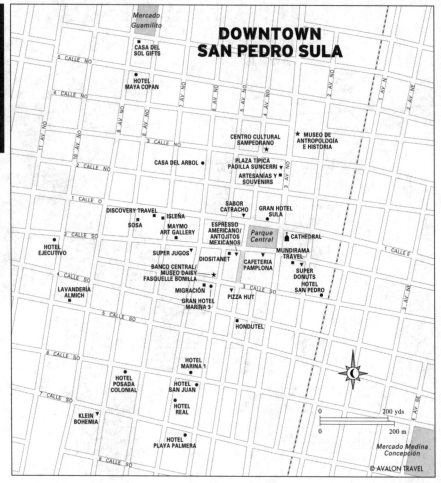

DOWNTOWN SAN PEDRO SULA

Pedro quickly faded in importance during the middle and late colonial period. After 1600, San Pedro was virtually abandoned, in part because of pirate and Indian attacks and also because colonists had moved on in the Spaniards' search for gold and silver in the highlands.

During the later part of the colonial era, San Pedro was a base for local cattle-ranchers and a collection center for sarsaparilla, a root that grew wild in the region and at the time was considered a miracle drug by Europeans, who believed it cured venereal diseases.

In the mid-19th century, San Pedro's fortunes took a turn for the better when commerce picked up at the port of Omoa, and San Pedro became a frequent stop-off point for goods on their way in or out of the country. But it was the growth of the banana industry and the reopening of Puerto Cortés in the late 19th century that jump-started San Pedro's economy, and it has continued growing steadily.

Orientation and Getting Around

San Pedro Sula is laid out in a straightforward

grid pattern, divided into northern and southern sections by 1 Calle and into eastern and western sections by 1 Avenida. Avenues *(avenidas)* run north–south, streets *(calles)* east–west. The central part of the city is ringed by Avenida Circunvalación. Addresses frequently refer to quadrants of the city: SO *(suroeste,* or southwest); SE *(sureste,* or southeast), NO *(noroeste,* or northwest), and NE *(noreste,* or northeast).

Casual visitors will likely spend the majority of their time in the western half of the city. There are numerous hotels near the downtown square, many restaurants and nightclubs in a southwestern section referred to as the *zona viva,* and a number of good hotels and restaurants, plus the city's two most popular shopping malls, just to the west of the Avenida Circunvalación. The old railroad track, which runs north–south along 1 Avenida Sur, is referred to as *la línea,* and venturing *abajo la línea* will quite literally put you on the wrong side of the tracks, where it is absolutely recommended to avoid after dark.

Most taxis charge up to US$3 for a ride within Circunvalación, more at night. Be sure to settle the price before you get in, as many *taxistas* will happily take advantage of unsuspecting foreigners. Those who wish to be cautious may prefer to get a radio taxi. Two radio taxi companies are **Radio Taxi** (tel. 504/557-5808) and **Central de Taxi** (tel. 504/557-4020), which are reliable but more expensive. *Colectivo* taxis charge only US$0.60 for the pleasure of being crammed into a cab following a set route with four other passengers and the driver. One useful *colectivo* leaves from 6 Avenida at 3 Calle SO and follows 6 Avenida out to Avenida Circunvalación to the highway exit to Puerto Cortés, in the northwest part of the city. Another, departing from 1 Avenida at 8 Calle, takes a winding route south from downtown all the way out to the Tegucigalpa highway, past the turnoff to Santa Rosa de Copán.

Buses are not particularly safe, nor is it easy to learn the routes; given that taxis are cheap they're generally the recommended way to move around. One exception might be getting to the bus terminal outside of town on the highway to the south. Those watching their lempiras can take a *rapidito,* a minivan bus, heading south on 7 Avenida, which should cost about US$0.40. A taxi to the bus station or the airport is about US$5.25.

Thanks to the grid layout, San Pedro Sula is quite easy to get around in a rental car. Note that many intersections in the center do not have any stop signs in any direction: north–south has the right of way over those traveling east–west.

SIGHTS
Parque Central

San Pedro's downtown *parque central* (central square), hopping with vendors, shoe shiners, moneychangers, evangelical preachers, and all manner of passersby, is a perfect spot to sit down and people-watch. The square often hosts impromptu music performances or other events. The adjacent *catedral* was built in 1949 and is not particularly interesting from an artistic standpoint, but it provides a relatively quiet place to sit for a minute, piped music notwithstanding. Running south from the center of the square is the *peatonal,* or pedestrian walkway, where moneychangers and a few jewelry sellers hang out.

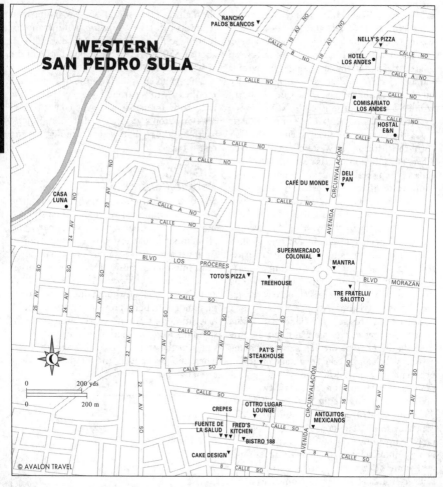

WESTERN
SAN PEDRO SULA

RANCHO
PALOS BLANCOS

NELLY'S PIZZA
HOTEL
LOS ANDES

COMISARIATO
LOS ANDES

HOSTAL
E&N

DELI
PAN

CAFÉ DU MONDE

CASA
LUNA

SUPERMERCADO
COLONIAL

MANTRA

BLVD LOS PRÓCERES

TOTO'S PIZZA

TREEHOUSE

TRE FRATELLI/
SALOTTO

BLVD MORAZÁN

PAT'S
STEAKHOUSE

CREPES

OTTRO LUGAR
LOUNGE

ANTOJITOS
MEXICANOS

FUENTE DE
LA SALUD

FRED'S
KITCHEN

BISTRO 188

CAKE DESIGN

0   200 yds
0   200 m

© AVALON TRAVEL

Museo de Antropología e Historia

A decent museum, the Museo de Antropología e Historia (3 Av. NO, between 3 and 4 Calles, tel. 504/557-1496 or 504/557-1798, 9 A.M.–4 P.M. Wed.–Mon., US$2) is the most notable cultural site in San Pedro. Its two floors of exhibits outline the development of the Valle de Sula from 1500 B.C. to the present. The displays (Spanish only) track Sula civilization from its earliest traces at the Playa de los Muertos site through the Lenca or Mayan settlements at Los Naranjos, to the colonial and modern eras. Interestingly, the foreign-owned banana industry, a crucial part of the valley's economy, is barely mentioned, perhaps in concession to nationalist sentiment.

Apart from the permanent historical exhibit, the museum has a gallery for rotating exhibits and a gift shop well stocked with T-shirts, calendars, books, cards, and artwork. Outside is a small patio cafeteria. A children's storytime is hosted on Saturdays, 10 A.M.–noon.

© AMY E. ROBERTSON

the clock tower of San Pedro's cathedral

Museo Daisy Fasquelle Bonilla

Located within the Banco Central, the Museo Daisy Fasquelle Bonilla (tel. 504/552-2741, 3 Calle SO at the corner with 5 Av., 9 A.M.–3 P.M. Mon.–Fri.), is a little-known museum that hosts rotating exhibits of paintings. Don't be intimidated by the bank guards; they are happy to let in museum visitors.

Museo de la Naturaleza

Located on 1 Calle at 12 Avenida NO, the Museo de la Naturaleza (8 A.M.–noon and 2–4 P.M. Mon.–Fri.) has rather unimpressive exhibits on Honduran nature, clearly geared to visits by school groups.

For Kids

There are two water parks just outside of town: **Wonderland** (tel. 504/559-9700, 11 A.M.–5 P.M. Fri., 9 A.M.–5 P.M. Sat.–Sun) is the bigger and better of the two, located on the *segundo anillo,* or outer ring road, opposite the Estadio Olímpico. **Zizima** is just off the highway to the airport and La Lima. The brand-new **Speed**

Racer Park (tel. 504/547-4081, noon–9 P.M. Mon.–Thurs., 10 A.M.–10 P.M. Fri.–Sun.), with go-karts, a skating rink, and mini-golf is conveniently located next door.

Mi Pequeño Sula is a children's museum that is slowly being developed, located next to the Municipal Gymnasium, on the highway to the bus terminal and Tegucigalpa. The planetarium has been completed, and there is a show Fridays at 4 P.M.

ENTERTAINMENT AND EVENTS
Bars, Lounges, and Dancing

The once-thriving disco scene in San Pedro has given way to the ubiquitous lounge, and there are lots of good ones. There are also plenty of more casual bars, and several bars and lounges have dancing.

Located in the hopping *zona viva,* the lounge **b412** (9a Calle and 16 Av. SO) is a great place to start out the evening, and its dance club **1201** downstairs plays mainly trance, techno, rave, and the occasional merengue or salsa.

Near the TGI Friday's on Boulevard Los Proceres (between 18 and 19 Av. NO) is **Treehouse,** an open-air restaurant/lounge that makes a great place to have a drink; there's dancing on weekend nights.

Living up to its name, **Klein Bohemia** (www.kleinbohemia.com, corner of 7a Calle SO and 8 Av., tel. 504/552-3172, 7 P.M.–1 A.M. Thurs., 7 P.M.–2 A.M. Fri.–Sat.) is where San Pedro's artists and intelligentsia come to have a drink amid rotating art exhibitions. Films are shown every Thursday night.

If what you're looking for is glam, head to **Ottro Lugar Lounge** (7 Calle SO between 18 and 19 Av.) just outside of the Circunvalación, or to **Luca Luca** (15 Av. SO between 8 and 9 Calle) in the *zona viva.* Another popular place for a dressed-up drink is **Salotto** (corner of 16 Av. SO and Blvd. Morazán), the bar inside of the Tre Fratelli Italian restaurant.

A popular but laid-back place for a brew is **Caribbean Bar** (16 Av. SO between 9 and 10 Calle, tel. 504/553-6149, open daily from 7 P.M. onward).

Two other spots popular with young *sampedranos* are **Le Loft** (16 Av. NO and 10 Calle), with two-for-one on vodka, rum, and whiskey on Wednesdays, and two-for-one martinis for ladies on Thursdays; and **The Cube** (10 Calle A, between 14 and 15 Av., www.thecuberestlounge.com), both with classic lounge and dance music.

Located in the *zona viva*, **Spot** (8 Calle SO between 15 and 16 Calle) is perhaps the only openly gay club in the country, usually packed with men getting down to disco and Top 40.

Casinos

The casino at the **Copantl** (16 Calle SO, off Boulevard del Sur) is popular. **Luxxor** (15 Av. SO at 8 Calle A) in the *zona viva* has blackjack, roulette, baccarat, and slot machines.

Movies

The three main malls in San Pedro—the MetroPlaza Mall just north of Avenida Circunvalación on the highway exit to Puerto Cortés; Multiplaza by the exit to Tegucigalpa; and MegaPlaza by the exit to El Progreso— each have at least three screens and better sound systems than the older cinemas in the center of town. Check the papers for the latest showings and times.

The Arts

The **Centro Cultural Sampedrano** (tel. 504/557-2575, 3 Calle between 3 and 4 Av. NO) downtown frequently holds concerts and dramatic performances, usually for US$3–4 per show. The cultural center also has a small library, stocked with books in Spanish and open to the public. The newer **Teatro José Francisco Saybe** (tel. 504/225-5117, Av. Circunvalación near 11 Av. NO) hosts the city's most fashionable performances, with ticket prices varying widely depending on the event.

SHOPPING
Arts and Crafts

San Pedro has one of Honduras's best handicraft markets at **Mercado Guamilito** (between

8 and 9 Av. and 6 and 7 Calles NO). The several dozen *artesanía* stalls sell a wide variety of handicrafts from across the country, including woodwork, paintings, sculptures, weavings, and more. Also here, you'll find a regular food market, many flower stalls, and several stands serving snacks and meals. It's a very pleasant place to shop—the salesfolk are friendly, and the market is spacious and safe.

A bit smaller, but with some interesting items (we picked up beer glasses made out of old Honduran beer bottles), is the covered market **Artesanías y Souvenirs** (8 A.M.–5 P.M. daily), a block behind the Gran Hotel Sula and conveniently located next to a great "food court" of ladies making fresh Honduran specialties.

Casa del Sol has excellent handicrafts shops in two locations, one in Mall Multiplaza (tel. 504/550-5711), the other in front of the Mercado Guamilito (on 6 Calle, between 8 and 9 Av. NO, tel. 504/557-1371, 7 A.M.–7 P.M. Mon.–Sat. and 8 A.M.–3 P.M. Sun.).

There is a branch of the jewelry store **Casa de Oro** in the Mall Multiplaza, selling its very popular, very expensive, and very nice silver necklaces, earrings, and bracelets in chunky Mayan designs.

Although quality varies, the best place in town to check out paintings by Honduran artists is at the art and frame shop **Maymo** (tel. 504/553-0318, 2 Calle SO between 6 and 7 Av., 8:30 A.M.–noon and 1:30–6 P.M. Mon.–Fri., 8:30 A.M.–noon and 2–5 P.M. Sat.). There's a second, slightly smaller branch on 1 Calle near the Crowne Plaza.

Cigar aficionados can stock up on *puros* (as well as excellent Honduran coffee) at **La Plazita** next door to Casa del Sol, or at **Casa de Puros** in the airport lobby.

Markets

The largest market in San Pedro is the **Mercado Medina-Concepción,** so named for the two neighborhoods in the southeast part of the city in which the sprawling market is located. The main market building is between 4 and 5 Avenidas and 6 and 7 Calles SE, but the surrounding streets are jammed with vendors

MAQUILAS: GOLDEN OPPORTUNITY OR EXPLOITATION?

The driving force behind San Pedro Sula's annual economic growth of 5-6 percent, and its status as one of the top earners in the national economy, is the couple of hundred export-oriented *maquila* factories in the region. The *maquilas* mainly assemble clothes from fabrics imported tax-free to Honduras, then re-export the finished product (again with no taxes) for sale in the United States. About 40 percent of the plants are owned by U.S. capital, 27 percent by Taiwanese, Korean, or Japanese capital, and the remainder by other international and domestic investors.

Maquila factories, a concept originally undertaken on a large scale along the Mexico-U.S. border, first arrived in Honduras in 1976, when the government passed the Puerto Cortés Free Zone law. Three years later, this was extended to Amapala, Tela, Choloma, Omoa, and La Ceiba. By 1998, further legal modifications allowed for the creation of free zones (called ZIPs) anywhere in the country, and now the majority of *maquilas* in Honduras are within a 50-kilometer radius of San Pedro Sula.

To many labor organizers outside Honduras, especially in the United States, the low wages and less-than-ideal conditions translate into a sort of modern slavery. Conditions in many *maquilas* are far from perfect. Verbal abuse, compulsory overtime, unreachable production quotas, and dismissal for pregnancy are all common. Nonetheless, local union leaders say many *maquilas* treat their workers with respect, subsidize lunch, provide transportation, and offer free medical care. Many female workers have developed a refined knowledge of the national labor laws and are quick to speak up for themselves and organize if treated unfairly.

The clamor in the United States passed right over like Honduras's annual tropical storms, and the *maquilas* continue attracting workers from all over the country, although growth is slowing. In 2008, 131,000 Hondurans worked in *maquilas*, up from 120,000 in 2004 and 100,000 in 2000. The local labor force continues its own struggle to improve conditions in the factories and gain wage increases (sometimes successfully), while the factory owners in turn do whatever they can to keep unions out of their shops and keep employee costs as low as possible. While *maquilas* typically offer just minimum wage, that salary easily beats the average wage as domestic help, and is three or four times what a woman might earn making tortillas to sell. There is still plenty to criticize about *maquilas* – for example, their exemption to the 60 percent increase in the national minimum wage mandated in 2009, although the US\$7 or so earned a day by *maquila* laborers is still nearly double what can be earned picking coffee or cotton or harvesting cane.

A 2008 World Bank study estimates that poverty levels in Honduras are slightly less thanks to employment by *maquilas*, particularly thanks to their employment of women, and the way women spend their income (typically with higher percentages going into family well-being than for their male counterparts). That's good news, since the *maquila* sector continues to grow – its largest project to date began operations in September 2008. The industrial park, ZIP Choluteca, is part of a larger project in the south that will include a commercial center, housing complex, recreational centers, and schools. It's a welcome addition to an economically depressed region of Honduras, and business owners love the chance to get away from the wage pressure in the economically stronger north.

of all variety. This is not an area all foreigners will feel comfortable walking around, even during the day, and it should definitely be avoided after dark. Just up 7 Calle at 9 Avenida SE is the smaller and newer **Mercado Dandy,** built in 1991 to ease the pressure on the main market.

Malls
U.S.-style malls are the latest retail rage to hit Honduras. The nicest is **City Mall** (Av. Circunvalación past 12 Calle SO), with over 200 stores, eight movie screens, and a couple of dozen restaurants. **Multiplaza** is at the intersection of Avenida Circunvalación and the exit to Tegucigalpa, behind the Hotel Camino Real (with a children's play area and wireless Internet in the food court).

The new, more upscale **Galerías del Valle** has opened in the northwest of the city as well. Perhaps the high vacancy rates (it was only about 25 percent occupied as of 2008) attest to the mall saturation in town.

Books and Newspapers
On the first floor of the City Mall, **Metro Nova** stocks a large selection of English books and newspapers, some books about Honduras, and books in Spanish by Honduran authors (among others).

The gift shop inside the Gran Hotel Sula has a small collection of books about Honduras, mainly in Spanish but with some in English, as well as a decent magazine selection.

SPORTS AND RECREATION
Golf
La Lima Golf Club (tel. 504/668-7816, www .clubcampestrelalima.com), 20 minutes from San Pedro off the highway to El Progreso, was originally built by United Fruit for its workers and guests but is now a private club open to anyone who will pay. Nonmembers may play 9 holes for US$16, or all 18 for US$21. Club rental is US$8. Generally, no reservations are necessary. To get there, look for the Colonia Tela entrance from the El Progreso highway, just east of the Río Chamelecón.

Also in San Pedro Sula is the 9-hole **Las Lomas Golf Club** (tel. 504/553-3106), which is open to nonmembers but does not have equipment rental.

Fútbol
For a taste of Honduras's national sporting passion, consider watching a soccer match at the **Estadio Olímpico,** southeast of the city, reached by a taxi for US$3–4. Local teams Motagua and Real España both play league games here, and frequently the national team does also. Tickets for regular season matches cost US$3–20, depending on where you want to sit. Crowds tend to be impassioned, but it's generally safe from hooligan-type violence, certainly not like watching a match in many European countries. Watch out for pickpockets, though.

Scuba Diving
Honduras Divers (tel. 504/9991-0778, www .hondurasdivers.com) arranges scuba outings to nearby Puerto Cortés and to the **Cayos Zapotillos** of Belize, as well as scuba classes at the Nautilus gym in town, and equipment sales. The shop is located at the Nautilus gym in northwest San Pedro. The basic diving course costs US$250, while the Dive Master course is US$600. A scuba tour of the Cayos is $110; diving near Puerto Cortés is much cheaper.

Spas
Two recommended spots are **Diva Spa** (tel. 504/521-6106, 7 Calle NO between 18 and 19 Av.) and **Salon and Spa Carmen Alicia Unisex** (tel. 504/552-2259, Av. Circunvalación, between 5 and 6 Calle), both of which offer salon services as well as spa treatments like massages and mud wraps.

At bare-bones **Fuente de Salud y Juventud** (7 Calle SO between 19 and 20 Av., tel. 504/552-0407), even penny-pinchers can indulge, given the rock-bottom price of US$8.50 for a one-hour massage. The health food shop-slash-massage parlor opens at 7 A.M. Sunday through Friday, closing in the late afternoon, except Fridays when it closes at noon.

ACCOMMODATIONS

San Pedro has a wide selection of hotels of all varieties and price ranges. There are a number of inexpensive hotels in the southwest quadrant of the city, within 10 blocks of the square. The cheapest are generally charmless, and cold water only, but those listed here were reasonably clean, while some of the midrange hotels are quite nice. If you're pinching your lempiras, take a look before you hand over your money, and keep in mind that it could be worth asking to see more than one room to find one with more light or less street noise. While many of the newer upscale hotels are generally located out on Avenida Circunvalación, a couple of nice boutique hotels have joined the Gran Hotel Sula downtown, and there are attractive midrange hotels in the center as well. Many hotels are often fully booked, so for all but the absolute cheapest, it is a good idea to reserve in advance. No matter where you stay, take taxis at night to go out and come back.

Under US$25

If you don't mind the prison-gray paint and have flip-flops for the shower, **Hotel San Juan** (5 Av. SO at 6 Calle, tel. 504/553-1488, US$5.25 s/d with shared bath, US$7 s, US$10.50 d with private bath, cold water only) is an acceptable cheapie. **Hotel Marina No. 1** (6 Calle SO between 5 and 6 Av., tel. 504/557-2953, US$7 s, US$8 d with fan and shared bath, US$4.50 more for a/c, cold water only) isn't necessarily nicer, but is at least painted in cheery yellow.

A big step up is the **Gran Hotel Marina No. 3** (3 Calle SO between 5 and 6 Av., tel. 504/557-8722), by far the top of the line in the Marina chain, with clean rooms, decent decor, and peach walls. Prices vary according to amenities: whether the room has hot or cold water, a fan or air-conditioning, a shower or a tub, and wireless Internet. A double with a fan and hot water goes for US$18.

Although its double rooms place it in a higher price category, the **Tamarindo Hostel** has dorm rooms for US$15 per person.

US$25-50

There are many great midprice hotels, including a couple that also offer cheap dorm-style accommodations.

Certainly the funkiest option in this price range is **Tamarindo Hostel** (9 Calle NO, between 10 and 11 Av., tel. 504/557-0123, www.tamarindohostel.com, info@tamarindohostel.com), in the trendy northwest section of the city, not far from the Guamilito Market and a number of good restaurants. Situated behind a security wall, Tamarindo, with its tidy little front garden, tropical birds, and colorful murals, is a virtual oasis. The downstairs common area includes a clean full kitchen with a stove and microwave, a TV lounge, and a large dining area with plenty of books, games, and tour brochures as well as Internet access (for a steep US$2/hour). Upstairs there are two dorms with bunk beds, private bath, warmish water, TV, fan, and air-conditioning for US$15 per person—these dorms are the best place in town to stay for that lively backpacker vibe. There are also four private rooms with bathrooms, warmish water, air-conditioning, and cable TV (US$45 s/d, US$60 t), but there are nicer places to stay if you are springing for a private room. The second-floor balcony hammocks make a nice place to relax, and lockers are available to stash your valuables. Owner Juan Carlos can help with pickup service from the bus terminal or airport.

Another clean, well-maintained hotel is **Hotel Real** (6 Av. SO, between 6 and 7 Calles, tel. 504/550-7929, US$17 s with fan, US$25 with a/c, US$28 d with a/c), decorated with plants, hanging Lencan pots, and peach paint. Rooms have TVs and private baths but, surprisingly at this price point, no hot water. Internet is available in the lobby for US$1 an hour, and breakfast is just $2, served until 10 A.M.

Hostal E & N (15 Av. NO at the corner with 5 Calle, tel. 504/552-5731, hostaleyn@amnethn.com, US$35 s, US$38 d) has two buildings on the same block, both with clean, simple rooms on a nice street in the northwest section of the city. Parking and breakfast are included, rooms have wireless Internet and air-conditioning, and the place is popular with groups, so try to book ahead.

◖ Hotel Posada Colonial (6 Calle SO between 7 and 8 Av., tel. 504/550-2763, posada colonial@hotmail.com, US$18 s, US$26 d) is a great little hotel with a nice atmosphere. Rooms have small tables, clean bathrooms, dark wood furniture, and wireless Internet. Free Internet is also available in the lobby. There is a parking lot, plus a small cafeteria next door. Laundry service is available for US$1 per item. The one drawback? It's not quite as centrally located as some of the other hotels. On the other hand, it's only a block from the groovy bar Klein Bohemia.

◖ Hotel Maya Copan (5 Calle NO, between 8 and 9 Av., tel. 504/552-1516, www.hotelmayacopan.com, US$37 s, US$45 d) has a good location just a block from the Mercado Guamilito. Some rooms are sunnier than others, and while the bathrooms are clean, a few have stinky pipes, so it can be worthwhile to take a look at more than one room. All are tidy, with air-conditioning and TV. There is purified water and Internet (US$1/hour) in the lobby, and parking is free.

The former Hotel Ambassador has been totally renovated and turned into the **Hotel Plaza Palmera** (7 Calle SO between 5 and 6 Av., tel. 504/557-6825, US$24 s, US$29 d). Although the location is a bit off the beaten path, the rooms are excellent value, with TV, air-conditioning, and chests, dressers, and headboards in dark carved wood. Some rooms have private balconies, while others share a balcony that overlooks a grassy pedestrian meridian on Avenida Los Leones.

US$50-100

One of the best additions to San Pedro's hotel selection in recent years is **◖ Casa del Arbol** (6 Av. between 2 and 3 Calles NO, tel. 504/504-1616, www.hotelcasadelarbol.com, US$81 s, US$99 d). Located in the heart of downtown, the 13-room hotel is a renovated wooden house copied from the banana plantations. A stone patio behind the house leads to more rooms that were built around a giant mango tree (*arbol* means tree, hence the name). Guest rooms have wood desks, chic linens, and classy Honduran artwork. Remarkable for a Honduran city hotel, significant efforts are being made to get green-certified, including solar panels to heat the water and run the lights, and low-flow toilets. A healthy breakfast buffet is included in the price.

The centrally located **Hotel Ejecutivo** (2 Calle at 10 Av. SO, tel. 504/552-4289, US$64 s, US$75 d) is a good choice for business travelers, with modern rooms with TV, air-conditioning, and a small table with two chairs, perfect for working or for a cup of coffee. Amenities include a gym and wireless Internet (the signal is best in the lobby), and the staff is friendly. Travelers checks are accepted here, as well as the usual cash and credit cards.

Oozing mod style is the nine-room **◖ Casa Guacamaya B&B** (16 Calle SO, off Boulevard del Sur, tel. 504/556-8406, US$63 s, US$70 d), opposite the Copantl. Rooms have white tile floors and white walls; bedding and chairs are in bright blues, reds, and greens. The furnishings are modern and hip, with flat-screen TVs, air-conditioning, and wireless Internet. Breakfast is a simple buffet including juice, ham, cheese and toast. Note that American Express and MasterCard *debit* cards are not accepted.

Just down the road and another excellent value is **Hotel La Cordillera** (16 Calle SO, off Boulevard del Sur, tel. 504/516-0405, www.boutiquehotellacordillera.com, US$75 s, US$99 d). Rooms are elegant, decked out in cream and pale green with accents of carved mahogany, flat-screen TVs, wireless Internet, and air-conditioning. Breakfast is included in the rates, served in the lobby restaurant, and there is a nice outdoor bar as well. It's a shame that the staff isn't always as gracious as the setting.

Reminiscent of U.S. chains such as Amerisuites, the 13-room **Suites del Valle** (6 Av. NO at the corner with 11 Calle, tel. 504/552-0134, www.suitesdelvalle.com, US$65 s, US$79 d) is a good choice for those looking for a little more space. Each comfortable room has a tiled kitchen area with a sink, microwave, coffeemaker, and dining table, set off from the carpeted sleeping area. There is wireless Internet throughout the hotel, and two computers are available for guest use in a large sitting area off the lobby.

In Colonia Trejo, and actually adjacent to the City Mall, is the **Apart-Hotel Monteverde** (12 Calle B SO at the corner with 16 Av., tel. 504/556-6239, www.aparthotelmonteverde .blogspot.com, hotelmonteverde76@yahoo .com, US$48 s, US$54 d). The rooms are better than the shabby hallways might lead you to believe, and they come with wireless Internet, a fridge, and a sink as well as the standard amenities. Some rooms have king-sized beds, and if you want a small stove and dishes, they're happy to bring them in. Conveniently, there is a laundromat in the same building.

US$100 and Up

For years *the* hotel in San Pedro, the **Gran Hotel Sula** (1 Calle at 4 Av. NO, tel. 504/545-2600, U.S. tel. 866/978-5025, www.hotelsula .hn, US$110 s/d, US$122 suite), facing the downtown square, has been surpassed in quality by the newer high-end hotels, but it is still favored by many business travelers and tourists for its central location and bustling vibe. The rooms all have private balconies (some with nice views), wireless Internet, and throw rugs over tile floors, and suites have large, separate kitchen/dining areas. The upscale **Granada Restaurant** serves lunch buffets and dinner à la carte, and the diner-style **Café Skandia,** with a patio overlooking the small pool, was long the city's only 24-hour restaurant, but alas, it has cut back to 6 A.M.–10 P.M. daily. The gift shop sells day-old U.S. newspapers and magazines and books in English, and there is a car rental agency in the lobby. Reservation requests made through the form on the hotel's website seem to get lost in cyberspace—better to call.

Another new boutique hotel in a converted home is **◖ Casa Luna** (2 Calle NO at 23 Av., tel. 504/510-1748, www.hotelcasaluna .blogspot.com, reservacionescasaluna@gmail

.com, US$81 s, US$104 d), located a few blocks beyond the Circunvalación in the northwest quadrant of the city. The seven spacious guest rooms are sleek and stylish, with high ceilings, queen beds, top-quality linens, and a tiny study with table and chair. Continental breakfast is included, and the restaurant is open 6 A.M.–10 P.M. The terrace is a comfortable place for a cup of coffee (brewed all day long) or a cocktail. The hotel can arrange a taxi to or from the airport for US$13.

An eight-story, modern pink tower in front of the Mall Multiplaza on the road heading out of town toward Tegucigalpa, **Hotel Copantl** (16 Calle SO, off Boulevard del Sur, tel. 504/556-8900, www.copantl.com, US$151 s, US$163 d) has 200 modern rooms with queen and king beds, ornate furnishings, TV, wireless Internet, and air-conditioning. The standout features of the Copantl are its many facilities, which include a beauty parlor, a tobacco and gift shop selling many English-language publications, a travel center/information desk, a convention center, a casino, two bars, three restaurants, an Olympic-size pool, a gym with Jacuzzi, and six tennis courts. A buffet breakfast is included with the room, as well as free shuttle service to and from the airport (on their schedule). The hotel is a favorite of traveling diplomats, aid agencies, and international organizations such as the United Nations. The seventh-floor open-air steakhouse, La Churrasquería (6 P.M.–midnight daily) is popular for its city views. Weekend rates (US$87 s, US$99 d) are a steal.

One of the finest in town is the **◖ Hilton Princess** (Av. Circunvalación at 10 Calle SO, tel. 504/556-9600, U.S. tel. 800/445-8667, www.hilton.com, US$128 s/d standard, US$162 s/d executive). The hotel's 124 rooms have all the amenities, including wonderfully powerful showers and an Internet hookup with the hotel's own server, and service is top-notch. Executive rooms include breakfast, butler service, coffee, tea, and juice in the afternoon, and express check-in/check-out. The hotel's location, in the main restaurant district and near the exit to Tegucigalpa, is convenient, and as it began its life as an independent hotel, the building has a lot more character than many international chains. Book through the Hilton website for the best rates.

Right next to the Mall Multiplaza south of downtown, at the highway exit to Tegucigalpa, is the **Inter-Continental** (Boulevard del Sur near Mall Multiplaza, tel. 504/545-2500, U.S./Canada tel. 888/424-6835, www.inter continental.com, US$166 s/d). The hotel always has Honduran and foreign businesspeople milling in its lobby. Executive level includes a welcome drink, an American breakfast, two laundry pressings, 6 P.M. snacks, and butler service. The hotel was upgrading its rooms at the time of writing and is likely to have the most luxurious rooms in town when it is done (and prices may rise accordingly). Amenities include a swimming pool, 24-hour gym, wireless Internet throughout the hotel, and a gift shop. Shuttle service to the airport costs US$10.

Long-Term Stays
The **Hotel La Cordillera** offers monthly rates of US$2,088–3,480, depending on the room and number of people. Just up the road is **Apart Hotel La Cordillera** (tel. 504/516-0520, www.aparthotellacordillera.com, US$70 s, US$81 d, US$20 more for suites with full kitchens). Although not quite as elegant as its sister hotel, it is still very nice, and a good option for those who will be in town for a while. The hotel has a minimart on-site, as well as a swimming pool, and all rooms have TVs, air-conditioning, and wireless Internet. There is also a two-story, three-bed penthouse suite available for US$319 per night. Discounts for long-term stays can be negotiated with the manager.

While they don't advertise monthly rates, the many suite-style hotels (such as Suites del Valle and Monteverde) in town can be good options for longer stays, and discounts for stays of a week or longer can likely be negotiated.

Near the Airport
The only airport hotel we can really recommend, and do wholeheartedly, is the **Banana Inn** (tel. 504/668-2501, US$64 s, US$81 d),

located less than 10 minutes from the airport in the town of La Lima. Rooms in this former *bananero* home are tastefully decorated, with dark wood furniture and carpeting. The 16 guest rooms often fill with airline crews, so book ahead, although a hotel expansion is in the works. A taxi here from the airport should be about $8, and the hotel will arrange one for you upon request.

If you've rented a car at the airport, to get to Banana Inn take a left onto the La Lima–San Pedro Sula highway, and take the La Lima turnoff after another minute or two. The road takes you straight to the central park, at the end of which you take a right (the park stays on your right when you turn). Follow this road over a bridge, around a curve to the left, and through a stoplight. Just after the stoplight, you'll see the entrance to Banana Inn on the left.

FOOD
Breakfast and Snacks
Super Donuts (2 Calle between 2 and 3 Av. SO, tel. 504/552-7812, 6 A.M.–8 P.M. daily), opposite the *catedral,* has an inexpensive and filling buffet breakfast.

Although the only thing Scandinavian about it is the Viking ship logo, **Pastelería Skandia** (7 A.M.–7 P.M. Mon.–Sat., 8 A.M.–3:30 P.M. Sun.), around the corner from the Gran Hotel Sula, has a tasty selection of pastries and good *licuados.*

The national chain **Espresso Americano** (tel. 504/552-4793, 6:30 A.M.–8 P.M. Mon.–Sat.), right on the corner of the *parque* and the *peatonal* pedestrian street, serves up a good espresso in a modern, coffee-bar atmosphere.

Among the several juice stands downtown is **Super Jugos,** at the corner of 2 Calle and 6 Avenida SO, open 8 A.M.–9 P.M. every day.

Cafés and Diners
Cafetería Pamplona (tel. 504/550-2639, 7 A.M.–8 P.M. Mon.–Sat., 8 A.M.–8 P.M. Sun.), on the square, always has a large crowd of cigarette-smoking, coffee-guzzling locals chatting or reading the newspaper at the Formica tables

while soft elevator music plays. The Spanish owner, who oversees the place from behind the bar, has decorated the interior with blown-up photos of the famed running of the bulls. The espresso is very good, and the extensive menu is moderately priced at US$2.50–4.50 for a full entrée. This is a good place to get an inexpensive meal: Breakfasts start at US$1.20 and run up to US$5.50, sandwiches are US$1.50–3.75, and pastas cost US$3.75–4.75. The menu tops out at the US$9 steak.

Café Skandia (6 A.M.–10 P.M. daily) in the Gran Hotel Sula has good service, an extensive menu, and reasonably priced food. It's always hopping, and resident expats meet here daily in the morning for a cup of coffee.

A ladies-who-lunch kind of place, **Cake Design's** (8 Calle SO at 19 Av., tel. 504/553-3167, 10 A.M.–9 P.M. Mon.–Sat.) has all manner of salads, quiches, sandwiches, and croissants for US$6–7, as well as daily soup specials and, of course, cakes.

Honduran

Our favorite new spot in town is **◖ Plaza Típica Padilla Sunceri** (7 A.M.–5 P.M. daily), the very clean, covered, market-style food court two blocks from the Gran Hotel Sula in the center of town. Whether breakfast, lunch, or dinner, a meal here will only set you back US$2–3. There is a wide selection of snacks and meals, including tamales, *pupusas,* and even *tapado olanchano* (beef stew). There are also several clean *comedores* in **Mercado Guamilito** (between 8 and 9 Av. and 6 and 7 Calles NO), serving inexpensive *comidas corrientes,* and you can expect (fast-moving) lines at the popular buffets. Check out the neighboring handicrafts markets before or after your meal.

A good choice in town for grilled meat or a *plato típico* is **Rancho Palos Blancos** (11:30 A.M.–1 A.M. daily), in an attractive, rustic wood and brick restaurant in the northwest section of town. Meals are well-priced at US$5–11, and there's live music on Saturdays.

A local legend for make-your-own *baleadas,* **◖ Baleadas Express** (Calle 13 NO, between

Av. Circunvalación and 11 Av., in Plaza Tropical, 7:30 A.M.–noon and 4–10:30 P.M. daily) looks a lot like a fast-food joint with its impersonal seating and plain lighting, but the tortillas are phenomenal and the assortment of meat fillings mouthwatering. Prices depend on the filling but an average *baleada* costs just US$1.

Very casual and centrally located downtown is the open-air **Sabor Catracho,** serving up tacos for US$1 each, *baleadas* for less, and set meals for US$3.20.

Italian

Nelly's Pizza (7 A.M.–9:30 P.M. daily) has moved to a new location on the Avenida Circunvalación, close to Hotel Los Andes. Despite the ornate fountain in an interior patio, the decor is rather spartan, but the pizza (US$7–11) is popular. Steaks are also available (US$8–10).

Tre Fratelli (tel. 504/557-3019, 11 A.M.–11 P.M. Mon.–Thurs., 7 A.M.–10 P.M. Fri. and Sat.), on Circunvalación at 1 Calle, in front of Mantra Disco, an upscale chain restaurant, serves up good Italian cuisine with a California touch in a homey atmosphere with blue-and-white checkered tablecloths, murals of rural Italy on the walls, an open kitchen, and a raised bar that sometimes hosts live music. Breakfasts include crepes and frittatas (US$4.50), and the lunch special is a good deal. The coffee and desserts are superlative. Inside is the bar Salotto, popular with young *sampedranos* on weekend nights.

At the Italian-owned **Trattoria Bel Paese** (5 Calle A NO between 13 and 14 Av.) the pasta (US$5–6) comes in great sauces but is cooked Honduran-style; that is, until limp. Be sure to ask for your dish *al dente.*

Asian

Macau (11 Calle at 14 Av. SO, tel. 504/553-4852, 10 A.M.–midnight daily) is among the more popular Chinese restaurants in the *zona viva* for its menu of large, reasonably priced dishes, even if they are unexceptionally flavored. The place is clean and charges US$4–5 per large entrée of *chap suey* or *chow min* with beef, chicken, pork, or shrimp.

Boc-Ga (13 Calle NO at 11 Av., tel. 504/9991-0077) has authentic if expensive Korean dishes such as kimchi soup (US$21–32), as well as many more reasonably priced choices such as beef teriyaki (US$8) and other kinds of soups (US$6–8).

Two blocks from the Hilton Princess on 14 Calle is **Bon-Sai,** serving up the best sushi in town, as well as Japanese specialties like tempura and *yakitori.*

Mexican

Antojitos Mexicanos serves slightly greasy but inexpensive Mexican-style *tortas, chilaquiles, huevos a la mexicana,* enchiladas, or tacos (US$1–2), with beer or soft drinks to wash them down. There are two locations: the *parque* above Espresso Americano (8 A.M.–8 P.M. daily) and on Avenida Circunvalación at 7 Calle SO (10 A.M.–6 P.M. daily, sometimes later on weekends). The latter also hosts occasional mariachi bands.

Seafood

In a converted house in the *zona viva* district is the ever-popular 【 **Arte Marino** (10 Calle SO at 15 Av., tel. 504/552-8046, 11:30 A.M.–11 P.M. Sun.–Thurs., 11:30 A.M.–midnight Sat.), serving excellent shrimp, ceviche, lobster, and fish fillets for US$9–14 per entrée.

Another recommended seafood restaurant is **Olabeto's,** located behind the Hilton Princess—ask at the Hilton for the exact address.

Other International

Considered one of the classier spots in town, although you might not believe it looking at the fake windmill out front, **Don Udo's** (13 Av. NO between 7 Calle and 7 Calle A, tel. 504/557-7991, 11 A.M. onward daily) offers a variety of international dishes and a sizable wine list. Through ownership has changed, it remains popular. There is indoor and patio seating.

Past its heyday but still popular with the local jet set and businesspeople with

expense accounts is **Pat's Steakhouse** (Av. Circunvalación at 5 Calle SO, tel. 504/553-0939, 11 A.M.–3 P.M. and 5:30–11 P.M. daily), generally thought to have the best cuts of beef in town. The *churrasco* runs US$17 for 8 ounces, US$21 for 12, with soup and a large salad, while the house specialty is the tenderloin (US$18–21). Quality fresh seafood is available also, and the wine list is extensive. The atmosphere is elegant with linens and dark wood, if a touch dated.

The menu at 【 **Bistro 188** (8 Calle SO, at the corner with 19 Av. SO, tel. 504/504-4815, noon–2 P.M. and 5:30–9 P.M. Mon.–Fri., noon–2 P.M. Sat.) may be short, but when each dish is this well-executed, who cares? Chef María José Rivera studied at the Johnson and Wales culinary school in Rhode Island, and her version of standards, such as niçoise salad, have flair (in this case, moist grilled salmon and dill sauce instead of the usual tuna and vinaigrette). An adjacent wine and tapas bar was under construction at the time of our visit.

In Barrio Los Andes **Deriva Wine Bar** is another chic eatery with a decent selection of Argentinian, Chilean, and French wines; a Peruvian-influenced menu including ceviches and seafood platters; and grilled meats (US$9–17).

Run by a Colombian woman, **Crepes** (7 Calle SO between 19 and 20 Av., tel. 504/553-5797) turns out its namesake dish in any number of sweet and savory versions, but also has Colombian snacks such as *arepas* (corn griddle cakes), as well as heartier dishes like chicken and steaks.

A laid-back place to get a tasty plate or ribs or even German sausage is **Jardines Café,** across the Río Piedras in the northwest corner of town, not far from the new mall Galerías del Valle. Thursday night is popular with local expats.

Vegetarian

Between pizza, pasta, and Chinese noodles, there are more options for vegetarians in San Pedro than in most of the country. But if vegetarian buffet with soy proteins is what you want,

THE ARABS OF HONDURAS

Arabic Christians began their emigration from Palestine to Latin America at the end of the 19th century, some seeking a freer environment for the practice of their religion, others lured by good deals the Honduran government was offering to foreign investors. Still others left their homeland around 1914, when the Ottoman Empire obliged Arabs to fight against the Allies. Many more arrived after World War II, escaping from the increasing hostilities between Muslims and Jews in the Middle East. Statistics on Honduras's Arabic population are hard to come by, but it's estimated that perhaps 200,000 of the country's 8 million people are of Palestinian descent – the highest proportion of any Latin American nation.

That's not even 3 percent of the nation's population. But many of the country's leading business and political families are Arab-Honduran. Honduras's first Arab immigrant is reputed to have been Constantino Nini, who arrived in 1893. He began as a dry goods peddler and ended up owning his own factory in La Ceiba, which produced mops and brooms. Countless more followed in Nini's footsteps: One local survey asserts that in 1918, Arab-Hondurans owned 41.5 percent of the businesses in San Pedro Sula. A few notable families are:

- **The Canahuatis:** You'll see this stamped onto the back of cars across the country, as Yude Canahuati owns the Ford dealerships in Honduras. Juan Canahuati is a free-zone and textile entrepreneur. Nawal Canahuati de Burbara is owner of Comisariato Los Andes, one of the largest supermarkets in Honduras. Mario Canahuati has served as ambassador to the United States, and in 2008 he campaigned to become the Liberal Party's candidate for president (but lost).

- **The Facussés:** Carlos Flores Facussé served as president of Honduras from 1998 to 2002. His mother hailed from Bethlehem.

- **The Kafatis:** The family originates from Beit Jala, a tiny Christian town near Bethlehem. The family business, Gabriel Kafati S.A., is the largest coffee roaster in Honduras, under the label El Café Indio. Oscar Kafati served as an ambassador to Egypt and Italy in the late 1990s, and then as the country's minister of industry and commerce. Eduardo Kafati is the president of Grupo INTUR, the conglomerate that owns all the Pollo Campero, Burger King, Popeyes, Little Caesars, Church's Chicken, Dunkin' Donuts, and Baskin Robbins chains in Honduras. He is also the owner of the Honduran franchises of the international chain Espresso Americano.

- **The Laraches:** Also from Beit Jala, Domingo Larach came to Honduras to escape Turkish control, arriving in San Pedro where he started out as door-to-door salesman. He founded Comercial Larach in 1900, and the family now owns a major hardware-store chain in San Pedro Sula and Tegucigalpa.

Arabic culture is at its strongest in San Pedro, which is home to the country's only Orthodox Christian church (consecrated in 1963), a English-Spanish-Arabic trilingual school, and, most famously, the Centro Social Hondureño Arabe, the country's poshest country club, by far. The luxurious dining room serving both Honduran and Arabic food is open to members only, but makes an exception for foreigners – just be sure to bring your passport.

head to **Fuente de Salud y Juventud** (7 Calle SO between 19 and 20 Av., tel. 504/552-0407, US$3.50), and you can get a dirt cheap massage while you're there.

Groceries

One good supermarket near downtown is **Supermercado Colonial** (Av. Circunvalación at 2 Calle NO, 7:30 A.M.–9 P.M. Mon.–Sat., 8 A.M.–8 P.M. Sun.). A bit less expensive is nearby **Comisariato Los Andes** (Av. Circunvalación at 6 Calle NO, until 8:30 P.M. daily).

INFORMATION AND SERVICES
Travel Agents

Two companies can arrange airline tickets. **Mundirama Travel Service** (2 Calle SO, between 2 and 3 Av. SO, tel. 504/550-0490 or 504/550-1192, fax 504/557-9022, 8 A.M.–noon and 1–5 P.M. daily), next to the cathedral, is also the American Express agent. A second option is **Cano Grand Tours** (1 Calle between 13 and 14 Av., tel. 504/553-4167 or 504/557-5760), near the stadium.

Banks

Just about any bank in town can change dollars, most have ATMs, and many will change travelers checks as well. The moneychangers on the square and along the *peatonal* are certainly a lot quicker and usually offer a better rate. It may seem shady to a foreigner, but there have been no reports of anyone getting robbed, and it's not illegal. Just be sensible: Make sure you have the exchange rate clear in your head, and count the money. If you have doubts on the numbers, borrow the changer's calculator and check it yourself.

MoneyGrams can be picked up at Banco Atlántida, while **Western Union** transfers are available at Banco del Occidente and Banco Ficohsa.

The American Express agent in San Pedro Sula is **Mundirama Travel Service** (2 Calle, between 2 and 3 Av. SO, tel. 504/550-0490, 8 A.M.–noon and 1–5 P.M. daily), right next to the cathedral downtown. Travelers checks are

available for sale to cardholders, and they can accept payments for U.S.-based or Honduran American Express cards.

Communications

The central **Hondutel** office, on the corner of 4 Avenida and 4 Calle SO, is open 24 hours a day, but after 9 P.M. a guard lets you in. This would be for emergency only, as Internet shops offer cheaper calls and this area isn't really safe at night.

Honducor (9 Calle at 3 Avenida SO, tel. 504/552-3183, 7:30 A.M.–5:50 P.M. Mon.–Fri., 8–11:50 A.M. Sat.) has express service. More reliable though significantly more expensive are **DHL** (Av. Circunvalación, between 10 and 11 Av. NO, tel. 504/552-2424) and **Federal Express** (17 Calle between 9 and 10 Av. SO, tel. 504/552-1717, www.fedex.com).

San Pedro Sula has innumerable Internet cafés for web surfing and international telephone calls. One most convenient café downtown with a fast connection is **Diosita.Net** (8 A.M.–8 P.M. Mon.–Sat., 9 A.M.–6 P.M. Sun., US$1/hour) with two locations, one right above the other in a small mall off the southwest corner of the central plaza behind the Espresso Americano. In City Mall there is a branch of the **MultiNet** chain, with Internet for US$1 an hour and cheap international phone calls (US$0.05/minute to the U.S. and Canada).

Laundry

You'll not find too many laundry shops near downtown, but one not too far away is **Dry Cleaning y Lavandería Almich** (5 Calle, between 9 and 10 Av. SO, tel. 504/553-1687, 8 A.M.–4 P.M. daily), charging US$0.50 per pound of clothes, washed and dried in the same day.

In Barrio Los Andes, in the northwest part of town near Hotel Los Andes, is **Lavandería Blanco Azul** (7 Calle, between 14 and 15 Av. NO, 8 A.M.–6 P.M. Mon.–Fri., 8 A.M.–1 P.M. Sat.), charging US$3 per 10 pounds for wash and dry. There is also a launderette at the **Apart-Hotel Monteverde** (12 Calle B SO at the corner with 16 Av., tel. 504/556-6239).

Spanish Classes

Geared more toward the professional community than the casual tourist, **Harris Communications** (tel. 504/552-2705, www.harriscom.org) is one option for private Spanish classes. They also have an office in La Ceiba.

Emergencies

If you need the **police,** dial 199 or call 504/556-5155 or 504/552-3171. The **fire department** can be reached by dialing 198, 504/552-5841, or 504/556-7644. For an **ambulance,** call the Red Cross at 194 or 504/553-1283. If you need to get in touch with a hospital, give a call to the **Clínica Bendaña** (tel. 504/553-1618 or 504/553-1614, 24 hours).

Immigration

The *migración* office (tel. 504/553-6928, 7:30 A.M.–3:30 P.M. Mon.–Fri.) is on 3 Calle, between 5 and 6 Avenidas SO, 2nd floor.

If your passport gets lost or stolen, there is a **U.S. Consul's office** (1–4 P.M. Mon., Wed., and Fri.) in San Pedro, on the 11th floor of the Banco Atlántida building on the central square, next to the Hotel Gran Sula.

Car Rental

The several car-rental agencies operating in San Pedro, all with offices in the city and at the airport, include **Maya Rent A Car** (in town at 3 Av. between 7 and 8 Calles NO, tel. 504/552-2670, or at the airport, tel. 504/668-3168), **Molinari Rent A Car** (at the Gran Hotel Sula, tel. 504/553-2639 or 504/552-2704), **Toyota Rent A Car** (3 Av. between 5 and 6 Calles NO, tel. 504/552-5498 or 504/552-0814), **Thrifty** (at the airport, tel. 504/668-3152 or 504/668-3153), **Hertz** (at the airport, tel. 504/668-3156 or 504/668-3157), and **Avis** (at the airport and in town at 1 Calle and 6 Av. NE, tel. 504/553-0888 or 504/552-2872).

GETTING THERE AND AWAY

San Pedro is the central transportation hub for northern and western Honduras and is frequently the gateway to the country for foreign visitors on their way to the north coast or Bay Islands. Most bus travelers in Honduras will eventually find themselves passing through San Pedro.

Air

Aeropuerto Internacional Ramón Villeda Morales, 13 kilometers from downtown San Pedro, has a branch of BAC Bamer bank for exchanging money and three ATMs, Casa de Puros for picking up cigars, Wendy's, Espresso Americano and DK'd Donuts, and several car rental agencies located in the international arrivals section. There are a couple of steeply overpriced gift shops. Taxis from town to the airport cost about US$10, and there's no way to get there by bus. If you're leaving the country on an international flight, be prepared to pay a US$34.04 departure tax (in dollars or lempiras, but change is given only in lempiras). Domestic flights are subject to a tax of US$1.50. There is also an office of the bus line **Hedman Alas** in the international arrivals area, with service to Tela, as well as to the main bus terminal in San Pedro Sula at 8:30 A.M., 9:30 A.M., 1:30 P.M., 2:15 P.M., and 5:15 P.M.

Isleña Airlines (tel. 504/552-8335, www.flyislena.com, 8 A.M.–noon and 1:30–5 P.M. Mon.–Fri., 8 A.M.–noon Sat.), with offices in the city at Avenida Circunvalación between 13 and 14 Avenidas in Barrio Los Andes, or at the airport, flies direct to Tegucigalpa twice daily (US$90 one-way) and to La Ceiba three times daily (US$65 one-way) with connections to the Bay Islands.

Sosa Airlines (tel. 504/668-3223 at the airport) flies daily to La Ceiba (US$73 one-way), with connections to Roatán and Utila. Sosa also has an office in town (tel. 504/550-6545 or 504/550-6548, 8 A.M.–noon and 1–5 P.M. Mon.–Fri., 8 A.M.–noon Sat.) at 1 Calle, between 7 and 8 Avenidas NO.

Central American Airways (tel. 504/688-4217, www.central-american-airways.com) is a great little airline with service only between San Pedro and Tegucigalpa, departing at 7 A.M. and 4 P.M. Monday–Friday. Its plane is also available for charter.

Taca Airlines (at the airport, tel. 504/668-

3333, www.taca.com) flies nonstop to New York, San José, Belize City, Miami, Guatemala City, and San Salvador, with connections to many more cities, including Houston, Los Angeles, Washington, D.C., Chicago, San Francisco, and Toronto. Taca has an office on Avenida Circunvalación, between 13 and 14 Avenidas NO in Barrio Los Andes (tel. 504/550-5268).

American Airlines (Av. Circunvalación between 5 and 6 Calle SO, tel. 504/553-3506, www.aa.com) has an office at the Banco Ficohsa office and flies twice daily to Miami.

Continental (tel. 504/557-4141, www.continental.com), with an office at Plaza Versalles on Avenida Circunvalación (tel. 504/557-8709) and another at the Gran Hotel Sula (tel. 504/552-9770), has a daily flight to Houston.

Delta (www.delta.com) has twice-weekly flights to San Pedro Sula direct from Atlanta.

Spirit (www.spiritair.com) has a flight at the ungodly hour of 2 A.M. to Fort Lauderdale, with connections to 10 other cities in the United States and Puerto Rico. Spirit occasionally has extraordinary deals.

Copa (tel. 504/506-2672, airport tel. 504/668-3210, www.copaair.com) has a daily flight at 6:40 A.M. to San José, Costa Rica, with onward travel to Panama City and connections from there to all over Latin America.

Aeromexico (www.aeromexico.com) has daily flights to Mexico City.

Maya Island Air (www.mayaislandair.com) offers service to Belize City, Belize.

Bus

The relatively new bus terminal (tel. 504/516-1616, www.grancentralhn.com) five kilometers south of downtown town on the highway that leads to Tegucigalpa has eliminated major headaches for anyone who needed to change buses in San Pedro. The terminal has a food court with chains like SuperJugos, Pizza Hut, and Antojitos Mexicanos; public restrooms; a health clinic and pharmacy; and a bunch of stores selling everything under the sun (in case you want to pick up a new fridge before hopping on the bus?). There

is a branch of **BAC Bamer** (9 A.M.–4 P.M. Mon.–Fri., 9 A.M.–noon Sat.), with an ATM, and a Banco Ficensa also with an ATM (9 A.M.–4 P.M. Mon.–Fri., 9 A.M.–noon Sat.), where Western Union transfers can be picked up.

Smaller companies that run buses to towns around the country have windows in the terminal, while the bigger luxury lines have their own private waiting areas (note that Congolón and Cotisa lines are tucked in the same side section as Sultana). The Hedman Alas office has a left-luggage service for its customers and an ATM. The schoolbus-style buses that go to the small towns surrounding San Pedro (known as *interurbanas* and *rapiditos*) do not have sales windows; the ticket is bought directly on the buses, which are lined up at the platforms (you have to ask around to find the one you need). There is a directory of companies and their destinations near the entrance.

Here is a sampling of schedules and prices current at the time of our visit (remember that these are always subject to change).

To **Choluteca:** The **Saenz** buses to Tegucigalpa continue on to Choluteca, charging US$29, with the 2 P.M. departure the latest one that continues on.

To **Cofradía, Cusuco National Park:** Frequent departures all day cost US$0.40.

To **Comayagua: Rivera** (tel. 504/558-0068) has hourly buses between 6 A.M. and 5 P.M. (US$4.20, three hours); the bus to Tegucigalpa with **Norteño** also stops here (US$3.70). **Transportes Diaz** runs frequent buses throughout the day, with stops in Taulabé and Siguatepeque (US$4.20). **Transporte Rivera** runs hourly buses between 6 A.M. and 5 P.M. for the same price.

To **Copán Ruinas and the border at El Florido: Hedman Alas** (tel. 504/516-2213, www.hedmanalas.com) has two first-class buses daily for US$17 to Copán Ruinas (2.5 hours). **Casasola** (tel. 504/516-2031, Copán Ruinas tel. 504/651-4078) has five buses a day that stop at La Entrada, Copán Ruinas, and El Florido, departing at 8 A.M. 11 A.M., 1 P.M., 2 P.M., and 3 P.M. (US$6, three hours).

To **El Progreso: Trasul** has buses that leave

every 40 minutes between 7:30 A.M. and 7 P.M. (US$1.30).

To **Gracias: Gracianos** (Gracias tel. 504/656-1403, departure at 2 P.M.) and **Toritos y Copanecos** (tel. 504/516-2086) both have one bus daily, charging US$5.25–5.75 for the five-hour ride. **Transportes Lempira/Coto** also has service to Gracias.

To **Jutiapa:** Buses to Trujillo with **Cotuc** also stop in Jutiapa (US$6.90).

To **La Ceiba: Hedman Alas** (www.hedman alas.com) first-class buses are a good option, costing US$17 for a comfortable, on-time ride four times daily. **Viana** also has first-class buses at 10:30 A.M., 1:45 P.M., and 5:30 P.M. (US$13, 2.5 hours). Less expensive is **Tupsa-Catisa-City** (tel. 504/509-0442), running buses hourly between 5:30 A.M. and 2:30 P.M., then two more buses at 4 P.M. and 5:30 P.M. (US$5.50, three hours), with a stop in Tela. The buses to Trujillo with **Cotuc** and with **Contraipbal** also stop in La Ceiba (US$5.25). **Mirna** has service to La Ceiba for the same price. Buses to Olanchito with **Emtraiol** and **Emtruiz** also stop in La Ceiba (US$5.25).

To **La Entrada: Congolón** (tel. 504/553-1174) and **Sultana** have hourly bus service for US$4 and US$4.80, respectively.

To **La Esperanza: Transporte Carolina-Joelito** (tel. 504/9713-5656) has 11 buses a day, between 5:30 A.M. and 1:50 P.M., US$5.25, 3–3.5 hours.

To **Lago de Yojoa:** To Pulhapanzak Falls, El Mochito, Peña Blanca, and La Guama, several buses leave between 10 A.M. and 4 P.M. daily (US$1.75–2).

To **Nueva Ocotepeque and the Guatemalan border: Congolón** (tel. 504/553-1174) has buses at 2 A.M., 6 A.M., and 11 P.M. to Nueva Ocotepeque (US$8.15) and on to Agua Calientes (US$9.60, or $12.40 for travel at night), six hours. **Sultana** has buses leaving roughly hourly between 6:15 A.M. and 6 P.M., charging US$8.30 to Nueva Ocotepeque and $9.60 to the border.

To **Olanchito: Emtraiol** (Olanchito tel. 504/694-3254) has buses at 6:30 A.M., 8:30 A.M., 10:30 A.M., 12:30 P.M., and 4 P.M.

(US$9). **Emtruiz** also services this route, for the same price.

To **Puerto Cortés: Impala** (tel. 504/553-3111 in Puerto Cortés) has buses every 20 minutes (US$2.50, one hour). Be sure to get on a direct bus—the frequently stopping regular is only pennies cheaper.

To **Sambo Creek:** Buses to Trujillo with **Cotuc** also stop in Sambo Creek (US$6.90).

To **Santa Bárbara: Cotisba** (Santa Bárbara tel. 504/643-2308) runs regular buses roughly every half hour between 5:20 A.M. and 6 P.M. (US$3.25, two hours). There are two direct buses at 8 A.M. and 4 P.M. (US$3.60, 90 minutes).

To **Savá:** Buses to Trujillo with **Contraipbal** also stop in Tocoa (US$7.50).

To **Santa Rosa de Copán: Toritos y Copanecos** (tel. 504/516-2086) runs buses between 4:30 A.M. and 5 P.M. daily for US$3.70 that take an excruciating four hours—it's better to check the time of the 2.5-hour *directo,* which costs US$5.70. **Congolón** (tel. 504/516-2253) has hourly bus service for US$4.65. The bus to Nueva Ocotepeque with **Sultana** stops in Santa Rosa, charging US$5.60—a bit more, but with more reliable service and fewer stops.

To **Siguatepeque: Transportes Diaz** runs frequent buses throughout the day, with a stop in Taulabé (US$3.15).

To **Taulabé: Transportes Diaz** runs frequent buses throughout the day (US$2.40). The bus then continues on to Siguatepeque and Comayagua. The bus to Tegucigalpa with **Norteño** stops here (US$2.70).

To **Tegucigalpa:** Direct bus rides to Tegucigalpa take 3.5 hours. **Rey de Oro** has direct buses leaving every two hours 6:30 A.M.–2:30 P.M., with a final bus at 5:30 P.M. (US$7.75); they arrive at Avenida Centenario by Casa Yaad and Hotel San Pedro in Comayagüela. **El Rey Express** (www.reye xpress.net) buses depart at 5:30 A.M., 6:30 A.M., 7:30 A.M., 9:30 A.M., 11:30 A.M., 1:30 P.M., 3:30 P.M., 4:30 P.M., and 6 P.M. (US$8.15), arriving at Barrio Concepción in Comayagüela, two blocks from the Central Bank, slightly closer to the center than the buses from Paisano or Gemenis. **Hedman Alas** (tel. 504/553-1316, www.hedmanalas.com) runs five "luxury" buses (their most basic) daily, with air-conditioning, TV, no bathroom, and a 25-minute stop in Siguatepeque, departing at 6:30 A.M., 9 A.M., noon, 4 P.M., and 5 P.M. (US$10.50). There are also four direct "executive" buses with air-conditioning, TV, and bathrooms daily at 5:45 A.M., 10:30 A.M., 3 P.M., and 5:50 P.M. (US$16), and at 8:30 A.M. and 2 P.M., the buses are "executive plus"—more expensive with larger seats that recline far and better footrests—similar to business-class seats on an airplane (US$18). Another first-class bus company, **Saenz** (tel. 504/516-2222), runs buses every two hours (except at noon) 6 A.M.–6 P.M. Monday–Saturday, and six on Sunday between 8 A.M. and 6 P.M. (US$18). Another first-class bus line with bathrooms, TV, and air-conditioning is **Viana,** with its regular buses at 6:30 A.M., 9:30 A.M., 1:15 P.M., 1:30 P.M., 3:30 P.M., and 6:15 P.M. (US$23) and Diamond class service available on the 6:30 A.M. and 3:30 P.M. buses for US$34. The 6:30 A.M. and 1:15 P.M. buses do not run on Sunday. **Sultana** (tel. 504/516-2048) runs buses every hour 6:30 A.M.–3:30 P.M. (US$5.80, 4.5 hours). **El Paisano** runs frequent buses with frequent stops, charging US$4.75 for the ride, which arrives in Barrio Lempira in Comayagüela, near where the buses leaving for Olancho are stationed. **Congolón** (tel. 504/553-1174) has a bus at 4:30 A.M. for US$5.70.

To **Tela: Tela Express** has five buses a day during the week (last at 5:45 P.M.), seven on Saturday (last at 6 P.M.), and six on Sunday (last at 6 P.M.), costing US$4.50. The bus to La Ceiba with **Tupsa-Catisa-City** (tel. 504/509-0442) also stops in Tela. Buses to Trujillo with **Cotuc** also stop in Tela (US$4.40). The bus to Trujillo with **Contraipbal** stops in Tela (US$4.40). **Mirna** has service to Tela for US$4.50. Buses to Olanchito with **Emtraiol** and **Emtruiz** also stop in Tela, charging US$4.30. **Hedman Alas** has service to Tela at 10:10 A.M. and 6:10 P.M. (US$16). These buses stop at the airport (so if your flight arrives with

a reasonable connection time, you don't even have to go into San Pedro if you prefer to just hit the beach).

To **Tocoa:** Buses to Trujillo with **Cotuc** also stop in Tocoa (US$8.85).

To **Trujillo: Cotuc** (tel. 504/520-7497) runs buses that stop at every city and town for a record 26 stops. Buses depart at 5:15 A.M., 6:45 A.M., 8:15 A.M., 9:45 A.M., 11:15 A.M., 12:40 P.M., 2 P.M., and 3:20 P.M. (US$9.65). **Contraipbal** runs a similar route but with 11 stops, at 6 A.M., 7:30 A.M., 9 A.M., 10:30 A.M., noon, 1:20 P.M., 2:40 P.M., and 3:40 P.M. (US$9.60).

International Bus

King Quality (tel. 504/516-2167, www.king-qualityca.com) runs one bus a day at 7 A.M. to San Salvador, arriving at San Salvador at 2 P.M. The bus is equipped with a bathroom, air-conditioning, and TV (whether you like it or not) for the 7.5-hour drive (US$41). The bus continues on to Guatemala city, arriving at 8 P.M. (US$63), and then on to Tapachula, Mexico (US$75).

Hedman Alas (tel. 504/553-1316, www.hedmanalas.com) has two direct first-class buses to Guatemala City at 9:50 A.M. and 2:30 P.M. daily via Copán Ruinas (US$45, 7.5 hours) and to Antigua, Guatemala (US$51, nine hours).

Tica Bus (tel. 504/516-2022, www.ticabus.com) has an office not far from the food court (8 A.M.–5 P.M. Mon.–Fri., 8 A.M.–noon Sat.–Sun.) with daily service to Nicaragua at 5 A.M. (US$32, eight hours). The same bus continues on to Costa Rica (US$52, two days) and Panama (US$87, three days).

Congolón (tel. 504/553-1174) has two direct buses a day to Guatemala City at 2 A.M. and 6 A.M. (US$31.50).

Fuente del Norte (tel. 504/9843-0507) has daily service to Río Dulce, Guatemala, for US$18, Guatemala City for US$26, and Melcho or Tecún Umán for US$40. The bus departs at 6 A.M., but customers can purchase their ticket the day before; the company's window is open 2:30–7 P.M. Connections are available to Belize City (US$40, eight hours).

Car

As the country's major industrial center, San Pedro Sula is well connected by paved road to the rest of the country. Highways to Santa Rosa de Copán, Nueva Ocotepeque, Copán Ruinas, Tela, La Ceiba, Yoro, and Tegucigalpa are all fairly well maintained and can be driven on safely most of the year. During the height of the rainy season, however, road conditions tend to deteriorate. In 2008 bridges on the main road to Trujillo washed out during the rains, but even if they haven't been repaired by now, there is an easy enough alternative route along a well-maintained gravel road.

PARQUE NACIONAL CUSUCO

Situated on the highest reaches of the Sierra Merendón, a north–south-trending mountain range in northwestern Honduras, Cusuco covers 23,440 hectares, of which 7,690 hectares fall in the core zone above 1,800 meters. The park forms part of the watershed for the Río Motagua, on the north and west sides, and for the Río Chamelecón, on the south and east. Cusuco encompasses the forests blanketing the highest peaks in the Merendón range, capped by Cerro Jilinco at 2,242 meters. Other peaks include Cusuco (2,000 meters), Cerro La Mina (1,782 meters), and La Torre (1,927 meters). In the 1950s, the forest around Cusuco was heavily logged by the Río Cusuco Company. Logging ended in 1959 when the region was declared a reserve on the recommendation of Venezuelan ecologist Geraldo Bukowski. The national park was established in 1987.

Cusuco is a popular park for both Hondurans and foreigners because of its proximity to San Pedro Sula and also for the great wealth of bird life in the cloud, pine, and subtropical forests. More than 200 species have been identified in the park, and it's estimated that up to 300 species may actually live there. The best months for bird-watching are October–March, to see many of the migratory species as well as the permanent residents. The reserve is also inhabited by some endangered mammals, including the park's namesake, the *cusuco* (armadillo), as well as white-faced and howler monkeys.

It's possible to get into Cusuco and hike around independently, but using a guide can be a good way to get to know the park better.

Getting to Cusuco

The main access to the Cusuco visitors center is by bus or car to Cofradía, a small town on the Santa Rosa highway 16 kilometers from the turnoff outside of San Pedro Sula. From Cofradía, continue 26 kilometers up a dirt road through pine forests with lovely views to the village of Buenos Aires, perched on a high ridge, and then on to the visitors center. The five kilometers between Buenos Aires and the visitors center can be treacherous if it has been raining, and one stretch is almost too steep to drive even when it's dry, so you may want to leave your wheels in Buenos Aires and walk the remainder. About halfway up to the park from Buenos Aires, at the 1,800-meter mark and the edge of the core zone, is a *tranca* (gate) that closes daily at 4 P.M. and on a few major holidays each year.

If you don't have a car, take one of the frequent buses from San Pedro to Cofradía. You can either get off at the town square and ask in the shops there for trucks heading up to Buenos Aires (they often leave in late morning or around noon), or stay on the bus to the end of the line, west of town, then walk a short distance to the start of the Buenos Aires road and hitch a ride with the first pickup to come by. From Buenos Aires, if no ride is available, it's a two-hour walk to the visitors center. There is a simple dorm-style guesthouse available in Buenos Aires.

Note: There have been reports of assaults on the road between Cofradía and Cusuco (especially closer to Cofradía), so walking the road is not without risk. It's better to drive or get a *jalón* to Buenos Aires.

It's possible to drive to the visitors center straight up into the hills behind San Pedro Sula, although finding the dirt road leaving the city from the Primavera neighborhood southwest of downtown is no easy task. Ask for the road leading to Las Peñitas or El Gallito, which ends up in Buenos Aires, and from there on to

Cusuco. This road is not in the best of shape but offers great views over the city and across the Sierra Merendón. By car it is 60–90 minutes away.

The park entrance is a hefty US$15 for foreigners.

Local Guides

Cusuco Expeditions (tel. 504/9907-4605 or 504/9771-9049, cusucoexp@yahoo.com) is a relatively new business, but its 40-odd community guides have been bringing people through the park for more than five years. Some guiding is available free of charge at the visitors center. Although guides are not necessary to navigate the main trails, they can be of use in helping spot animals and birds. Cusuco Expeditions can also provide information on transportation to and from the park.

Hiking in the Park

An informative visitors center at the end of the entrance road, with maps and displays on local flora and fauna, is the place to start your tour of the park. After looking at the displays and descriptions of the local flora and fauna, choose from a small network of six trails to hike around in the park. Ask the *vigilante* here to tell you where to find the three well-known bird-watching spots. The trails—Cantiles (two kilometers), El Danto (two kilometers), El Quetzal (one kilometer), La Mina (2.5 kilometers), El Pizote (two kilometers), and Colorado (five kilometers)—are well marked and not too steep or strenuous, but they can be muddy, so bring boots and watch your footing. Wildlife is very timid at Cusuco, so it takes patience, luck, and good binoculars to spot anything, but the forest is lovely to walk in regardless. At the northern end of Sendero El Danto is a small hut housing a local family that makes its living cultivating and selling cloud-forest plants in a small outdoor nursery.

Early morning bird-watchers, or those who simply want to spend a night in the forest, may camp in one of four designated areas on the entrance road, just before the visitors center.

The topographical maps covering the park are the 1:50,000 *Cuyamel-San Pedro Sula 2562 I, Valle de Naco 2562 II, Quimistán 2562 III,* and *Cuyamelito 2562 IV.*

Mountain Biking in the Sierra Merendón

The Sierra Merendón is crisscrossed with dirt roads and trails that make for great mountain-bike adventuring. From San Pedro, bikers can simply head west on 1 Calle past Avenida Circunvalación, through La Primavera neighborhood right into the forest, and up steep dirt roads into the mountains. Some roads eventually end up in Buenos Aires and Cusuco National Park, while others branch off northward to Puerto Cortés.

EL PROGRESO

An unattractive, hot agricultural city of 115,000 on the east bank of the Río Ulúa, El Progreso offers little to interest tourists. Most foreigners who find themselves in El Progreso are changing buses on their way between San Pedro Sula and Tela. The only reason to delay your departure might be to check out two souvenir shops in town. The large **Turiplaza-Imapro** shop (tel. 504/647-2200, www.imapro-honduras.com, 7:30 A.M.–5 P.M. Mon.–Sat., 10 A.M.–5 P.M. Sun.), at the exit to Tela, has a large selection of Honduran handicrafts and tourist collectibles, particularly large hand-carved wood items (check them out on the website before you go out of your way to the store, as the style is pretty distinctive, and may or may not be to your liking). **Mahchi** (tel. 504/647-0221), a block from the main highway junction, has some good-quality Honduran paintings, folk art, and clothing.

Accommodations and Food

The **Hotel Plaza Victoria** (tel. 504/647-0222, US$21 s, US$29 d) is popular with missionary groups and medical brigades. It has parking, a swimming pool, and even English-speaking staff.

Another "upscale" hotel is **Hotel Casa Blanca** (tel. 504/647-1954, US$24.50 s, US$30.50 d), on the highway exit toward Tela, with 58 large and quiet rooms, each with air-conditioning, TV, hot water, and private bathroom. A swimming pool is on-site.

Culinary adventurers will be glad to hear that El Progreso is reputed to be home to the tastiest grilled bull nuts *(huevos de toro)* in the country; the famous no-name grill, or *parrilla* (which also, by the way, has excellent chicken and other non-genitalia menu items) is found by walking from the main park back toward the highway; look to your left right next to the DIPPSA gas station.

There are a number of good steak restaurants in town; look for **Kactus,** along the highway, or **La Parrilla** (tel. 504/647-2433), outside of downtown on the road to Santa Rita, next to a DIPPSA gasoline station.

About 10 minutes outside of town on the highway toward Tela is **Centro Turístico La Cabana,** a large open-air restaurant with two nice swimming pools (US$3 pp for use of pools).

Information and Services

Dollars and travelers checks can be changed at **Banco Atlántida** (which also receives MoneyGrams), right in the center of town, and there is a Western Union office at **Banco del Occidente** along the highway. The latter is next door to **Supermercado Antorcha,** a good place to pick up supplies.

Getting There and Away

Trasul (tel. 504/647-3366) runs buses every 40 minutes between 6 A.M. and 6 P.M. (US$1.30, 30 minutes), departing from behind the Panadería Hawit. Buses to San Pedro Sula and Yoro also depart from the main bus terminal, just off the square. San Pedro buses leave frequently all day long until 6:10 P.M. (US$1, 30 minutes). Buses to Yoro leave every hour or so between 5 A.M. and 5 P.M. (US$2.50, 3.5 hours), and to Morazán (for Pico Pijol) they leave every hour 6 A.M.–6 P.M. (US$2, two hours).

Transportes Ulúa (tel. 504/647-3270) runs five direct buses a day to Tegucigalpa (US$8, four hours).

Buses to Tela leave from a different stop, four blocks west of the main terminal. Direct buses leave at 3 P.M. and 4:15 P.M. Monday–Friday, 8 A.M. and 8:45 A.M. Saturday–Sunday (US$2, 45 minutes). Try to plan on the direct bus, as local buses take about two hours and seem to stop every kilometer.

El Progreso is connected to San Pedro by a 28-kilometer, four-lane highway passing La Lima and the airport. Continuing north to Tela, the highway narrows to two lanes but is still in fairly good condition. East and south, a road cuts from El Progreso back to the San Pedro Sula–Tegucigalpa highway at La Barca, passing **Santa Rita.** From Santa Rita another two-lane paved road winds up into the mountains to Morazán and Yoro. At Santa Rita, on the turn to Yoro, is the very good **Comedor El Triángulo,** a favorite stop for La Ceiba–Tegucigalpa buses for the inexpensive and hearty buffet. It's open 6 A.M.–6 P.M. daily.

Lago de Yojoa and Vicinity

Honduras's largest natural lake, Lago de Yojoa, is roughly 16 kilometers long by eight kilometers wide, at an altitude of 635 meters, right along the San Pedro Sula–Tegucigalpa highway. Lake depth varies between about 18 and 25 meters, depending on season. The setting, backed by the majestic cloud-forested mountains of Santa Bárbara and Cerro Azul/Meámbar (both protected as national parks), is spectacular. Formerly overlooked by many Central America travelers, Lago de Yojoa is growing in popularity as a spot well worth visiting for a few days of hiking, ruins exploration, bird-watching, or just soaking up the glorious scenery.

The shores of the lake are dotted with innumerable ruins, mostly believed to be of Lenca origin, including Los Naranjos. Along with

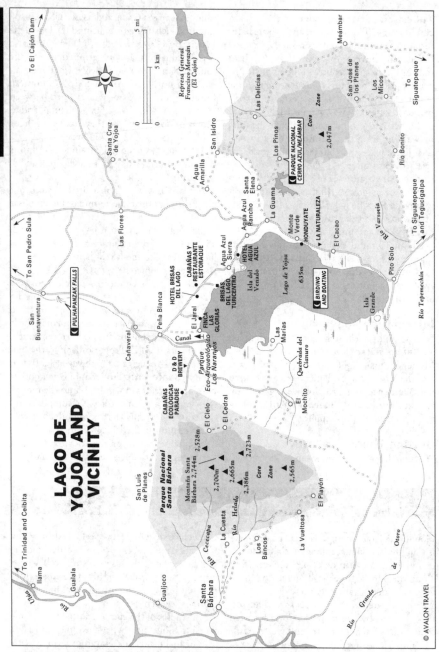

LAGO DE YOJOA AND VICINITY

To El Cajón Dam

To San Pedro Sula

To Trinidad and Ceibita

To Siguatepeque

To Siguatepeque and Tegucigalpa

To El Cajón

Represa General Francisco Morazán (El Cajón)

Las Delicias

Meámbar

San José de los Planes

Los Micos

Río Bonito

PARQUE NACIONAL CERRO AZUL/MEÁMBAR

Core Zone

2,047m

Santa Cruz de Yojoa

San Isidro

Los Pinos

Santa Elena

Agua Amarilla

La Guama

Monte Verde

HONDUVATE

LA NATURALEZA

El Cacao

Río Varsovia

Las Flores

Agua Azul Rancho

Agua Azul Sierra

HOTEL AGUA AZUL

PULHAPANZAK FALLS

San Buenaventura

HOTEL BRISAS DEL LAGO

CABAÑAS Y RESTAURANTE ESTORAQUE

Peña Blanca

El Jaral

BRISAS DEL LAGO TORCENTRO

FINAS GLORIAS

Isla del Venado

Lago de Yojoa

635m

Isla Grande

BIRDING AND BOATING

Pito Solo

Río Tepemechín

Cañaveral

Canal

D & D BREWERY

Parque Eco-Arqueológico Los Naranjos

Las Marías

Quebrada del Cianuro

CABAÑAS ECOLÓGICAS PARADISE

El Cielo

El Cedral

El Mochito

San Luis de Planes

Parque Nacional Santa Bárbara

Montaña Santa Bárbara 2,744m

2,528m

2,700m

2,665m

2,723m

2,386m

2,565m

Core Zone

Río Helado

Río Cececapa

La Cuesta

Los Bancos

El Playón

La Vueltosa

Gualjoco

Ilama

Gualala

Santa Bárbara

Río Ulúa

Río Grande de Otoro

© AVALON TRAVEL

5 mi

5 km

0

0

© AVALON TRAVEL

© AMY E. ROBERTSON

tranquil Lago de Yojoa

the Valle de Sula, Lago de Yojoa is thought to have been one of the most heavily populated areas in Honduras in pre-Columbian times, used as a home by the Lenca, Maya, and perhaps other groups.

The lake is drained naturally on the south side by Río Tepemechín, which leads eventually into the Río Ulúa, and on the north by the Río Blanco, which has been partly channeled to power a hydroelectric plant at Cañaveral. Along the Río Lindo, a tributary to the Río Blanco, is Pulhapanzak Falls, an easily visited and very beautiful 43-meter waterfall.

Regular buses ply the roads around the lake, between Peña Blanca and El Mochito, La Guama, and Pulhapanzak Falls. If no buses are immediately apparent, just stick out your thumb—hitchhiking is fairly reliable.

◖ BIRDING AND BOATING ON LAGO DE YOJOA

The extensive marshes and forests around Lago de Yojoa, located in the transition zone between the Valle de Sula and the central highlands, boast the country's largest variety of bird species. One count put the number of species at 407. Whatever the exact number, the lake and surrounding forests are a birder's paradise. One particularly good spot is at Hotel Agua Azul or the nearby Isla del Venado; another is the foothills of Santa Bárbara near San Luis de Planes.

Largemouth bass fishing in the lake was once legendary, attracting anglers from across the globe, but the bass population has declined due to overfishing. Much more common nowadays is tilapia, a nonnative species. Large fish farms on the lake produce as many as 20 tons of harvested fish per day. Yacht and fishing trips with equipment can be arranged on the lake by contacting Richard Joint of **Honduyate** (www.honduyatemarina.com). Local fishermen, especially at Las Marías on the west side of the lake, will also be happy to arrange trips. If you go this route, it's best to come equipped with your own gear.

A few locals stationed along the canal between Peña Blanca and the lake also rent rowboats for a nominal fee (usually around US$2) for tourists to paddle out onto the lake. One spot to look for them is about two kilometers from Peña Blanca on the El Mochito road, where the road takes a sharp turn. Here a path leads down to the canal's edge. There is also a sign advertising boats for rent *(se aquila lanchas)* just before the D&D Brewery, and the *turicentro* run by the Brisas del Lago hotel is open to nonguests as well. This is a good way for bird-watchers to patrol some of the wetlands around the edge of the lake. Boats are also available at the lakeside hotels Agua Azul, Los Remos, and Finca Las Glorias, which are also lovely settings for lunch.

AROUND THE LAKE
◖ Pulhapanzak Falls

Of the several *balnearios* along the Río Lindo, a tributary of the Río Blanco north of Peña Blanca, by far the most popular is the 43-meter-high Pulhapanzak Falls (Cascadas de Pulhapanzak). The falls are located just off the road leaving Peña Blanca to the north, connecting to the San Pedro Sula highway. To get to the falls, take a bus from either Peña Blanca or San Pedro Sula, and get off at San Buenaventura, which is 12.5 kilometers from the San Pedro Sula–Tegucigalpa highway and 10 kilometers from Peña Blanca. From San Buenaventura, walk one kilometer to the signposted turnoff to the falls. If in doubt, ask a local to point the way.

The dirt road dead-ends at a gate, where visitors pay an entrance fee of US$2. Beyond are a parking lot and a few small changing rooms to put on bathing suits. There is a broad pool along the Río Lindo, just above the falls, which is great for a swim—just don't swim too close to the drop-off! On both sides of the river are plenty of shady places to take a rest.

To properly admire the falls, follow the steps down along the edge of the river to a viewpoint below. The land around this part of the river is private property and is still covered with dense forest, a visually pleasing background for the falls. Those interested in a naturalist explanation can hire a guide for US$5.25.

Warning: The wet, steep paths leading down and around the falls are treacherous, especially during rainy weather, requiring great balance

© AMY E. ROBERTSON

Water plunges 43 meters from the lip of Pulhapanzak Falls.

and careful footing. People have literally fallen to their deaths here.

A very-sketchy looking zipline *("canopi")* has been set up that zigzags across the river, with one thrilling cross just after the waterfall drop-off (US$16).

A horde of local boys, some of whom speak smatterings of more than three languages, will offer their services to guide visitors to a cave behind the falls, where Mayan artifacts are reputed to have been found. The boys will also show you a couple of great places to jump out into the water, if you dare to follow them—they are fearless and extremely sure-footed.

Back up by the gate is a snack bar/restaurant and large open field, in the center of which are a few mounds covering what are thought to be Mayan-era ruins. The owners are happy to have people camp out for a nominal fee, either with a tent on the lawn or in a hammock among the trees. The area is usually packed on weekends and deserted during the week.

Between San Buenaventura and Peña Blanca is the hydroelectric power plant at **Cañaveral.**

In front of the office are two sculptures from the Los Naranjos site, one a headless statue and the other a large dish, which were unearthed during the construction of the Río Blanco canal in 1962. Next to them is an example of one of the turbines used in the power plant.

Parque Eco-Arqueológico Los Naranjos

Along the jungly northwestern shores of Lago de Yojoa, not far from the village of El Jaral, are the unexcavated ruins of Los Naranjos (tel. 504/9946-9482, 8 A.M.–4 P.M. daily, US$5), a pre-Hispanic settlement thought to be of Lenca origin, although much archaeology remains to be completed. The site began to be settled around 800 B.C. and was at its height in the couple of centuries on either side of the birth of Christ. Stylistic features of buildings and pottery suggest some Olmec influence in the early period and interaction with Mayan culture in later times.

The main entrance to Los Naranjos is at the end of a newly refurbished road that branches off the Peña Blanca–La Guama road, just past Peña Blanca (look for the large sign). After purchasing your US$5 entrance, stop to take a look at the small display of pottery and obsidian arrowheads in the museum, before heading down the pathways to the ruins themselves.

While the ruins themselves are not visually spectacular, they are worth checking out for those with an interest in Mesoamerican culture. And even casual visitors will be enchanted strolling down the well-maintained pathways through the lovely jungle foliage, with a veritable symphony of birds on all sides. Early morning is a particularly good time to watch for birds. A wooden walkway branches off to one side, making a loop through a wetland area at the edge of the lake, or visitors can head straight for the ruins themselves—basically just several large mounds, with some exposed rock. Excavations and reconstruction will likely be underway for years as scientists learn more about this enigmatic site. Walking the four miles or so of raised pathways through the lush forest, one can easily understand why

an indigenous group would want to settle here—it seems about as close to the Garden of Eden as you can imagine. The largest ruin, a 20-meter-high building, is actually outside of the park, on private property nearby that the government may purchase in the future. The park also features a cafeteria, bathrooms, and a souvenir shop.

Be forewarned that the paths can be closed at the height of the rainy season due to flooding, and if the main paths are closed, there can be absolute swarms of mosquitoes on the back paths. Don't forget your binoculars and mosquito repellent or long-sleeved shirt and pants.

Peña Blanca

Not much of a town itself, Peña Blanca lies at a major crossroads near the northwest corner of the lake. From here, roads continue to El Mochito around the west side of the lake, to Agua Azul and La Guama along the north side, and along the Río Lindo past Pulhapanzak Falls to the San Pedro Sula–Tegucigalpa highway to the north. Visitors will find no compelling reason to stop at Peña Blanca other than for transportation purposes. There are a few *comedores*, but save your appetite for one of the hotel restaurants nearby.

There are two basic options in town for accommodation. **Hotel Maranata** (tel. 504/650-0106, US$10.50 s with shared bath, US$13 s and US$16 d with TV and private bath, cold water only) is on the main road before the turnoff to Los Naranjos. Rooms are clean, and the hotel also offers laundry services to its guests. The largish rooms at **Hotel La Finca** (US$18.50, cold water only) are a slight step up. There is one with a mural of the lake, perhaps to make up for its town location. Reservations can be made by contacting the sister property Finca Las Glorias (tel. 504/566-0461, www.hotellasglorias.com).

Of the several low-priced *comedores*, **Cafetería y Repostería Candy** (8 A.M.–6 P.M. daily), just across the canal heading toward Agua Azul, is about the best. It offers decent breakfasts, lunches, and dinners for about US$2 per meal.

There are a couple of Internet cafés in town; just ask around if you don't spot them.

Buses leave Peña Blanca daily in late morning to **San Luis Planes,** a village set high on the northern flanks of Santa Bárbara Mountain, where you can find guides to take you into the cloud forest. The road to San Luis turns off just north of Peña Blanca and takes a bit under an hour to drive in a private vehicle.

A few kilometers outside of Peña Blanca, before you arrive at Los Naranjos Ecological Park, is the peach and ochre **Hotel Colonial** (tel. 504/9827-9524, US$21 s, US$26 d), with pleasant tile-floor rooms with air-conditioning, TV, and a fan. Amenities include a very small swimming pool and washers and dryers that guests can use. Room number 6 has a view. On the same road is **Comidas La Champa,** an open-air restaurant of wood and thatch.

San Luis de Planes

While **Parque Nacional Santa Bárbara** is often accessed from the villages near the town of Santa Bárbara, it's also possible to explore via San Luis de Planes, a small town 14.5 kilometers west from the Cañaveral–Peña Blanca road. Ornithologist Malcolm Glasgow, based at the D&D Brewery, is happy to take naturalists on guided bird tours of the cloud forest for US$16–32 per person, including a stop for coffee in the village (D&D can pack a lunch for you). Sketch maps are on the back of the D&D Brewery, and hikes through the cloud forest make for a great day out.

Lakeshore Lodging and Food

Leave it to an Oregonian bluegrass picker to set up Honduras's first microbrewery and hostel in the middle of the God-blessed jungle. What better excuse can you come up with to trek over to the west side of the lake, than to lounge in hammocks in the middle of a coffee plantation, swilling a dark mug of porter? Also available are a variety of ales, a rotation of fruity brews (including mango and coffee), and homemade root beer, blueberry soda, and cream soda. This is the **D&D Brewery** (tel. 504/9994-9719, www.dd-brewery.com), the

vision of Robert Dale, who is also always looking for fellow guitarists to come by and pick with him. There is one large cabin with several small guest rooms (US$9.50 s, US$13 d) that are rather basic (each has a private bathroom, which in some cases just means the toilet is tucked behind a shower curtain inside the room), but all have fans and hot water. Tucked into the foliage are three private cabins, still fairly simple, but each has a nice porch with a hammock (US$26 for two people, US$37 for four). There are also dorm-style accommodations, or those really saving their lempiras can use a hammock or pitch a tent for US$2, with use of a hot shower and bathroom facilities. An open-air restaurant lines the small swimming pool, where Bob and his Honduran wife serve heaping burger plates, chicken quesadillas, corn dogs, and more, for US$2.50–6. Although few rave about the beer, the chocolate chip cookies are out of this world, and locally made breads, jellies, wines, homegrown coffee, house-made sodas, and even hibiscus champagne are also sold out of the restaurant. Bob can set you up with top-notch bird-watching trips on the lake and in the Santa Bárbara park, rents mountain bikes for US$5.25 a day, and can arrange fly-fishing excursions as well. D&D is a couple kilometers up a spur road in the town of Los Naranjos, three kilometers south of Peña Blanca near the lake. From San Pedro Sula, buses to El Mochito go right past the entrance to the brewery (US$1.60). From Tegucigalpa, buses to Las Vegas pass in front of it as well. From Peña Blanca, buses and taxis charge US$0.40 to drop you off a few minutes' walk away at the end of the road. Resident ornithologist Malcolm Glasgow can take visitors on **guided bird tours:** US$8 per person for a local walk, US$9–12 per person for a tour by rowboat on the lake, or US$16–32 pp for a hike in the cloud forest of the Santa Bárbara National Park. There's plenty of good birding for non-experts, with easily spotted hawks and herons on the lake, and a good chance of seeing a toucan.

A little farther down the dirt road that passes D&D are the **Cabañas Ecológicas Paradise** (tel. 504/602-9743, US$50 s/d), two recently built wooden cabins high on stilts. The rather overpriced cabins each have a lovely enclosed porch with rustic furniture, and a cramped bedroom with a fan and a mini-fridge. The cabins are located within the lush Centro Turístico Paradise, next to coffee fields, a gurgling stream, and a jarringly unkempt staff house. The resort gets packed with day visitors during Semana Santa, when it is decked out with flowers.

In a spectacular setting on the north shore of the lake, along the highway between Peña Blanca and Agua Azul, located 1.5 kilometers off the highway down by the lakeshore, is the more upscale **Finca Las Glorias** (tel. 504/566-0461, www.hotellasglorias.com, US$46 s, U$49 d), renting attractive but worn cabins and apartments set on a grassy lawn by the water's edge, each with air-conditioning, fans, TV, and porch hammocks. During the rainy season there can also be an outrageous number of bugs in the rooms. Come for a day visit instead: The restaurant is good (US$6 for tilapia from the lake, US$4.50 for a buffet breakfast), horseback rides are available, and the hotel has a small marina where you can rent boats. There is also a gift shop, a little bit of play equipment for tots, and a murky swimming pool.

About a kilometer east of the Las Glorias entrance is **Brisas del Lago** (tel. 504/608-7229, Tegucigalpa tel. 504/237-0194, San Pedro tel. 504/557-1433, US$32 s, US$39 d), with institutional-looking concrete buildings painted a cheery yellow set on a hillside well away from the lakeshore. The spacious rooms, which feature air-conditioning and small balconies or patios, are quite nice, although the buildings in which they are contained are decidedly unattractive. There is a swimming pool and children's play equipment on the grounds, and horseback riding is available. Brisas operates a *turicentro* a kilometer away on the lakeshore with pools, small boats, kayaks, canoes, sports fields and a restaurant. The *turicentro* (tel. 504/608-7229 or 504/9992-2937) is open to the public as well as hotel guests.

Just past the entrance to Brisas on the highway heading toward Agua Azul, on the opposite side of the road, is the **⬤ Cabañas y Restaurante Estoraque** (tel. 504/608-3669 or 504/9992-9807, normawari2004@yahoo .es), run by a Honduran-American couple. There are four cute cabins set back from the road in a garden (US$18 s to US$26 for four people), each with a private bathroom, fan, and TV. While there isn't any waterfront, guests can head to the nearby *turicentro* at Brisas del Lago, to the Hotel Agua Azul, or to Finca Las Glorias, for use of their marinas. The restaurant (8 A.M.–9 P.M. Wed.–Sun.) has a simple menu of burgers (US$2), fish dinners (US$6), and barbecued chicken (US$4), prepared with care in a spotlessly clean, screened-in kitchen. The cabins are frequently occupied, so book in advance.

Four kilometers east toward La Guama from Brisas del Lago is **Hotel Agua Azul** (tel. 504/9991-7244 or 504/608-3671). The attractive wooden cabins on a small rise above the lake are slowly being updated, with rustic wood furnishings, TV, and air-conditioning; the two rooms closest to the lake have been renovated and cost US$33 per night for up to four people. The remaining 16 rooms are quite basic inside, with a fan and hot water, and rent for US$22 a night. Five two-bedroom cabins that can sleep up to five people cost US$40 per night. The reasonably priced food is good, and although service can be slow, the wooden-porch restaurant with its two pool tables offers stunning views out over the lake, making time pass quickly. Kayaks, fishing trips, and boat trips around the lake are available. The swimming pool is a disappointment, with more vegetation than water inside. The nearby **Isla del Venado** and the rocks at **La Venta** are good places to watch birds.

At kilometer marker 161 on the San Pedro–Tegucigalpa highway, in the village of Monte Verde on the east side of the lake, is the pricey **Honduyate Marina** (tel. 504/990-9386 or 504/990-9387, www.honduyatemarina.com, US$79 s, US$89 d, US$115 suite), a marina/restaurant/hotel. The owners can arrange water-ski and fishing trips, and they hire out their nine-meter yacht for full-day cruises with picnic lunch and bar service for US$120, or you can rent a sailboat, motorboat, or rowboat. The hotel's five rooms are not luxurious, but quite nice, if a bit cutesy, with wireless Internet (for a charge), TV and DVD player, and air-conditioning; the doubles have small balconies as well. There are also two small cabins with air-conditioning (US$30 for a double bed, US$44 for a double plus a twin). Shoestringers can stay in a large cabin with bunkbeds for US$15 per person or arrange to camp on-site. Nonguests can use the swimming pool for US$3.50 (US$2 kids). The on-site restaurant is closed Tuesdays.

A couple of kilometers toward Tegucigalpa from Honduyate, also right on the lakeshore, is a strip of (at last count) an astounding 53 fish restaurants crammed up against one another, all serving reasonably priced fresh fish and *comida típica*.

La Naturaleza, a buffet restaurant on the east side of the San Pedro Sula–Tegucigalpa highway near the village of Monte Verde, has a bilingual photo display and small museum regarding the Cerro Azul/Meámbar National Park, the lake, and the surrounding area. Other features include a good butterfly house, children's play equipment, and a Kobs ice-cream shop. (This is a great stop on a road trip with kids.) Plans for a hotel are underway. You can occasionally get good information on the national park from the people here, but your best bet is up in Los Pinos.

At the southeast corner of the lake, where the Santa Bárbara road meets the San Pedro–Tegucigalpa highway, is the village of **Pito Solo.** The only rooms available are actually just before town at **Los Remos** (tel. 504/9959-9812, los-remos@hotmail.com, US$26 s/d with fan, US$37 s/d with a/c), a one-level, ranch-style place reminiscent of, in the words of one guest, the Bates Motel. Rooms are none too great, but facilities include a pool, a small restaurant, and rental rowboats. With its lake views from the restaurant it's a great place to stop for lunch (although service is exceptionally slow), and if you decide to go for a row,

there is some good birding here (spottings include lesser yellow-headed vulture, wood stork, fork-tailed flycatcher, American wigeon, lesser scaup, muscovy duck, and both the fulvous and black-bellied whistling ducks).

Getting to the Lakeshore

There is frequent bus service to the lake both from San Pedro Sula (take a bus to Peña Blanca or El Mochito) and from Tegucigalpa (take a bus to La Guama). To get to D&D and the Cabañas Paradise, take a bus to El Mochito and get off 2.3 kilometers after Peña Blanca when you see the Los Naranjos soccer field on the right. Take the second right-hand turn after the football field; it's maybe half a kilometer to D&D, a full kilometer to Cabañas Paradise.

To reach the hotels along the northeastern border of the lake, there are frequent buses between Peña Blanca and La Guama—just let them know where you want to get off (it's about US$0.50 from La Guama to the Los Naranjos park, US$0.40 from Peña Blanca).

From Pito Solo, it's 157 kilometers to Tegucigalpa, 97 kilometers to San Pedro Sula, and 53 kilometers to Santa Bárbara.

◖ PARQUE NACIONAL CERRO AZUL/MEÁMBAR

Looming over the eastern side of Lago de Yojoa, and frequently shrouded in clouds, is a sheer-walled massif of mountain peaks cloaked in lush green forests, protected as Parque Nacional Cerro Azul/Meámbar, or PANACAM. The park covers just over 400 square kilometers, ranging between 415 and 2,080 meters, supporting (from lower to upper elevations) coffee plantations, lowland humid forests, pine forest, and cloud forest. On one of the highest peaks in the center of the park is a rare elfin forest, similar to the one in Sierra de Agalta, Olancho, a bizarre ecosystem of stunted oak and pine trees, covered with moss and lichen.

Because of its location at the transition from the hot northern lowlands to the cooler, more arid mountain country of central Honduras, Cerro Azul/Meámbar supports an unusually diverse animal population, though the wildlife faces severe pressure from its human neighbors, who usually view animals either as pests or potential meals. But even in the coffee plantations on the lower stretches of the mountains, many of the park's 200 or so bird species can be seen screeching noisily and flitting about in the trees. And in the park's upper sections, reachable only by a multiday hike, at least 50 (and possibly more) species of mammals make their homes.

Cerro Azul/Meámbar plays a vital role in Honduras's electric power generation, supplying some 80 percent of the water used by the huge El Cajón dam to the east, and 20 percent of the water to Lago de Yojoa, which in turn supplies the smaller hydroelectric plant at Cañaveral.

Recognizing the importance of the mountain's ecosystem to the national economy, the Honduran government has turned over administration of the park, temporarily at least, to Proyecto Aldea Global (Project Global Village), a nonprofit organization linked to the Mercy Corps, a U.S.-based relief agency. Aldea Global began working in the area in 1984. A highly-respected NGO, Aldea Global funds a host of socially oriented projects in the 42 communities located within the park limits, in an effort to increase environmental awareness and protect the park, as well as to improve the standard of living of the local residents.

While a good portion of the forest around the cabins is secondary growth, it is in good condition and thriving with birds and other animal life; 134 species of birds have been spotted in the park, as well as ocelots, deer, armadillos, agoutis, white-nosed coatis, and 28 types of snakes. The upper sections of forest along the trails go through primary cloud forest, vibrant and beautiful. The area is often socked in with clouds and rain, so be prepared to get wet.

Pulpería La Guama, just at the highway, is a good spot to stock up on food and drink and ask about transportation to the park.

Los Pinos

While there are several signs for the park along the highway, the only one that leads to the park entrance and **Los Pinos visitors center** (tel. 504/9865-9082, panacam@paghonduras.org) can be reached by following the signs at the town of La Guama. From there it is seven kilometers uphill on a mostly well-maintained road, although there are a few rough patches that require four-wheel drive during the rainy season. (If you're worried your car can't make it, the park can sometimes arrange for a pickup from **La Naturaleza,** five kilometers south of La Guama.) Park entrance is US$2 for Hondurans and foreigners alike, and it is open 8 A.M.–4 P.M. Monday–Friday, an hour later on the weekend.

The visitors center contains a restaurant and a small selection of crackers, soft drinks, and some bottled water. Sunday lunch is regularly offered, but visitors other days may find the restaurant closed or with insufficient supplies if they just show up; call first and reserve if you are hoping for a meal, which run US$5–7. Wireless Internet is also available at the restaurant, and a computer for visitor use may be installed in the future.

While it's an easy day trip from either San Pedro Sula or Tegucigalpa, there are also cabins and campgrounds for anyone who wants to stay overnight. Camping is US$5.25 per person—you must bring your own gear. The ▄ **PANACAM Lodge** (tel. 504/9865-9082, panacam@paghonduras.org) consists of dorm-style accommodations for large groups (US$8.50 pp, minimum 10 people, cold water only) or very nice cabins that can sleep up to 4, for US$30–50, depending on the number of people and beds (park entrance is included with the cabins). The wood cabins have thick towels, classy bathrooms, and hot water. Solo travelers and small groups may be able to negotiate a stay in the dorms if they are unoccupied, by speaking with the park caretaker. Perched high on the side of the mountain overlooking Lago de Yojoa, the cabins are a lovely place to go if you'd like to experience a Honduran mountain forest but don't have the gear, time, or inclination for a full-on camping trip.

Rapiditos (minibuses) run between La

Guama and Santa Elena every 15 minutes or so, charging US$0.40 for the ride, and then you can walk the remaining four kilometers to the cabins (it's all uphill, and takes about an hour), or call ahead to the park caretaker for a pickup. Alternatively, the people who manage the minibuses will take up groups all the way to the cabins for about US$10 and can come pick you up whenever you arrange.

From the cabins, three trails lead into the forest for exploration. The shortest, Los Vencejos, takes visitors to a small waterfall in just 20 minutes, perfect for less-spry travelers. Sendero Venado, just over a kilometer long, takes about an hour round-trip. The longer Sendero El Sinai loop trail is seven kilometers, with some steep sections, fantastic views if the weather permits, and three waterfalls on the way. It's possible to camp out on the high point of the trail, enjoy a night in the forest, and catch the views at sunset and sunrise. Climbing farther up into the mountains on this side is quite difficult, though not impossible if you hire a guide at the visitors center (US$10–20/day). Summiting the 2,080-meter *cerro* is possible with a guide; expect to spend 2–3 days and to pay for your guide's food and drink on top of the guiding fee.

The regular trails are well maintained (a Herculean task from the looks of it) and no guide is needed, but if your Spanish is up to it, local guides can be extremely informative and charge US$10 for a several-hour walk around the trails.

Elsewhere in the Park

Los Pinos is by far the easiest entrance to the park, and the only one with significant tourist facilities, but it is also possible to hike in from several communities on the north, east, and south sides of the mountains. One route is via the village of Cerro Azul, eight kilometers from the San Pedro Sula–Tegucigalpa highway, turning off at the village of Bacadias. There are coffee plantations and a guesthouse; more information can be found by contacting the Tegucigalpa office of Aldea Global (tel. 504/239-8311, pagcent@paghonduras.org).

From **Las Delicias,** guides can lead the way to the summit, exiting the park through Los Jicaques. Contact PANACAM at Los Pinos (tel. 504/9865-9082, panacam@paghonduras .org) to arrange a guide for this route.

Another very good contact is Danilo Rivera, a resident of the *aldea* of **San José de los Planes,** on the south side of the park, right at the edge of the park's core zone. San José is reached by a rough dirt road from Siguatepeque. There are many forks along the way—just keep asking for the road to Los Micos, a village shortly before San José, then ask around for Danilo.

Park Information

The best source of information on the park is the caretaker who lives on-site (tel. 504/9865-9082, panacam@paghonduras.org), although Aldea Global's central office in Tegucigalpa (tel. 504/239-8311) and website (www.pag honduras.org) also have some information.

Topographical maps covering the park are 1:50,000 *Taulabé 2660 III* and *Santa Cruz de Yojoa 2660 IV.*

El Cajón Dam

On the eastern side of Cerro Azul/Meámbar, gathering a large part of the mountain's water, is the massive Represa General Francisco Morazán, otherwise known as El Cajón Dam. Completed in 1985, this huge dam on the Río Humuya supplies a good portion of the country's electric power. The watershed of El Cajón is severely deforested, a fact that gravely threatens the long-term viability of the dam. The absence of trees reduces the amount of water captured by the surrounding watershed and has also led to massive soil runoff from the deforested hillsides, which can destroy the dam machinery. Despite tree-planting campaigns and the almost superhuman efforts of Aldea Global, the situation shows little sign of improving.

Though perhaps not on top of the list for most tourists, the dam may hold some interest for anyone with some time on their hands or a particular interest in monumental engineering. The dam administration offers tours of the dam's inner workings on weekends—get there by 10 A.M. on Saturday or Sunday, and ask the guard to call ahead for a tour. The tours, guided by young engineering students, are reportedly quite fascinating for those so inclined.

Word has it that a couple of tour boats now cruise the lake behind the dam every day, although no details were available.

The easiest way to reach the dam is by private car, turning off the San Pedro Sula–Tegucigalpa highway 56 kilometers from San Pedro, toward Santa Cruz de Yojoa. Just before reaching Santa Cruz, a well-maintained side road turns toward the dam, 23.5 kilometers farther on. After 12 kilometers, at the crest of where the road crosses a ridge into the Río Humuya watershed, you'll reach an Army gate, where visitors must register and receive a written pass. Show the pass at a second Army post, 3.5 kilometers down the hill, and continue down to another gate, which the guard will open to let you pass. Just below the gate is a fork—turn to the right and wind up and around the edge of a hillside to the top of the dam, four kilometers farther. Here you can park your car, wander out across the top of the massive structure, and peer over the side for heart-stopping views down to the dam's base, well over 200 meters straight down. At one side

of the entrance to the walkway is a monument to the 25 workers who died during the dam's five-year construction. Guards can be a bit reluctant at times to let in visitors; PANACAM can arrange tours for groups.

It is possible to reach the dam by bus from Santa Cruz de Yojoa, though visitors must stop to register themselves at the first army post, then wait for another bus or a *jalón* farther on.

CUEVAS DE TAULABÉ

Approximately 17 kilometers south of Pito Solo, at kilometer marker 140, are the Cuevas de Taulabé (8 A.M.–4 P.M. Mon.–Fri., until 5 P.M. Sat.–Sun., US$2), which have been mapped and explored to a depth of 921 meters without hitting the bottom, though it is believed that exits from the caverns exist as far away as Lago de Yojoa, Santa Bárbara, and Copán. The first 300 meters of the cave have been lit and have railings and steps, taking anywhere from 25 minutes to an hour to explore, depending on your pace. Beyond that, bring a flashlight and watch your footing. It might be best to hire a guide for exploring beyond the main path, as it's easy to get lost; rates are negotiable, typically US$3–4 for an hour. Ask about the legendary *bandito* who hid out in the caves for months. Locally made honey is sold along the highway near Taulabé.

Santa Bárbara and Vicinity

At the foot of the towering Montaña de Santa Bárbara, cupped in the lush, hot lowlands not far from the Río Ulúa, is the town of Santa Bárbara, capital of the department of the same name. The emerald-green mountain country around Santa Bárbara, dotted with little villages, is well worth exploring. The region produces large quantities of coffee and is famed for making hats, baskets, and other crafts from the local *junco* palm.

SANTA BÁRBARA

The mercantile town of Santa Bárbara is either a large town or a small city, depending

on your point of view. There's not a lot to do in town except chat with the friendly locals, but it's an easy place to while away a few hours strolling around or hiking up to the hillside castle visible from town. As a point of reference, the church is on the east side of the park.

History

Santa Bárbara was founded in 1761 by several families who moved to the region from Gracias, reputedly escaping usurious priests. A large portion of the settlers were of Jewish

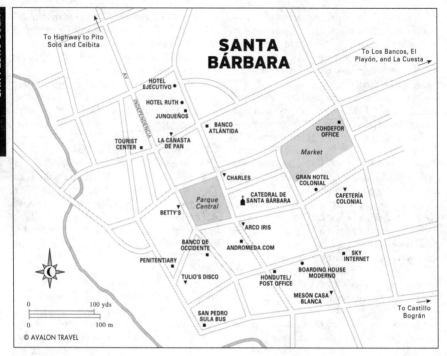

background. Santa Bárbara remained relatively small until April 1815, when the nearby town of Tencoa, one of the first Spanish settlements in Honduras, was flooded by the Río Ulúa. Tencoa's surviving inhabitants moved to Santa Bárbara, and the combined population made it the biggest town in the area.

Sights

The 115-year-old **Catedral de Santa Bárbara** facing the town square *(parque central)* features an intricately carved wooden altar with painted statues of saints. At the time of writing, the park, unfortunately, was completely closed off, presumably for renovations.

Just outside of town are two *balnearios* (swimming holes) in rivers coming off the mountain, called **La Torre** and **Santa Lucía.**

A visit to the long-abandoned **Castillo Bográn** in the hills above Santa Bárbara is a pleasant way to pass the day. From the square,

look for (or ask any local to point out) the castle, visible on a ridge southeast of town. The castle is four kilometers from Santa Bárbara on a dirt road leading to the village of Las Crucitas. Pickups occasionally drive the road and will give you a lift for a few lempira, or you can walk it in one or two sweaty hours, depending on your pace. Up close, the deserted castle is not as impressive as it looks from below, but the views are majestic.

Shopping

Handicrafts from the Santa Bárbara region are best purchased in surrounding villages, although there is a shop or two in town. Roadside stands sell hammocks and straw products including hats and baskets a few kilometers north of Santa Bárbara.

Accommodations

Most hotels in Santa Bárbara are on the lower

end of the price scale, and comfortable rooms can be found without difficulty.

Gran Hotel Colonial (tel. 504/643-2665, US$29 s or US$34 d), 1.5 blocks from the square going toward the hills, has 52 clean rooms spread over three buildings. Prices range depending on the size of the room and whether or not it has a TV and air-conditioning. The more expensive rooms come with complimentary breakfast across the street at Cafetería Colonial.

Another option is the **Hotel Ejecutivo** (tel. 504/643-2206, US$16 s, US$29 d), 1.5 blocks north of the park. The rooms have tiled floors and are surprisingly cool, even on hot days, along with fan, TV, and private bathroom. The hotel closes its doors at 10 P.M., unless you let them know if you're going to be out late. The upstairs rooms, with their front balconies, are nicer.

For less money, neighboring **Hotel Ruth** (tel. 504/643-2632, US$13 s, US$16 d, another US$8 for a/c) has slightly dingy rooms with fans and private bathrooms.

Similar in price to Ruth but quite a bit nicer is **Boarding House Moderno** (tel. 504/643-2203, US$13 s, US$18.50 d), one block southeast of the square. The large, quiet building has tidy rooms with hot water and private bathrooms, and with air-conditioning for about double the price. Some rooms are pretty dark, but you can always ask to see more than one. The front desk sells sodas and fruit juices, and even has a little gift shop.

The nicest rooms around are outside of town, near the exit to Juanjuco, where the **Hotel Antony** (tel. 504/643-0486, US$32 s, US$42 d) opened in early 2009 (same owners as the Colonial). Amenities include a pool, restaurant, and Internet access, and fancier rooms (US$47 s/d) have Jacuzzi tubs, plasma TVs, and mini-fridges. As of writing, the hotel was open for business, but had not yet been officially inaugurated, and prices were expected to go up a bit after inauguration.

Food and Entertainment

One great meal in town can be had at **Mesón Casa Blanca** (tel. 504/643-2839, 7:30 A.M.–8 P.M. Mon.–Sat.), an unusual setup.

Food is served in the house of a Santa Bárbara family, two blocks southeast of the square. The house is decorated with paintings, old photographs, and sculptures, and it feels a bit like eating in your grandmother's house. Lunch is a buffet and runs US$6, including a drink, while breakfast and dinner are à la carte.

Also very good, and less expensive, is **Betty's Cafetería y Repostería** (tel. 504/643-3006, 8 A.M.–9 P.M. Mon.–Fri., 8 A.M.–noon Sun.), on the park, with great juice drinks and massive *baleadas* for under US$1.

With heaping platters of mouthwatering *pollo asado* and fried plantains, **Charles** (tel. 504/643-2433, 8 A.M.–9 P.M. daily), a clean, tiled restaurant on the northwest corner of the park, beckons customers with the tantalizing aroma of roasted chicken for a reasonable US$2.50, as well as Honduran tacos, *típico* meals, and a number of natural juices and pastries.

Arco Iris (tel. 504/643-2348, 9 A.M.–10 P.M. daily), on the southeast corner of the square, adjacent to the cathedral, has inexpensive fresh juices, *licuados,* and ice cream. Across the street from Hotel Colonial and down the street a bit is **Cafetería Colonial** (tel. 504/643-2812, 6 A.M.–9 P.M. daily), with reasonable, inexpensive *comida típica, pupusas,* and burgers with fries.

A noteworthy addition to Santa Bárbara's dining scene, the spotless **La Canasta de Pan** (tel. 504/608-6179, 8 A.M.–4 P.M. Sun.–Thurs., 8 A.M.–2 P.M. Fri.) is the town's first vegetarian restaurant. Breakfasts are US$2.50, lunch US$3, and *licuados* top out at a dollar. Fresh whole-grain breads, soy products, and a number of health-food items are sold, and interestingly, Swedish massages are also available for absolutely rock-bottom prices (US$4 for 30 minutes, US$6 for 60).

Tulio's Disco, a block west of the park, is a popular spot for weekend dancing.

Information and Services

Hondutel (7 A.M.–5 P.M. Mon.–Fri.) receives faxes at 504/643-2550. *Correos* (the post office) is right next door, a block south of the square. **Banco de Occidente** and **BGA** will usually change dollars but not always travelers checks. **Andromeda.com** (tel. 504/643-2678, 8 A.M.–9 P.M. Mon.–Sat., 8 A.M.–noon Sun.), half a block southeast of the park, charges US$0.65 per half hour and US$1 per hour of Internet use on its 10 computers and offers international phone calls at US$0.20 per minute to the States.

Information on the city and surrounding region is available at the helpful tourist office, known as the **Centro Cultural Hibueras** (tel. 504/643-2905 or 504/643-3174, 8 A.M.–noon and 1–4 P.M. Mon.–Fri., 8 A.M.–noon Sat.), located north of the park and west of Avenida Independencia, which also sells local handicrafts.

Getting There and Away

Santa Bárbara buses headed for Tegucigalpa leave from the terminal two block west of the park. **Junqueños** (tel. 504/643-2113) runs three buses (US$7.25, 4.5 hours) Monday–Saturday to Tegucigalpa (times vary from day to day, but the last one leaves at 2 P.M.) and two buses on Sunday (8:30 A.M. and 2 P.M.). Junqueños tickets are sold next to Hotel Ruth on the second floor.

Buses to San Rafael, a village in the mountains south of Santa Bárbara, leave from the same terminal at noon, US$1.50, three hours. From San Rafael, you can continue by hitching to Gracias. The bus returns from San Rafael at 4:30 A.M.

Three blocks south is the **Cotisba** terminal (tel. 504/643-2383), which runs direct buses to San Pedro Sula every 20 minutes between 4 A.M. and 5 P.M. daily (US$2, two hours).

From San Pedro Sula or Santa Rosa de Copán, the road to Santa Bárbara turns off at Ceibita, between kilometer markers 32 and 33. From Ceibita, it's another 61 kilometers of well-maintained road to Santa Bárbara, through beautiful countryside. The junction at Ceibita is invariably lined with local *campesinos* selling luscious fresh fruit of all varieties in big piles on the roadside.

If you're coming the opposite direction,

north out of Santa Bárbara, and heading toward Copán Ruinas or Santa Rosa de Copán, take a right at the first T, then left at the second.

East out of Santa Bárbara, the highway leads to Pito Solo, where it meets the San Pedro Sula–Tegucigalpa highway. This 53-kilometer stretch of road is not as frequently traveled as the one toward Ceibita, but it is also a scenic drive.

NEAR SANTA BÁRBARA
◖ Villages near Santa Bárbara

The department of Santa Bárbara is filled with colorful colonial villages infrequently visited by foreigners. Many, such as Gualjoto, El Níspero, Los Bancos, and San Vicente, are known for producing good quality *artesanías* (handicrafts). **Ilama,** on the road toward Ceibita and San Pedro Sula, is famous for its *junco* goods. Unfortunately, its lovely colonial church was severely damaged by an earthquake in May 2009. San Luis, also off this road, is a pleasant little town set in the cool hills 1,000 meters above Santa Bárbara. Also well known for handicrafts are La Arada and Nueva Celilac.

VILLAGES NEAR SANTA BÁRBARA

© AVALON TRAVEL

Set high on a mountain divide separating Santa Bárbara from the Gracias region is **San Rafael,** a scenic town dating from colonial times. A daily bus from Santa Bárbara travels past El Níspero up the dirt road to San Rafael, and the adventurous can continue onward to Gracias by hitchhiking down the far side of the mountains. No hotels exist in San Rafael, but locals will rent rooms for a night.

Up in this direction, south of Santa Bárbara toward Gracias, is **Cerro Pucca,** one of the highest mountains in this part of Honduras and reportedly affording some of the finest views in the country, across five departments on a good day. The mountain is reached through the community of El Cile, via a 12-hour hike from the village, or El Lepaera. In both villages, you'll find locals more than happy to guide you the right way for a negotiable fee (usually US$8 a day or so).

Trinidad, on the highway toward Ceibita, has a lovely central park where a marimba band plays live every Sunday evening after Catholic mass. The town hosts a number of festivals throughout the year, including beautiful colored sawdust carpets for Holy Week as well as unusual papier-mâché "chimneys" in mid-December, which are ritually burned to make way for the new year.

Just outside of Trinidad is **La Estancia El Pedregal** (tel. 504/552-6365, www.estancia -elpedregal.com, US$35 d cabin, US$55 cabin sleeping up to eight), a working farm on a beautiful hillside that also takes guests seeking a taste of rural Honduran lifestyle. Rooms are in log cabins with porches with hammocks, air-conditioning, and hot water, and some come with a kitchen. The restaurant also serves tasty locally produced food. There's great hiking all around, and plenty of activities on the farm if that's your thing. The owner will collect you in Trinidad if you arrange beforehand.

Swimming

About 20 minutes outside of town on the road to Pito Solo is **Balneario Bella Vista,** with three pools, an open-air bar and restaurant, and plenty of grassy areas for kids to run around or to have a picnic (US$1 admission).

© AMY E. ROBERTSON

traditional corn grinders, on display at La Estancia El Pedregal, outside of Santa Bárbara

Parque Nacional Santa Bárbara

Surrounding the peak of Santa Bárbara, the second highest in the country at 2,744 meters, Santa Bárbara National Park covers about 13,000 hectares of cloud, pine, and semihumid tropical forest. Montaña de Santa Bárbara is not part of any major mountain range but an anomalous, solitary massif rising up between the town of Santa Bárbara and Lago de Yojoa. The inaccessible, rarely seen forest on top of the mountain is reputed to be dense and wild, full of weird rock formations and lots of wildlife.

The park was created by the government to protect this precious watershed, but local *campesinos* have been increasingly encroaching on the forest, cutting old-growth trees and planting illegal coffee with virtual impunity in this completely unenforced reserve. Venturing into the park is only for the most adventurous, machete-wielding souls, as there is no established trail system. Nonetheless, those who've been there rate it as one of the finest cloud forests in the country.

It's possible to get into the forest from several of the villages around the edge of the mountain, if you're willing to make the effort. From Santa Bárbara, you can catch a ride on a truck or drive 20 minutes by dirt road to the villages of La Cuesta, Los Bancos, and El Playón and look for guides. In El Playón, Mario and Reino Orellano are usually willing to take visitors into the forest for a negotiable fee.

Another route into the forest is via **San Luis Planes,** a village set in a high valley on the north side of the park; you can get there by bus from Peña Blanca on Lago de Yojoa. (Ornithologist Malcolm Glasgow at D&D Brewery leads hikes and bird-watching tours.) The road from Peña Blanca is best negotiated by four-wheel-drive vehicle and takes about an hour to drive. The forest starts just beyond San Luis, though it would take more than a couple of days of hiking to get up to the peak, and you'd need a guide. Shorter hikes into the lower parts of the forest are easily possible here, and you could make a serviceable campsite not far from San Luis without difficulty.

A third option, also reach from Peña Blanca, is via the village of **Los Andes.** Take the road to El Mochito, and at the highest point (maybe 10 kilometers from Peña Blanca), look for a dirt road turning right uphill, signposted for Los Andes. The rough dirt road is about five kilometers long. In Los Andes, ask around for someone to guide you into the forest.

From El Mochito, on the south shore of Lago de Yojoa, you can get a truck to El Cedral and continue on foot or horseback to El Cielo, where guides can be found to lead you up to the higher reaches of the park. The extremely determined could probably find a way over the top and back down the far side to Santa Bárbara. As with most places in Honduras, guides generally charge about US$10 a day, plus expenses for food.

For more information on the park and access to it, stop in at the Santa Bárbara COHDEFOR office. The topographical map covering the park is 1:50,000 *Santa Bárbara 2560 I.*

Siguatepeque

Set in a pine-forested highland valley midway between San Pedro Sula and Tegucigalpa, Siguatepeque (pop. 53,000) enjoys a cool and comfortable climate—a pleasant change for those coming from the steamy north coast. In spite of its long history—the town was one of the first bases for the Spanish in their conquest of Honduras—little colonial-era architecture remains in Siguatepeque. There are few attractions per se to interest foreign visitors, though the invigorating climate and fine countryside may inspire you to spend a couple of days hiking around the hillsides. Many highway drivers stop in Siguatepeque to eat at the Granja d'Elia, Don Tiki, and Betania buffet restaurants on the highway. A new minimall of sorts right on the highway has clothing stores, a Wendy's, a Banco Atlántida

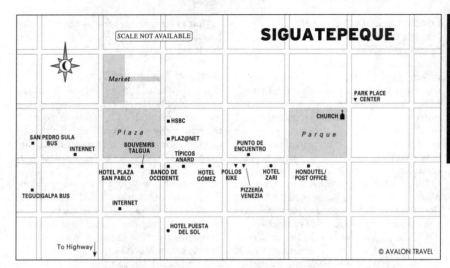

SIGUATEPEQUE

SCALE NOT AVAILABLE

Market

PARK PLACE ▼ CENTER

■ HSBC

CHURCH ⚐

Plaza

■ PLAZ@NET

Parque

SAN PEDRO SULA ■ BUS
INTERNET ■

SOUVENIRS TALGUA

PUNTO DE ENCUENTRO

TÍPICOS ANARD

HOTEL PLAZA SAN PABLO

BANCO DE OCCIDENTE

HOTEL GÓMEZ

POLLOS KIKE

HOTEL ZARI

HONDUTEL/ POST OFFICE

TEGUCIGALPA BUS ■

INTERNET ■

PIZZERÍA VENEZIA

HOTEL PUESTA DEL SOL ●

To Highway ↓

© AVALON TRAVEL

with ATM, and an Espresso Americano coffee shop.

ORIENTATION AND SIGHTS

Siguatepeque has two main squares: The one with the church on it is known as the *parque,* while the other, two blocks west, is called the *plaza.* The center of town is about 1.5 kilometers off the San Pedro Sula–Tegucigalpa highway. The park has been redone with lots of lovely plants and flowers, as well as a rather bizarre, UFO-like concrete structure, which does not deter the townsfolk from congregating daily. The plaza, on the other hand, looks completely abandoned, overgrown with tall weeds and sporting an unfinished rebar and cement structure of some sort.

About four kilometers down the highway west to La Esperanza is the village of **El Porvenir,** a local center for Lenca pottery, sold out of several houses on the road.

PRACTICALITIES
Accommodations

There is an abundance of places to stay in Siguatepeque, starting with **Hotel Zari** (tel. 504/773-0015, US$9 s, US$14 d), just off the southwest corner of the park, with reasonably clean and well-equipped rooms

(cable TV, private bath, fans). Some of the hotel's 53 rooms are in a second building across the street.

◖ **Hotel Gómez** (tel. 504/773-0868) has two types of rooms set around the parking lot—the older ones have a fan (US$9 s, US$16 d), while those in the new wing have air-conditioning and are modern and spacious (US$21 s, US$27.50 d), with wireless Internet connection. Some English is spoken.

Hotel Plaza San Pablo (tel. 504/773-0700/4020, www.hotelplazasanpablo.com, US$23.50–26 s, US$36 d), on the plaza, is popular with business travelers. Its 37 modern rooms have all the amenities, including air-conditioning, TV, telephone, and private bathroom. The massive triple suite goes for US$63. The staff is pleasant, and the hotel has Internet service and a fine rooftop terrace. They can arrange a taxi service for about US$1 to the highway.

Another relatively upscale hotel (for Siguatepeque) is **Hotel Puesta del Sol** (tel. 504/773-3179, US$16 s, US$26 d with fan, US$24 s, US$32 d with a/c), located a block and a half south of the plaza. The 46 rooms are rather small, but colorful and tidy. Suites are available for US$53–63, and Internet for US$0.50/hour. The hotel can also book massages.

Food and Entertainment

Pizzeria Venezia (10 A.M.–9 P.M. daily) has decent pizza (US$7–8 for a large), as well as a large selection of fresh *licuados*. There is a second branch out on the highway, catering to passing motorists, with better pizza than the original. Next door is **Pollos Kike,** a roast chicken restaurant with a little more style than the usual joint.

Another good spot is the restaurant at **Park Place Center,** a sort of downtown shopping center next to the park.

Del Corral Steak Ranch on Francisco Morazán is renowned for its steaks, while **Del Corral Snack Bar** is a popular place for snacks and coffee in the Del Corral Supermarket.

On the highway to San Pedro, at kilometer marker 118, is a deli-supermarket, **Granja d'Elia.** All sorts of vegetables, meats, cheeses, and other goodies are available daily until 8 P.M. The adjacent restaurant, very popular with motorists driving between San Pedro and Tegucigalpa, serves a decent buffet with a wide selection of breakfasts, appetizers, meat and vegetarian entrées, and salads, open 6 A.M.–9 P.M. daily. Right next door is **Don Tiki,** and a couple of kilometers farther up the road toward Siguatepeque is **Betania,** two other good buffet restaurants.

Local farmers come from the villages on Thursdays and Saturdays to sell their goods in the **San Juan market.**

Information and Services

Hondutel on the *parque* is open daily 5:30 A.M.–9 P.M. Right next door is **Honducor,** with express mail service available.

Banco de Occidente, HSBC, and **Banco Atlántida** will change dollars and travelers checks. The latter two also have cash machines.

Opposite Pizzeria Venezia is **Punto de Encuentro,** an Internet and ice cream shop. There is another Internet shop, **Puntonet,** near the San Pedro and Tegucigalpa bus stations. A third option is **Plaz@net Cyber Café** (9 A.M.–9 P.M. daily), on the east side of the plaza.

Típicos Anardá has a few souvenirs, as does **Souvenirs Talgua #1,** next to the Hotel Plaza San Pablo.

Getting There and Around

Siguatepeque is 125 kilometers from San Pedro and 117 kilometers from Tegucigalpa, with well-maintained highway in both directions. Driving toward Tegucigalpa, the steep, winding stretch of highway down into the Valle de Comayagua is known locally as Cuesta La Virgen.

The easiest way to get to San Pedro or Tegucigalpa is to take a US$1 taxi ride out to the highway and catch the next bus that comes by in your direction. If you don't feel like waiting on the highway, however, both **Transportes Maribel** (tel. 504/773-0254) and **Empresas Unidas** (tel. 504/773-0149) run buses to Tegucigalpa from at 5:15 A.M., 6:15 A.M., 7:15 A.M., 9:15 A.M., 11:15 A.M., 12:15 P.M., 1:15 P.M., and 3:15 P.M. (US$2.50, 2.5 hours). Buses also stop in Comayagua (US$1) and Palmerola (US$1.30).

Etul (tel. 504/773-0033) has buses to San Pedro Sula at 4:50 A.M., 5:20 A.M., 6 A.M., 7:10 A.M., 7:40 A.M., 8:20 A.M., 8:50 A.M., 9:45 A.M., 10:30 A.M., and then every 40 minutes until 4 P.M. (US$3.30, two hours).

To get to La Esperanza, take a US$1 taxi ride to the highway turnoff, a couple of kilometers from the Siguatepeque turn on the way to San Pedro. From the gas station at the La Esperanza turn, buses leave roughly every two hours, charging US$3 for the 90-minute ride. If you don't see any buses around, just stick out your thumb. The road to La Esperanza is 67 kilometers, dropping down into the Río Otoro (upper Ulúa) valley, past the town of Jesús de Otoro, and climbing back up into the mountains to La Esperanza.

To get to Jesús de Otoro, catch the bus next to Hotel Puesta del Sol, hourly between 10 A.M. and 4 P.M., US$1.60 for the 40-minute ride.

A taxi to the highway should cost US$1.60; in town a ride should cost about US$0.40, although it's possible to walk everywhere.

Comayagua

Comayagua, Honduras's original capital city, is on the northwestern edge of the broad Valle de Comayagua, the largest flat region in central-western Honduras. The 390-square-kilometer valley lies roughly equidistant between the Caribbean and Pacific coasts. Comayagua (pop. 60,000) lies at the junction of the Río Chiquito and the Río Humuya. With help from the Spanish government, the small city has spruced up many of the fine architectural monuments and museums. Comayagua is well worth stopping at for a day, particularly for the colonial buffs, and more adventurous types can visit a nearby cloud forest, waterfalls, and a couple of small pre-Hispanic ruin sites.

After more than three centuries as the country's political and administrative center, Comayagua has a wealth of colonial monuments. City authorities have in the last decade begun promoting an ambitious project known as **Comayagua Colonial,** which entails renovating many old buildings, recobbling the streets, and enforcing strict building codes. The *parque central* and Plaza San Francisco are reaping the benefits of this program. While Comayagua is unlikely to become the next Antigua, Guatemala, the renovation projects are certainly a welcome change.

Comayagua is home to Honduras's most renowned festivals during **Semana Santa,** the week leading up to Easter, with sawdust carpets on the streets and processions throughout the week. Hotels usually raise prices and establish minimum stays of 3–4 nights. Another interesting time to visit is in early February, to catch the famous **Baile de los Diablitos** performance.

Just outside of town, in the middle of the valley, is the Enrique Soto Cano Air Force Base, better known as Palmerola, used by the U.S. military. With the closing of the U.S. bases in Panama Canal Zone, activity at Palmerola has increased substantially. In another boost to the local economy, a ZIP (free trade zone) carries on business just outside of town. The surrounding region survives mainly on agriculture, particularly coffee grown around La Libertad, fruits like peaches and apricots, and many vegetable farms.

History

The broad, fertile Valle de Comayagua attracted settlers long before the Spanish arrived in the region in 1537. For centuries, the valley had been a bastion of the Lenca, but during the years before Columbus, Nahuatl-speaking migrants from central Mexico moved into the region, apparently coexisting peacefully with the original inhabitants. The attractions of the area were obvious and are further illustrated through the name Comayagua, which is thought to mean "abundance of food" in Maya.

It's unclear exactly when the first conquistadors passed through the valley, but Alonso de Cáceres founded Santa María de Comayagua on December 7, 1537, under orders from Francisco Montejo. The first city was destroyed shortly thereafter by Indians in the region, who rose with Lempira in revolt against the Spaniards. In fact, the valley was the last bastion of Indian rebellion to be put down, holding out until the first months of 1539.

Comayagua was reestablished the same year, and by 1557 the crown recognized it as a *villa* (city). Not long after, veins of silver were found nearby, further encouraging Spaniards to settle there. By 1573, Comayagua was the most important city in the province, surpassing Gracias a Dios. It was made the administrative capital of the colony, which it remained through the rest of the colonial period.

Comayagua was a center for intrigue and a target for attack during the wars of independence and Central American union. The town was pillaged and burned several times in the mid-19th century, most notably in 1837 by Guatemalan General José Justo Milla. When Honduras was established as an independent country, Comayagua was declared the capital. The rise of Tegucigalpa in the late 19th century

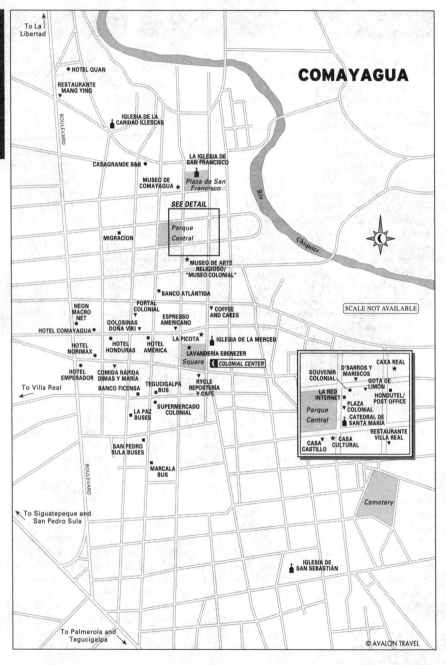

COMAYAGUA

To La Libertad

● HOTEL QUAN

RESTAURANTE MANG YING ▼

BOULEVARD

IGLESIA DE LA CARIDAD ILLESCAS ▪

CASAGRANDE B&B ●

LA IGLESIA DE SAN FRANCISCO ▪

MUSEO DE COMAYAGUA ★

Plaza de San Francisco

SEE DETAIL

Parque Central

■ MIGRACÍON

Río

Chiquito

★ MUSEO DE ARTE RELIGIOSO/ "MUSEO COLONIAL"

SCALE NOT AVAILABLE

▪ BANCO ATLÁNTIDA

NEON MACRO NET ▪

PORTAL COLONIAL ▪

▼ COFFEE AND CAKES

GOLOSINAS DOÑA VIKI ▼

ESPRESSO AMERICANO ▼

HOTEL COMAYAGUA ▼

LA PICOTA ★   ♦ IGLESIA DE LA MERCED

HOTEL NORIMAX ▪

HOTEL HONDURAS ▪

HOTEL AMÉRICA ▪

LAVANDERÍA EBENEZER

Square   Ⓒ COLONIAL CENTER

HOTEL EMPERADOR ▪

COMIDA RÁPIDA DIMAS Y MARÍA ▪

TEGUCIGALPA BUS ▪

RYCLE REPOSTERÍA Y CAFÉ

To Villa Real

BANCO FICENSA ▪

LA PAZ BUSES ▪

SUPERMERCADO COLONIAL ▪

SAN PEDRO SULA BUSES ▪

MARCALA BUS ▪

BOULEVARD

↖ To Siguatepeque and San Pedro Sula

[Detail inset]

SOUVENIR COLONIAL

D'BARROS Y MARISCOS ▼

CAXA REAL ★

LA RED INTERNET ▪

GOTA DE LIMÓN ▼

HONDUTEL/ POST OFFICE ▪

Parque Central

PLAZA COLONIAL ▼

CATEDRAL DE SANTA MARÍA ♦

RESTAURANTE VILLA REAL ▼

CASA CASTILLO ▪

★ CASA CULTURAL

Cemetery

IGLESIA DE SAN SEBASTIÁN ♦

To Palmerola and Tegucigalpa

as a center for gold and silver production led to a bitter rivalry between the two cities, which was finally settled in 1880 when President Marco Aurelio Soto changed the seat of government to Tegucigalpa.

Since then—a black day for Comayagua—the city slid into a sort of genteel poverty, trying to retain the pretensions of a capital but without the economic or political power base. These days, Comayagua mostly survives on the valley's agriculture and cattle industries, as well as on money derived from the nearby Palmerola Air Force Base and the new industrial park. The U.S. military presence in town is quite noticeable if you stick around for a couple of days; several ex-military personnel operate businesses in town.

Orientation

Downtown Comayagua is a couple of kilometers off the San Pedro Sula–Tegucigalpa highway, connected by a divided avenue known as El Bulevar (The Boulevard). Comayagua is centered around the broad downtown square *(parque central)* and, one block to the north, the more dilapidated **Plaza San Francisco.** Four blocks south is the smaller **Plaza La Merced.** All the main sights in town are located within walking distance of the square, but a taxi might be desired to get out to the highway or to the bus stations.

SIGHTS
◖ The Colonial Center

As the capital of Honduras for more than 300

HOLY WEEK IN COMAYAGUA

Normally a sleepy colonial town, Comayagua explodes with life during Semana Santa (Holy Week), the week between Palm Sunday and Easter.

Although not on the scale of its more famous neighbor, Antigua, Comayagua also has a long tradition of processions over brilliantly colored sawdust carpets. It's a sight well worth seeing if in Honduras over Easter week; just be sure to reserve your hotel room well in advance. Exact times are certainly subject to change from year to year, but hopefully the guidelines here will at least help you get to the right place at the right time.

· **Palm Sunday:** The procession of the Señor de la Burrita (Lord of the Little Donkey) begins at La Caridad church at 7 or 8 A.M., accompanied by music and hundreds of palm-waving celebrants.

· **Maundy Thursday:** Church altars are elaborately set in remembrance of Jesus' Last Supper, open for admiring at 5 P.M. At 6:30 P.M. there is a procession of the Holy Sacrament around the Parque la Libertad, arriving at the monument at the cathedral. Then at 9 or 10 P.M. a silent procession begins in memory of Jesus' incarceration, starting at La Merced and ending at dawn inside the cathedral.

· **Good Friday:** The procession of Via Crucis begins at 8:30 A.M., at the San Francisco church, replete with pointy-capped penitents and cross-bearing Jesuses. The procession crosses the sawdust carpets throughout the city, ending with a reenactment of the crucifixion at the cathedral at noon.

· **Easter Vigil:** The all-female procession of the Virgin Mary of Loneliness begins at 4 P.M. at the cathedral.

· **Easter Sunday:** A procession called the Carreritas de San Juan (Saint John's Races) begins at La Caridad church at 8 A.M., with the Virgin of La Caridad, Mary Magdalene, Veronica, and Saint John searching for Jesus throughout town. (Veronica is a woman said to have wiped Jesus' face with a cloth during his walk to Golgotha, an act that is remembered at the sixth station of the cross, the sixth stop on the Via Crucis procession.) The images are brought together in front of the Casa de la Cultura, to later enter the cathedral at the start of Easter mass at 10 A.M.

years, and the religious seat of the colony under Spanish rule, Comayagua boasts many colonial structures and works of art. Don't miss the ornate *catedral,* right on the downtown square, along with two interesting museums, one of colonial religious art and the other of regional archaeology.

Formerly, most were in rather sad condition, but recently Comayagua has begun a major overhaul of its colonial past in an effort to boost itself as a tourist destination, in part with the help of money from the Spanish government. Both the main *parque* and the Plaza La Merced have been given complete facelifts, with very positive results. The bustling central park has been rebuilt with cobblestones and is filled with all sorts of lovely plants, trees, and flowers, along with freshly painted benches, a bandstand, and a beautiful fountain. Numerous kiosks set up a fair every 15 days to sell souvenirs and traditional Honduran food. Note the outline of the cathedral, which lines up with the church's shadow once a day, drawn on the stones of the park in front.

CATEDRAL DE SANTA MARÍA

The imposing Catedral de Santa María, also known as La Iglesia de la Inmaculada Concepción, was built on the site of the original Comayagua plaza over the course of more than a century, between 1580 and 1708. The prolonged construction stemmed from problems obtaining funds and the need to rebuild the church's foundation in the 17th century.

The church's facade, which recently underwent thorough renovations, is decorated with sculpted columns and eight statues set in niches. The tower, built in 1650, holds one of the oldest known clocks in the world. The Reloj Arabe, as it is known, was made around 1100 and graced the side of La Alhambra in Granada, Spain, before it was donated to Comayagua by King Felipe II.

Inside the cathedral are three extraordinarily elaborate *retablos* in baroque style, with sculptures by Andrés y Francisco de Ocampo dating from the 1630s. Many colonial religious paintings hang on the walls inside. The cathedral is

CAPITAL RIVALRY

Comayagua's colonial history is illustrious. In 1540 it became the capital of the Honduras district of New Spain. Once independence was gained in 1821, Comayagua remained the capital of the state of Honduras in the United States of Central America. After Honduras became an independent republic in 1838, the capital alternated between Comayagua (preferred by the Conservative party) and Tegucigalpa (preferred by the Liberals).

This alternating system deepened a rivalry between the two cities, based on Comayagua's perception of itself as refined, educated, and superior, and Tegucigalpa's resentment of that attitude.

Tegucigalpan and Liberal Marco Aurelio Soto assumed Honduras's presidency in 1876. He divided his time between the two cities until 1880. It is said that the high society of Comayagua publicly snubbed his indigenous Guatemalan wife. According to legend, the First Lady's birthday was approaching and President Soto was planning a party in her honor – and decided to permanently move the capital to Tegucigalpa to put an end once and for all to the slights his wife suffered at social occasions.

Others point out that President Soto was an important partner of the Rosario Mining Company, based in San Juancito some 40 kilometers from Tegucigalpa. Naturally, a Tegucigalpa base served his business interests.

Whatever the reason, President Soto permanently moved the nation's capital in 1880 to the mountainous city of Tegucigalpa, leaving Comayagua to suffer a long, slow decline.

normally open 9:30 A.M.–noon and 2–5 P.M. weekdays, and of course Sundays for mass.

MUSEO DE ARTE RELIGIOSO (MUSEO COLONIAL)

One of the highlights of colonial Comayagua was the Museo de Arte Religioso, a small museum which housed an eclectic and occasionally fascinating collection of religious art from Comayagua's five churches, including paintings, chalices, statues, vestments, old documents, and an impressive wooden confessional. The building housing the pieces, the old Bishop's Palace dating from 1735, was devastated by a fire in April 2009, and the museum temporarily closed. Over 80 percent of the collection was saved, however, and the museum will hopefully soon reopen here or elsewhere in town. Our favorite pieces are the small silver hand-held shields, used for the exchanging of peace during mass during the time of the plague, as a way to avoid actually shaking hands and thereby transmitting or catching any contagious diseases (a precaution that seemed timely once more as H1N1 flu broke out).

MUSEO DE COMAYAGUA AND LA IGLESIA DE SAN FRANCISCO

One block north of the square is the Museo de Comayagua (8:30 A.M.–4 P.M. daily, US$1),

facing the Plaza San Francisco, in a 16th-century building that was Honduras's seat of government for a short time in the 19th century. There is an interesting collection of pre-Hispanic pottery, as well as well-done exhibits on local culture and traditions. Labels are in English and Spanish.

Next to the museum is the Plaza San Francisco, with the Iglesia de San Francisco on the north side. The church, originally called La Iglesia de San Antonio, was built in 1574 in a simple style and rebuilt completely between 1610 and 1620. An earthquake in 1784 badly damaged the structure, and the roof collapsed in 1806. Three years later, another quake knocked down the bell tower. A second reconstruction was completed in 1819. No wonder the church attracts faithful worshipers—after all those disasters, it's a miracle it's still standing!

The church has an ornate carved *retablo* and a gory statue of Christ. Hours vary—ask around for the caretaker to let you in if it's closed. He may let you go up into the three-story bell tower,

© AMY E. ROBERTSON

the gardens of the Museo de Comayagua

but watch out for the rotten wood planks if you go up.

CAXA REAL

Around the corner from the Plaza San Francisco are the crumbling remnants of the colonial Caxa Real, or tax-collection house, built between 1739 and 1741. Destroyed by the earthquake in 1809, it now consists only of a front portion of the original building—and that has a small garden growing on top and is leaning at a precipitous angle. The inscription above the door states that the building was constructed under direction of Lt. Col. Don Francisco de Parga, under orders of Royal Field Marshal Don Pedro de Rivera Villalón, to serve as the Royal Treasury for King Felipe and Queen Isabel.

IGLESIA DE LA MERCED

The first church built in Honduras, construction on La Merced began in 1550, on the reputed site of the first mass spoken in the valley. Its baroque facade is thought to date from the early years of the 18th century. Many of the paintings and sculptures in the church were made in the 17th century.

Across the street, there's a small square with a pillar in the center, known locally as **La Picota.** It was erected in 1820 in honor of the liberal Spanish Constitution of 1812—illustrating Comayagua's loyal colonial sentiments when the rest of the country, and indeed the continent, was heading toward independence from the mother country.

Outside the Colonial Center
IGLESIA DE SAN SEBASTIÁN

Some 10 blocks south of the square stands Iglesia de San Sebastián, built in 1581 as a site for blacks and Indians in the city to pray. The towers were added in later years and rebuilt in 1957 in a rather unattractive style. The church's architecture is fairly elemental, but the 16th-century image of Saint Sebastian with 15 silver arrows over his body is worth a look. The remains of Honduran president and general José Trinidad Cabañas are buried under the church floor, marked by an engraved

stone. In early February the church is the stage for the **Baile de los Diablitos,** which remembers the persecution (and death) of Sebastian, a Christian saint and martyr who died during the Roman persecution of Christians in the 3rd century A.D. In the dance, Sebastian begins as one of the persecutors, converts to Christianity, and becomes one of the persecuted, eventually dying by arrows. In a local twist, the *diablitos* or devils are believed to represent a native Lenca priest who converts to Christianity.

IGLESIA DE LA CARIDAD ILLESCAS

Several blocks northeast of the square, La Caridad was also intended during the colonial era for use by the *mestizo,* black, and Indian populations in the neighborhood. Construction on the church began in 1629. Of the several religious artworks within, of particular note are the gold- and silver-lined *retablo* dedicated to Santa Lucía and the statue of the Señor de la Burrita, the Lord of the Little Donkey.

SHOPPING

Souvenir Colonial, just around the corner from the main square, has a nice selection of *artesanías* from Honduras, including mahogany carvings, cigars, pottery, stone sculpture, and some paintings.

RECREATION

The **Comayagua Golf Club** (tel. 504/715-0116, www.comayaguagolfclub.com) has a nine-hole course, as well as apartments and cottages for rent. The course is open to the public; it's US$10.50 to play and US$5.25 for club rental. The cottages are one-, two- and three-bedroom, with fully kitchens, air-conditioning, and TV, renting for US$81/night, including breakfast. (If you are staying in a cottage, there is no charge to play golf.) To get there, take a right from the highway just after Hotel Santa María when heading north, then the second right off the boulevard.

ACCOMMODATIONS
Under US$25

A block east of the boulevard and three blocks west of the Iglesia La Merced plaza, **Hotel**

Norimax (tel. 504/772-1210, US$16 s, US$18 d) is a pleasant hotel in a two-story building, with checkered tile floors and a small shared balcony. The rooms have worn linens and paint, but clean bathrooms and air-conditioning, and the staff is cheery.

Hotel Emperador (tel. 504/772-0332, US$16 s, US$17 d, or US$24 s, US$ 26 d for rooms with microwave and fridge), on the Boulevard, a block north of the Metro Plaza, has unexceptional but clean rooms with air-conditioning, TV, and telephone. A few rooms have balconies. Monthly stays can be arranged for US$300 a month, plus the cost of electricity.

Hotel Quan (tel. 504/772-0070, hquan@hondutel.hn, US$14 s, US$19 d with fan, US$21–47 s, US$29–55 d with a/c; all with breakfast), on the block behind Restaurante Mang Ying, has a wide variety of rooms with hot water and TV. The older section is cheaper and basic, with mismatched linens, but clean. Across the street, the hotel has a motel-style building around an aboveground pool with nicer rooms, equipped with air-conditioning, TV, and refrigerator. Those on the second floor have hammocks on the breezeway. The hotel is kept clean, the management is very helpful, and the neighborhood northwest of downtown near La Iglesia de la Caridad is quiet.

If you really need to save money, **Hotel Honduras** (tel. 504/772-1893, US$6 s and US$8 d, cold water only) has cramped rooms. The shared bathroom is not very clean.

US$25-50

The best midrange hotel in town is ◖ **Hotel América** (tel. 504/772-0360, Hotel-AmericaInc@yahoo.com), close to the center. Located in an attractive colonial building, the hotel has a nice lobby, a clean swimming pool, and a cafeteria. In the older part of the hotel, rooms (US$15 s, US$26 d, more for a/c) have TV and fans. There is a small shared living room if you want to get out of your room for a while. In the newer part of the hotel, all rooms (US$27 s, US$44 d) have air-conditioning and are spacious, with

desks and new bathrooms. Triples are available in both sections of the hotel. The pool (8 A.M.–9 P.M. daily) can be used by nonguests for US$2.50, or for free if you have a meal in the little restaurant.

A block off the *bulevar* is **Hotel Comayagua** (tel. 504/772-1209, hotelcomayagua10@yahoo.es, US$21 s, US$29 d), with good if simple little rooms, acceptable baths, and Formica floors. The place could use a paint job, but it has a shared balcony with a sofa and a couple of chairs, and overall a fairly airy feel. Rooms have TV and air-conditioning, and there is a cafeteria on-site.

A 15-minute walk from the center (across the boulevard into town) is the **Hotel Villa Real** (tel. 504/772-1751, www.villarealcolonial.com, US$37 s, US$49 d, breakfast included). The hotel, which looks so promising from the website, is a little disappointing in person. Some rooms are great, with colonial-style furnishings (the best is number 9, for US$58), but others are rather plain, with dated furniture (number 5 is a big letdown). There is a small but clean pool, along with some children's play equipment (with a laundry line full of drying clothes strung across the yard during our visit).

US$50-100

Cozy and charismatic, ◖ **Hotel Casagrande B&B** (7a Calle NO, tel. 504/772-0772, casa grandecomayagua@yahoo.es, US$50 s, US60 d, breakfast included) is a nine-room colonial hotel with carved wood furniture and bathrooms decorated with hand-painted tiles. It's reminiscent of the colonial hotels in places like Antigua, Guatemala, and we wish there were more places like this. There soon may be, as Casa Grande is planning an annex across the street. One more plus? Although they do raise rates during Semana Santa, it's only by about US$10.

Modern, and a bit overpriced considering the so-so service, is the motel-style **Hotel Santa María** (tel. 504/772-7872 or 504/772-8934, fax 504/772-7719, US$58 s/d), on the San Pedro–Tegucigalpa highway just outside of town. Rooms have air-conditioning, hot water, telephone, and cable TV.

FOOD
Snacks and Light Meals

For cheap *licuados,* sandwiches, and baked goods, plus outdoor tables on a pleasant plaza, try the **Rycle Repostería y Cafe** (tel. 504/772-2331, 8 A.M.–8:30 P.M. daily), right across from the Iglesia de la Merced. One block north of there, **Coffee and Cakes** (tel. 504/772-1729, 7:30 A.M.–5:30 P.M. Mon.–Fri., 8 A.M.–6 P.M. Sat.) smells delicious as you walk by and also serves meals like roast chicken. A nice place to cool off with an ice cream is **Helados Eskimo** (8 A.M.–10 P.M. daily), located between the Catedral de Santa María and the municipality building on *parque central.*

The ubiquitous **Espresso Americano** is near the Iglesia de la Merced.

Honduran

The nicest place to eat in town, both for the setting and the food, is ◖ **Villa Real** (tel. 504/772-0101, restvillareal@yahoo.com, 11 A.M.–10 P.M. Tues.–Sat.), a block east of the Catedral de Santa María. Tables are set around a grassy courtyard garden, attractively lit up at night, in a restored colonial Comayagua house just off the *parque.* The restaurant owners are gracious hosts, happy to show visitors around the different rooms of the house either before or after eating, to admire colonial furniture, decorations, and art. The kitchen makes very good traditional Honduran food, and a nice *sopa Villa Real* with chicken, toasted tortilla, tomato, cheese, and cream.

Right next to the church is **Plaza Colonial** (7:30 A.M.–9 P.M. daily), one of the more atmospheric restaurants in town and always busy. The Honduran standards (namely, grilled meats) are US$5–8, while the set meal (at breakfast, lunch, or dinner) is just US$3. Another attractive midrange restaurant with Honduran standards is **Gota de Limón** (9 A.M.–midnight Mon.–Sat., 6 P.M. onwards Sun.), with *pupusas* for US$2.50 and steak or chicken entrées for around US$7.

On the south side of the main square, in a restored building, is the rather ordinary buffet-style **Casa Castillo** (11 A.M.–9 P.M. Tues.–Sun.), which has low-priced breakfasts, *comida corriente, baleadas,* and other munchies.

Around the corner from the main square is **D'Barros y Mariscos** (tel. 504/771-6184, 9 A.M.–3 A.M. Tues.–Sun.), with wood tables, and everything from US$3 sandwiches to US$8 shrimp dishes. (Don't believe that the late hours are kept on weekdays, despite what we were told.)

There are countless inexpensive eateries around town; one with a bit of charm is the **Portal Colonial** (8 A.M.–5 P.M. Mon.–Thurs., 8 A.M.–9 P.M. Fri.–Sat.), serving typical breakfasts (eggs, beans, and tortillas) as well as lunches and dinners of things like tacos, pork chops, and beef roast for US$2.50.

Around the corner is **Golosinas Doña Viki,** serving Honduran "snack" food: enchiladas, tacos, *baleadas,* and blended fruit-milk drinks.

Packed with locals is **Comida Rápida Dimas y María,** with a similar menu of Honduran standards.

International

Restaurante Mang Ying (9 A.M.–9:30 P.M. daily), on the boulevard near Hotel Quan, serves up heaping plates of chop suey, chow mein, and other dishes at reasonable prices.

Out on the highway, about one kilometer south of Comayagua, is **El Torito** (tel. 504/772-7113, 11:30 A.M.–2:30 P.M. and 5:30–10 P.M. daily), serving up very good and hugely portioned beef, pork, and chicken dishes at midrange prices.

Groceries

If you want to pick up some groceries or other supplies, try the **Supermercado Colonial,** by the Tegucigalpa bus terminal.

INFORMATION AND SERVICES
Information

The municipality has trained high-quality guides, available at the *alcadía,* or mayor's office. They can offer a lot of information about the local churches and museums. We really enjoyed our walk around town with Mito, who can also be contacted directly at tel. 504/3369-1871.

Some limited tourist information is available at the **Casa Cultural Comayagüense** (also known as El Portal de los Encuentros, tel. 504/772-2028, 9 A.M.–5 P.M. Mon.–Thurs., 9 A.M.–9 P.M. Fri., 8 A.M.–noon and 5–9 P.M. Sat.), which can also help find local guides, such as Ermis Banegas (tel. 504/3369-1871), who can take visitors on day trips to the Montaña de Comayagua National Park for US$20 a day. A small *guía turística* (tourist guide) can be purchased at the Museo de Comayagua.

Banks

BGA, Banco de Occidente, Banco Atlántida, and others will exchange dollars or travelers checks. Banco Atlántida has a cash machine, which works only with Visa cards, and receives MoneyGrams. Wires from Western Union can be picked up at **Banco Ficensa** (8 A.M.–4 P.M. Mon.–Fri., 8 A.M.–noon Sat.).

Communications

Hondutel is behind the Catedral de Santa María (7 A.M.–8:30 P.M. daily). Next door is **Honducor,** with EMS fast-mail service available (8 A.M.–noon and 1–4 P.M. Mon.–Fri., 8 A.M.–noon Sat.).

Among the several Internet places in town are **La Red Internet** (8 A.M.–10 P.M. daily), next to the cathedral on the park, charging US$1 per hour. On the boulevard are **Neom Macro Net** (tel. 504/772-4495 or 504/772-2418, 8 A.M.–10 P.M. daily) and **Oficom Internet** (8 A.M.–8 P.M. Mon.–Fri., 11 A.M.–5 P.M. Sun., next to the Hotel Emperador), offering international and domestic calls as well as Internet. Not far from the main square is **Café Net.**

Laundry

Laundry can be washed at **Lavandería Ebenezer** near the Iglesia de la Merced.

Emergencies

For medical problems, **Centro Médico San Rafael** (tel. 504/772-0068, 24 hours) has a competent doctor and is not too expensive.

GETTING THERE AND AWAY
Bus

Buses to **Tegucigalpa** are offered by **Transportes Catrachos,** five blocks south of the square. The buses run every half hour 5 A.M.–5 P.M. (US$2, 90 minutes). Buses to **La Paz** can also be caught here (US$0.70, one hour). **Transportes Rivera** (tel. 504/772-1208), a block farther south on the same street, has buses hourly to **San Pedro Sula** 5 A.M.–4 P.M. (US$2, three hours). Alternatively, you can take a taxi out to the highway and flag down a bus headed in either direction with minimum hassle.

Empresa San Miguel (tel. 504/772-0611), half a block south of the Rivera terminal, runs buses to **Marcala** five times a day 6:30 A.M.–2 P.M. (US$2, 2.5 hours, or less to La Paz or San Pedro Tutule for Guajiquíro).

Car

From Comayagua, the highway west to Siguatepeque (32 kilometers) and San Pedro Sula (160 kilometers) and east to Tegucigalpa (85 kilometers) is kept in fairly good condition all year. In either direction, the road ascends steeply into the mountains ringing the Comayagua Valley.

NEAR COMAYAGUA
Parque Nacional Montaña de Comayagua

Only seven kilometers from Comayagua is the edge of Montaña de Comayagua National Park, covering 30,094 hectares, of which 6,600 hectares form the core zone. The highest point in the park is **El Portillo,** 2,407 meters. The cloud forest is not one of the country's finest, certainly nothing compared to Celaque or Sierra de Agalta, but sizable patches of cloud forest remain, populated by quetzals, toucans, eagles, deer, monkeys, and a few pumas. You can hike into the park from the villages of **Río Blanco** and **Río Negro,** both reached via dirt road from **San Jerónimo,** 12 kilometers from Comayagua by dirt road. (It's about an hour's drive from Comayagua to Río Negro.) In San Jerónimo, ask for the Gonzalez family for more information.

Near Río Negro is a lovely waterfall hidden

amid the dense forest, about a two-hour hike round-trip from Río Negro, along a clearly marked trail. Several other hikes nearby are also possible, with guides (easily found in Río Negro, or the park caretaker may be able to help). Off the road to La Libertad, you can also enter through **Tres Pinos** or **Zona Helada.** Reputedly, two trucks leave Comayagua daily to Río Negro, one shortly before and one shortly after midday—ask around near the market for more information. It's also possible to get out on the road early in the day and look for a *jalón.*

Ermis Banegas (tel. 504/3369-1871) is a guide who can also arrange transportation, or call the Casa Cultural Comayagüense for more information (tel. 504/772-2028). Private transportation to the park is a hefty US$63, for anywhere up to 10 people, and guiding is another US$20 a day. There are well-marked trails, so a guide is really optional. If you decide to stay the night, there are simple cabins in the park for US$6 per person (meals are available too). Independent travelers who don't have a car should plan on staying the night, as rides up leave around 11 A.M. or noon, and rides back aren't available later in the afternoon.

Topographical maps covering the park are 1:50,000 *Comayagua 2659 II* and *Agalteca 2759 III.*

Enrique Cano Soto Air Force Base (Palmerola)

For much of the 1980s, Palmerola was essentially a U.S. military enclave, from which the Contra war against the Sandinista government in Nicaragua was directed. More recently, the base has been used in the war against drugs.

Growing pressure from Honduran citizens and politicians against U.S. presence has led to a reduction in the number of personnel at the base. In 1995, more than 2,000 U.S. military were housed here; that number dropped to 450 by 1996. At last report, the number of military personnel at the base was around 1,000. Despite de facto U.S. control, the base—a couple of kilometers southeast of Comayagua on the highway toward Tegucigalpa—is now officially under the Honduran flag.

La Paz

The capital of the department of the same name, La Paz has little to interest the casual traveler. It's a frequent stop-off point for those visiting the mountain country south around Guajiquíro and toward the Salvadoran border. Near La Paz are the ruins of **Yarumela and Chircal,** believed to be two of the oldest ruins sites in Honduras. Reportedly only a few mounds are visible at both sites.

One block from the market (turn north at the Banco de Occidente) is **Hotel y Restaurante Alis** (tel. 504/774-3179, US$5 d with shared bathroom and fan, US$10.50 d with private bathroom, fan, and TV), with decent accommodations and food. **Las Champas,** one block north of the soldier statue near the entrance to town, has inexpensive *comida corriente* and snacks.

Six buses daily leave to Marcala between 5 A.M. and 2 P.M. (US$1.50, two hours on a paved road). To Guajiquíro, one bus leaves daily at noon, takes the Marcala road for half an hour, then turns into the hills for another bumpy 2.5 hours, US$1. Buses to Comayagua leave all day until late afternoon, US$0.70, one hour. All buses leave several blocks north of the square, between the market and the soldier statue.

San Pedro de Tutule and Guajiquíro

Roughly 30 kilometers southwest of La Paz on the road to Marcala, set two kilometers off the highway, is the town of San Pedro de Tutule, a market town for the villages in the surrounding mountains. San Pedro de Tutule, along with the region around La Esperanza, is one of the last bastions of pure Lenca Indians in the country. Should you find yourself in this lovely, rustic little town, **Hospedaje San Pedro** (tel. 504/933-0599, US$2 pp) has four basic rooms. The attached restaurant serves a generous *plato típico* with truly delectable hot pepper–flecked white cheese for US$1.25.

High in the mountains above Tutule, about two hours by rough dirt road, is Guajiquíro. The quiet Lenca village with a simple parish church is perched on the hillside, with an impressive view across the valley below. From here, you can hike up into the **Reserva Biológica Guajiquíro,** covering 67 square kilometers of pine and cloud forest, interspersed with patches of farmland and small ranches. The highest part of the reserve rests on a high mesa, with several small peaks of more than 2,200 meters. While hardly in a pristine state, the park is nonetheless a scenic and relaxed mountain area for a couple of days of hiking, camping, and bird-watching. Plenty of small mammals, including foxes, wild pigs, deer, and even a few cats live in the thickest patches of forest. The forests of Guajiquíro are famed for having all the different pine species found in the Honduran highlands, sometimes even visible all on a single hillside. On clear days, from the more southerly peaks around Guajiquíro are dramatic views of the volcanoes across the border in El Salvador. A region near here called Opatoro is also reported (by Robert Gallardo) to have fine cloud forest and bird-watching territory, as well as a decent dirt road driving as high as 1,800 meters.

Topographical maps covering the reserve are 1:50,000 *Opatoro 2658 III* and *San Pedro Tutule 2658 IV.*

MARCALA

South of the Valle de Comayagua, the highway winds up into the mountains to Marcala, the main town in an area that produces some of the finest coffee in Honduras. Marcala is a pleasingly tranquil Honduran town with friendly townsfolk. There's not much in the way of tourist sights per se in town, but it's a great base from which to go on a tour of an organic coffee farm, or to go walking through very lovely and safe countryside, dotted with several waterfalls and patches of cloud forest.

This is one of the last areas of indigenous Lenca culture, a stretch of mountain country extending north to La Esperanza and Gracias. Marcala is an excellent starting point for an exploration of **La Ruta Lenca,** and there are direct buses that take passengers the 36 kilometers to La Esperanza (10 of which are paved), from where one can connect with

transportation to San Juan and on to Gracias. Marcala is also on the way to an infrequently used and picturesque route to cross between Honduras and El Salvador, although this route may be challenging in the rainy season.

Most of Marcala's life revolves around **coffee.** The strict control of altitude around Marcala provides the beans with an export quality rare in Honduras. An organic cooperative in town is the first Honduran organization to have exported coffee to international locations, starting with Germany and quickly expanding to other countries (including having sold beans to that most famous of coffee shops, Starbucks). To witness the coffee-picking season at its height, it is best to visit from mid-November to the end of March. A movement was afoot with coffee growers to re-institute the formerly annual Feria del Café in February.

Marcala's yearly Feria Patronal (Patron Saint Festival) is held during the last two weeks of September, with religious ceremonies, street parades, food stands, carnival games, and more. The church, **San Miguel Arcangel,** merits a peek inside, with tall wood pillars that hold up a soaring ceiling shaped like a boat's hull.

Local volunteers have organized an active tourism committee to promote Marcala and the vicinity, which has built an information kiosk in the downtown park.

Marcala's climate is usually not too hot during the day but cool in the evenings. The June–October rainy season brings regular afternoon and evening downpours. Nothing a good spirit and raincoat can't handle, but better yet take the attitude of the locals, who calmly resign themselves to another cup of coffee and sweet bread until the storm passes.

Cooperatives

Local cooperative **RAOS** (tel. 504/764-5181, mielpez37@gmail.com, 8 A.M.–4 P.M. Mon.–Fri., 8 A.M.–11 A.M. Sat.) has its office two blocks from the park, where you can pick up bags of their organic coffee, handmade soaps, and local honey. RAOS can arrange tours of members' **organic coffee farms** (US$5 pp, less

© AMY E. ROBERTSON

Coffee grown around Marcala is widely considered to be the best in the country.

for a group), with a day or two notice—either contact them directly or ask at the tourist office for information. Lunch on the farm or even a night in the farmer's simple but clean home can also be arranged. A visit during harvest season (approximately November 10 through March) can be especially interesting.

The **Cooperativa Unidas Para Progresar** (tel. 504/764-5946, www.coomupl.org) is a type of women's credit union where you can pick up bags of organic coffee, jams, honey, pottery, fruit wine, and other products, as well as arrange for visits to micro-businesses and organic farms. Another women's cooperative that sells locally made products and can arrange for outings to farms is **Cooperative Mujeres de la Sierra** (tel. 504/764-5029).

Accommodations

By far the nicest digs in town are at **Casa-Hotel Frissman** (tel. 504/764-5854, US$26 s, US$29–47 d), with clean and spacious rooms in a big orange building (with parking) on the outskirts of town. Prices vary depending on the room layout, but all have attractive wood

furniture and nice bathrooms. A pot of coffee is set out in the mornings.

Three kilometers outside of town on the road to La Esperanza, in a bucolic forest setting, is **La Casona Hotel Campestre** (tel. 504/764-5718, US$18 s, US$23 d), decent for those who have their own wheels or really like being out in the woods in peaceful surroundings. *Casona* means big house, which is exactly what this is, with a shared living room complete with piano. Additional rooms have been built in a newer wing, but the place remains dated and rather worn. There's a swimming pool (filled only during the summer months, roughly March–May, and no restaurant, so be prepared to head into town for all meals.

Of the cheaper hotels, **Hotel Nueva Jerusalen** (tel. 504/774-5909, US$16 s, US$18–21 d) is best, with tile floors and reasonably clean rooms. There are 40 rooms set up motel-style around a parking lot, with another 8–10 in the works.

Less expensive but also acceptable is **Hotel Roxana** (tel. 504/764-5866, US$10 s, US$16 d), across from the post office and the street market. Each room has a private bath with hot water (although you should make sure your hot shower works before settling in), cable TV, and private parking. Bring your flip-flops for the shower. The hotel also operates a cafeteria, although you can get a better meal elsewhere in town. Roxana has a 10 P.M. curfew, but it's hard to imagine a reason to be out later than that in Marcala.

Food

Driven El Mirador (tel. 504/764-5540, open until 9 P.M. daily) offers local Honduran cuisine, including breakfasts, steak, chicken and fish, and light snacks like simple sandwiches and salads, and accordingly high prices. Since the owner also runs the Hotel La Casona, outside of town with its very own set of tilapia fish ponds, locals swear by the fried-fish platters.

The buffet-style **Casa Gloria Restaurante** (tel. 504/764-5869) is a good bet for quick, filling, and good meals, with an array of meats, chicken, rice, vegetables, and other side dishes during lunch, and eggs, beans, cheese, and ham typical for dinner. The restaurant, right in the central park, is decorated with paintings, pottery, and sculptures by local artists.

Newcomer **Malú** has quickly established itself as the top restaurant in town, although the menu is filled with the standards, such as *plato típico* (US$3.70), burgers (US$3), tacos (US$2.50), and *anafre* (US$1.50). The place is clean and cute, and there is a "traveler's bookcase" where you can exchange that paperback you've just finished reading.

Comedor Mexicano, on the main street a block and a half down from Banhcafe, serves up tasty burritos, enchiladas, hamburgers, and Honduran dishes at reasonable prices. The owner lived in the United States and happily speaks English to tourist customers and serves up tasty Mexican burritos, American-style hamburgers, beef plates, enchiladas, and typical Honduran dishes for a reasonable price. It's a good place to watch a sports match on TV and drink a beer.

Local legend **Pupuseria El Paso Colegial** (late afternoon and early evening) serves up *pupusas,* the standard Salvadoran snack, cooked by a gregarious *señora* on the front patio of her house on the main entrance road to town.

If you're looking for a change of cuisine, **Palacio Chino** near the Hotel Nueva Jerusalen serves up Chinese standards 10 A.M.–10 P.M. daily.

For good pastries, fruit juices, and even baguettes at low prices, head to **La Princesita,** just off the main *parque.*

Information and Services

A **tourist information kiosk** (10 A.M.–7 P.M. Wed.–Mon.) has been built in the town *parque.* It has maps and information on things to visit and do in the surrounding area.

There are no ATMs in town and credit cards are not accepted anywhere, but you can change dollars at Banco de Occidente. To make phone calls, go to **Hondutel** (tel. 504/764-5398) on the main street, or use one of the public phones outside with phone cards purchased from local stores. Two of the many Internet shops in town, both of which also have low-price international phone calls, are **Café Internet** (tel. 504/764-5630), a block from the park, and **Global Online,** one block west of the church.

Honducor (tel. 504/764-5758, 8 A.M.–noon and 2–5 P.M. Mon.–Fri., 8 A.M.–noon Sat.) is next to the church. The **police** can be contacted at 504/764-5715, and the station is a block north of the church. One good private clinic for general medical concerns is **Clínica Moreno** (tel. 504/764-5478, open daily), one block from the police station, attended by a friendly female doctor. **Farmacia Lamar** (tel. 504/764-5214) and **Medicinas La Economía** (tel. 504/764-5303) are both located on the main street, one block past Hotel Roxana.

Getting There and Away

Lila (tel. 504/764-5729) runs six buses to Tegucigalpa between 4:30 A.M. and 2 P.M. (US$4 for the 3.5–4 hour ride), and one bus to San Pedro Sula that departs at 5:15 A.M. (US$8, five hours). Buses to Comayagua leave at 6:30 A.M., 8 A.M., 11 A.M., 1 P.M., and 2 P.M. (US$3, three hours). There are two buses to La

Esperanza each morning (US$3, 1.5–2 hours) and one bus to the border with El Salvador that leaves at 5 A.M. daily (five hours). Check where to catch the bus to the border, but for the rest you can flag them down at the Texaco gas station on the edge of town.

Excursions near Marcala

The small community of **La Estanzuela** is about 10 kilometers outside of Marcala, three kilometers off the paved road that leads toward La Esperanza. Visitors will find well-marked trails through pine forests, coffee farms, fishponds, and a high waterfall with shallow bathing pools. Nearby is **La Cueva del Gigante,** or the Cave of the Giant, located a couple of kilometers above the waterfall, with vestiges of a very early Mesoamerican settlement. More information on the cave and the pools can be found through Señora Alba Luz Guevara at her house next to the soccer field, who can also help set up horseback tours, or by calling 504/783-2141. A guesthouse has been set up in the community as well. To reach La Estanzuela by car, take the highway to La Esperanza, then turn left on a dirt road after seven kilometers. After another 200 meters you will reach a sign; take a right. Follow the road by some houses, reaching the town after 2.5 kilometers. Cars can be left in the soccer field. The pools *(balnearios)* are a little more than one kilometer from the field.

El Chiflador is an impressive waterfall located in a patch of cloud and pine forest above Marcala. It provides the town's water. To get there, either drive or walk up the road toward El Salvador and ask in Barrio La Victoria for the turnoff uphill. About four kilometers from town look for a wire fence with a gate on the right, where a steep trail heads down to the top of the waterfall.

Another waterfall, with more facilities for tourists, is **Las Orquideas,** a small forest reserve with a high waterfall, and also with changing rooms, a picnic area, and walking trails. Trails allow visitors to appreciate a wide variety of rare flora, including the national flower, the orchid. It's located 1.5 kilometers

Hikes in the countryside near Marcala lead to coffee farms and waterfalls.

© AMY E. ROBERTSON

VICINITY OF MARCALA

To La Esperanza

LA ESTANZUELA ★

To San Pedro de Tutule →

LA CHORRERA ★

■ MARCALA ○

LAS ORQUÍDEAS ★

EL CHIFLADOR ★

0   5 mi
0   5 km

© AVALON TRAVEL

To El Salvador

past the town of Chinacla, which is 2.5 kilometers from Marcala on the road to La Paz. Six hundred meters after the entrance to Chinacla, there is a dirt road next to the church. Follow the dirt road, taking a right at any and all turnoffs, and you should reach the pools after 1.2 kilometers.

The closest waterfall to town is **La Chorrera,** near a pine forest, and with changing rooms and an area for camping. Four kilometers down the road to La Esperanza take a right on a dirt road, where you will see a sign for a school. La Chorrera is just half a kilometer along the road.

If you have your own transportation, these routes are better approached with a four-wheel-drive if your visit coincides with the rainy season.

SOUTH OF MARCALA TOWARD EL SALVADOR

Beyond Marcala, the road continues through lovely scenic countryside of coffee and corn farms and pine forest down into the lower,

hotter canyon country near the Salvadoran border. About two hours' drive from Marcala toward the border are two traditional Lenca communities worth visiting, **Santa Elena** and **Yarula.** Santa Elena is known for the local corn festival in October, as well the Baile de los Negritos in March, a traditional dance that mixes a Christian homage to the town's patron saint, Santiago, with local Lencan traditions.

Near Santa Elena, a couple of hours' hike past the village of Azacualpa (local guide required), are a series of cave paintings well worth a visit. Yarula is well known for its delicious yellow corn and tortillas. There are a couple of eateries but no accommodations in either town, so plan on a day trip back to Marcala or onward to El Salvador. A bus from Marcala heads this direction, or you can seek a *jalón.*

Also in this area is **Nahuanterique,** once part of the disputed territory between El Salvador and Honduras left over from the 1969 Soccer War. Nearby are pine forests, bird-watching, rare flora, lakes, and waterfalls. An active indigenous organization was at last check building no-frills (no electricity) tourist cabins. For more information, inquire with the organization CONDREZAFH (tel. 504/764-5411), or visit their office in Marcala.

The Salvadoran Border and Perquín

Farther down the road in the hot lowlands, the dirt road crosses a remote border post, with a Honduran official on one side but no one from El Salvador on the other (at last report). The Honduran agent (a friendly fellow) will stamp your passport and let you back in if you come on the same route. Farther along you will come to a Salvadoran police checkpoint, where your passport will be scrutinized. Tourists should not have to pay a fee at either point; however, if you leave El Salvador by another border, you will likely have to pay a small fine for not having a proper entry stamp.

The first town across the border is Perquín, a picturesque little town with camping areas and nature centers nearby, and a very interesting

Museo de la Revolución dedicated to the civil war. The annual **Festival de Invierno** (Winter Festival), in August, is famous all over Central America for its music, artists, and crowds enjoying the fun. Perquín and Marcala are working to jointly develop tourism in the area, and information on the region is available at www .marcalaperquin.org. There is a small tourist booklet on the region surrounding Perquín available at Marcala's tourist kiosk. Perquín is about three hours away from Marcala by car or bus.

Pico Pijol and Yoro

The cowboy towns of Morazán and Yoro are the gateways to infrequently visited cloud forest parks of Pico Pijol and Montaña de Yoro, as well as the back door to the wild, rugged Olancho territory.

MORAZÁN AND PICO PIJOL
Morazán
Morazán, a dusty town of 8,500 set two kilometers off the Yoro highway, is 45 kilometers from Santa Rita in the middle of the Valle de Cataguana, below the Sierra de Pijol. Morazán makes a good base for visiting Pico Pijol National Park, as it's the closest town with lodging and supplies. Located a kilometer or so off the highway, Morazán is strung along a bumpy east-west dirt road, with a DIPPSA gas station in the middle to serve as a reference point.

There are one or two small hotels, *comedores,* and a Hondutel office. There is also a local COHDEFOR office, one block uphill from the gas station, then one block to the left, with some limited information on Pico Pijol (on the whole the office is not geared for prospective campers and hikers, but is your best bet for help in finding a guide).

Campers will find several stores in town offering the usual assortment of packaged foods, while a good selection of fruits and vegetables can be found in the many stands lining the main street.

Parque Nacional Pico Pijol
In this little-explored cloud-forest reserve, the sheer-walled mountains of Pico Pijol are a major water source for the El Cajón reservoir and San Pedro Sula. The land has been set aside as a protected area more in the interests of resource conservation than tourism. No trails have been developed in the 11,206-hectare park, apart from those used by local hunters, but it is possible to explore the upper reaches of the forest with the help of guides and a machete. The imposing rock massif has several peaks, the highest being Pico Pijol, at 2,282 meters. On the western edge of the massif rises Cerro Mulato, 1,852 meters, from which you can see San Pedro Sula on a clear day. Four major rivers flow off the mountains: Río Pijol, Río Pataste, Río Chilistagua, and Río Jacagua. The forest boasts 237 wildlife species, including a significant quetzal population.

Much of the mountains' lower-elevation forest cover has been cut down to make room for coffee plantations, *milpas* (cornfields), or grazing land, but the core zone of the park, above 1,800 meters, is still in good shape. The south side of the Río Pijol valley is particularly pristine, due to the precipitously steep mountain slopes.

Hikers aiming to get into the central, highest section of the park can choose between several potential access routes. From Morazán, the quickest way is from the village of Porvenir de Paya, reached by pickup truck or foot via Mojimán. Another option is to go in from the southeast side of the park, from the *aldea* of Alto Pino, the end of a dirt road turning off the Morazán–Yoro highway several kilometers east of Morazán. Near the village of Tegucigalpita, before Alto Pino, is a major cave system of unknown depth, with wide chambers and an underground waterfall near the cave mouth. An aboveground waterfall can be visited by hiking in from Tegucigalpita.

PARQUE NACIONAL PICO PIJOL

Morazán

Río Cuyamapa

Mojiman

Río San Juan
Nueva Esperanza

Triunfo
Cuyamapa

Río Cuyamapa

Patuste

San Juan Camalote

El Porvenir de Paya

Los Murillos

Río

El Ocotillo
Pajarillos

▲ Cerro Pajarillos 1,575m

▲ 1,790m

Río Pijol

Core

Cuevitas

Zone

▲ 1,821m

▲ 2,015m

▲ 2,142m

Pico Pijol 2,282m

Linda Vista

Cerro El Sargento 1,852m ▲

Alto Pino

Río Chilistagua

Santa Marta

Tegucigalpita

Río Jacagua

0   2 mi

0   2 km

© AVALON TRAVEL

Along the Río Pijol, reached from the village of El Ocotillo, is a triple waterfall called **Las Piratas,** an excellent swimming spot surrounded by forest, a short 20-minute walk from the road. Visitors can get out to Las Piratas and back to Morazán in the same day without any difficulty by catching rides on pickup trucks or walking from Morazán via San Juan Camalote. Buses do go out to some of the villages in the park from Morazán, but the schedule changes regularly, so you have to ask in Morazán for departure times.

Guides can be arranged through the AECOPIJOL office in Yoro and are highly recommended given the lack of established trails. The COHDEFOR office in Morazán has a large topographical wall map that can give you an idea of the park's geography. Topographical maps covering the park are 1:50,000 *El Negrito 2661 I* and *Las Flores 2661 II.*

"No-see-ums," or tiny biting gnats, are abundant at Pico Pijol, so be sure to bring heavy-duty repellent.

YORO AND VICINITY

Beyond Morazán, the highway winds up into the hills to the east before descending on the far side into the Valle de Yoro. At the eastern end of the valley is Yoro, a major market town for the region and a pleasant rural Honduran town. This is the end of the paved road, some 110 kilometers from Santa Rita. Many of Yoro's streets are dirt, although several have been paved in recent years (thus depriving local shoe-shine boys of good business). The church in Yoro holds the remains of Padre José Manuel Subirana. Known as La Santa Misión, he was a tireless missionary and protector of the native Tolupán in Yoro; he died on November 27, 1864. Subirana is still revered among the *campesinos* of central Honduras, many of whom consider him a saint.

There's not much for tourists in Yoro itself, but it serves as a base to visit the nearby Montaña de Yoro National Park and the colonial mission church of **Luquigue.** Nights are cool in Yoro, a pleasant change from the heat of lower-lying Progreso and San Pedro to the west in the Sula Valley.

The town's best annual party is held every June to coincide with the Lluvia de Peces. Villagers come from all parts to dance in the central park on the big night.

Accommodations and Food

The **Hotel Marquez** (tel. 504/671-2805, US$22 s, US$29 d) on the main street is the about the nicest place in town, although that's not saying much. Rooms have air-conditioning, cable TV, and hot water. The restaurant (also about the best in town) is open 7 A.M.–10 P.M. daily.

Less expensive but a decent value is **Hotel**

THE RAIN OF FISH

One and a half kilometers southeast of the town of Yoro, a swampy field called El Llano del Pántano is the site of a most unusual annual rainstorm, according to local legend. During the height of the rainy season, usually sometime in mid-June, a fierce storm will hit in the middle of the night, and in the morning, residents find the fields full of flopping fish! The annual event has become known as the **Lluvia de Peces**, or Rain of Fish.

More skeptical minds have theorized that the fish come upriver from a tributary of the Río Aguán and use the inundation of heavy rain to reach the marsh, where they are accustomed to laying their eggs. Reportedly, some Japanese scientists traveled to Yoro not long ago to solve the mystery – and came away mystified. The devout attribute the phenomenon to the Spanish Catholic missionary Father José Manuel Subirana, who lived in Honduras from 1856 to 1864. Seeing the poverty in which the people of Yoro lived, he prayed for three days and three nights asking God for a miracle to help the poor people by providing food. The Rain of Fish is said to have occurred ever since.

One of Yoro's best annual parties is held to coincide with the special night every June, with villagers from all around coming down to dance on the town square at night.

Palace (tel. 504/671-2229, US$13 s, US$26 d), just down from the Hotel Marquez, which offers clean rooms with private baths, cable TV, and fans.

Another low-price option is the three-story **Hotel Nelson** (tel. 504/671-2269, US$9.50 s, US$10.50 d), in front of the municipal market. The view from the top floor of the Nelson, out across the surrounding valley and mountains, is very fine.

A great spot to sit in the open air under a *champa* and have a nice lunch or dinner and a *cerveza* or *jugo natural* is **Rancho Típico,** two

blocks from the park. The rotisserie chicken is the specialty (US$3 for the dinner with sides), and hamburgers, steak, and fish are also available.

The best cheap food in Yoro is the *baleadas* (US$0.60) at **El Triunfador Restaurante,** three blocks from the park. **Expreso del Rancho** on the park serves a variety of coffees and pastries. **La Tortuga Veloz** on the park will change dollars and serves hamburgers and *licuados.*

Information and Services

On the second floor of the kiosk in the middle of the square is **AMY,** or Asociación de Amigos de la Montaña de Yoro (tel. 504/671-2199), where visitors can get some information on the nearby park, but they're not especially helpful to casual travelers. Better to contact the office of **AECOPIJOL,** the Asociación Ecológica para la Protección del Parque Nacional Pico Pijol (tel. 504/691-0412 or 504/9720-3454, or aecopijol@yahoo.es), located opposite the park. They welcome visitors on their own research trips and can help provide information and arrange a guide (strongly recommended) if they're not going out anytime soon.

Banco Atlántida on the east side of the square can change dollars and now has a functioning ATM. Across the street are **Hondutel** (7 a.m.–9 p.m. Mon.–Fri, 7 a.m.–noon Sat.) and the post office. Internet is available at **Businessnet** in front of the Hotel Marquez or at **Emagic** near the studio of Radio Yoro, both US$1.25 per hour or US$0.75 for a half hour.

Getting There and Away

Buses to San Pedro Sula depart at 4:45 p.m., 7 p.m., 9 p.m., 11 p.m. and 12:20 a.m. with **Transportes Urbina,** charging US$6 for the three-hour ride. Buses from Yoro go via Sulaco and Cedros to Tegucigalpa once daily at 7 a.m. (US$8), or else take a bus to Santa Rita and catch a Tegucigalpa-bound bus from the highway there.

Buses run east through the mountains to Mangulile and La Unión in Olancho, near La

Muralla National Park, but not with a regular schedule, and depending on the road conditions (both in terms of potholes and banditry). Private pickups still run the route and will take passengers on the three-hour ride, usually leaving by late morning at the latest. Ask at the market on the main street. The road to La Unión has exceptionally lovely scenery, and its safety is reported to have improved in recent years. Check with locals, preferably the local police, before taking this route.

The scenic dirt mountain road to Olanchito (101 kilometers) via Jocón is generally in good condition and takes two hours in a private car. Be sure to check in Yoro on the current state of the road, as the rains sometimes cut off through traffic.

Parque Nacional Montaña de Yoro

Just south of Yoro is this broad, forest-blanketed mountain, in theory reserved as a national park and a protected important local watershed. Environmental protection, however, is limited in practice, with an average estimated 309 hectares deforested annually since 1987, when the park was inaugurated. Local authorities have failed to enforce prohibitions on the growth of communities at the edge of the park, and deforestation continues unchecked. The park covers 15,366 hectares, about one-third of which falls in the department of Yoro and the remainder in the department of Francisco Morazán. Although the cloud forest atop the mountain (2,282 meters) is fairly intact, wildlife is scarce, what with the local *campesinos* frequently venturing up to hunt game.

Tourist infrastructure is pretty much nonexistent, but it is possible to get into what's left of the forest with local guides. The best access to the park is via the beautiful little village of **San José Machigua,** visible from Yoro high on the mountain, where COHDEFOR maintains a small cabin that can house visitors, with prior arrangement through AMY in Yoro. To get there, catch a ride or walk three kilometers from Yoro to the Presa de Yoro, a small dam on the Río Machigua. From here, it takes three hours to walk to San José, located at

the transition between pine and broadleaf forest. A fun way to get to San José de Machigua is on horseback with Cristóbal Vásquez (tel. 504/671-2864 in Yoro). He has a coffee plantation just below San José and charges US$6 per day for use of his horses. He is very knowledgeable about the area. In Machigua, visitors can hire a guide (US$7 a day, plus food for the guide) to take them up to the summit in a full day's walk. A variety of flora can be found in the park, including mahogany, fruit trees, and medicinal plants; fauna is rare. It's best to avoid the eastern and southern sides of the park, which are known for marijuana production.

For more information on the park, either stop in at the AMY office on the second floor of the kiosk on Yoro's central square or go to COHDEFOR's natural resources office (tel. 504/671-2355) outside of town, just off the El Progreso road.

South of Yoro

Some 25 kilometers west of Yoro on the highway to Santa Rita, just before the village of Punta de Ocote, a dirt road turns southward to Yorito and Sulaco. At Yorito, 12.5 kilometers down this road, a side road continues six kilometers farther to **Luquigue,** a colonial mission church established in 1751 by Franciscan missionaries in an effort to convert the Tolupán Indians who lived in the region at that time. The friars were generally unsuccessful; the Indians were kept there only by force and fled whenever possible. The mission was abandoned shortly after independence from Spain in 1821. The single-domed, whitewashed church, seemingly long forgotten in this isolated little village surrounded by pine-forested mountains, is worth seeing more for the atmosphere and surrounding countryside than the structure itself. Ask around for the *mayordoma,* who will give you the key to go inside to see two simple, carved wooden *retablos* (altarpieces).

The next major town south of Yorito is San Antonio, known for a lovely natural bridge with a river cutting through it, called **Puente Natural de San Antonio.** The bridge, about

THE TOLUPÁN OF MONTAÑA DE LA FLOR

Formerly one of the most widespread indigenous groups in Honduras, the Tolupán – or Jicaque, as they are called by *ladinos* – numbered at last count (the 2001 census) approximately 10,350. In preconquest times, the Tolupán lived across a wide swath of present-day Honduras from northern Olancho almost all the way to the Guatemalan border. Unlike the Pech, a neighboring indigenous group who came originally from the jungles of South America, the Tolupán are thought to have migrated to Honduras from the southwestern United States, as their language, Tol, is closely related to that of the Sioux. Now the Tolupáns are found primarily in the department of Yoro, with a small number in the northernmost corners of Comayagua and Francisco Morazán, and the westernmost tip of Olancho.

Because the Tolupán refused to convert to Catholicism, opting to fight or retreat into the mountains rather than accept Spanish rule, they were a constant target of colonists needing laborers. Many thousands are thought to have died in the construction of the fortress at Omoa, and countless others were enslaved or perished working in dye factories or transporting sarsaparilla.

By the mid-19th century, only about 8,000 Tolupáns still clung to their traditional ways in the mountains of Yoro, living in villages surrounded by wooden palisades deep in the forests and avoiding contact with outsiders whenever possible. Unfortunately for these remaining communities, they happened to live in an area rich in sarsaparilla; in the 1860s, the world market for this root boomed when adding it to beverages became all the rage. The governor of Yoro, Jesús Queróz, ordered his soldiers to force the Tolupáns to gather the root year-round, even in the torrential rainy season, and march it to the coast at Trujillo or Tela.

This bleak period of slavery, which continued into the 20th century, is burned deep into the minds of the surviving Tolupáns. They still speak of how, when an Indian died from exhaustion or disease while carrying sarsaparilla, the soldiers only stopped the column long enough to redistribute the dead man's load, but not long enough to bury him.

A handful of Tolupán families, desperate to flee the Yoro soldiers and live in peace, learned of an unpopulated forest on the far side of the Montaña de Yoro, out of the jurisdiction of the Yoro governor. They escaped there in 1864, just ahead of pursuing soldiers. The small group, led by men who had taken the names Juan Martínez, Francisco Martínez, Pedro Soto, and León Soto, settled in a region called Montaña de la Flor, at that time raw forest.

The villages of Montaña de la Flor now have about 700 inhabitants, all descendants of those first three families, and they are the only Tolupán communities retaining some of their original traditions and language. Most villagers still speak Tol, although all also speak Spanish. They do not drink alcohol, do not practice Catholicism, and for the most part disdain surrounding *ladino* villagers and their money-oriented ways. It is said that the Tolupáns of Montaña de la Flor are the only ones to still observe the traditional death rite of keeping vigil with the deceased in the kitchen for 24 hours, the body wrapped in a sheet, while those who keep watch quietly contemplate the life of the deceased.

The communities are also some of Honduras's poorest, plagued by extreme poverty.

How long their traditional ways will continue is uncertain, as Montaña de la Flor can now be reached by road from nearby *ladino* villages and towns, and some Tolupáns have married with *ladinos*. One can hope they will fare better than their former compatriots in Yoro, who only vaguely remember their Tolupán past.

six meters high and some 20 meters long, is a kilometer outside of San Antonio—ask anyone in town to point the way. Keep an eye out for a large ceiba tree, which marks the spot. Inside the cave are fine spots to swim in the Quebrada Los Anises, as well as thermal waters cascading down from the roof! It's a lovely spot to camp, and no one will bother you, except during Holy Week, when locals come to enjoy the waters.

The mountains on either side of the Yoro-Sulaco road are the last bastion of the Tolupán, who once lived from the Guatemalan border to Olancho. In many of the mountain villages, a few elders still speak the language, but it is fast disappearing except in a few isolated communities, particularly around Montaña de la Flor. The best way to get to the main settlement at Montaña de la Flor is via Cedros, north of Tegucigalpa.

Chalmeca

A tiny village on the banks of the Río Jalegua some 15 kilometers northeast of Yoro, Chalmeca is home to a simple chapel containing a carved wooden black Christ statue, venerated by the many inhabitants of Yoro and surrounding parts of north-central Honduras. According to the local legend, the statue miraculously appeared at the foot of an oak tree next to the river at an unknown date in the past and was found by José María Solórzano, who built the chapel to house the statue. By the time Padre José Manuel Subirana arrived in Yoro in the mid-19th century, the Cristo Negro was already famed in the region, and story has it the *padre* paid a visit to Chalmeca to see the statue for himself. On the first of January each year, pilgrims from Yoro and nearby parts of Olancho come to Chalmeca to pay their respects and hold the annual festival for the Cristo Negro.

TEGUCIGALPA AND SOUTHERN HONDURAS

Tegucigalpa and Southern Honduras don't attract many international tourists, but travelers with a little time and an adventurous spirit can find plenty to explore. Set in the mountains at 1,000 meters, Tegucigalpa is the country's capital and a sprawling metropolis, complete with restaurants, luxury hotels, shopping malls, and traffic—as well as attractive colonial churches and interesting museums in the walkable downtown. The cloud forests of La Tigra National Park are a short drive away, and a number of colonial villages are close enough for easy day trips.

Southern Honduras is composed of the departments of El Paraíso, Choluteca, and Valle, and is the country's least visited region. Although not much explored by the average tourist, there are hidden attractions tucked away in the mountains and coastal plains worth seeking out, especially for those passing through on their way to Nicaragua or El Salvador. Highlights include the colonial mining town of Yuscarán, the cigar factories of Danlí, the cloud-forested reserve of La Botija, and the beaches of Isla del Tigre.

PLANNING YOUR TIME

An afternoon downtown and a meal out will be enough to satisfy most travelers' curiosity about the country's capital. An hour from the capital is Parque Nacional La Tigra, with a network of trails through its cloud forest ranging from an easy 45-minute walk to all-day treks that can turn into relaxing overnighters at the ghost mining town of El Rosario. Nearby are the colonial villages of Santa Lucía and Valle

© AMY E. ROBERTSON

HIGHLIGHTS

《 Tegucigalpa's Colonial Center: With its busy *parque central*, colonial churches, and fine museums tracing Honduras's artistic and political history, a stroll through Tegucigalpa's center is obligatory for anyone passing through town (page 376).

《 Valle de Ángeles: This colonial town, set in cool pine forests about the capital, makes a perfect day trip to have a good meal in one of the several restaurants, shop for handicrafts, or just take a stroll (page 403).

《 Parque Nacional La Tigra: Energetic nature-lovers can hike around a network of well-maintained trails through a mountaintop cloud forest and stop off on the way to visit the deserted mining town of El Rosario (page 408).

《 Yuscarán: This classic Honduran colonial mining town, complete with a whitewashed *catedral* and cobblestoned streets, is built on the side of a hill honeycombed with old mines and topped with a cloud-forest reserve (page 416).

《 Danlí: If you're passing through on the way to Nicaragua, Danlí deserves a look to check out one of the several cigar factories in and around town, or come for the **Festival de Maíz,** to watch a rodeo show and try corn in seemingly infinite incarnations (page 419).

《 Isla del Tigre and Amapala: In the Golfo de Fonseca, Isla del Tigre and its only town seem trapped in some sort of time warp and make an unusual sort of beach trip (page 430).

《 Parque Nacional La Botija: Tucked into a remote corner of Honduras, right up against the Nicaraguan border in the mountains above Choluteca, is the infrequently visited, dry tropical forest of La Botija, known for its plentiful wildlife, including white-faced monkeys (page 438).

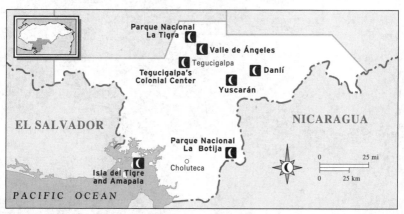

LOOK FOR 《 TO FIND RECOMMENDED SIGHTS, ACTIVITIES, DINING, AND LODGING.

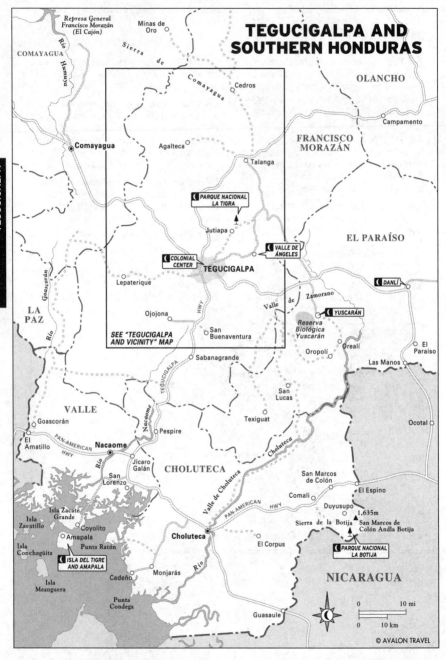

TEGUCIGALPA AND SOUTHERN HONDURAS

COMAYAGUA

Represa General
Francisco Morazán
(El Cajón)

Río Humuya

Minas de
Oro

OLANCHO

Sierra   de   Comayagua

Cedros

Campamento

Comayagua

Agalteca

FRANCISCO
MORAZÁN

Talanga

🏕 PARQUE NACIONAL
LA TIGRA

Jutiapa

EL PARAÍSO

🏕 VALLE DE
ÁNGELES

🏕 COLONIAL
CENTER   TEGUCIGALPA

🏕 DANLÍ

Lepaterique

Valle   de   Zamorano

🏕 YUSCARÁN

Guascorán

Río Guascorán

LA
PAZ

Ojojona

HWY

Reserva
Biológica
Yuscarán

Orealí

El
Paraíso

SEE "TEGUCIGALPA
AND VICINITY" MAP

San
Buenaventura

Oropolí

Las Manos

Sabanagrande

VALLE

Goascorán

TEGUCIGALPA

Nacaome

San
Lucas

Texiguat

Ocotal

El
Amatillo

PAN-AMERICAN   HWY

Nacaome

Jícaro
Galán

Pespire

CHOLUTECA

Valle de Choluteca

Choluteca

San Marcos
de Colón

El Espino

San
Lorenzo

Río Nacaome

PAN-AMERICAN   HWY

Comali

Duyusupo

1,635m

Isla Zacate
Grande

Isla
Zacatillo

Coyolito

Amapala

Punta Ratón

Sierra de la Botija

San Marcos de
Colón Andla Botija

Isla
Conchagüita

🏕 ISLA DEL TIGRE
AND AMAPALA

Choluteca

El Corpus

🏕 PARQUE NACIONAL
LA BOTIJA

Cedeño

Monjarás

Río

NICARAGUA

Isla
Meanguera

Punta
Condega

Guasaule

0   10 mi

0   10 km

© AVALON TRAVEL

de Ángeles, the latter a mecca for handicraft shopping.

Farther afield are Ojojona, Cedros, and Yuscarán, all of which make for entertaining excursions from the city. Yuscarán is especially charming, one of the prettiest little towns in the country, with plenty of cloud forest, petroglyphs, and abandoned mines to keep visitors busy for a day or two.

The highway past Yuscarán continues to the Nicaraguan border at Las Manos via Danlí, a mid-sized town with a few colonial structures and several cigar factories worth a day's visit.

Isla del Tigre, or Amapala, as it is more often referred to, is a popular if off-beat getaway for residents of Tegucigalpa. An island with a volcanic cone in the center and a dozen beaches around it, it takes an overnighter to get a proper taste of the place, and to have time for a boat ride through the other islands and mangrove forests around the Golfo de Fonseca.

The other larger cities of the south—Choluteca, San Lorenzo, and Nacaome—have limited tourist appeal. On the other hand, a couple of the smaller towns are great jumping-off points for explorations of the countryside. El Corpus is a quiet mining village just 17 kilometers—but a world away—from the bustling streets of Choluteca, and an interesting outing if you'r in the neighborhood. Farther east, clo⸱ to the Nicaraguan border and well worı going out of your way for, is the small town of San Marcos de Colón, a base for great hikes in the dry tropical forests of La Botija. Visits to the forest are doable with one night camping out from San Marcos, but it's better to plan for at least two nights to have more opportunity to explore. The towns that produce the famous black and white clay pottery are also located close to Nacaome.

Avoid having to spend the night in any of the border towns discussed in this chapter, as facilities are minimal.

Tour Operators

Greko Tours (tel. 504/239-5998 or 504/239-5999, cell 504/998-0304, www.grekotours .com) runs one-day tours of Tegucigalpa (US$36 solo, or US$18 pp with a group), Valle de Ángeles and Santa Lucía (same prices), La Tigra National Park (US$54 solo or US$21 with a group), as well as farther afield to Comayagua, Amapala, Lago de Yojoa, Olancho, and Copán at reasonable rates for two or more people. Buses with drivers are available for special group trips.

Arrecife Tours (tel. 504/239-1782 or 504/239-1783, www.arrecifetours.com) has similar city and regional tours costing about the same as Greko. It also runs a three-day, two-night tour of Tegucigalpa and vicinity, with hotels included.

Explore Honduras (in Edificio Medicast, Ste. 206, Blvd. Morazán, tel. 504/236-9003 or 504/236-7694, www.explorehonduras.com) is a third company with city and area tours, at slightly higher costs than the other two.

Destinos de Éxito (tel. 504/236-9651, www.destinosdeexito.com) also offers tours of the city, La Tigra, Santa Lucía, and Valle de Ángeles.

TEGUCIGALPA

Tegucigalpa

Honduras's capital, a city of just over one million inhabitants, occupies a high mountain valley around 1,000 meters above sea level, with the Río Choluteca running right down the middle. The valley is ringed by mountains, with a narrow opening to the north allowing the Río Choluteca to continue on its convoluted course to the Pacific Ocean 130 kilometers away.

Opinions of Tegucigalpa—called "Tegus" (Tay-goose) by locals—vary wildly. Some visitors are uninspired and can't wait to catch the next bus out of town, while others are charmed by the mix of colonial and modern buildings, the mountain setting, and many services.

Among Tegucigalpa's tourist attractions are several colonial churches, three museums, a number of markets, and plenty of handicraft stores, most in the downtown area.

Because of its altitude, Tegucigalpa has a pleasant climate year-round, generally warm during the day and cool at night, and the mean annual temperature is 28°C (82°F). September through November can be a bit cooler with some rain, and the coldest month is January, when *frentes fríos,* cold north winds, pass through town. Pollution can get heavy in March and April, the time in which farmers in the hills follow centuries-old slash-and-burn agricultural techniques.

History

Both archaeological work and historical records suggest the Tegucigalpa Valley was not a major population center, at least in the years shortly before the Spanish conquest. It's postulated that the mainly Lenca population was dependent on the larger settlements in the nearby Comayagua Valley. Many believe the city's name derives from the Lenca words meaning "land of silver," but the Lenca had no interest in silver and are not likely to have named a place because of it. Others have suggested

the urban panorama of Tegucigalpa

© AMY E. ROBERTSON

TEGUCIGALPA

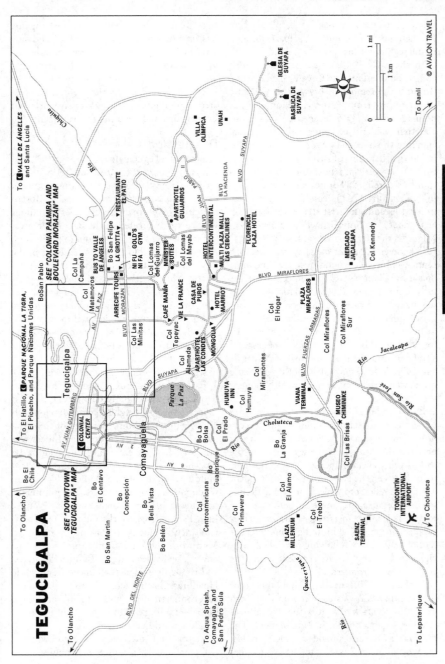

© AVALON TRAVEL

To Danli

IGLESIA DE SUYAPA

BASÍLICA DE SUYAPA

1 mi
1 km

UNAH

VILLA OLÍMPICA

BLVD SUYAPA

AV PABLO

BLVD JUAN

BLVD LA HACIENDA

APARTHOTEL GUIJARROS

RESTAURANTE EL PATIO

Bo San Felipe

BUS TO VALLE DE ÁNGELES

▼ To VALLE DE ÁNGELES and Santa Lucía

Chiquito

Río

BoSan Pablo

Col La Campaña

Col Matamoros

SEE "COLONIA PALMIRA AND BOULEVARD MORAZÁN" MAP

LA GROTTA ▼

NI FU NI FA

GOLD'S GYM

Col Lomas del Guijarro

MINISTER SUITES

Col Lomas del Mayab

HOTEL INTERCONTINENTAL

FLORENCIA PLAZA HOTEL

MULTI PLAZA MALL/ LAS CEBOLLINES

MERCADO JACALEAPA

Col Kennedy

BLVD MIRAFLORES

ARRECIFE TOURS

AV MORAZÁN

CAFÉ MANÍA

CASA DE PUROS

VIE LA FRANCE

PLAZA MIRAFLORES

Col El Hogar

Col Miraflores

Río Jacaleapa

BLVD LA PAZ

Col Las Minitas

Col Tepeyac

MONGOLIA ▼

HOTEL MARRIOT

APARTHOTEL LAS CONDES

Col Alameda

BLVD SUYAPA

Col Miraflores Sur

BLVD FUERZAS ARMADAS

Río San José

PARQUE NACIONAL LA TIGRA, El Picacho, and Parque Naciones Unidas

Parque La Paz

HUMUYA INN

Col Humuya

Col Miramontes

VIANA TERMINAL

MUSEO CHIMINIKE ★

Col Las Brisas

To El Hatillo,

Tegucigalpa

SEE "DOWNTOWN TEGUCIGALPA" MAP

AV JUAN GUTEMBERG

Comayagüela

Choluteca

Bo La Granja

TONCONTÍN INTERNATIONAL AIRPORT ✈

To Choluteca

COLONIAL CENTER

Bo La Bolsa

Col El Prado

Río

To Olancho ▶

Bo El Chile

2 AV

6 AV

Guacerique

Bo

To Olancho

Bo San Martín

Bo El Centavo

Bo Concepción

Bo Bella Vista

Col Centroamericana

Col Primavera

Col El Álamo

Col El Trébol

SAENZ TERMINAL

Bo Belén

PLAZA MILLENIUM

BLVD DEL NORTE

To Aqua Splash, Comayagua, and San Pedro Sula

Guacerique

Río

To Lepaterique

"place of the painted rocks" and "place where the men meet." The ending "galpa," common in the region, means "place" or "land."

In the early 1540s at the latest, Spanish conquistador Alonso de Cáceres likely passed through the region on his way to Olancho under orders from Francisco Montejo, but he made no report on the valley. It's probable that residents of Comayagua, who were combing the new colony for precious metals, found the first veins of silver near Santa Lucía by 1560. An official report to the Spanish authorities dated 1589 states silver was found in Tegucigalpa 12–15 years prior. According to local legend, the first strike was made on September 29, Saint Michael's day; hence, San Miguel is the city's patron saint.

Whatever the exact date, by the late 16th century, miners were building houses and mine operations along the Río Choluteca and in the hills above. Tegucigalpa had no formal founding, like Comayagua, Gracias, or Trujillo, but grew haphazardly and remained a small settlement of dispersed houses connected by trails for the first years of its existence. The original name for the settlement was Real de Minas de San Miguel de Tegucigalpa, but by 1768 the mines were producing enough wealth to merit the title "Villa."

By the end of the colonial period, the city's mineral wealth eclipsed Comayagua in economic importance. Because of the rivalry between the two cities, the legislature of the short-lived Central American Republic alternated between the two, and in 1880 President Marcos Aurelio Soto moved the capital definitively to Tegucigalpa. Some say Soto made the move out of anger toward the Comayagua aristocracy for snubbing his indigenous wife, but more likely he was following his liberal principles by locating the government where the economy was strongest.

In the early 20th century, Honduras's economic expansion was centered on the north coast, and the lack of a cross-country railroad left Tegucigalpa behind in development. The mines at El Rosario provided some stimulus, but most of the profits went to New York rather

than Tegucigalpa. To this day, Tegucigalpa has no major industry to speak of and survives mainly through the government, the service industry, a small financial community, and a handful of *maquilas* on the outskirts of town. In 1932, the Distrito Central was created, bringing neighboring Comayagüela and Tegucigalpa under a unified government.

Orientation

Downtown Tegucigalpa is arranged around the *parque central* (central square), with the Parroquia de San Miguel Arcángel (known simply as *la Catedral*) on the east side. Most of the city's government and business buildings were formerly located in the downtown area, but many have since moved out to Miraflores, Avenida Juan Pablo II, and other parts of the city, no doubt partly to escape the abysmal traffic. Most of the sights of interest to tourists are within walking distance of *parque central*. Because of the city's broken geography and haphazard construction over the centuries, Tegucigalpa does not have an ordered street plan and can be a bit confusing to navigate at first (a problem vastly compounded by the lack of street signs in many neighborhoods).

East and uphill from downtown are Barrio San Rafael and Colonia Palmira, the first modern, wealthy neighborhoods developed in Tegucigalpa and home to many of the city's embassies, high-priced hotels, and nicer restaurants. Farther east continue Avenida La Paz, home to the imposing U.S. Embassy building, and the parallel Boulevard Morazán, with many shops, restaurants, and minimalls. Southeast of downtown extends Avenida Juan Pablo II, where the Clarion and Inter-Continental Hotels and the newly expanded Mall Multiplaza are located, and Boulevard Suyapa, which leads to the Basílica de Suyapa and the Universidad Nacional Autónoma de Honduras. Cutting across the south part of the city, connecting the San Pedro Sula exit to the highway leading east to Danlí, is the fast-moving Boulevard Fuerzas Armadas.

Across the Río Choluteca from downtown is Comayagüela, a noisier and poorer sister city to Tegucigalpa. The main city market and almost all of the long-distance bus stations are in Comayagüela. Some travelers may find it convenient and inexpensive to stay in Comayagüela, but avoid walking around at night (and be on alert during the day).

Most budget travelers will end up staying in downtown Tegucigalpa, where inexpensive accommodations and food are available, and head over to Comayagüela for transport in and out of town. Travelers with a bigger budget, or those in Tegucigalpa for work, will spend most of their time in Colonia Palmira, on Boulevard Morazán and Avenida Juan Pablo II, for the higher-end restaurants and hotels.

Getting Around

The main sights downtown can easily be covered on foot, but buses or taxis are needed to get to many of the bus stations and far-flung parts of the city. Taxis in Tegucigalpa are more expensive than in smaller towns, usually charging US$2.50–3 around town, depending on where you're going, or US$5 out to the airport or to El Hatillo. Always ask the price before you get in. Street taxis are generally safe in Tegucigalpa, but two relatively reliable radio taxi services are **Radio Taxi Pionero** (tel. 504/225-5563 or 504/225-1555) and **Radio Taxi Mall Multiplaza** (tel. 504/232-2352 or 504/232-4067). Another excellent option for larger groups is to make arrangements with one of the **minivan taxis** that form part of the airport cooperative. One recommended driver is Josué Sanchez Reyes (tel. 504/9952-7516), who can be hired by the hour, by the day, for tours, and for multiple days, as well as simply for a ride to or from anywhere in town.

Colectivo (shared) taxis run set routes and charge only US$0.60, but figuring out which taxis go where requires lots of questions and walking around. That said, all *colectivos* have the center as their starting or end point, so you should be able to find any route you need by asking around downtown. One useful *colectivo* drives between Puente La Isla near the stadium out to Colonia Kennedy. Another departs from a block behind La Merced and the Galería

Nacional de Arte and drives past the Honduras Maya out past the Clarion crossing Avenida Juan Pablo II and on to Plaza Miraflores. A third *colectivo* leaves from the corner of Avenida Cervantes and Calle Salvador Mendieta and crosses Comayagüela via 4 Avenida, going out past Mercado Mayoreo to Carrizal, by the exit to San Pedro Sula and Olancho. To head out Avenida La Paz past the U.S. Embassy to San Felipe at the exit to Valle de Ángeles, *colectivos* leave from Calle Palace just north of the *parque central.*

Most city buses (invariably old school buses) cross from the south or west, passing through Comayagüela by the Mercado Mayoreo and continuing through Tegucigalpa out to the north or east. Some pass right by the *parque central,* while others cross the river farther upstream and pass by the Penitenciaría or the Estadio Nacional. Two oft-used buses are the "21 Tiloarque-La Sosa," which runs from Mercado Mayoreo up 6 Avenida in Comayagüela, through downtown, and out Avenida La Paz to where the Valle de Ángeles and Santa Lucía buses leave, and the "32," which goes from Comayagüela out Boulevard Suyapa to the National University. Safety is a major concern on the buses—it is not unheard of for armed robbers to board buses for a quick robbery—should you be unlucky enough that this happens to you, just hand over whatever they ask for, and consider springing for a taxi the next time.

Traffic can be excruciatingly slow in downtown Tegucigalpa and in Comayagüela. Armed with a decent map, these are the easiest parts of the city to navigate, but the long waits, especially during rush hour, require plenty of patience. The eastern avenues, like Morazán, Juan Pablo II, Suyapa, and Miraflores, as well as the southerly loop road Boulevard Fuerzas Armadas and the *periférico,* or ring road, can also get congested during rush hour but are usually smooth at other times of day.

Safety

Like any big city in a poor country, Tegucigalpa can be a dangerous place. The great majority of visitors will have no problems at all. Pickpockets and (less frequently) muggings are a concern throughout the city. Be aware that the upscale neighborhood Colonia Palmira has become a popular spot for muggings, where would-be thieves are especially on the lookout for people with cell phones or laptops, and people walking alone. Comayagüela is well known as the most dangerous part of the capital, although the worst areas are neighborhoods where travelers are unlikely to visit, such as Carrizal along the hillside—walking on the main streets during the day shouldn't be a problem, but the market is a bit sketchier. Avoid walking around at night anywhere in the city.

One mugging tactic is to have two persons on a motorcycle, which slows as it passes you, and the rider yanks your purse or pack off your shoulder. Keep packs on both shoulders and purses with the strap over one shoulder and crossing your body, or keep your bag on the shoulder away from the street to make yourself less of a target for this type of mugging.

The smaller towns and countryside areas near Tegucigalpa mentioned in this guide, like Santa Lucía, Valle de Ángeles, Ojojona, Cedros, and La Tigra National Park, are all very safe.

SIGHTS
◖ The Colonial Center
PARQUE CENTRAL
Tegucigalpa's bustling downtown square is a great place to people-watch. It's invariably full of city folk walking around, buying newspapers, selling odds and ends, or just hanging out. Beware of sitting under the trees as you may find yourself the object of target practice from the pigeons above. Tourist police hover in the square, so while flaunting valuables is never recommended, the park is fairly safe.

A *peatonal,* pedestrian street, extends several blocks west of the square and is lined with (rather ordinary) shops and restaurants. There are also banks where you can change money and money changers lurking nearby for those who don't want to wait in line at the bank

(but please don't flash your cash; remember that US$100 is a *lot* of money in Honduras). The money changers are legitimate and generally honest, but make sure you have an idea of the current exchange rate just to be on the safe side. Street vendors once clogged the *peatonal* and the plaza at Iglesia Los Dolores but have been moved to the covered market next to the church. The *peatonal* has been renamed Paseo Liquidámbar, for the American sweetgum tree that grows in Honduras.

PARROQUIA DE SAN MIGUEL ARCÁNGEL
Otherwise known as *la Catedral,* the *parroquia* was built between 1765 and 1782 on the site of a simpler wooden church and is a fine example of late colonial architecture. Although the design is relatively simple, the vaulted ceiling and domed altar are impressive. The incredibly intricate gold-and-silver altarpiece sculpted by Guatemalan artist Vicente Gálvez is the church's artistic highlight. Presiding over the altar is a statue of San Miguel, the patron saint of Tegucigalpa. Several sculptures and paintings decorate the interior, including ones by famed colonial artist José Miguel Gómez.

The cathedral was damaged so badly in the earthquake of 1808 it was practically abandoned for almost 30 years before being reinforced. A 1975 earthquake caused further damage, which has since been repaired. The church's exterior was restored in 2009 and repainted peach, its original color. Inexplicably, picture-taking is not allowed inside here, nor in La Merced or Los Dolores.

LA MERCED AND GALERÍA NACIONAL DE ARTE
One block south of the square is a large building that houses both La Iglesia de La Merced and the Galería Nacional de Arte. Originally a convent built in 1654 by the Order of Our Lady of Mercy *(merced),* the property was seized by the Honduran government in 1829, when a secularization of convents was declared, and converted into a university. Over the next century and a half the building saw various

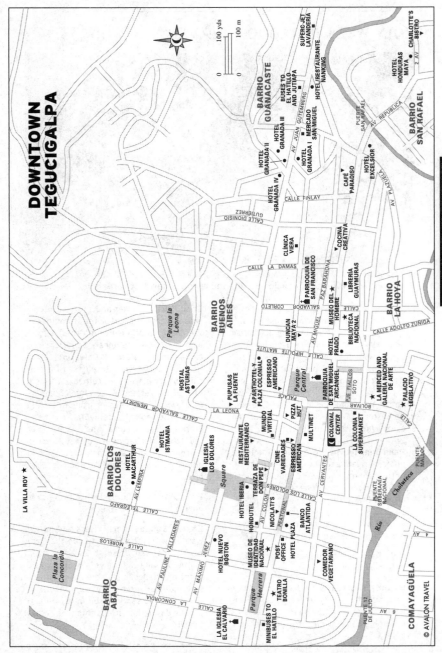

DOWNTOWN TEGUCIGALPA

TEGUCIGALPA

0   100 yds
0   100 m

LA VILLA ROY ★

BARRIO ABAJO

Plaza la Concordia

BARRIO LOS DOLORES

BARRIO GUANACASTE

BARRIO BUENOS AIRES

Parque la Leona

BARRIO SAN RAFAEL

BARRIO LA HOYA

COMAYAGÜELA

LA IGLESIA EL CALVARIO ★

MINIBUSES TO EL HATILLO

CALLE LA CONCORDIA

AV. PAULINE VALLADARES

CALLE MORELOS

AV. MÁXIMO JEREZ

Parque Herrera

TEATRO BONILLA

HOTEL NUEVO BOSTON

MUSEO DE IDENTIDAD NACIONAL

POST OFFICE

HOTEL PLAZA

COMEDOR VEGETARIANO

BANCO ATLÁNTIDA

NICOLATI'S

PEATONAL

AV. COLÓN

CALLE TELÉGRAFO

AV. LEMPIRA

HOTEL MACARTHUR

HOTEL ISTMANIA

CALLE SALVADOR MENDIETA

IGLESIA LOS DOLORES

Square

RESTAURANTE MEDITERRÁNEO

TERRAZA DE DON PEPE

HOTEL IBERIA

HONDUTEL

CALLE LOS DOLORES

CINE VARIEDADES

ESPRESSO AMERICAN

AV. CERVANTES

HOSTAL ASTURIAS

PUPUSAS LA FUENTE

LA LEONA

APARTHOTEL PLAZA COLONIAL

ESPRESSO AMERICANO

MUNDO VIRTUAL

PIZZA HUT

MULTINET

COLONIAL CENTER

LA COLONIA SUPERMARKET

CALLE HIPÓLITO MATUTE

Parque Central

PALACE

PARROQUIA DE SAN MIGUEL ARCÁNGEL

PJE FIALLOS

SOTO

BOLÍVAR

LA MERCED AND GALERÍA NACIONAL DE ARTE

PALACIO LEGISLATIVO ★

CALLE

PUENTE MALLOL

Río Chiluteca

PUENTE SOBERANÍA NACIONAL

4 AV.

6 AV.

PUENTE 12 DE JULIO

CALLE LA DAMAS

DUNCAN MAYA 2

CALLE HIPÓLITO MATUTE

AV. MIGUEL

CALLE PAZ BARAHONA

SALVADOR CORLETO

PARROQUIA DE SAN FRANCISCO

MUSEO DEL HOMBRE ★

LIBRERÍA GUAYMURAS

HOTEL PRADO ●

BIBLIOTECA NACIONAL

CALLE ADOLFO ZÚÑIGA

CLÍNICA VIERA

COCINA CREATIVA ▼

CAFÉ PARADISO

HOTEL EXCELSIOR

AV. PLAZUELA

CALLE FINLAY

CALLE DIONISIO GUTIÉRREZ

HOTEL GRANADA IV

HOTEL GRANADA II

HOTEL GRANADA III

HOTEL GRANADA I

AV. JUAN GUTENBERG

MERCADO SAN MIGUEL

BUSES TO EL HATILLO AND JUTIAPA

HOTEL/RESTAURANTE NANKING

SUPER-JET LAVANDERÍA

PUENTE SAN RAFAEL

AV. REPÚBLICA

2 AV.

HOTEL HONDURAS MAYA ●

CHARLOTTE'S BISTRO ●

© AVALON TRAVEL

HOLY WEEK IN TEGUCIGALPA

Traditions are revived in Tegucigalpa with the laying of sawdust carpets for Holy Week.

Although many of the capital's residents flee the city to the beach during Semana Santa (Holy Week), the city has been working hard in recent years to revive its once-dying traditions of processions throughout the week that tell different parts of the biblical Easter story – a real boon for anyone around during an otherwise very, very quiet period. You might be able to confirm the schedule in the weeks leading up to Easter on Tegucigalpa's municipal website, www.lacapitaldehonduras.com.

- **Palm Sunday:** The Procession of the Triumphant Arrival, recalling Jesus' arrival into Jerusalem on a donkey, begins at **Iglesia El Calvario** in Parque Herrera at 7 A.M. The crowds brandish palm leaves, which are blessed in the *parque central* an hour later in front of the cathedral, when the primary mass of the day begins.

- **Holy Tuesday:** The procession for the Lord of Humility begins at 6 P.M.

- **Maundy Thursday:** The silent, and rather ominous, men-only Procesión de Prendimiento begins at 11 P.M., in remembrance of when the Romans incarcerated Jesus.

- **Good Friday:** Flower and sawdust *alfombras* (carpets) are laid on the street for the Via Crucis (Stations of the Cross), beginning at 9 A.M. at the **Iglesia San Francisco** and ending at **Iglesia El Calvario** (Parque Herrera). Commemorative acts of the crucifixion take place at the cathedral at noon. At 5:15 P.M. a statue of the Virgen Dolorosa (Sorrowful Virgin) is taken from the **Iglesia San Francisco** to the cathedral, in remembrance of Jesus' burial. The procession of the Holy Burial begins at 5:30 P.M. At 10 P.M. there is a somber all-female procession in honor of Mary, La Virgen de la Soledad (Virgin of Loneliness).

- **Holy Saturday:** An Easter vigil service is held at 8 P.M. in the cathedral.

- **Easter Sunday:** Early risers will be rewarded with the chance to see the **Carreritas de San Juan** at 6 A.M., when a statue of Saint John meets with a statue of the arisen Jesus, who then meets with a statue of the Virgin Mary. Mass follows at 6:30 A.M., and services continue throughout the day in the various churches across the city.

incarnations, including as a barracks and as a cockfight arena. The building became an art museum in 1985 and has housed the National Gallery of Art since 1994.

La Iglesia de La Merced features a beautiful gilded altarpiece flanked by two smaller *retablos*. The Galería Nacional de Arte (Plaza La Merced, tel. 504/237-9884, 9 A.M.–4 P.M. Mon.–Sat., 9 A.M.–2 P.M. Sun., US$1.30 admission) is a small but fine art museum, perhaps one of the best in Central America. A printed guide in English is available to borrow during your visit.

The gallery traces the evolution of Honduran art, beginning downstairs with rooms dedicated to prehistoric pictographs and petroglyphs, stone and ceramic art from the Mayan era, and a stunning collection of colonial paintings, sculptures, and gold and silver religious art. The pieces were all chosen for their visual beauty as much as (if not more than) for their historical importance. Be sure not to miss the three works by José Miguel Gómez, considered the most important Honduran painter of the colonial era. Upstairs, several rooms contain paintings from classic Honduran artists Pablo Zelaya Sierra, Carlos Zuñiga Figueroa, and José Antonio Velásquez, as well as lesser-known painters and sculptors, such as Virgilio Guardiola and Aníbal Cruz.

For such a small, economically deprived country, Honduras has produced an unusual number of fine visual artists, and the museum is an excellent tour of the country's artistic history. The artwork is laid out tastefully and with good lighting, and the historical progression

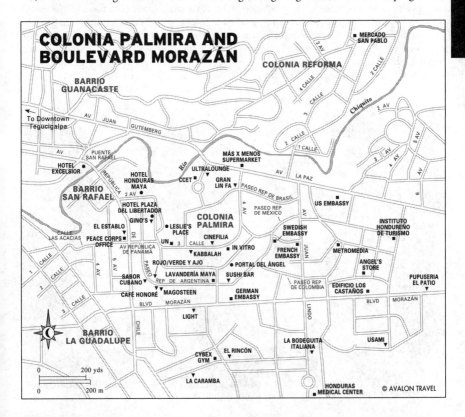

allows visitors to appreciate the development of Honduran art. Art aficionados should not miss this museum.

Next to the church and art gallery is the **Palacio Legislativo,** or National Congress. It's known laconically by locals as El Sapo (The Frog) because the bizarre architecture makes it seem as though the building is about to hop away.

MUSEO DE LA IDENTIDAD NACIONAL

Facing the Correo Nacional at the far end of the pedestrian street is the Museo de la Identidad Nacional (corner of Calle El Telégrafo and Av. Miguel Barahona, tel. 504/238-7412, www.min.hn, 9 A.M.–5 P.M. Tues.–Sat., 10 A.M.–4 P.M. Sun., US$2.60), the newest attraction in Tegucigalpa's historic center. The museum's permanent installations recount Honduras's geologic, cultural, and political history, while other rooms offer temporary art exhibitions. A 20-minute video (in Spanish) showing a virtual tour of the Mayan ruins of Copán is included in the admission price (shown at 10 A.M., 11:30 A.M., 2 P.M., and 3:30 P.M. Tues.–Sat., and at 11:30 A.M., and 2 P.M. Sun.). While the permanent exhibitions include a significant amount of text printed on the wall, English-speaking guides are available free of charge, and they do an excellent job of pulling out the most compelling facts and bringing them to life. The museum is housed in a beautifully restored 125-year-old building that began as the General Hospital and then became the government Ministries Palace, prior to its conversion into the museum. School groups can visit free on Tuesdays and Thursdays, and do in droves—other days of the week you might have the museum to yourself.

PARROQUIA DE SAN FRANCISCO

Facing a small, shady park three blocks east of the square is the oldest extant church in the city, first erected in 1592 and rebuilt in 1740. Inside the church are a gilded altarpiece and several colonial-era religious paintings, although the doors have been closed for ages,

Schoolchildren line up to enter the Museum of National Identity.

reputedly for renovations. The building next door, formerly the Franciscan monastery, is now used by the army for a rather sad military museum that will hopefully improve when its current renovation is completed.

MUSEO DEL HOMBRE

Housed in the recently renovated building on Avenida Cervantes, four blocks east of the *parque,* is a quiet, modest museum-slash-gallery (tel. 504/238-3198, 8:30 A.M.–noon and 1:30–5 P.M. Mon.–Fri., free admission) with rotating exhibits of varying quality, as well as a permanent collection of paintings that recount Honduras's history (the staff will happily explain the paintings if you ask). The house once belonged to Independence hero Ramón Rosa and later served as the national Supreme Court. The museum has frequent receptions and events. In the back of the museum is one of Honduras's principal art restoration workshops.

PARQUE HERRERA AND TEATRO NACIONAL MANUEL BONILLA

Six blocks west of the square is the attractive but slightly seedy Parque Herrera, in front of which stands the Teatro Nacional Manuel Bonilla (tel. 504/222-4366), inaugurated in 1916 and built at the behest of the eponymous general. Bonilla tried to get the theater built during his first administration in 1906, but a flood swept the new building away, and he had to wait until he returned to power to see the building inaugurated, 10 years later. The facade is reputedly designed in the style of the Athenée of Paris, and the ornate interior is crowned by a panoramic painting of the Tegucigalpa valley from the mountain of El Berrinche by famed Honduran painter Carlos Zuñiga Figueroa. The theater seats 600 in rows on the ground floor and box seats above. For information on upcoming performances, ask at the box office or check local newspapers. If you can't make a show, check if the doors are open and peek inside for a glimpse of the beautifully restored interior.

At the northwest corner of the park is **La**

Iglesia El Calvario, dating from the mid-18th century and housing several *retablos* and an image of the Virgen de la Soledad.

IGLESIA LOS DOLORES

Dominating a large square, Los Dolores is a large, bright-white church with a relatively plain facade but featuring several beautiful pieces of religious art inside, including relief paintings of the stations of the cross, a gilded, carved altarpiece, and the painted interior dome. Unfortunately, it is often closed—visit on a Sunday or else try asking at the office on the side of the church for a peek inside. The church, built in 1732, is a few blocks northwest of the downtown square. The street vendors that formerly mobbed the square have been moved into a covered market area on the east side of the plaza. The street to the west of the church and behind it right around the church are none too safe at night but house a number of very cheap "hostels" for those running low on cash. The tiny pedestrian street that runs along the eastern side of the church is filled with ladies selling homemade tortillas.

LA VILLA ROY AND PLAZA LA CONCORDIA

La Villa Roy, a mansion perched on a hillside just west of downtown Tegucigalpa, was donated to the public in 1974 by the wife of ex-president Julio Lozano Díaz. The gesture seems remarkably patriotic, considering her husband was deposed by a military coup in 1956. The mansion now houses the **Museo de Historia Republicana** (tel. 504/222-1468, 8 A.M.–4 P.M. Mon.–Sat., US$1 admission), which traces the development of the Honduran republic from its birth at the end of the Spanish colonial era in 1821 to the present.

Though the museum is not particularly gripping, the mansion has been nicely restored, and people with at least a passing interest in Honduran history will find several displays to hold their attention, especially if they can read the Spanish labels. The well-worn boots and trusty Eveready flashlight of great Honduran geographer and cultural historian Jesús Aguilar

TEGUCIGALPA

Giant replicas of Mayan stelae watch over park-goers at Plaza La Concordia.

Paz, who created the first accurate map of Honduras in 1933 and compiled voluminous journals during his endless trips around the country on oral history, local legends, and observations on flora and fauna, are enshrined in a glass case. The rooms upstairs dedicated to the early part of the 20th century, complete with many old photographs and paraphernalia, are quite informative, but the history of the Carías era and the second half of the 20th century are bland.

On your way out, take a look at the fleet of black presidential vehicles parked in the garage, including a couple of wicked-looking Cadillacs.

Just below the museum, on the way back into downtown and one block west, is the small, leafy **Plaza La Concordia,** featuring several impressive replicas of Mayan stelae (sculptures).

Outside the Colonial Center

PARQUE LA LEONA

Set among the winding cobblestone streets and colonial houses of the picturesque Buenos

Aires neighborhood just west and uphill from the square, Parque La Leona makes a pleasant spot to take a rest and admire the views over downtown and the valley. The park is a 15-minute walk from the square up a steep hill. Keep an eye peeled to admire the many colonial and 19th-century mansions lining the road on the way up—and the other eye on the people around you, as these side streets aren't the safest. There is a small café where you can have a Coke and enjoy the view.

PARQUE LA PAZ

Atop Juana Laínez hill in the center of Tegucigalpa, near the Estadio Nacional, is Parque La Paz, commemorating the peace treaty ending the so-called Soccer War between El Salvador and Honduras in 1969. Although the views are nice enough, this is a dangerous area, and walking here is not recommended.

THE SUYAPA CHURCHES

Honduras's patron saint, La Virgen de Suyapa, is venerated in a simple, white-plaster chapel set on a small square on the eastern outskirts of Tegucigalpa, near the National University (Universidad Nacional Autónoma de Honduras, or UNAH). The **Iglesia de Suyapa,** built in 1749, houses the six-centimeter-tall statue of the virgin in a wooden case behind the altar (bring your binoculars if you really want a good look). The church sees a constant flow of worshippers from across the country praying to the diminutive virgin.

A short distance from the chapel, set on a hillside and dominating the skyline in the eastern part of the city, is the **Basílica de Suyapa,** a massive, cavernous church built in 1958. It's painted in bright colors and covered with pictographic stained-glass windows.

FOR KIDS

Inaugurated in 2003 and funded by the World Bank, **Chiminike** (tel. 504/291-0339, www.chiminike.com, 9 A.M.–noon and 2–5 P.M. Tues.–Fri., 10 A.M.–1 P.M. and 2–5 P.M. Sat.–Sun., US$2.50) is an excellent interactive children's museum, housed in a bright blue

SUYAPA, THE PATRON SAINT OF TEGUCIGALPA

Far larger than the cathedral downtown is the **Basílica de Suyapa,** a mammoth white- and blue-trimmed church on the eastern edge of town – a rather large home for a six-centimeter saint.

Although the *basílica* is new, the image it was built to venerate dates from 1747, when a humble laborer, Alejandro Colines, was heading home to the village of Suyapa after a day working the corn fields in the town of El Piligüín. Night fell before he could reach home, and he lay down on the ground to sleep. Alejandro felt what he thought must be a stone under his back, but found instead a wood statue. It is said that the Virgin Mary became *catracha* (Honduran), in the form of the tiny, dark-complexioned cedar statue Alejandro found.

Alejandro lived with his mother, Isabel María, who upon seeing the statue promptly built a small altar in their home. The *suyapenses* would visit her over the next 20 years, asking for comfort, health, and help with all problems. In 1768 it came to Isabel María's attention that an important military captain, José de Zelaya y Midence, was suffering terribly from kidney stones, and no doctor had been able to help. The statue was loaned to Zelaya, who prayed fervently for healing. Three days later, he passed three kidney stones and was healed. This is considered the virgin's first miracle, and

a chapel was built for her in Suyapa shortly thereafter.

In 1925 Pius XI declared Our Lady of Suyapa a saint, and named her the patron saint of Honduras. February 3 was selected as her feast day. The festival in Tegucigalpa spans January 25–February 4.

An estimated two million pilgrims come to pay homage to the diminutive saint during her festival, and the large church was built in 1958 to accommodate the worshippers. Originally intended to be her permanent home, the tiny statue disappeared shortly after being placed in the church, only to reappear in the small chapel in Suyapa a block away. (She disappeared a second time in 1986, stolen from the chapel, and reappeared in the men's restroom of a downtown restaurant a few days later – presumably stolen for the valuable gemstones that adorned her dress.) Apparently, she understands the problems of crowd control, however, and consents to be on display in the basilica during the festival.

The celebrations primarily consist of hourly masses, and there's unbelievable traffic to reach the church, but a few small performances (a folklore dance group, the national police's marimba band) are sprinkled throughout, for which the schedule can be found on the chapel's website, www.virgendesuyapa.hn.

Suyapa is everywhere, even on the radio.

and purple building on Boulevard Fuerzas Armadas, right near the Supreme Court. Displays include large-sized replicas of the human body, the environment, a grocery store, and Honduran culture, among others. Check out the tilted room, where you can play being a human yo-yo (for an extra charge). Displays are all in Spanish. Each room has people there to help visitors, although their primary purpose is to assist the endless stream of school groups that come through on weekdays. The odd name derives from a well-known Honduran children's song about a frog; hence all the frog statues and symbols around the museum.

The **zoo** (9 A.M.–5 P.M. daily, US$1) at the Parque Naciones Unidas is another hit with smaller children. There is a depressed jaguar in a heart-rendingly small cage, but the monkeys and peacocks are impressive and, oddly enough, in larger cages. There is also some children's play equipment and plenty of room to run or bike around in the park.

To cool off on a hot day, head to **Aqua Splash** (tel. 504/224-1584, US$8) water park, on the way out of town toward San Pedro Sula (visible from the highway, so easy to find). The water is not heated, so the park can get chilly on an overcast day.

PARQUE NACIONES UNIDAS/EL PICACHO

On the top of Montaña El Picacho off the road to El Hatillo, Parque Naciones Unidas (8 A.M.–5:30 P.M. daily) commands views over the entire Tegucigalpa Valley. Opened in the 1940s, the pine-forested park is a fine place to escape the noise of the city for a while and breathe clean air. The park also features a frequently used soccer field, a small zoo, a children's play area, and (the most recent addition) the Cristo del Picacho, similar in style to the Christ statue over the harbor in Río de Janeiro. Buses to El Picacho leave from behind Los Dolores church on Sunday only—during the week, take an El Hatillo bus, get off at the intersection, and walk 1.5 kilometers into the park, or take a cab, which should cost about US$5 from downtown. Park entrance is US$1.

On the way to the park, just under a kilometer from the turnoff from Avenida Jeréz, is the imposing white Universidad Católica de Honduras building, visible from around the city. The wide-open university parking lot makes a great place not too far from downtown to catch views over the city.

ENTERTAINMENT
Dancing

Sabor Cubano (tel. 504/235-9947, 11 A.M.–11 P.M. Mon.–Thurs., 11 A.M.–2 A.M. Fri.–Sat.) continues to be the city's top spot for salsa dancing. The restaurant with a dance floor is right among all the restaurants in Colonia Palmira on Avenida República de Argentina. Run by a Cuban woman, it's a Caribbean-style restaurant during the day and most nights, but the real reason to come here is for the dancing, which starts at 9 P.M. on weekends. The music isn't live, except for special occasions, but the dancers are good and the vibe is fun. Dance lessons are available (5–7 P.M. Tues. and Thurs.); just show up and negotiate rates directly with the instructor.

As in any city, the popular discos in town are continually changing, making it hard to keep track, but they are always in the same part of town, and in fact they're often in the same building, just with a new name. A reasonably up-to-date website with disco and bar listings is www.quehacertegus.com.

Tegucigalpa's glitterati are currently enamored with **Light** (tel. 504/9941-7994), near the western end of Boulevard Morazán opposite Wendy's, and **La Grotta** farther east on Morazán. Both have plenty of lounge-style seating as well as music and dancing until late (or early, depending on how you view it).

Kabbalah (on Avenida Rep. de Panamá in Colonia Palmira, half a block from the United Nations building) is another possibility. The ultimate lounge in town is the eponymous **UltraLounge**, a Euro-style hangout that plays techno, trance, dance, house, and other progressive rave music.

A gay-friendly disco is **Metropolis,** opposite La Curacao store off Boulevard Suyapa.

Bars

Lounges are increasingly popular in Tegucigalpa, one of the most popular being **Río** in the shopping center Los Proceres. While **El Rincon** (tel. 504/235-4551) in Colonia Rubén Dario, a few blocks from Morazán, is technically a restaurant, it has a very large and glamorous lounge area that is packed on weekends and serves a mean martini. The **Nau** lounge at the Inter-Continental hotel is another chic spot to sip cocktails, at the edge of the hotel pool.

Downtown, the top floor terrace of **La Terraza de Don Pepe** (tel. 504/237-1084) grants a view with its beers and has karaoke on weekends. Up the hill in Colonia Palmira, the **Mirador** (tel. 504/280-5000) bar at the Hotel Honduras Maya has a lovely outdoor terrace with a great view of twinkling lights along the hills in the evening—and two-for-one beers during happy hour.

A good place for a casual beer is **Pupusería El Patio** on Boulevard Morazán (a block east of McDonald's). Beer is cheap, and there is often live music, dancing, and/or karaoke. People usually show up every night of the week, but like everywhere in Tegucigalpa, it's the weekend nights that are packed. **La Caramba,** a couple of blocks off Boulevard Morazán, is another place for a drink and live music, usually of very good quality, with salsa music on Fridays.

There are a number of bohemian spots for a drink, where the city's artists and intelligentsia congregate. **Cinefilia** (on Av. Rep. de Panamá) is a popular spot for after-work drinks, and it has a large selection of international films for rent. Downtown not far from Hotel Excelsior is **Café Paradiso** (Av. Miguel Barahona 1351, tel. 504/222-3066), which offers a bit of everything—food and drink, free wireless Internet, poetry readings, film screenings, and live music. Call ahead for a schedule, or sign up for event listings via email by writing to paradiso@cablecolor.hn.

TEGUCIGALPA

A NIGHT ON THE TOWN

While San Pedro Sula and La Ceiba have bigger reputations as party towns, there is plenty happening in Tegucigalpa if you know where to look. Weekends are naturally the busiest nights out, while on Sundays and Mondays you're better off just getting a good night's rest in your hotel room. Here are a few places to pop into on the weekend:

· **Budget:** For a cheap beer and meal, hop a cab to Pupusería El Patio, where locals pack the place on weekends for a casual beer accompanied by live music, dancing, and karaoke. Those really wanting to get their Latin groove on should check out the salsa dancing (no cover!) and mojitos at Sabor Cubano.

· **Cultural:** The first order of business is to check if anything is playing at the Teatro Nacional Manuel Bonilla, a beautifully restored theater that hosts performances from jazz to opera, ballet to classic theater (the best way to do this is by stopping in). Barring a performance at the theater, poke into Café Paradiso in the center, which hosts film screenings, poetry readings, and the like. Still haven't found something to grab you? Check with Caramba, a bar a few blocks south of Boulevard Morazán, for live music, hosted regularly on the weekends.

· **Glam:** Head to the outdoor patio of the Honduras Maya Hotel at twilight to enjoy a drink with the backdrop of glittering city lights. From there head to El Rincon and dine on pizzas and pastas accompanied by fine wines or apple martinis. If it's still early, make one more stop at the stylish Río bar in Los Proceres shopping center, for the ubiquitous lounge experience. When you're good and ready, head to one of the city's several discos; one hot spot is Light, on Boulevard Morazán.

Casa de Puros in the Casanoble shopping center on Juan Pablo II has a small bar and restaurant (with an excellent ventilation system) in case you want to sip and nibble while you smoke a cigar. Specialty cocktails and some interesting wines are available, as well as gourmet toasted sandwiches.

Cinemas

Movie theaters in Tegucigalpa showing first-run movies include **Variedades** right downtown and **Cinemark** at the Mall Multiplaza on Avenida Juan Pablo II. Movies for adults are often shown in English with subtitles in Spanish *(subtitulado),* while children's movies are typically dubbed *(doblado)*—check at the box office.

The bookstore and coffee shop **Café Paradiso** (tel. 504/237-0337, 10 A.M.–10 P.M. Mon.–Sat.), on Avenida Miguel Barahona in Barrio Guanacaste, shows independent films on Tuesday nights at 7:15 P.M. for free.

The Cuban restaurant and salsa club **Sabor Cubano** (tel. 504/235-9947) shows Cuban movies on Thursdays at 8 P.M.

Fútbol

Two first-division *fútbol* (soccer) teams, Olimpia and Montagua, play their games in the Estadio Nacional (National Stadium) near downtown. Matches are frequently held on weekends, with ticket prices running US$1.25–8 for normal league games and US$2–10 for national team matches. It's often possible to buy tickets at the box office right before the game, but for big matches it might be better to buy a day in advance. (Beware that big games can mean big drinking for fans—smaller games will be less rowdy.) In the rare event that a game sells out, the *revendedores* will be out in front of the stadium, reselling tickets at a (usually minimal) markup.

After any victories by the national team, known variously as La Bicolor or El Equipo de Todos, the favored place to cruise and celebrate is on Boulevard Morazán. Should either of the local teams win a national championship, victory celebrations can also be expected.

Theater/Expositions

The Manuel Bonilla Theater downtown and the Plaza Millenium on Boulevard Fuerzas Armadas regularly host plays and other performances. The best way to get a schedule of events is to visit http://rds.hn and click on "Eventos" along the top—it will bring you to a calendar that lists events of every kind. *Concierto, exposición,* and *obra teatral* mean concert, exposition, and play, respectively, and clicking through leads to the details of when, where, and cost, if any.

The Centro Cultural de España en Tegucigalpa (CCET for short) is another great source for cultural activities, regularly sponsoring cultural events around the city. To get on their email list, contact them at info-ccet@aecid.hn.

SHOPPING
Markets

From Seattle to San Pedro Sula, Taxco to Tegucigalpa, markets can be a fascinating way to get a glimpse into a city. The most important in town is the **San Isidro Market** just over the bridge in Comayagüela, between 5 and 7 Avenidas and 1 and 2 Calles, worth a visit to check out the hustle and bustle. Commerce is hardly confined by the actual market building, though, with thousands of vendors of all variety lining the surrounding streets, bridges, and sidewalks. Absolutely everything seems to be for sale: pencils, erasers, T-shirts, toothpaste, toilet paper, dried herbs still on the stem or ground in plastic bags, cheap silverware sets, pocket calculators, wristwatches, freshly slaughtered pork and beef, cheeses from Olancho, and myriad other sundries—really an astounding assortment of products. Most people in the market seem cheerfully amused by foreign visitors. Take a chance and go inside the market building itself—it looks daunting from outside, but you'll generally find it a lot quieter and less hectic than the streets.

The **Mercado Mayoreo** is also located in Comayagüela, on the road toward Carrizal and the highway, and a number of intercity buses leave from the streets around the market.

Less intimidating and easier to each is the much smaller **San Miguel Market,** located on Avenida Gutemberg near the Nan King hotel and restaurant. This is a good place to pick up fresh fruit—look for mangoes and the *azucarrón* pineapple when they're in season. Located next to the Estadio Nacional, **La Feria del Agricultor** (Fri.–Sat.) is the place where small farmers sell their goods. On a Friday morning it's the best place in the city to buy fish—by Saturday afternoon it may well be the worst, as testified by the stench and the swarms of flies. Fruit is an excellent buy and the fresh cheese vendors have a good reputation—but we don't suggest eating at the fried food stands unless you have a large stock of Imodium with you.

Any obvious foreigner is a natural target for pickpockets, so come with little to lose, and be aware of your surroundings at all markets.

Gifts and Handicrafts

Commonplace handicrafts stores are conveniently located next to one another at the far end of Avenida Cervantes east of the square (close to the Hotel Excelsior). Similar-quality shops can also be found next to the Hotel Iberia near Iglesia Los Dolores, at the corner of Avenida Cervantes and Calle Adolfo Zuñiga, and in and around the Hotel Honduras Maya. The gift shop at the Museo de Identidad Nacional has a limited but interesting selection of higher-quality souvenirs, such as candles made by a women's cooperative and stylish handmade leather purses.

High-quality souvenirs can be found in the upscale parts of town. **In Vitro** (2139 Av. República de Panamá, tel. 504/232-3452, 8 A.M.–7 P.M.) in Colonia Palmira sells finely made glass and wooden trays, placemats and table runners made of *tuno,* and handmade paper, among other items. All the products in the store are made by cooperatives, in San Juancito (near Valle de Ángeles) and the Mosquitia. The gift shop at the Marriott hotel, **Bahía** (tel. 504/235-6949), also sells well-made products from both cooperatives and individual artisans. Look for the Lencan pots with tiny lizards, cloth handbags, shell necklaces, and leather cigar and passport cases.

On the street behind Los Castaños shopping center is **Angel's Store,** which among the usual displays of Lencan pottery and Copán coffee also has some unique pewter pieces and Mayan motif jewelry.

At the Mall Multiplaza, **Casa D'Oro** sells beautiful silver jewelry with Mayan designs—a pair of fairly simple earrings can sell for US$30–35, while the more elaborate bracelets and necklaces go for several hundred dollars.

If your travels haven't taken you to the cigar meccas of Danlí and Santa Rosa de Copán, you can pick up top-notch smokes at **Casa de Puros** in the Casanoble shopping center opposite the Casa Presidencial on Juan Pablo II (there's also a branch in the airport).

Books

Metromedia (Edificio Casa Real, Av. San Carlos, tel. 504/221-0770 or 504/221-0771, 10 A.M.–8 P.M. Mon.–Sat., noon–5 P.M. Sun.), near the U.S. Embassy, sells a slew of English-language magazines, newspapers, novels, and even this illustrious travel guide. It has branches in the Mall Multiplaza (tel. 504/232-1294) and in the airport (tel. 504/234-5128). There is an Espresso Americano in the main branch if you want to sit and flip through magazines. It also rents movies.

About the best Spanish-language bookstore in Honduras is **Librería Guaymuras** (tel. 504/237-5433, 8:30 A.M.–noon and 1–6 P.M. Mon.–Fri., 8:30 A.M.–noon Sat.) on Avenida Cervantes, which stocks an extensive collection of novels, poetry, and books on Honduran and Central American history, society, and politics. Look for works by Roberto Quesada, Dario Gonzalez, Ramón Amaya Amador, and Rocío Tábora, for a few interesting reads.

Maps

The best places to pick up a city map are the souvenir shops downtown and in the hotels—although only the names of major boulevards are identified. (Look for a sign in the window saying "City Maps.") The airport also has a free map at the information desk that has all of Honduras on one side and city maps for half a dozen major Honduran cities on the back. Topographical, road, mineral, resource, and other maps published by the Honduran government can be purchased at the **Instituto Geográfico Nacional** (tel. 504/225-0752 or 504/225-2759, 8 A.M.–4 P.M. Mon.–Fri.), at the Secretaría de Transporte (SECOPT) in Comayagüela, 15 Calle one block east of 1 Avenida. The office stocks a large though not complete selection of 1:50,000 and 1:250,000 topographical maps, but the staff will often make a photocopy of ones not available for sale. Maps are inexpensive, bureaucratic hassles are nonexistent, and the staff is knowledgeable and friendly.

SPORTS AND RECREATION

Defying categorization is the massive **Villa Olímpica,** located at the end of Juan Pablo II. While the complex is showing signs of age, it houses a stadium, open-air track, covered pool, and other facilities. The track can be accessed for free and is the one safe place in town for walkers and runners, who turn out in droves early in the morning. They also offer very low-cost music and sports lessons for kids, and there are paved paths perfect for taking children for a spin on their bikes. While the complex is generally safe, there's no need to tempt fate by flashing cell phones, money, jewelry, and the like. A few helpful phone numbers are: 504/231-0566 for swimming; 504/235-7334 for gymnastics; 504/265-3754 for tennis; and 504/250-0421 for martial arts.

Runners can also contact the local chapter of Hash House Harriers, which meets sporadically. To find out about any upcoming runs, check their blog at http://hashtegucigalpa .blogspot.com.

Health Clubs and Swimming Pools

Those after a good workout in Tegucigalpa can head to **Cybex** (tel. 504/239-5132), a couple of blocks off Morazán, in Colonia Minitas. The gleaming gym has a 25-meter pool (the only covered pool in town), basketball court, squash and racquetball courts (although you need your own racquet), a sauna and steam room, and plenty of the Cybex machines you may be familiar with from gyms at home. One-day visits cost US$16. A number of classes (dance, Pilates, spinning) are offered, as well as swimming, basketball, tae kwon do, and soccer for children.

Another, much cheaper option is **Gold's Gym** (tel. 504/236-7120), off Morazán almost toward the end, with a full gym (including sauna) and a 25-meter outdoor pool. Regular membership is US$35 to join, then US$37 per month, but visitors can pay US$8 for a one-day visit, US$26 for one week.

Metta Studios is a new Pilates studio a block off Boulevard Suyapa that also has regular gym equipment and a small room for exercise classes.

It is possible to become a member of the pool and gym at the Honduras Maya Hotel, or simply have lunch or drinks poolside and use the pool for the day. The Marriott also offers membership to its health club and pool. You can also get a massage at either hotel. Use of the pool at the Hotel MacArthur downtown costs US$5 for the day.

Dance Classes

Plaza Garibaldi (tel. 504/232-0017, open every day) teaches Latin dance: Classes are held three times in the morning, once at midday and three times in the late afternoon/evening. For US$40 per month you can take as many classes as you want, and "nutritious food" is included.

A private teacher is on-site at **Sabor Cubano** (5–7 P.M. Tues. and Thurs.), no appointment needed—just show up.

Golf and Tennis

Tegucigalpa offers two nine-hole courses. The **Tegucigalpa Country Club** (tel. 504/227-4546) is nothing fancy, at all, but is conveniently located just off Boulevard Fuerzas Armadas in the western end of the city. The more pleasant **Villa Elena** (tel. 504/224-0400) is a half an hour outside of town on the road to

San Pedro Sula, and has a swimming pool, a poolside restaurant, and somewhat run-down tennis courts as well.

Biking

There are a number of great spots outside of the city for biking. **Hondubikes** (tel. 504/239-2192, www.hondubikes.com) is an excellent bike shop that should also be able to help connect you with other riders. The shop is hard to find, so be sure to print out the map on the website even if you're planning to get there by taxi.

Horseback Riding

Out of the city to the northeast on the way to Valle de Ángeles is **La Herradura.** Contact Karen Atole at 504/265-9032 for more information.

ACCOMMODATIONS

As you would expect from a capital city, Tegucigalpa offers a wealth of hotel rooms in all price ranges. Most visitors on a budget will want to stay in the downtown area, which is where many inexpensive and midrange hotels are located. More well-heeled travelers can choose from quality hotels in Colonia Palmira and out on Boulevard Juan Pablo II, southeast of downtown. Comayagüela, across the Río Choluteca, also has plenty of hotels in the budget and midrange categories. While Comayagüela is not the safest or most interesting neighborhood, it could be an option for travelers arriving late or departing early by bus, since many bus companies have their depots here.

Under US$25

Combining bargain-basement prices with an ultra-convenient location, the best value in town is ❪ **Hotel Iberia** (on the small street leading to Iglesia Los Dolores, tel. 504/237-9267, US$7 s, US$10.50 d with shared bath, US$11.50 d private bath), centrally located between Avenida Colón and the church—a more desirable location now that the street vendors have been moved into a separate covered market. There is a pleasant, sunny common area with TV on the second floor, and hot water 6–8 A.M.

Another good choice is the American-owned **Hotel Nuevo Boston** (Av. Máximo Jeréz 321, tel. 504/237-9411, US$12 s, US$19 d), just west of Los Dolores church in Barrio Abajo. Very quiet rooms are set around two small courtyards. The rooms have fans and hot water; the larger rooms facing the street cost a bit more. No TVs in the rooms, just the one in the comfortable sitting room next to the reception desk.

If those two are somehow full, a third option in the same price range is the **Nan King** (Av. Gutemberg, a block east of the San Miguel market, tel. 504/237-1226, US$10 s, US$16 d with fan, more for a/c and TV), attached to a busy Chinese restaurant. The rooms are somewhat dark and the linens are shabby, but the bathrooms are clean enough and the owners speak English. They have big rooms that can sleep up to 10 people, and they are planning to install wireless Internet.

Also nearby is **Hotel Istmania** (1438 5a Av., half a block north of the Iglesia Los Dolores, tel. 504/237-1914, lahasbun@hotmail.com, US$22 s, US$24.50 d, $2.50 more for a/c), an aging but comfortable and clean multistory hotel. A few rooms have tiny balconies and views (try room 701), and you can catch a wireless Internet signal from the upper rooms (Internet is also available in the hotel lobby).

Hotel Granada I (Av. Juan Gutemberg 1401, tel. 504/237-2381, US$14 s/d), in Barrio Guanacaste, is something of a Tegucigalpa institution, attracting an eclectic assortment of travelers and Hondurans with its three floors of clean, inexpensive tile-floored rooms. All rooms have private baths and fans, and some have TV or two beds for a bit more money. Check mattresses as some are much the worse for wear. Drinking water is free and the reception desk sells soft drinks. Around the corner and up the hill are the **Granada II** (Subida Casamata 1326, tel. 504/237-4004) and **Granada III** (Subida Casamata 1325, tel.

504/237-0798), with about the same prices. Ask for a room that does not face the street for a more peaceful stay.

US$25-50

Hotel MacArthur (Av. Lempira 454, tel. 504/237-9839, www.hotelmacarthur.com, US$35 s, US$40 d, US$10 more for a/c) is a reliable hotel in Colonia Dolores, a residential neighborhood downtown, featuring clean, modern rooms with hot water, telephone, and TV. The highlight of the well-managed hotel is its common areas—a nice swimming pool (long enough to do laps), a reasonably priced restaurant, and an interior parking lot. Some rooms have more windows and better light than others, so don't hesitate to ask to see more than one before deciding. All in all, it's a good value for the money.

❰ Aparthotel y Plaza Colonial (Av. Jeréz between Calles Matute and Palace, tel. 504/222-7727, aparthotelcolonialhn@hotmail.com, US$38 s, US$49 d) is a surprisingly charming find smack in the center of downtown, perfectly located for explorations of the churches and museums nearby. True to its name, the small building has some colonial charm, with tile floors and an inner courtyard, but all finishings are brand new. Rooms are spacious and include a kitchenette, while apartments offer a bit more space for US$10 more.

The newest addition to the Granada empire is the **Granada IV** (Subida Casamata 1323, tel. 504/237-4004, US$26 s, US$ 42 d, all rooms with a/c), on the same street as II and III. Rooms are bigger and nicer than in its siblings, and there are computers with Internet access in the lobby.

Two hotels that don't have much going on for them beyond location are **Hotel Prado** (tel. 504/237-0121, US$33 s, US$38 d), across Avenida Cervantes from the cathedral, and **Hotel Plaza** (tel. 504/237-2111, US$35 s, US$47 d), at the western end of the *peatonal*. Neither is terribly clean, and the Prado is rather dark as well, but their central positions may appeal to some travelers.

US$50-100

❰ Linda Vista (Calle Las Acacias 1438, tel. 504/238-2099, www.lindavistahotel.com, US$49 s, US$65 d) is an attractive bed and breakfast with six cozy, tastefully decorated rooms, each with TV, direct-dial telephone, air-conditioning, and wireless Internet. There is a small but lovely colonially furnished common area with tile floors, with a computer for Internet access. Living up to its name, Linda Vista has a beautiful view from its garden.

Leslie's Place (tel. 504/220-7494, www.dormir.com, US$70 s, US$87 d), on the other side of Hotel San Martín in a converted house with a patio, offers eight rooms decorated with new furniture and equipped with TV, direct-dial telephone, and modem Internet.

An excellent midrange option run by a Honduran-American family, five minutes from the airport in the southeast part of the city, at Colonia Humuya 1150, is the **Humuya Inn** (tel. 504/235-7275, www.humuyainn.com, US$75 s, US$87 d), with nine spacious rooms and three suites, all with wood beams and tile floors, cable TV, air-conditioning, free wireless Internet access, and walk-in showers. Five efficiency apartments with full kitchens are available for US$1,100 per month. The only drawback (not a drawback at all, for some) is that there's not much in the way of restaurants or nightlife in the quiet residential neighborhood well away from downtown or Boulevard Morazán, but the hotel offers a simple buffet breakfast with the price of the room, and lunch and dinner are also available. It can fill with mission groups, so try to book ahead.

Those who want the amenities of a larger hotel can consider the fairly new **Florencia Plaza Hotel** (tel. 504/232-3800, www.florenciaplazahotel.com, US$69 s, US$81 d), conveniently located on the Boulevard Suyapa, not far from the Mall Multiplaza. The hotel has a pool, bar, and restaurant, and rooms have TVs, Internet, and mini-fridges (suites with sitting areas are also available). Rates include breakfast.

US$100 and Up

The rates quoted here are the normal rack rates. Less expensive weekend, corporate, or group rates are often available on request or through the website. As well, many of the higher-end hotels (in particular the Honduras Maya) will offer their smaller rooms for as low as US$60 d when business is slow.

The best service and rooms in downtown are at **Hotel Excelsior** (tel. 504/237-2638, US$99 s, US$110 d, suites also available), on Avenida Cervantes two blocks toward the *parque* from the Hotel Honduras Maya. The staff is attentive and most speak English well. The rooms have orthopedic mattresses and even hypoallergenic sheets! Hotel services include wireless Internet, a swimming pool, and a casino.

On a hill overlooking downtown from the east, the **Honduras Maya** (Av. República de Chile, tel. 504/280-5000, www.hotelhondurasmaya.com/english.html, US$104 s, US$135 d) has long been the hotel of choice for wealthy guests both foreign and local. Its central location in Colonia Palmira makes for an easy walk or short cab ride to many popular restaurants and bars, and with its Mayan motif it has the most local character of the big high-end hotels. The Maya has 164 rooms with all the amenities (including free wireless Internet), as well as more expensive executive suites and 18 apartments. The downstairs restaurant is nothing special, but the outdoor patio at the Bar Mirador is a great place to have a drink with a view. Other services include a lovely outdoor pool, a couple of souvenir shops, travel agent, hair stylist, a decent masseuse, and a large convention center. Many staff—including front desk—speak limited English. Prices here seem to be especially subject to fluctuation depending on how full the hotel is. Next door, under different ownership, is the **Casino Royale,** Tegucigalpa's best-known casino.

A few blocks east of the Honduras Maya is the boutique hotel **Portal del Angel** (Av. República de Perú 2115, tel. 504/239-6538, www.portaldelangel.com, US$128 s, US$145 d, $35 less for weekend nights). Set in an attractive mansion, with a restful dining room/sitting area, the hotel has 14 rooms on two floors with tile and wood floors, carved wooden furniture, tasteful decorations, and all the amenities, including an outdoor pool. Room prices include continental breakfast and airport transfer.

East of downtown are the high-end Inter-Continental and Marriott hotels. **Hotel Real Inter-Continental** (tel. 504/290-2700, U.S. tel. 888/424-6835, www.ichotelsgroup.com, weekday rates start at US$135 s/d, with significant discounts available on weekend nights), directly across from the Mall Multiplaza on Juan Pablo II, is the most prestigious in town, with a spacious atrium and adjacent outdoor patio with pool, 157 rooms, and seven suites. Their concierge services are the best in town.

Nearby, also on Avenida Juan Pablo II (although neither the mall nor much of anything else is within walking distance), is the **Marriott Tegucigalpa** (tel. 504/232-0033, www.marriott.com, US$159 s/d), a looming 12-floor structure of glass and concrete with 154 rooms, full-service restaurant as well as a bar, outdoor pool, and exercise room with machines and free weights. Shuttle service to the Mall Multiplaza is available. Again, much lower rates are offered on the weekend.

Comayagüela Accommodations

While acceptably safe by day, central Comayagüela is no place to be hanging out at night. But if your bus arrives late and you have an early bus connection the next morning, you might as well avoid trekking over to the other side of the river for your accommodations.

The █ **Hotel Condesa Inn** (12 Calle and 7 Av., tel. 504/237-7857, US$15 s, US$18.50 d) is a good choice, nearby several bus companies, with clean, pleasant rooms. A restaurant and laundry service are on-site.

A few blocks away, the four-story **Hotel San Pedro** (tel. 504/222-8987, US$5 s/d communal bath, US$9 s/d private bath), on 6 Avenida between 8 and 9 Calles, is as basic as it gets, but popular for its ultra-cheap, clean rooms.

Just across the street, the **Hotel Plaza Real** (tel. 504/237-0084, US$10.50 s, US$13 d, about US$4 more for private bath) is a step up, with 27 rooms around a leafy courtyard and free coffee served all day long.

Along the lines of the Condesa (but not quite as nice), is the **Hotel Centenario** (tel. 504/222-1050, US$18 s, US$37 d) on 6 Avenida between 9 and 10 Calles. All rooms have TV and telephone, and well-worn sheets and mattresses.

Apartments and Long-Term Accommodations

If you are in town for a longer stay, many of the hotels also have apartments available: **Hotel Istmania** (US$316/month), **Hotel Prado** (US$620/month), **Humuya Inn** ($1,100/ month), **Hotel Excelsior** (US$1,450/month), and **Hotel Honduras Maya** (US$104/night). The apartments range in amenities, and in size from suites to two-bedrooms, so inquire carefully to avoid any surprises.

There are also a number of *aparthotels* in town, typically offering a bit more space, and many with all the amenities of a hotel.

Run by a friendly Spanish-Honduran, the (**Hostal Asturias** (tel. 504/238-3866 or 504/923-0257, ediber@edured.net, US$210/ month) is in a rambling converted house on the quiet street up to Parque La Leona in Barrio Buenos Aires, a residential neighborhood north of the *parque central* that is popular with young expats. Rooms differ in size, and some have small kitchens and TVs. All are very comfortable, with private baths and hot water. Upstairs is a communal kitchen, TV, and sitting area (for those without them in the room), with a fine balcony overlooking the city. This is a really good deal for a longterm stay. Best to check ahead if you want to stay here, as the nine rooms sometimes fill up with groups.

Apart-Hotel Guijarros (tel. 504/235-6851, www.guijarros.com), in Colonia Lomas del Guijarro in front of the American School, is popular with business travelers and their families for its central location between Mall Multiplaza and Boulevard Morazán. Rooms on the lower floors can be dark due to shade from the pool-side palm trees, but those on the upper floors are airy. Two-bedroom apartments are available for US$130 a night and have full kitchens as well as washers and dryers. Standard rooms with a mini-fridge and microwave are also available (US$60 s, US$65 d). There are discounts for extended stays, which can sometimes be negotiated significantly. The *aparthotel* has an outdoor pool, an exercise bike and treadmill, and pleasant staff.

Also in Lomas del Guijarro, **Minister Suites** (2a Av., Eucarinas 3601, tel. 504/239-6195, www.ministersuites.com, US$70 standard, US$94 executive) has sleek rooms with small kitchenettes. Standard rooms have one double bed, while the executive rooms can sleep up to four in two double beds. Discounts are available for stays of a week or more.

Nearby in Colonia Tepeyac is **Aparthotel Las Condes** (Calle Yuscarán 2402, tel. 504/235-6198, www.lascondeshotel.com). One-bedrooms start at US$46, two-bedrooms at US$60, and rates drop slightly for stays longer than 15 days. Internet is available for an additional charge.

FOOD

Tegucigalpa could hardly be considered a culinary mecca, but with a little poking around you'll find a variety of different cuisines and price ranges to suit all tastes. Apart from the restaurants described here, travelers will find an inordinate number of American chain restaurants across the city (many of which have indoor play areas for children, which can be a plus if you're traveling with little ones). Perhaps worth mentioning is the free wireless Internet at McDonald's and Pizza Hut.

Snacks and Light Meals

At the northwest corner of the *parque* (and again a few blocks down the pedestrian walkway) is **Espresso Americano,** serving up a decent espresso (and cappuccino, latte, or macchiato) in a Starbucks-like atmosphere. You'll see outlets of the same chain all over town, and in fact all over the country.

On the main road in Colonia Tepeyac, **Café Manía** (6:30 A.M.–9 P.M. Mon.–Thurs.,

6:30 A.M.–10 P.M. Fri.–Sat., and 7 A.M.–9 P.M. Sun.), near the Honduras Medical Center, has equally good coffee and a better selection of pastries, plus sandwiches and desserts. Magazines and newspapers are available for browsing, and there is free wireless Internet and a small children's play room.

Also along Colonia Tepeyac's main road is **Vie La France** (tel. 504/235-7643), a Japanese-owned French chain bakery with pastries, sandwiches, quiches, and absolutely delicious chocolate croissants.

A new addition to the businesses along the *peatonal* is **Nicolati's,** a coffee shop and creperie. The crepes come in both sweet and savory varieties; small ones run US$1.50–3.50, large US$2.35–5.50.

For fresh fruit smoothies and fruit salads, look for countless little businesses advertising *licuados.* There's one at the northwest corner of the *parque,* another opposite Hotel Prado on Avenida Cervantes, and a couple more along Avenida Colon. *Licuados* are typically US$1.25–2.

Cafés

The quiet **Café Paradiso** (Av. Miguel Barahona 1351, tel. 504/237-0337, 10 A.M.–10 P.M. Mon.–Sat.) serves coffee, snacks, sandwiches (US$1.50), and standard lunch and dinner fare (US$4.75) amid a small but interesting collection of Spanish-language books. The café is popular with the local intelligentsia and frequently hosts poetry readings or other cultural events.

Café Honoré, in Colonia Palmira on Avenida República de Argentina, has pricey but flavorful deli-style sandwiches, homemade soups, salads, and pastries. Try the hearty corn chowder, with potatoes and bacon, or the artichoke dip. A hot or cold sandwich will set you back US$8–10 for a large or US$4–6 for a small, while soups cost US$3–5 for a bowl or US$1.75–3 for a cup. Lining shelves around the walls of the café are all sorts of gourmet crackers, jellies, spices, and other goodies, while imported cheeses and cold cuts are for sale at the deli counter.

Honduran

A tasty, inexpensive way to fill up is with *pupusas,* tortillas stuffed with cheese, beans, and/or pork. **Pupusas La Fuente** is conveniently located downtown on Calle La Leona. **Pupusería Paseo Universitario,** on Boulevard Morazán, has a bit better atmosphere, while our favorite is ❰ **Pupusería El Patio** (also on Boulevard Morazán, across from McDonald's), with great *pupusas,* tacos, and *baleadas.* Depending on the restaurant, *pupusas* cost US$0.70–1 each—two is a light meal, while eating four requires a hearty appetite.

Penny-pinchers can also find a good deal at **El Establo** (Av. República de Chile 781, tel. 504/239-6016), with soups, sandwiches, meat dishes, and so forth, for US$2–4.

A perennial favorite among budget travelers for its low-priced Honduran standards is ❰ **La Terraza de Don Pepe** (8 A.M.–10 P.M. daily), on the second floor of a building on Avenida Colón, three blocks west of the *parque.* If you go to eat there, don't fail to take a look at the colorful shrine by the bathrooms, where in 1986 the statue of the Virgen de Suyapa, Honduras's patron saint, appeared wrapped in newspaper, after being stolen some weeks earlier from its church. Breakfasts are a steal at US$1, while lunch or dinner of chicken, steaks, shrimp, and the like will set you back US$4–6. There's karaoke on the third-floor terrace 6–11 P.M. on the weekends.

Repostería Duncan Mayan, a block and a half off the park on Avenida Colón, is, despite the name, not a pastry shop but a relaxed diner-bar popular with both locals and a few foreigners, who crowd the 112-year-old establishment's many tables, tipping their Imperials until the 10 P.M. closing time. The food here, though just the usual steak–pork chop–chicken fare, is well prepared and hearty, and will set you back US$5–8 per meal. There is live music Thursday–Saturday. A second branch has opened in a restored colonial home a few blocks away.

One of the longest-operating upscale traditional Honduran restaurants in town is ❰ **El Patio** (tel. 504/221-4141, 11 A.M.–midnight daily or until everyone leaves), near the eastern end of Boulevard Morazán, not to be confused with its sister *pupusería* down the street. Here the kitchen serves up choice cuts of beef (US$8–15), *pinchos* (US$12), and tasty *anafre,* a great hot bean-and-cheese dip, in huge portions, all in a cavernous restaurant decorated in Mayan kitsch, with servers wearing traditional Honduran costumes.

Vegetarian

While Hondurans are big meat-eaters, it is easy enough to find vegetarian snacks such as beans and tortillas and cheese *pupusas.* Beyond that, the options are limited. **Comedor Vegetariano** (10 A.M.–2 P.M. Mon.–Sat.), near the western end of Avenida Cervantes, is dark and unappealing at first glance, but the fragrant smells coming from the kitchen quickly erase any doubts. A plate of vegetarian food with a drink goes for US$2.30.

Not strictly a vegetarian restaurant, but with several veggie meals available like soya burgers and salads, is **Cocina Creativa** (Av. Miguel Barahona tel. 504/222-4735, 8 A.M.–4 P.M. Mon.–Sat.), two blocks east of the *parque.* Breakfasts run US$1.50, and lunches (buffet except on Saturdays) are US$2.50.

The Lebanese restaurant **Gyro's,** in the Los Castaños shopping center on Boulevard Morazán, is not exclusively vegetarian either but has a number of tasty Middle Eastern veggie options like falafel and tabbouleh.

Mexican

ℂ Los Nopalitos (República de Uruguay 219, tel. 504/221-0684, noon–11 P.M. Tues.–Sat., 10 A.M.–5 P.M. Sun.), on a side street not far from the U.S. Embassy, is hands-down the most authentic Mexican restaurant in town. Three-course lunch specials plus beverage are available Monday–Friday for US$10, but the best time to visit is for a weekend lunch, when Mexican specialties such as *cochinito pibil* (Yucatan-style pork) or *barbacoa de borrego* (lamb barbecue) are prepared.

For inexpensive Mexican breakfasts, *tortas,* tacos, *burritas,* tostadas, and *garnachas*

(US$2–4), try **Tortas Locas,** on the *peatonal,* or **Turimex,** a block east of the *parque* on Avenida Colón (the latter also offers *licuados*).

Los Cebollines near Mall Multiplaza is a pricier Guatemala-based chain in an atmosphere like a Mexican-style Tony Roma's (which happens to be next door), but the food is actually good and the margaritas are great.

Italian

A cross between an imported Italian goods store and a little café restaurant, **ℂ La Bodeguita Italiana** (tel. 504/231-0374, noon–3 P.M. and 6–9 P.M. Mon.–Sat., 9 A.M.–5 P.M. Sun.) whips up quality pastas (US$9–12) with a glass of Chianti, or other daily specials like salmon carpaccio and an excellent steak. The small restaurant, with red-and-white checkered tablecloths set right in front of the shelves of imported pastas, sauces, olive oil, and wines, is at a small traffic circle *(redondel)* a couple of blocks south of Boulevard Morazán in Colonia Minitas.

Gino's (tel. 504/238-1464) in Colonia Palmira across from the Hotel Plaza San Martín, also serves up reliable pasta, at similar prices. The chocolate dessert is heavenly. Too bad the restaurant is only open for lunch (Mon.–Sat.), except Wednesdays, when it's open until 9 P.M.

Cheesy pizza with a thick and crunchy olive-oil crust is the specialty at **Tito's** (along Boulevard Morazán, by McDonald's). Ranging from US$9–13, they are not cheap, but they are worth it. Note that the large is a lot more pizza for just a little more money, and will serve two hungry people.

Chinese

There are any number of Chinese restaurants in Tegucigalpa, testifying to the city's sizable Chinese population. Most are known for low prices and large portions. One decent joint downtown is **Restaurante Nan King** (Av. Juan Gutemberg, 11 A.M.–10 P.M. daily), on the ground floor of the hotel of the same name, offering a monster chop suey and other dishes in a spacious dining room. Prices for most plates are US$4–10, and burgers are available for US$2.25.

More upscale, and easily spotted with the bright-orange plastic palm trees out front, is **Gran Lin Fa** (tel. 504/232-2271), in the Colonia Palmira at the corner of Calle Palmira, with a large selection of Chinese specialties (all large portions on large plates) at US$6–10 per entrée.

Harder to find but for many the best in town is **Mongolia** (tel. 504/232-6907), tucked away behind the Church's Chicken on Juan Pablo II.

Japanese

By consensus, the best sushi in the city is at **C Usami** (tel. 504/221-0505, noon–2:30 P.M. and 6–9 P.M.Mon.–Sat.), on a residential street of Castaños Sur in Colonia Minitas, a few blocks south of Boulevard Morazán. Take a seat in the wooden tables in the cool, tile-floored dining area and choose from the extensive menu of sushi, sashimi, tempura, and other Japanese specialties. Prices are high but not outrageous (US$5–9 for most sushi rolls) considering the quality.

Sushi Bar (tel. 504/239-3233, noon–2 P.M. and 5:30–10 P.M. Mon.–Sat.), in the Bakery Center on Avenida República de Argentina in Colonia Palmira, a block off Boulevard Morazán, is easier to find, but their sushi is pricier than at Usami and there is less selection.

Other International

C Mangosteen (noon–10 P.M. Mon.–Sat.), in Colonia Palmira on Avenida República de Argentina, is a sleek restaurant that opened in the spring of 2009 and quickly became the new favorite in town. The menu is fusion, with several Thai curries alongside more typical Continental fare. Those in the know make meals of the outstanding appetizers, which include mozzarella in panko, Peruvian ceviche, salmon and beef carpaccio, and our favorite, the *tiradito de pescado,* a twist on ceviche served with crispy banana chips. Appetizers are in the US$8–12 range, and mains US$10–20. Try to snag a table in the romantic courtyard.

Rojo, Verde y Ajo (República de Argentina, tel. 504/232-3398, noon–11 P.M. Mon.–Thurs., until midnight on Fri. and Sat.), set in a converted house, is the place to see and be seen for Honduran politicians. The menu is on the pricey side (US$12–15 for most main courses), but quality is good. Try the *corvina a la belle meuniere,* white sea bass with mushroom, butter, and lemon sauce, or the *medallones al cognac,* beef medallions in cognac sauce.

Back downtown, **Restaurante Mediterraneo** (tel. 504/237-9618, 10 A.M.–8 P.M. Mon.–Sat.) has an extensive menu with a variety of Honduran and Greek specialties—recipes that the owner learned from her Greek husband's family, such as *fakés,* lentil soup (US$3), and lamb in wine sauce (US$10). The house specialty is the "garbage sandwich," a belly-busting sandwich with an entire chicken drumstick inside (US$3.50). There are also numerous vegetarian options. The diner-style restaurant, on Calle Salvador Mendieta three blocks from the *parque,* is a popular place for office workers to have drinks and talk, and the waitresses will bring you an endless supply of *boquitas* (snacks) while you drink. The US$4–5 daily set meals are a good value.

Steaks and Burgers

The Inter-Continental's new restaurant, **Factory,** is certainly the fanciest place in town, in a beautiful setting around the hotel's pool. Both domestic and U.S.-imported cuts are available—and while the imported steaks are admittedly top-notch, the domestic cuts are also good, and about $10 cheaper (steaks US$18–30, sides sold separately).

Even Argentine expats love the beef at the Argentine-style chain steakhouse, **Ni-Fu Ni-Fa** (tel. 504/221-2056), on Boulevard Morazán. The steaks are around US$15, which also includes a trip to the salad bar. Head to their deli in Los Proceres butcher shop for an inexpensive *entraña* (skirt steak), steak sandwich, or meat to take home to the grill.

Café La Milonga (Rep. de Argentina 1802, tel. 504/232-2654) in Colonia Palmira is a café in the Argentine tradition with delicious *empanadas* and grilled meats, a decent wine selection, and a pleasant courtyard. The café occasionally hosts live music and performances, as well as tango dance classes.

The best deal in town for meat-lovers can be found at large, family-friendly **Asados El Gordo** (tel. 504/221-0152) on Boulevard Morazán, where a steak meal will only set you back US$6.

If you're craving a burger, ignore the international chains and head straight to the Honduran **Bigo's,** which has combos (burger, fries, and soft drink) for US$3–5. One convenient location is in the Colonia Palmira, a block from the Hotel Honduras Maya, with outdoor seating; another is on the northern side of the *parque central.*

Out of the City
Far up on the mountainside above Tegucigalpa, on the road to El Hatillo, is **La Cumbre** (tel. 504/211-9000 or 504/211-9001, 6–10 P.M. Tues.–Sat., noon–3 P.M. Sun.), a restaurant that would be worth going to just for its spectacular views over the city but thankfully has good international food. Bring a sweater or jacket—it can be cool up in the hills. Reservations recommended.

If you're heading northeast out of the city toward Valle de Ángeles, look for **Clarita's** on the right-hand side of the road, about halfway between Tegus and Santa Lucía. It sells authentic Mexican soft tacos along with a variety of Mexican handicrafts.

Groceries
Más X Menos (pronounced Mas Por Menos, 8 A.M.–9 P.M. Mon.–Sat., 8 A.M.–8 P.M. Sun.), on Avenida La Paz below the U.S. Embassy, is a full-service grocery with all manner of imported and domestic packaged goods. A convenient downtown supermarket is **La Colonia** (7 A.M.–8 P.M. Mon.–Sat., 8 A.M.–6 P.M. Sun.), one block west from the park on Calle Bolivar. There's also a branch in Comayagüela on 6a Avenida between 9 and 10 Calles, and the branch on Boulevard La Hacienda and the Mega-Colonia on Boulevard Suyapa carry a wide selection of imported products. **Mercado San Miguel,** next to the Hotel Granada in Barrio Guanacaste, has a decent selection of fruits and vegetables and is considerably easier to navigate than the larger market in Comayagüela.

INFORMATION AND SERVICES
Information
The **Instituto Hondureño de Turismo** (tel. 504/238-3974 or 504/222-2124, fax 504/222-6621), on the fifth floor of Edificio Europa, Avenida Ramón Ernesto Cruz behind the U.S. Embassy, can be of some use if you have a specific query but is generally unaccustomed to dealing with individual travelers.

Travel Agents
Two travel agents that can arrange plane tickets and take care of other basic services are: **Mundirama Travel** (tel. 504/232-3909 or 504/232-3943, fax 504/232-0072), in Edificio Ciisca on the corner of Avenida República de Chile and Avenida República de Panamá; and **Travel Express** (tel. 504/220-0010, 9 A.M.–5 P.M. Mon.–Fri., 9 A.M.–noon Sat.) on Av. Colón next door to Hotel Prado. (They also have a branch on Morazán near the DHL office.)

Banks
Any of the dozen or so banks downtown will change your dollars, and most will change travelers checks or put a cash advance on a credit card. During off-hours you may want to consider one of the men waving thick wads of lempiras and dollars along the *peatonal.* Though it may appear shady, the "black market" moneychangers are legal, and generally honest businesspeople—it's more a question of whether you want to pull out your cash in full view of everyone on the street, as it's always recommended you count your money right then and there.

Banco Atlántida (9 A.M.–4 P.M. Mon.–Fri., 9 A.M.–2 P.M. Sat.) will do cash advances on a Visa and has ATMs—Visa only. **Banco del**

Occidente is open 8 A.M.–7 P.M. daily (changing dollars only), and there are branches of Citibank and HSBC all over town. If you need to change some money at the last minute before getting on a bus in Comayagüela, there is a branch of **Banco Atlántida,** on the corner of 6 Avenida and 11 Calle.

ATMs are located all over the city, with terminals linked to international networks. For safety's sake it's best to take care of ATM transactions inside of malls, banks, or grocery stores (in that order)—and in better neighborhoods as well.

The American Express agent in Tegucigalpa is **Mundirama Travel** (tel. 504/232-3943 or 504/232-3909, fax 504/232-0072, 8 A.M.–noon and 1–5 P.M. Mon.–Fri., 8 A.M.–noon Sat.), Edificio Ciisca on the corner of Avenida República de Chile and Avenida República de Panamá. They will sell checks to American Express cardholders.

Communications

The main **Hondutel** office (7 A.M.–8:30 P.M. daily) is on Avenida Colón west of the square. It charges US$0.10 per minute for calls to the United States. The office receives faxes at 504/237-9715.

A much quicker and less expensive option is to make calls from one of the myriad Internet shops anywhere in town, where calls to the United States are typically US$0.05 a minute, or twice that to Europe.

The downtown *correos* (8 A.M.–6 P.M. Mon.–Fri., 8 A.M.–1 P.M. Sat.) occupies an attractive old building at the end of the *peatonal,* opposite the Museo de Identidad Nacional. In Comayagüela, the *correos* is next to Hondutel on 6 Avenida (open the same hours). Express service is available at both offices.

DHL (tel. 504/264-1300) is on Boulevard Morazán between McDonald's and República de Chile. **UPS** (tel. 504/232-7121) is in Edificio Palmira right across from the entrance of the Honduras Maya. **Federal Express** (tel. 504/221-2010) is at the end of Boulevard Morazán.

There is an Internet café on just about every other block in Tegucigalpa. **MultiNet** charges US$1 per hour, with webcams, fax service, and phone booths (US$0.05/minute to U.S. and Canada) available too. There is a branch on the *peatonal* (8:30 A.M.–7 P.M. Mon.–Sat., 9 A.M.–5 P.M. Sun.) and another at the Plaza Criolla on Boulevard Morazán (8 A.M.–8 P.M. Mon.–Sat., 9:30 A.M.–7 P.M. Sun.). There's a branch in the Mall Multiplaza as well.

Mundo Virtual (7 A.M.–10 P.M. Mon.–Sat., 9 A.M.–8:30 P.M. Sun.) is another well-located café, at the corner of Calle Salvador Menieta and Avenida Colón downtown, charging US$1.10 an hour.

Immigration and Car Papers

The central *migración* office (tel. 504/245-6491, www.migracion.gob.hn, 9 A.M.–5 P.M. Mon.–Fri.) is now on the *anillo periférico,* the city's ring road, opposite the Universidad Tecnico de Honduras. Ninety-day visas are now automatically being issued, but this is the *only* immigration office where visitors can renew the visa for an additional 30 days, for a US$20 fee.

Should you have a foreign car in Honduras and need to renew the papers, the place to go is the **Banadesa** building (tel. 504/220-1138, 8 A.M.–noon and 1:30–5 P.M. Mon.–Fri.) in Comayagüela, a block from the Parque Obelisco, to an office on the street (not the main offices upstairs), which is in charge of foreign car permits.

Laundry

The oddly named **Superc Jet Lavandería** (8 A.M.–6:30 P.M. Mon.–Sat.), on Avenida Juan Gutemberg, just west of where it crosses a bridge and becomes Avenida La Paz, charges US$2 to wash and dry seven pounds of dirty duds the same day you drop them off.

In Colonia Palmira, just off Boulevard Morazán on Calle Maipu, is the more expensive **Dry Cleaning y Lavandería Maya** (7 A.M.–6 P.M. Mon.–Fri., 8 A.M.–4 P.M. Sat.), charging US$4.50 to wash and dry up to 10 pounds.

Spas and Salons

For a truly transporting experience, head to **Yoga Garden** (tel. 504/236-9139, www.yogas gardenspa.com) about 7 kilometers outside of town on the road to Valle de Ángeles. Te spa offers massages, water therapies and acupuncture, as well as yoga classes in a relaxed, forest setting. The steam room or sauna is US$26, while a massage costs US$42.

In town, **Stetique Plaza Azul** in Lomas Del Guijarro (tel. 504/235-3635) and at the Marriott (tel. 504/239-1033) is another popular place for massages, skin treatments and salon services (nails, hair), with special chocolate and Dead Sea packages. Massages are also available at the Hotel Honduras Maya.

With branches on Av. La Paz (tel. 504/221-0237) and Boulevard La Hacienda (tel. 504/235-4950), **Ivonne's** is a popular place for a haircut or to get "done up" before a night on the town.

Spanish Schools

Despite the number of foreigners living here, there are not many Spanish schools in Tegucigalpa, and a number of those that exist are of questionable quality. One that seems to be well-regarded is **GlobalTec,** located in Colonia Minitas next to the Argentine Embassy. Several languages are available.

Emergencies

To call the **police,** just dial 199. For the **fire department,** dial 504/232-1183 or 504/239-3479, or 198. If you need an **ambulance,** call the Red Cross at 504/227-7474 or 504/227-7575, or dial 195. The **Clínica Viera hospital** can be reached 24 hours at tel. 504/237-3156 through -3160.

Medical Attention

The private **Clínica Viera** (tel. 504/237-3156 through -3160), downtown on Avenida Colón just east of Calle Las Damas, stays open 24 hours, can take care of most health problems, and has top-notch doctors. It's not cheap, so it's best to come here if you have insurance (which will reimburse you when you get back home)

or are in serious trouble (standard doctor visits can set you back US$30–40). The newer and fancier **Honduras Medical Center** (admissions tel. 504/280-1560, emergency room tel. 504/280-1201, www.hondurasmedical center.com) has similar prices. Hospital Escuela is notorious for its lack of hygiene, and so cannot be recommended except in the most dire of emergencies (a visit there should only set you back a dollar or so).

Should you need a pediatrician, Dr. José Berlioz (tel. 504/221-1939, office hours 2–6 P.M. Mon.–Fri.) is fluent in English and used by many expat families.

There are several 24-hour pharmacies around town, including **Kielsa** on Juan Pablo II across from the Inter-Continental hotel.

The Red Cross **ambulance** can be reached by dialing 195 or 504/227-9344. There is also a private ambulance service called Rescate Medico Movil, at 504/239-9999 (emergency only) or 504/232-6999 (nonemergencies). The latter is a membership service, and it will charge US$250 or more for use of the ambulance for nonmembers.

Car Rental

The best time to rent a car in Tegucigalpa is when you're headed out of town, to avoid the maddening confusion of traffic and winding, unnamed streets in the city. Should you need a car when you arrive into the country, there are a dozen agencies with booths at the airport, including the international companies **Avis, National, Budget, Alamo, Thrifty,** and **Hertz;** book in advance through their websites. Both Budget and Avis also have offices on Boulevard Suyapa, and Avis also has a desk at the Inter-Continental hotel. Rates for these companies start at about US$20 per day for compacts, US$30 per day for intermediate-sized cars, and US$50 a day for SUVs. If you plan to spend much time outside of the cities, four-wheel-drive is a wise choice. Prepay only as many days as you are sure you want—unlike in the United States, you will be charged for unused days if you turn the car in early.

Other companies at the airport include

Payless (www.PaylessCarRental.com), **Inverze** (tel. 504/239-9374), **Honduras Rent-a-Car** (tel. 504/233-0922), **Cars 24/7** (tel. 504/234-7011, rentacar24-7@hotmail.com), and **EuroAmerican** (tel. 504/280-9191). There is also a car rental agency across the street from the Hotel Honduras Maya.

A word of safety: Holdups when stopped for a streetlight are not unheard of, but simply keeping your windows rolled up is an effective deterrent (would-be muggers like to be able to verbally threaten, and will choose a different target if your windows are closed). This is not a problem outside of the major cities.

GETTING THERE AND AWAY

While a great number of tourists fly in to San Pedro Sula because of its proximity to the north coast and the Bay Islands, Tegucigalpa remains one of Honduras's two principal transportation hubs. Bus travelers trying to find their way out of town will find themselves tracking down dozens of privately owned terminals scattered all over the city, mostly in Comayagüela. Remember that schedules and prices are subject to change, and always double-check if possible before heading to the terminals.

Air

Toncontín International Airport, six kilometers south of downtown on the highway leading out to Choluteca, is infamous among airline pilots for having an unforgivingly short runway. There has been talk for 20 years about building a different airport or accommodating the airstrip at Palmerola for commercial travel, vigorously renewed after a 2008 accident at Toncontín (although the final reports on the accident showed pilot error). The runway is currently being extended a few hundred meters more, and the move seems to be on hold for now.

The terminal recently benefitted from a facelift, and there are numerous car rental agencies, a McDonald's and two Espresso Americanos, a branch of the Metromedia bookstore and of Casa de Puros, and a few good, albeit pricey,

souvenir shops. There are two banks on-site, Banco Fichosa and BAC Bamer, which will exchange dollars and travelers checks, as well as advance money on a Visa card. There are two more ATMs on the ground floor close to the check-in area. Moneychangers hang around after most international arrivals, are actually authorized by the airport, and are a good way to avoid the lines at the banks. The banks close by five, and the moneychangers leave an hour or two later, so if you are arriving on a small regional flight in the evening, ATMs may be your only option. (There is a sign just before customs indicating Money Exchange, but don't be fooled—there isn't actually any counter there.) Outside the main arrivals door is a small tourist information booth that has a decent map of the country with several city maps on the other side.

Apart from the limited food available at the airport, a Burger King, Pizza Hut, and Church's Chicken are right across the street.

Airport taxis cost US$10 to anywhere in the city, payable in dollars or lempiras. If you don't have much luggage and you're on a budget, it's much cheaper to walk right out front to the main road and catch a bus there. All the buses passing in front of the airport to the north go to downtown. You can also catch regular cabs there, but be prepared to negotiate the price before getting in, and expect to pay a premium given it's obvious you're coming from the airport—you're only likely to save US$3–4 over the cost of the airport cab.

If you're leaving the country on an international flight, be prepared to pay a US$34.04 departure tax in dollars or lempiras. No matter which currency you pay in, any change will come back in lempiras. Domestic flights have a US$1.50 tax.

Taca/Isleña, offices in town at the Plaza Criolla center on Boulevard Morazán (tel. 504/234-2422 for TACA, 504/236-8778 for Isleña, www.taca.com or www.flyislena .com) and at the airport (tel. 504/233-2192), has national flights on Isleña direct from Tegucigalpa to San Pedro Sula and La Ceiba, with connections to the Bay Islands, and international flights with Taca to San Pedro Sula and San Salvador, connecting to cities across the Americas. **Sosa,** at the airport (tel. 504/233-7351 or 504/234-0137) and in town on Boulevard Morazán near the corner of Calle Maipu (tel. 504/239-0757), flies to San Pedro Sula and La Ceiba, with connections to the Bay Islands and the Mosquitia. **Central American Airways** (tel. 504/233-1614, www.central-american-airways.com) is a great little airline with service only between San Pedro and Tegucigalpa, departing at 8 A.M. and 5 P.M. Monday–Friday. Its plane is also available for charter.

Continental has offices in Edificio Palic in Colonia Palmira on Avenida República de Chile, in the Hotel Clarion (tel. 504/220-0999, www.continental.com), and at the airport (tel. 504/233-7676 or 504/220-0999), and flies to Houston daily. **American Airlines** (toll-free tel. in Honduras 800/220-1414, www.aa.com) flies daily to Miami, and **Delta** (toll-free tel. in Honduras 800/791-9000, www.delta.com) has flights to Atlanta.

Buses to Central and Western Honduras

To **San Pedro Sula:** Direct buses to San Pedro take about 3.5 hours; those with stops can take 4–4.5 hours. Offering frequent direct regular (US$10.50) service at 5:45 A.M., 7 A.M., 9 A.M., 10 A.M., noon, 1:30 P.M., 3 P.M., 3:45 P.M., 4:30 P.M., and 5:30 P.M. is **Hedman Alas** (tel. 504/237-7143, www.hedman alas.com), on 11 Avenida between 13 and 14 Calles. Hedman Alas also runs much nicer *"ejecutivo"* and *"ejecutivo plus"* buses for US$16 and US$18, respectively. Hedman Alas also has a bus station on Boulevard Suyapa at the Hotel Plaza Florencia (tel. 504/239-0468), but only one bus a day departs from there. Less expensive but also direct is **El Rey Express** (tel. 504/237-8561, www.reyexpress.net), on 12 Calle and 7 Avenida, which departs at 5:30 A.M., 7:30 A.M., 9:30 A.M., 11:30 A.M., 1:30 P.M., 3:30 P.M., and 6 P.M. (US$8.15). **Saenz** (tel. 504/233-4229), at 6 Avenida and

9 Calle at Centro Comercial Perisur with departures at 6 A.M., 8 A.M., 10 A.M., 2 P.M., 4 P.M., and 6 P.M., charges US$18 for first-class service. **Rey de Oro** has direct buses leaving every two hours 6:30 A.M.–2:30 P.M., with a final bus at 5:30 P.M. (US$7.75), departing from Avenida Centenario by Casa Yaad and Hotel San Pedro in Comayagüela. Another first-class bus line with bathrooms, TV, and air-conditioning is **Viana** (tel. 504/225-6583), with its regular buses at 6:30 A.M., 9:30 A.M., 12:30 P.M., 1:30 P.M., 3:30 P.M., and 6:15 P.M. (US$23), and Diamond-class service available on the 6:30 A.M. and 3:30 P.M. buses (US$34). Their stop is on Boulevard Fuerzas Armadas, by the Esso gas station and Mall Las Cascadas. Half a block away from the terminal for Rey Express is **Sultana** (tel. 504/237-8101), with frequently stopping but much cheaper buses (US$5.80).

To **Siguatepeque: Empresas Unidas** (tel. 504/222-2071), on 7 Avenida between 11 and 12 Calles, has frequent departures 7 A.M.–5 P.M. (US$2.50, 2.5 hours).

To **Comayagua:** Half a block away from the terminal for Rey Express is **Sultana** (tel. 504/237-8101), with frequent service, charging US$6.75 for the 90-minute ride.

To **La Paz and Marcala: Lila** (tel. 504/237-6870) has six buses a day, leaving from the corner of 13 Calle and 8 Avenida, charging US$4 for the four-hour ride. For La Paz the charge is US$3, and the ride takes two hours.

To **Santa Bárbara: Transportes Junqueños** (tel. 504/237-2921), at 8 Avenida between 12 and 13 Calles, has buses at 7 A.M., 10:30 A.M., and 2 P.M. every day except Sunday, when there are only two, at 8:30 A.M. and 2 P.M. (US$7.25, four hours).

To **Santa Rosa de Copán, Nueva Ocotepeque,** and **the Guatemalan border: Toritos y Copánecos,** at the corner of 8 Avenida and 12 Calle, tel. 504/237-8101, has hourly buses to Santa Rosa de Copán between 6 A.M. and 1:30 P.M. (US$13, six hours), while the bus that continues on all the way to the border at Aguascalientes (US$16.40, nine hours) departs at 10 P.M.

Buses to the North Coast and Olancho

To **El Progreso: Transportes Ulúa** (tel. 504/238-1827), from its terminal at the corner of 6 Avenida and 18 Calle, offers four direct buses daily (US$8, three hours), the last in midafternoon.

To **La Ceiba: Cristina** (tel. 504/220-0117), on the corner of 12 Calle and 8 Avenida, has eight buses a day 7:30 A.M.–3 P.M. (US$11.50). **Kamaldy** (tel. 504/220-0117) also has frequent service for the same price, with its terminal on 8 Avenida between 12 and 13 Calle.

The bus line **Viana** (tel. 504/239-8288 or 504/239-9988) runs luxury, nonstop cruisers to La Ceiba with two movies in English, a meal, and coffee, nice but not cheap at US$29. Two buses depart daily at 6:30 A.M. and 1:30 P.M. from its terminal on Boulevard Fuerzas Armadas, just west of the exit to the airport and Choluteca, next to Mall Las Cascadas. **Hedman Alas** (tel. 504/237-7143, www.hedmanalas.com) also has first-class buses for US$23, connecting in San Pedro Sula. Service to Tela is also possible, always connecting through San Pedro.

To **Trujillo: Cotraipbal** (tel. 504/237-1666), 7 Avenida between 11 and 12 Calles, has two direct first-class buses a day to Trujillo via Comayagua and La Ceiba, departing at 7:30 A.M. and 10:20 A.M. (US$15, 10 hours). There are no buses straight to Trujillo via Olancho anymore; if you want to go that way, first go to Juticalpa and then catch a bus onward the next day from there.

To **Juticalpa** and **Catacamas: Discovery** (tel. 504/222-4256), on 7 Avenidas between 12 and 13 Calles, offers hourly bus service starting at 6 A.M. (US$8.50 to Juticalpa, 2.5 hours). **Aurora** (tel. 504/237-3647), on 8 Calle between 6 and 7 Avenidas, runs local buses to Juticalpa and Catacamas at 5 A.M., 6 A.M., 7 A.M., 9:30 A.M., 10:30 A.M., noon, 3 P.M., 4 P.M., and 5 P.M., charging US$4.50 for direct and US$3 for local service to Juticalpa, US$5.75 for direct and US$4 for local service to Catacamas.

Buses to the East and South

To **Danlí** and **El Paraíso: Discua/Contreras** (tel. 504/230-0470) operates direct buses to Danlí every hour between 5:30 A.M. and 6 P.M., departing from the Mercado Jacaleapa (US$3 direct, two hours; US$2.40 with stops). Five of these buses continue on to El Paraíso for US$5.50, and two (leaving Tegucigalpa at 6:30 and 11:30 A.M.) go all the way to the Nicaraguan border at Las Manos (US$6). **Rapiditos del Oriente** has faster minivan service to Danlí, departing from the DIPPSA gas station in Colonia Kennedy (along Boulevard Miraflores, near the supermarket La Colonia) for US$3.15. *Colectivo* taxis run out past Mercado Jacaleapa from Puente La Isla, between downtown and the stadium, for US$0.50.

To **Yuscarán:** Buses leave from Mercado Jacaleapa, just up from the Contreras station, three times daily, charging US$1.70. Two buses daily go via Danlí to Nueva Palestina and Patuca in Olancho, in frontier territory at the upper reaches of the Río Patuca (US$4.25, seven hours).

To **Choluteca** and **the South: Mi Esperanza** (tel. 504/225-1505) has direct service four times a day to Choluteca for US$3.90, the last at 6 P.M., from its terminal on 7 Avenida at 23 Calle, a block from the Instituto de Seguro Social. **El Dandy** (tel. 504/225-2596), at 20 Calle between 6 and 7 Avenidas, has service to Choluteca for US$3.40, continuing on to San Marcos Colón (four hours) and Guasaule (4.5 hours). **Saenz** (tel. 504/233-4249), at 6 Avenida and 9 Calle at Centro Comercial Perisur, charges US$11.40 for the ride. Buses direct to El Amatillo (four hours) and El Salvador also leave from Mercado Mayoreo, southwest of Comayagüela on the main highway exit toward Olancho (reached by local buses marked "Carrizal" or via a US$3 taxi ride). There are also many buses leaving to Choluteca from here. Catch *colectivo* taxis to Mercado Mayoreo from Avenida Cervantes a block west of the *parque central* for US$0.60.

Buses near Tegucigalpa

To **El Hatillo** and the **Parque Naciones**

Unidas: Minibuses leave to El Hatillo frequently until 8 P.M. from Parque Herrera west of the *parque central* (US$0.30).

To get to the **Jutiapa** visitors center of **La Tigra,** catch one of four buses leaving daily from Avenida Colón in Barrio Guanacaste next to a DIPPSA gas station, near the Hotel Granada, the last at 2 P.M. (US$0.75). Sometimes you can catch more frequent buses to El Hatillo and hitch from there, but traffic is unreliable, so it's better to try to catch the Jutiapa bus.

To **Santa Lucía, Valle de Ángeles** and **San Juancito (La Tigra):** Buses originate at the Mercado San Pablo but can be caught much more conveniently at the end of Avenida La Paz by Los Proceres shopping center, opposite Hospital San Felipe. (It's US$0.50 to Santa Lucía and US$0.75 for the 45-minute ride to Valle.) For San Juancito, look for buses going to Cantarranas (also called San Juan de Flores). You can catch *colectivo* taxis to San Felipe from Calle Palace on the north side of the *parque* in downtown Tegucigalpa for US$0.60. There are also *rapiditos,* nonstop vans, to Valle de Ángeles near Clínicas Viera downtown, charging US$1 for the 30-minute ride.

To **Ojojona:** Buses leave as soon as they fill up from the 6 Avenida near the corner of 7 Calle (US$0.65, 45 minutes); last bus leaves to Ojojona at 6 P.M.

To **Cedros** and **Minas de Oro:** Three buses a day, the last in early afternoon, make the two-hour trip from Mercado Mayoreo, on the highway exit toward Olancho, for US$5. Buses also go onward from Cedros all the way to Yoro on a much-improved road.

International Buses

Hedman Alas (tel. 504/237-7143, www.hedman alas.com), on 11 Avenida between 13 and 14 Calles, has *ejecutivo* buses connecting via San Pedro Sula and Copán Ruinas to Guatemala City (10 hours, US$52) and Antigua, Guatemala (11 hours, US$64).

Tica Bus (tel. 504/220-0579, www.tica bus.com), at 16 Calle between 5 and 6

Avenidas, runs one southbound bus a day to Managua, Nicaragua (US$20, eight hours); San José, Costa Rica (US$40, 15 hours); and Panama City, Panama (US$65, 31 hours). There is also one northbound bus a day to San Salvador, El Salvador (US$15, seven hours); Guatemala City, Guatemala (US$30, 12 hours bus time plus an overnight in Guatemala); and Tapachula, Mexico (US$45, 17 hours bus time plus the overnight in Guatemala). Both depart at 5:30 A.M.

King Quality (tel. 504/225-5415 or 504/225-2600, www.kingqualityca.com) has one *ejecutivo*-class bus departing at 5:30 A.M., with breakfast, TV, and paperwork help at the border, to San Salvador, El Salvador (US$37 regular, US$50 "king," six hours), or Guatemala City, Guatemala (US$63 regular, US489 "king," 14.5 hours), continuing on to Tapachula, Mexico (US$75 regular, US$94 "king"). A second, regular bus drives to San Salvador only, departing at 2 P.M. The bus to Managua, Nicaragua (US$38 regular, US$63 "king," eight hours), and San José, Costa Rica (US$57, 16.5 hours), also departs at 5:30 A.M. This bus stops in Jícaro Galá, a more convenient place to catch it if you're coming from somewhere in the south. The terminal is on Boulevard Comunidad Económica Europea (next to PAGSA), in Barrio La Granja, south of Comayagüela.

Car

Four principal highway exits lead out of Tegucigalpa. West to San Pedro Sula, the easiest route out of town is from the western end of Boulevard Fuerzas Armadas, while the exit to the east and Danlí departs Tegucigalpa from the eastern end of the same boulevard, where it crosses the *anillo periférico,* the city's ring road. South to Choluteca, follow Boulevard Comunidad Europea (sometimes referred to as the Boulevard Miraflores) south from downtown, past the airport. You can also access this highway from the *anillo periférico* and avoid some of the city traffic. To Olancho and the north, follow either 6 Avenida through Comayagüela and out Boulevard del Norte, or (much faster) get to Barrio Abajo, northwest of downtown near Parque Concordia, and look for the road exit crossing a bridge (Puente El Chile) and heading uphill to Cerro Grande, where it meets the Olancho highway. If you're heading to the San Pedro Sula exit from downtown, it's often easier to leave via this route and loop back to the San Pedro exit, thus bypassing Comayagüela.

If you're coming back into the city from the south or west and want to get to downtown, it's usually quicker to loop around farther east along Boulevard Fuerzas Armadas and the *anillo periférico* and come into the downtown area via Avenida La Paz, rather than coming through crowded Comayagüela.

One secondary road leaves Tegucigalpa to the northeast along Avenida La Paz to Santa Lucía and Valle de Ángeles, while another leaves Avenida Juan Gutemberg in Barrio Guanacaste up to El Hatillo and villages on the west side of La Tigra.

Near Tegucigalpa

The capital city is ringed on all sides with pine-forested mountains, interspersed with numerous towns and villages to visit in day trips, as well as **Parque Nacional La Tigra,** a cloud forest reserve easy to reach for casual hikers.

◖ VALLE DE ÁNGELES

Valle de Ángeles, 23 kilometers east of Tegucigalpa, leads a sort of double life. It's part playground for wealthy Tegucigalpa residents and tourists, and part rural Honduran mountain village. The town is lively on weekends, with a camera-toting, handicraft-buying crowd, but tough-looking cowboys still clomp around the cobblestone streets on horseback on their way into the surrounding pine forest. Weekdays you practically have the town to yourself, and may find some of the restaurants closed.

As its name (Valley of Angels) suggests, the town is beautifully set in a high mountain valley at 1,310 meters, surrounded by mountains on three sides and dropping off into a valley on the fourth. Apart from enjoying the atmosphere and breathing the clean mountain air, many visitors come to Valle de Ángeles to shop for handicrafts in the couple of dozen shops. Among the handicrafts sold in town are woodcarvings, ceramics, pewter, tapestries, furniture, paintings, and many other items from across the country. Despite the promising market name, the **Mercado Municipal de Artesanías,** in the market building where the Tegucigalpa buses turn around, has a less-interesting selection of handicrafts than the many stores in town. Across the street is **Lesandra Leather,** a small store with fine leather purses and wallets. Note that many stores also carry items from elsewhere in Latin America, so if Honduran origin is important to you, be sure to ask where the piece came from before you buy.

Accommodations

Right in town is **Posada del Ángel** (tel. 504/766-2233, US$20 s, US$35 d), offering 20 rooms around a large courtyard with a pool in the middle. The property has charm, making the rather dark and bare-bones rooms a disappointment. They do have hot water and cable TV, and there's also a restaurant, parking lot, and conference rooms. It's best to reserve for a weekend visit, as they often fill up. The pool is also available for day use for US$2.50.

Hospedaje Los Naranjitos (tel. 504/7666-3138, US$16 s, US$21, cold water only), a couple of blocks beyond Posada del Ángel, has very plain rooms, some without even windows, and no water in the hotel 6 P.M.–4 A.M. Although exorbitantly priced for what you get, the rooms are clean enough if the Posada del Ángel is somehow full.

Just outside of town, a kilometer up the road toward San Juancito, is **Villas del Valle**

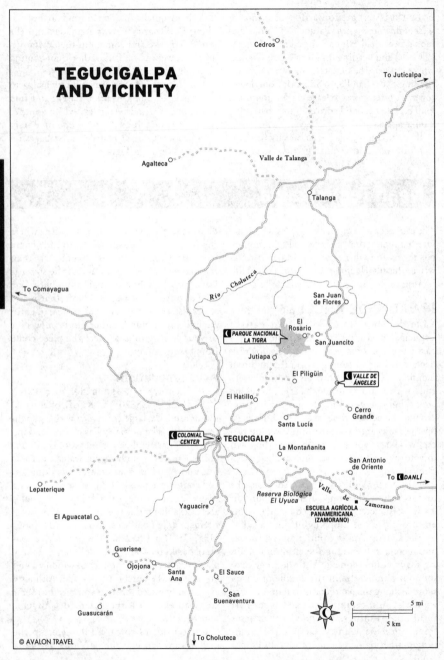

TEGUCIGALPA AND VICINITY

Cedros

To Juticalpa

Agalteca

Valle de Talanga

Talanga

To Comayagua

Río Choluteca

San Juan de Flores

El Rosario

PARQUE NACIONAL LA TIGRA

San Juancito

Jutiapa

El Piligüin

VALLE DE ÁNGELES

El Hatillo

Cerro Grande

Santa Lucía

COLONIAL CENTER ✦ TEGUCIGALPA

La Montañanita

San Antonio de Oriente

To DANLÍ

Lepaterique

Reserva Biológica El Uyuca

Valle de Zamorano

El Aguacatal

Yaguacire

ESCUELA AGRÍCOLA PANAMERICANA (ZAMORANO)

Guerisne

Ojojona

Santa Ana

El Sauce

San Buenaventura

Guasucarán

To Choluteca

0   5 mi

0   5 km

© AVALON TRAVEL

(tel. 504/766-2534, www.villasdelvalle.com, standard cabins US$32 s, US$36 d, US$51 family). The brick cabins each have fans, hot water, refrigerators, and TV, and most have a hammock hanging out front. There is also one "apartment" cabin that has a kitchenette and two-person dining table wedged into the room. There is a small aboveground pool and some children's play equipment. It's nothing fabulous, but decent.

La Casa San Martin (tel. 504/9716-3542, www.lacasasanmartin.com) is also outside of town, a country home with amenities like a Jacuzzi, renting rooms for US$30–35 per person per day, all meals included. They can organize activities such as trekking or learning handicrafts or Spanish.

Food

Because of the high number of day-trippers coming through Valle, visitors will find several decent places to eat in different price ranges. Certainly the most atmospheric place to eat in town, and also the best food, is (**La Casa de las Abuelas** (9 A.M.–5 P.M. Thurs.–Sun.), set in a cozy old adobe house dating from the mid-19th century and restored by the owners. They specialize in steaks for US$14–17 per plate but also have delicious *anafres,* sandwiches, and breakfasts for about US$6.

Half a block from the park, **El Asado Don Juan** has a menu of *anafre,* meat *pinchos,* and shrimp, and an appealing second-story terrace for eating open-air. Next door is **Epocas,** offering similar food in a unique antique-filled setting.

El Portal, half a block from the park, is in a lovely colonial building from 1851, formerly the weekend home of 19th-century president Dr. Maurelio Soto. The dishes are standard Honduran fare for US$8.50–10 a plate, and the restaurant is open daily until 8 P.M.

Pupusas Toñita on the way into town has a pleasant garden in which to munch the ubiquitous stuffed corn tortilla *pupusa.* Other good places to snack are the *pupusa* and *licuado* shops on the street to the right after the church (look for **Virginia's Pupusas**), or at the

Espresso Americano (10 A.M.–7 P.M. daily) on the square.

On the road out of town toward Tegucigalpa is **Restaurante La Florida** (tel. 504/766-2121, 10 A.M.–8 P.M. daily, later on weekends), with hearty meat and poultry dishes that run about US$15 each, sandwiches, and a couple of good soups like the *tapado olanchano,* a thick stew with steamed meat, yucca, and plantain. The place fills up on weekends with family groups that come not only for the food, but also for the giant outdoor children's play area with swimming pools and pony rides (a separate US$1.50 charge).

Services

Near the church is **Aroma del Café Ciber-Net** (9 A.M.–7 P.M.) for Internet and coffee.

There square has an ATM, and there's a **Banco del Occidente** (8:30 A.M.–4 P.M. Mon.–Fri., 8:30 A.M.–11:30 A.M. Sat.) a couple of blocks from the square, although it is only able to change dollars into lempiras. Most places in town would likely accept dollars anyway.

An interesting option for learning Spanish is offered by **Koinonia** (tel. 504/766-2555, www.escuelavalledeangeles.org), a nonprofit organization that runs a Spanish school as a way to fund its work with disadvantaged children in Tegucigalpa. Twenty hours of classes per week is US$180 for private lessons, or US$140 for small group classes, plus a US$60 registration fee and US$25 contribution to the organization. Lodging and food can be arranged for an additional US$70–110 per week.

Getting There and Away

To catch a bus to Valle, follow Avenida La Paz east past the U.S. Embassy and catch the bus by Los Proceres shopping center, opposite Hospital San Felipe, at the gas stations at the end of Avenida La Paz. Buses leaving Valle back to Tegucigalpa leave daily until 5:30 P.M. (Saturdays until 6 P.M.), charging US$0.75 for the 45-minute ride. You can also catch a *rapidito,* a nonstop van, near Clínicas Viera, charging US$1 for the 30-minute ride.

If you are on the eastern edge of Tegucigalpa and leaving to Olancho, it's just as fast, if not faster, to go via Valle and San Juan de Flores to reconnect with the main highway at Talanga, rather than through the center of Tegucigalpa.

Three kilometers from Valle toward Tegucigalpa on the left side of the highway is **Parque Turístico,** where you'll find picnic tables among the pine trees. The park recently had a face-lift, and the facilities (pool, restaurant, bathrooms) are all much improved. Horses are available for rent here.

SANTA LUCÍA

A picturesque colonial village of red tile roofs and cobblestone streets perched on a hillside 13 kilometers above Tegucigalpa, Santa Lucía is a growing destination for Hondurans and a few expatriates looking for a quiet, cool escape near Tegucigalpa. Along with nearby Valle de Ángeles, it's a popular weekend day-trip destination for city residents.

For much of the colonial period, Santa Lucía was home to some of the richest mines in Honduras. The town produced so much wealth for the crown that King Felipe II sent a wooden statue of Christ in appreciation, which can still be seen in the attractive whitewashed church, which is usually only open on Sundays (at other times you can try checking if anyone is in the office on the side of the building who could let you in). Several other icons, including the town's patron saint, are also kept inside the church. You may notice a number of young Americans in town—since the 1980s, Santa Lucía has served as the training center for the Peace Corps, where new volunteers spend their first few months in-country before moving out to their sites around the country.

Apart from having a meal, enjoying the views, and admiring the colonial church, there's not much to do in Santa Lucía, but it's a pleasant place to spend an afternoon wandering around.

The dirt road continuing past the church and turning uphill into the forest offers a route to hike along for great views over the town, Tegucigalpa below, and La Tigra forest. The road supposedly continues across the

the whitewashed church of Santa Lucía

mountaintop to the Danlí highway, reached in 2–4 hours walking, where you could hail a passing bus down to Tegucigalpa. However, there are a lot of dirt roads up here, and not always people to ask for directions, so be sure you have your bearings if you head out this way. This pine-forested mountain offers great scenery and clean air, and it is quite safe. The road would also be a great mountain-bike ride.

A trail descends from Santa Lucía to Tegucigalpa, but it lets out into some tough shanty villages on the outskirts of the city, and robberies have been reported, so that walk is not recommended.

Accommodations

The fanciest hotel in Santa Lucía is the **Hotel Santa Lucía Resort** (tel. 504/779-0540, hotel -santalucia-resort@yahoo.com, US$28–56 s/d), set on a leafy hillside 1.2 kilometers before arriving in town. The rambling main building, made with lots of brick and wood, with a tile roof, has various rooms ranging in price depending on size and amenities. There is a nice restaurant serving Honduran and international dishes (US$8–10) with both patio and indoor seating, and live music at Sunday lunch. The hotel has children's equipment, a sauna, and wireless Internet.

Also on the road into town (a 5–10-minute walk from the center) is **Brisas de Santa Lucía** (tel. 504/779-0597, hotelbrisasdesanta lucia@gmail.com), a bed-and-breakfast with clean, tastefully decorated rooms and pleasant common areas. There are 14 rooms in different configurations that can sleep 1–6 people, for US$16 per person.

Right in town not far from the church is 【 **La Posada de Doña Estefanía** (tel. 504/779-0441, meeb8@yahoo.com, US$25 s/d), a small inn with just four rooms and a charming garden. Rooms 1, 2, and 3 are all very tastefully turned out in colonial style, and rooms 1 and 2 have a stunning view of the church and hillside below. Room 4 doesn't have much going for it beyond its size—it can sleep up to five people and costs an extra US$10.

Food and Drink

There are a number of good restaurants in town, serving the city folk who come for a weekend escape. Right by the central park is **Típicos Lelys** (11 A.M.–10 P.M. daily), a block-long restaurant with open-air seating. *Plato típico* (US$8) is served daily, while *pupusas* (US$2 for a plate) are reserved for Friday–Sunday, and soups like *mondongo* (US$1.50) and *sopa marinera* (US$8) are only available on Sunday. There is children's play equipment in between the two seating areas.

Don Quijote (tel. 504/239-7920) recently changed digs from Valle de Ángeles to a house on a tree-shaded hill near the entrance to Santa Lucía. The Spanish restaurant is famous for its *paella* and also serves up fish and beef dishes (US$15–20). A basketball court and long slide might keep kids from getting bored while they wait for their food.

Glorieta Carmen, a little blue shack just down the hill from where the buses stop going toward the church, cooks up simple meals (fried chicken, burgers, tacos) and soft drinks or beer. For lighter refreshment, pick up a *paleta* (popsicle) at one of the home vendors near the church.

Before reaching Santa Lucía, about half a kilometer from the Tegus-Valle highway, is the bohemian-hipster hangout **El Jaguar,** famous for specialty drinks such as Mayan Orgasm and tamarind liqueur, and serving plenty of good food, such as shrimp and avocado quesadillas, to accompany the cocktails.

Services

A few handicrafts are available at **Artesanías Ondina** just past Típicos Lelys on the same side of the street as the park.

Internet, phone, and fax are available at **Telecentro Santa Lucía,** half a block downhill from the church, underneath the public library.

There is a Spanish school, the **Centro Hondureño de Español** (tel. 504/779-0445 or 504/239-3930) on the edge of town.

To get to Santa Lucía by car, drive from downtown out Avenida La Paz; at a junction known as San Felipe (just past a gasoline station and just before heading on to the *periférico*), turn left uphill, following signs to Valle de Ángeles. The well-marked Santa Lucía turn-off is 11 kilometers from Tegucigalpa, and the town itself is two kilometers in from the highway. Buses leave for Santa Lucía every 30–45 minutes from the Hospital San Felipe, at the eastern end of Avenida La Paz (US$0.50). The last bus back down to Tegucigalpa leaves around 5 P.M.

◖ PARQUE NACIONAL LA TIGRA

The first protected area in Honduras, La Tigra was established as a reserve in 1952 and declared a national park in 1980. It covers 23,571 hectares across the top of the mountains above Tegucigalpa, of which 7,571 hectares form the core zone. A visit to the park makes for a refreshing day trip from Tegucigalpa.

Because of the proximity to the El Rosario mines, the forests in La Tigra were heavily logged around the turn of the 20th century, so only a few patches of primary cloud forest remain. The mining company cut a dirt road across the mountain from El Rosario to Tegucigalpa, which exposed the heart of the forest for the exploitation of its precious woods for use in mines and surrounding villages. In spite of the depredations, La Tigra has recovered into a healthy cloud forest and offers a good opportunity to admire the flora and fauna, especially for those who don't have the time or desire to venture farther afield to Celaque, Sierra de Agalta, or other, better-preserved forests. Being a drier cloud forest than many others in Honduras, La Tigra is also an opportunity for bird-watchers to view species not easily seen elsewhere in Honduras, such as the blue-and-white mockingbird, rufous-browed wren, garnet-throated hummingbird, and wine-throated hummingbird, as well as the ever-popular resplendent quetzal.

La Tigra has a well-developed trail system, enabling casual hikers to enjoy a day or two wandering about the woods at their leisure, without fear of getting lost—one of the

© FUAD AZZAD

A flower vendor peddles his wares along the road to La Tigra National Park.

principal reasons for the park's popularity. Several mines are along the dirt road, some blocked off and others still open. If you want to go exploring, take good care and be advised the mines are usually full of water. Between the Hondutel towers and El Rosario, the road has been allowed to deteriorate and is now no more than a wide footpath.

Besides the road, there are seven well-marked footpaths ranging in length 600–6,600 meters. Unsurprisingly, these offer more opportunity to spot wildlife and enjoy the atmosphere of the forest. Though the dirt road does reach the highest accessible point in the park—Rancho Quemado at 2,185 meters—the views are limited by trees. The best spot to catch glimpses of the valleys below is next to the Hondutel towers on a ridge above the road. The shortest loops are near the Jutiapa visitor's center. The waterfall is closest to El Rosario and requires a fairly good fitness level to negotiate the steep inclines.

Other peaks in the park include Cerro La Estrella (2,245 meters), Cerro La Peña de

Andino (2,290 meters), and Cerro El Volcán (2,270 meters). Some of the most pristine stretches of cloud forest remain in the region south of the trails, around Cerro El Volcán, but unfortunately, the area is off-limits to visitors.

Practicalities

The entrance fee for the park is a tad high at US$10 per person (US$1.50 for nationals and residents). There are cabins with very basic rooms at both entrances to the park, charging an exorbitant US$25 per person (children US$10 pp), or you can pitch a tent at either Jutiapa or El Rosario for US$7.50 per person, the only two places camping is allowed. To reserve a space, contact **Amitigra** (tel. 504/238-6269, www.amitigra.org, amitigra@cablecolor .hn), the nonprofit that maintains the park. For a last-minute reservation at the visitors center at El Rosario, try contacting Melvin, the young caretaker, directly, at 504/9865-7016. As with Cusuco near San Pedro Sula, you're paying for the proximity to a major city and a well-maintained, though modest-sized, network of trails. Some backpackers have had luck showing up at El Rosario, pleading poverty, and negotiating a discount, but don't count on it.

Spanish-language guides, some with limited English as well, knowledgeable about the plants and animals of the park, can be hired at the visitors centers at either side of the park for US$5–15 depending on the length of the trip. Guides should be arranged in advance, again through Amitigra.

If you are traveling by bus, the best way to see the park in a day is to get up early in the morning to catch the 7 A.M. bus up to Jutiapa from Tegucigalpa, leaving plenty of time to hike across the park and down to San Juancito, where you can catch the last bus back to Tegucigalpa at 3 P.M. The park is closed on Mondays, and open 8 A.M.–5 P.M. other days. Visitors are not allowed in after 3 P.M.

El Rosario

The town of El Rosario is a collection of turn-of-the-20th-century mining buildings clinging to the precipitous hillside, some in ruins and others in good condition. The old cemetery is an interesting place, filled with the tombstones (all written in English) of the international vagabonds who worked in the mines in the 19th and 20th century. The old mine hospital houses the visitors center (where you can pay your entrance fee, get a trail map, and look at the displays on local wildlife and geography) and the *eco-albergue,* with eight clean rooms, some with private bathrooms. A cafeteria can be opened when requested by guests (US$3.15 breakfast and dinner, US$3.70 lunch), or you can bring your own food. As groups sometimes fill the place up, it would be wise to call ahead to Amitigra if you want to be sure of having a room.

Far more appealing accommodations can be found at **◖ Mirador El Rosario** (tel. 504/767-2141 or 504/9987-5835), run by a German couple, Monika and Jörg. They have built a simple wood cabin onto the steep hillside, which has two rooms that rent for US$26 each (s/d). The views from the cabin porch and the dining room (inside Monika and Jörg's home) are spectacular. Meals are not included and all food is vegetarian—dinner (US$5–6) at the candlelit table is especially romantic. There is a very clean outhouse with shower next to the cabin, and the owners can pick visitors up from San Juancito for a US$12 charge. Homemade jams and fruit wine are also available for purchase.

If the Mirador is booked, the **Chalet-Cabañas La Montaña** (tel. 504/235-5084) up the road by the school is an intermediate option. There are a couple of *pulperías* in town for stocking up on basic supplies.

To get into the park from the east side, drive, hitch, or take a bus out to San Juancito from Valle de Ángeles, 10 kilometers on a newly paved road. Buses to Cantarranas (San Juan de Flores) from Valle de Ángeles will drop you off at the *desvio* to San Juancito, from which you can walk 15 minutes into town. The steep canyon in which San Juancito sits became a raging river during Hurricane Mitch, sweeping away a great many buildings

EL ROSARIO: THE NEW YORK AND HONDURAS ROSARIO MINING COMPANY

High up on a mountainside above the town of San Juancito, on the far side of La Tigra National Park from Tegucigalpa, lie the vestiges of what was for a time the richest mine in the western hemisphere – the New York and Honduras Rosario Mining Company, better known as El Rosario.

With the active encouragement of Honduran president Marco Aurelio Soto, El Rosario was formed in 1880 by Julius J. Valentine and his four sons, Washington S., Ferdinand C., Louis F., and Lincoln. A firm believer in the need to develop the Honduran economy with foreign capital, Soto offered the Valentines tax breaks and incentives so generous that, for fear of nationalist backlash, he kept the details of the contract secret for 17 years. By 1888, El Rosario was far and away the most powerful economic concern in the country, exporting US$700,000 in bullion annually. To ensure a continued free hand to operate as they pleased, mine owners led by Washington Valentine assumed an increasingly important role in national politics, going so far as to engineer the re-election of President Luis Bográn in the 1888 presidential vote. The company was so closely identified with the U.S. presence in Honduras that for a short time the U.S. embassy was located in the mine complex at El Rosario.

The political machinations paid off handsomely, as the government invariably sided with the company in disputes with local villagers and small-scale Honduran miners over land, water, timber, and limestone. The government also repeatedly helped round up reluctant workers for the chronically understaffed mines.

Over the course of its 74 years of operation, El Rosario produced some US$100 million of gold, silver, copper, and zinc from slightly less than 6.5 million tons of ore. In the process, the mine's U.S. owners and shareholders became extremely wealthy. The benefits, though, were less evident in Honduras. In spite of the relatively high wages paid to miners, abysmal working conditions led to constant labor shortages as workers fled to their homes – many only to be rounded up by local militia and brought back to the mines. The owners' cold-blooded view of Honduran workers is evident in a letter written to shareholders by Washington Valentine in 1915 about "the severe drought which occurred during the year past": "While undoubtedly a great hardship upon the country as a whole, for the Company it had its great advantages.... [It] induced many people to seek work in San Juancito thus there was an abundance and even a surplus of labor."

In its insatiable thirst for timber, the company almost entirely denuded the forests on the San Juancito side of the mountain, and eventually punched an adit (horizontal mining tunnel) clear through the far side of the mountain to access virgin stands of wood. Much of the original cloud forest at La Tigra was destroyed by the mines, and almost all of the flora seen along the trails in the park today is secondary growth.

By 1954, the richest veins of ore were spent, and when the miners struck to support the banana workers' strike on the north coast, it was enough to convince the New York owners to shut down most of their operations. The deserted buildings of the mines, standing starkly empty on the bare hillside above San Juancito, are eerie reminders of the mine's boom years.

---

in the center of town, as well as a huge ceiba tree that was a town landmark. There is not much happening in town almost all year, with the exception of an excellent music festival at the end of April, typically the last weekend.

From San Juancito, a dirt road continues up the hill to El Rosario, the former mining complex. It's only a couple of kilometers up to the mines, but because of the steep grade, it's a stiff 1.5-hour walk, especially with a pack, so hope one of the workers passes by in a truck to give you a lift. You may also be able to convince someone in town to take you up in a pickup for about US$10. By car, the road may be impossible in the rainy season without four-wheel-drive.

Jutiapa

Less visually dramatic than the mining complex at El Rosario, but easier to get to from Tegucigalpa, is the western entrance to the park, via the village of Jutiapa.

The very easy Sendero Las Granadillas starts here—good for small children or those who want to take it easy, walkable in 45 minutes at a slow place—as does the more challenging Sendero Bosque Nublado, which is still kid-friendly but has a few inclines and takes 2–3 hours depending on your pace.

There is a tiny *pulpería* selling lollipops, gum, and the like at the visitor's center. For a more substantial meal, stop at **Ecos de la Montaña,** a few kilometers before reaching the park, for tasty *anafres* and tacos in a woodsy setting. There are ping-pong tables, pony rides, and children's play equipment, as well as a few pleasant rooms should you decide to stay the night.

To get to the Jutiapa visitors center without a car, catch one of four buses leaving daily from Avenida Colón in Barrio Guanacaste next to a DIPPSA gas station, near the Hotel Granada, the last at 2 P.M. (US$0.75). Sometimes you can catch more frequent buses to El Hatillo from near Teatro Bonilla downtown and hitch from there, but traffic is unreliable, so it's better to try to catch the Jutiapa bus. The bus schedule varies, so check the day before to find out the exact hours. At last report, one bus left at 7 A.M., allowing the entire day to hike through the park to San Juancito and catch a bus back to Tegucigalpa the same day. It's possible to hire a taxi up to Jutiapa from Tegucigalpa for around US$12, though you may have to look around for a taxi driver who knows the way.

If you're driving, take the paved road leaving Tegucigalpa from Avenida Juan Gutemberg in Barrio Guanacaste uphill past Parque Naciones Unidas, then through the town of El Hatillo. Continue just under two kilometers on the now-dirt road to a junction marked with a sign

pointing to the right to Jutiapa and La Tigra, 10 kilometers farther on.

Mountain Biking and Rappelling

Although biking in the park itself is prohibited, the mountainsides around the park, especially in the vicinity of El Hatillo and farther north, are crisscrossed with hundreds of trails and dirt roads suitable for mountain bikers. One local rider declared, his eyes shining in quasi-religious rapture, that the region around Tegucigalpa *"es un paraíso"* (it's a paradise) for mountain biking. Amitigra (tel. 504/238-6269, www.amitigra.com) can provide information about routes; some are outlined (in Spanish) on their website (look under Ecotourism/ Actividades/Ciclismo).

Amitigra can also help organize rappelling for a mere US$12 a day, not including food or transport.

CEDROS

Another fine colonial mining town near Tegucigalpa, less often visited than Valle de Ángeles or Santa Lucía, Cedros is a collection of whitewashed, tile-roofed houses clinging precariously to the edge of a pine-forested mountainside, 26 kilometers from the Olancho highway turning off some 60 kilometers north of Tegucigalpa, just past the town of Talanga. Cedros was founded in 1537 by Spanish conquistador Alonso de Cáceres Guzmán and has experienced several different gold-mining booms throughout its history. Locals like to say it was the capital of the country for 24 hours, when Honduras's first national assembly met there on August 28, 1824. The building in which the historic meeting took place still stands, a block up from the *parque,* and it is marked with a small plaque. The town's main church, **San José de Cedros,** is a beautiful chapel with a gleaming white facade and bell tower, and two carved wooden *retablos* trimmed with gold inside. The church's roof was damaged during Hurricane Mitch but was restored by 2001.

The small **Casa de Cultura** on the *parque* next to the police station, with books on

Cedros and general Honduran history, was also recently renovated. Don't fail to walk up the low hill called El Cerrito right behind the square, which offers fine views over the town and surrounding hills.

The lively local *feria,* now quite safe since liquor and gambling were banned in 1998, is held January 8.

In the surrounding hills are many old mines, including two quite close to town that were in operation until recently, both run by small-scale foreign miners. The town residents, a singularly mellow and friendly bunch, seem to have little interest in striking it rich themselves, instead scraping out a living with coffee and other farm products.

It's possible to spend the night in Cedros at **Dona Elinda's guesthouse,** behind the church. The guesthouse has clean rooms with a shared bath available for just a few dollars per night. Standard Honduran fare is available at **Restaurante Típicos,** kitty-corner from the *alcaldía.*

Three buses a day ply the route between the Cedros *parque* and Tegucigalpa (at the Mayoreo market in Comayagüela, US$4, two hours), the last one leaving in both directions in the early afternoon. You can also catch one of the Minas de Oro buses from the same market in Tegucigalpa and walk the 1.5 kilometers uphill to Cedros from the turnoff.

Fossil hunters will be interested to know that there's a spot where you can stop and look for pieces of fossilized forest, right along the edge of the road—ask locals for directions.

Northwest of Cedros, the dirt highway continues out to Minas de Oro, reportedly another attractive colonial mining town, with frequent buses from Tegucigalpa, and beyond on a well-maintained road to Yoro. Other roads branch off beyond Minas de Oro toward Olancho. Though the towns and people out here are generally *tranquilo* and the mountain scenery superb, it's a bit risky to drive in your own car toward Olancho on these roads, as highway holdups have been reported. The well-traveled road to Cedros and Minas de Oro, and on to Yoro, is quite safe, however.

RESERVA BIOLÓGICA EL CHILE

A modest reserve of pine and cloud forest atop a broad mountain bordering the departments of Francisco Morazán and El Paraíso, El Chile covers 61 square kilometers. Much of the forest on the lower flanks of the mountain has long since disappeared and turned into coffee plantations, but good-sized patches of intact cloud forest can still be found in the highest part of the park, a plateau ringed with several peaks of around 2,100 meters. The highest point in the park is Pico de Navaja (2,180 meters).

Transport into the park is not easy. Hikers can get to the reserve from either the north or the south, though the northern route is usually a bit quicker. Catch any Juticalpa bus as far as **Guaimaca,** a large town about an hour from Tegucigalpa set in a broad farming valley. From Guaimaca, a side road in relatively good condition heads south into the hills to the village of **San Marcos,** an hour or so by pickup truck. In San Marcos is a small visitors center with information about the park, and guides can be hired for trips of varying length into the forest and to nearby waterfalls. A half-day trip costs around US$5, more for a full day.

It's also possible to visit the south side of the park by driving or catching a bus (from Mercado Jacaleapa in Tegucigalpa) to **Teupasenti,** a large coffee town with several hotels and restaurants located about 25 kilometers north of the highway to Danlí. From Teupasenti, catch a ride on a pickup 2.5 hours up to the village of El Chile, on the side of the mountain of the same name, and ask around for guides into the forest. Reportedly, a lake is tucked into a high valley on the south side of the reserve.

VALLE DE ZAMORANO

The highway from Tegucigalpa east to Danlí winds up into the mountains above the city, crossing a pass before continuing down to the Valle de Zamorano. The highest peak on the south side of this mountain pass, quite close to the highway, is the **Reserva Biológica Cerro de Uyuca,** a small patch of cloud forest.

PETROGLYPHS AND PAINTED CAVES

Of the several petroglyph sites in the vicinity of Tegucigalpa, one of the most impressive and easiest to visit is near El Sauce, a couple of kilometers east of the Choluteca highway. The turnoff is at the same gas station as the Ojojona turn, but on the opposite side of the highway. The dirt road, leading to San Buenaventura, heads across open fields, then winds down off the plateau to a valley below. At the bottom of the hill is El Sauce, and a 40-minute walk from there, you'll find the petroglyphs. Once in the village, turn left off the main road at the only turn, and then left again through the first gate. Continue to the small rancho at the end of this road, and ask someone to point the way to **Las Cuevas Pintadas** (The Painted Caves), as the site is known locally. The trail follows the edge of a small valley for about 15 minutes, reaching a point where another, smaller valley runs into it. At the junction is a small, usually deserted hut. Another five minutes up the side valley, look for rock overhangs – facing upriver, there's one on the right side and three on the left. Each is filled with dozens of etched images and designs. Some modern graffiti has been added, but thankfully very little.

No one is sure how old the carvings are, but recent studies they are perhaps about 600 years old, not thousands of years old as first believed. They make for an interesting sight nonetheless.

If you don't feel like spending too much time wandering around looking for the caves, ask one of the local kids to show you the way for a few lempiras, or stop by the municipal offices in Ojojona and ask for Oscar Pineda (tel. 504/767-0161), who speaks English and will guide a walk to the caves for US$5. Apart from the caves, the valley is a beautiful place for a walk in the countryside. In this same valley are the remnants of a small colonial-era mine works, including a mill and canal.

There's some nice hiking in the reserve, but visits must be arranged through the school in Zamorano.

Past the turn to Tatumbla, the highway continues up and over the pass at **La Montañita,** where a side road turns north to Santa Lucía. On the far side of the pass, the highway snakes down the mountains into the fertile Valle de Zamorano, one of the richest agricultural regions in central Honduras. In the center of the valley, along the edge of the highway, is the **Escuela Agrícola Panamericana** (tel. 504/776-6150, www.zamorano.edu), more commonly referred to simply as Zamorano, set up in the 1940s by the United Fruit Company under the directorship of William Popenoe. The school trains farmers from across Latin America and is one of the best-respected schools in the region. Students receive hands-on experience in the fields and gardens around the attractive campus. Anyone interested in agricultural research may want to stop into the school's library or bookstore, or stop in at the small plant nursery and grocery store selling local produce (vegetables, meats, cheeses), open 8 A.M.–5:30 P.M. daily. **Banco de Occidente** also has an ATM here. There is an on-site hotel, the Kellogg center, which is especially suited for conferences. Arrangements must be made in advance if you want to tour the grounds or stay at the Kellogg Center.

A dirt road turning off the highway opposite the school leads to **San Antonio de Oriente,** a colonial village that was the subject of many paintings by its most famous son, Honduran artist José Antonio Velásquez.

OJOJONA

An attractive colonial village near Tegucigalpa is Ojojona, 32 kilometers from the capital on the crest of the mountains sloping down toward the Pacific Coast, at an altitude of 1,390 meters. Thought to have been settled by the Spanish in 1579 on the site of a Lenca village, Ojojona played a larger and more important role than Tegucigalpa for much of the colonial era because of the rich mines of El Aguacatal,

© AMY E. ROBERTSON

Ojojona is known for pottery, made in surrounding villages and sold in town.

Guasucarán, El Plomo, and Las Quemazones in the nearby hills.

Among the many colonial buildings in the now-sleepy rural town are three churches: Iglesia San Juan Bautista (1824), Iglesia de Carmen (1819), and Iglesia del Calvario. In the Iglesia del Calvario, a few blocks from the square, hangs a colonial-era painting titled "Sangre de Cristo" (Blood of Christ). Quite a vision of gory religious symbolism, it depicts an agonized Christ on the cross, his blood gushing down onto a flock of sheep placidly grazing below—but you'll have to visit on a Sunday if you want to peek inside any of the churches. The house with the wooden pillars on the square is the oldest structure still standing in Ojojona, built in 1723. For a time, the house was owned by the family of Honduran painter Pablo Zelaya Sierra, and is now under renovation.

Ojojona is known for the simple earthenware pottery made in surrounding villages and sold in a couple of shops in town.

Near Ojojona is **Cerro de Ula,** a traditional region known for its terraced hillside farming, a practice thought to date from pre-Columbian times.

Accommodations and Food

The simple **Hotel Ojojona** (tel. 504/767-0485, US$20 s, US$25 d) is currently the only place to stay in town, up a steep hill near the entrance to town. The rooms are pleasant and have hot water and private bathrooms. There is an American-owned bed and breakfast in the works.

Restaurant Joxone (9 A.M.–4 P.M. daily) just off the square serves beef pork and chicken (US$2.50–5), as well as small plates such as *enchiladas catrachas, chilaquiles* and *baleadas,* for US$0.60–1.30. Near the entrance to town, **Comedor Típica La Choza** is open later, with similar food and prices. The best snack in town is just over the Puente El Cuzuco, the footbridge out of the main square, where a little shack sells three tasty tacos for a buck (lunch only).

Services

There is an Internet café (9 A.M.–noon and 1–6 P.M. Mon.–Fri., 9 A.M.–noon Sat.)

just off the main square, facing the Palacio Municipal.

Buses leave for Tegucigalpa every 30 minutes 4:30 A.M.–9 A.M., and every hour thereafter until 5 P.M., charging US$0.65 for the 45-minute ride. If you miss the last bus, you can hire a *mototaxi* for US$2.50 to take you to the *cruce*, the intersection with the main highway, where you can flag down any bus heading to Tegucigalpa. Leaving from Tegucigalpa, catch the bus on 5 Avenida in Comayagüela, at the Mercado Mayoreo, near the Centro Comercial La Norteña. Buses leave Tegucigalpa every hour 6:30 A.M.–8:30 P.M.

To get to Ojojona by car from Tegucigalpa, take the highway toward Choluteca until you reach a DIPPSA gas station at a mountain crest, 24 kilometers from the capital. From here, a road turns right and leads eight kilometers to Ojojona, passing through Santa Ana, where there is a colonial church with a lovely painted dome.

Guarisne and Guasucarán

The village of Guarisne, six long and bumpy kilometers from Ojojona, is a traditional Lenca community and a center for ceramics. Near the town of Guasucarán, 16 kilometers by rough dirt road from Ojojona, is one of the country's best examples of a colonial mining complex. One worker with the Instituto Hondureño de Antropología e Historia reports that several of the large *hornos* (ovens) stand near the old mine, their chimneys still intact. To get there, drive or hitch a (rare) ride to Guasucarán, and from there, hire a guide for the several-hour hike. A bus drives out to Guasucarán once a day from Ojojona. There's nowhere to stay in town, but you could probably find a bed without difficulty if you ask around, or you could camp. Bring your own food.

WEST OF TEGUCIGALPA
Zambrano

Some 35 kilometers west of Tegucigalpa on the way to Comayagua, in a high valley ringed with pine forest, is the roadside town of Zambrano. About 1.5 kilometers from Zambrano, along the dirt road to La Catarata Escondida (Hidden Waterfall), is **Casería Valuz** (tel. 504/898-6755 or 504/239-2328, caseriovaluz@hotmail.com, US$40–60 d/t), an attractive lodge built with lots of wood trim, with 15 rooms of varying sizes and a kitchen/dining room downstairs. Rooms each come with hot water and many have balconies and a fireplace. Food packages cost US$25 per person for three meals. Out back are two cabins, each equipped with two bedrooms, and a kitchen. The surrounding countryside is lovely and the air is pure—a good place to get away for a few days, if that's what you're after. Be sure to book your visit ahead of time to help arrange transport. Owner Jorge Valle Aguiluz, an avid outdoorsman, can arrange horseback trips nearby or driving trips farther afield in the surrounding mountain country.

On the highway just past Zambrano going toward Comayagua, at kilometer marker 36, is **Parque Aurora** (daylight hours Tues.–Sun.), a wooded area with fields and benches for picnicking, a small lake, and horses to rent; US$0.75 for adults, US$0.35 for children under 12.

Refugio de Vida Silvestre Corralitos

About 15 kilometers north of Zambrano as the crow flies is this little-visited forest reserve similar in character to El Chile and covering 6,926 hectares of mountainside. While the pine and broadleaf forests are facing serious pressures from loggers, hunters, and farmers, plenty of intact forest still graces the upper slopes of Montaña de Corralitos (2,117 meters), in the heart of the reserve. To get there, take a dirt road leaving the San Pedro highway just outside of Zambrano to the mountain town of **San Francisco Soroguara;** ask around there for someone who can guide you into the forest or at least give some directions on where to start hiking. This is a friendly and safe rural region, where the villagers have strong ideas on the importance of hospitality. You'll have no problems getting directions from families in their tidy, painted *ranchos* dotting the lovely mountain countryside.

For more information on Corralitos and suggestions on possible guides, contact **Fundación Educa** (tel. 504/239-1793 or 504/239-1642) in Tegucigalpa, Colonia Las Minitas, just off Boulevard Morazán. Jorge Valle Aguiluz, owner of Casería Valuz in Zambrano, may also have ideas on how to get into the park. Topographical maps covering the reserve are *Zambrano 2758 IV* and *Agalteca 2759 II*.

Department of El Paraíso

The rolling hills and broad plains of the El Paraíso department in southeastern Honduras have long been favored by Hondurans for their rich agricultural potential and mineral wealth. The valleys of Jamastrán and Moroceli are dotted with farms, cattle ranches, and tobacco fields, and the surrounding hills are filled with coffee plantations.

The climate in El Paraíso is generally temperate and comfortable, with most villages and towns located between 800 and 1,000 meters in elevation. Several major river systems are either born in or pass through El Paraíso, including the Río Choluteca, the Río Coco on the border with Nicaragua, and the Río Guayambre, one of the major tributaries of the Río Patuca. Adventurers can begin trips in the department of El Paraíso into Olancho and Gracias a Diós, along either the Río Patuca or Río Coco.

◖ YUSCARÁN

A charming colonial mining town, Yuscarán is a jumble of twisting cobblestone streets and tile-roofed plaster buildings perched on the edge of a mountain at an elevation of 850 meters. The town centers around an inviting square filled with trees and flowers. The climate is semitropical and the surrounding area is pleasingly lush. Yuscarán makes a great place to spend a night or two, enjoying the relaxed colonial ambience or taking a hike in the surrounding mountains.

Gold was discovered above Yuscarán in the late 17th or early 18th century, and the town was officially founded in 1744. After hitting an early peak toward the end of the 18th century, the mines went into decline until the last decades of the 19th century, when there was a brief revival.

The charming cobblestone streets are thanks to forced labor from the penitentiary, a century-old custom that ended in 1998 when Hurricane Mitch washed the penitentiary building away and it was rebuilt elsewhere. (The municipality now takes responsibility for maintaining the stone streets.)

Yuscarán is home to various events throughout the year, notably the **Mango Festival** held in May or June. This is a major mango-producing area, and the entire population descends upon town to enjoy music, dancing, and drinking. The other big local party is the town *feria,* in honor of the Immaculate Conception of María. Held in early December, the *feria* is notable for (in addition to attending special masses) people getting drunk and lighting off *bombas,* and a bizarre and hysterical type of polo contest using donkeys instead of horses, suggested by a Peace Corps volunteer a few years back.

Although only about 2,000 people live in Yuscarán, the town is the capital of the El Paraíso department.

Sights

The central square is a great place for people-watching, flanked on one side by the simple **Iglesia de San José** on the park, finished in 1768 and usually referred to as the *parroquia.* The main sight of note in town is **Casa Fortín** (8 a.m.–4 p.m. Mon.–Fri.), a family house built in 1810 and abandoned in 1910 when family members contracted tuberculosis and left for Tegucigalpa. The two-story house, declared a national monument, serves as the town museum but due to limited funding is pretty rundown. If it's closed, ask at nearby houses for the owners, who will let you in. You'll find many mineral samples, as well as mining and farming tools from the past century. The person in charge of the *casa,* Carlos Rodriguez, is very knowledgeable about Yuscarán's history and surroundings. He works with a local group that built a few trails in Monserrat and cleared out a couple of old mines for tourists to visit, and is one of a couple of guides in town who can show the way.

After visiting Casa Fortín and the church, it's easy to spend an hour or two walking around the town admiring the rustic colonial architecture and cobbled streets. Don't be surprised if an older gentleman named Oscar Lezama approaches you in the park—he's another Yuscarano eager to share his wealth of knowledge with visitors, and he can also help arrange for guides.

The best-known *aguardiente* liquor in Honduras, more commonly known as *guaro,* is produced here at the **El Buen Gusto** and **Monserrat** factories. Curiously, Yuscarán *guaro* is technically illegal to sell in town (other forms of alcohol are perfectly legal), but it can still be found if you know which *pulpería* to ask in. Better yet, get a free tour of one of the distilleries, at the end of which you're usually handed a bottle. For a tour of El Buen Gusto (7 A.M.–4 P.M. Mon.–Fri., 7 A.M.–11 A.M. Sat.), just make your way to the distillery, a couple of blocks from the park—visitors are welcome any time. Tours are in Spanish, but even if you don't understand the language it's worth taking a peek to see a few of the 22,000 daily liters in production.

For more information on hiking in the mountains above town, stop by **Fundación Yuscarán** (tel. 504/793-7158, fundacion yuscaran2005@yahoo.com, 8 A.M.–4 P.M. Mon.–Fri.), a local tourism and natural resources NGO located next to the town hall building on the park.

The small white sanctuary of **Santa Anita,** perched atop 78 wide stone steps a 15-minute walk from the park down the road to Oropolí, is a fine hilltop viewpoint under an enormous ceiba tree, also the village's favored make-out spot. It's a great place to walk to anytime, but sunsets are particularly fine. An all-night vigil with music and singing is held at the sanctuary the night of December 9 to celebrate the Day of the Virgin of Guadalupe.

Accommodations

(Casa Colibrí Hospedaje (tel. 504/793-7611, US$20 s, US$24 d) is a cozy hotel in a colonial building facing the park. Tastefully decorated with wood furniture and Guatemalan bedspreads, the two guest rooms have private bathrooms and share a pleasant common room with a sitting area and book exchange. The hotel also has a very complete folder on local hikes, guides, and restaurants.

Next door in another attractive colonial building is **Hotel Colonial Yuscarán** (tel. 504/3294-9399, US$13 s, US$16 d). The rooms here are much simpler, but clean and with TVs, fans, and private baths.

Apart-hotel Nolasco (tel. 504/793-7139, carlosnolascohn@yahoo.com, US$35 one bedroom, US$41 two bedroom) has two brand-new fully-equipped (even a washer and dryer!) apartments a block from the square. The one-bedroom can sleep up to three people, and the two-bedroom sleeps up to four, plus sofa-beds that can squeeze in more.

A cheaper option is **Aparta-hotel Ochoa** (tel. 504/793-7199, US$18 s/d), three blocks from the *parque central* down the road to the right of the church. It has a tiny swimming pool, four basic but clean rooms, and one apartment that rents for US$26.

Hotel Carol (tel. 504/793-7143, US$7 s, US$11 d), right at the entrance to Yuscarán, is a last-resort choice with saggy beds and grubby bathrooms.

Food

Be prepared for simple and inexpensive Honduran *comedor* fare anywhere you go in Yuscarán. The only exception is **Restaurante Kim Fu,** next to Hotel Carol, with Chinese food for US$3–5 a plate.

Comedor Lita, facing the **Casa Fortín,** is popular with locals and offers typical Honduran plates for US$2–3. On the outskirts of town on the road to Oropolí is another good choice, **Típicos Monserrat,** which also offers breakfast, and *sopa de res* in addition to the standard meat and chicken, each US$2.50.

Information and Services

A good place to find out what's happening in Yuscarán, particularly the festival dates, which can change from year to year, is the town's website, www.yuscaranhonduras.com.

The only bank, **Banco de Occidente** (8 A.M.–4 P.M. Mon.–Fri., 8 A.M.–11 A.M. Sat.), changes dollars and can give you an advance on a credit card. There is slow Internet service available in the town library.

Hondutel (7 A.M.–8 P.M. Mon.–Fri., 8 A.M.–6 P.M.Sat.–Sun.) and **Honducor** (the post office) are half a block from the *parque central* up the street to the right of the Hotel Colonial Yuscarán.

Getting There and Around

Usually eight buses a day drive the 68 kilometers between Yuscarán and the Mercado Jacaleapa bus station in Tegucigalpa, the first leaving at 5:30 A.M. and the last at 4 P.M., charging US$1.70. Two buses a day head to Danlí, at 6:15 A.M. and 7:40 A.M., also charging US$1.70. It's also possible to get a pickup truck ride up the 17-kilometer paved spur road to the Danlí–Tegucigalpa highway at El Empalme and flag down a passing bus to either Danlí or Tegucigalpa. For getting around town or to nearby destinations, *mototaxis* are plentiful (US$0.25 for a ride in town, and trips all the way out to the Danlí–Tegucigalpa highway can be negotiated).

There is a direct bus to Danlí daily at 6:15 A.M. (US$1.70) and another bus that comes from Oropoí, passing through Yuscará at 7:40 A.M. on its way to Danlí.

Carlos Rodríguez (tel. 504/9790-5710, cultura yuscaran@yahoo.com) and Carolina de Lezama (tel. 504/793-7160) can guide visitors around town, the mines, to the petroglyphs,

and on the trails. Carlos charges US$5 for a tour around town, US$10 for the petroglyphs, and US$15 on the trails, transportation not included. Gustavo Pavón (tel. 504/9851-0961, guenpaga@yahoo.com) is another naturalist guide certified in tourism and able to lead and make arrangements for large groups (and charges accordingly).

Reserva Biológica Yuscarán

The highest parts of the mountains looming above town form a biological reserve covering 4,187 hectares. Peaks inside the reserve include El Volcán (1,991 meters), El Fogón (1,825 meters), and Monserrat (1,783 meters). From Yuscarán, take the road out toward the Tegucigalpa highway and look for a dirt road turning steeply up to the left (west) just outside of town, past a small *quebrada* (stream) and little wood house. The road winds precipitously up the mountainside seven kilometers to the Hondutel radio tower atop Cerro Monserrat. Suitable for four-wheel-drive only, and unnervingly steep even with that, the road is walkable in a couple of hours (or an hour by car). Totally exposed in places on the bare hillside, the road offers spectacular views east over the Río Choluteca Valley and into Nicaragua and south down to the Pacific Ocean.

The uppermost part of the mountain is covered by a modest cloud forest, much of it secondary growth. An easily spotted trail leaves the dirt road from just below the Hondutel radio tower and heads down into the forest, where you can look out for the many noisy birds living in the reserve. Visitors could pitch a tent easily enough either near the tower or in the woods below. Try to convince the Hondutel *vigilante* to let you into the compound on the mountaintop for the view across to the forest-covered peak of **El Volcán** to the west.

A saddle, now cleared of its forest and used as pasture, connects Cerro Monserrat to the main section of the reserve around El Volcán. Beware of camping out in this pasture as the ticks are plentiful—stick to the forest near the Hondutel tower. No obvious trails continue west from the saddle up into the forest toward El Volcán. El Volcán is reportedly best accessed from the *aldeas* of La Granadilla and La Cidra, on the north side of the reserve. Take the road out of Yuscarán toward the highway, and look for a well-traveled gravel road turning left (west) three kilometers from town. Off this road, which leads eventually to Guinope in the Valle de Zamorano, a side road turns off left (south) up toward El Volcán. The only trails out this way will be from local hunters.

The trail system in the reserve and to surrounding attractions can be confusing. To avoid getting lost (and to create local incentive to preserve the forest), consider hiring a local, trained guide. Contact one of the guides in Yuscarán or the **Fundación Yuscarán** (tel. 504/793-7158, fundacionyuscaran2005@yahoo.com), with an office just off the park, for guides and also for general information about the reserve, the town, and surrounding areas. They can provide you with a map of the five trails they maintain. It's possible to visit several old mines perforated into Cerro Monserrat and the surrounding hills, as well as take day hikes to a beautiful lake (there's a photo on display in the Fundación Yuscarán office) and two waterfalls, La Cascada Aurora and La Cascada El Barro.

Elsewhere near Yuscarán

Two sets of petroglyphs are located south of Yuscarán, one near the junction of the Río Oropolí and the Río Choluteca, past the town of Oropolí, and the other near the village of Orealí, closer to Yuscarán. Along the banks of the Río Choluteca near Orealí are a series of swimmable hot springs. As the Río Choluteca here is downstream of Tegucigalpa, it would seem advisable not to take a cooling-off dip in the river, but the springs themselves are clean. Two buses drive between Yuscarán and Oropolí daily, and hitchhiking is not difficult, especially early in the day.

The petroglyphs of Aguacates was recently discovered near town, a 25-minute walk or 10-minute in a *mototaxi,* but you'll need a guide to find them as the trail is not yet marked and involves dodging through some barbed wire fences.

Off the Tegucigalpa–Danlí highway, near the Yuscarán turnoff, is **Teupasenti,** once a bustling market town for the many coffee growers in the area. Unfortunately, post-Mitch, the market never revived. Going farther up this road takes you to the village of El Chile and the southern side of the **Reserva Biológica El Chile,** a small patch of cloud forest. Buses to Teupasenti leave Tegucigalpa's Mercado Jacaleapa twice a day, and truck *jalones* up to El Chile are not hard to find.

The town of **Moroceli,** also off the Tegucigalpa highway near Yuscarán, west of Teupasenti, has a large cigar factory right in the center of town, run by a Cuban expatriate who is reportedly happy to take visitors on a tour of his shop.

◖ DANLÍ

Founded in the late 1600s, Danlí is a sizable city of 68,000, though still with a small-town feel. It lies in the center of the Valle de Cuzcateca, which extends south to the town of El Paraíso, and is not far from the rich Valle de Jamastrán. Apart from the cigar industry in Danlí, cattle-ranching and coffee production are the region's economic mainstays. Danlí is a relaxed town with a couple of colonial sights worth spending a couple of hours walking around in if your travels take you in this direction. The town explodes to life during the annual Festival de Maíz (Corn Festival), with daily music and dance performances, rodeo shows, and food stands selling corn in every imaginable form.

Sights

La Iglesia de la Inmaculada Concepción, on the *parque central* and pleasingly flanked by palms and other verdant trees, was built between 1810 and 1817, at the end of the colonial era. Inside are five simple wood and gilt *retablos* (altarpieces). On the opposite side of the square is the **Museo del Cabildo** (8 A.M.–noon and 1–3:45 P.M. Mon.–Fri., US$0.50), housed in a two-story building built in 1857 and showing its age. It features an odd assortment of pre-Hispanic and colonial-era trinkets, and the old

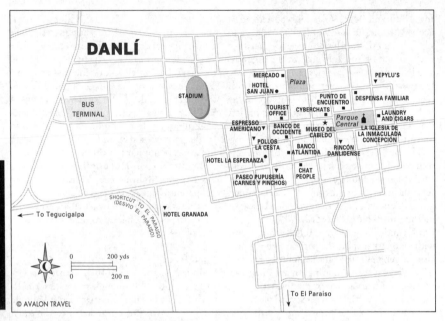

caretaker will happily tell you about them if your Spanish is up to it.

Acuaducto Los Arcos are the minor ruins of Honduras's second potable water system, built in 1770 and located in the Barrio Los Arcos, a 25-minute walk from central Danlí, only worth visiting if you're a die-hard archaeology buff.

Danlí is home to a burgeoning cigar industry. A dozen or so factories operate in and around the city, including Honduran Cuban Cigars, Cuban Honduran Tobacco, Plasencia Tobacco, Central American Cigar, Tabacalera Occidental, and Puros Indios, most of which welcome visitors—just knock on the door. **Puros Indios** (tel. 504/763-1486, 8 A.M.–4 P.M., Mon.–Fri.), an excellent hand-rolling factory on the road leading from town to El Paraíso, will happily give tours (in Spanish) of its factory, which produces 25,000 cigars a day. Boxes of cigars are available for purchase direct at the factory for about half their U.S. price (starting at US$42 and up, payable in lempiras or dollars). City maps indicating cigar factories (as well as hotels, restaurants, and Internet cafés) are available at the tourism office.

This is also a cowboy town, and you'll see several *talabarterías* (leather goods stores) selling saddles, hats, and other items. They can turn out good-quality products with several days' advance order.

The **Festival de Maíz,** held annually the last week of August, is Danlí's major yearly party. Featured are music (usually including many of Honduras's top artists), dancing, bullfights, a parade, and many different corn products for sale. Next door to the tourism office is an office dedicated solely to the festival that can provide a detailed schedule of events (tel. 504/9834-8613, eliohe@yahoo.com).

Hikes near Danlí

Beyond Acuaducto Los Arcos is the approach to La Piedra de Apagüiz, a nearby mountain that can be hiked up in a couple of hours. Another worthwhile day hike is to Montaña San Cristóbal, about 10 kilometers outside

Danlí, a short car ride or one-hour walk to the base of the mountain. Take the road to Mineral de Agua Fría and ask around for the trail. Continuing on this road will bring you to the ruins of the Agua Fría mines.

Accommodations

Hotel La Esperanza (tel. 504/763-2106, US$15 s, US$24 d with fan, US$21 s, US$35 d with a/c), near the gas station three blocks west and two blocks south from the *parque* toward the exit to El Paraíso, has about the best low-price rooms in town, distributed around a one-story interior courtyard and all with TV and fans. Parking is available.

A spartan but clean option is the **Hotel San Juan** (tel. 504/763-2655, US$11 s, US$22 d), three blocks west and a block and a half north of the *parque*. The largish rooms have TVs, fans, and hot water. The **Hotel Apolo** is best avoided unless you've run out of money— a grimy single room with shared bath is just US$5 (you get what you pay for).

On the highway bypassing Danlí between Tegucigalpa and El Paraíso is **Hotel Granada** (tel. 504/763-2499, US$30 s, US$41 d with fan), a one-story, motel-style building favored by visiting businesspeople, with comfortable rooms with cable TV and hot water. The hotel has a restaurant.

Food

Of the several restaurants in the center of town, **Rincón Danlidense** (7 A.M.–9 P.M. Tues.–Sun.) is about the best. A block south from the *museo*, the restaurant offers a large menu of reasonably priced Honduran standards, like *anafre* (bean-dip appetizer, US$4), *plato típico* (US$4), or *tacos catrachos* (US$2.50). Full meals with chicken, pork, or beef with sides go for US$5–6.

Pepylu's (tel. 504/763-2103, 7 A.M.–10 P.M. daily), one block north of the church, has similar meals for similar prices, with tables in a quiet indoor courtyard.

Popular with locals, **Paseo Pupusería**, located across from the gas station, is a pleasant place for the namesake *pupusas*, as well as beef and *pinchos*.

EATING CORN IN DANLÍ

Having created an entire festival around corn, it's only fitting that *danlidenses* have come up with a host of drinks and snacks made from this humble grain.

Those made of fresh corn can be found in found stands around the park during the festival, in particular:

- **tamalitos** – small tamales made of fresh corn normally served with a dollop of cream

- **montucas** – larger tamales of fresh corn with pork or chicken

- **atol** – a corn pudding served warm, thin, and drinkable; warm, thick, and eaten with a spoon; or cooled and cut into chunks

- **guirilas** – fat tortillas of fresh corn

- **elotes** – corn on the cob

Other corn-based products popular year-round include:

- **chicha** – corn liquor

- **tortillas de maíz** – tortillas of dried corn flour

- **tamales** – made of dried corn, usually without meat inside

- **nacatamales** – like a *tamal*, but with meat (typically pork or chicken)

Restaurante Kuan Ming (tel. 504/763-2105, 9 A.M.–10 P.M. daily), two blocks from the square on Calle Canal, serves decent Cantonese food (or the Honduran version thereof, at least) for US$3–5 per meal.

On the main avenue between the square and the bus terminal is **Pollos La Cesta** (8 A.M.–4 P.M. and 5–11 P.M. daily), serving tasty chicken in a fast food environment.

There's an outpost of **Espresso Americano** three blocks west from the park. A popular street snack in Danlí is *alboroto* or *sopapo*,

THE CIGAR CAPITAL OF HONDURAS

© AMY E. ROBERTSON

a cigar roller's workstation

Because of its reliable climate, with an average temperature of 24°C (75°F) and an average 75 percent humidity, the region surrounding Danlí is considered a natural humidor, perfect for cigar production. Taking advantage of these ideal conditions are a dozen or so factories, capitalizing on the boom in cigar smoking in the United States and Europe.

A few of the factories use mainly locally grown leaves to make a midrange, inexpensive cigar, while others use only the premier leaves of the local crop, and blend in leaves at times from Brazil, Panama, Ecuador, the Dominican Republic, Nicaragua, and even Italy to create a hand-rolled, top-quality stogie, prized by connoisseurs and highly rated in *Cigar Aficionado* magazine.

Wherever the leaves were grown, when they first arrive at the factories, they are stacked in *pilones* (piles), sprayed with water, and left to sit for several months. Because of a chemical reaction in the leaves, the *pilones* literally cook themselves, reaching temperatures of 45°C (113°F). Each factory has its own master in charge of the *pilones*, who decides when the leaves have been properly cured and are ready to roll. This idiosyncratic process is probably the most crucial in establishing a certain cigar's flavor – two factories can buy the same leaves at the same time and, because they cure them differently, produce completely different-tasting cigars.

After taking them from the *pilones*, work-ers remove the veins by hand from the leaves in a separate room, and the leaves are again sprayed and stacked. Rolling is accomplished in two stages: First, the filler leaves, usually four of them, are rolled and cut to shape, and then put in a mold overnight. The next day, the wrapper leaf – often an Ecuadorian Sumatra or Connecticut broadleaf – is put on, and the cigar is moved into the humidor room for storage.

Most cigars rolled in Danlí are exported and are very difficult to come by in Honduras, one exception being those produced by Puros Indios, which sells to the Casa de Puros stores in San Pedro Sula and Tegucigalpa (the company accountant, José Manuel Espinoza, gladly gives tours – in Spanish – of the factory). Lower-grade cigars are available in many tourist gift shops (sometimes along with cigars rolled at the Flor de Copán factory in Santa Rosa de Copán). Finding your way into a *bodega* in one of the factories around Danlí is the best way to buy a box of your choice (even the *bodega* at Puros Indios has many cigars not available in-country).

One top-rated cigar to come out of the region is the Rocky Patel Decade Torpedo, made by the Paraíso cigar factory in neighboring El Paraíso. For a well-regarded cigar made of exclusively Honduran leaves and wrapper, look for the Camacho Corojo Toro made by Tabacos Rancho Jamastrán.

sorghum that is toasted and popped like popcorn and served with honey.

A good spot to pick up groceries is at **Despensa Familiar,** a block north of the church.

Information and Services

The tourist information office is two blocks west of the park, just past the office for the Festival del Maíz, and is open until 4 P.M. weekdays.

There is a dry-cleaners/laundry service located just behind the church that, conveniently, also sells cigars at what they claim are wholesale prices. It even accepts credit cards.

BGA, Banco de Occidente, and Banco Atlántida all change dollars and sometimes travelers checks. **Hondutel** and **Honducor** (the post office) are just off the park. There are numerous Internet shops in town for checking the web and placing inexpensive international telephone calls.

Emergencies

To reach the **police** dial 199, 504/763-2224, or 504/763-2253; for the **fire department** dial 198 or 504/763-2340. For an ambulance, call the **Red Cross** at 504/763-2295.

Getting There and Away

All buses leave Danlí from the central bus terminal near the exit of town toward Tegucigalpa. **Discua/Contreras** (tel. 504/763-2217) runs buses every hour or so to Tegucigalpa 5:30 A.M.–6 P.M. (US$2.40 for the local service and US$3 for express). Nonstop *rapiditos* (minivans) leave from half a block from the bus terminal every two hours 6 A.M.–5 P.M. The *rapiditos* charge US$3.15 and arrive in Colonia Kennedy in Tegucigalpa, at the DIPPSA gas station on Boulevard Miraflores, from where it's possible to find a *colectivo* into town.

Frequent buses ply the route back and forth to El Paraíso for US$1.15. **Transportes Mi Empresa** has three buses a day from Danlí to Nueva Palestina (where boats can be found down the nearby Río Patuca into the Mosquitia), US$4.20 for the 4.5-hour ride.

Tegucigalpa is 98 kilometers from Danlí by a well-maintained, two-lane highway. Continuing past Danlí toward Nicaragua, the smooth paved road continues through El Paraíso to the Nicaraguan border at Las Manos, 30 kilometers from Danlí.

Taxis from the terminal to anywhere in town cost US$0.65–0.80.

EL PARAÍSO AND THE NICARAGUAN BORDER

A midsized agricultural town 18 kilometers from Danlí at one end of the Valle de Cuzcateca, El Paraíso is the last stop before the Nicaraguan border at Las Manos, 12 kilometers up the road.

El Paraíso is the heart of a major coffee-producing region (20 percent of the country's coffee production), and if you visit during the November–February harvest season, you can learn about the picking, drying, and toasting processes.

Should you happen to be in the vicinity during the week around May 15 (the city's anniversary), consider stopping by to check out the dancing, food, and cultural events during the **Festival Cultural El Paraíso.**

The most centrally located hotel in town is certainly **Hotel Isis** (tel. 504/US$9 s, US$14 d), right on the park, with basic comfy rooms with fan, hot water, and TV. If the Isis is somehow full, head four long blocks south of the park, to the **Hotel Quinta Avenida** (tel. 504/893-4298, US$9 s, US$15 d), which is similar but with saggier beds. The owner speaks a bit of English.

Just across from the Quinta Avenida is El Paraíso's newest and fanciest hotel, the **Hotel Mario Chavez** (tel. 504/793-4345, hotelmario chavez@yahoo.com, US$26 s, US$37 d), named for a late congressman from the town. The pleasant rooms have TVs, hot water, air-conditioning, and wireless Internet, and there is a decent pool and a small kids' play area. A restaurant is in the works. The hotel can fill with groups at times, so making a reservation in advance is smart.

Típicos La Galera (7 A.M.–10 P.M. daily) is

TEGUCIGALPA

a decent, inexpensive place on the park serving well-made Honduran standards as well as burgers, *pupusas,* and *baleadas.* A meal here will set you back just US$2–3.

One block from the park past the UNAH building is the clean and modern **Comedor Campestre** (7 A.M.–8 P.M. daily), with similar meals and prices, and their breakfast selections include pancakes and corn flakes.

Restaurante Chen's, half a block from the park past Comercial San Cristobal, serves up huge portions of chop suey, fried rice, sweet and sour any kind of meat goes, US$2–6 depending on how big a portion you want.

Only open for dinner Friday–Sunday, **Café D'Palo** has good (though not huge) Honduran meals for US$2–3, but the main attraction is the live music on Saturday nights only, well worth checking out if you are in town.

Espresso Americano is on the corner of the park. The second-floor terrace of **Refresquería Nancy,** facing the park, is another pleasant place to have a coffee and snack.

A kilometer or two out of town on the road to Danlí, **Mi Pequeño Jardín** (9 A.M.–10 P.M. daily) serves up pasta and pizza as well as shrimp, fish, and breakfasts in a grassy setting with a few outside tables. Pasta starts at US$4, while large pizzas and shrimp dishes will set you back US$10–12.

Banco Atlántida (8 A.M.–4 P.M. Mon.–Fri. and 8 A.M.–noon Sat.) on the park will change U.S. dollars or provide a cash advance on a credit card (there is no ATM). The best bet for changing to or from córdobas is at the border itself.

There are a number of Internet cafés in town where you can also place international calls, including **Cafetos.com** half a block from the park past Farmacia Mi Esperanza.

Minibuses to the border leave every hour or so from the terminal until 4 P.M., charging US$0.50. *Colectivo* taxis fitting four passengers will go for US$5.

Buses to Danlí leave every 20 minutes between 6 A.M. and 5:40 P.M., charging US$0.85. Buses to Tegucigalpa leave every half hour starting at 4 A.M. and ending at 3 P.M. and charge US$3.80. Buses to Las Manos leave every 40 minutes starting at 6:30 A.M. and ending at 4 P.M., charging US$0.75.

Las Manos

The Nicaraguan-Honduran border at Las Manos is a collection of huts along the highway with a large gate across the middle, in the midst of green hills dotted with fields of coffee. Both the Honduran and Nicaraguan immigration and customs offices are theoretically open 24 hours a day, but sometimes it can be difficult to roust people at late hours so it's best to come through during the day. The Honduran officials take a half-hour lunch break at noon.

Services at the border comprise a Hondutel office, *casa de cambio, comedor,* and *pulpería.* Official and freelance exchangers have basically the same rate. Buses continue into Nicaragua every hour or so from the border until 6 P.M. It takes about an hour to get to the next big town in Nicaragua, El Ocotal, and costs US$3. The entire trip from Tegucigalpa to the border can be accomplished in three hours by bus, if you don't have to wait long at El Paraíso for a bus to Las Manos. Taxis out to the border from El Paraíso run US$5, for up to four people. The last bus returns to El Paraíso from the border at 5 P.M.

The Pacific Coast

Honduras's Pacific coast is a hot plain facing the Golfo de Fonseca (Gulf of Fonseca), which it shares with El Salvador and Nicaragua. Coastal beaches do exist, most notably at Cedeño and Isla del Tigre near Choluteca, but they can't compare with those in nearby El Salvador or on Honduras's Caribbean coast. Set back from the coast is cooler hill country, dotted with dry forests and old mines. Aridity along the coastline is traded in for humidity during the rainy season (June through September), while the hills remain fairly green year-round. The region's struggling economy, one of the poorest in the country, is dominated by shrimp-farming and cattle-ranching.

Three major rivers—the Choluteca, Goascarán, and Nacaome—trisect the narrow Choluteca Plain. The country's only volcanoes, the termination of the volcanic chain of the Colinas de Juacarán beginning in El Salvador, are found here. Isla del Tigre (Amapala) is an example of one of these extinct volcanoes.

Much of the Pacific coastline is, or was, covered with mangrove swamps, but in recent years the growing shrimp-farming and cattle-ranching industries have severely threatened these fragile ecosystems. The **Bahía de Chismuyo,** not far from the El Salvador border, is a protected area of mangroves in name, but shrimp farmers have been clamoring to be allowed to clear more land there. One of the country's most forceful environmental groups, the Comité para la Defensa y Desarrollo de la Flora y Fauna del Golfo de Fonseca (Committee for the Preservation of the Fauna and Flora of the Gulf of Fonseca, or CODEFFAGOLF), wages an unending fight to halt the expansion of the shrimp farms.

The Choluteca Plain and surrounding hills have been heavily farmed for years, and the deforestation and massive use of pesticides and fertilizers have combined to wreak havoc on the land. Desertification is advancing relentlessly in the south, and many *campesinos* have been forced to migrate to other parts of the country because the land is no longer arable.

One unavoidable fact about Choluteca coastline is the heat. For much of the year, especially outside of the May–October rainy season, it is extremely hot, often reaching temperatures as high as 40°C (104°F). Rainfall on the Pacific coast is not as intensive as on the Caribbean side, and the wet and dry seasons are much more clearly defined. The rains start in April or May and continue until November, while the remaining months are invariably cloudless.

CHOLUTECA

Although it's the fourth-largest city in Honduras, with 154,000 residents, Choluteca feels more like an overgrown village. The small colonial downtown area remains much as it was a few centuries ago, with its *parque central,* narrow cobblestone streets, and one-level, tile-roofed colonial buildings, most of which are in a sad state of disrepair. Sights in Choluteca are limited, but it can be an interesting place to spend half a day, especially if you are traveling between Honduras and Nicaragua or El Salvador.

The name Choluteca, which is thought to mean "broad valley," derives from the preconquest inhabitants of the region, the Chorotega Indians. The Chorotega, related to the Toltec, were relatively recent arrivals themselves, having migrated from Chiapas, Mexico, sometime around A.D. 1000.

The area around Choluteca was first explored by the Spanish under the command of Andrés Niño, as part of a 1522 expedition led by Gil González Dávila up the west coast of Central America from Panama. Capt. Cristóbal de la Cueva founded Xérex de la Frontera—later called Choluteca—in 1541.

During colonial times, Choluteca grew quickly, its economy driven by the active Pacific seaport and the rich mines of El Corpus, in the hills above Choluteca. The town was originally settled on the west side of the Río Choluteca, but after pirates sacked and torched the town in the 17th century, colonists relocated to the present site.

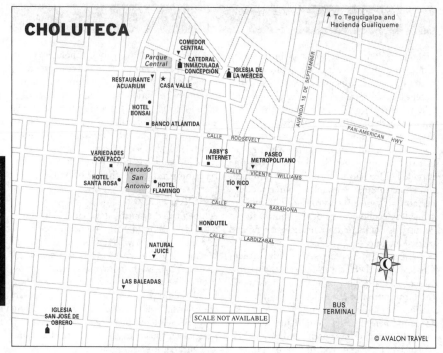

CHOLUTECA

To Tegucigalpa and
Hacienda Gualiqueme

COMEDOR
CENTRAL

Parque
Central

CATEDRAL
INMACULADA
CONCEPCIÓN

IGLESIA DE
LA MERCED

RESTAURANTE
ACUARIUM

CASA VALLE

HOTEL
BONSAI

BANCO ATLÁNTIDA

CALLE ROOSEVELT

PAN-AMERICAN HWY

VARIEDADES
DON PACO

ABBY'S
INTERNET

PASEO
METROPOLITANO

AVENIDA 15 DE SEPTIEMBRE

Mercado
San
Antonio

HOTEL
SANTA ROSA

HOTEL
FLAMINGO

CALLE VICENTE WILLIAMS

TÍO RICO

CALLE PAZ BARAHONA

HONDUTEL

CALLE LARDIZABAL

NATURAL
JUICE

LAS BALEADAS

IGLESIA
SAN JOSÉ DE
OBRERO

SCALE NOT AVAILABLE

BUS
TERMINAL

© AVALON TRAVEL

Anyone interested in the history and legends of Choluteca and the region, and who reads Spanish, should look for three books published in 1996, *Por Cuentas, Aquí en Choluteca, Por Cuentas, Aquí en El Corpus,* and *Por Cuentas, Aquí en Nacaome.*

Local officials talk about restoring many of the colonial buildings downtown in an effort to boost the town's meager tourism potential, but they've yet to take action. The annual **Feria Patronal** of Choluteca, held December 6–14, is reputed to be quite a bash, with lots of good food, drinking (lots and lots of drinking), music, dancing, and fireworks on the last night.

Orientation and Getting Around

Choluteca is essentially a one-story city, extending along dusty (or muddy, depending on the season) streets from the downtown square. It's built along the east bank of the Río Choluteca, and the highway to Tegucigalpa leaves Choluteca across an impressive-looking suspension bridge, one of the few bridges in southern Honduras to survive the wrath of Hurricane Mitch in 1998.

The highway from Tegucigalpa, called the **Panamericana,** continues east, bypassing downtown on its way to the Nicaraguan border. The city has two markets: The main, older one, **Mercado San Antonio** (usually called Mercado Viejo), is two blocks south of the square; the other, **Mercado Nuevo,** is six blocks farther south. Although Choluteca covers a lot of ground, most places of interest to travelers are within walking distance of the square in the northwest quadrant. One exception is the bus station, a dozen or so blocks southeast of the square. Taxis to the terminal and around town cost US$0.75.

Sights

The **Catedral Inmaculada Concepción** on the square dates from at least 1643, the date on the baptismal font, but is thought to be older.

JOSÉ CECILIO DEL VALLE: PHILOSOPHER OF CENTRAL AMERICAN UNITY

Known among Hondurans as *"El Sabio,"* or "The Wise One," José Cecilio del Valle is renowned as one of Central America's first great intellectuals, a sort of Thomas Jefferson to Francisco Morazán's George Washington. Del Valle was born on November 22, 1777, to a wealthy landowning family. As a youth, he moved to Guatemala for his education, and at the age of 23, he graduated as a lawyer from the Universidad de San Carlos. At that time, the first calls for independence from Spain could be heard echoing through Central America, and Del Valle quickly plunged into the nascent movement with a passion, founding the pro-independence newspaper *El Amigo de la Patria* and leading the Partido Evolucionista.

When independence was officially declared on September 15, 1821, Del Valle was on the scene at the Palacio de Guatemala and was one of the writers of the Act of Independence. He initially opposed the annexation of Central America by Mexico under Iturbide but agreed to act as a deputy to the congress in Mexico.

As a relentless defender of the rights of Central America, Del Valle irritated Iturbide, who had him thrown in jail for six months. When the empire fell in 1824, Del Valle regained his freedom and was elected deputy in the new congress of the Central American Union.

Conservative Manuel Arce then appointed El Sabio as vice president, but he refused to accept the office, campaigning against the illegitimacy of Arce's regime. When Arce was overthrown in 1829, Del Valle competed against independence hero Francisco Morazán for the Central American presidency but lost. Del Valle finally won the 1833 elections but died before he could take office.

Throughout his career, Del Valle was legendary for his intelligent and humanitarian proposals and his tireless efforts to unite the Americas. In 1822, he published a manifesto on his Pan-American beliefs, which ends with the words: "America from this moment will be my exclusive occupation – America by day when I write, by night when I think. The study most worthy of Americans is America."

TEGUCIGALPA

The wood-paneled ceiling resembles the hull of a boat. In 1917, the facade was rebuilt to its present form. If you can find the woman who takes care of the premises, it is possible to persuade her to let you climb the (almost-functioning) clock tower for expansive views of the surrounding area.

Two blocks east of the cathedral is the older **Iglesia de La Merced,** also built at an unknown date but thought to have been erected in the middle or late 16th century. It features eye-catching twisted ("salomonic") columns on the outside. In colonial times, the surrounding neighborhood housed the city's Indian and black population, who prayed at the church. The church is normally only open on Saturday.

The colonial building on the southwest corner of the square is the former home of famed native son José Cecilio del Valle (1777–1834).

Check out the back of the 100 lempira bill for a picture of this historical building, which now houses the local library. It's possible to enter the house through the *turismo* office on the side of the house (just past the library entrance), although there's not much to see inside (nor much information to be had at the tourism office). The statue in the middle of the square is of Del Valle.

If you have nothing but time (and preferably your own transportation since it's a bit far), check out **San José de Obrero** on the southwest side of town for a more unusual church experience. There is a refuge for injured animals on the church grounds. Although the cages are quite small, the animals, including monkeys and white-nosed coatis, are treated well. Inside the church is an impressive, modern mural (painted in 1982) full of political symbolism.

Accommodations

Of the less expensive hotels in town, **Hotel Santa Rosa** (tel. 504/782-0355, US$5 s, US$8 d with fan, or US$12 s, US$18 d with TV and a/c), next to the old market, is the best value. There are hammocks lining the inner patio, perfect for a midday break from the heat. **Hotel Bonsai** (tel. 504/782-2648, US$14 s with fan, US$20 d with a/c, all with TV), half a block south of the square, has a nicer courtyard, but in some rooms the bath is only partially enclosed. On the east side of the Mercado Viejo is **Hotel Flamingo,** an absolutely spotless hotel with a friendly manager (tel. 504/782-4342, Hotel_flamingoch@yahoo.com, US$18 s, US$24 d with TV and a/c). Both Santa Rosa and Hotel Flamingo face the market, and many buses leave from spots around there. Choluteca is the hottest city in Honduras, so springing for air-conditioning here might be a wise choice.

There are several motel-style hotels along the Panamericana, convenient for those traveling through with a car and popular with people in Choluteca on business. **The Southern Paradise Hotel** (tel. 504/782-9291, www.paradise hotel.cholutecaenlinea.com, US$37 s, US$53 d) along the road heading to Guasaule is modern and nicely furnished. All rooms have air-conditioning and TV, its pool is the cleanest in town, and it has a small restaurant. Two kilometers farther south is the **Hotel Casa Real** (tel. 504/782-8529, US$40 s US$58 d). Its spacious rooms are perhaps showing a little age, but that's more than made up for by the large pool with three slides and the free Internet (two computers in the lobby and wireless Internet throughout the hotel). There is a restaurant as well.

For something homier, try the **Las Tres Marías** (tel. 504/9985-2369 or 504/782-3363, memp1116@hotmail.com, US$30 s, US$40 d), a family-owned bed-and-breakfast that opened in early 2009 in the Brisas del Sur neighborhood, on 1 Calle (from the Instituto Jose Cecilio del Valle take a left and go 2.5 blocks). The home is comfortable, and the family has a property on the beach as well for those interested in soaking up the sun.

By far the classiest and most expensive setup in town is **Hacienda Gualiqueme** (tel. 504/782-2750, fax 504/782-3620, www.hotelgualiqueme .com, US$67 s, US$90 d), just across the suspension bridge on the highway toward Tegucigalpa, on the right side. Rooms are spread across extensive grassy grounds, each with stained wood beams, tile floors, and high ceilings. Besides the standard amenities, there is a pool and children's play equipment. At the time of writing, the restaurant served breakfast, but lunch and dinner were available only for groups.

Food

One of those classic general store–restaurants where everyone stops in to catch up on the local gossip, **Comedor Central** (6 A.M.–8 P.M. Mon.–Sat. and on Sun. morning) on the square is a good place for snacks, breakfasts, light meals, and beers. Breakfasts and the *comida corriente* go for $2.

One of the most popular places to eat with locals is ◖ **Las Baleadas** (7 A.M.–3 P.M. daily), an outdoor café six blocks south of the central park and then a half-block west. Las Baleadas seems to be where all the city's taxi drivers take their lunch. In addition to countless variations of the ever-popular *baleada,* there is a daily hot plate selection. Lunch here will set you back US$1–2 a plate. Olman, the man who runs it, couldn't be nicer to foreigners and is always happy to help out.

For a classier meal, try **Restaurante Acuariun** (closed Mondays) across the street from the Valle house, serving dishes such as seafood soup and breaded shrimp. **Tío Rico** (9 A.M.–5 P.M. Mon.–Thurs., open until late Fri.–Sat.), on the main west-running street in town, two blocks from the Panamericana, has burgers, meat, and seafood (US$2–6 a plate) in a relaxed setting. Friday and Saturday nights it turns into one of Choluteca's best places for a drink and some dancing. **Paseo Metropolitano** is kitty-corner from Tío Rico's, and its *pupusas* and *pinchos* are two for one on Tuesday and Wednesday.

For a change of pace, **Hong Kong** has standard Chinese fare in a relatively upscale environment for US$4–8 a plate.

Licuados Frutas Tropicales (7 A.M.–6 P.M. Mon.–Sat.), five blocks south of the central park, is the best place in town to grab an ice-cold drink, either a *licuado* or a fruit-filled *natural*. For US$1–2 they will mix anything you want in a blender with juice and ice. They often have most everything on hand (orange, banana, watermelon, apple, papaya, carrot, etc.), although some fruits are seasonal. Another great drink is *morro*, made from *semilla de jícaro* (calabash seed) and sold on the street in little plastic baggies with straws.

The best supermarket in town is **Maxi Bodega** next to Pizza Hut on the Panamericana.

Services

Banco Atlántida will exchange dollars but not travelers checks, while BGA will exchange both. Several banks around town have internationally linked ATMs. **Honducor,** several blocks southeast of the square, has express mail service. Next door is **Hondutel,** which can receives faxes.

Internet shops seem to be popping up all the time in Choluteca, and are easily found downtown. Most of them offer the same high-speed Internet and international phone calls. Prices are usually US$1 per hour of Internet and US$0.05 per minute to call the States. One of the best places on the main road in town is **Abby's Internet,** with 15 computers.

Half a block east of the park is **Hotelito and Variedades Don Paco.** There are far better hotel choices in town, but they have a good selection of **souvenirs** if you're looking to pick something up.

In case of an emergency, you can always reach the **police** by dialing 199, 504/782-0701, or 504/782-0785, and the **fire department** by dialing 198 or 504/782-0503. **Policlínica Ferguson** (tel. 504/782-0281 or 504/782-0300), on 3 Calle and Avenida Central, can help with basic health problems.

Getting There and Away

Mi Esperanza (tel. 504/782-0841) has inexpensive regular buses to Tegucigalpa from a private terminal a couple of blocks north of the main terminal, charging US$3.90 for the three-hour ride. Buses run every two hours 4 A.M.–5 P.M. **El Dandy** (tel. 504/782-0204) has buses that depart every 45 minutes from the main Choluteca terminal, a dozen blocks southeast of the square, to the Mercado Mayoreo in Comayagüela (Tegucigalpa). The four-hour ride costs US$3.40. **Astrasur,** also located at the terminal, has similar prices and services.

For express, **Líneas de Lujo** has an office a block from the terminal and charges US$10 for the 2.25-hour drive. **Saenz** (tel. 504/782-2712) has buses at 6 A.M., 10 A.M., 2 P.M., and 6 P.M., and charges US$11.40.

Direct buses to Guasaule on the Nicaraguan border leave from the terminal daily every half-hour between 5:30 A.M. and 6 P.M., charge US$1.50, and swing by the main terminal to pick up passengers before leaving town. It's a 1.5-hour ride, and the bus drops passengers off right at the bridge over the border. A *microbus* from the terminal costs just 10 cents more for the nonstop ride. They operate 6 A.M.–5 P.M. and leave as soon as the van is full, about every half hour.

Buses leave the main terminal for San Marcos de Colón frequently between 4 A.M. and 6 P.M. for US$1. From San Marcos, you can continue on to the Nicaraguan border at El Espino. Buses also frequently leave the main terminal heading to El Amatillo at the Salvadoran border.

Buses to El Corpus leave regularly between 5:30 A.M. and 6 P.M. from the terminal and markets, charging US$1.50 for the one-hour ride (look for buses marked El Triunfo).

Many buses also have stops around the Mercado Viejo. Buses to Tegucigalpa leave from in front of El Nilo on the east side of the market between 6:30 A.M. and 5 P.M., charging US$3.40, and buses to El Amatillo leave from the corner south of Hotel Santa Rosa. The first bus heads out at 3:30 A.M., and they leave roughly every 25 minutes thereafter until 5:50 P.M. The ride takes two hours. (It's not advisable to hang around the market before dawn, but if you were staying at the Hotel

Santa Rosa you could lurk in its doorway until the bus appears.)

All buses leaving from the terminal invariably take a spin through town to look for more passengers, so if you can't get to the terminal, it's often possible to flag one down. Taxis to the terminal cost US$0.75 from the square.

The main highways leaving Choluteca toward Guasaule (47 kilometers), San Marcos de Colón (56 kilometers), El Amatillo (85 kilometers), and Tegucigalpa (142 kilometers) are all paved and in relatively good condition.

CEDEÑO

The Pacific coast town of Cedeño is a low-budget Honduran beach getaway, a fairly seedy collection of worn wooden buildings lining a reasonably decent stretch of sand. Its popularity is due principally to the fact that it's the closest decent beach to Tegucigalpa. The few restaurant/discos in town are usually packed on the weekends and deserted during the week. In spite of being on the protected gulf, waves can get fierce, depending on the tide and the season. Better beaches than the one in town lie within walking distance, just a few minutes in either direction. If you happen to be visiting in December, January, or February, consider staying to watch an amazing golden sunset over the Pacific Ocean. The rest of the year the sun sets over El Salvador.

Four direct buses leave Cedeño daily for Tegucigalpa, the last in early afternoon, charging US$2.30. Buses frequently depart for Choluteca, US$1. The last bus out of town to Choluteca leaves at 4:30 P.M.

The turnoff to Cedeño is five kilometers west of Choluteca at Santa Elena on the Panamericana Highway. The 34-kilometer, newly paved road to the highway passes through sugar and melon plantations and the town of Monjarás.

PUNTA RATÓN

Along the road to Cedeño is the turnoff to Punta Ratón, where a nice beach can be found if you can get a ride out there and back. Punta Ratón is also home to a local sea turtle conservation project. During the months of August, September, and October, sea turtles land on the beaches nearby to bury their eggs, which then hatch in October and November. Those tiny hatchlings that survive make their way out to sea and begin the cycle again. The sad truth is that a large portion of the turtle eggs end up as appetizers in this poor region. However, a local group has organized a project to gather eggs after the mother buries them, protect them while they gestate, and put them down on the beach by the water when they hatch. Volunteers are welcome September 1–25 and can stay for no charge at a very bare-bones cabin—with mattresses, water, and electricity—in exchange for their assistance. (A charge may eventually be applied as a way to upgrade the accommodations.) Contact the mayor's office (*alcaldía*) in Marcovia (tel. 504/787-4001) for details, and ask for Roni Umansor.

◖ ISLA DEL TIGRE AND AMAPALA

The 316-square kilometer volcanic island of Isla del Tigre is hardly more than spitting distance from the Honduran mainland, but it has a few decent beaches, some good seafood, and an appealing lost-in-time feel. Amapala is its only town, and Hondurans often refer to the whole island by the town's name.

Amapala was once Honduras's primary Pacific port, but it has long since been superseded by Puerto de Henecán near San Lorenzo.

COCKTAIL DE CURILES

Curiles are black clams, typically served in a ceviche-style cocktail. While delicious, they can unfortunately be contaminated with high levels of *E. coli*, particularly those harvested near the shores of Cedeño. (The same can be said for oysters harvested from the Golfo de Fonseca.) Do yourself a favor and eat them cooked.

the volcanic Isla del Tigre, in the Golfo de Fonseca

Amapala is now a decaying 19th-century relic, looking for a way to survive. The primary attraction in the town itself is the well-restored church, dating from the late 1800s. The surrounding water is warm (although rather dark from mud stirred up from the sea floor), and several beaches around the island are worth checking out. Tourism is perhaps the island's best hope for survival, and so far it's enticing 1,000 cruise shippers a year to visit.

Andrés Niño first sighted Isla del Tigre in 1522, but the Spanish didn't settle there initially. Pirates used the island as a hideout until 1770, when the governor of San Miguel, El Salvador, ordered a town built. For a short time during the presidency of Marco Aurelio Soto, Amapala functioned as the capital of Honduras.

Although subject to the same heat as the Choluteca plain, the island is often graced by an ocean breeze, making the climate more hospitable. Isla del Tigre is six kilometers in diameter, and the volcanic peak is 783 meters high. Until the early 1990s, a U.S. Drug Enforcement Agency (DEA) contingent staffed a base at the peak, but now it's deserted.

A small tourist office at the dock in Amapala can help answer questions about where to go on the island—when it's open that is (8 A.M.–noon and 2–5 P.M. Mon.–Fri., 8 A.M.–noon Sat.).

Around the Island

A 17-kilometer dirt road rings Isla del Tigre, so named for one of the island's long-extinct animal denizen—it makes for a great bike ride, although you'll need to bring your own bike. Many extremely poor *campesino* families live in simple huts along the road, scraping a living from little agricultural plots on the mountainside. From Amapala heading southwest (counterclockwise), about 20 minutes from town by foot and just past the Honduran military post, a dirt road turning inland leads to the top of the volcano, the site of the now-deserted DEA base. The walk takes about two hours of hard hiking, and the views, especially in the early morning when the sky is clear, are superb. (It's also smart to get your hike in as early as possible before the heat really kicks in.) It's possible to spend the night if equipped with tent, water, and food—sunrise is usually lovely.

About 45 minutes from Amapala on foot, not far past the mountain road, is **Playa Grande,** a swath of black sand facing El Salvador and lined with several fish restaurants. At the north end of the beach is La Cueva de la Sirena, a bat-filled red volcanic rock cave with two entrances, one on the ocean. Local legend has it that Sir Francis Drake hid a stash of his ill-gotten booty here.

Of the popular beaches, **Playa Negra** is by far the cleanest, and it's actually possible to see through the water to your feet if the water is calm. Many other less obvious and usually deserted beaches are located around the island, awaiting exploration. Playa El Zapote is one of the only white-sand beaches on the island (white from crushed shells) and there is a hotel, but there are also a lot of biting *pulgas de mar* (water fleas). From Playa Caracol on the west side, you can walk across the shallow water to the barely inhabited Isla el Pacar, where you can pitch a tent, or navigate around the outcropping to the right for a beach all for yourself.

© FUAD AZZAD

A boat awaits its fisherman on the shores of Isla del Tigre.

The waters virtually lap the edge of the restaurants at Playa Grande and Playa El Burro during high tide, so plan accordingly. Avoid swimming at the beaches where fishermen work, as manta rays and jelly fish like to swim nearby in search of fish discards.

Accommodations

Keep your expectations low. One of the best places to stay is at **Mirador de Amapala** (tel. 504/795-8483, www.miradordeamapala.com, US$30–45 d), a few minutes' walk from the main dock. *Mirador* means lookout, which is a bit deceiving, since only one or two of the 30 rooms have a view of the sea just across the street. The modern-style hotel, with air-conditioning, TV, and hot water, also has an adequate restaurant, a murky pool with a water slide, and free transportation via *mototaxi* to and from Playa Grande (imperative, given that the beach right at the hotel is unswimmable). Promising new rooms are being built right along the shoreline that look like they will truly have spectacular views. Room prices seem to vary according to how much business they have.

Directly on Playa Grande is the **Hotel and Restaurant Dignita** (tel. 504/795-8707, US$26 s/d without a/c, US$42 with a/c). The three simple rooms come with two double beds and private bath—but no view of the sea.

Hotel Playa Negra (tel. 504/220-1183 for the owner Roxani in Tegucigalpa, or 504/795-8027 to contact the hotel directly, US$79 s/d), up the hill from the beach of the same name, seems to have recovered from its nadir of disrepair. While the grounds are still somewhat run-down, rooms and the pool were clean during a recent visit. Reports since then have been hit or miss. The spacious rooms have two double beds and a small sofa, and there is a restaurant on-site with a nice view of the water. Kayaks can also be rented for a row in the sea.

There are a couple of places to stay at Playa El Burro. **Aquatours Marbella** (tel. 504/795-8050, US$42 s/d) has humid rooms with two double beds, private baths, and air-conditioning. They also charge nonguests US$2 a person to use their "entertainment center," which consists of a cloudy pool, broken-down patio furniture, billiards, music, raggedy hammocks, and beach games. The next-door restaurant, **Veleros** (tel. 504/795-8040, US$16 s/d), has three simple but tidy rooms.

Locals also claim that the island is safe enough for camping right on the beach, if you should be so inclined.

Food

Dignita on Playa Grande has the best seafood in town, with excellent seafood soup and "lobster" (more like giant prawns) (US$6–12). There are also a number of shacks along the beach selling simple and cheap dishes like fish *carnitas.*

El Faro Victoria (lunch and dinner Fri.–Sun., dinner only the rest of the week), next to the dock, has decent burgers, fish, chicken, shrimp, and lobster for US$3–10 per meal. The friendly owner, who speaks a bit of English, also rents out two tiny guest houses two blocks from Playa El Burro for US$10.50 a night.

Veleros is a good restaurant serving sandwiches (US$1.50), fish (US$3–6), and lobster (up to US$18 for the largest), with a deck right on the beach at Playa El Burro. The restaurant at the **Hotel Playa Negra** also has a nice view of the sea.

Practicalities

There isn't a bank in town, but most businesses will accept dollars if you don't have anything else. It's often a good idea to bring a lot of change in lempiras, as breaking big bills on the island can be a problem. There are two Internet shops in town, one of which (by the health clinic) does international telephone calls too.

To get to the island by public transport, get off a Choluteca–Tegucigalpa bus two kilometers west of San Lorenzo to the dirt road turnoff to Coyolito. Here, hop one of the hourly buses or hitch a ride the 30 kilometers to Coyolito. Alternatively, you can get a bus to San Lorenzo and catch a Coyolito-bound bus from the center

of town. *Colectivo* boat rides from Coyolito to Amapala cost US$1.30, or US$7 for a private boat ride. These same boats charge about US$26 for a half-day tour around the island or varying prices to specific destinations (other nearby islands, mangrove forests, etc.). For more information, check with the **Capitanía del Puerto** in Amapala (tel. 504/795-8643). One direct bus goes to Tegucigalpa at 3 A.M. each day, but it's easy to take a bus to the main highway and catch a passing bus to either Tegucigalpa or Choluteca.

One bus circles the island each day early in the morning, and there's some traffic in the morning—good for hitching rides—but in the afternoon, it's usually deserted. Pickup trucks stand in for taxis on the island, and rides can cost US$3–7 depending on the destination.

SAN LORENZO AND THE TEGUCIGALPA HIGHWAY
San Lorenzo

A hot, modern town of 17,000 on the gulf, San Lorenzo's main reasons for existence are nearby Puerto de Henecán, the country's third-largest port after Puerto Cortés and Puerto Castilla, and the shrimp-packing plants in town. Visitors to San Lorenzo are generally there for one of two reasons: for business or to feast on the freshest seafood in southern Honduras. Check out the random assortment of cement sea creature statues along the highway. The beaches in San Lorenzo are a bit drab, but El Guyabo, 26 kilometers away and easily accessible by bus, has many hammocks and lots of relaxation (US$1 entrance fee to private beach).

Should you need to stop in San Lorenzo for the night, one of the better hotels is the American-owned **Villa Concha Mar** (tel. 504/781-2332), which has a wide variety of rooms ranging from US$21 for the most basic single to US$57 for an apartment. The hotel has a clean pool, Internet available, and a rooftop restaurant with a great view (serving international and Honduran fare). They can also arrange very expensive (US$350–400) yacht trips for up to 12 people through the gulf.

TEGUCIGALPA

© AMY E. ROBERTSON

San Lorenzo

The waterfront **Hotel Miramar** is in serious disrepair, outrageously overpriced, and cannot be recommended at this time. The public pier next door is a pleasant little spot, however.

One decent midpriced option by the town square is **Hotel San Lorenzo Rivera** (tel. 504/881-3025, US$26), with spacious, albeit barren, rooms, TV, air-conditioning, and private baths.

Several restaurants beyond Hotel Miramar in a waterfront area called La Cabaña serve up great seafood, about the best of which is the lively **Porto del Golfo.** The business, owned by the packing company Empacadora de San Lorenzo, is now a co-op of sorts where the same employees that staff the daily operations also make administrative decisions as well. Because the packing and shipping is their main business, the eatery has a very warehouse feel. If they sense that you will be staying for a while, they also serve complimentary seafood appetizers. There are plenty of basic, cheaper *comedores* in the center of town.

The owners of **Las Arenas Discoteque** claim it is "the most" popular dance club in southern Honduras—if you enjoy women wrestling in chocolate.

Both Banco Atlántida and Banco de Occidente will change dollars.

Buses running between Choluteca and El Amatillo pull into the town market. If you're looking to catch a Tegucigalpa bus, it's best to go out to the highway and flag down one coming from Choluteca.

Many casual travelers may end up in San Lorenzo in order to get a bus to Coyolito, where boats cross the bay to Amapala. The buses leave the town market daily every 90 minutes between 8:30 A.M. and 4:30 P.M. (US$0.50).

Jícaro Galán

Jícaro Galán is little more than a few buildings at the junction of the Tegucigalpa highway and the Panamericana, which runs from El Salvador through Choluteca and on to Nicaragua. On the Tegucigalpa side of the junction is **El Oasis Colonial** (tel. 504/795-4007, US$40 d) with motel-style, air-conditioned rooms around a pool. Jícaro Galán is 43 kilometers from Choluteca and 99 kilometers from Tegucigalpa.

Nacaome

If you're passing through to El Salvador, the colonial town of Nacaome is an interesting stop. Nacaome means "two races," named after its founding in A.D. 148 on a peace pact between the Chola and Chaparrastique tribes. Spaniards arrived in 1535, and built the town's church—which was rebuilt in 1867, into a domed church on the *parque central*. If you need a place to stay, try the **Hotel Real Vista Hermosa** (tel. 504/795-5160, US$52 d) or the **Hotel Sunset** (tel. 504/795-3359, US$24 d).

El Amatillo

A blastingly hot and unattractive border post in the midst of desolate hills, El Amatillo is a place to depart as quickly as possible. Expect short and fast lines on the Salvadoran side, but mystifyingly long and slow ones on the Honduran side. The folks that approach you to help you fill out your immigration form often have horrible handwriting, but they can expedite the process by cutting in the front of the line for you, for a negotiable fee, of course.

The border is open daily 6 A.M.–10 P.M. The nearest town in El Salvador is Santa Rosa de Lima, reached by frequent bus until late afternoon. Most buses to Tegucigalpa (4.5 hours on the direct bus, longer by the local bus) and Choluteca (three hours, local bus only) run 4 A.M.–5 P.M. Sometimes (with smooth skills) it's possible to talk your way onto one of the *lujo* (luxury) buses to Tegucigalpa. One bus runs direct from the border to San Salvador every day around noon (US$5, 3.5 hours). If you do get stuck, there's **Hotel y Comedor Remar,** near the Texaco gas station. El Amatillo is 42 kilometers from Jícaro Galán on a paved two-lane highway.

Pespire

Set in a river valley just above the Choluteca plain, 82 kilometers from Tegucigalpa, Pespire is a small, quiet colonial town with a lovely domed church and a historic two-story government building, both on the square.

Hotel Palmeras (tel. 504/776-1345, US$25 s, US$32 d) is a clean, modern hotel on the main road through town. It frequently hosts groups, so it is best to reserve in advance if possible. The three-story hotel has 20 pleasant rooms, all with TV, air-conditioning, and

TEGUCIGALPA

LENCAN POTTERY

In the Lencan highlands surrounding Gracias, traditional pottery is hand-molded, baked in the sun, and usually painted a brick-color, if it's painted at all. But across Honduras, gift shops sell a different kind of "Lencan pottery" – made of pale clay that is fired in a kiln, and then the black outer stain is rubbed off to create black and white patterns.

This pottery originates in the Lencan communities of southwest Honduras, in the department of Valle. The techniques used to produce the pottery are centuries old, and the designs got a big boost in the 1980s when an Italian anthropologist resident in Honduras began giving aesthetic advice. One women's cooperative in Valle that is renowned for its work is **Magu-Alfarería Lenca** (Magu is short for Manzanarez Gutierrez, two common last names in the area).

For information on Magu, contact Maria Magdalena at 504/3347-2201. The cooperative is based in the tiny community of La Arada, Goascorán, along the highway heading west from Nacaome, close to the border town El Amatillo and the border with El Salvador. Visitors are welcome, and the prices at the source are unbeatable.

Alternatively, pick up a piece from any of the myriad shops across Honduras selling it, including the shop Alfar in the Clarion hotel in Tegucigalpa, where new twists on the traditional design (pottery colored by vegetable dye or gold dust) are available for purchase.

The pottery is a beautiful souvenir, but quite fragile, so be careful how you pack it.

© AMY E. ROBERTSON

the quiet streets and three-domed church of Pespire

private bath. **Comedor Palmeras** is a bit further down the street, owned by the hotel owner's sister, and there's an Internet café across the street.

The frequent buses running between Choluteca and Tegucigalpa will drop you and pick you up at a set of steps along the highway that lead down into Pespire, for $1.75 either direction.

Sabanagrande

Farther up into the hills, 42 kilometers from Tegucigalpa, is Sabanagrande, a town of 4,000. In precolonial times, the town was known as Apacunca, meaning "place with washing water" in Lenca. The Spaniards first settled the town in the late 18th century, as an extension of the mining boomtown Ojojona. The **Iglesia de Rosario** on the square has an elegant wooden roof and balcony. You'll notice lots of places advertising *rosquillas* in town and along the highway—this is a crunchy bread snack eaten with coffee, for which the town is known. Buses to Tegucigalpa cost US$0.75 and pass frequently on the highway.

EL CORPUS AND SANTA ANA DE YUSGUARE

For an offbeat adventure, a jaunt up the dusty roads to the colonial mining town of El Corpus is a worthwhile day trip while in southern Honduras. During the colonial era, the town became the center of one of the richest mining regions in the country, and some mines in the surrounding hills still operate. The colonial church is currently being restored, and one old mine is located directly behind it. No formal hotels operate in the small town, but you can find inexpensive and basic lodging if you ask around. One *comedor* selling fried chicken and tortillas is just off the main square, next door to the Tigo business, and there are a number of *pulperías*.

The cobblestone streets and colonial architecture are reason enough to see El Corpus, but the surprisingly lush countryside all around the town adds to its feel of being an oasis in the dry Choluteca plain. Many paths lead up into the hills, including to a viewpoint where you can see out over the Golfo de Fonseca, into Nicaragua, and sometimes as far as El Salvador. Two particularly good hikes are to **Cerro**

Calaire, 2–3 hours away, or a longer hike via the *aldea* of **Agua Fría** to **Cerro Guanacaure.** From the top of Cerro Guanacaure, covered with a sort of dry tropical forest, hikers have great views over the volcanoes of Nicaragua and the Golfo de Fonseca. Agua Fría is a two to three-hour hike from El Corpus, and the mountaintop is another hour or two farther. Locals will be happy to point the way.

The turnoff to El Corpus is from the new loop road between the exits to San Marcos Colón and to Guasaule. The bumpy dirt road to El Corpus is 15 kilometers long. Buses to Choluteca leave every hour 5:30 A.M.–6:30 P.M. for the hour-long ride, charging US$1.

It's possible to take a bus directly to Agua Fría from Choluteca—they leave from Campo Cabaña near the Mercado Viejo, usually at 11 A.M. and 1 P.M. daily (and charge US$1.50), but during the rainy months or if one of the buses happens to be out of service, there is just one bus at noon. Unfortunately, the only bus back to Choluteca from Agua Fría leaves early in the morning and there are no hotels, but you can likely find a villager willing to put you up for the night if needed.

If traveling by car, head out of Choluteca on the Panamericana toward San Marcos de Colon. At the large roundabout at the edge of town, take a right, heading south toward Guasaule, and you will see the turnoff for El Corpus shortly thereafter. It doesn't take more than half an hour to get from the center of Choluteca to El Corpus by car.

Santa Ana de Yusguare is en route to El Corpus, five kilometers from the highway turn-off. Its colonial church has been beautifully restored, and there is a big restaurant and recreation area outside of town called **Rincón del Valle** (tel. 504/782-3010), with a swimming pool, children's play area, and mini-zoo.

SAN MARCOS DE COLÓN AND LA BOTIJA

San Marcos de Colón, a small town set at an elevation of 960 meters, is mainly visited by travelers on their way through to Nicaragua, but it is perhaps the south's best-kept secret (well, at least it was until this book hit the shelves). The colonial town is very well-preserved (and has been described as Honduras's cleanest city). There are fine forests in the area, most notably

San Marcos is nestled into the hills of the Sierra de la Botija.

cloud forest and dry tropical forests at La Botija mountain. This is a great, infrequently visited area for day walks or multiday hikes. The climate is surprisingly cool, a refreshing change from the hot lowlands around Choluteca.

In addition to wandering around town and visiting the nearby forest, travelers may be interested in checking out **El Fuerte Perez,** the ruins of an old fort just five minutes away by car or taxi. To get there, drive straight past the *alcaldía,* take a left when the road comes to a T, then the next right. Located on a hilltop, it is a good spot for a view of town.

Accommodations

The fanciest joint in town is **Hotel Barcelona** (tel. 504/788-3870, US$13 s, US$18 d), a modern two-story hotel facing the market. Rooms are clean although the linens are a touch dingy, and there is a restaurant with a nice view. **Hotel Colonial** (tel. 504/788-3822, US$13 s, US$14.50 d), two blocks west of the central park toward the highway, has a bit more charm, and the rooms have air-conditioning. **Hotel Shalom** (tel. 504/788-3643, US$12 s, US$15 d) is on the same street four blocks east of Banco BGA (uphill). It's a little more bare-bones, but there is a great city view from the top floor conference room. **Hotel Ipanema** (tel. 504/788-3091) is a similar option with similar prices.

Twenty kilometers away on the highway back toward Choluteca, at kilometer marker 173, is **Hotel Monte Lorenza** (tel. 504/887-4819, US$26–32 per cabin), a small rustic spot perched on the hillside with great views from its restaurant and the two-bedroom cabin. The restaurant is decked out as if for a wedding reception, but it provides typical Honduran fare at standard prices.

Food

Right near the bus station is **La Exquisita,** serving delicious fried chicken, enchiladas, and tacos for US$2–4. **Restaurante Típico Garomar** (7 A.M.–9 P.M. daily), one block off the square, has *licuados,* juices, *baleadas, comida corriente,* and burgers at low prices, in a rustic, plant-filled setting. Both restaurants will help organize trips

to La Botija. The other upscale restaurant in town is **Bonanza** (8 A.M.–9:30 P.M.) one block south of the church, with a good selection of international and Honduran dishes, including omelets for breakfast, sandwiches, chicken and beef for dinner, and even a mushroom brochette (US$3.50) for vegetarians.

A few kilometers out of town on the road back to Choluteca is **El Portillo,** a restaurant and recreation spot with horseback rides and children's play equipment.

Services

Típico Garomar also runs an Internet café at the corner next to the restaurant, called **CIFS** (7 A.M.–10 P.M. daily), and international calls can be made from here as well. The **Hondutel** and **Honducor** offices are next to the market. There are several banks in town, including **Banco Atlántida** and **HSBC,** which will change dollars but no travelers checks or córdobas (8:30 A.M.–3:30 P.M. Mon.–Fri. and 8:30–11:30 A.M. Sat.).

Getting There and Away

Mi Esperanza runs buses from San Marcos to Choluteca (US$1.30) at 6 A.M., 7:45 A.M., 10 A.M., 12:30 P.M., 2:15 P.M., and 4 P.M. Its office is facing the market, and you can buy tickets through to San Lorenzo, Jícaro Galán, and Tegucigalpa (US$2.15, US$2.25, and US$4.20, respectively). **Blanquita Express** has buses at 7:15 A.M., 11:15 A.M., and 3:15 P.M.

Parque Nacional La Botija

This little-known forest mountain region near the border of Nicaragua is one of the great hidden secrets of southern Honduras. Much of the 19,100-hectare forest is pine, oak, and the hardwood quebracho, while seven peaks above 1,500 meters have patches of cloud forest on top. On the lower slopes descending into Nicaragua are patches of primary tropical dry forest, a rare find these days in Honduras. The highest elevation is the Jilguero peak at 1,735 meters. The mountains here give birth to the Río Coco, Central America's longest river.

The forests of La Botija are excellent for spotting birds of all kinds, blue morpho butterflies, white-tail deer and white-faced monkeys (the latter most easily spotted February–March when they collect *ojoche*, the highly nutritious maya nut. The occasional puma is even spotted (or makes itself known by raiding a farm), although your guide will be none too thrilled help you to meet up with one in the forest. Several waterfalls are found in the sierra, including **La Cascada de la Mina**, near an old mine shaft, and **La Loma del Salto.** Another popular destination is **Las Tres Pilas,** three natural baths.

A Peace Corps volunteer, working with a group of locals, built an interpretive trail up to one of the forest-covered peaks, Cerro de Águila, but the markings have since disappeared. Plenty of less well-trod trails crisscross the forest, and having a guide is a good idea.

Doña Marta Garomar, of the Típicos Garomar restaurant in San Marcos, can provide information on the sights both in La Botija and elsewhere around San Marcos, and can organize a variety of half-day excursions into the park, either walking with guides (US$2.50) or on horseback (US$7.75). It's ideal to notify her a few days in advance, to set up horses and guides, but something can usually be arranged by the following day. The best way to reach her is by calling the restaurant, at 504/788-3466.

Alternatively, you can contact Dr. Ángel Enrique Sándoval Lopez at his restaurant La Esquisita (tel. 504/788-3505), who can provide the same kind of information and contacts as Doña Garomar. In fact, both use the guide Javier Terceros in the village of Duyusupo, 11 kilometers from San Marcos, at the foot of the reserve. Javier is enthusiastic about preserving the beauty of the setting around him, and about using tourism as a way to both enjoy and protect the reserve. If you are interested in spending more time out in the reserve, you can rent a two-bedroom cabin on his property for US$26 a night, or even pitch a tent on his property (you'd have to bring your own equipment). Javier's friendly wife will make breakfast for US$2 or lunch for US$3. If you speak Spanish, you can call Javier directly at 504/754-5691.

To get to Duyusupo, there are two buses a day, leaving San Marcos at 7 A.M. and 1 P.M.,

taking 45 minutes. The buses return to town at 8:30 A.M. and 2:30 P.M. If you have your own wheels, head up the hill past the church and take a left after Hotel Shalom. From there follow the paved road as it curves around to the right and becomes dirt. The 11-kilometer road is well-maintained and takes about half an hour by car.

THE NICARAGUAN BORDER
Guasaule

A Nicaraguan border town in the lowlands near the coast and not much more attractive than El Amatillo on the Salvadoran side, Guasaule is easier and more popular than the El Espino crossing into Nicaragua from Choluteca. Buses (US$1.50) drive frequently between Choluteca and Guasaule daily between 6 A.M. and 10 P.M., which are also the operating hours of the border offices. Direct buses to Tegucigalpa leave several times a day until early afternoon, charging US$2. Minibuses run directly between Guasaule and El Amatillo, US$5, for those just transiting through Honduras.

Should you be forced to spend the night in Guasaule, **Hotel Los Tres Hermanas,** the last building on the Honduran side, is not too bad. Across the street, decent food can be found at **Cafetería La Aurora.**

Just past town is the border bridge, over the Río Guasaule. Half a kilometer farther is the Nicaraguan border post, then at another five kilometers is the town of Somotillo. From here, other buses continue elsewhere inside Nicaragua.

El Espino

These border offices, infrequently used compared to Guasaule (much to the chagrin of the local officials), are open daily 8 A.M.–6 P.M.

Minivans provide bus service to the border at El Espino, 11 kilometers away by paved road, and cost US$0.60, although drivers will often try to charge you more returning to town from the border. They run all day and usually leave when they fill up. From San Marcos, the minivans leave from next to the market, right by the buses.

BACKGROUND

The Land

Honduras is located at the great bend where Central America sweeps east into the Caribbean from the base of Mexico and then takes an abrupt 90-degree turn southward before trending eastward again to link with South America. The second-largest country in Central America, after Nicaragua, Honduras covers 112,491 square kilometers, an area about the size of England. While one imaginative geographer likened Honduras's shape to that of "a sleeping basilisk," the more prosaic-minded among us see an inverted triangle, the apex pointing due south into the Pacific Ocean and the base (bulging on the eastern side) facing north into the Caribbean Sea.

The country's perimeter consists of a 342-kilometer border with El Salvador, a 256-kilometer border with Guatemala, a 922-kilometer border with Nicaragua, 735 kilometers of north-facing Caribbean coastline, and 153 kilometers of southern, Pacific coastline. At its widest point—between Cerro Montecristo, on the border with El Salvador and Guatemala, and Cabo Gracias a Dios, bordering Nicaragua—Honduras extends 675 kilometers.

The main landmass of Honduras sits roughly between latitude 16° N on the north coast and 13° N at the Golfo de Fonseca, and between longitude 83°15' W at Cabo Gracias a Dios and 89°20' W near Nueva Ocotepeque. Honduras's

Caribbean possessions, the Swan Islands, lie at latitude 17°30' N.

Approximately two-thirds of Honduras is covered by rugged mountain ranges, or *cordilleras*. These mountains are the country's principal defining geographic feature and have played an important role in shaping Honduran history.

Flat areas are found mainly along the narrow north and south coastal plains, the jungle-covered lowland plains of the Mosquitia, and a very few inland valleys.

GEOGRAPHY
Geological Setting

About 75 million years ago, in the mid-Cretaceous geological era, the tectonic plate on which Honduras sits constituted itself in the mid-Pacific Ocean and began drifting in a northeasterly direction. By the Miocene era, this plate—called the Caribbean Plate—had plugged itself neatly into an existing gap between the North American and South American Plates, forming a land bridge between the two continents. But as it happens, the gap wasn't as big as the landmass, so the Caribbean Plate has been gradually pinched by its two larger neighbors—a principal factor shaping Honduras's tumultuous topography. Although the pinching has slowed its progress, the Caribbean Plate obstinately continues moving east and northeast at a rate of 2–4 centimeters a year. At that rate, Honduras should be nudging up against Cuba in 25 million years or so.

Crashing into the Caribbean Plate from behind is the Cocos Plate, the culprit in a great deal of seismic and volcanic activity in Mexico and on the western coast of Central America. The Cocos Plate, apparently propelled with a great deal of energy, is thrusting under the Caribbean and parts of the North American Plates, forcing these landmasses upward and creating the region's steep Pacific slope mountains. Tiny slips between these plates, pushing up against one another with unimaginable force, unleash regular earthquakes and volcanic activity.

Situated on the northwestern part of the Caribbean Plate, Honduras forms part of the border (geologically speaking) against the North American Plate. Offshore, the Bay Islands and, farther off, the Swan Islands are located right at the edge of the fault—which at that point is a deep undersea trough called the Bartlett or Cayman Trench. Because the two plates are slipping past each other here, rather than meeting head-on, this fault is less prone to geological activity than the Cocos.

Although plate tectonics are a prime factor in creating Honduras's tortured topography, the country is largely free of volcanoes, and earthquakes are rare. That said, spring 2009 brought a series of significant earthquakes, most notably a quake off the coast of Roatán that registered 7.1 on the Richter scale. Incredibly enough for a quake of such a magnitude, damages were relatively mild—five deaths, and some structural damage, but nothing devastating.

Mountain Ranges

After glancing at a topographical map of Honduras, one is tempted to say that the entire country is one big mountain range and leave it at that. In Mexico and other Central American countries, the *cordilleras* are long, parallel rows. But because Honduras is at the junction of the Caribbean, North American, and Cocos Plates, its landmass has been geologically squeezed, resulting in a jumble of small mountain ranges and isolated massifs zigzagging across the country in all different directions and in no apparent order.

In fact, however, the mountains are divided fairly clearly into two "groups." The first, caused by the pushing between the Caribbean and North American Plates, consists of several ranges roughly trending west to east or southwest to northeast. Forming the border with Guatemala, right on the south side of the Motagua Fault, is the ancient and well-worn range known variously, over the course of its run from the southwest corner of the country to its plunge into the Caribbean Sea by Omoa, as the **Cordillera del Merendón, Sierra del Espíritu Santo,** and **Sierra de Omoa.** The

Bay Islands are actually an expression of this same range, where it pops its head up again offshore and forms the edge of Honduras's continental shelf in the Caribbean. In northern Honduras, the **Sierra Nombre de Dios** parallels the north coast between Tela and Trujillo, forming a narrow coastal plain and reaching an elevation of 2,480 meters at Montaña Corozal in Parque Nacional Pico Bonito. Farther east, **Sierra de Agalta** begins in the center of the Olancho department and extends northeast into the Mosquitia, though its name changes to **Sierra del Carbón** and **Sierra del Río Tinto** as it heads north. This range, along with the smaller **Sierra La Esperanza** to the west, forms the principal boundary on the western side of the Mosquitia, an isolated lowland region in northeastern Honduras. Branching off from the Agalta range just to the east is a jumbled cluster of mountains and high ridges known as the Montañas del Patuca or Montañas de Punta Piedra. Beginning in the El Paraíso department is the aptly named **Cordillera Entre Ríos,** which runs northeasterly between Ríos Patuca and Coco. Farther north into the Mosquitia, this range is known as the Montañas de Colón.

The second group of mountains in Honduras is a series of short, rugged ranges running parallel to one another roughly northwest–southeast, extending from El Salvador into the center of the country. Closest to El Salvador is the tallest, **Sierra de Celaque,** topped by Cerro de las Minas, the highest peak in the country at 2,849 meters. Farther northeast are the **Cordillera Opalaca, Cordillera Montecillos, Montaña Meámbar, Montaña de Comayagua,** and **Sierra de Sulaco** in Yoro. Beyond Sierra de Sulaco, these mountains run into conflicting geological formations, resulting in the crazy labyrinth of ridges and valleys in western and central Olancho.

Isolated ranges include Montaña de Santa Bárbara, at the edge of Lago de Yojoa—the country's second-highest peak at 2,744 meters—and several mountains in the vicinity of Tegucigalpa.

Except for a few eroded cones in the Golfo de Fonseca, none of the mountains in Honduras are volcanic—in sharp contrast to neighboring Guatemala, Nicaragua, and El Salvador.

Valleys and Rivers

Crisscrossing this mountainous countryside are several major river systems and countless smaller ones. Honduras shares the largest river in Central America, the Río Coco, with Nicaragua, but contains the second largest, the Río Patuca, completely within its borders. Because the continental divide is quite far south in Honduras, most big rivers drain to the north, into the Caribbean Sea, though four sizable rivers do flow south to the Pacific.

In the western part of Honduras, long a center of human settlement and economic activity, is the broad **Valle de Sula,** through which flow the 200-kilometer **Río Chamelecón** (born in the hills by the Guatemalan border near the ruins of Copán) and the much bigger **Río Ulúa,** draining a huge area of western Honduras in its 400-kilometer course to the north coast. The flat, flood-prone lower part of the Valle de Sula, particularly around El Progreso and La Lima, is one of the principal banana regions of the country.

East of the Río Ulúa, several short but furiously intense rivers pour off the steep flanks of the coastal Sierra Nombre de Dios, notably the **Río Cangrejal,** near La Ceiba, a favorite among rafters and kayakers. Gathering the waters from the south side of the Sierra Nombre de Dios as well as the mountains of Yoro and western Olancho, the 200-kilometer **Río Aguán** cuts its path in a northeasterly direction to the Caribbean. The banana companies maintain extensive plantations in the wide, rich Valle del Aguán.

The wild Mosquitia region, in the far northeast corner of Honduras, is home to several large rivers, born in the mountains far to the south. The 215-kilometer **Río Tinto** and its largest tributary, the **Paulaya,** both begin in the Sierra de Agalta of central Olancho, and pass through what was once rainforest but is now mostly pastures and small farms. Just east is the smaller **Río Plátano,** still blanketed by virgin jungle and protected as a biosphere reserve. The mighty **Río Patuca,** still farther east, courses over 500 kilometers from as far south as the departments of El Paraíso and Francisco Morazán, not far from Tegucigalpa, through Olancho and down to the Mosquitia. Several of the Patuca's tributaries, including the Guayape, Guayambre, and Wampú, are known for producing gold. The **Río Coco,** even longer than the Patuca, forms a large part of the land border between Honduras and Nicaragua on its 550-kilometer route to Cabo Gracias a Dios.

On the south side of the country, the largest river system is that of the **Río Choluteca,** which takes a convoluted horseshoe route starting off in a northerly direction through Tegucigalpa, then coming around in a sweeping 180-degree turn to empty into the Golfo de Fonseca on the Pacific. West of the Choluteca are the smaller **Río Nacaome** and the **Río Goascorán,** the latter forming part of Honduras's border with El Salvador.

The so-called Honduran Depression cuts a lowland gap through the country, following the Río Ulúa, up the Río Humaya into the Valle de Comayagua, over a low pass and down to the Pacific along the Río Goascorán. For many years, successive Honduran governments hoped to build a transcontinental railway along this route, which at its highest point, on the continental divide, is only 870 meters. Another major tributary to the Ulúa, the Río Otoro, also almost meets the Pacific-flowing Río Lempa, separated by a pass of 1,050 meters.

Numerous intermontane basins of varying sizes, usually between 300 and 900 meters above sea level, are located throughout Honduras. The larger ones, like the Valle de Comayagua (Comayagua), Valle de Catacamas (Olancho), Valle de Jamastrán (El Paraíso), and Valle de Sensetí (Ocotepeque), are intensively worked for crops or cattle, or both.

Lakes and Lagoons

The only natural lake of any size in the country is **Lago de Yojoa,** 16 kilometers long by 8 kilometers wide at an elevation of 635 meters. With the construction of El Cajón dam,

a larger man-made lake was created along the Río Humuya.

On the north coast, and particularly in the Mosquitia, are many lagoons and freshwater wetlands, separated from the ocean by narrow sandbars. Among the larger lagoons are **Laguna de Alvarado** behind Puerto Cortés; **Laguna de los Micos,** near Tela; Cuero y Salado, just west of La Ceiba; and **Laguna Guaymoreto,** outside of Trujillo.

Farther east in the Mosquitia, these lagoon systems are much more extensive. The largest is **Laguna Caratasca,** measuring 66 kilometers long by 14 kilometers wide and linked by waterways to the adjacent Laguna de Tansin and Laguna de Warunta. Other large lagoons in the Mosquitia include **Laguna de Brus** and **Laguna de Ibans.** In fact, one could reasonably consider the entire Mosquitia coastal area one huge wetland system, as networks of canals and seasonal waterways extend basically from the Río Coco all the way to Palacios.

Coastal Plains

Considered an inhospitable, malarial swamp by the Spaniards, Honduras's northern coastal plain has for the past century been the country's most intensively exploited region, mainly producing bananas and pineapples for foreign fruit companies. For most of its length, the plain is quite narrow, in places only a couple of kilometers separating the ocean from the Cordillera Nombre de Dios.

The only places the plain extends inland a significant distance are the valleys of the Ríos Ulúa, Chamelecón, and Aguán and in the broad expanse of the Mosquitia. The Mosquitia plain, in the northeast corner of the country, encompasses more flat land than the rest of the country combined, but because of its thin, acidic soil, the region is unsuitable for agriculture.

The Pacific lowlands are on average only 25 kilometers wide, composed mainly of heavily cultivated alluvial soils tapering into mangrove swamps at the edge of the Golfo de Fonseca. After years of deforestation and poor farming techniques, the once-rich soils of these plains have long since eroded.

Islands

In the Caribbean, the three main Bay Islands (Islas de la Bahía) of Utila, Roatán, and Guanaja, plus many smaller cays, are considered a continuation of the Sierra de Omoa, a northeast-trending mountain range that meets the Caribbean west of Puerto Cortés. Farther north are the smaller Swan Islands (Islas del Cisne), also thought to be part of the same geological formation.

Honduras owns several small islands in the Golfo de Fonseca (Gulf of Fonseca), the largest of which are Isla del Tigre and Isla Zacate Grande, both eroded volcanoes at the southern end of a mountain chain that begins in El Salvador.

CLIMATE
Temperatures

Honduras is situated completely within the tropics—south of the Tropic of Cancer and north of the Tropic of Capricorn—and as in most tropical countries, temperature is defined more by altitude than by season. Generally, temperatures change little from month to month in the same location, apart from slight cooling during the rainy season. January and February are the coolest months, while March and April are the hottest, although temperatures rarely vary more than 5°C on average throughout the year.

The Caribbean and Pacific lowland regions are both known as *tierra caliente* (hot land), where average daytime high temperatures hover between 28° and 32°C (82–90°F) throughout the year. Rain and strong ocean breezes offer some relief and are often present on the north coast, the Bay Islands, and the islands of the Golfo de Fonseca. Interior lowland regions, such as the Valle de Ulúa or the Valle del Aguán, are often extremely hot and humid, and the Choluteca plains are downright scorching for much of the year, particularly during the dry season, with daytime temperatures occasionally hitting 40°C (104°F).

Much of central Honduras, between 500 and 1,800 meters elevation, is *tierra templada* (temperate land). Here temperatures usually

stay comfortable throughout the year, pleasantly warm but not overly hot during the day and cool in the evening. Tegucigalpa, in a sheltered valley at about 1,000 meters elevation, is a classic example of such a climate zone; daytime highs average 24°C (75°F) in January and 29°C (84°F) in April, while lows in those months average 14°C (57°F) and 18°C (64°F), respectively.

The mountain country, above 1,800 meters elevation, is called *tierra fría* (cold land), where temperatures average 16–20°C (61–68°F) during the day and can drop to freezing at night. Strong winds, mist, clouds, and tree cover help keep temperatures down. The highest, cloud forest–covered peaks are the coldest locations in Honduras. Hiking these forests can be pleasantly cool during the day, but be ready for the evening chill. Regions particularly known for their cold weather are in the departments of Intibucá, Lempira, and La Paz, in the mountains of southwest Honduras.

Precipitation

Honduras is a humid place, which is why it has such lovely green countryside. The country averages around 82 percent humidity, with the dampest areas being the north coast and the Mosquitia, and the driest on the Pacific coast.

In some regions, particularly in the south, center, and west of Honduras, the wet and dry seasons are quite well defined. Usually the *invierno* (rainy season) begins in May or June and continues to November or December. This wet period is often broken in August or September by a three- to four-week dry spell called *la canícula* or sometimes *el veranillo de San Juan*. During the rainy season, skies are often clear in the morning, and clouds start to build around midday, leading to an afternoon shower, which usually passes by evening—but, particularly later in the rainy season, there can come several days at a time when the drizzle doesn't stop and the world is gray and wet.

In much of the north of the country, the seasons are much less predictable, and rains can come at any time of year. On the north

THE PITILESS PATH OF HURRICANE MITCH

Late in the day on Monday, October 19, 1998, meteorologists monitoring the Caribbean Sea took note of a tropical low forming not far from the coasts of Colombia and Panama. By October 22, with the barometer falling below 1,000 millibars, meteorologists dubbed the 13th tropical storm of the year Mitch.

Meteorologists expected that Mitch would continue northward toward Mexico, Cuba, Jamaica, and the U.S. Gulf of Mexico. But on October 24, with winds of 160 kph and classified as a Category 2 hurricane, Mitch began to slow down and veer off to the west, toward the coast of Belize and the southern Yucatán Peninsula.

By Monday, October 26, Mitch was a Category 5 hurricane, with sustained winds of 290 kph, gusts over 350 kph, and a barometer reading of 906 millibars — the second-lowest reading recorded in the 20th century in the Atlantic. On the morning of October 26, Mitch turned again, appearing to come around the corner of Central America and take aim at Honduras.

The first inhabited land in the hurricane's path, and the only place to feel the storm's full wind power, was the easternmost Bay Island of Guanaja. The effects were devastating. The small fishing community of Mangrove Bight, built right on the water's edge on Guanaja's northeast shore, was completely wiped off the map by 10-meter waves and howling winds. Luckily, the locals were able to flee to higher ground before the storm struck, and no one in town died. Passing right over the top of Guanaja, the awesome winds of Mitch flattened all the vegetation on the island and removed most of the rooftops in Bonacca Town and elsewhere on the island.

As Mitch ran into the steep mountains lining Honduras's north coast, the storm slowed its forward movement and began dumping immense volumes of rain. Rivers across the country flooded over their banks with terrifying and lethal suddenness, swollen by all the water pouring off the water-logged mountains. Entire towns were left underwater in the Río Aguán valley, and coastal villages at river mouths were practically swept away. Choluteca, on the Pacific side, was also completely submerged.

Bridges fell throughout north-central Honduras, cutting off many coastal Garífuna villages and large areas in central Yoro, which had to be supplied by helicopter and boat for weeks after the storm.

In Tegucigalpa, it was as if a flood poured down from the heavens, resulting in massive flooding in the middle of the night along Río Choluteca and its tributary, the Río Chiquito, which join together in downtown. Mudslides dropped several neighborhoods down steep hillsides into the valley below, and destruction was massive. The two main bridges connecting downtown Tegucigalpa to Comayagüela, which normally have about 13 meters of clearance between the river and the top of the arches, were completely covered during the night. The city water pipes all burst due to excessive water pressure, leaving city residents without water for two weeks.

Finally, by the night of October 31, Mitch left Honduras for Guatemala, continuing as a tropical depression across Mexico and into the Gulf of Mexico. The exact loss of life caused by Mitch will never be known, but it was certainly one of the worst natural disasters ever to hit Honduras, killing over 7,000 people, according to government estimates. A further 8,058 people were reported missing, another 12,000 were injured, and 33,000 homes were washed away. Although Honduras faced the greatest death toll from the storm, another 4,000 people perished in Nicaragua and about 400 more in Guatemala and El Salvador.

coast or in the Mosquitia, the season is not so much dry and wet, but rather wet and wetter still. The rainiest parts of the year on the north coast are usually September–November, when the tropical storms and hurricanes developing over the Atlantic rip through the Caribbean, and December–February, when *nortes,* northern cold fronts, make their way down from Canada and the United States, often bringing with them days of gray skies and rain. Because of the high humidity and the backing wall of the Sierra Nombre de Dios, the north coast is drenched by tropical storms just about every month of the year.

Hurricanes and Tropical Storms

Major tropical storms typically strike Honduras every decade or so, leaving thousands homeless and sometimes dead. The devastating Hurricane Mitch of 1998 was one of the worst natural disasters of the 20th century to hit Honduras. Although not as powerful as Mitch, 1974's Hurricane Fifi devastated the region around Choloma, in northwest Honduras.

In general, though, Honduras lies off the regular hurricane path in the Caribbean. Most storms come from the southeast and travel northwest, passing through the western Caribbean toward the Gulf of Mexico, to the north of Honduras. But it's best to try to avoid the north coast of Honduras during the August–November hurricane season. Even if the hurricanes themselves don't reach the shore, they bring heavy rains; flooding is an annual ritual and can seriously disrupt travel. Cases of cholera and other diseases are also more common during this time. Pacific hurricanes rarely strike Honduras.

Other Travel Considerations

During the rainy season, expect road conditions to deteriorate severely. Major highways are reasonably well maintained all year (some better than others), but often the government will not bother patching other roads during the rains. As a result, many dirt roads become totally impassable, even with four-wheel-drive.

Also during the rains, water visibility for scuba diving is diminished on the Bay Islands. But because the islands don't have the high mountains like the mainland to catch precipitation, rainfall tends to be considerably lower than on the north coast. February–March and July–September are usually two good times of year for the islands.

Hiking in the mountains of central Honduras is possible year-round, but it's less muddy during the dry season, especially in the south part of the country. In places like Pico Bonito, Cusuco, or Sierra de Agalta, it rains all year, so just come prepared to get wet. If you're planning on rafting or river-boating, the best time of year is after the rains, in December or January, when water levels are high.

Flora and Fauna

FLORA

First-time visitors to Honduras may be surprised to find out that this modest-sized country houses a bewildering diversity of nearly 10,000 vascular plant species in a variety of ecosystems. Although many nature-lovers aren't aware of it, Honduras has much more extensive intact cloud forest and rainforest than its more heralded neighbors, Costa Rica and Guatemala. Honduras also offers huge expanses of pine forest in the central highlands, kilometers of coastal mangrove forests, and even patches of rare dry tropical forests. All told, Honduras contains over a quarter of all the wildlife-rich forests in Central America.

According to a 2005 estimate, Honduras has 4.65 million hectares—or 42 percent of its territory—of forest cover. Of this total, 32.5 percent is primary forest, a combination of pine and broadleaf forest. This is similar to its neighbor, Nicaragua, which has the largest amount of forest cover in Central America with

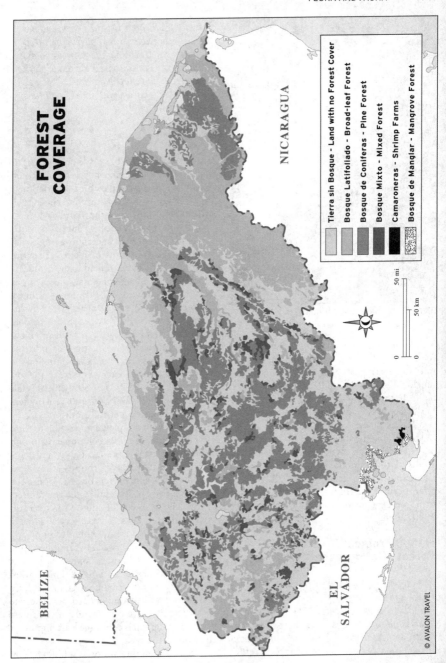

FOREST COVERAGE

Tierra sin Bosque - Land with no Forest Cover
Bosque Latifoliado - Broad-leaf Forest
Bosque de Coníferas - Pine Forest
Bosque Mixto - Mixed Forest
Camaroneras - Shrimp Farms
Bosque de Manglar - Mangrove Forest

BELIZE

NICARAGUA

EL SALVADOR

© AVALON TRAVEL

50 mi
50 km

© FUAD AZZAD

Birds of paradise are abundant in Honduras.

tiny leaves rising to great heights, and the ferns in between. I had always pictured jungle as suffocating spaghetti tangles, drooping and crisscrossed, a mass of hairy green rope and clutching stems.... This was more like a church, with pillars and fans and hanging flowers and only the slightest patches of white sky above the curved roof of branches.

Paul Theroux was a bit weak on Honduran geography in his popular novel *The Mosquito Coast*—the Río Aguán, which his fictional American family followed up into the jungle, actually leads into one of the most heavily cultivated valleys in Honduras. But his description of tropical rainforest certainly rings true. These forests, which once blanketed the entire north coast of Honduras, tend to move observers to religious metaphor, so awe-inspiring is their majestic beauty. Walking in a primary rainforest, one is indeed surprised with how little undergrowth exists between the immensely tall trees, sometimes more than 60 meters high, with huge buttresses looking for the world like flanking supports on a medieval cathedral.

5.2 million hectares of forest (43 percent of the country), followed by Guatemala, with 3.9 million hectares (36 percent of its land). The much-ballyhooed Costa Rica is second to last on the list, with only 2.4 million hectares, beating out only tiny, overpopulated El Salvador (which has a meager 0.3 million hectares).

Unfortunately, illegal logging is rampant, and deforestation rates have risen since the 1990s, with an annual deforestation rate estimated at 2.88 percent for the 2000–2005 time period, leading to an estimated loss of 37 percent of forest cover for the period 1990–2005.

Humid Tropical Forest (Rainforest)

This jungle, the start of the high forest, was tall and orderly. Each tree had found room to grow separately. The trees were arranged in various ways, according to slenderness of leaf size, the big-leafed ones on the jungle floor, the towering trees with

The annual average temperature in the forest hovers around 25°C (77°F), while rainfall averages between 200 and 400 centimeters a year, making it a natural hothouse, a perfect environment for plants to develop to their most efficient level. The evolutionary triumph of the rainforest is that almost all its nutrients are concentrated above ground—the forest has only a few centimeters of dirt. Under the dirt lies a mass of white threads, the rootlets of trees living in conjunction with a certain type of fungus. These act as a sort of garbage collector of the forest, quickly decomposing any organic material and providing nutrients to the trees, which in turn supply the products of photosynthesis to the fungus. This is what plant biologists call a "mature system." As little as one-tenth of 1 percent of nutrients penetrate below the first five centimeters of the forest floor, meaning soil is one of the least important elements to the cycle.

The wealth of the rainforest is hidden from

human observers, far above in the upper stories of these great trees, where an entire world of plants and animals exist without ever coming down to the ground. Roaming around in this elevated ecosystem of vines and ferns are snakes, monkeys, lizards, sloths, macaws, toucans, and literally thousands of species of insects, each living in their own particular niche. On the top is the canopy itself, an unbroken field of green leaves soaking up the generous sun and photosynthesizing for all they're worth. So complete is the canopy that practically no sun at all penetrates down to the jungle floor, unless a fallen tree opens a temporary gap. But the open space is invariably colonized in short order, with vines and new tree shoots moving in so fast you can practically watch it happen. The jungle is so vibrant it seems at times to be a single living creature rather than a collection of individual plants.

The rainforest is composed of a dizzying variety of trees and plants, although to the untrained observer, many trees in the rainforest look strikingly similar. It is thought that at least 2,000 vascular plants, probably more, live in the rainforest, making it by far the most diverse ecosystem in Central America. Tree types include mahogany, cedar, laurel, rosewood, strangler fig, tamarind, oak, ceiba, almond, cacao, nance, and San Juan, to name just a few. Rarely are several trees of the same species grouped together, which makes identification all the more difficult. As naturalists Adrian Forsyth and Ken Miyata put it in their book, *Tropical Nature,* "A naturalist in New England can easily learn all the species of native trees in the region in a single summer, but there are few people who, even after a lifetime of study, can confidently identify most of the trees in a patch of tropical American rainforest."

Because the rainforest offers so many lovely hiding places, trying to spot the abundant wildlife in it can be frustrating, especially on hikes. The jungles of the Mosquitia may support 80 percent of the mammal species in the country, but good luck finding all but a few of them. You won't have too much trouble running across the occasional troop of noisy monkeys, but most other creatures have excellent camouflage and stay well hidden. Many are nocturnal. Rainforest birds in particular are difficult to find, as their nests are extremely well hidden to avoid predators. One good way to look for birds and mammals in the jungle is along a river, where you can look into the upper stories of trees.

Until the beginning of the banana industry at the start of the 20th century, most of the north coast of Honduras was covered by rainforest. Most of the forest west of Trujillo has long since fallen victim to the machete, although healthy stretches still exist in Parque Nacional Pico Bonito, near La Ceiba, and smaller ones in Parque Nacional Capiro y Calentura, near Trujillo. But farther east in the remote, isolated Mosquitia region is the largest chunk of remaining rainforest in Central America, protected by the biosphere reserves of the Río Plátano and Tawahka Asagni. For anyone who wants to experience a true rainforest in all its expansive, wild splendor, a trip out to the Mosquitia is mandatory.

Cloud Forest

A unique sort of high-altitude jungle atop the highest peaks in Honduras, the cloud forest is a fairy-tale world of oak and wild avocado covered in vines, huge ferns, orchids, and bromeliads. A perpetual mist creates a spooky stillness broken only by the plaintive call of a quetzal or the scurry of a fox. It seems nothing short of miraculous, after walking up through the much drier pine forests below, how much moisture the cloud forest retains. Although cloud-forested peaks do not receive significantly more rainfall than surrounding regions, temperatures (6–12°C/43–54°F on average) and evaporation levels are markedly lower, so the forest retains a great deal more water, much of it in the form of the near-permanent airborne mist.

The result is a dense, towering forest that appears similar to lowland rainforest in its exuberance but is totally different in composition. The number of tree species is quite low compared to the rainforest, but the profusion of epiphytes covering the trees to gather the

HONDURAN NATIONAL SYMBOLS

- **tree** – ocote pine
- **flower** – orchid (Rhyncholaelia digbyana)
- **animal** – white-tailed deer
- **bird** – scarlet macaw
- **flag** – three horizontal stripes of blue, white, blue, with five blue stars in the middle white stripe. The stars represent the members of the former Federal Republic of Central America: Costa Rica, El Salvador, Guatemala, Honduras, and Nicaragua.

moisture blowing through the forest is astounding. Although epiphytes passively live on the cloud forest trees and are not parasitic, they can sometimes colonize a tree so successfully it literally collapses under their weight.

Trees in the cloud forest don't reach the same heights as in the lowland rainforest, both because of the climate and because of the invariably steep slopes they grow on, and the undergrowth is often thick. But in a few places, for example the plateau atop Celaque, you'll find stately stands of towering oaks, spaced widely with few plants underneath. The cloud forest provides a home for many of the same mammals that live in the rainforest, such as jaguars, sloths, monkeys, and peccaries, but has a unique bird population not seen in lower, hotter forests. The quetzal is certainly the most famed of the cloud forest birds, and it is joined by other types of trogon as well as the odd-sounding three-wattled bell bird and the emerald toucanet, among many others.

Two types of cloud forest exist in Honduras. In the southern and western part of the country, "true" cloud forest has developed. Here the geographic position of the mountains, in the prevailing wind patterns, has captured a constant cap of clouds, from which the forest sucks its moisture. The true cloud forest is located at elevations of roughly 1,800–2,800 meters and is isolated by a ring of drier pine or liquidambar (sweet gum) forest. Because these forests are biological islands, a variety of endemic plant and animal species are found within them.

In northern Honduras, another type of cloud forest is found at lower elevations. These forests receive more direct rain than those in the south and rise directly out of the tropical forest below them with only a small intervening band of pine, if any at all. These cloud forests are more accurately characterized as mountain rainforests and are sometimes found as low as 1,000 meters. The forests of Pico Bonito are a prime example.

In a few places at the highest elevations, notably in the Sierra de Agalta, strong winds and high moisture levels have combined to create bizarre and rare **elfin forests.** Here gnarled, stunted pine trees only a couple of meters tall grow among a profusion of mosses, lichen, ferns, and shrubs.

A sort of transitional stage between the cloud forest and rainforest is the **subtropical wet forest,** which receives about the same amount of rainfall but hosts an intermediate mix of species. Because this climate is ideal for coffee-growing, subtropical wet forests are under heavy pressure from small-scale plantations, especially in Olancho, Yoro, Santa Bárbara, and around Lago Yojoa. Were you to hike the very difficult route up the side of Pico Bonito just outside of La Ceiba, you'd walk up through, successively, tropical, subtropical, and montane wet forests—one of the few places in the Americas where this is possible.

As the sources of Honduras's rivers, cloud forests are vital to ensure the country's water supply. Unfortunately, they are also natural targets for *campesinos* who live in the valleys below, hungry for wild game, land, or wood. It was in recognition of cloud forests' critical importance that the Honduran government enacted the 1987 law creating the national park system, which was aimed primarily at protecting the cloud forests. While the laws have been of use in defending better-known parks like La Tigra, Cusuco, or Celaque, the destruction continues unabated in many remote, less-visited forests.

Highland Pine Forest

Probably the most extensive type of forest in the country is the pine forest of the central highlands, technically known as a subtropical moist forest. The most common of the several pine species is the *ocote (Pinus montezumae),* but the Caribbean pine *(Pinus caribaea)* is common also. Ocotes generally occur between 600 and 1,400 meters, depending on the region. In wetter areas, they grow in dense forests laced with epiphytes. In drier areas, the ocotes are more widely spaced, often sharing the forest with *encino* or *roble* oak trees, particularly around water sources, and frequently with many broadleaf shrubs underneath.

Dry Forest

In lowland regions on both the Pacific and Atlantic coasts where rainfall levels are not high enough to support rainforest, deciduous tropical forests were once common but are now rarely found. Acacia and copa trees are common, often mixed in with tree cacti, agaves, and a variety of drought-resistant shrubs. A superb example of a deciduous tropical forest can be seen in Sierra de la Botija, in the area around San Marcos de Colón and El Corpus, near Choluteca; other patches are found along the valleys of the Ríos Ulúa, Humaya, Otoro, Choluteca, and Goascorán, around Olanchito in the Río Aguán Valley, and in a few places on the Bay Islands. The forest of El Boquerón in Olancho, with its gliricidia, ceiba, walnut, and fig trees, is a subtropical dry forest.

Savannah

Surprising to casual tourists, as well as a few plant biologists, is the presence of grassland savanna over large portions of the Mosquitia. The grasslands, dotted with stands of Caribbean pine, receive the same amount of rainfall as the adjacent rainforest and are often submerged during the wettest parts of the year.

A drier type of savanna supporting grasses and occasional stands of acacia and

© FUAD AZZAD

the orchid *Rhyncholaelia digbyana*, the national flower of Honduras

cactus covers parts of Olancho and El Paraíso. Biologists believe these areas were originally forested.

Mangrove Wetland

Much of the Honduran coastline, both Pacific and Caribbean, was once fronted by marshy tidal wetlands supporting extensive mangrove swamps. While cultivation and ranching have wiped out much of the former wetlands, several sizable mangrove areas remain. An unusual tree able to withstand high levels of salt, the mangrove thrives at the boundary between land and sea, where no other tree species can live. Most common close to the ocean are red mangroves, while farther inland, on drier ground, black and white mangroves predominate.

Rather than having their root structure buried in dirt, as most trees do, the mangroves appear to be standing on tippy-toes in the water, supported by a network of roots. Amidst these root networks is a safe, nutrient-rich nursery of sorts for many fish and shellfish species. The mangroves are important in protecting many low-lying coastal areas from the worst ocean storms, and they also help filter sediment out of river runoff, thus actually helping to build new land. The mangrove swamp, along with the coastal tropical forest often behind it, provides a home to troops of monkeys, sea and land birds, manatees, and crocodiles.

Due to expanding fruit cultivation and ranching on the Caribbean coast, and shrimp-farming on the Pacific, many of Honduras's mangroves have been wiped out. Patches remain in the protected areas of Punta Sal, Punta Izopo, Cuero y Salado, Laguna Guaymoreto, and the Bahía de Chismuyo in the Golfo de Fonseca. But by far the largest reserve of mangroves still largely unmodified by humans in the country is along the coastline of the Mosquitia, in far northeastern Honduras.

MAMMALS

Because of Honduras's rugged topography, a number of isolated regions remain refuges for numerous wild species extinct elsewhere. The larger national parks, in particular Pico Bonito and Sierra de Agalta, and the rainforest of the Reserva de la Biosfera del Río Plátano are the most likely places to encounter rare mammals.

Monkeys

Among the larger wild mammals in Honduras's forests, the three monkey species indigenous to the country—*mono aullador* (howler), *mono cara blanca* (white-faced), and *mono araña* (spider)—are unquestionably the easiest to spot. Noisy and very visible as they roam the upper stories of rainforests and cloud forests, the intelligent and social creatures hang out together in groups ranging from just 3–4 to more than 25. Good places to scout for monkeys are Cuero y Salado and Pico Bonito, near La Ceiba; Punta Sal and Laguna de los Micos, near Tela; Sierra de Agalta and La Muralla in Olancho; and all over the Mosquitia.

Howler monkeys are the largest and the loudest of the three. A stocky beast with dark fur weighing as much as seven kilograms, the male howler is owner of an unusually large set of vocal cords, contained in the bulging sac in his neck. After warming up with a series of loud grunts, the male howler lets loose with an unearthly roar echoing out over the jungle, which can be heard for several kilometers. The howlers' favorite time to howl is in the early morning and sometimes in the late afternoon, also. Despite their intimidating cries, howlers are fairly passive and sedentary, and they live on a diet of fruits and plants.

Impressively acrobatic but shy and elusive, **spider monkeys** are named for their long, slinky limbs perfectly designed for cruising through the upper stories of tropical jungle. The tail of the spider monkey is astoundingly dexterous, equipped with sensitive pads like on the tips of fingers to better probe and grip with. Spider monkeys flee from human settlements and are much less frequently seen than other monkeys. But should you run across a group, for example, out in the forests of the Mosquitia or in Sierra de Agalta, expect them to aggressively screech, fling twigs and nuts at you, rattle branches, and create a ruckus until you move on. Like the howlers, spider monkeys subsist principally on fruits and leaves, though they may occasionally eat insects also.

Diminutive but remarkably intelligent, the **white-faced** or **capuchin monkey** stands only 40 centimeters tall or so, with a distinctive tuft of white hair around its head. Unlike the spider and howler, the white-faced monkey is an omnivore, quite content to raid a bird's nest for its eggs or gobble a slow-footed lizard that happens by. If it finds a fruit too hard to gnaw into, a white-faced monkey will industriously bash the food against a tree or rock until it relinquishes its nourishment. White-faced monkeys were once quite bold near the Sierra de la Botija, in southern Honduras near the Nicaraguan border, but reprisals from farmers whose corn they would steal have caused the monkeys to retreat deeper into the forest.

Cats

Five different feline species still stalk the hills and forests of Honduras, though in a much-reduced habitat from former years. These animals are mainly nocturnal, so unless you go hiking at night or stumble across their den, it's very unlikely any of Honduras's cats will ever cross your path.

The king of cats is unquestionably the **jaguar,** called a *jaguar, tigre,* or *pantera* in Honduras. The largest cat in the Americas, jaguars measure up to two meters in length and can either be brown with black spots or flat black. These majestic, powerful animals are impressive hunters, known to drag off horses and cattle and even go fishing for crocodile or manatee. But jungle mammals such as monkeys, wild boars, or deer are their most common prey.

Though in grave danger from hunters and habitat loss (each jaguar needs 25 square kilometers of territory to hunt), jaguars can show up in the oddest of places. In 1995, an evidently confused adult female wandered out of the forests of Pico Bonito, through pineapple plantations, across the La Ceiba–Tela road, and into a house in the village of San Juan. The inhabitants, somewhat perturbed by their new guest, closed up the house with the animal inside and called for help. After it had thoroughly trashed the inside of the house, local environmentalists eventually managed to get the jaguar into a wooden cage, which was then put into the back of a truck and driven back up to the forest. As the "rescuers" arrived at the edge of the forest, the enraged (or terrified) jaguar managed to destroy its cage and leap to freedom.

A bit smaller than jaguars and with an unspotted brown coat are **cougars,** also known as pumas or mountain lions (*león* in Spanish). While the jaguar sticks close to humid forests, cougars are quite happy in much more arid environments, like the mountains of southern and central Honduras. Cougars have unusually large back paws, which help make them gifted jumpers. Without much of a start, a cougar can easily clear 7–8 meters in a single leap, and they have been seen to jump from heights of up to 20 meters. Not standoffish when it comes to domestic animals, cougars are happy to raid the local farm for a tasty sheep, chicken, or pig to supplement their normal repast of wild pigs, raccoons, or other small wild mammals. Because of this proclivity, the rural folk of Honduras vilify cougars and hunt them down whenever they can.

Slightly smaller than the cougar, and often confused with it, is the **jaguarundi,** which can appear both in a rust color and in black. Smaller still, both about the size of a very large house cat and with spotted coats, are the **ocelot** and **margay** (both called *tigrillos* in Spanish).

Baird's Tapir

The largest mammal in the country, the tapir is an odd-looking creature related to the rhinoceros, measuring more than two meters long and weighing up to 300 kilograms. Found in both lowland and highland forests, and even sometimes secondary forest, the tapir—called *danto* in Honduras—is a frequent target of hunters, both human and feline, for its meat. Tapir are invariably found near lakes and rivers, and if frightened, they will beat a furious stampede straight to the water, flattening anything in their path and letting out an odd grunting sound as they run. Living on a steady diet of leaves, the tapir stuffs its small mouth with an odd, elongated, mobile snout, a sort of proto-trunk.

Armadillos, Anteaters, and Sloths

With the common trait of having no teeth, these three foraging animals are united under the taxonomic order *Edentata*. The *hormiguero* (great anteater), up to a meter long, is the largest of Honduras's anteaters, followed by the more common *tamandu* (lesser anteater) and the smaller silky anteater, which rarely ventures out of trees and is seen infrequently. Anteaters spend much of their lives prowling the forests at a leisurely pace in search of ants and termites. After ripping up a termite or ant mound with its strong forearms and sharp claws, the anteater probes the mound with its most unusual tongue, a sticky appendage up to half a meter long that gathers up ants by the dozen. Biologists have estimated that anteaters can munch upwards of 30,000 ants a day. To defend themselves against the vicious stinging ants that live in Honduras's forests, anteaters have remarkably tough fur and hides, which local *campesinos* insist cannot be cut through by a machete. While not particularly agile or speedy, the anteater is known to defend itself so well with its vicious hooked claws that even jaguars prefer to look for easier prey.

Also subsisting on a steady diet of ants and termites, with a few other insects thrown in for variety, are two species of armadillo, the *cusuco* (nine-banded) and *pitero de uña* (naked tailed). Looking like baby dinosaurs, these curious creatures are equipped with calcified armor plates to defend themselves from attack as they waddle their ungainly way around the forest floor. A larger ancestor of the armadillo, the glyptodon, once lived in Honduras, as evidenced by fossils found near Gracias, Lempira.

If armadillos and anteaters seem unusual, the sloth is downright hilarious. Inching its way in slow motion along the undersides of tree branches in the perpetual quest for more leaves, the sloth is certainly the most relaxed mammal you're likely to run across in the forest. With an unusually slow metabolism, sloths simply don't have much get up and go. What stirs biologists to wonderment is that these proverbially lazy animals, seemingly so badly adapted to the pitiless wild, have managed to survive to the present day! Sloths are a favorite target of jaguars and harpy eagles, which literally pluck them out of trees. Perhaps to help keep an eye out for this constant threat, the sloth has an extra neck vertebra, allowing it to peer directly over its own back. And with their algae-covered fur and slow movement, the animals are difficult for predators to spot. Two species live in Honduras, the *perezoso de dos dedos* (two-toed sloth) and the *perezoso de tres dedos* (three-toed sloth). Despite the extra digit, the three-toed sloth is the slower of the two. Sloths come down from their tree homes every week or so to take their *toilette,* relieving themselves of some 30 percent of their body weight into a carefully prepared hole, which the sloth neatly covers with leaves before climbing back up for the rest of the week. While sloths are slow movers in the trees, on the ground they are practically invalids, barely capable of locomotion. A sloth clawing its way laboriously along the ground, over to a tree, and up the trunk to the safety of the branches looks like an actor in a really bad melodramatic movie, gravely wounded but still valiantly struggling across the ground. Because they are so easy to hunt, the inoffensive sloth has not fared well at the hands of man and is now seen only in more remote areas like Sierra de Agalta in Olancho or the Mosquitia.

Peccaries

If during a forest hike you should hear much grunting and furious activity nearby, you may have stumbled into a group of peccaries, called either *quequeo* or *chancho de monte* (mountain pig) in Honduras. A gregarious animal, the peccary forages in large groups of up to 30 or 40 animals, rummaging around in underbrush for plants, fruit, small animals, insects, or whatever else comes across their path. While peccaries have no interest in confronting humans, they are notoriously unobservant, not always seeing hikers just a few meters away on an open trail. Jaguars and cougars hunt these temperamental, aggressive animals, but the cats have been known to come out on the losing end of a run-in with an irate band of peccaries.

The smaller collared peccary is extremely adaptable and is found in any type of forest, including lowland jungle, dry tropical forest, pine forest, cloud forest, and even secondary forest and farmland. The larger white-lipped peccary, which runs in larger groups across more territory and is much more sensitive to human presence, is less frequently seen in Honduras.

Bats

The mammal with by far the most representatives in Honduras is the bat, with 98 species registered at last count. Most common and one of the country's largest species is the **Jamaican fruit-eating bat,** which lives on figs, bananas, and mangoes. More insidious is the **vampire bat,** loathed by *campesinos* in Central America not so much because the bat might suck their blood, but rather because it often kills off valuable livestock with paralytic rabies. An interesting sight is the **greater bulldog bat,** the only species in the Americas capable of catching fish, for which it is known as *murciélago pescador* in Honduras. These bats, with remarkably large wingspans and long claws, frequent the waterways on the north coast. They hunt by skimming over the water, locating their prey with a nifty little sonar system, and pouncing when the small fish or crustaceans near the surface. Other species include the **northern ghost bat** and the **Honduran white bat,** both with white coloring, and the **tent-making bat,** which, as its name suggests, builds itself a personal chalet of leaves and twigs to bed down.

Other Land Mammals

The adaptable **white-tailed deer** *(venado)* is seen in many different ecosystems throughout Honduras, despite being a favorite target among hunters for both its meat and valuable pelt. Considerably smaller, and with a reddish coat, is the **brocket deer** *(tilopo* or *venado colorado),* rarely seen and considered in danger of extinction. Both the **gray fox** and **coyote** still roam the mountain country in all parts of Honduras, particularly the west around Ocotepeque and the east in Olancho and El Paraíso.

The **kinkajou** *(mico de noche),* which looks like a cross between a cat and a small monkey with bulging eyes, is utterly unfazed by human presence and will come out for a look if you walk by in its cloud forest home. Found all over Honduras are the *pizote* (white-nosed coati), a rat-like critter with razor sharp teeth; the *mapache* (bandit-faced, omnivorous raccoon); *zorro espín* (porcupine); *conejo* (rabbit); *ardilla* (squirrel); several species of *zorro* or *zorrillo* (skunk) and *guazalo* (opossum); and a myriad of smaller rodents.

Marine Mammals

Otherwise known as the sea cow, the **West Indian manatee** *(manatí* or *vaca marina* in Spanish) is a huge, slow-moving, and gentle creature that resides in freshwater canals and lagoons near the ocean. The manatee, which can grow up to four meters long and weigh 700 kilograms, leads a lazy existence, resting for long periods with only its nose above water and nourishing itself with various aquatic plants. With their oversized lungs, manatees can stay under water for up to 15 or 20 minutes, propelling themselves with their single tail fluke and two slide flippers.

Once found all along the Caribbean coast of Central America, manatees are now in serious danger of extinction. The animal is hunted by both Miskito and Garífuna, who prize its meat (the Miskito claim it has seven distinct flavors in different parts of the body). Slow-moving as they are, manatees are also frequently hit by boats cruising around the coastal waterways, and they are often caught in fishing nets. As a result of these depredations, manatees are no longer common on the north coast, and their slow birth rate (one calf every three or four years) is not helping replenish the population. The waterways of Punta Sal, Punta Izopo, and

Cuero y Salado are thought to harbor only a few dozen manatees, while more live in the remote lagoons of the Mosquitia.

In the waters around the Bay Islands, you might spy **spinner** and **Atlantic bottle-nosed dolphins,** which often cruise through the surrounding waters in their patrols around the Gulf of Mexico and Atlantic Ocean. A dolphin program and research station at Anthony's Key Resort on Roatán can offer visitors an opportunity to scuba dive or snorkel with specially trained bottle-nosed dolphins. Much more rarely seen, sticking to the deeper waters of the Cayman Trench north of the Bay Islands, are **sperm, humpback, pilot,** and **killer whales.** Columbus spotted **tropical monk seals** during his stop at Guanaja in 1502, but the last confirmed sighting of a monk seal was on the Serranillas Islands (which now belong to Colombia) in 1952—the seal is thought to be extinct.

The **neotropical river otters,** called *nutria* or *perro de agua,* were once common in the rivers and lakes of mainland Honduras but seem to be going the way of their seal cousins due to excessive hunting and pollution in rivers and lakes. These inoffensive creatures are extremely intelligent and even funny, prone to playing with one another. The otter can still be seen in the rivers of the Mosquitia and in a few protected areas on the north coast like Pico Bonito and Punta Sal.

BIRDS

With such an amazing number of diverse ecosystems and sheer quantity of remaining forest cover, Honduras is a true paradise for tropical birders. There are 30 distinct cloud forests, huge swaths of tropical jungle, pine forest, mangrove wetlands, arid and thorn forests, and other habitats. The most up-to-date count is 714 species, and with the country only gradually being thoroughly investigated, that number is going up every year.

Cloud forests, such a rare and unique high-altitude environment of oak and avocado trees covered in bromeliads and vines and wreathed in mist, attract a number of

unusual avian residents. Everyone's favorite is of course the brilliantly colored resplendent quetzal, hard to find in Guatemala and Costa Rica but easily spotted in a couple of dozen locations in Honduras. At La Tigra, right outside of Tegucigalpa, seasoned birders can look for specialties like the blue-and-white mockingbird, rufous-browed wren, wine-throated hummingbird, bushy-crested jay, and green-breasted mountain-gem. The more dense forests at Celaque are home to the highland guan, slate-colored solitaire, black robin, spotted nightingale-thrush, mountain trogon, and numerous hummingbirds, while the lucky birder may encounter rarities like the blue-throated motmot, slaty finch, and maroon-chested ground-dove.

Out in the forest reserves at Sierra de Agalta or La Muralla in the far-flung Olancho region, resplendent quetzals are a dime a dozen. More unusual species include the three-wattled bellbird, spectacled and black-and-white owls, the king vulture, 12 woodcreeper species, crested and highland guans, the great curassow, tody and broad-billed motmots, and a host of relatively tame cloud forest birds.

The **rainforests** of the Mosquitia contain more than 500 species, including at least 45 at the northern limits of their ranges. These include the harpy eagle (largest of New World eagles), great green and scarlet macaws, the agami heron, jabiru (a stork with a three-meter wing span), black-and-white hawk-eagle, rufous motmot, great jacamar, white-fronted nunbird, green-and-rufous kingfisher, snowcap, and chestnut-mandible toucan. The easily accessible botanical gardens at Lancetilla, near Tela, and at Pico Bonito, are packed with toucans, trogons, motmots, tanagers, orioles, parrots, eagles, owls, and all manner of obscure (and entertainingly named) specialties like rufous piha, lovely cotinga, purple-crowned fairy, great potoo, and many others.

Transition zones between highland forests and the tropical lowlands, in particular the area around Lago de Yojoa, are superlative places to spot species from both areas, as well as local species like various ducks, tanagers,

© MIKE JONES

Cloud forests at La Tigra and Celaque are home to numerous hummingbirds.

orioles, motmots, toucans, and many others. The trails in Cerro Azul/Meambár, right next to the lake, are one of the best places to spot the keel-billed motmot, one of Central America's most sought-after birds.

The **mangrove wetlands and coastline** of northern Honduras, especially at Punta Sal and Punta Izopo near Tela and Cuero y Salado near La Ceiba, are another favored environment for birds. These coastal wetlands are havens for large numbers of pelicans (white and brown), roseate spoonbills, white ibis, magnificent frigatebirds, herons, egrets, gulls, terns, plovers, sandpipers, and rare rails and crakes.

The best source of information about birds and birding in Honduras is www.birdinghonduras .com, put together by veteran Honduran birders Mark Bonta and David L. Anderson. Bonta, in particular, supplied the great majority of information on birds and places to bird for this travel guide. Bonta and Anderson lead birding tours and also wrote the *Birder's Guide to Honduras,* with extensive bird-finding tips and the official checklist of Honduran species. Another

great resource is Robert Gallardo, who also has an excellent website, www.birdsofhonduras .com. Gallardo also leads birding tours and organized a Mesoamerican Bird Festival in February 2009 at Lago de Yojoa that he hopes to make an annual event. Other useful resources include the *National Geographic Field Guide to the Birds of North America,* by Jonathan Alderfer and Jon L. Dunn, and *Birds of Mexico and Central America,* by Ber van Perlo, both published in 2006.

FISH AND CORAL

The greatest variety of fish in Honduras is undoubtedly found in the reefs and surrounding waters of the Bay Islands, which contain an estimated 96 percent of all the marine life found in the Caribbean. Fish of all sizes, from tiny chromides to the whale shark, the world's largest fish, are found near the islands.

A list of smaller fish species in the Caribbean waters off Honduras, with all the distinct species living on the reef, in deeper water, and along the coast, would go on for pages. A few of the colorful favorites on the reef include grouper, butterfly fish, barracuda, yellowtail snapper, Goliath fish, and angelfish. Other marine animals often seen on the reef are eagle and manta rays, green moray eels, sea horses, octopi, and sea turtles, to name just a few of the more prominent residents.

In their 100–150-year life span, **whale sharks** can grow up to 15 meters long, with a weight of nearly 12 tons. Daunting though they may be, whale sharks are harmless to humans, living off plankton and tiny shrimp, which they filter through their gill rakers as they cruise the deep waters north of the Bay Islands. The blunt-snouted, speckled fish are equipped with two sets of dorsal fins toward the tail and a pair of larger pectoral fins. The Bay Islands region is one of the few places in the world where whale sharks can be seen all year, most commonly in the waters near Utila, particularly February–April and August–September. Utila's population is made up of whale sharks roughly 6–10 meters in length, and 15–20 tons in weight.

Other inhabitants of the deeper waters around the islands and off the north coast are wahoo, king and Spanish mackerel, bonito, blackfin tuna, kingfish, and marlin, while famed fighting fish such as snook and tarpon live in the lagoons along the coast, at the intersection of fresh and salt water.

Sharks, such as hammerhead, nurse, and blacktip, frequent the deeper waters along the Caribbean coast of Honduras. The waters of the Mosquitia are particularly notorious for hammerheads, and more than a couple of Miskito lobster divers have stories to tell about unpleasantly close encounters with these aggressive sharks. Don't go swimming out beyond the waves in the Mosquitia! While sharks frequent the waters around the Bay Islands, there have been no reports of divers being attacked. A variety of other sharks live in the Pacific near Honduras, but they rarely make it into the Golfo de Fonseca. If they do, local fishermen promptly catch them and turn them into fillets.

Several species of shellfish are found in Honduran waters, particularly lobster, shrimp, conch, and a kind of crayfish found in the lagoons and swamps of the north coast. Lobster- and shrimp-fishing is a major industry on the north coast and in the Bay Islands, and shrimp-farming is also big business on the Golfo de Fonseca.

Resident freshwater fish include tilapia (found particularly in Lago de Yojoa), largemouth bass, catfish, mollies, minnows, and mojarras. Mountain trout and related native species, like guapote, tepemechin, and the endangered cuyamel, still live in Honduran rivers. This last fish, very meaty and tasty, once abounded in the rivers all along the north coast but has been fished to near extinction everywhere except a few places in the Mosquitia and Olancho.

The temperate waters surrounding the Bay Islands are an optimal habitat also for coral, of which some 73 types have been identified, along with 41 species of sponge. Staghorn and elkhorn corals, widely decimated in the Caribbean during the 1980s, are still relatively plentiful near Roatán. The reef forms part of the Mesoamerican Barrier Reef.

REPTILES AND AMPHIBIANS

Honduras is home to some 20 species of **lizards,** including the common iguana and the larger and more intimidating basilisk lizard. Two places especially well known for their huge and numerous lizards are the region around Brus Laguna (in the Mosquitia) and the Bay Islands, although they are seen less and less frequently due to hunting. Several lizard species on the islands are found nowhere else in the world, though they are in danger of extinction from overhunting.

Well over 100 species of **snakes** slither through the forests and pastures (and sometimes swim in the waterways) of rural Honduras, and almost all of them are harmless. Among the poisonous species are the dreaded fer-de-lance (called *barba amarilla,* yellow beard, for the bright yellow patch on its neck); the *coral* (coral snake) with its distinct bands of red, black, and white; and the noisy *cascabel*

© FRANKLIN RAMIREZ, GUARUMA.ORG

Few of Honduras's 100-odd species of snakes are poisonous.

(rattler). All of these species are found throughout the country, so watch out for them. When hiking in rural areas, it's always advisable to watch where you put your feet, particularly when walking among rocks, logs, or tall grass. Less dangerous are **boas,** which can grow up to three meters long. Although not poisonous, boas have sharp teeth and don't hesitate to bite if threatened.

Crocodiles and their smaller relatives, the **caymans,** inhabit the many lagoons, swamps, and waterways all along the Caribbean coast. So perfectly adapted to their environment that they have barely evolved since the age of the dinosaurs, crocodiles still maintain a healthy population in Honduras, despite the depredations of hunters after their meat and hide, or just avenging the loss of a pig or favorite hunting dog. Out in the Mosquitia, swapping legends of huge crocodiles is a favorite pastime among the Garífuna and Miskitos. A pilot flying a small plane over Laguna de Ibans not long ago thought he saw an abandoned canoe on one of the small islands in the middle of the lagoon. Swooping down for a closer look, he saw that it was in fact a monster of a crocodile, fully four meters long, basking placidly in the sun. Villagers living in Cocobila, Belén, Raistá, and other communities nearby still insist on swimming and bathing in the lagoon, even though a croc will take someone's arm or carry off a baby every year or two.

Sea turtles, especially hawksbill and green ridley but also loggerhead and leatherback, once regularly beached themselves on the north coast and in the Golfo de Fonseca to lay their eggs, but merciless hunting has devastated their populations. As a result of limited protection programs on a few beaches—for example, Plaplaya in the Mosquitia and Punta Ratón on the Golfo de Fonseca—workers patrol beaches at night during the season when females come in, collect the eggs and protect them in incubators until they hatch, and then release them directly into the sea.

Spending almost their entire long lives at sea, only female turtles come to shore, and then only for as long as it takes to laboriously

© JUAN VELASQUEZ, GUARUMA.ORG

one of the smaller species of lizard in Honduras

dig a nest, deposit their eggs, and struggle back into the water. The turtles arrive at night, often shortly before dawn, and leave between 70 and 120 eggs, each about the size of a golf ball, with an odd leathery skin that feels fragile but is actually quite resilient. Left to their own devices, the eggs take about two months to hatch, sometimes less, at which point the tiny hatchlings struggle out of the sand and directly into the ocean. But rarely are eggs left

alone these days, as they are considered a local delicacy and can fetch a good price. *Hueveros,* or "egg men," walk up and down the beaches at night during the season, raiding nests and frequently killing the defenseless mother for meat as well. While the number of turtles is but a fraction of what it was 30 years ago, protection programs in Honduras and other countries offer some hope that the populations can rebound.

Environmental Issues

Honduras has managed to retain such valuable natural patrimony not because of any far-sighted planning on the part of the government or a particularly enlightened eco-consciousness on the part of the inhabitants—far from it, in fact. Rather, it has been the country's daunting topography, lack of arable land, and comparatively low population density that have spared the forests. But as in many other poor, underdeveloped

countries, Honduras's population is growing explosively, and the consequent pressures on the remaining forests are increasing hand in hand with it, at a vertiginously accelerating rate and in a variety of ways. Most obvious is logging, a notoriously inefficient and wasteful industry in Honduras. Modern forestry techniques are practically unheard of, and with lax, corrupt forestry officials and little police support, loggers pretty much cut as they please. The government estimated in 2004 that some 100,000 hectares of forest are lost each year, or about 2 percent of the forest cover. Formerly concentrated on the pine forests of central Honduras, loggers have in the last couple of decades mounted an invasion of the southern edges of the Mosquitia's rainforests, where they destroy entire stands of forest just to get at a single mahogany, worth a pretty penny in wealthy western countries. A 2005 report by the Environmental Investigation Agency, *The Illegal Logging Crisis in Honduras,* details with damning evidence the rapacious practices of several well-connected lumber companies, particularly in Olancho and the Mosquitia, to export mahogany, pine, and other woods to U.S. companies, Home Depot among them. So next time you buy lumber, check the tag to see where the wood comes from, and if it's from Honduras, don't buy it.

Close on the heels of the loggers, at least in Olancho and the Mosquitia, invariably come an army of *colonos,* invading peasants determined to hack out a small farm and later try to convince the government (often successfully) to regularize their de facto holdings. Large-scale ranchers are often next in line, snapping up huge holdings from the *colonos.* Because Honduran ranchers use very elementary cattle-raising techniques, their productivity is remarkably low, wasting huge amounts of land.

The 30-odd patches of cloud forest in highland Honduras face their own variety of threats. While the smaller trees don't attract loggers, their wood works just fine for the *carboneros,* who chop down whatever tree happens to be at hand to make charcoal. Just as ominous is the continual encroachment of coffee plantations into the lower reaches of the cloud forest, which provide the perfect climate for high-quality arabica coffee beans. The mangrove wetlands on both coasts are a prime source of firewood, and those in the Golfo de Fonseca are ceding to the expansion of coastal shrimp farms.

In the face of governmental apathy (not to say complicity), dozens of grassroots environmental groups have sprung up across the country, most dedicated to protecting a specific local natural area. True, some NGOs receive criticism as being little more than sponges for foreign aid money. But others are well-organized, noisy defenders of the environment, not afraid of speaking up against the wealthy interests often behind environmental destruction. And this has not come without a cost, as these interests invariably have well-armed young thugs ready to make threats or carry them out. Just two of the better-publicized cases in the 1990s involved the still-unsolved murders of activists Jeanette Kawas and Hector Rodrigo Pastor Fasquelle. More recently, Padre Tamayo in Salamá, Olancho, has risked his life to take brave public stands against the illegal logging and drug-running by well-connected people (and was nominated for the 2008 Front Line award for Human Rights Defenders at Risk, in recognition of his efforts). His colleagues from the Movimiento Ambientalista de Olancho (Environmental Movement in Olancho), Heraldo Zuñiga and Roger Ivan Cartagena, were killed execution-style in 2006 by members of the national police, after having received death threats for their environmental work.

A more recent development in Honduras has been the increased participation of individuals, groups, and government missions from other countries in protecting the environment. Because suspicions of Honduran corruption run (justifiably) very high in other countries, many donors are paying close attention to environmental programs and even getting involved themselves. Two examples are Finnish foresters sent to help replant the island of Guanaja, which lost most of its vegetation when Hurricane Mitch ran over it, and the binational German-Honduran projects in the Río Plátano and at Celaque. Private foreign groups are involved also, such as Proyecto Aldea Global from the United States, to which the Honduran government has turned over administration of Parque Nacional Cerro Azul/Meámbar. One can hardly expect foreigners to be the miracle cure for Honduras's environmental problems, but they can use their aid money in a persuasive fashion, act as witnesses to what's happening in the countryside, and help curb some of the worst abuses.

History

All things considered, history has not been particularly kind to Honduras. The list of foreigners taking advantage of the country and its peoples begins at least as early as the incursion of Mesoamerican warriors shortly after the time of Christ, who would found the Mayan dynasty in Copán, and continues through the Spanish conquistadors down to the banana companies and *maquila* factories of today.

With its daunting mountainous topography, and lacking the fertile volcanic soils of its Central American neighbors, Honduras never spawned a "home-grown" agricultural society of any significant size during the Spanish colony and modern era. No elite class based on coffee or cattle like those in neighboring Guatemala, Nicaragua, and El Salvador developed in Honduras during the colonial era, and the wealth produced from the gold and silver mines was quickly shipped abroad. Instead, Honduras remained a land of *milpa* farmers, who cultivated small patches of land planted with beans, corn, and vegetables to satisfy the immediate needs of their families.

Lacking any wealthy class of its own or a strong central government to defend itself, Honduras was an easy target for U.S. mining and banana companies, who arrived at the beginning of the 20th century and in effect became the country's first ruling class. These days, Honduras finds itself struggling to get by, one of the poorest nations in the Americas and stuck in a seemingly endless cycle of debt and anemic economic growth.

Yet, despite this relentless cycle of underdevelopment and exploitation, Honduras somehow managed to maintain overall social peace for most of the 20th century, a remarkable feat considering the appallingly violent civil wars elsewhere in Central America. Some social disturbances did occur, most notably the Great Banana Strike of 1954 and, later, land-invasion movements by *campesinos*. But because Honduran authorities did not view their society through the prism of a rigid class divide,

political and military leaders did not react with the blind opposition characteristic of their more repressive neighbors. Labor unions were legalized and their limited demands met; the military even undertook a modest agrarian reform program when in power in the 1970s, which helped defuse a potentially explosive situation in the countryside. It may come as a surprise that Honduras has the longest existing two-party political system in the hemisphere outside of the United States and Uruguay. True, they were both set up originally by the banana companies and are now basically ideological empty vehicles for political ambition and patronage. But for all its defects, the Honduran system has proved remarkably flexible in accommodating the needs of its people.

PRE-COLUMBIAN HISTORY
The First Hondurans

It remains a matter of conjecture whether the earliest settlers in Honduras arrived over land from Asia via the Bering Strait, as many believe, or on rafts from the South Pacific islands. Whatever route they took, the first people to live in what is now Honduras had arrived by about 10,000 B.C.

Next to nothing is known about these early Americans. Archaeologists hypothesize the earliest of them were hunters and gatherers who may have spent only a short time in the region before continuing on to South America.

Early Honduran Societies

Because of its position in the center of the Americas, Honduras was a crossroads for pre-Columbian indigenous cultures, a border zone of sorts where Mesoamerican and South American indigenous peoples met.

At some point between 3000 and 1000 B.C., the region was populated by migrants from both the north and the south. Linguistic evidence indicates that the ancestors of today's Pech and Tawahka migrated up from South America, while the forebears of the Tolupán appear related to the Sioux of North America. Because the Lenca language as well as dozens of other idioms previously spoken in Honduras have been lost, it's impossible to determine where the other pre-Hispanic inhabitants came from. The earliest evidence of settled society in Honduras found thus far dates from 2000 to 1500 B.C. It appears that localized cultures developed simultaneously in the Valle de Sula, at Yarumela in the Valle de Comayagua, and in Olancho. The level of interaction between these different societies is a matter of debate, but judging from pottery remains, some intergroup trading took place. A great deal of investigation remains to be done in Honduras, where numerous ruins of unknown origin are still untouched by archaeologists. Olancho and the inland parts of the Mosquitia, in particular, are filled with ruins large and small.

Around or shortly after the time of Christ, several indigenous groups from Mexico and Guatemala migrated into Honduras. The Toltec-speaking Chorotega are thought to have first settled in western Honduras and later continued southward to the Choluteca plain, where they were living at the time of the Spanish conquest. The Nahuatl-speaking Pipil migrated south from Mexico at about the same time.

Not long thereafter, another group moved into western Honduras from Mexico and Guatemala and set the foundations for an explosion of development. These people—who would become the Maya—went on to build one of the greatest civilizations ever known in the Americas.

The Maya

An unknown people, thought to have links with the Teotihuacán culture in Mexico, crossed the Sierra Espíritu Santo from Guatemala into the valley of Copán around A.D. 100, conquering the Maya-speaking inhabitants of the region. After a slow beginning, these new rulers consolidated their local control over the next three centuries and began construction of the city of Copán by the 5th century.

The first positively dated glyph at Copán was made in A.D. 426 to mark the accession of Yax K'uk' Mo' to the city's throne. Thus began the ruling dynasty of Copán, which spanned four centuries, ending sometime around A.D. 822. While Copán clearly had links to other cities in Guatemala and Mexico, it was just as often in war as in trade, in the tumultuous Mayan world of independent city-states.

For reasons not entirely clear, Copán was the greatest center for arts, astronomy, and science among the Maya. The elaborate stelae erected at Copán are unparalleled anywhere in Mesoamerica, and the city's royal astronomers calculated planetary movements, eclipses, and the yearly calendar with a precision equaled only by modern science.

Built gradually over the course of 400 years, with old temples buried and new ones built over them, the city of Copán is an impressive testament to the wealth and vision of the Mayan rulers, and their ability to marshal large numbers of laborers. Some 24,000 people are thought to have lived in and around Copán at its height.

Mysteriously, classic Mayan civilization abruptly collapsed in the Yucatán, Guatemala, and Honduras around A.D. 900. The collapse is all the odder considering Mayan cities were not part of one great centralized empire. One widely accepted explanation for the demise of Mayan civilization is that the population simply grew too big for the surrounding lands to support. This certainly seems to be the case at Copán, where recent studies confirm massive deforestation and soil erosion just before the city's collapse. Although Mayan-speaking people continued to live in the Valle de Copán and still do so today, the city was abandoned entirely.

Honduras in 1502

In regions outside of Mayan control, and after the decline of the Maya, Honduras was a complex mosaic of tribes, subtribes, and chiefdoms. There were only vague borders between them, and all were busy trading, bickering, and frequently warring among one another when Columbus first arrived on the scene in 1502.

Western and south-central Honduras in

1502 were dominated by the Lenca, a broad grouping composed of several different and often hostile subtribes, including the Potón, Guaquí, Cares, Chatos, Dules, Paracas, Guajiquíros, and Yaras.

The historical account of which languages were spoken by which Lenca tribes is extremely muddled. It's possible the same groups were given two different names by different witnesses, and that others were not Lenca at all. Some tribes were exclusively hunter-gatherers, while others cultivated maize and other crops in the mountain valleys of Comayagua and Sensetí, and around Lago de Yojoa.

In far western Honduras, the Chortí Maya held sway over the mountain region along the border with Guatemala west and south to El Salvador and were organized in local chiefdoms.

Throughout Honduras at the time of the conquest were trading outposts maintained by the Aztecs. Not far from present-day San Pedro Sula, the city of Naco—the largest urban center in the country when the Spanish conquest began—is thought to have been one such outpost, although others argue it was a Chortí Maya city.

Most of central and north-central Honduras was occupied by the Tolupán in 1502, while farther east in present-day Olancho and Mosquitia were the Pech and the Tawahka. Each of these tribes survived by hunting, fishing, and limited agriculture. Settlements were small and frequently temporary, and groups moved often to find fresh game and rich soil for planting.

Unquestionably, these various indigenous groups interacted with one another often, either through trade or warfare. In several places, they lived side by side in relative harmony, especially in the valleys of Comayagua, Catacamas, and Agalta, and around Lago de Yojoa. No group possessed the strength to exercise hegemony over the others, a fact that greatly helped Spanish invaders.

CONQUEST AND COLONIZATION
Columbus's Fourth Voyage

In July 1502, on the fourth and final voyage of Cristóbal Colón (Christopher Columbus), the famed admiral sailed from Hispaniola along the Caribbean coast of Central America and came upon the island of Guanaja, where he met with the local people and waylaid a trader's canoe laden with axes, copper goods, cacao, and pottery.

Despite the fact that the canoe was seen approaching from the west, Columbus continued east from Guanaja, which he named the Island of Pines. His first stop was at Punta Caxinas, near present-day Trujillo. The first mass spoken on the mainland of the Americas was held at Punta Caxinas. A weather-beaten concrete cross now marks the reputed site.

East of Trujillo, Columbus stopped again at the mouth of a large river, which may have been the Aguán, Sico, or Patuca. Because this was the place chosen to claim the lands for the Spanish crown, Columbus named the river Río de la Posesión.

Continuing farther east along the coast of the Mosquitia, Columbus's fleet was buffeted by severe storms until rounding the easternmost point of Honduras and reaching calmer waters off present-day Nicaragua. In honor of the better weather, the point was christened Cabo Gracias a Dios, a name it retains today.

The Conquest Begins

Following this uneventful first visit, the Spaniards ignored Honduras for the next 20 years, apart from a possible scouting trip by explorers Juan Díaz Solís and Vicente Yáñez Pinzón in 1508. Occupied with consolidating their newfound possessions in the Caribbean, the conquistadors did not return to Honduras until 1522–1523, when Gil González Dávila led an exploratory expedition up the Pacific coast from Panama, reaching the Golfo de Fonseca.

In the following couple of years, six Spanish expeditions converged on Honduras, each headed by ambitious soldiers after wealth and glory, just as predisposed to fight each other as the indigenous people. Not an auspicious start to colonization, it presaged the trend of placing personal power over group interests—the rule in Honduran government ever since.

González Dávila, with the approval of the

PIRATES IN THE CARIBBEAN

The hidden coves and protective cays of the Bay Islands and the secluded lagoons of the Mosquitia made ideal hideaways for marauding pirates in the late 16th and 17th centuries, a debauchery often supported by the British, who were fighting with the Spanish for the region's riches. Large fleets stayed at Port Royal, named for the famous Jamaican port, while smaller groups would often anchor in the cays of Guanaja, and many notorious pirates passed through what is now Honduras.

Henry Morgan was born around 1635 in Wales, but made his way to Jamaica as a young man, where his uncle was lieutenant governor. He began his career as a privateer: a sailor on a private warship authorized by a country's government to attack foreign shipping (the ship and loot were stolen rather than sunk). It's likely that he was the "Captain Morgan" who joined the fleet of Christopher Myngs in 1663, which sailed to capture the Spanish settlement at Trujillo, as well as two settlements in Mexico. From privateering it was just a short step to piracy, and Morgan was dexterous at using the conflicts between England and its enemies to his advantage, enriching himself and his crews with England's support. Morgan quickly became infamous not only for his prowess in taking over settlements, but also for the cruelties and excesses with which they were taken.

Likewise, **John Morris** sailed the Caribbean under privateering commissions granted by Sir Thomas Modyford, governor of Jamaica. He often sailed with Morgan. (Indeed, he was one of the commanders in an explosion that occurred during a wild party onboard Henry Morgan's flagship in 1670.) Morris served again under Morgan in his raids against Portobelo, Maracaibo, and Panama in 1671 – raids that breached the newly signed peace treaty between England and Spain. Morgan was arrested, and in a near-comical twist of fate, former privateer Morris was then commissioned as a pirate hunter, instructed to arrest privateers who continued acts of piracy against Spain. Morgan's fate was likewise turned on its head – several times. Morgan was taken to England after his arrest, where he was able to prove that he had no knowledge of the treaty. Instead of going to prison, Morgan was knighted, and he returned to Jamaica in 1675 to take up the post of lieutenant governor, a position he held onto until 1681. Morgan died in 1688, diagnosed with "dropsie" (although there is much speculation about liver failure from his binge drinking).

John Coxen (sometimes spelled Coxon) was another English privateer, but as England was technically at peace with Spain, he sailed at times under French commissions, and other times with out-of-date English commissions to support his ransacking and booty-taking throughout the Caribbean and the coast of Central America. As acting governor, Henry Morgan even issued a warrant for Coxen's arrest around 1679 for his plundering of Spanish towns. John Coxen reputedly lived on Roatán from 1687 to 1697, perhaps in an effort to escape the warrant for his arrest. Coxen's Hole wasn't founded until 1835, by immigrants from the Cayman Islands.

crown, was the first to land on Honduran shores, establishing a small town near the mouth of the Río Dulce, in what is now Guatemala. The explorer marched into the heart of Honduras toward Nicaragua in early 1524. Shortly thereafter, Mexican conqueror Hernán Cortés sent an expedition of his own led by Cristóbal de Olid, who arrived on the north coast in May and quickly set up a settlement at Triunfo de la Cruz (which was later resettled by the Garífuna, who remain there still). It is said that the Aztecs told Cortés they received their gold from the mountains of Honduras. Thus it may have been no accident that the conquistadors made directly for the gold-rich rivers of Olancho.

Olid wasn't totally loyal to Cortés, and once on his own he tried to claim the province for himself. When word of this reached Cortés in Mexico, he promptly dispatched a second expedition, led by Francisco de las Casas, to ensure his authority. Further complications occurred from the incursions of Pedro de Alvarado and Hernando de Soto, who entered Honduras from Guatemala and Nicaragua, respectively. Amid the bickering and fighting, in which Olid literally lost his head, the first permanent settlement was established in the country, at Trujillo.

Impatient with reports of fighting among these various factions, and not trusting anyone, Cortés personally led an expedition to Honduras. Beginning in late 1524, he undertook an incredible several-month overland trek through the jungles of the Yucatán and the Guatemalan Petén, reaching Honduras in the spring of 1525. Although Cortés briefly took control of the situation in Honduras, by the time of his departure in April 1526, his long absence from Mexico had undermined his position in the royal court, and he never again held a position of power.

Displeased with the turbulent course of conquest and wanting to ensure direct control over the new colony, the Spanish crown sent Diego López de Salcedo to act as royal governor of Honduras. López de Salcedo anchored off Trujillo on October 24, 1526, and after a few days of negotiations with suspicious colonists loyal to Cortés, he was allowed to land and take office.

Rebellion and Consolidation

The 15 years after López de Salcedo took over as governor were chaotic for the nascent colony and catastrophic for the indigenous people. Continued infighting, conflicting royal *cédulas* (orders giving authority to conquer and govern a given area), and repeated revolts by native peoples prevented the Spaniards from significantly extending their control across the country.

Several localized attacks against Spanish settlements took place around Trujillo and in the Valle de Sula in the early 1530s, and in 1536, mass rebellion broke out across most of western and central Honduras. Led by the Lenca warrior Lempira, for whom the national currency is named, thousands of Lenca and allied tribes took up arms against the Spaniards. The hostile tribes kept the colony in a precarious position until 1539, when Lempira was assassinated by the Spanish. Localized rebellions continued after Lempira's death, especially in the Valle de Comayagua, but the Spanish put them down easily.

Victory over the Lenca served the Spanish well, both eliminating further native resistance and uniting the conquistadors in the colonial project. Establishing the towns of Gracias a Dios, Comayagua, San Pedro Sula, Choluteca, and Tencoa in the late 1530s, the Spaniards laid the foundation for extending control throughout the region.

As always, gold and silver proved the main impetus for new Spanish settlements. Deposits were discovered early near Gracias a Dios and Comayagua, and not long after in Olancho and in the hills above the Golfo de Fonseca.

In the early colonial era, the province was divided into two sections: Higueras, which comprised present-day western and central Honduras, and Honduras proper, which covered Trujillo, the Mosquitia, Olancho, the region around Tegucigalpa, and the Golfo de Fonseca.

Indigenous Population Declines

In the first decades after the conquest, the indigenous population of Honduras went into a precipitous decline, devastated by both the constant fighting and European plagues. Diseases for which the indigenous people had no tolerance actually preceded the Spaniards, communicated by infected Indians coming to Honduras from Mexico and Caribbean islands. When the conquistadors arrived in person, the plagues picked up force, ravaging local populations. An estimated 500,000–800,000 native people lived in Honduras before 1492, but by 1541 colonial reports put the number of Indians under Spanish control at just 8,000. Although this figure does not include the populations of Tolupán, Pech, and Tawahka outside Spanish influence, it still represents an almost unimaginable decline in population.

While this unintended biological weapon certainly facilitated the conquest, it also posed serious problems for the Spaniards, who needed laborers to work the mines and provide them with food. Indigenous populations would not recover from the plagues and begin to grow again for more than 50 years.

The Poorest Colony

Because of labor shortages and the rapid depletion of the richest veins of gold and silver by the end of the 16th century, Honduras quickly became a colonial backwater. Since the possibilities for getting rich were slim, able governors did their utmost to be stationed elsewhere, leaving Honduras with incompetent administrators who were eager to leave at the first opportunity, with whatever they could take with them.

Spain's control over Honduras, as with many other regions of Latin America, was through *encomiendas,* a method in which Spaniards received awards of land and the right to use the native people who lived on the land for labor in return for religious instruction.

Farming was difficult; Honduras lacked the rich volcanic soils of its neighbors and the rugged terrain made bringing produce to markets even harder. Because of these hardships, would-be colonists looked elsewhere for land. In the early years of the colony, the only industries of any importance were ranching, often for local consumption, and gathering sarsaparilla, thought at the time to be a cure for venereal disease.

In addition, the developing colony was faced with the constant threat of pirate attacks against coastal towns on both the north and south coast, and later with British settlers in the Mosquitia and the Bay Islands. These Shoremen (as they were called), helped by their Miskito allies, made living on the north coast a dangerous undertaking, effectively sealing off the Caribbean coast from Spanish control for the better part of two centuries.

Late in the colonial era, improved technology led to a renewed though short-lived boom in mining, particularly in the mines of Santa Lucía, above Tegucigalpa, and El Corpus, near Choluteca. Farmers in the region of Copán and Gracias also exported large quantities of high-quality tobacco to Europe and other colonies. Nonetheless these were mostly small-scale ventures compared to the wealthy coffee plantations of neighboring Guatemala and El Salvador, to say nothing of the fabulously rich mines of Mexico and Peru. Thus it comes as no surprise that Honduras did not attract significant migration or experience significant economic development during the colonial period.

INDEPENDENCE AND 19TH-CENTURY HONDURAS
Mexican Empire and Central American Federation

Rather than fighting for their independence from the Spanish empire, Central Americans had it handed to them without a struggle when colonial authority completely collapsed in the early 1820s. On September 15, 1821, representatives of the former colonies of Honduras, Costa Rica, Nicaragua, El Salvador, and Guatemala jointly declared independence from Spain in the government palace of Guatemala.

Brief struggles followed within the new countries over how to govern themselves. In Honduras, the two principal cities of Comayagua and Tegucigalpa split on the issue, the former opting to join with Mexico and the latter preferring a union of Central American republics.

By early 1822, the issue had been decided, and the countries declared themselves loyal to Iturbide, the new emperor of Mexico. This would-be empire lasted just over a year, at which point Iturbide was deposed and Central American nations joined together to become a federation, separate from Mexico.

The United Provinces of Central America was a fine idea in theory but in practice foundered on the unpleasant realities of local rivalries, suspicions, and the split between partisans of the Conservative and Liberal trains of political thought. Broadly, Conservatives favored the church, the land-owning elite, and a paternalistic attitude toward indigenous people

FRANCISCO MORAZÁN: CENTRAL AMERICA'S GEORGE WASHINGTON

Honduras's national hero, Francisco Morazán is one of the most revered characters in Central American history, recognized as a visionary thinker and politician, a humane individual, and one of the finest soldiers ever to fight on American soil. Because of his appreciation for the American Revolution and his tireless efforts to promote Central American unity, Morazán is sometimes called the George Washington of Central America.

Morazán was born October 3, 1792, to an upper-middle-class colonial family in Tegucigalpa. Gifted both physically and intellectually, and imbued with strong self-discipline, he was largely self-taught. He received his only formal education from a priest in the town of Texiguat, at that time the only school near Tegucigalpa. Morazán taught himself French so he could read Rousseau's *Social Contract*, and he continued with Tocqueville, Montesquieu, and the history of Europe.

When Central America declared independence from Spain in 1821, Morazán put himself under the orders of Dionisio de Herrera, then mayor of Tegucigalpa. Morazán's first command was at the head of a group of soldiers sent to Gracias in 1822 to transport a load of silver and mercury. He was captured by soldiers from Comayagua but managed to talk his way out of being detained by claiming he was traveling on business. After the Central American provinces broke away from Mexico and created their own union, Morazán took up arms for the Liberal side. He lost his first battle, defending Comayagua from Conservative troops, and was forced to flee to El Salvador to escape a prison term.

After this inauspicious start, Morazán's fortunes improved dramatically. In 1827, Morazán traveled to Nicaragua, where he gathered an army to invade El Salvador and fight off Conservatives attacking from Guatemala, which he did the following year. In 1829, he continued by taking Guatemala; in elections the next year, Morazán was voted president of the Central American Federation. With one brief interruption, Morazán held this post until 1838. Although the federation experienced constant strain from internal opposition, Morazán managed to institute farsighted reforms in bureaucracy, public education, taxation, freedom of religion, the judicial system, infrastructure, and the development, albeit temporary, of democratic institutions.

Morazán's Liberal policies antagonized the church and elite landowners in all five Central American countries. The forces pulling them apart proved stronger than those holding them together, and in spite of his best efforts, the union fell apart shortly after he left office. Morazán was forced into exile in Peru in 1840, but he returned two years later. He led a coup in Costa Rica, with the idea of using that country as a base to reestablish the union. His forces were defeated by Conservatives in September 1842, and on September 15 – ironically, the anniversary of Central American independence – Morazán was executed. He was given permission to order his own execution. After correcting the firing squad's aim, he called out, *"¡Ahora bien, fuego!"* ("Ready, fire!"). According to legend, he was heard to say, *"¡Estoy vivo!"* ("I'm alive!"), and a second volley killed him.

With Morazán's death died any real chance at Central American union, in spite of the obvious advantages of such an alliance. The idea resurfaced repeatedly over the following century and a half, and may even reappear today in the form of trade agreements among some Central American countries.

and *campesinos,* while Liberals supported economic modernization, education, eradicating the power of the church, and a policy of erasing indigenous culture and homogenizing the population. By 1838, after 16 years of nonstop infighting among its members, the Central American union was dead, and each province became a sovereign nation.

The Birth of Honduras

After a few months of vacillation, Honduras declared itself independent on November 15, 1838, and enacted the first of many constitutions in January 1839. Between this time and 1876, Honduras experienced a period of extreme instability and precious little economic or social development.

Rivalries between Liberals and Conservatives dominated the political landscape across Central America during this era, and when one side was in power in one country, rulers of the opposite persuasion organized invasions or coups from their territory. Being in the middle of Central America, Honduras was a frequent target of and participant in these schemes and aggressions.

As if the squabbles between its Central American neighbors weren't enough, Honduras also had to cope with the machinations of North Americans and British, both private citizens and government officials. American agent E. George Squier and British representative Frederick Chatfield abused their power to advance the interests of their respective countries, most particularly regarding a much-discussed but never realized transcontinental railroad or canal.

Even more ominous were the activities of private American and British citizens in Honduras. From the United States came the messianic, slightly lunatic "gray-eyed man of destiny," William Walker. Convinced he was the savior of Central America, and backed by wealthy U.S. financiers, Walker invaded Nicaragua and declared himself president in 1855. Although his rule was short-lived, Walker performed the heretofore impossible task of uniting all the Central American republics—at least for as long as it took them to defeat and expel the hated gringo. Undaunted, Walker returned to Honduras in 1860 with the idea of retaking Central America, only to be captured near Trujillo by the British, turned over to Honduran troops, and summarily executed.

Ever more subtle than North Americans, British power brokers contented themselves not with outright invasion but with contracting a series of debts with the Honduran government. This made a few British bankers and several corrupt Hondurans rich but crippled the country before it had a chance to get started in its modernization. In one of the shadier transactions in financial history, British bankers lent Honduras a bit less than £6 million to help construct a national railroad. The government eventually saw merely £75,000, the rest remaining in sticky fingers on both sides of the Atlantic. By 1871, only 92 kilometers of track had been laid, and even that was shoddily built and soon collapsed. Unable to cope with even the interest on the loan, successive governments tried to forget it existed until 1916, by which time Honduras owed US$125 million and had to plead for the loans to be renegotiated.

The Liberal Years

One of the first forward-thinking governments in Honduran history began in 1876, with the inauguration of President Marco Aurelio Soto, a Liberal. A firm believer in modernization, Soto and his successor, Luis Bográn, did what they could to lay the foundations for development.

Between 1876 and 1891, when Bográn was deposed, successive administrations regulated state finances, started free primary education, and reformed the legal code. Convinced of the need for foreign capital to lift Honduras out of poverty, Soto also promoted mining among U.S. investors.

His campaign's most notable success, if it can be termed as such, was the founding of the New York and Honduras Rosario Mining Company in 1880, which quickly became the most profitable and productive mine in the western hemisphere during that period.

Although the company provided jobs for a thousand Honduran workers and was for a time the most important economic and political player in Honduras, all profits went directly to New York; in the long run, Honduras saw little benefit for the concessions it offered.

The Banana Companies

The railroad and mining episodes gave merely a taste of the foreign domination that was to come with the advent of the banana industry on the north coast. U.S.-bound freighters were buying bananas from local producers as early as 1860, but in 1899 the Vaccaro brothers—later Standard Fruit, and now Castle and Cooke—set up the first foreign-controlled plantations on the mainland near La Ceiba. They were quickly followed by United Fruit and Cuyamel.

Once these foreign companies moved in, small-scale Honduran producers were forced out of business either through land buyouts or crude threats. Thus, by the beginning of World War I, the three largest companies, all foreign-owned, controlled huge portions of land, the country's only railroads, and more than 80 percent of the Honduran export trade. Large chunks of rich bottom land were literally given away to the companies in return for the construction of railroads, which for the most part they never built.

The banana companies showed no compunction about bribing and cajoling government officials and army officers. When quieter tactics proved unsuccessful, financing a revolution was not entirely out of the question, and disputes were often decided in the end by U.S. military intervention.

Reviewing this inglorious period, one historian observed that "North American power had become so encompassing that U.S. military forces and United Fruit could struggle against each other to see who was to control the Honduran government, then have the argument settled by the U.S. Department of State."

THE DEVELOPMENT OF MODERN HONDURAS
The Cariato

The perennial instability proved a distraction to the banana companies and the U.S. government, and after the merger of United and Cuyamel in 1929, the political situation in Honduras changed. Political strongman Tiburcio Carías Andino, who belonged to the newly born Partido Nacional (National Party), was able to seize power in 1932—and retained in for 16 years.

LEGENDARY LEE

Born in Livingston Parish, Louisiana, in 1863, **Lee Christmas** decided to try his fortunes abroad in 1894 and moved to Puerto Cortés, Honduras. Captured by rebels in 1897, Christmas joined their cause — at least for a couple of years, until he decided to defect to the government army. Despite his turncoat history, he was made a colonel and later appointed chief of police of Tegucigalpa, in 1902. His loyalties didn't last long, and in 1903 Christmas switched sides again, becoming an aide to rebel general Manuel Bonilla. Bonilla became president of Honduras in 1904 and appointed Christmas a general.

Bonilla was overthrown in 1907, and, a rebel once more, Christmas led successful battles on Trujillo, Ironia, and La Ceiba — successful in large part due to his U.S.-supplied machine guns. Bonilla resumed the presidency, but at his sudden death in 1913, Christmas was forced to flee, and he remained at large in Latin America for the next 10 years.

Many legends surround Christmas, including a story of having seized Utila from the Honduran government. He is said to have walked around the island turning heads in his cream-colored suit, climbing Pumpkin Hill every day to check if Honduran gunboats were coming for him. Some say Christmas was killed, others that he made it back to Louisiana, as penniless as he'd left.

Carías, who began his career as a military cook, was a classic example of an uneducated yet extremely shrewd and ruthless *caudillo* (political boss). Social developments were minimal under his rule; the military was professionalized, the opposition and media suppressed, and the fruit companies—particularly United—given a free hand.

The Cariato was the kind of time when, in the words of historians Donald Schulz and Deborah Sundloff Schulz, "members of the opposition were forbidden to travel in automobiles, the First Lady sold tamales at the Presidential Palace, and the president of Congress justified Carías' long rule by noting that 'God, too, continues in power indefinitely.'"

Following the end of World War II, Central American dictators had become an unnecessary embarrassment to the United States, and Carías was forced from office in 1948 in favor of protégé Juan Manuel Gálvez. Gálvez ruled for six years and began the long process of economic modernization by developing a central bank, starting a system of income tax, and expanding public works.

The Great Banana Strike

The landmark Great Banana Strike of 1954 represented the birth of Honduras's organized labor movement, the most powerful in Central America. Although sporadic strikes occurred on banana plantations and docks as early as 1916, the 1954 strike was the first large-scale labor action that could not be quickly bought off or put down with force.

Appropriately, the actions leading to the strike began on Labor Day, May 1, 1954. A group of dock workers in Puerto Cortés asked United Fruit officials for double pay for work on Sunday, which was mandated by law. Their request was put off for several days, and in the meantime United fired their designated spokesman.

In response, the dock workers went on strike. They were soon joined by all 25,000 United workers and 15,000 Standard Fruit workers, an expression of pent-up frustration at abysmal working conditions, low pay, and cavalier treatment by banana-company officials.

The strike was supported by Hondurans throughout the country, and workers of several other industries struck out of solidarity. Lasting 69 days, the strike was eventually broken by a combination of limited concessions, payoffs to labor leaders, and the establishment of company-friendly unions in competition with the more militant ones. The American Federation of Labor (AFL) played a prominent role in setting up these "stooge" unions.

Although direct gains from the strike were minimal, it was a watershed for the nascent labor movement. By negotiating with the unions, both the government and the banana companies tacitly accepted their right to exist, and the following year laws were passed on union creation, collective bargaining, and the right to strike. While this may seem like a commonplace gain by a labor movement anywhere in the world, these rights were impossible to even contemplate in any of the countries neighboring Honduras.

Growth of Military Power

At the same time, a political watershed was taking place in Honduras. In the face of an incompetent and unpopular government, and partly spurred by the banana strike, a group of military officers organized a successful coup d'état on October 21, 1956.

Though elections were held the following year and the military duly turned power back over to civilians, the coup marked the beginning of military influence in the country's politics, a defining characteristic of Honduran government for the next four decades. One indicator of this influence was two clauses in the new constitution written by the military during its brief stay in power. One allowed the head of the military to disregard orders from the president that he considered unconstitutional, and the second gave him control over all military promotions.

Following the 1957 elections, the Constitutional Assembly chose Liberal Ramón Villeda Morales as president. He quickly

THE SOCCER WAR

For more than two centuries, Honduras and El Salvador have disputed portions of the border between them in a remote mountain region and in the Golfo de Fonseca. This conflict, along with land shortages and immigration pressures, contributed to the outbreak of the so-called Soccer War in 1969.

The war seemed to be sparked by a World Cup soccer match between the two countries. While sporting passions do run high in Central America, the real reasons behind the fighting were much more serious. For years, land-hungry *campesinos* from overpopulated El Salvador had been crossing the mountainous border and setting up small farms and businesses in Honduras. By the late 1960s, Salvadoran immigrants made up roughly 20 percent of Honduras's rural population – this at a time when Honduras had begun feeling land pressures of its own. Wealthy Honduran landowners began waging a cynical propaganda campaign that distracted from the country's internal problems and fueled a growing hatred for the Salvadorans.

In April 1969, the Honduran government gave Salvadoran settlers 30 days to return to their country; by June, some 20,000 had fled. (Others were victimized by irate Hondurans and the Mancha Brava, a Partido Nacional vigilante squad.) That same month, the two countries faced one another in elimination matches to qualify for the 1970 World Cup.

The first match was held on June 8 in Tegucigalpa. As is common practice, loyal hometown fans gave the visiting team a sleepless night by screaming, honking horns, and setting off firecrackers in the streets below its hotel. The following day, the Salvadoran squad predictably lost, 1-0. A young Salvadoran girl shot herself in grief over the loss, furthering the drama and tension, and tens of thousands of Salvadorans – including the country's president and the soccer team – marched to her funeral.

A week later, for the second match, the Honduran team traveled to San Salvador. This time, of course, the Salvadoran fans kept the Honduran team awake all night; at the game, they booed the Honduran national anthem and ran a rag up the flagpole instead of the Honduran flag. Honduras lost the match 3-0, and violence erupted. The Honduran team had to be escorted to the airport by the military, and visiting Honduran fans were beaten (dozens were hospitalized, and two died).

Because of the violence, the deciding third match was postponed. A month later, on July 14, the El Salvador military bombed several locations inside Honduras and launched a surprise land attack. The Salvadoran Army made it deep into Honduras, but, when the Honduran Air Force destroyed the Salvadorans' main fuel depot, the Salvadorans were unable to advance. The war lasted 100 hours. Some 2,000 people, mostly Honduran *campesinos*, were killed, and 130,000 Salvadorans returned to their country. Apart from releasing nationalistic frustrations on both sides, the war accomplished nothing. The final soccer match was eventually held June 26 in Mexico City; El Salvador won 3-2.

instituted much-needed social reforms, such as literacy projects, public health care, road-building, and agrarian reform. The agrarian reform, in particular, made Honduran landowners and fruit companies nervous (this all in the wake of the coup in Guatemala, engineered by the banana companies and the U.S. government because of agrarian reform in that country). When it appeared an even more radical Liberal would win elections after Villeda, the military again took control on October 3, 1963. Colonel Oswaldo López Arellano assumed leadership of the country, and apart from a democratic hiatus in 1971–1972, the military stayed in formal power until 1978.

The first half of military rule, until the 1969 Soccer War with El Salvador, was characterized by a suppression of communist groups and *campesino* organizations, but at the same time tentative agrarian and social reforms.

Following the war and the failed democratic interlude of 1971–1972, López Arellano returned to power, this time convinced of the need for real agrarian reform. Between 1973 and 1976, 31,000 families received 144,000 hectares of land through the Instituto Nacional Agrario (National Agrarian Institute). Although it did not eliminate the problems of landless workers, it was a large step in the right direction and a reform that would have been completely unimaginable in El Salvador, Nicaragua, or Guatemala at that time.

Following a scandal involving bribes paid by the banana companies to government officials, López Arellano was forced from power in March 1975. His replacement, Colonel Juan Alberto Melgar Castro, slowed the pace of reform. Melgar Castro was ousted in 1978 by a junta led by General Policarpo Paz García, who organized elections in 1981 that nominally returned civilian politicians to power.

Reagan and the Contras

Two external but related developments of extreme importance to Honduras took place shortly before the 1981 election of Liberal Roberto Suazo Córdova: the victory of the Sandinista revolution in Nicaragua and the inauguration of U.S. president Ronald Reagan. Viewing the world through the paranoid prism of communist-capitalist conflict, President Reagan could not tolerate the presence of the socialist-leaning Sandinistas in "his" hemisphere, and Honduras was the perfect launching pad for the U.S.-financed and -directed counterrevolution.

With the complicity of Suazo Córdova and the fascistic armed forces commander General Gustavo Álvarez Martínez, the CIA at first overtly and later covertly directed a stream of training, funds, and weapons to an army of anti-Sandinista Nicaraguans living along the Honduras-Nicaragua border in Olancho and El Paraíso.

Along with the Contras, as the fighters were known, came U.S. military personnel by the hundreds and CIA agents by the dozen, using Honduras as a base not only for the Contra war but also to help the Salvadoran military in its own struggle against leftist rebels. The country had become a virtual appendage of the U.S. military.

Concurrently, the Honduran military tightened its hold over society, although the country was still a formal democracy. Álvarez ruthlessly imprisoned, tortured, killed, or "disappeared" labor activists, peasant leaders, priests, and other opponents, often using the infamous hit squad Battalion 3–16. Though the repression never reached the heights it did in El Salvador or Guatemala—victims here numbered in the hundreds rather than thousands—these strong-arm tactics were unheard of in Honduras and created widespread discontent even within the military. In 1984, Álvarez was exiled by fellow officers, and his successor, Walter López Reyes, put an end to the blatantly unsavory acts of repression. Nevertheless, the military remained in firm control behind the scenes.

By 1988, the Contra war began winding down, due to U.S. congressional opposition, the Iran-Contra affair, the Central American peace process, and Honduras's growing unhappiness with having the Contras based inside its borders. The Contras were disbanded by early 1990, following the election of Violeta Chomorro in Nicaragua.

It bears noting that a new national constitution (Honduras's 16th since its independence from Spain) was implemented in 1982. In an effort to close the door on dictatorships, presidential terms were reduced from six years to four. This constitution also established that the president cannot be reelected, and that certain articles—including those on the presidential term and reelectability—cannot be amended.

The 1990s

In the 1989 elections, Partido Nacional candidate Rafael Leonardo Callejas was swept into office by a large margin, promising a program of economic modernization.

Young, smooth Callejas believed the only way to pull Honduras out of the hole was a heavy dose of economic adjustment; that is, selling off public industries, laying off public employees, floating the exchange rate, and encouraging foreign investment. A superbly gifted politician, Callejas managed to push these measures through and generally see them through to the end of his term in 1994, in spite of widespread public and political opposition.

The results were mixed, at best. Unemployment and absolute numbers of people living in poverty rose, but defenders claim it was a necessary price for putting the country's fiscal book in order. Critics also contend corruption and cronyism were rife throughout Callejas's term.

The 1993 elections brought Liberal Carlos Roberto Reina to power, a long-time politician respected for his personal honesty. He took office in 1994 promising a "moral revolution" to clean up the corrupt political system. His success was limited. Corruption continued, of course, though perhaps at a lower level than before. While posting some impressive growth numbers during his term (mainly as a result of Callejas's policies), Reina made no significant moves to cope with his country's exploding debt.

Reina's one great success, which came to fruition under his successor, was beginning the process of placing the nation's then-autonomous military under civilian control.

Offering a "new agenda" of economic growth after years of neoliberal hardships, Liberal candidate Carlos Flores Facussé won the presidency in November 1997. Scion of an extremely wealthy Honduran family of Arab descent and brother of one of the country's top businessmen, 47-year-old Flores had been assiduously building his power base within the Liberal Party for nearly two decades. Among Flores's many business interests is ownership of *La Tribuna* newspaper, which has long been his mouthpiece.

Flores took office in January 1998 and spent his first year trying to gain a reprieve on the country's seemingly impossible financial burdens. In part at the behest of the World Bank and the IMF, Flores implemented a package of austerity measures, gambling that the combination of these measures and expected debt relief would be enough to reactivate the economy. But if there ever was any hope that

these measures would succeed, Hurricane Mitch blew them away in short order. Between October 1998 and the end of the presidential term, the Honduran government found itself in a near-permanent state of crisis management, unable to look beyond meeting immediate needs and trying to get the country back on its feet. Inevitably, accusations of corruption and mismanagement in reconstruction aid money were rife, despite efforts to improve transparency and implement civilian oversight.

One development, already underway before the hurricane but accelerated in its aftermath, was the increasing presence of international organizations, bilateral missions, and private foreign groups in everyday Honduran life. It seems that everywhere you turn in Honduras is a group of German resource managers, or Japanese and Cuban doctors, or agriculture projects sponsored by the IADB, USAID, DFID, GTZ, or myriad other mysterious acronyms.

The Maduro Administration

Nationalist Ricardo Maduro Joest won the elections held in November 2001 by a vote of 55.2 percent over his rival, aging Partido Liberal stalwart Rafael Pineda Ponce, with 44.2 percent, and he assumed power January 27, 2002. Fifty-five years old when he took office, Maduro presented a charismatic, modern image, complete with an attractive Spanish wife, that many Hondurans initially found very appealing.

Maduro was born in Panama to a Panamanian father and Honduran mother, a fact that the Partido Liberal tried unsuccessfully to use against him during the election campaign. His main election platform was a crusade against the country's increasing criminality and insecurity, especially in Honduran cities. The fact that Maduro's son was kidnapped and killed in 1997 lent credence to his impassioned rhetoric about making the streets safe again.

As president, Maduro made some moves against crime, like a dramatic upswing in high-visibility patrols in cities and on the main roads, often with police and military working together. The effect on crime rates, however, was minimal. A disciple of former president Rafael Callejas, Maduro followed fairly strict economic policies during his term.

Maduro ended his term in late January 2006 in a sorry state, disliked by much of the population for oddly personal reasons rather than his record per se. He clearly made efforts against crime, although with limited success. The economy did not exactly boom, but it didn't bust either, and Maduro did help win the free trade agreement with the United States. It's hard to say what it was that rubbed Hondurans the wrong way about him. Perhaps the very things that appealed to them about Maduro in the first place: his slick good looks, charm, and Spanish wife.

Perhaps it was symbolic then that his wife, Aguas, gave an interview to the Spanish magazine *Hola,* published the day before the end of his term, saying that she planned to divorce Maduro. The couple attended President Zelaya's inauguration in the Estadio Nacional in Tegucigalpa and were forced to stoically face a chorus of boos when they walked in. Despite his ignominious exit, Maduro remains a highly influential member of the Partido Nacional.

Manuel "Mel" Zelaya

Manuel Zelaya Rosales of the Liberal Party won the November 2005 elections, beating National Party rival Porfirio Lobo Sosa. Scion of an Olanchano family from Catacamas, Zelaya is considered a sharply intelligent man, although he quit school before obtaining his college degree.

The election victory was narrow, with only 3.7 percent of the vote separating the two, and the Liberals fell short of a majority in Congress, meaning several smaller parties may well hold inordinate power in passing legislation. Zelaya's "people power" campaign stressed a more transparent democracy, including a greater decentralization of decision-making power in the political system. However, his victory likely had a lot more to do with the public dislike of outgoing Maduro, as well as the excessively hard-line anticrime campaign of

Lobo (spurred by an American political consultant, Mark Klugmann).

Campaign promises included a doubling of the national police force and the development of a rehabilitation program for gang members, neither of which has occurred. Instead, crime has risen notably during his tenure, linked to the increased penetration of organized crime. Some of his closest collaborators have been involved in corruption scandals.

Somewhat unexpectedly, Zelaya has moved to align himself with the leftist movement in Latin America, most notably signing the ALBA pact with Venezuela in August 2008 (described by Zelaya as a move to the center-left). *Alba* means "dawn," and the initials in Spanish stand for Bolivarian Alternative for the Americas. Honduras became the sixth country to sign, joining Venezuela, Bolivia, Cuba, Nicaragua, and Dominica. Sponsored by Hugo Chavez, the treaty is meant to represent a trade alternative to free trade

"Mel" gained popularity with local unions when he signed the ALBA pact, an alternative to free trade agreements with the United States.

agreements with the United States. In early 2009, Honduras received 100 tractors from Venezuela that had been promised as part of the ALBA deal.

Zelaya and his administration have faced an enormous economic challenge during his tenure: A food crisis amplified by the sharp increase in fuel prices during 2007–2008 was compounded by the worldwide economic crisis that began in the United States in late 2008.

In 2009, Zelaya campaigned heavily for a *cuarta urna,* or fourth ballot box, through which Hondurans would vote on the installation of a National Constituent Assembly. While the idea follows in the footsteps of the political reform seen in recent years in countries like Bolivia and Ecuador, many within Honduras perceived the fight for a constituent assembly as a naked attempt by Zelaya to change the constitution so that he might stay in power for longer. A coup in June 2009 removed Zelaya from power, and the president of the Honduran Congress, Roberto Micheletti, stepped up.

At the time of writing, the political impasse generated by the coup had not been resolved, despite international mediation efforts. Presidential elections remained scheduled for November 2009. The two principal candidates are Zelaya's old rival Porfirio "Pepe" Lobo and Elvin Santos, Zelaya's vice president from January 2006 to December 2008, when he resigned from the post in order to run for president.

Government

POLITICAL SYSTEM

Remarkably, Honduras has the oldest two-party system in the western hemisphere (after the United States and Uruguay). Apart from brief interludes of military rule, presidents from either the Liberal or National Party have governed the country since the beginning of the 20th century. Even during the dictatorship of the Partido Nacional's Tiburcio Carías (1932–1948), the Partido Liberal continued to participate (meekly) in the political system. Not that this means Honduras is any paragon of democracy. Rather, it points to the fact that both parties are cut from the same cloth and have managed to institutionalize a system permitting them to alternate turns skimming off a healthy slice of Honduras's national wealth. Venal though Honduran politics may be, the system has at least provided a surprising degree of social peace in the desperately poor and underdeveloped country.

Since 1982, with the passage of its 16th constitution, Honduras has simultaneously elected a president, three vice presidents, and the 128-member unicameral Congreso Nacional (National Congress) every four years. During the last election, some 1.8 million Hondurans were registered to vote, about 46 percent of eligible voters. Honduran elections are a very peaceable affair, with violence and open vote fraud almost unheard of.

The president, who cannot be reelected, is by far the most powerful figure in the country. In theory, the Congress has wide authority; in practice, almost all policy initiatives come from the executive office. Until 1998, Congress was always controlled by the president's party and generally acted as a rubber stamp. However, under election rules in place since 1998, voters now vote for separate parties for different posts. Thus far, congressional independence has improved judged in terms of the noise factor, but not as much in terms of actual policy design control.

Honduras is divided into 18 departments *(departamentos):* Atlántida, Choluteca, Colón, Comayagua, Copán, Cortés, El Paraíso, Francisco Morazán, Gracias a Dios, Intibucá, Islas de la Bahía, La Paz, Lempira, Ocotepeque, Olancho, Santa Bárbara, Valle, and Yoro. Each has a governor who is appointed and removed at the discretion of the president.

Every four years, the country's 297 municipal governments hold elections for *alcalde*

© AMY E. ROBERTSON

the Casa Presidencial, or President's House, in Tegucigalpa, the capital of Honduras

(mayor) and municipal council on the same day as the national elections. Until the 1993 elections, local officials were on the same ballot as national ones, but now voters may split the ticket between different parties. Rural *municipios* are further divided into *aldeas* (villages) and *caseríos* (hamlets).

POLITICAL PARTIES

For more than a century, Honduran politics has been formally dominated by two parties: the Liberals and the Nationals. The Partido Liberal was created first, in an effort to institutionalize the modernizing liberal reforms of Marco Aurelio Soto and Luis Bográn. The Partido Nacional was born as a splinter group of the Liberals in 1902 at the behest of Manuel Bonilla, who later became the party's first president.

Since their inception, little has distinguished the two parties in terms of policy. For many years, the Nationals were linked closely to the military, but that was more an accident of circumstance than a true ideological stance,

evidenced by the close cooperation of successive Liberal presidents Suazo Córdova and Azcona with the military in the 1980s.

For the most part, the parties have been vehicles for personal ambition, a fact never much disguised. Campaigns are invariably long on mudslinging and personal accusations and woefully short on political proposals.

Despite lacking clear ideological differences, each party has certain core areas of support—the Nationals in the rural departments of Copán, Lempira, Intibucá, and Gracias a Dios and in the southern departments of Valle and Choluteca, while the Liberals are more popular in the urban areas and the north coast. Political scientists have suggested that party allegiance is often merely passed down over generations, much like support for a favorite soccer club, rather than being a real assessment of the options.

Smaller parties have tried to break the grip of the big two, but with little success. Both the Christian Democrats (Partido Demócrata Cristiano de Honduras, PDCH) and the reformist Innovation and Unity Party (Partido de Innovación y Unidad, PINU) constituted themselves in the late 1960s and received an initial burst of support after the 1969 Soccer War. While both parties began as very critical of the two major parties, these days the PINU and PDCH are basically part of the system, generally allying with either the Nationals or Liberals. In the 2005 election, PDCH won four seats in Congress (out of 128) and PINU won two.

The only truly unique political party on the scene is the beleaguered Democratic Unification Party (Partido Unificación Democrática, PUD), comprising land-rights activists, leftists, and even a few ex-guerrillas. The PUD is particularly strong in conflictive areas like the Valle del Aguán and faces regular repression from landowners and ranchers. PUD mayoral candidate Carlos Escaleras looked likely to win the November 1997 election in Tocoa, but he was shot dead on October 18. Several other PUD members have been killed, and many more have been threatened into putting aside their activism to save their lives. In the most recent national election, PUD took four seats in Congress and can provide potentially important swing votes.

THE MILITARY

Until the mid-1990s, it could be reasonably argued that Honduras's official political system was nothing more than window-dressing for the country's true power broker, the armed forces. After taking direct power for the first time in 1956, the military maintained a watchful eye over civilian politicians, who, knowing the rules of the game, were careful not to tread on any boots. While technically under civilian authority, the military was in reality fully independent, answering to no one. Changes in military leadership, the result of behind-the-scenes maneuvering, were presented to surprised politicians as fait accompli, and the Congress duly ratified the new leader without question.

Nonetheless, this independence did not automatically lead to military repression. The Honduran military is a curious animal. The officer corps is not made up of wealthy elites, as is the case in neighboring countries. It's much more egalitarian. In fact, in the absence of a strong homegrown elite, the military became an elite class itself, with its own interests and agenda sometimes quite different from the country's politicians, business leaders, and landowners. For this reason, the military has never been as rabidly conservative or repressive as other regimes in the region. When in direct power in the early 1970s under Colonel Oswaldo López Arellano, the military actually embarked on a far-ranging agricultural reform program, a far more radical measure for the countryside than those considered by civilian politicians.

During the height of the U.S.-sponsored Contra war, the military assumed a more sinister role, engaging in torture and disappearances similar to the abuses in neighboring El Salvador, Guatemala, and Nicaragua, but never on the same scale. Even opponents concede that fewer than 200 activists were killed by the authorities during the 1980s, compared to the tens of thousands elsewhere in Central America. But opposition to even these relatively few transgressions came from within the military itself, and with the winding down of the Contra war, complaints of military abuses declined.

The first steps taken to put civilians firmly in control of the Honduran military came from President Reina, who began by abolishing mandatory service in 1995, and then transferred the police to civilian authorities in 1997. The transition was completed on January 27, 1999, when President Flores demonstrated his control by replacing Armed Forces chief General Mario Hung Pacheco with Colonel Daniel Lopez Carballo, then appointing lawyer and journalist Edgardo Dumas Rodriguez as the new Defense Minister (Ministro de Defensa). While the position of Defense Minister had existed previously, changes in Article 15 of the Constitution effectively gave the minister power to control military leadership.

Although numbering only 13,000 soldiers, half the number it had reached at the height of the 1980s buildup, the military is still a powerful force in Honduras society. To cope with falling military budgets and the curtailing of U.S. military aid, the military has started to develop its own financial base. It has been so successful that its investment arm, the Instituto de Previsión Militar (IPM), is one of the largest investors in the country. The IPM owns hotels, shrimp farms, a cement factory, and a range of other holdings thought to be worth US$100 million. However, many of these holdings were put under civilian control in late 1999, and for the first time, the army now has a civilian paymaster.

One ominous tendency in recent years is the increasing incidence of military personnel involved in drug-trafficking, robberies, and the executions of street children and gang members. Officers have been implicated in drug-running, and in January 2000, a sergeant was caught red-handed holding up a taxi in Tegucigalpa. In 2006, members of the national police executed two environmental activists in Olancho.

Military support was also critical to the ousting of Manuel "Mel" Zelaya in June 2009, when soldiers arrested the president and put him on a plane to Costa Rica.

Economy

Honduras is an extremely poor country. Annual per capita income was US$1,330 in 2007 and a staggering 59 percent of the population lives below the poverty line, with 35 percent in extreme poverty (unable to meet basic needs). There has actually been a significant reduction in poverty in recent years, but clearly there's still a long, long way to go.

The development of Honduras is a litany of bright ideas and fond hopes foundering on the realities of the country's difficult circumstances in the world economy and ineffective, corrupt leadership. The Spaniards, quickly put off by endless mountains and precious little easy wealth, left it a colonial backwater of mainly self-sufficient farmers supplemented with limited mining and agricultural exports. The first real economic development came in the form of British and American mining concerns in the mid-1800s, followed by the banana companies of the early 20th century. The banana companies completely transformed the economy of the north coast in particular, basically creating the cities of La Ceiba, Tela, and Puerto Cortés, and fueling San Pedro Sula's rise as the country's main business city.

This economy of basically subsistence farming along with mining and banana exports by foreign firms continued until the 1950s, breaking down on growing competition in bananas and the depletion of most large mineral deposits. During the 1960s and 1970s, the Honduran economy grew steadily, following a policy of import-substitution and promotion of nontraditional exports. This policy essentially banked on an economic boom to offset the inevitable fiscal difficulties, but the region's military conflicts during the 1980s sent investment and production into a tailspin.

After the end of the Contra war and the implementation of fiscal reforms by President Callejas, Honduras became a favorite for foreign investors, particularly Asians building tax-free export factories, called *maquilas*. The growth in *maquila* exports, combined with growing exports of coffee, bananas, sugar, and shrimp, fueled growth rates of 3 percent a year or better beginning in 1995.

Hurricane Mitch was a major setback for the Honduran economy. Growth for 1998 had been projected at 5 percent, and even though the storm hit with only two months left in the year, damage pulled the number down to 2.9 percent. The following year, when the full effects of the destruction were felt, saw the economy shrink by 2.5 percent. In terms of overall development, the widely held view is that the country was set back 25 years.

After a reconstruction-led rebound of 5 percent in 2000, the slowing U.S. economy

ECONOMIC FIGURES

	2000	2001	2002	2003
GDP per capita (in US$)	1,130	1,172	1,174	1,200
Exports (in millions of US$)	1,291	1,200	1,159	1,288
Family Remittances (in millions of US$)	440	574	765	842
Inflation (percent)	10.1	8.8	8.1	6.8
Public Foreign Debt (in billions of US$)	4.4	4.0	4.0	4.4
Budget Balance (in millions of US$)	-128	-60	-9	-194

and falling international coffee prices combined to pull GDP growth down to 2.5 percent in 2001 and 2002. Growth since then had been on the rise, up to 6.3 percent annually in 2006 and 2007, but fell to 3.8 percent in 2008 and is projected to drop further, to 2 percent, in 2009.

In terms of the economy's structure, it's a telling sign that remittance income—money sent back home from Hondurans working abroad, mainly in the United States—is the biggest foreign currency earner, exceeding US$2.5 billion in 2008. Number two is the *maquila* export factories, which earned more than US$800 million in 2004. Agricultural products, led by coffee and bananas, are third in terms of export earnings nowadays, totaling around US$650 million in 2004. Tourism earnings are on the rise at US$360 million, and mining still generates significant income, at US$127 million. Thus while the outlook for the Honduran economy is improving, it still fluctuates in large measure to foreign rhythms over which it has no control, principally those of commodity prices and the U.S. economy.

FOREIGN DEBT

One of many factors that have hampered the Honduran government's ability to stimulate growth and spend more on social programs is a massive load of debt, inherited from generations of improvident former governments. Honduras's debt hovered between US$3 billion and US$4 billion dollars, well over half of the tiny country's GDP, for most of the 1990s. At the end of 1999, the total was around US$4.6 billion, not including several hurricane relief loans. Interest and service payments on the debt gobble up at least 30 percent of the annual budget, money that could be used to address many unfilled and critical needs.

Even before Hurricane Mitch struck, the creditor nations of the Paris Club—Canada, Denmark, France, Italy, Japan, Germany, Holland, Spain, Switzerland, and the United States—and the World Bank were considering including Honduras under the Highly Indebted Poor Countries (HIPC) initiative, which aims to forgive large portions of basically unpayable debt owed by poor countries to the World Bank and the IMF. The

	2004	2005	2006	2007
GDP per capita (in US$)	1,262	1,356	1,470	1,635
Exports (in millions of US$)	1,567	1,829	1,974	2,192
Family Remittances (in millions of US$)	1,138	1,776	2,329	2,561
Inflation (percent)	9.2	8.8	5.3	8.9
Public Foreign Debt (in billions of US$)	4.8	4.0	2.8	1.8
Budget Balance (in millions of US$)	361.8	186.9	311.2	-161.8

Banco Central de Honduras

proposal will likely include 41 countries, of which 33 are in Africa, 4 are in Asia, and 4 are in Latin America (Bolivia, Nicaragua, Guyana, and Honduras).

By 2005, Honduras had arrived at the HIPC "completion point," and the debt was reduced by US$1.2 billion in 2006. By the end of 2007 the debt was reduced by another billion, dropping to US$1.8 billion. Since then it has crept up to US$2.15 billion as of February 2009.

AGRICULTURE

Agriculture, both for export and internal consumption, is the largest single segment of the Honduran economy. In 2004, it accounted for 13.3 percent of GDP, worth just under US$1 billion, although it employed nearly half the country's workforce. As in other parts of Latin America, an increasing number of people are leaving the countryside to look for work in the cities or emigrating to Mexico and the United States.

In spite of the large percentage of people living and working in the countryside, land ownership is dramatically skewed in Honduras. In 1993, more than 60 percent of the country's arable land was in the hands of the Honduran government and the two largest foreign banana companies, Chiquita and Castle and Cooke. By contrast, 80 percent of the country's farmers owned less than 10 hectares of land each, and the average parcel size is 2.5 hectares.

Honduras has a complex system of land ownership and tenancy. While some farmers own their land outright, it's much more common to work the land under some other arrangement. An *arrendamiento* (rental) is a straightforward rental of land for a preset amount. *Aparcería* is an arrangement whereby the farmer is obliged to give a part of the harvest—usually the famed *quinto,* or fifth part, dating from colonial times—to the property owner. A *colonato* is a mixed system, in which the farmer is required to work land for the *patrón* for a wage, while having rights to work a piece of land for himself at the same time. Farmers working under this very common setup are called *colonos.* This term is also used to denote any small-scale farmer hacking out a homestead from virgin land, like the flood

© AMY E. ROBERTSON

Diving for lobster, a major Honduran export, is a lucrative, albeit risky, business.

of migrants moving into the southern fringes of the Mosquitia rainforest. An *ejido* is a piece of land owned by the local municipal government but granted to a certain person or persons to use for a defined length of time. *Tierra comunal* (communal land) is also owned by a municipality and is open for use by any of its inhabitants.

King among staple crops in Honduras is *maíz* (corn), cultivated in just about every corner of the country. As the base of the tortilla, corn is considered the staff of life in Honduras, as in many other Latin American countries. If the weather gods are smiling, corn fields produce twice a year, first in May–August and then again in November–February. The exact time of harvest varies greatly, depending on the region and that year's climate. *Frijoles* (beans), yucca, potatoes, and rice are also common additions to the family plot, or *milpa*. No discussion of staple crops would be complete without a mention of the ever-present *plátano*, or plantain, that bready version of a banana served fried with just about every Honduran meal.

Luscious fruits grow in bewildering variety in the tropical climates of Honduras, providing a reliable, healthy, and low-cost addition to the local diet. Among the most common fruits are the orange, watermelon, lemon, grapefruit, mango, banana, pineapple, guava, papaya, plum, and, of course, the decadently rich favorite, the avocado.

Agricultural Exports

Over the past 10 years, **coffee**—grown in many of the highland regions of central Honduras—has overtaken bananas as the country's top export cash crop. Plunging international coffee prices in the early part of the decade (in good part due to increased global production, particularly in Vietnam) led export earnings to fall from US$339 million in 2000 to US$161 million in 2001, but coffee made a quick comeback and production has increased yearly since 2001. Between the increased production and rising prices, coffee exports reached historic levels in 2008, bringing roughly US$623 million into the country. As of 2008, Honduras was the second biggest producer of coffee in Central America (a close second to Guatemala),

HONDURAN EXPORTS

- **coffee:** US$404,000,000

- **bananas:** US$250,900,000

- **shrimp and lobster:** US$205,600,000

- **lead and zinc:** US$124,500,000

- **gold:** US$79,900,000

- **palm oil:** US$66,200,000

- **soap and detergent:** US$42,000,000

- **wood:** US$37,500,000

- **cantaloupe and watermelon:** US$34,400,000

- **sugar:** US$30,500,000

- **Total export volume:** US$1,929,500,000

Banco Central de Honduras, 2006

and the 10th largest in the world. Germany is its number one buyer.

The department of Santa Bárbara produces nearly a quarter of the country's coffee, followed by El Paraíso, Comayagua, La Paz, and Copán. The best coffee in Honduras is considered to be from Marcala, La Paz. Favored climates are between 1,000 and 1,600 meters in elevation, often right at the lower edges of cloud forests. Almost all coffee grown in Honduras is of the arabica variety, which is shade-grown, rather than the lower-quality robusta bean. Many coffee farmers are small-scale, more than half with plots of two hectares of less. Around 70,000 people are employed in coffee production, many organized in local cooperatives.

Coffee trees begin bearing fruit two years after planting, and they usually produce for at least 10 years, unless infected by bean bores or other plant diseases. Normally, plants yield two harvests a year, one in February and the second in April or May. The harvest varies considerably from region to region.

Although much Honduran coffee is of high quality, the sorting and grading process is so lackadaisical that sacks of Honduran coffee beans are regularly discounted US$10 or US$15 on the international market. Fine quality coffee cannot have more than 5 percent of its beans off-grade, and many Honduran cooperatives run more like 10 percent or 15 percent off-grade. Nor do Honduran growers sort by altitude—a major factor in coffee quality. So, for the time being at least, Honduras remains well below El Salvador, Costa Rica, and the regional leader, Guatemala, in the coffee market. Interestingly, the Honduran press reports that large amounts of Honduran coffee have been smuggled into Guatemala in recent years, to then be re-exported as "Guatemalan" coffee.

The original "banana republic," Honduras still depends in large part on **bananas** as part of its export earnings. The two big banana companies, Chiquita (United) and Dole (Standard), still maintain large plantations in Honduras and have diversified into pineapple and palm oil, though continued trade disputes with the Europeans and production problems after Hurricane Mitch have slowed business of late. Both companies—which together control half the world banana market—took major losses in 1999, as did the significant sector of independent producers, with total Honduran banana exports down almost 80 percent from the previous year. In an effort to placate unhappy stockholders, the big companies shed several thousand workers but hired some back after protests from unions and the government.

After registering an abysmally low export figure of US$38 million in 1999, after Hurricane Mitch, the banana trade has recovered somewhat, to US$124 million in 2000, US$208 million in 2004, and US$384 million in 2008—but bananas remain a much smaller portion of Honduran exports than in previous years. Other agricultural exports of note include African palm oil, pineapple, sugarcane, and a few nontraditional exports, such as melon, black pepper, ornamental flowers, ginger, Chinese peas, and sweet onions. The **shrimp-farm** industry on the Golfo de Fonseca grew steadily since its inception in the 1980s, but in recent years it has leveled out at around US$200 million per year. On the Caribbean coast and in the Bay Islands, lobster, conch, and shrimp fishing are mainstays of the local economy.

Cattle and Lumber

In spite of taking up 30 percent of the country's arable land, much of it suitable for agriculture, the cattle industry plays a proportionally small part in the national economy. In part, this is because ranchers rely on traditional cattle-raising methods dependent on rainfall and pasture feed, which result in unreliable, low yields. A few powerful landowners control most of the ranching.

Considering the great wealth of forests in Honduras, judicious logging holds potential for providing jobs and good income. However, much of the country's forest wealth has been wasted through over-logging, corruption, and mismanagement. Nearly seven million hectares of land retained forest cover in 1964. By 2005, that figure had dropped to 4.65 million, with the forests disappearing at an estimated rate of 2.88 percent each year. Groups such as the Environmental Investigation Agency have recommended not purchasing lumber from Honduras (sold in places such as Home Depot), given the ease with which illegally harvested timber enters the market, and the challenge in verifying the legality of the wood. Taking a different approach, the Rainforest Alliance certifies companies with sustainable harvesting practices, and in early 2009, 10 Honduran companies had received certification.

The problems of erosion and desertification that go along with logging have hit most of the country but are particularly severe in the south. In search of valuable mahogany and other hardwoods, pirate loggers have even been cutting dirt roads into the periphery of the Río Plátano Biosphere Reserve.

Almost half the legal board-feet of wood cut in Honduras comes from Olancho, followed at a distance by Francisco Morazán, El Paraíso, Yoro, and Comayagua. Pine is still by far the biggest legal logging wood.

INDUSTRY AND TRADE
Maquilas

The nation's most dynamic economic sector is the *maquila* industry of San Pedro Sula and the north coast. The *maquila* boom began with the passage of the Puerto Cortés Free Zone law in 1976, which was extended to Amapala, Tela, Choloma, Omoa, and La Ceiba three years later. By 1998, further legal modifications allowed for the creation of free zones (called ZIPS) anywhere in the country.

Taking advantage of the favorable laws, as well as inexpensive labor and a strategic location close to the United States, some 180 factories, mainly clothing producers, have since opened. While the first factories were in Puerto Cortés and Choloma, with a few in La Ceiba, new ones have begun springing up in La Lima, Villanueva, Comayagua, Naco, and Choluteca, and more are planned. Growth has been explosive, with *maquilas* increasing their contribution to Honduras's balance of payments from US$96 million in 1994 to US$510 million in 1999 and US$800 million in 2004. By 2007, *maquilas* employed 130,000 workers (two-thirds women). CAFTA will likely give a significant shot in the arm to the export-manufacturing sector.

The Lempira

Honduras's national currency, the lempira, has dropped steadily in value over the past several years due to the country's bleak economic outlook, but does enjoy periods of relative stability from time to time. Inflation put a severe strain on Hondurans, and those who can afford it took to buying dollars as a safeguard. It is now possible to hold dollar accounts in local banks. Dollars are widely accepted at tourist establishments in Roatán and can often be used in a pinch elsewhere. At the time of writing, the lempira was trading at 19.1 to the dollar. A good website for checking the current rate is www.xe.com.

The People

DEMOGRAPHICS

Honduras has a growing population, approaching eight million. The annual growth rate was 2 percent for the period 2000–2005, a rate that is expected to hold for the second half of the decade. Just over 50 percent of the population is under 18 years old. Despite this growth, Honduras still has a relatively low population density, averaging around 70 people per square kilometer for the entire country and dropping as low as 5 per square kilometer in the wild Mosquitia region.

Although roughly half of the population still lives in rural areas, the country is experiencing rapid urbanization rates, centered on Tegucigalpa, the north coast cities, and San Pedro Sula, one of the fastest-growing cities in Latin America.

ETHNIC DIVERSITY

Travelers coming south from Guatemala to Honduras may be surprised at the overwhelming nonindigenous nature of the population. More than 90 percent of Hondurans are *mestizos*, also

SO YOU'RE FROM . . .

If you're from:	Then you're a:
Comayagua	*comayagüense*
Danlí	*danlidense*
Gracias	*graciano*
Juticalpa	*juticalpense*
La Ceiba	*ceibeño*
San Pedro Sula	*sampedrano*
Santa Rosa de Copán or Copán Ruinas	*copaneco*
Tegucigalpa	*capitalino*
Utila	*utilian*
Yoro	*yoreño*

called *ladinos* (persons of mixed European and Central American Indian ancestry). Only 5 percent of the people, or about 410,000, claim to be Amerindian, while less than 1 percent are black and 2 percent are white.

Because Honduras was only partially controlled

© FUAD AZZAD

Ladinos, people of mixed European and indigenous ancestry, comprise most of the population of Honduras.

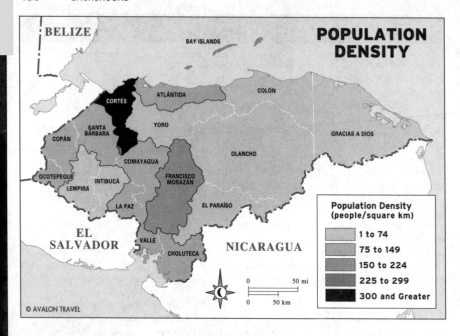

POPULATION DENSITY

Population Density (people/square km)

- 1 to 74
- 75 to 149
- 150 to 224
- 225 to 299
- 300 and Greater

© AVALON TRAVEL

by the Spanish during the colonial era, the north coast, the Bay Islands, and the Mosquitia have a culture markedly different from that of the country's interior. English and North American influences have left their mark on the coast; English is spoken as often as Spanish, and the culture is more closely related to the Caribbean islands than the rest of Honduras.

Indigenous Groups

While the number of minority ethnic groups in Honduras is a mere 6 percent of the total population, certain regions of the country are strongly marked by these pockets of ethnic and cultural diversity. The largest indigenous group in the country is the **Lenca,** who number around 300,000 people living in villages and towns throughout western and southern Honduras. Perhaps because they provided the stiffest defense to the Spanish invaders, the Lenca are, in a way, the emblematic tribe of the country, idealized in the national myth not unlike the Aztecs in Mexico. Nonetheless, the Lenca language is now lost entirely, and only a few traditions continue.

Tucked into the far western corner of the country along the Guatemalan border are an estimated 37,000 **Chortí Maya.** While Chortí traditions and language were on the decline for many years, in recent years the group appears to have reasserted itself, creating a strong and vocal Chortí organization.

Once living across large areas of central Honduras, the **Tolupán** have practically ceased to exist as a cultural group. Only one village in the mountains of northern Francisco Morazán still speak their language, though 10,000 *campesinos* in rural Yoro call themselves *tribu* and organize their villages in a communal fashion.

Farther east in Olancho and the Mosquitia are two former rainforest tribes now living in rural villages, the **Pech** and **Tawahka.** The Pech number around 4,100 people and are split into two regions, one around El Carbón along the highway from San Esteban to Tocoa, and the second northwest of Dulce Nombre de Culmí. The even smaller Tawahka, with a population of only about

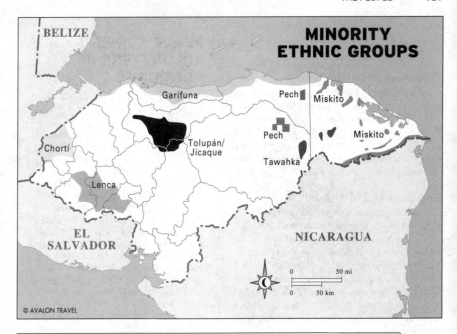

HONDURAN ETHNIC GROUPS

Name	Estimated Population	Location
Lenca	300,600	Intibucá, Lempira, and La Paz
Miskito	55,000	Gracias a Dios
Garífuna	49,950	North Coast
Chortí Maya	37,050	Copán
English-speaking blacks	13,300	Bay Islands
Tolupán	10,350	Yoro and Francisco Morazán
Pech	4,100	Olancho, Gracias a Dios, and Colón
Tawahka	2,650	Río Patuca in Gracias a Dios and Olancho

These groups together make up roughly 6 percent of Honduras's population.

Instituto Nacional de Estadística, 2001 Census

2,650, live along the Río Patuca, near the border of the Gracias a Dios and Olancho departments.

True to Honduras's propensity to join in collective action (which is perhaps in part derived from the communal tendencies of the indigenous groups), the Chortí Maya, Lenca, Tawahka, and Pech are in frequent contact with one another and with Garífuna and Miskito organizations to work together for their common cause, fighting against repression and governmental neglect.

Garífuna and Miskitos

Few ethnic groups in the world can trace their birth to specific historic events, but Honduras is home to two that can: the Garífuna of the north coast and the Miskito, in the northeast. These two unique ethnic groups were created from the mixing of African slaves who escaped from two shipwrecks with two different indigenous peoples early in the colonial era. Rather than fade in the face of modernization, both these groups appear to have grown stronger. According to the 2001 census, the Miskito numbered over 55,000, while the Garífuna totaled nearly 50,000, with another 13,300 English-speaking blacks on the Bay Islands categorized into a separate group.

PEACE CORPS VOLUNTEERS IN HONDURAS

Nearly 200 U.S. Peace Corps volunteers, one of the highest numbers of any country in the world, perform their two-year tour of duty in Honduras. Peace Corps participation in the country began in 1962 and was boosted during the mid-1980s as part of a good-relations program intended to show Honduras's importance in U.S. regional policy – over 5,000 volunteers have passed through the country since then. Although numbers have been scaled back recently, volunteers still work in most parts of the country, but particularly in western, central, and southern Honduras. Volunteers mainly concentrate on agriculture, public health, water quality, small business development, and tourist promotion, with an emphasis on the newly created national park system. Peace Corps volunteers are invariably eager to talk about their sites and are excellent sources of information on their particular regions and the country as a whole.

Culture

ARTS
Literature

Honduras may not be the most prolific country in Latin America's literary world, but it has produced two of the most famous early modernist writers in the region: poet and essayist Juan Ramón Molina and historian and journalist Rafael Heliodoro Valle.

Along with Nicaraguan Rubén Dario, Molina (1875–1908) was one of the founders of modernist Latin American poetry and is considered Honduras's national poet. Much of Molina's poetry expresses his existential anguish and a struggle with deep philosophical themes. Although he did not write extensive prose, what he did produce is beautifully lyrical. Shortly after Molina's death from a morphine overdose, his collected works were published in a volume titled, *Tierras, Mares, y Cielos* (Lands, Seas, and Skies).

One of the most influential Latin American journalists of his era, Rafael Heliodoro Valle (1891–1959) was a prolific writer who published regularly in newspapers across the Americas and wrote extensive histories on the region. In one of his most famous professional coups, Valle in 1945 interviewed reformist Guatemalan president Juan José Arévalo in the

Mexican newspaper *Excélsior*. Arévalo candidly discussed the backwardness of his country and the obstacles in the way of development. After Valle's death, his most wide-ranging and reflective work, *Historia de las Ideas Contemporáneas en Centro-América* (History of Contemporary Thought in Central America), was published, a landmark in regional historical philosophy.

Modern Honduran literature of note is limited mainly to short stories. Three well-respected authors are Víctor Cáceres Lara, Marcos Carías, and Eduardo Bahr. The latter in particular is known for his politically oriented stories. One exceptional Honduran social novelist is Ramón Amaya Amador, who in 1950 wrote the famed "Prisión Verde" (Green Prison), a story about life as a banana plantation worker.

Visual Arts

Honduras has produced a number of top-quality visual artists, the most famous of which are the so-called "primitivists": Pablo Zelaya Sierra, Carlos Zuñiga Figueroa, and especially José Antonio Velásquez, who painted classic Honduran themes, such as tile-roofed villages and rural scenes in a colorful and almost childlike style. Velásquez, a self-taught artist, spent much of his time painting the lovely colonial village of San Antonio de Oriente, near Tegucigalpa in the Valle de Zambrano.

More recent, innovative artists include Dante Lazzaroni, Arturo López Rodezno, Eziquiel Padilla, Anibel Cruz, and Eduardo "Mito" Galeano. Galeano, who works in the town of Gracias, is known for painting Lenca-oriented themes.

Architecture

Modern Honduran architecture is generally unremarkable. A wealth of colonial buildings still stand, particularly in Tegucigalpa, Comayagua, Gracias, and innumerable other small towns and villages.

Typically, the most visually interesting buildings are the cathedrals and churches of the 18th century. Most are built in a Central American style known as "earthquake baroque," which adapted the dominant styles of Spain to local conditions. Earthquake baroque is known for squat, ground-hugging structures built to resist frequent quakes. The buildings' solidity is relieved by intricate columns, sculptures, and decorations.

Churches built in the 16th and early 17th centuries, most of which have not survived, tended to be much simpler, while those erected in the late colonial period were much more elaborate. One particularly Honduran characteristic in colonial church architecture is the use of folded or pleated patterns on exterior columns.

The interiors of larger churches and cathedrals are invariably decorated with elaborate paintings and sculptures and are dominated by a carved and often gilded *retablo* (altarpiece). Smaller churches, especially in rural areas, are often painted in a more rustic style.

Large, airy wooden houses with porches are common in the north coast banana towns of Puerto Cortés, Tela, and La Ceiba, where North American influences predominated at the turn of the 20th century.

Music

The traditional indigenous music of the Lenca, Pech, Tolupán, and Maya has dwindled in importance over the centuries and is infrequently played, outside of special ceremonies. In many rural areas of Honduras, the venerable *conjunto de cuerda*, or string group, is always around to strike up a tune with guitars, bass, and violin.

One native Honduran music of note on the north coast is *punta*, the traditional music of the Garífuna. Original *punta* is a stripped-down music form based around a thumping drum accompanied by singing, blowing a conch shell, and dancers performing physics-defying miracles with their hips.

Honduran pop music consists primarily of Caribbean merengue, salsa, and *cumbia*, with a dash of American pop thrown in. Islanders and many of the Garífuna on the north coast also listen to a lot of Jamaican reggae.

A handful of singers are maintaining Honduran ballads and folkloric music, the most widely known being Guillermo Anderson and Karla Lara. Guillermo Anderson is from the north coast, and his albums always include a healthy dash of *punta* in their rhythms. Rising star Polache (short for Paul Hughes, born to a German father and Honduran mother) from La Ceiba seems to be following in their footsteps, with a bit of a rocker's edge. In Olancho, Mexican-style *ranchera* music is the local favorite, particularly as sung by "El Charro" Velasquez from Juticalpa. CDs by any of these artists are usually available in any store that sells CDs (try the mall if you have to).

Reggaeton, rap in English and Spanish laid over a sort of slowed down, Caribbean-style techno music with a reggae bass line, is also wildly popular, particularly in the dance clubs, while standard American pop music seems to rule the airwaves. Don't be surprised to hear plenty of Madonna, George Michael, Bon Jovi, and Guns N' Roses, among others. Country music is also surprisingly popular, especially on the Bay Islands and the north coast.

CRAFTS

Although not as well known as Guatemala for handicrafts, Honduras does offer several unique *artesanías* for tourists to purchase during their trips. Several villages near Tegucigalpa, especially Valle de Ángeles, are known for their woodcarvings and leatherwork, while Ojojona is a good place to buy simple pottery. Painted "Lenca pottery" with black and white designs can be found all around the country and is cheapest outside of Nacaome, where it is produced, while authentic brick-colored Lencan pottery can be bought in Gracias and the surrounding villages.

The region around Santa Bárbara is famed for producing *junco*-palm goods, from simple mats to baskets and hats. When buying *junco,* take a good look at the weave—the tighter the weave, the finer the quality and the higher the price.

On the north coast, you can buy traditional drums of the Garífuna, along with carvings, paintings, and recordings of *punta* music. Items made in the Mosquitia out of *tuno,* a beaten bark, can be found in gift shops across the country.

LANGUAGE

Anyone visiting Honduras after Mexico or Guatemala will be immediately struck by the faster, softer cadences of Honduran Spanish, more similar to the Spanish spoken in Nicaragua and the Caribbean. Words are not as strongly enunciated and are often cut off at the end, with one word running into another. It takes a little getting used to, and you may find yourself saying *"más despacio, por favor"* (slower, please) or *"repita, por favor"* (repeat, please).

Generally, Honduran Spanish is similar to that spoken elsewhere in Latin America, with a few exceptions, particularly the use of *vos* instead of *tú* (see the *Spanish Phrasebook* for more on this usage). Because of British and North American influence, broadly accented Caribbean English is the dominant language on the Bay Islands, particularly in Utila, although Spanish is increasing with the influx of Latinos from the mainland. Some English is also spoken along the north coast and in parts of the Mosquitia.

Garífunas and Miskitos mainly use their own languages amongst themselves, but almost all are bilingual and many are trilingual, speaking Spanish and/or English as well. Other indigenous languages are fading, but some communities still speak Pech, Tolupán, Mayan, and Tawahka. Lenca has fallen out of use entirely.

RELIGION

Honduras is an overwhelmingly Roman Catholic country, although Evangelical Protestant churches have been growing very quickly in recent years. A 2002 poll found that 63 percent of Hondurans reported themselves as Catholic, 23 percent as evangelical Christians, and 14 percent as "other" (or did not answer).

Traditional Amerindian religious practices have been all but forgotten, except for a few ceremonies still practiced in rural areas. A belief in magic and witchcraft is common among Hondurans in both rural and urban areas.

A FEW HONDUREÑISMOS

Here are some words and phrases unique to Honduras and a few others used in Central America only. The **bolded** words are the ones you're likely to hear over and over again during your stay.

adiós – literally, goodbye, but often used in villages and the country as a casual salutation when passing someone on the street or trail

a pata – by foot (as in *voy a pata*, "I'm going by foot")

arrojar – to throw up

a todo mecate – really fast

bolo – drunk

burra – a working class lunch of tortillas, beans, and eggs

burro – someone who doesn't pay attention

cachimbón – great, excellent

catracho – Honduran, used either as a noun or adjective (e.g., *comida catracha* means "Honduran food")

catrín – sharp dresser

chabacán – someone who is always joking, or who always uses swear words

chamba – job

chasta – really bad

chepear – to cheat, copy an exam

chepos – "cops" or police officers

cheque – cool, all right, okay

chichí – baby

chigüín – small child

ichiva! – "watch out!" or "heads up!"

choco – blind

chunche – thing

cipote – kids, children (used more in the cities)

coco – intelligent

cususa – home-brew liquor, more commonly called *chicha*

guachi – watchman, guard (short for *guachimán*, which is also used)

guarizama – machete

guaro – *aguardiente*, a low-quality, high-proof liquor (the principal brands are Yuscarán and Tatascán)

güirros – kids, children (used more in rural areas)

hule – out of money (as in *estoy hule*, "I'm broke")

jalón – a ride (as in ¿*Me da un jalón?* "Will you give me a ride?")

juma or *goma* – a hangover

Los USA – the United States (pronounced "los YOO-sa")

macaneo – mess, scandal

macanudo – excellent, cool

maleta – literally, suitcase, but in slang means stupid (e.g., *sos maleta* means "you're stupid")

mama – frequently used to refer to someone you don't know

mami – a piropo, like "hot mama"

mara – gang (and a gang member is a *marero*)

mata de... – field of (e.g., *mata de maíz* is a field of corn)

mentar la madre – insult

mírave – literally, look-see, used *not* to point out something to look at, but when something is being explained

muchacho – an adolescent or young adult

neles – no way, forget it (often *neles pasteles*)

paila – pickup truck

paja – literally, straw; but in slang, made-up stories, just hot air or lies

pisto – money

puchica – an interjection to show surprise, like "wow!" or "man!"

pulpería – small store, like a minimart (also often referred to as *la pulpe*)

¡Que pinta! – an exclamation, like "right on!"

reventado – ruined, messed up

un turismo – a small sedan car (as opposed to four-wheel-drives or trucks)

vaya pues – used after nearly every sentence, as an all-inclusive "okay" or "understood"

yuca – literally, yucca or cassava, used in slang to mean difficult

zopilote – vulture

The Catholic Church

The Catholic church in Honduras has traditionally been one of the poorest and most understaffed in Central America. Approximately 300 ordained priests minister to a population of nearly eight million, and most of the priests are from other countries. In the face of this difficulty, the church began a program called Delegates of the Word, in which men and women of the laity are trained to be spiritual leaders of a given parish. Now some 30,000 Delegates of the Word live in Honduras, and the movement has spread through much of Central America. A small Jesuit mission continues in the central province of Yoro, run mainly by foreign missionaries.

Unlike other Catholic churches in the region, notably in El Salvador, the Honduran church has not been a major force for social activism. For a time during the 1960s and early 1970s, church leadership allowed priests and delegates to pursue the "social option for the poor" and take an activist stance. But the massacre of 10 *campesinos,* two students, and two priests in Olancho in 1975 at the hands of wealthy landowners put a fast end to the campaign. Since the mid-1980s, the church has once again begun to speak up on social issues but is not considered activist.

Protestants

Moravian missionaries were the first foreign religious group to come to Honduras, arriving in the Mosquitia region in the 1930s. Since the 1980s, evangelical groups, many sponsored by North Americans, have been growing rapidly.

© FUAD AZZAD

Honduras is an overwhelmingly Catholic country, as evidenced by elaborate Holy Week celebrations.

Denominations include the more traditional evangelical Baptist and Adventist churches, and Pentecostal churches such as the Assembly of God and the Church of God. The Moravian presence remains strong in the Mosquitia (although most Miskitos still identify themselves as Catholics), while Baptist churches can be found in nearly every town in the South. A 2002 poll found that nearly a quarter of the Honduran population responded that they are evangelical Christians, and that number is on the rise.

ESSENTIALS

Getting There

BY AIR

Several airlines fly directly to Honduras from other countries. From the United States, **Continental** (U.S. tel. 800/231-0856, www.continental.com), **American** (U.S. tel. 800/433-7300, www.aa.com), **Delta** (U.S. tel. 800/241-4141, www.delta.com), and **Taca** (U.S. tel. 800/400-TACA—800/400-8222, www.taca.com) all fly directly to Honduras from either Houston, Miami, or Atlanta into Tegucigalpa, San Pedro Sula, and Roatán. Taca also connects with all of Central America plus Mexico via San Salvador, while **Copa** (U.S. tel. 800/FLY-COPA—800/359-2672, www.copa air.com) flies from Mexico City and Panama City. There are daily connections to Roatán via La Ceiba on **Taca/Isleña** (tel. 504/552-9910, www.flyislena.com), and in January 2009 Taca/Isleña initiated a nonstop flight from San Pedro Sula to Roatán on the weekends. **Sosa** (tel. 504/550-6545 in San Pedro Sula, aerososa@psinet.hn) offers flights Monday–Saturday to Utila and Guanaja, daily to Roatán, all via La Ceiba. (Sosa does not have a website and may be difficult to book outside of Honduras, but is a relatively reliable airline.) A new company, **C.M.** (tel. 504/234-1886, cmairlines@yahoo.com) also has direct flights to Roatán from Tegucigalpa.

Standard round-trip airfare between the United States and San Pedro Sula is roughly US$550 from any of the departure cities above,

© AMY E. ROBERTSON

US$800 if you're departing from elsewhere, though better deals can occasionally be found in advance through travel agents or, even better, the many airline ticket websites on the Internet. Of the many agencies helpful at finding tickets to Latin America, one good one is **Exito Travel** (tel. 800/655-4053, www.exitotravel.com). It's always worth checking directly with the airlines also, as they often will give the best rates.

BY LAND

If you're planning to visit just Honduras and not spend time touring nearby countries, getting there by land isn't the most practical way to go. From the U.S. border, it takes at least three days on buses through Mexico and Guatemala to reach the closest Honduran border post at Aguas Calientes. Those who are on longer trips, however, and have some interest in spending time in Mexico or Guatemala should certainly consider getting there by bus or car. If you're on your way directly to San Pedro, the north coast, or the Bay Islands, the quickest route from Guatemala is via Chiquimula, Guatemala, to the border at El Florido and on to Copán in Honduras. The other main route, preferable for those intending to visit Santa Rosa de Copán and Gracias, is via Esquipulas to Aguas Calientes, near Nueva Ocotepeque. It's also possible to travel by well-paved road via Puerto Barrios Guatemala and Omoa, Honduras, if you are in the north.

For those headed to Tegucigalpa or other points south, the fastest route is via El Salvador. Depending on your destination in Honduras, travelers coming from El Salvador will want to cross at El Poy, near Nueva Ocotepeque, or at El Amatillo on the Pacific coast. El Poy is the fastest way to get to the north coast, while El Amatillo is the quickest for Tegucigalpa. A more scenic route is via La Esperanza through canyon country to Perquín, a remote border town in El Salvador.

If you're coming from or are on your way to Managua, Nicaragua, or farther south, the quickest border crossing is through Las Manos, beyond Danlí.

A slightly sketchier but still possible crossing is between Puerto Lempira, in the Gracias a Dios department (the Mosquitia) through the border town of Leimus to Puerto Cabezas, Nicaragua. No firsthand information is available on the crossing, but *migración* officials in Puerto Lempira say they have a post at Leimus.

Car

Coming down from the United States with your own vehicle is not unduly difficult, though it's a long way. Get through the huge expanse of Mexico on the quickest route possible to get to Tapachula, Chiapas, and cross into Guatemala at Tecún Umán. Driving through Guatemala via Escuintla and Guatemala City to the Honduran border at either El Florido or Aguas Calientes takes approximately 8–9 hours. Alternatively, those with time on their hands can take the more scenic but considerably slower route through San Cristóbal de las Casas, Mexico, through the highlands of Guatemala, and on to Honduras. Some information is available on the website www.go-panamerican.com, but real details are specified in the e-book available at www.drivemeloco.com.

International Buses

Three bus companies run daily trips between Honduras and other parts of Central America. **King Quality,** in San Pedro (tel. 504/553-4547) at 2 Calle, between 9 and 10 Avenidas SO, and in Tegucigalpa (tel. 504/225-5415 or 504/225-2600), runs daily first-class buses to Managua, San Salvador, and Guatemala City; **Tica Bus,** in San Pedro (tel./fax 504/556-5149, www.ticabus.com) at the Texaco station on Boulevard del Sur and in Tegucigalpa (tel. 504/220-0579 or 504/220-0590, www .ticabus.com) at 16 Calle between 6 and 5 Avenidas, has buses to Mexico, Guatemala, Nicaragua, Costa Rica, and Panama every day; and **Hedman Alas,** in San Pedro (tel. 504/553-1316, www.hedmanalas.com) on 3 Calle between 7 and 8 Avenidas and in Tegucigalpa (tel. 504/237-7143) at 11 Avenida between 13 and 14 Calles, has daily buses to Guatemala City and Antigua.

BY SEA
From Belize
One boat a week, the **D-Express** (tel. 504/ 9991-0778, info@hondurasdivers.com), plies the waters between Placencia, Belize, and Puerto Cortés, charging US$53 for the 2–3-hour trip.

Getting Around

BY AIR
Because Honduras is fairly small, flying between destinations in most of the country is not really necessary, with a few exceptions.

Two areas where it's not a bad idea to arrive by plane are the Bay Islands and the Mosquitia. The islands are serviced by a less-expensive ferry, but plane flights from La Ceiba are also cheap and quick. **Isleña** (tel. 504/552-9910, www .flyislena.com) charges US$37 to Roatán and US$52 to Guanaja, one-way, while **Sosa** (tel. 504/550-6545 in San Pedro Sula, aerososa@ psinet.hn) charges US$56 to Roatán and has service to Utila and Guanaja as well. In January 2009 they also initiated nonstop service between San Pedro Sula and Roatán on Saturday and Sundays. A new airline, **C.M.** (tel. 504/234-1886, cmairlines@yahoo.com) has nonstop service between Tegucigalpa and Roatán.

Flying cuts travel time between La Ceiba and Brus Laguna in the Mosquitia from 12 hours to 90 minutes. Round-trip flights are US$225, departing Mondays and Fridays with Sosa. Flying saves about two days of travel time by bus, pickup truck, and boat between La Ceiba and Puerto Lempira (again with Sosa), although most tourists won't have reason to go there, and if you have a group of seven or more, you can also charter a flight with Sosa to a number of the other villages. Based in La Ceiba, **SAMI** (tel. 504/433-8032), also known as Honduras Air, has flights to a number of villages in the Mosquitia, although it is famously unreliable (a five-hour delay is not unusual). C.M. has nonstop flights between Tegucigalpa and Puerto Lempira, and can be chartered.

If you're in a rush or absolutely hate buses, flights between the two main cities, San Pedro Sula and Tegucigalpa, cost US$66 one-way on either Isleña or **Taca** (tel. 504/550-8222 in San Pedro Sula, 504/234-2422 in Tegucigalpa, www.taca.com). **Central American Airways** (tel. 504/233-1614) also services this route on weekdays (it is their only route), and typically has fewer delays. Flying between La Ceiba and Tegucigalpa can save a couple of hours of travel time, and is possible on both Isleña and Sosa.

BY BUS
Buses are the most widely used means of transportation for Hondurans. Buses are often essential to visit the more out-of-the-way destinations, and budget travelers will be happy to hear most buses are relatively comfortable and inexpensive. For example, the four-hour direct bus ride between San Pedro Sula and Tegucigalpa costs only US$8 for regular service, US$18 for first-class.

Direct, first-class bus service is available between main cities and destinations like San Pedro Sula, Tegucigalpa, La Ceiba, and Copán. Of the different companies operating these routes, **Hedman Alas** is considered far and away the best, with new, comfortable buses, each equipped with bathrooms and providing on-time service. But you won't find luxury on any but these few routes. Many buses to smaller towns are converted U.S. school buses, with bench seating designed for children, so if you're tall, expect a bit of discomfort.

The designated bus station in most towns is called simply the *terminal de buses*. In Tegucigalpa and Comayagua, each company runs its own terminal, and unfortunately, they're not centrally located. The terminal at San Pedro Sula is few minutes outside of town, and the convenience of being able to switch buses without leaving the terminal more than makes up for any inconvenience in getting to and from the station.

TOUR OPERATORS

Most tourist destinations in Honduras do not require any guides. For some hiking, boating, or other naturalist or cultural trips, specialized guides may be worth the extra cost, and these are discussed in the relevant chapters.

Several companies offer more general services, like tours of the main highlights or particular regions of the country, that may appeal to those in a group, on a limited schedule, or who simply want everything arranged ahead of time to ensure a smooth trip. Transportation services like chauffeured buses or cars are also available. Those listed below have been in operation for a number of years and cover essentially all parts of the country.

MesoAmerica Travel (tel. 504/557-8447 or 504/557-3258, www.mesoamerica-travel .com), in San Pedro Sula.

Maya Temple Tours (tel. 504/509-0555, U.S. tel. 877/467-1692, www.mayatempletours .com), in San Pedro Sula.

Greko Tours (tel. 504/239-5998 or 504/239-5999, www.grekotours.net), in Tegucigalpa.

Explore Honduras (tel. 504/236-9003 or 504/236-7694, www.explorehonduras.com), in Teguicigalpa.

Arrecife Tours (tel. 504/239-1782 or 504/239-1783, www.arrecifetours.com), in Tegucigalpa.

Using a national operator can ease travel planning, and naturally you pay more for the service. Regional tour operators are listed in their respective chapters, have unbeatable knowledge of their area, and often charge lower prices.

Determining bus departure times for most (non-first-class) buses can be a bit of a guessing game. Some buses leave only when full, which means you should get there early, while others leave at the appointed time, full or not. Generally, long-distance buses leave on a regular schedule.

When you arrive at a station to catch a bus, expect to be accosted by *ayudantes,* or helpers, who will tell you in urgent tones that the bus you want is just out the door and you must buy a ticket immediately. You may then get on the bus and wait another hour before leaving. Another common trick is to tell you the bus is a *directo* (direct) when in reality it stops whenever it sees another potential passenger (or "whenever a chicken flaps its wing on the side of the road," as one long-suffering local put it).

In some buses, you are expected to buy a ticket at the station beforehand, while in others the *ayudante* will come around and collect the fare after the trip has begun. If the latter is the case, you will be asked how far you are going, and your fare will change accordingly. Hold on to ticket stubs, as the drivers sometimes collect them at the end of the ride.

In the converted school buses, backpacks and other luggage that does not fit in the overhead racks is stowed in the back, where a couple of seats are normally removed to add space. More expensive buses have compartments below, but if your bag is stashed there by an *ayudante,* keep a close eye on the door until the bus pulls out. Buses in San Pedro Sula in particular have been notorious for having bags ripped off while the unsuspecting victims are on board, awaiting departure. Hedman Alas is a notable exception to this—they take good care of the security in all of their terminals.

Apart from the rare express buses, it's customary to flag down a passing bus anywhere along the route—extremely convenient for those traveling in rural areas. Don't bother trying to look for a designated bus stop; just get out on the road and stick out your hand when a bus comes by.

When planning a trip by bus, remember that schedules can change, and prices will fluctuate with changes in the price of fuel. If the price of gas has gone up lately in the United States, you can be sure that bus prices will have gone up in Honduras as well.

On rare occasions, buses will be stopped by police and all men will have to get off and line up to be cursorily frisked and have their identifications checked.

HITCHHIKING

Travelers looking to get out into the backcountry of Honduras should be sure to learn the crucial word *jalón*. This literally translates to "a big pull," but in Honduras, it means hitching a ride. In many rural areas, hitchhiking is the only way to get around, and pickup trucks with room invariably stop to let another passenger pile into the back. In fact, pickup trucks often serve as local buses and use set routes, times, and prices.

Not only is hitching safe and convenient in rural Honduras, but riding in the open air in the back of a pickup beats being crammed into a hot bus for a few hours. Many budget travelers and Peace Corps workers prefer hitching even when buses are available. While it is generally very safe for solo females to hitch in the pickups described above, traditional hitching and getting into random cars is never recommended, particularly for women alone.

Hitchhiking is common only out on back roads, not on main highways. Some budget travelers insist on hitching everywhere, and it's usually possible, but hitching on main highways is both less common and less safe than in rural areas.

BY TAXI

Taxis are omnipresent in most towns and cities. Meters aren't used, and there's usually a going rate within a certain area. It may be tricky figuring out the going rate. US$0.75–1 usually gets you around within the downtown area of most towns. In Tegucigalpa taxis charge US$2–3 to most destinations and US$4 to the airport or to the park at El Pichacho, while US$3 should get you anywhere in San Pedro. For rides farther afield, expect to negotiate.

A good technique is to ask a local the prices before hailing a cab, or to reject the first cab and hail a second one, then compare prices.

Taxis are generally collective *(colectivo)* in

© FUAD AZZAD

Mototaxis (auto rickshaws) are plentiful in places like Copán Ruinas and Tegucigalpa.

Honduras, meaning they stop and pick up passengers along the way and drop them off according to whichever destination is closer. If you're in a hurry and want a nonstop trip, tell the driver and expect to pay extra. Despite being paid in nothing but small change, a taxi driver almost certainly won't have change to give you if you pay with a 500-lempira bill; make sure you have a note of 100 or less.

In San Pedro and Tegucigalpa, several *colectivo* taxis run fixed routes from a certain point downtown to the outskirts of the city, usually charging US$0.60 or so for the pleasure of being crammed in with four passengers and the driver.

Taxis are invariably found at the downtown square of any town or city, or at the bus station. If you hear someone honking at you as you walk through a town, more than likely it's a taxi—the driver's letting you know he's free if you're looking for a ride.

BY BOAT
To the Bay Islands

The ferry MV *Galaxy Wave* (www.safeway maritime.com) runs regularly scheduled trips throughout the week to the islands of Roatán, and the much-smaller and less-nice *Utila Princess* (www.utilaprincess.com) goes to Utila from the Cabotaje dock outside of La Ceiba.

On the islands, several outfits and resorts offer a variety of boating and fishing trips. It's also possible to hire local fishermen to take you on freelance trips.

The Mosquitia

In the Mosquitia, a variety of canoes known as *canoas, tuk-tuks, pipantes,* and *cayucos* (depending on the exact size and shape of the boat, whether poles are involved in steering, and whether the motor is inboard or outboard) are the only transportation available for getting upriver from the coast into the rainforest.

BY CAR

Renting a car in Honduras allows you to explore large areas of the country accessed only with difficulty by public transportation.

Foreign driver's licenses are sufficient for renting; International Driver's Licenses are not required.

Road Conditions

Driving in Honduras is a bit of mixed bag, and road conditions change with the seasons, as heavy rains not only wash out dirt roads and weaker bridges, but also create massive potholes. Ruts on back roads can be so deep at times that only high-riding SUVs like Land Rovers can pass.

When driving in cities, keep a close eye on signs indicating one-way streets. Most large towns and cities are not difficult to navigate, except Tegucigalpa. The traffic in downtown and in the Comayagüela district can be horrific and the streets confusing. Better to leave your car at a hotel and get around downtown by taxi or on foot during your stay.

It's absolutely essential that foreign drivers drive very defensively, not expecting anyone else on the road to obey the laws or even act logically. Trucks in particular take positive glee in passing around blind curves on Honduras's many mountain highways, so don't take your eyes off the road and always be ready to dodge out of the way. Keep a close eye on pedestrians and bicyclists, as they seem to be so fatalistic as to actually take delight in meandering around in the road and forcing cars to get out of their way.

Particular items that highway drivers should watch out for, which may indicate trouble ahead, are oncoming cars flashing their lights at you (usually an indication of trouble on the road ahead), a pile of sticks or a cone in the road (usually to signal a car stuck in the road), a large branch sticking straight up in the middle of the road (to indicate a large pothole), or anyone in another car or on the side of the road waving a hand up and down, palm facing down, indicating "slow down!" And, of course, it goes without saying to be always on the lookout for random livestock crossings, axle-eating potholes, or stray objects on the pavement.

Be prepared for very reckless passing

techniques on mountain roads, including passing on blind curves, and the improvisational invention of third lanes in the middle of the highway to avoid collisions.

Driving at night is not recommended in any part of the country. As in Mexico and the rest of Central America, there are just too many potential hazards to make it worth risking, in particular drunk drivers, cars that don't use headlights, and those pesky potholes. If you absolutely must drive for some reason, watch closely for cattle, potholes, and other random obstacles in the road. Keep an eye out for signs warning of upcoming *túmulos* (speed bumps). Driving Honduran highways in the rain can be treacherous as well and is not for the faint of heart.

The great majority of roads in Honduras are dirt, and anyone who wants to get out to rural areas will find themselves spending a lot of time bumping along unpaved roads of widely varying quality. Many roads are passable only with four-wheel-drive.

Police checkpoints—little yellow-and-gray shacks on the side of the road, usually with a police officer sitting in a chair out front, watching the day pass by—are common throughout Honduras. Slow down as you pass—usually, you will be waved through or ignored entirely. But sometimes the officer will make it clear you should stop. Do so without hesitation, and break out your papers. Your car permit, driver's license (a foreign one will do), and passport must always, always be with you. If not, expect hassles and fines, and possibly the retention of your driver's license. (You will be given a slip of paper in return, to take with you when you pay the fine, in order to get your license back.) It is rare to have problems if everything is order, but if you are still asked to pay some kind of fine on the spot, asking to see the police officer's badge and writing down his name can be an effective way for the fine to suddenly become a "voluntary contribution," which you can then decline to make. While most of these checkpoints are pro forma, it seems like every week or so they will suddenly stop every car coming and thoroughly check your papers, and maybe even examine your car. This can be either due to a stolen car the police have been alerted to look for, or merely an effort to make their presence felt.

Rules of the Road

Traffic rules in Honduras are fairly self-explanatory and similar to rules in the United States. Speed limits are not obeyed, but if you want to be safe, follow them anyway. Seat belts are mandatory, and police are increasingly cracking down on their use. It is illegal to talk on a cell phone while driving, and police don't hesitate to pull you over for that infraction. Turning right on a red light is sometimes allowed and sometimes not, so don't risk it. One oddity is that no left turns are permitted at any stoplight that does not have a left-turn arrow indicator. Another is that no smoking is allowed while driving.

If you are pulled over for a traffic offense, your license will be taken. You can try to pay a bribe to get it back, but remember, the official fines are usually cheaper than a bribe. If you ask for a ticket, you will be given one, and then you have 72 hours to go to the *tránsito* (traffic police) office to pay the fine and reclaim your license. In Tegucigalpa, the office is the Dirección General de Tránsito in Colonia Miraflores. Usually, the officer who takes your license will turn it in the same day, and by the next morning you can go to *tránsito*, pay your fine, and pick up your license again— a remarkably painless process. If you are on the move and don't want to stick around for a day, you may try to pay a bribe, but keep in mind that not all Honduran police officers are corrupt, and encouraging corruption is not the most moral way to behave as a tourist.

In Case of Accident

If you have an accident with another car, tell someone to get *tránsito*, the traffic police. Don't move your vehicle or leave the scene of an accident before *tránsito* arrives—if you do, you will automatically be considered partly at fault for the accident. It does not matter if your accident blocks the entire street or highway.

While waiting, get all information possible about the other driver. When *tránsito* arrives, the officers will talk to both drivers separately, then write out a description of events for both to sign and date.

An appointment will then be assigned at the Juzgado de Tránsito (Traffic Court), where a monetary arrangement will be made. Few people carry insurance in Honduras, so the judge will arbitrate between the two parties to arrive at an agreement. If no agreement is reached, either party can sue.

In the case of an accident involving a pedestrian, again, call the police immediately and do not leave the scene. You may have to spend up to a week in jail, but no more. It's very likely you will be forced to pay all medical bills, as well as a fine to the victim in case of injury, or to the family of the victim in case of death, regardless of who was at fault.

Do not even consider fleeing the scene of an accident. This only creates more serious trouble for you. It's best to follow the process through to its conclusion.

Fuel and Repairs

Regular (leaded) gas is no longer available in Honduras. Gas stations, including many U.S. chains like Texaco and Shell, are common throughout the country, and in places with no gas stations, gas is sometimes sold out of barrels. Be sure to fill up whenever you're planning a trip into rural Honduras. It is not uncommon to be overcharged for gas, so be sure to check that the reader is reset to zero before the gas starts flowing, and take a second to look at the pump at the end before paying, to verify the total.

Mechanical help is relatively inexpensive, but parts can be costly depending on your vehicle. Toyota is the unquestioned king of the road here, particularly the four-door, four-wheel-drive diesel pickups. There are also plenty of Mitsubishis, Nissans, Hondas, and Kias.

Be sure to get your vehicle thoroughly checked before leaving for Honduras, and consider bringing a few basic spare parts such as filters (gas, air, and oil), fan belts, spark plugs

and spark-plug wires, two spare tires (instead of one), fuses, and radiator hoses. Recommended emergency gear for vehicles includes a tow rope, extra gas cans, water containers, jumper cables, and, of course, a jack and tire iron. According to Honduran law, you are required to have a fire extinguisher and reflective triangles in your car at all times, and the police will occasionally ask at their checkpoints if you have them.

Many drivers in Honduras do not have insurance, which makes driving defensively that much more important.

Car Rental

Renting a car in Honduras is not cheap. Expect to pay at least US$45 per day minimum with unlimited mileage, more with insurance. About a dozen different agencies, including several international companies like **Hertz** (U.S. tel. 800/654-3001, www.hertz.com), **Budget** (U.S. tel. 800/472-3325, www.budget.com), **Avis** (U.S. tel. 800/331-1212, www.avis.com), and others operate in Honduras. The best rates can usually be obtained by booking through the company's website. Note that it is impossible to get full-coverage insurance with rental companies. The best you can get is a policy that will leave you, the renter, fully covered for other cars and passengers, but liable for the first US$3,000 of damage to the rented car. If your credit card has insurance for cars reserved and paid for with the card, you may be able to save yourself US$12 a day on insurance—check your credit card policy before you leave home. Whether you scratched up the car through bad driving, or whether some malevolent passerby keyed it, it doesn't matter—you pay. So make sure you always find safe parking for a rental car. Car-rental agencies of course have extensive and expensive insurance available. Also, many car rental agencies, including reputable international companies, operate with a prepay system that does not allow for refunds on cars returned early.

BY BICYCLE
Bicycle Touring
Remarkably, cyclists rate Honduras as the best

Central American country to tour by bicycle. The main highways are in decent condition and are relatively wide, and highway traffic is low.

Bicycle touring may seem specialized, but it's actually a wonderful way to really see a country. There's no need to race—determine a comfortable pace for your group and plan your journey accordingly. Drawbacks to biking in Honduras include the extremely mountainous terrain, which will wear you down, and the lack of good quality spare parts. Riding in a group is best.

One (perhaps the only) good resource for bikers in Honduras is the bike shop **Hondubikes** (tel. 504/239-2192, www.hondubikes.com) in Tegucigalpa.

Mountain Biking

Mountain biking is a nascent but growing sport among the wealthy in Honduras. Few trails have been developed, but there are plenty of rugged logging roads to explore. Both the Sierra Merendón, right behind San Pedro Sula, and the mountains north and west of Tegucigalpa are fantastic for mountain biking, crisscrossed with trails and dirt roads through pine, tropical, and cloud forests and rural farming country.

Visas and Officialdom

VISAS
Tourist Requirements

Citizens of the United States, western Europe, Canada, Argentina, and Chile are not required to have a visa and are issued a tourist visa on arrival in Honduras. Authorities are currently granting 90-day visas, and any extensions (30 more days are available) must be taken care of at the immigration office in Tegucigalpa. Citizens of all other countries are required to obtain visas before entering Honduras. Cost usually depends on what that country charges Hondurans for visas. Sometimes it's free, and sometimes it can cost up to US$20.

Tourists are granted a 90-day visa upon entry. One 30-day renewal is allowed, for a US$20 fee. Renewals can no longer be processed at the immigration offices across the country but must be submitted in Tegucigalpa. You should be able to get the form at least at the *migración* office in most large cities. The immigration office (www.migracion.gob.hn) in Tegucigalpa is on the *anillo pereférico,* opposite the UTH (Universidad Tecnico de Honduras). Sometimes you may be asked to get a certain amount of *timbre* stamps, available at a local bank, as payment, and you will need to leave your passport for 1–3 days.

The fine for overstaying a visa is calculated at immigration upon exiting the country; airport officials are accustomed to doing this, and no one else seems to be able to say in advance how much it will be. One report is that there is a US$32 fine for the first month and 20 percent of the minimum salary (US$290) for each additional month. Others have been charged more.

Foreigners are required to carry their passports with them at all times, but rarely if ever will it be checked. Be sure to keep photocopies in your hotel room or, better still, just carry the photocopies.

CUSTOMS

Travelers entering Honduras are allowed to bring with them anything needed for a vacation, including any sports equipment, plus 200 cigarettes, 100 cigars, half a kilogram of tobacco, and two quarts of spirits. When leaving the country, be sure not to have any pre-Columbian artifacts, endangered animals, or coral, particularly black coral, as these could be confiscated in either Honduras or your home country; you could even wind up in jail.

If you have to declare anything over $300, you may find yourself at the mercy of airport customs officials who may try to take advantage of unsuspecting foreigners by levying some

EMBASSIES AND CONSULATES

EMBASSIES IN TEGUCIGALPA

- **Argentina:** Colonia Rubén Darío, Avenida José María Medina 417, tel. 504/232-3376

- **Belize:** bottom floor of Hotel Honduras Maya, tel. 504/238-4614

- **Brazil:** Colonia Palmira, Calle República de Brasil, tel. 504/221-4432

- **Canada:** Colonia Payaqui, Edificio Financiero Uno, Boulevard Juan Pablo II, tel. 504/232-4551

- **Chile:** Colonia Rubén Dario, Avenida Las Minitas 501, tel. 504/232-2114

- **Colombia:** Edificio Palmira, 3rd floor, across from Honduras Maya, tel. 504/239-9709

- **Costa Rica:** Residencia El Triángulo, 1 Calle 3451, tel. 504/232-1768

- **Cuba:** Colonia Florencia Sur, Calle Principal 4313, tel. 504/239-5993

- **Dominican Republic:** Colonia Miramontes, in front of Banco Continental, tel. 504/239-0130

- **Ecuador:** Colonia Altos de Castaño, Sendero Senecio 2968, tel. 504/221-4906

- **El Salvador:** Colonia Rubén Dario, 2 Avenida and 5 Calle, tel. 504/239-0901

- **Guatemala:** Colonia Lomas de Guijarro, Alfonso XIII 3716, Edificio El Faro, tel. 504/231-1543 or 504/232-5018

- **Mexico:** Colonia Lomas de Guajirro, Calle Eucalipto, tel. 504/232-8712

- **Nicaragua:** Colonia Lomas del Tepeyac B-M, tel. 504/232-1966

- **Panama:** Edificio Palmira, 3rd floor, across from Honduras Maya, tel. 504/239-5508

- **Peru:** Colonia Linda Vista, Calle Principal 3301, tel. 504/236-7994

- **United Kingdom:** Colonia Payaqui, Centro Financiero Uno, 3rd floor, tel. 504/239-8218

- **United States:** Avenida La Paz, tel. 504/236-9320, http://honduras.usembassy.gov

- **Venezuela:** Colonia Rubén Darío, Circuito Choluteca B 2116, tel. 504/232-1886 or 504/232-1879

CONSULATES IN TEGUCIGALPA

- **Jamaica:** Avenida Los Proceres, Edif. Luis Kafie, tel. 504/236-5159

- **Paraguay:** Colonia Las Minitas, Sendero Las Palomas, tel. 504/239-5178

CONSULATES IN SAN PEDRO SULA

- **Belize:** Kilometer marker 5 on highway to Puerto Cortés, tel. 504/551-6191

- **Chile:** Colonia Bella Vista, 2 Calle between 33 and 34 Avenidas, tel. 504/552-4223

- **Dominican Republic:** Barrio Suyapa, tel. 504/553-6356

- **El Salvador:** Barrio Guamilito, Edificio Park Plaza, 11 Avenida between 5 and 6 Calles NO, tel. 504/557-2718

- **Guatemala:** Colonia Trejo 24 Avenida and 12 Calle SO, tel. 504/556-9550

- **Mexico:** 2 Calle and 20 Avenida SO, #205, Barrio Río Piedras, tel. 504/553-2604

- **Nicaragua:** 21 Avenida and 11 Calle, Colonia Trejo, tel. 504/550-3394

- **United Kingdom:** Colonia Moderna, 2 Calle between 18 and 19 Avenidas NO, tel. 504/550-2337

- **United States:** (American Citizens Services Office) Banco Atlántida Principal Office, 11th floor across from the *parque central*, tel. 504/558-1580 (1-4 P.M. Mon., Wed., Fri.)

CONSULATES IN CHOLUTECA

- **El Salvador:** Barrio El Centro, tel. 504/780-0199

outrageous tax in order to claim your goods. There are a number of private *agencias aduaneras* (customs agencies) that can help prevent this. If you contact an agency in advance of your trip, they can meet you right at the airport and help ease the process. One agency with offices in both Tegucigalpa and San Pedro Sula is **Agencia Aduanera Arhsa** (Tegucigalpa tel. 504/239-2452, San Pedro tel. 504/557-2419, www.arhsa.com).

Cars

Foreign cars are allowed into Honduras for a total of six months. Travelers overstaying the limit will be fined. When arriving at the border, be sure to have your title, license, and passport (with visa, if necessary). Insurance is not required. Cross during the week, or early Saturday morning, as it is necessary to make a payment at the bank, which is closed Saturday afternoon and Sunday.

Three-month permits are issued initially, for a US$50 fee. Sometimes you may be offered only a 30-day permit, but firmly request three months. Prices should be clearly posted on signs at border offices, and receipts should be given for every fee. If a border official will not give you a receipt, the fee is probably not required.

At border posts you will be pestered by *tramitadores* (people who help with official paperwork) offering their services. All *tramitadores* should have identification approved by the government—don't hire someone who is not wearing identification. If the border offices are crowded, or if you're not confident in Spanish, *tramitadores* can be quite useful in helping facilitate your way through the paperwork. But if you speak Spanish reasonably well and there aren't too many people around, the procedures are not difficult to navigate alone. Basically, you first get your passport stamped by *migración,* then proceed to the *aduana,* or customs, where you must show your title, registration, driver's license, and passport. After filling out a form, go to one of usually two or three banks at the border, pay a fee, and return to the *aduana* to receive your papers. As you leave the border entering Honduras, stop at the police station, where they will inspect your papers and register your car's presence in the country. You are under no obligation to leave through the same border post—leave wherever you like. The entire process usually takes an hour or so, on an average day.

If you'd like to renew your permit when the time expires, to a maximum of six months unless you receive a work visa in the country, go to the Dirección Ejecutiva de Ingresos in the Banadesa building in Comayagüela, a block from Parque Obelisco, tel. 504/220-1138. Normally, if your papers are in one day before noon, you can pick them up the next day by early afternoon. Fines for not renewing your car papers run up to thousands of lempiras very quickly, so make sure you don't let your permit lapse.

If you want to drive a car to Honduras and sell it there, you will have to pay some hefty taxes, around 35 percent of calculated vehicle value for passenger cars or 22 percent for pickup trucks. The same office in Comayagüela will help you through the process. Cars older than 10 years cannot be imported, and at the time of writing, there was a moratorium on the import of SUVs. (But you can certainly purchase both old cars and SUVs once in country.)

Motorcycles

For information on touring through Central America and crossing Honduran borders on motorcycle, www.horizonsunlimited.com is your definitive information source. Permit regulations are similar to those for foreign cars and trucks.

BORDER CROSSINGS

Official border crossings into Honduras are El Poy and El Amatillo from El Salvador; Aguas Calientes, El Florido, and Cuyamelito from Guatemala; and Las Manos, El Espino, Guasaule, and Leimus (near Puerto Lempira) from Nicaragua. Several unofficial crossings are regularly used along the more remote reaches of the Salvadoran border and across the Río Coco to Nicaragua.

Entering and leaving Honduras by land is generally quick and easy. The best time to arrive is midmorning, well before lunch break, but most border posts are open until 5 P.M. or 6 P.M. You may be asked to pay a US$3 fee when crossing into Honduras by land, and you should be given a receipt if you do. There are no exit fees.

Those leaving Honduras by airplane are required to pay an exit fee of US$34.04.

Conduct and Customs

Generally speaking, Honduran society features customs and traditions similar to those in other countries in the region. Family is of paramount importance, although marriages are often informal due to the expense of weddings and the scarcity of priests. The majority of Hondurans are Catholic, though not necessarily strict ones.

When traveling in Honduras, don't plan on being in a hurry to get anywhere. Things happen at a leisurely pace, and no one rushes. Trying to pressure people to act with haste will get little result other than stress. Take it easy.

Hondurans are fairly laid-back about clothes in general, but wearing shorts will certainly draw some odd looks in rural villages in the interior. Generally, beachwear should be left to the north coast and the Bay Islands. Public nudity, including swimming naked, is illegal in Honduras (although Paya Bay resort on Roatán has "naturalist" weeks on its private beaches).

The litter level in Honduras is disturbingly high. Don't be surprised to see locals toss garbage on the street or out the bus window.

SEXUAL POLITICS

As in most of Latin America, Honduran women must cope with a host of sexist, macho attitudes from men, especially in rural society where women are expected to stay indoors and keep quiet when matters of business are being discussed. A budding feminist movement has taken root but has a long way to go to combat the ingrained *machismo*. According to government estimates, some 500,000 women suffer from physical abuse at the hands of men. Honduras has many single mothers; it's very common for women to have one or two children by age 20. Many marriages are informal, and men have little compunction about leaving their wives for another woman. And men who do stay married are practically expected to sleep with prostitutes (legal in Honduras) or have affairs.

Despite the social obstacles, women have become more active in Honduran public life of late. Women have begun to play an increasingly important role in civil organizations in the last decades. Some of the most effective social organizers, labor leaders, and environmental activists in the country are women. Women play an ever-larger role in the country's labor force, as they account for nearly all the workers in the rapidly growing *maquila* factory sector. Several Honduran women also hold highly visible roles in Honduran politics, such as past Tegucigalpa mayor Vilma de Castellanos and the highly respected president of the Honduran Central Bank, Gabriela Núñez de Reyes.

For an excellent and at times harrowing account of life as a woman in rural Honduras, read Elvia Alvarado's *Don't Be Afraid, Gringo: A Honduran Woman Speaks from the Heart.*

FEMALE TRAVELERS

Foreign women will likely find themselves the object of a certain amount of unwanted attention while traveling in Honduras. Honduran men tend to view women as either pure, chaste mother figures or as objects of sexual attention. Due in part to representations of women in western media, most foreigners are viewed as the latter.

One way to cope with the situation is to dress and act conservatively. Tank tops, short skirts, and other skimpy garments do not help in this regard, though certainly on the north coast beach towns and in the Bay Islands, these are accepted.

If you are not looking for male attention, avoid looking men in the eye—this is considered an invitation for the man to introduce himself and try to pick you up. Whether you handle forward men rudely or try to ignore them is up to you. As a general rule, the more you talk to them (regardless of what it is you're actually saying!), the more encouraged they will be.

The flip side is that Honduran men have an ingrained consideration toward women and will often go to ridiculous lengths to do a favor for a lady. Since you have to put up with the bad side of *machismo* all the time, it seems perfectly legitimate to make use of its chivalrous tendencies when appropriate.

While men are often annoyingly persistent and need to be clearly told to go away, rarely are they actually dangerous. Nonetheless, rape is certainly an issue to keep in mind in Honduras, as in any country. The north coast beach towns are particularly dangerous spots. Women are better off going to discos in male company or at least in a group of women. *Cantinas* are exclusively the domain of men, as are pool halls, although shooting some pool with a co-ed group of friends in the afternoon shouldn't bring you any trouble.

Of course, plenty of female travelers may, in fact, be very attracted to Honduran men. In which case, you will not have a difficult time at all finding a guy to spend time with. But (at the risk of sounding alarmist) be aware that AIDS is a serious problem in Honduras, so bring condoms and be prepared to do some convincing to make Honduran men use them. UNAIDS considers Honduras to have a generalized epidemic on the north coast, concentrated in certain populations—men who have sex with men, sex workers, prisoners, and the Garífuna—that have prevalence rates of greater than 5 percent.

Should you fall victim to an assault or rape in Honduras, you cannot expect a great deal of sympathy or help from the police. Services like counseling and special health care for rape victims are nonexistent. The best bet for medical help is to go to one of the better private hospitals (not the government hospitals or the small clinics) in the cities of Tegucigalpa, San Pedro Sula, or La Ceiba. For legal help, contact your embassy in Tegucigalpa or consulate in San Pedro Sula.

On a more positive note, female travelers will, if they make the effort, find wonderful opportunities to get to know the many strong, worldly wise matrons who sometimes seem like the most sensible people in the country. And because women travelers seem less threatening than men, Hondurans of both sexes frequently open up more to them. With a little looking around, interested travelers will find hundreds of grassroots social organizations that, if not strictly feminist, are run mainly by women.

MALE TRAVELERS

Like foreign women, male travelers can expect plenty of attention from the opposite sex. Many Honduran women see foreign men with a combination of idealization of the *gringo* and a mercenary attitude about the possibilities of marrying one or getting some of their money.

Most of this attention comes in the form of giggling from groups of women you happen to pass by. But often a single woman will catch your eye, or even boldly walk up to you and introduce herself, something women rarely do with Honduran men. If you stop to chat with a woman, even if she's a complete stranger, asking her out for a date is perfectly acceptable. And in the uncomplicated sexual culture of the Caribbean, if you go out on a date, it's just a small step to go to bed together. What you wish to do about this state of affairs is of course entirely personal, but should you end up in bed with a *hondureña*, be sure to bring your own protection and use it, as AIDS is rife in Honduras. Honduran women rarely insist on a condom.

It's not uncommon, especially in north coast beach towns, to see an older foreign man escorting around a young Honduran woman. While this may seem distasteful to some, it's also true that many of these women are fully aware of their situation and what they are doing, at times a lot more than the men.

This assumes, of course, that both individuals are of consenting age—a much more sinister phenomenon is when an older foreign man goes for an underage Honduran girl. Despite the fact that this is illegal, the dire poverty and lack of opportunity in Honduras, along with a sickeningly large number of willing rich foreign clients, have made child prostitution a growing social problem in Honduras, as in Cuba and Thailand.

TRAVELING WITH CHILDREN

With its opportunities for exploring and learning, traveling with children in Honduras can be a wonderful experience—especially since discounts are given on domestic flights and in hotel rooms, making it more affordable as well. Hondurans are generally very accepting of children in restaurants or elsewhere (don't be surprised if the staff offer to whisk your baby away to the kitchen while you eat), and young kids often become icebreakers between travelers and Hondurans.

Unfortunately, in the cities where crime rates are highest (San Pedro Sula, La Ceiba, and Tegucigalpa), children are seen as a vulnerability to would-be muggers, so be on greater alert for pickpockets and muggers when you're with little ones. Teens often hang out in the malls without an adult, but it is not recommended that they do so elsewhere in these cities. And while there are never any guarantees, taking an afternoon stroll *sans* chaperone in places like the West End, Roatán, is considered perfectly safe.

Sports and Recreation

HIKING AND BACKPACKING

Blessed with more rugged mountain country and intact forest cover than anywhere else in Central America, Honduras offers fantastic possibilities for wilderness. Not that the country's natural areas have much in the way of tourist infrastructure. Apart from the national parks of Celaque, Cusuco, Cerro Azul/Meámbar, and La Tigra, wilderness areas generally don't feature marked trails or informative visitors centers. What hikers will find are dozens of unexplored patches of cloud forest across the mountains of central Honduras, huge areas of lowland tropical forest near the Caribbean coast, and several less extensive but unique ecosystems like mangrove wetlands and dry tropical forest. Each of these environments is well stocked with its own varieties of vibrantly colorful tropical birds, stealthy predators, and a myriad of other creatures seen only by those who have the energy to get out into their habitat and the patience to wait quietly for them to appear.

Not only is hiking in Honduras the best way to fully appreciate the country's natural beauty, but it also brings foreigners in contact with rural Hondurans, who are some of the most decent, open-hearted people you are likely to ever run across. The rule (replicated, no doubt, in most of the world) seems to be the farther one goes out into the *campo,* away from cities and roads, the friendlier people get. You may find yourself stopping repeatedly on the trail to share a cup of coffee at the friendly insistence of some *campesino* in his hut.

While most people logically prefer to head into the woods during the dry season (roughly January–April, depending on the part of the country), hiking during the rains has its own appeal. The trails turn into muddy bogs (which they often are for most of the year anyhow, within the forest), but the electric green brilliance of the foliage often makes up for the discomforts.

Etiquette and Ethics on the Trail

The role of foreign visitors is extremely important in helping preserve Honduran natural resources. The concept of protected areas is new in Honduras and viewed with great skepticism, especially by the rural folk who live near (or sometimes actually within) these areas. Left to their own devices, the desperately poor, often literally starving *campesinos* use the wilderness to supplement their paltry income by chopping wood for fuel, cutting out badly needed new farmland, or hunting wild game.

By providing some form of economic benefit to the people who live nearby, foreigners can help encourage locals to view a natural area as a resource worth protecting, as it can attract tourists. This economic benefit can come from hiring a local guide, buying a meal from a family, or paying a few lempiras to pitch a tent outside a farmer's hut. Those going on a trip with a tour company are not exempt from this—you must be sure that the company you go with leaves some money behind, rather than using their own guides, transportation, food, etc. Just imagine how a self-sufficient trip must look to the locals—here come these unfathomably wealthy foreigners out enjoying themselves in our forest that we are no longer supposed to touch, and they don't leave us a lempira! And after that, they really expect us *not* to go hunting to feed our families?

Navigation

Hikers will find trails crisscrossing the hillsides all over rural Honduras, created and used for many centuries by local *campesinos*. Several principal trails, well-beaten and wide, act as "trunk roads" for an area, while smaller footpaths branch off in all directions. Once you arrive at the edges of farming and grazing land, wanting to enter the forest, trails are harder to find and often disappear entirely, used only by the occasional hunter. Sometimes forest trails can be found crossing from one side of the mountains to another, usually over a low pass rather than across the mountaintops, where the thickest forest is invariably found.

A few main trails are marked on the 1:50,000 topographical maps sold by the Instituto Geográfico Nacional. But when faced with the reality of dozens of trails, you will want to have a command of at least basic Spanish to ask directions from locals.

Most valleys, ridgelines, or other logical routes in rural Honduras have a path along them. If an apparently feasible route has no trail, that's probably for a good reason, like an impassable section out of sight ahead. Real trouble starts when you get off the trail, thinking you know better. Bushwhackers should be fully prepared with topographical maps, a compass, and a sharp machete.

Hiring a local guide is an excellent idea when hiking in Honduras, for a variety of reasons. First and foremost, of course, he will relieve you of the difficult task of finding a route. Also, guides are often very good at spotting wild animals (and killing them—they're usually hunters, which is why they know the forest so well), and if your Spanish is up to it, they can tell you all sorts of interesting information about the forest and region. The best place to find a guide is invariably in the last village at the very end of the dirt road, near the edge of the forest. Sometimes you can ask the local Corporación Hondureña de Desarollo Forestal (COHDEFOR) forestry office for advice on guides, or just start asking around town. Rates are usually around US$10 per day, plus food for the guide.

Safety

The countryside of Honduras—areas accessible by foot only, not by vehicle—is normally quite safe from criminals, which only stands to reason: What kind of thief is going to bother venturing out into the mountains to rob dirt-poor *campesinos?* Once you are on the trail, you can stop worrying about *banditos* and start paying attention to finding your way and enjoying the scenery.

It is true, however, that certain rural highways are known for holdups and assaults. Particularly bad spots include western Olancho, northeastern Olancho around Dulce Nombre de Culmí, the highway in Olancho near San Esteban, parts of the north coast, and northern Francisco Morazán. These concerns are discussed in more detail in the destination chapters, and it is always smart to ask about current conditions when you arrive.

Natural dangers are always present when hiking and are no different in Honduras than most parts of the world. Bring sufficiently warm and dry clothes, enough food and water, a first-aid kit, a good tent to protect you from the elements and creepy-crawlies (or at least a jungle hammock), and—the basic rule of hiking—watch where you step!

Protected Areas

According to the government, the country's 107 actual or proposed protected areas—*parques nacionales* (national parks), *refugios de vida silvestre* (wildlife refuges), *reservas biológicas* (biological reserves), and the two *reservas de la biosfera* (biosphere reserves)—make up 24 percent of Honduran territory. Though this may seem an astoundingly large percentage for such a poor, undeveloped country, the reality is that many of the "protected areas" are merely lines on a map in some bureaucrat's office. Faced with a chronic lack of staff and enforcement ability, the government department in charge of most reserves, COHDEFOR, does little to stop the invasion of land-hungry peasants, cattle herds, and loggers into protected areas. Luckily, Honduras's rugged mountains and relatively low population have helped where the authorities have come up short, but that won't work for many more years. NGOs have started to spring up to help protect specific reserves, and their very existence seems like a positive sign for the future of the parks.

Most of the natural reserves were established in 1987, when Congress passed a law declaring all land above 1,800 meters in elevation to be a national park. The reserves are composed of a central *zona nucleo* (core zone), meant to be untouchable, and a surrounding *zona de amortiguamiento* (buffer zone), where some agriculture and hunting are allowed, depending on the area.

A number of the Peace Corps volunteers in Honduras—there are hordes of them—are involved with developing certain protected areas as tourist attractions. They have been hard at work drawing up maps, marking trails, building visitors centers, and training guides. The volunteers are often the best sources of information on ways to get into a certain forest and on the flora, fauna, and other sights to look for there.

Cloud Forests

A dense mountaintop forest with towering trees covered with lianas, vines, bromeliads, mosses, and ferns, all wrapped in mist and dripping wet most of the year, the cloud forest is a unique and magical ecosystem. Although the cloud forests of Costa Rica and Guatemala receive more publicity, Honduras has conserved considerably more virgin cloud forest than either of those countries.

Probably the most-visited cloud-forest parks in Honduras, because of the ease of access, are **Parque Nacional La Tigra,** just outside of Tegucigalpa, and **Parque Nacional Cusuco,** near San Pedro Sula. Both parks have visitors centers and clearly marked trails, allowing even inexperienced hikers to enjoy the forest and look for birds without fear of getting lost. The forests at La Tigra and Cusuco are not the most pristine, having been logged earlier in the century, but sizable, dense forest has returned, along with nearly 200 species of birds (including the popular quetzal), a variety of mammals, and countless reptiles and insects.

Four much more impressive cloud-forest parks with developed trails that offer varying degrees of difficulty are **Parque Nacional Celaque,** near Gracias, **Parque Nacional Cerro Azul/Meámbar,** next to Lago de Yojoa in central Honduras, and **Parque Nacional Sierra de Agalta** and **Parque Nacional La Muralla,** both in Olancho.

Celaque has a broad stretch of primary cloud forest on its high plateau and can be accessed by casual backpackers along a well-marked trail with two campsites on the way. The highest peak in the country, Cerro de las Minas (2,849 meters), is in Celaque. The well-managed Cerro Azul/Meámbar has four developed trails, several nice cabins at the edge of the forest, and a visitors center with restaurant, all easily accessed from the San Pedro Sula–Tegucigalpa highway.

Sierra de Agalta is Honduras's most extensive cloud forest, followed closely by La Muralla, and, because of their remoteness, these truly spectacular forests and their animal inhabitants have been little disturbed by humanity. Getting to these parks is not so easy, but doable for those willing to rough it for a few days. **Parque Nacional Santa Bárbara,** just across the lake from Cerro Azul/Meámbar, also has pristine cloud forests in its core zone, but access is difficult. Smaller reserves in central Honduras, like **Corralitos, El Chile, Yuscarán, Guajiquíro,** and **Montaña Verde,** all harbor patches of little-visited cloud forest easily reached in an overnight hike.

On the lower edges of most cloud forests in Honduras, hikers will pass through stretches of pine and oak forest and small coffee plantations planted in the traditional style, among lots of wild fruit trees providing shade. Take the time to look around—patches of open area are often excellent places for spotting birds and small mammals.

Hiking sandals can be ideal for conditions in the Mosquitia.

The Mosquitia Reserves

The fabled Mosquitia jungles, the largest remaining broadleaf rainforest in Central America, are without argument the most incredible adventure travel destination in Honduras. The Mosquitia is in far northeastern Honduras, not connected (or only barely) by road to the rest of the country. Most trips to the Mosquitia begin by flying into Brus Laguna and then taking a boat trip upriver into the forest. Once in the rainforest, travelers will want to admire the incredible variety of plants and animals through a combination of cruising the river and taking side treks deeper into the forest.

Created in 1980, the **Reserva de la Biosfera del Río Plátano** covers 815,000 hectares of the densest, most inaccessible sections of tropical rainforest in the Mosquitia. The easiest way for visitors to get into the Río Plátano Biosphere Reserve is with one of the guide outfits leading tours into the Mosquitia. Trips can last anywhere from three days to two weeks; they include boating up the Río Plátano to the

village of Las Marías and then into the rainforest beyond, often combined with short hiking forays into the forest. La Ruta Moskitia is a community-based organization that provides quality tours. Two companies, La Moskitia Eco-Aventuras and Omega Tours, run rafting and hiking trips from the southern mountains of Olancho down the headwaters of the Río Plátano to the coast, an epic two-week trip.

Freelance trips into the reserve are very possible for adventurous travelers who aren't on a tight schedule. The best way to get there is to fly to Brus Laguna from La Ceiba and contract a boat across the lagoon and up the Río Plátano to Las Marías, where guides can be found to take you farther upriver or into the jungle. Trying to cross over from Olancho into the reserve independently with local guides is, however, simply unwise, both for the daunting natural obstacles and the rural violence prevalent in that part of northern Olancho.

East of the Reserva de la Biosfera del Río Plátano, along two sections of the Río Patuca in the Mosquitia and Olancho, are the

Reserva de la Biosfera Tawahka Asangni, covering 233,000 hectares of homeland for the small Tawahka indigenous group, and **Parque Nacional Río Patuca,** covering 376,000 hectares. Created in December 1999, these reserves are home to expanses of rainforest similar to the Río Plátano. The best place to go for guided trips into the rainforest on the Patuca is Krausirpe, the unofficial Tawahka capital, where you can find guides. Krausirpe can be reached either by a combination of plane to Ahuas and boat upstream from there, or downstream from Nueva Palestina in Olancho. Expensive charter flights into the Patuca region can also be arranged.

Tropical Forest Reserves

Just behind La Ceiba is **Parque Nacional Pico Bonito,** the largest park in the country after the Río Plátano Biosphere Reserve. Towering Pico Bonito (2,435 meters) is blanketed with some of the densest tropical jungle in the country. Almost no trails exist in the park, making it serious adventure territory. The jagged terrain and thick jungle hide a wealth of wildlife rarely seen by tourists. A much smaller coastal mountain reserve good for an easy hike is **Parque Nacional Capiro y Calentura** behind Trujillo.

Other patches of lowland tropical forest can be seen in the wonderful **Jardín Botánico Lancetilla** near Tela, around the shores of **Lago de Yojoa,** and behind the north coast wetland reserves of **Parque Nacional Jeanette Kawas (Punta Sal), Refugio de Vida Silvestre Punto Izopo,** and **Refugio de Vida Silvestre Cuero y Salado,** though these last three are usually visited by boat, not by foot.

Infrequently visited by foreigners, the highlands on the south side of the country near the Golfo de Fonseca and the Nicaraguan border contain some of the best-preserved **dry tropical forests** in the region. **Sierra de la Botija,** near San Marcos de Colón, has seven peaks over 1,500 meters, each with a small patch of cloud forest on top and primary dry tropical forest on the mountain flanks descending into Nicaragua. This almost totally unknown area, which may soon be declared a 10,000-hectare reserve, is the birthplace of the Río Coco, Central America's longest river, and is filled with waterfalls and wildlife.

Maps

Topographical maps of scale 1:50,000 covering the entire country are published by the **Instituto Geográfico Nacional** or IGN (tel. 504/225-0752 or 504/225-3755, 8 A.M.–4 P.M. Mon.–Fri.). Though accurate for terrain, the maps are not totally reliable when it comes to trails. The ones shown often (but not always) exist, but usually many more trails exist also.

The maps cost US$2 each and can be purchased at the IGN's central office in Comayagüela (Tegucigalpa) at the Secretaría de Transporte (SECOPT) on 15 Calle, one block east of 1 Avenida. Some sheets are out of print, but the office staff will usually make a photocopy for you. If your Spanish is up to it, you can write or call ahead for the maps; the staff will send you copies of the sheets you need (have the names handy) if you send advance payment for the cost of the maps and shipping.

It's also possible to get IGN topographical maps through **Omni Resources** (1004 S. Mebane St., P.O. Box 2096, Burlington, NC 27216, tel. 336/227-8300 or 800/742-2677, www.omnimap.com/catalog/int/honduras .htm) in the United States for US$10–15 per sheet. Its stock of 1:50,000 topos is about as good as at the IGN—about half of the series is available.

Equipment

While a visit to the coastal communities of the Mosquitia does not require much special gear, expeditions farther into the region do. Generally, no special equipment is needed for camping in the cloud-forest reserves. Just keep in mind it rains more in cloud forests than in the surrounding lowlands, so come prepared with rain gear, heavy boots, and a change of warm clothes kept in a waterproof bag. Tents are sometimes more practical than hammocks for sleeping because of the frequent rain. Specially designed jungle hammocks with mosquito-netting and plastic roofs are fairly ingenious devices, however, and many jungle trekkers swear by them because of the ease of finding a place to sling them and the comfort.

Machetes are not necessary for hiking the main trails in the more developed national parks, like Cusuco, Celaque, or Cerro Azul/Meámbar, but they are an invaluable tool to anyone really heading into the bush. You can pick one up in just about any *ferretería* (hardware store) for about US$3—and a *lima* (file) to keep your blade sharp for another US$0.75. Machetes are all fairly similar, with black plastic hand-grips, but vary somewhat in blade size.

Snakebite kits are a good idea, particularly in the coastal, tropical forests. Mosquitoes are everywhere in Honduras, especially in the lowlands and on the coast, so come prepared with repellent.

Canned food, pasta, and dried soups are available in local *pulperías,* but carry a few freeze-dried meals if you're planning a long trip away from civilization. Running water in the upper reaches of cloud forests is often drinkable, as long as you're definitely above any settlements or cattle-grazing areas, but use a filter or purification tablets anyway to be safe. A couple of drops of bleach in each quart of water also works to kill bacteria (but not necessarily all parasites).

White gas for camp stoves is difficult to come by in Honduras, so it's best to bring a stove that runs on gasoline or kerosene (like the excellent MSR XGK stove), or bring your own fuel. Be aware that airlines flying to the United States are growing increasingly difficult about taking camp stoves, and they are not easy to come by in Honduras.

BOATING
Wetland Reserves
In times past, almost the entire Pacific and Caribbean coasts of Honduras were lined with a maze of wetlands and mangrove forests, the majority of which have long since fallen victim to the machete. The remaining wetland areas provide habitats for howler monkeys, parrots, crocodiles, manatees, and myriad other creatures that hide in the tangle of vegetation along the waterways. Most tourists will want to take a guided boat trip, either with an organized tour outfit or by hiring a local boat, but it's totally feasible to explore these reserves independently in sea kayaks or canoes. Only a couple of places on the north coast rent sea kayaks, although with luck that number will increase soon. If all else fails, you could always find a local fisherman willing to rent you a wooden *cayuco* for a nominal fee.

On the north coast, on each side of the wide bay around Tela, are **Parque Nacional Jeanette Kawas (Punta Sal)** and **Refugio de Vida Silvestre Punta Izopo.** Between Tela and La Ceiba is **Refugio de Vida Silvestre Cuero y Salado,** on land formerly owned by Standard Fruit Company. Though not protected as an official reserve, the wetlands farther east in the **Mosquitia** are immense and in much better condition than wetlands anywhere else in the country. Boat tours are easily arranged in Puerto Lempira or Palacios.

Tucked into the more isolated fingers of the Golfo de Fonseca is **Refugio de Vida Silvestre Bahía de Chismuyo,** protecting a singularly dense and tall mangrove forest, well worth a day trip to visit if you're in southern Honduras. Boats can be found in Coyolito, near Amapala.

Rafting and Kayaking
Several of Honduras's many rivers have extensive rapids ranging from Class II–V and above (i.e., unrunnable), tumbling through boulder-strewn gorges lined with tropical forest, excellent for white-water adventuring. The best season for river-running is right at the end of the rains, December–February, but it's possible to raft just about any time on the north coast, which receives rain all year. Rafting and kayaking guide companies are all based in La Ceiba. While visiting kayakers can rent all the gear they need, they may wish to bring their own helmet or spray skirt along with them.

The best-known river in Honduras, and

one of the finest rafting and kayaking rivers in Central America, is the **Río Cangrejal,** right outside of La Ceiba, with four distinct rapids sections of varying difficulty and great beauty. Most rafters stick to the lower, "commercial" section, while kayakers head upriver to try their hand at the more treacherous and thrilling rapids, falls, and chutes of the other three sections.

Several other, smaller rivers pouring off the flanks of the Pico Bonito range near La Ceiba offer shorter but equally intense runs, like the **Río Zacate,** or the **Río Coloradito,** both just west of La Ceiba off the Tela highway. Getting to the put-in at the Coloradito takes a bit of hiking, but it's well worth it for five tumultuous kilometers of Class III–V rapids, suitable for kayaks only and with lots of scouting. East of La Ceiba, passing through the town of Jutiapa, is the **Río Papaloteca,** with several Class IIIs and a couple of Class Vs on its course toward the Caribbean.

Inland from La Ceiba, through the Río Aguán valley and up a dirt road heading south into the Olancho mountains, is the **Río Mame,** requiring at least two full days and support with pack animals. The river has several sections on its long course down into the Valle del Aguán, the upper ones with Class III–V rapids, for kayakers only, while the Class II–III lower stretch is okay for rafts. Roughly parallel to the Mame, some 40 kilometers to the west over the mountains in Yoro, is **Río Yaguala,** similar but with a heart-stopping *subterráneo* section, almost a full cave. Trips to the Yaguala take at least three days and are for kayakers only. The countryside out this way is spectacular.

Farther east, in the jungle-clad Mosquitia region, multiday trips lead down the **Río Sico,** starting in Olancho and coming out near the highway crossing at La Balsa. This is a good rafting trip, with some exciting but not too intense rapids and interesting scenery of homestead farms and cattle ranches amid remnant sections of tropical rainforest. Deeper into the Mosquitia are the **Río Plátano, Río Patuca, Río Mocorón,** and **Río Coco,** to name just the main rivers. All of these are great for multiday adventure rafting through tropical rainforest.

The Río Copán in western Honduras has a decent 12-kilometer run of Class III rapids running right past the Mayan ruins, a one-day rafting trip.

Yachts

Although not the top destination on the Caribbean boating circuit, Honduras has some wonderful places accessible only by private boat, like kilometers of unexplored reef in more remote parts of the Bay Islands and dozens of little-known cays off the Mosquitia.

Boaters will find only one full-on **marina** in all of mainland Honduras, Lagoon Marina right outside of La Ceiba, although it is up for sale and might not last long. There are 120 meters of jetty, with room for 20–25 sailing boats. Services include a fuel station, repair shop, and restaurant and bar on the weekends.

Out on the Bay Islands, yachts can tie up at the **Barefoot Cay** on Roatán, or at **Graham's Place** on Guanaja.

Elsewhere on the Bay Islands or in the ports on the north coast, boaters are advised to tie up at the main dock and look for the *capitanía del puerto* (port captain's office) to inquire about where to moor and find boat services.

The only inland body of water worth sailing is **Lago Yojoa,** 16 kilometers long by 8 kilometers wide and around 20 meters deep on average. Occasional regattas are held on the lake—contact Richard Joint at **Honduyate** (www.honduyatemarina.com) for more information.

SCUBA DIVING AND SNORKELING

Probably the most popular form of recreation with foreign visitors to Honduras, in terms of absolute numbers, is scuba diving and snorkeling on the Bay Island reef system. The diving around the three main islands and countless cays is unquestionably world-class, rated by some as the finest in the western hemisphere.

Another advantage to diving the Bay Islands

is the extremely low cost of certification courses and dive packages. Utila in particular has become a mecca for budget travelers looking for inexpensive explorations of the underwater world.

BEACHES

Although it has two coastlines, Honduras's prime beaches are all on the north, Caribbean coast. Truly superb stretches of powdery sand lined by coconut palms can be found all along the coast, from Guatemala to the Mosquitia region near Nicaragua.

The best "urban" beaches, where tourists can stay at decent hotels, are at Tela and Trujillo. Both have clean beaches right in town and easily accessible excellent beaches just outside of town. La Ceiba and Puerto Cortés have city beaches, but they're dirty and not particularly attractive. A nice beach, Playa Cienaguita, can be found just a few minutes outside of Puerto Cortés, on the road toward Omoa.

Visitors willing to take day trips or to rough it a bit in less-than-ideal accommodations will find the country's best beaches at villages between these four main towns. Many Garífuna villages are situated along idyllic beaches, including (from west to east) Bajamar, Miami, Tornabé, Triunfo de la Cruz, Sambo Creek, Río Esteban, Santa Fe, and Santa Rosa de Aguán. Basic hotel rooms are available in all these villages.

Much of the Mosquitia is lined with kilometers of wide open, deserted beach, though facilities are minimal. The Bay Islands also boast lovely stretches of beach. West Bay Beach in Roatán is about as fine a patch of tropical beach as you could hope to find, and the island has a couple of dozen others along its coastline. Utila only has a couple of small beaches on the main island, but several sandy cays just offshore. The north side of Guanaja has fine stretches of powdery sand, and the less-visited Cayos Cochinos are postcard perfect.

GAME SPORTS
Fishing

Honduras boasts some of the finest deep-sea, flats, and lagoon fishing in all of Central America, rivaling its better-known neighbor Costa Rica. Not many tournaments are staged in Honduras, nor have world records been posted off its coasts, but some gargantuan tarpon are known to be lurking in the waterways around the Mosquitia in eastern Honduras, and hefty sailfish abound in the waters around the Bay Islands.

Fishing charters are easily arranged in the Bay Islands, either with outfits specifically catering to tourists, or less formal day trips (bring your own gear) arranged with local boats. Frequent catches include kingfish, marlin, king and Spanish mackerel, bonito, wahoo, blackfin tuna, red snapper, barracuda, and the occasional shark. Flats fishing is also excellent in shallow sandy areas around the islands, like south of Barbareta of eastern Roatán. Favorite targets are bonefish, 2–4 kilos of wily, recalcitrant muscle, and permit, as well as snapper and tarpon.

The dedicated sport fisher out for really big fish may want to consider a weeklong trip to the Mosquitia, going for one of those 45-kilo tarpon frequently caught (and released) there. The best tarpon season is February–May. Snook are also common in the Mosquitia, and while not as big as tarpon, they put up quite a fight for their size. **Team Marin Honduras** (www.teammarinhondurasfishing.com) offers organized trips in the region.

The best inland fishing is at Lago de Yojoa, Honduras's largest natural lake. Tilapia were introduced to the lake years ago and a sizable population took hold. Then the lake became a major fishing destination and overfishing depleted stocks. Because of stricter regulations, the population is on the rebound. The only place offering organized fishing trips on the lake is **Honduyate** (www.honduyatemarina.com) on the San Pedro Sula–Tegucigalpa highway right on the lakeshore, at highway kilometer marker 162 near the village of Monte Verde. Honduyate has fishing gear available to use. Trips might also be arranged at the **Hotel Agua Azul** (tel. 504/9991-7244 or 504/608-3671). Those with their own gear can negotiate trips with local boats in the village of Las

Marías or Peña Blanca, on the west and north sides of the lake.

Hunting

Hunting for game in Honduras is more a practice of survival for local *campesinos* than a sport, but foreigners are permitted to hunt in certain areas. National parks are off-limits. The Pacific plains around Choluteca are legendary hunting grounds for white-winged dove, but dwindling populations of the birds have led to restrictions. Hunting is now allowed only for migrant doves and only in certain areas. Deer, quail, wild turkey, and boar are common game in other parts of the country, particularly the Olancho and El Paraíso departments. Hunting season normally runs from the end of November to March 15.

For more information on hunting seasons, locations, and permits, check with the Instituto Hondureño de Turismo (Honduran Tourism Institute, tel. 504/238-3974 or 504/222-2124, www.letsgohonduras.com).

SPECTATOR SPORTS
Fútbol

More of a national religion than merely a sport, *fútbol,* known to North Americans as soccer, is played just about everywhere in the country. Players range from shoeless young men whacking a half-deflated playground ball around a dirt lot to first-division professional teams and beloved La Bicolor, the white-and-blue clad national team.

Honduras's league, composed of 10 teams, is one of the more competitive leagues in Central America, frequently sending players off to the Mexican league and even to Italy's fabled *calcio.* Going to a match is an inexpensive way to catch a glimpse of the fiery spirit lurking inside otherwise tranquil Hondurans. The league has two mini-seasons, February–June and August–October, with a championship determined through playoffs. The best teams perennially are Olympia and Motagua, from Tegucigalpa, and España, from San Pedro Sula.

When discussing the national team, watch out. Don't even think about making jokes about the team's ineptitude—this is no

laughing matter. Honduras is usually on the cusp of getting into the World Cup finals tournament, but not quite doing it (as in the 2008–2009 qualifiers for World Cup 2010).

A ragingly popular subset of Honduran soccer madness, *futbolito* is a miniature version of its sister sport. It is played with a small ball on a shortened field, often on paved basketball courts, and uses small cages as goals. Indeed, the sport moves more like basketball than soccer, with more importance placed on footwork and technique than strength and running. It is played in most towns, big and small, and leagues exist throughout the country.

Béisbol and Basquetbol

Both baseball and basketball are gaining popularity in Honduras. Bay Islanders are particularly fanatical about baseball and can be heard endlessly discussing the latest stats on major-league players in the United States. Surprisingly, a national basketball league was formed recently.

ENTERTAINMENT
Discos

It's a sorry town that doesn't have at least one disco where the locals can boogie until the daylight hours on Friday and Saturday. Larger towns and cities invariably have several, often near each other, and many are hopping Wednesday–Sunday. The north coast towns of Tela and especially La Ceiba are famed for their nightlife, and any visitor with a partying spirit should be sure to go out at least one weekend to check out the scene.

The favored music in discos is salsa, merengue, *punta,* American pop, *reggaeton,* and the occasional slow country tune. A few lounges in San Pedro Sula and Tegucigalpa play techno/house.

Discos usually don't get cranking until midnight or later, though in some smaller towns, festivities can start earlier. Fistfights and the occasional knifing are not uncommon but rarely involve foreigners, unless they do something exceptionally stupid like insult someone or try to pick up someone else's date. Almost all the attention you receive will be friendly, some perhaps unusually friendly. Male travelers shouldn't be surprised if they're approached by very forward young women in the discos. As you will be quick to note, unless you've had a few drinks, many are prostitutes. Foreign women can also expect to get plenty of attention in a disco, even if accompanied by a man. As long as you keep your wits about you and fend off the overzealous men with good humor, all will be well. Going to discos alone is not a great idea if you are a woman.

Pool Halls

Salones de billar, as pool halls are known, are common all over Honduras. They're not always the cleanest of places, and sometimes the players are a bit rough-looking but are usually friendly to the occasional foreigner who stops in for a couple of games and beers.

In the most common game played, simply called "pool," players line up the 15 balls around the side of the table, potting them in numerical order. The shelves on the wall are for each player to keep track of the balls he or she has sunk, and at the end, players add up their point total based on the face value of the balls. Any number of people can play. Eight-ball is common enough for most pool halls to have a triangle, but it is not the game of choice. Players from the United States will notice the unforgiving narrowness of the table pockets.

Accommodations

Rooms in Honduras range from five-star luxury spreads in Tegucigalpa, San Pedro Sula, and the Bay Islands where you will be waited on hand and foot to a straw pallet in a hut in rural mountain areas. Most places to stay are somewhere in between, and vary in price mainly according to whether or not rooms come with fans, a/c, TV, private bathroom, and extra amenities. One new development is several ecolodges, from the luxurious to the backpacker, springing up in the beautiful countryside around La Ceiba and in the Mosquitia. Let's hope the trend continues, as this is just the sort of place Honduras could use more of. Lower-priced hostels for international travelers are also starting to become more common.

Tax on hotel rates is a whopping 16 percent. As a general rule, the tax is included in the rate in lower-end establishments, and added to the quoted rate at more expensive places. There are, of course, always many exceptions to any rule. For ease of comparison, we have calculated the tax for those who do not included it in their quotes, and added it in. *Note:* Some establishments charge the tax only if you are paying by credit card, not if you pay with cash.

Camping is possible and safe in many rural areas (always ask first), but designated campsites and RV hookups are nearly nonexistent.

HOSPEDAJES, HOSTELS, AND LOW-PRICED HOTELS

The vast majority of hotels in Honduras charge between US$3 and US$25 per night per person. In cities and large towns, the hotels—called *pensiones, hospedajes,* or simply *hoteles*—are often grouped near each other in the downtown area. In many smaller towns and villages, rooms at the lower end of the scale are the only choice. *Hospedajes* are often the bottom of the lot, and not necessarily clean or safe. Take a good look around before deciding to stay.

Rooms in cheaper hotels are extremely basic, often merely cement cubes with a fan, a light bulb dangling from a wire, and a bed of wildly varying quality. Take a look before you pay—key elements to check for are a good mattress, a working fan, hot water if you're supposed to have it, a quiet location, and, of course, cleanliness. With heat and mosquitoes common in many parts of Honduras, especially the north coast, a fan can be a key component to a restful night. Overhead fans are usually preferable as they stir up the air in the entire room and keep the nasty bugs at bay.

Budget hotels frequently offer the choice of *baño privado* (private bathroom) or *sin baño* (without bathroom; that is, shared bathroom). Taking a room *sin baño* is a good way to save a few lempiras, but be sure to wear sandals into the communal bathroom to avoid athlete's foot or other fungi.

The better quality low-priced hotels—there's usually at least one in every town—send maids out every day to scour the rooms and place fresh sheets on the beds. Many also have free purified drinking water in the lobby and provide pitchers for guests to fill up and bring to their rooms.

When a hot shower is offered, it's often in the form of an in-line water heater attached to the shower head called an *electroducha,* affectionately known among frequent travelers as "suicide showers." These contraptions usually (but not always) provide a stream of scalding water. Don't get too close to all those dangling wires unless you're looking for an unpleasant zap. The units can be so poorly wired they manage to electrify the entire showerhead. Beware.

Haggling over room price won't get you too far in the lower-end hotels, as prices are rock-bottom as it is, but it's worth it to ask if there's anything less expensive (*¿Hay algo más económico?*) than the first price quoted, since owners often assume a foreigner wants the best room.

While there are many cheap hotels, there are few that are backpacker-style hostels, with notable exceptions in San Pedro Sula, the Bay Islands, and Copán.

MIDRANGE HOTELS

Formerly limited to cities and major tourist destinations only, a growing number of good quality hotels falling into the inexpensive and moderate categories, charging between US$25–100 per night, have been springing up in Honduras in recent years. Most large towns have at least one moderately priced spot with air-conditioning, TV with cable, clean bathrooms, decent mattresses, private parking, and a restaurant or cafeteria of some type.

Travelers won't have much luck trying to negotiate a better deal for one or two nights, but discounts are frequently available for stays of a week or longer. It's usually best to talk to the owner or manager, rather than a receptionist, in attempting such negotiations.

Apart from the standard hotels and motels, more cozy bed-and-breakfasts and apartment-style hotels can also be found, particularly in San Pedro Sula, Tegucigalpa, and La Ceiba.

Prices don't vary much throughout the year in most of the country, but during Semana Santa (Holy Week, or Easter), and often over Christmas/New Year's, rooms are more expensive in the north coast beach towns of Trujillo, La Ceiba, Tela, Omoa, and Puerto Cortés, and on the Bay Islands. In La Ceiba, prices rise dramatically for the long weekend around the Feria de San Isidro, a famed carnival held each year in mid-May. Rates are higher in Comayagua during its famed Holy Week celebrations.

HIGH-END HOTELS AND RESORTS
Luxury Hotels

Full-service, top-class hotels are few and far between in most of Honduras, found only in Tegucigalpa, San Pedro Sula, Copán, and the Bay Islands. In the capital and in San Pedro, well-heeled travelers have plenty of options to choose from, including Marriott, Clarion, Camino Real, and others, as well as a couple of small, high-quality boutique hotels like Portal del Ángel in Tegucigalpa. Rates run anywhere from US$100 to US$1,300 for the finest suites. Rack rates are usually quite a bit higher than corporate rates, which are often available to ordinary travelers on request. Also, it's worth noting that many luxury hotels have weekend deals sometimes half the normal price, as many of the hotels' usual clients are businesspeople coming through during the week. Some of the more down-at-the-heels luxury spots, like the Honduras Maya in Tegucigalpa or the Gran Hotel Sula in San Pedro Sula, frequently offer their smaller rooms at a considerable discount if you ask.

Dive Resorts

Some of the finest accommodations in Honduras are to be found in these often supremely tasteful and blissfully relaxed resorts on the Bay Islands. Most offer weeklong packages including three meals a day, two boat dives a day, and unlimited shore diving for US$1,000–1,800 per person. Rooms are often freestanding *cabañas* set next to the ocean to catch the sea breeze, making air-conditioning happily unnecessary. As these resorts are eager to attract repeat vacationers, service is frequently extremely attentive. There are several resorts on Roatán, Utila, and Guanaja, and one on the Cayos Cochinos.

Beach Resorts

Although they've been talking about it for years, the north coast of Honduras facing the Caribbean Sea has yet to realize its promise as a tourist mecca. Very few high-end resorts are to be found on the north coast, though this will soon change as the Los Micos project west of Tela becomes a reality. The only currently existing large beach resorts in Honduras are the Palma Real Beach Resort, a luxury beach resort 20-odd kilometers east of La Ceiba, and La Ensenada resort near Tela.

Ecolodges

La Ceiba has become the location of choice for ecolodges in Honduras, and it's not hard to see why. In few places is a large city with excellent transport connections so close to several very fine natural areas, in particular the jungle-clad Pico Bonito National Park and the Río Cangrejal. The Lodge at Pico Bonito is the best-known ecolodge, but there are many others, at all price points. Rustic ecolodges have also been established on the coast of the Mosquitia near Brus Laguna, owned and operated by community cooperatives.

SLEEPING IN RURAL HONDURAS
Camping

Campsites and RV hookups have not yet made it to Honduras, so come prepared for primitive camping. In most areas in rural Honduras, this is no problem. Generally speaking, the countryside is the safest part of the country, and the worst hassle you can expect is to get pestered repeatedly by local *campesinos* to come have a cup of coffee and a chat with them.

When looking for a spot to pitch a tent, it's best to check around and see if you're about to set up on someone's farm. If so, ask permission: *"¿Está bién acampar aquí?"* Offering a few lempiras, or perhaps inviting the owner over to your camp for a bite to eat, is also polite.

The few campsites in the country can be found in some of the national parks, such as La Tigra, Cusuco, Celaque, Pico Bonito, La Muralla, and others. Camping is regulated in Cusuco and La Tigra but fairly laid-back in the other parks. If in doubt, stop in at the local COHDEFOR office and ask.

No special gear is needed for camping in Honduras; just come prepared for the conditions. Tents are best to shelter yourself from the frequent rain and cold weather common in the mountains, though jungle hikers may prefer jungle hammocks.

"Dar Posada"

In many villages in the central and western mountains, a few Garífuna beach villages, and in some parts of the Mosquitia, no hotels are available for travelers. No worries: Just ask around to find a family willing to put you up for the night. The key phrase is *"dar posada,"* or "offer lodging." Often one family is known to have an extra room and is in the habit of renting it out to travelers for a few lempiras (US$1–4).

Food

Honduras isn't known for its culinary specialties, but the discerning traveler will find plenty of ways to fill the belly and satisfy the taste buds at the same time. With the infinite variations on *plato típico,* the national dish, seafood dishes of the north coast, and the omnipresent and addictive *baleadas,* Honduran cooks do surprisingly well with limited resources.

Hondurans eat a light *desayuno* (breakfast) when they get up, a decent-sized *almuerzo* (midday meal) between noon and 2 P.M., and *cena* (supper) between 6 and 8 P.M. This, of course, pertains only to those Hondurans who can afford it—a good-sized portion of the population makes do on little more than some beans, rice, tortillas, and, with luck, a small piece of meat or vegetable.

WHERE TO EAT

Those restaurants in Honduras where you can expect table service and a menu are called *restaurantes.* In large towns and cities, you'll find high-priced restaurants offering international-style food, or at least creatively prepared Honduran standards. In smaller towns, hotel restaurants are often the best places to get a good meal.

Simpler places offering set meals at inexpensive prices are known as *comedores* (eateries) or *merenderos.* The best way to judge a *comedor* is to check the number of locals eating there—the more, the better.

Common in many larger Honduran towns, and on highways servicing buses and other drivers, are *buffet* restaurants, which are just what they sound like: an array of different dishes to choose from, priced depending on what you get, but typically around US$4 for a meal with rice, beans, salad, a main dish, and a fruit drink. These are often great places to fill up on veggies, if you're getting tired of all that meat and tortillas. It's always a good idea to get to buffet restaurants soon after they put the food out, when it's fresh and hot. If you don't drag yourself in for breakfast until 9:30 A.M.,

you may find the eggs looking rather haggard after sitting there for three hours.

Most town markets have a section with a few stalls inside serving inexpensive and typically good-quality breakfasts and lunches.

Ordering and Paying

Most sit-down restaurants will have a menu, called *la carta* or *el menú,* but smaller establishments often just serve what they happen to have. To find out the day's pickings, ask, *"¿Qué hay para comer?"* ("What is there to eat?").

When you are done eating, ask for *la cuenta* (the bill), or if the restaurant is a small eatery or food stand, ask *"¿Cuánto es?"* or *"¿Cuánto le debo?"* ("How much do I owe you?"). Tips are not common in most simple eateries, but 10 percent is expected at any midrange or more expensive restaurant. Some of the better restaurants will add a 10 percent gratuity to the bill, so check before you leave another tip.

WHAT TO EAT

The main meal in any Honduran restaurant is without doubt the *plato típico,* a standard combination of ingredients that can vary dramatically in quality but is always relatively inexpensive.

The centerpiece of the *plato típico* is always a chunk of beef, accompanied by fried plantain, beans, marinated cabbage, rice, a chunk of salty cheese, and a dollop of sour cream. Possible variations might include saffron rice instead of plain rice, well-prepared beans instead of canned refrieds, or yucca instead of plantain. Tortillas, usually corn, are served on the side.

A relative of the *plato típico* is the *comida corriente* or *plato del día,* also a set meal and usually a bit less expensive than the *plato típico.* The main course can be fish, chicken, pork, or steak, depending on whatever the cook got a good deal on that day. Fixings are similar to the *plato típico.*

In a country with a major cattle industry, it's

© AMY E. ROBERTSON

Most Honduran meals come heavy on the starch.

no surprise that beef is a staple of the Honduran diet. Called *bistec* or *carne asada,* the country's grilled beef is not always the finest quality—as with many products, the best is reserved for export. The country's second-most-popular meat is *cerdo,* or pork. You'll often run across a pretty mean *chuleta de cerdo* (pork chop) in Honduran restaurants.

Pollo frito (fried chicken) is also one of the most common dishes in Honduras. It's a rare bus stop or small town that doesn't boast at least one restaurant specializing in fried chicken. One of the more creative and tasty Honduran meat dishes is *pinchos,* a sort of shish kebab typically made with skewered and grilled vegetables and chunks of marinated beef.

A good appetizer is *anafre,* an ingeniously heated clay pot holding refried beans with cheese and cream, to be eaten with *tostadas* (toasted tortilla chips).

A favorite Honduran soup is *tapado,* a vegetable stew often served with beef or sometimes fish. Another, which the squeamish will want to avoid, is *mondongo,* or tripe (intestine) stew

served in beef broth with cilantro and potatoes or other vegetables.

When on the north coast, the Bay Islands, or near Lago de Yojoa, be sure to take advantage of the very tasty *pescado frito,* or fried fish. Some of the Garífuna villages on the north coast also whip up a superb grilled red snapper with rice and vegetables. On the Bay Islands, locals are fond of skewering a variety of fish and making a stew called *bando* with yucca, other vegetables, and lots of spice. Another traditional Garífuna fish soup is *machuca,* with bananas and plantains.

Langosta (lobster), *camarones* (shrimp), and *caracol* (conch) are all commonly eaten on the north coast, though supply may be limited by the tight restrictions recently adopted to protect the dwindling shellfish population. One superb north-coast specialty is *sopa de caracol,* or conch stew, made with coconut milk, potatoes, and sometimes curry. Several restaurants in Tela make mouthwatering *sopa de caracol.*

Main meals are almost always served with a basket of warm tortillas, thin dough pancakes

THE SWEET AND THE SOUR

Those poor souls who have only tasted the pineapples imported to the United States and Europe are in for a taste sensation after slicing into their first fresh Honduran *azucarrón* pineapple.

The name – which roughly translates as "super-sugary" – hints at the mouthwatering pleasures to come. Many foreigners, long convinced they didn't like pineapple at all, have been known to become utterly addicted to the *azucarrón*, buying a fresh one at the market every morning and getting deliciously messy gobbling it down. The high sugar content that gives the *azucarrón* its succulent taste is also the reason it never makes it out of the country. The sugar content is so high that the fruit ripens quickly and can't survive the journey to foreign markets without going bad. Fruit companies have long tried to develop varieties that taste the same but won't ripen so fast, but have yet to succeed.

Don't have a sweet tooth? Don't worry, Honduras certainly has the fruit for you. The nance is a small yellow-orange fruit that grows in clusters on a tree; it's deceptively cute and harmless-looking. Bite in. It's been called "cherry's evil twin." We find the most accurate description of its flavor to be "like vomit in your mouth." Try it if you dare.

usually made from corn but sometimes from wheat flour. The unaccustomed palate often needs time to adjust to corn tortillas, but once converted, the taste buds will crave the solid, earthy taste. Beans and rice are also frequent accompaniments to a meal.

On the north coast, North American and Garífuna influences have made tortillas less common, and you may find meals accompanied by delicious *pan de coco* (coconut bread), a Garífuna specialty.

Breakfast

The standard Honduran breakfast consists of *huevos* (eggs), tortillas, a chunk of salty cheese, a slice of fried ham, and a cup of strong, sweet Honduran coffee. Eggs are normally cooked *revueltos* (scrambled) or *estrellados* (fried).

Western innovations like corn flakes and pancakes, frequently served with honey instead of syrup, are on the rise in Honduras but are not common in smaller towns.

A reliable, low-priced breakfast is a cup of strong black coffee with a sweet bread or *tamal*.

Snacks

Travelers searching for the Honduran equivalent of the Mexican taco will be pleased to discover *baleadas,* the snack food of choice. *Baleadas* are flour tortillas filled with beans, crumbly cheese, and a dash of cream, then warmed briefly on a grill. Sometimes they throw in scrambled eggs and/or guacamole for a bit extra. Cheap and filling, *baleadas* make a good, light midday meal.

Also common are *pupusas,* a snack of Salvadoran origin consisting of thick tortillas filled with sausage and/or cheese, and tamales (also *nacatamales*), cornmeal stuffed with pork, olives, or other ingredients, then wrapped in a banana leaf and boiled. North American–style *hamburguesas* are extremely popular, especially on the north coast. And Mexican munchies like tacos, *tortas,* and quesadillas are common.

Rosquillas, crunchy bread rings, are popular for dunking in the omnipresent cup of strong black coffee. The town of Sabanagrande, between Tegucigalpa and Choluteca, is particularly known for *rosquillas.* And just about every town in Honduras has a *repostería,* a sweetbread bakery that also serves coffee and sodas, perfect for an afternoon break.

Often sold in street stands are *tajadas,* fried plantain chips served in a small bag with a slice of lime or a dash of salsa. *Tajadas* are also sometimes served in restaurants with a salad of cole slaw and salsa. Sliced fresh fruit, such as pineapple and mango, is commonly sold at street stands, along with bags of nance, a small fruit described by one journalist in Honduras as "cherry's evil twin."

Vegetarian Food

With a population of dedicated meat eaters, finding vegetarian food in Honduras is not an easy task, but it's not impossible unless you are vegan (in which case, plan on cooking a lot). Quesadillas and *baleadas* provide excellent snacks, as does fresh fruit sold cut up and ready to eat by street vendors (try to get just-cut pieces). For main meals, you can often request plates of rice, beans, and cooked vegetables. Most cooks are happy to cook without oil if you ask them—it just never occurs to them that people might like it that way!

BUYING GROCERIES

The first word to learn when looking for groceries in most towns and villages in Honduras is *pulpería*. These all-purpose general stores might carry just a few canned goods, drinks, and candy, or might offer a full range of foodstuffs. Almost every population center of any size has a *pulpería*—in fact, if a village has only one business establishment, it's always a *pulpería*.

Every town of size also has a *mercado* (market), where you can find a wide variety of fruits, vegetables, and meats—the squeamish should brace themselves for the sight of raw flesh covered with flies. Produce is sold in *libras* (pounds) just as often as in kilograms, if not more so; be sure you know the weight before buying. When buying food by the pound, don't just pick up a couple of pieces and ask how much it costs—that's simply an invitation to get ripped off. Check the price per pound or kilogram and watch it being weighed. It's often worth asking a couple of stalls their prices before buying. Although prices are normally standard, some vendors are not above trying to skim a few extra lempiras out of a naive-looking foreigner.

Western-style *supermercados* (supermarkets) are found only in large towns and cities. The produce here is often not as good as at the local

Look for groceries at the ubiquitous *pulpería*, or general store.

Every town of size has a market, with a variety of vegetables, fruits, and meats.

market, but their draw is a large selection of packaged foods, especially imported ones.

Tortillas can be bought in bulk at neighborhood *tortillerías,* which make them fresh daily. Good bread is not always easy to come by in Honduras; what's available can be found in *panaderías.* Sweet breads and cookies are more common than sandwich-style loaf breads, as most Hondurans eat tortillas.

BEVERAGES
Nonalcoholic Drinks

The coffee addict will be pleased to hear that Hondurans brew a mean cup of joe, most often served black with lots of sugar. In contrast to that in Guatemala, most of the coffee is actually brewed from beans; even in inexpensive *comedores,* a fresh cup is more common than Nescafé. If you take milk, be sure to ask for it on the side, as it is not normally served. Tea is much less common but can be found in better restaurants.

Freshly squeezed fruit juices, sometimes blended with milk or other ingredients, called *licuados,* can be found all across the country and make a filling midday snack that could be substituted for lunch. Often, they're served with a sprinkle of nutmeg or cinnamon on top and a healthy dose of sugar. If you don't want either, be sure to advise the proprietor beforehand. Generally, the milk is prepackaged and pasteurized, but you may want to check first to be sure. You can also get *combinados,* various fruits mixed with orange juice or other juices, or with add-ins like peanuts, corn flakes, and wheat germ.

Refrescos can refer to soda pop as well as to fresh fruit juice mixed with water and sugar. In most establishments these are mixed with purified water, but again, check first. Two particularly tasty mixes are *mora* (blackberry juice) and *horchata,* a rice drink with cinnamon. Cartons of processed orange juice are available all over the country, but fresh-squeezed orange juice is surprisingly hard to find. Better to do what most Hondurans do—buy the cheap oranges sold everywhere on the street, cut in half and with most of the rind shaved off to allow better squeezing as you suck out the contents. Oranges usually cost two or three lempiras, 10 or 15 cents.

Tap water is rarely safe to drink in Honduras, outside of a few luxury hotels that have their own in-line purifiers. In rural areas, most towns chlorinate their water, meaning the majority of buggies are dead, but treatment seems to be haphazard. One Peace Corps volunteer working in water sanitation commented that sometimes the person in charge won't get enough money from the town for chlorine one month or just might not get around to using it. So while drinking the water might usually be safe, it hardly seems worth the risk, considering the dysentery and other nasty ailments common in Honduras.

Many hotels, even less expensive ones, buy large bottles of purified water and keep them in the lobby for guests. Agua Azul is a popular brand of purified water sold in containers of various sizes. Be environmentally aware: Don't buy lots of small plastic bottles and throw them away. It's better to buy a gallon or liter jug and fill it up at your hotel (ideally, bring a high-quality water bottle from home to use, as the low-quality bottles available in Honduras aren't great for longer-term use). This saves you money and saves Honduras a lot of plastic garbage, of which it has plenty already.

Alcohol

All the main brands of *cervezas* (beers) brewed in Honduras are made by the same company, Cervecería Nacional. Port Royal is a lager sold in a green bottle with a colorful label, and the heavier Salva Vida ("Lifesaver") is sold in a dark-brown bottle. Brewed in Tegucigalpa, Imperial is the beer of choice for the cowboy country of central Honduras and Olancho. Going into a *cantina* in Olancho and asking for a Port Royal or Salva Vida is like walking into a cowboy bar in the western United States and asking for a wine cooler. Also popular are the imported beers Heineken, Corona, and Budweiser.

Several varieties of *ron* (rum) of reasonable quality are distilled in Honduras, but other local spirits, such as gin and vodka, are nauseatingly bad. The local rot-gut liquor is *aguardiente,* either made in local stills and sold by the jug, or bottled by low-budget distillers and sold in liquor stores. The most popular variety is El Buen Gusto, also called Yuscarán for the town where it's made.

Local wines are not worth mentioning, but several foreign varieties can be found in better supermarkets and liquor stores. Avoid them on the north coast as they don't hold up well when stored in the heat.

A word about drinking establishments: Waiters in *cantinas* or inexpensive restaurants often leave the empty beer bottles on the table when you order more. This is merely a way to help with accounting at the end of the night.

Those who venture into the more remote parts of rural Honduras, particularly in the central and western regions, will note that many small towns and villages are dry. However, you can often find a *pulpería* selling beers on the sly if you ask around.

Tips for Travelers

VOLUNTEERING IN HONDURAS

An increasing number of foreign visitors to Honduras are coming not for a tropical vacation, but for a trip with more meaning. Honduras is a very poor country, and the motivated will find plenty of opportunities for volunteering time in a myriad of settings. Teams of doctors and nurses from Canada, the United States, and elsewhere frequently come to poorer parts of the country to offer basic medical care. Volunteers help out running orphanages and homes for street children, installing computer systems in local town governments, building housing and clean water systems, or teaching in local schools. Those with particular skills, like

RESPONSIBLE TOURISM

The North American Center for Responsible Tourism suggests that travelers keep the following guidelines in mind on their trip:

- Travel with a spirit of humility and a genuine desire to meet and talk with local people.

- Be aware of the feelings of others. Act respectfully and avoid offensive behavior, particularly when taking photographs.

- Cultivate the habit of actively listening and observing rather than merely hearing and seeing. Avoid the temptation to "know all the answers."

- Realize that others may have concepts of time and attitudes that are different from – not inferior to – those you inherited from your own culture.

- Remember that you are only one of many visitors. Do not expect special privileges.

- Learn local customs and respect them.

- Instead of looking only for the exotic, discover the richness of another culture and way of life.

- When bargaining with merchants, remember that the poorest one may give up a profit rather than his or her personal dignity. Don't take advantage of the desperately poor. Pay a fair price.

- Keep your promises to people you meet. If you cannot, do not make the promise.

- Spend time each day reflecting on your experiences in order to deepen your understanding. Is your enrichment beneficial for all involved?

- Be aware of why you are traveling in the first place. If you truly want a "home away from home," why travel?

health care, construction, computer skills, or the like, are most appreciated, but anyone willing to work hard can find a place to put themselves to use, and any native English speaker can find a place to teach English. Most situations will require volunteers to pay their own way, although some minimal housing and food may be provided.

Coming with an attitude for learning, rather than one of "benefactor," will open up many doors. Hondurans complain of volunteers that make no effort to interact with the locals or try local cuisine. The cost of a volunteer trip is often as much as a Honduran earns in six months. The best way to make sure that money is well-spent is by learning as much as possible and bringing that knowledge home to share.

One excellent clearing house for information on volunteering in Honduras is www.volunteerhonduras.com, with links to dozens of opportunities to work with NGOs and social projects in Honduras, as well as homestays with families accustomed to hosting foreigners. An international volunteer website with many links in Honduras is www.idealist.org. Many of the more socially active churches in other countries run projects in Honduras for any number of different causes.

People who volunteer their time quickly realize that lending a useful hand opens up an entirely different manner of relating with Hondurans, one that offers emotional and spiritual rewards far beyond a mere vacation.

STUDYING SPANISH IN HONDURAS

After the raging success of language schools in neighboring Guatemala, it's no surprise several Hondurans have set up schools of their own. Language schools can be found in Copán Ruinas, Santa Rosa de Copán, La Ceiba, Utila, and Roatán. Generally, the schools rate as fairly good to excellent, although teacher quality can be more varied. Prices are around US$150–220 per week, including five days of one-on-one classes, and around US$220 if room and board with a local family is included.

GAY AND LESBIAN TRAVELERS

Although legal, homosexuality is Honduras is a closeted affair. There are few resources for gay and lesbian travelers, and the attitude of many locals toward homosexuality is strongly informed by anti-gay Catholic and/or *machista* perspectives. Gay marriage and adoption were officially banned in Honduras in 2005, by a constitutional amendment written in backlash to the government's formal recognition of three gay civil rights groups a few months earlier.

There are eight gay rights groups in Honduras, with roughly 5,000 members. Comunidad Gay Sampedrana in San Pedro Sula is Honduras's oldest LGBT organization (they have organized an annual pride march since 2001), and it shares office space with the lesbian-rights organization Mujer Sin Límite.

San Pedro and Tegucigalpa each have a gay bar. While Roatán and Utila do not have any gay or lesbian bars, the international atmosphere in West End and Utila Town, if not exactly gay-friendly, is at least gay-tolerant, and may be a more comfortable environment for same-sex couples than much of the mainland.

There are a number of transgender sex workers in Honduras's major cities, and three transgender activists were killed in late 2008 and early 2009 in Tegucigalpa, raising fears of increased violence against the transgender community.

Organizations

Comunidad Gay Sampedrana and **Mujer Sin Límite** (tel. 504/550-6868, 2 Calle between 8 and 9 Avenida, Barrio Concepción) are in San Pedro Sula. You can also try contacting the director, Suyapa Portillo, via email at aisportillo@hotmail.com. Other activist groups include **Grupo Prisma** (tel. 504/232-8342, prisma@sdnhon.org.hn) and **Colectivo Violeta** (tel. 504/237-6398, alfredo@optinet .hn), both in Tegucigalpa.

Tours

Undersea Expeditions (U.S. tel. 800/669-0310, www.underseax.com) leads gay and lesbian dive tours to Roatán. Their tours are booked at the **Inn of Last Resort** (tel. 504/445-4113, U.S. tel. 888/319-3255, www .innoflastresort.com), which was on the market for a while but did not sell. Hopefully the resort will stay as gay-friendly as ever if the business changes hands.

WOMEN TRAVELING ALONE

While Honduras shares some of the *machista* culture widespread in Latin America, it is a reasonably comfortable place for a woman to travel alone, especially in the more touristed areas. Walking alone at night is not recommended in Tegucigalpa, La Ceiba, or San Pedro Sula, more because the vulnerability of a solo woman makes an attractive target for would-be muggers, rather than the possibility of sexual assault (which is certainly a possibility, but a much rarer occurrence). Day or night, purses or bags that can be carried across your body, rather than over one shoulder, are a good choice in San Pedro and Tegucigalpa, as they foil motorcycle-riding purse-snatchers.

As in much of Latin America, North American and European women are often considered easy conquests. Don't exchange glances or accept drinks if you're not interested. Going to bars or discos alone is certainly possible, but it's important to be sure that you'll be able to easily get a taxi when you're ready to go home. While plenty of Honduran women wear tight-fitting clothes and low-cut blouses, similar attire on a *gringa* will certainly attract attention, usually limited to cat-calls and whistles.

For those who haven't found a travel mate but aren't sure about going it alone, **Journeys International** (U.S. tel. 800/255-8735, www .journeys.travel) is an ecotourism company that organizes tours to many countries around the world, including Honduras. Some of the trips are women-only, and all tours welcome solo female travelers. **Scuba Diving Divas** (www.scubadivingdivas.com) is another

FESTIVALS IN HONDURAS

Attending a festival can be an excellent way to experience local culture. Just bear in mind while travel planning that some of the festivals occasionally change the date they are celebrated.

JANUARY

January 6: Reenactment of the Arrival of the Three Kings, in Ajuterique, Comayagua.

January 8: Town festival of Cedros, near Tegucigalpa, with no alcohol allowed (and hence very safe).

January 15: *Guancasco* between Ilama and Gualala, in Gualala, Santa Bárbara.

January 15: *Guancasco* between Gracias and Mejicapa, in Gracias.

January 17: Town festival of Belén Gualcho for San Antonio Abad, in western Honduras.

January 19-20: Town festival of Erandique held in honor of San Sebastián, with the Baile de los Negritos.

January 25: *Guancasco* between Ojojona and Lepaterique, in Ojojona.

January 25-February 4: Celebration of the Virgen de Suyapa, Honduras's national saint, culminating in a massive celebration at the basilica in Tegucigalpa.

FEBRUARY

February 2: *Guancasco* between Ilama, Gualala, and Chinda, in Ilama, Santa Bárbara.

February 2: *Guancasco* between Lejamaní and Comayaguela, in La Cuesta, Comayaguela.

February 8-10: Baile de los Diablitos, Comayagua, in honor of San Sebastián.

February 8-10: Coffee Festival, El Suyatal Village, near Cedros.

February 22: Town festival of La Campa in honor of San Matías, one of the best known in western Honduras, still with traditional Lenca elements.

February 23: *Guancasco* between La Campa and Belén, including the famous Baile del Garrobo, in La Campa.

February 24: Baile de los Negritos, Santa Elena, La Paz.

MARCH

March 2-19: Las Enramadas de San José Chiquito, in Nacaome, Valle.

March 19: Town festival of Copán Ruinas in honor of San José; starts the week previous to the 19th.

Third Sunday in March: Indigenous Music Festival, Nueva Celilac, Santa Bárbara.

Last week of March: Coyol Festival, Catacamas.

APRIL

Semana Santa (Holy Week): Easter (in March or April) is quite a spectacle in several cities in the country, frequently with elaborate parades throughout the week and beautiful carpets of colored sawdust and flowers on the streets for the processions to walk on. The culminating parade is the Via Crucis on Friday morning, with "Jesus" carrying his cross in a solemn procession. Places particularly known for Semana Santa celebrations are Santa Rosa de Copán in western Honduras and Comayagua in central Honduras. Tegucigalpa is working to revive its traditions as well. In the Garífuna towns along the north coast, you may be able to find the traditional dance Baile de las Tiras on the day before Easter. Yuscarán is famous for its Carreritas de San Juan (St. John's Races) early in the morning on Easter Sunday.

April 5-15: the Festival del Pino is celebrated in Siguatepeque.

Second week of April: Blackberry Festival in Opatoro, La Paz.

April 12: On this day in 1797, some 4,000 Garífuna were unceremoniously dumped on Roatán by the British, the beginning of their settlement along the Honduran coast. The anniversary marking this arrival is cause for great celebration in Punta Gorda, Roatán, with Garífuna from all over Honduras attending the event.

April 24: the Gran Romería Lenca is celebrated in Taulabé, Comayagua.

Last Sunday of April: Cantarranas hosts a festival of traditional foods, specifically ones that are in danger of becoming lost. Cantarranas is a short distance beyond Valle de Angeles. The town of San Marcos in the municipality of Santa Bárbara celebrates a family-friendly festival of traditional games, with lots of dancing and music.

MAY

May 3: There are celebrations in many cities and towns across Honduras for the Day of the Cross, but especially in the Garífuna town of Triunfo de la Cruz.

Second week of May: The Coffee and Flower Festival is celebrated in Las Selvas, El Paraíso.

Second Saturday of May: The Hammock Festival is celebrated in Langue, Valle.

Mid-May: Feria de San Isidro is *the* party in La Ceiba – a several-day bash culminating in a blowout Saturday night that attracts some 200,000 revelers from across Honduras and the Caribbean. The country may have other national celebrations, but the *feria* is Honduras's time to cut loose.

May 15: The city anniversary of El Paraíso is cause for celebration, with dancing, food, and cultural events during the Festival Cultural El Paraíso.

May 23 and 24: The Flower Festival is celebrated in Santa Lucía, Francisco Morazán.

End of May, beginning of June: Yuscarán, near Tegucigalpa, holds an annual Mango Festival, when the entire population of the area descends upon town to enjoy music, dancing and a hysterical type of polo contest using donkeys instead of horses.

JUNE

June 11: *Guancasco* between Villa San Antonio and Yarumela, held in Villa San Antonio.

Second week of June: Although the exact date varies from year to year, it is around this time that the Rain of Fish is celebrated in Yoro.

June 24: Town festival in Trujillo in honor of San Juan Bautista.

Last weekend of June: La Esperanza celebrates the Festival Gastronómico del Choro y el Vino, which celebrates two regional specialties: wild mushrooms and fruit wines.

JULY

Late July: The National Garífuna Festival is held each year in Bajamar, drawing Garífuna from Belize, Guatemala, and Honduras for a party of dancing and music. (Typically on the third weekend of July.)

July 25: *Guancasco* between Lepaterique and Ojojona, held in Lepaterique, Francisco Morazán.

July 26: The Milk Festival is celebrated in La Ceiba.

AUGUST

August 22: The Corn Husk Festival is celebrated in Nueva Celilac, Santa Bárbara.

Last Week of August: The Festival de Maíz (Corn Festival) is celebrated in Danlí.

Last Saturday of August: The Rosquilla Festival is celebrated in Sábanagrande.

SEPTEMBER

Second week of September: The Festival of the Milpa (Family Farm) is celebrated in Sulaco, Yoro.

Second half of September: Town festival of Marcala, with religious ceremonies, street parades, food stands, carnival games, and more.

OCTOBER

October 3: *Guancasco* between Texiguat and Liure, in Texiguat, El Paraíso. There is also a *guancasco* between Yarumela and La Villa San Antonio, held in Yarumela, La Paz.

October 12: Día de la Raza is celebrated throughout Honduras, in commemoration of Columbus's arrival to the Americas. There is also a Lenca festival of song and dance on this day in Intibucá.

October 17: The Fish Festival is celebrated in Amapala.

October 18: The Corn Festival is celebrated in Santa Elena, La Paz.

(continued on next page)

FESTIVALS IN HONDURAS (continued)

NOVEMBER

November 2: The Danza del Cikin is performed in the Chortí region around Copán Ruinas and Cabañas.

Third Sunday in November: The Bread Festival is celebrated in La Paz.

DECEMBER

December 6-14: Town festival of Choluteca, a fairly uninhibited bash with lots of food, music, and drinking.

December 7-14: Town festival of Juticalpa, in honor of the Immaculate Conception of María.

December 7-14: Town festival of Yuscarán, notable for (in addition to attending special masses) getting drunk, lighting off *bombas*, and a skinny dog contest.

December 8: Choluteca celebrates the National Festival of Cultures.

December 12: *Guancasco* between Gracias and Mejicapa, in Mejicapa, Gracias. Also, several towns host a Procesión de los Inditos.

December 13: *Guancasco* between Yamaranguila and San Francisco de Opalaca, Intibucá.

December 17: *Guancasco* between Lejamaní and La Cuesta, in Lejamaní, Comayagua. This day Lejamani also hosts the presentation of the Baile del Gigante.

---

company that organizes women-only diving trips to Roatán.

TRAVELERS WITH DISABILITIES

Anyone traveling with a disability in Honduras will quickly realize that there are very few allowances made for anyone less mobile. The international chain hotels in the major cities are the best bets for wheelchair-friendly rooms (one lovely exception is **La Casa Rosada** in Copán Ruinas, which does have one wheelchair-accessible room).

Internal travel by plane or bus can be a challenge, although flight attendants on local puddle-jumpers are certainly accustomed to helping those with physical disabilities on and off the planes. Hiring a van with a driver is an easy option in Tegucigalpa, San Pedro Sula, La Ceiba, and Roatán.

Given that medical care is not on a par with that in the United States, any kind of emergency could be much more difficult to address.

Flying Wheels Travel (U.S. tel. 877/451-5006, www.flyingwheelstravel.com) is a full-service travel agency that can make customized travel plans for travelers with disabilities who are traveling with able-bodied companions.

WHAT TO TAKE

Everyone has their own style of packing, depending on taste and what sort of traveling might be on the agenda. Packing light is always a good idea, especially if you're planning a lot of bus transport, but it's not such a big deal if you're planning on staying in one place or have a rental car. In terms of clothing, shorts, T-shirts, and lightweight shoes or sandals are standard equipment for the hotter lowlands and coast, along with a couple of loose-fitting, long-sleeved pants and shirts, both to fend off mosquitoes and to look presentable. In the higher elevations, pants and a sweater or light jacket for evenings are useful. Honduran dress code is fairly relaxed, but as with anywhere in Latin America, looking clean will get you a long way with officialdom and the like. Shorts are fine on the coast, but long pants are more common in most inland parts of the country, and women wearing short shorts will likely attract unwanted attention if worn anywhere other than on the beach.

Recreation Equipment: All scuba diving equipment is easily rented in any Bay Islands dive shop, but veteran divers will want to bring their own properly fitting masks and fins, and other specialty gear like prescription masks or your favorite gauge. For any hiking or boating excursion in Honduras, mosquito repellent, sunscreen, and a hat are musts. Rain can hit at any time in most of the country, so bring some type of light waterproof shell. Hiking trips require the requisite camping gear, most commonly a tent and lightweight sleeping bag. Hammocks (with fitted mosquito nets) can also be convenient, especially in hilly forests where it can be difficult to pitch a tent. If you're planning a hike, expect lots of mud.

Day hikes can often be done with sneakers, but boots are essential for multiday expeditions. Locals use cheap rubber Wellington-style boots, which are an option, though surely not orthopedically ideal. Campers will also want to bring some way to purify water, and plastic bags to keep things dry in the pack. Quality photographic supplies are expensive and rare in Honduras, so it's best to come with all you need.

Health and Safety

As an extremely poor, underdeveloped country, Honduras has its share of health and safety risks, and it doesn't have the best doctors and police to help its citizens or foreign visitors cope with them. Nonetheless, with a few basic precautions, travelers can greatly reduce their risk of falling ill or victim to crime.

Travelers might consider purchasing travel insurance before going to Honduras. Several types of insurance are available from many companies in the United States and Europe, covering different amounts of medical expenses and stolen luggage replacement.

COMMON AILMENTS

As in just about every country in Latin America, it's essential to watch carefully what you eat and drink. Tap water is absolutely never safe to drink; be sure to check that any water served at a restaurant or hotel is *agua purificada*. Be particularly aware of salads and uncooked vegetables, and make sure meat, especially pork, is well cooked. Eating street food is standard practice for many veteran travelers, but someone just coming to Honduras for a short stay may want to avoid it and save themselves a possible case of **diarrhea.**

If you do develop diarrhea, two courses of action are available: Eat as little as possible, drink a lot of water, and let the bug run its course (literally), or take medications such as Pepto-Bismol or Imodium. How effective Pepto is depends on what the problem is, while

Imodium essentially serves as a cork—not really what your body needs, but extremely useful when you have to go on a bus or plane ride when sick.

Food poisoning is also relatively common. Although it may appear severe at first, with vomiting and uncontrollable bowels, the bug will pass in about a day. Hole up in a hotel room with a good book, a bottle of water, and maybe a few pieces of bread, and expect to feel a bit weak for a couple of days following the illness. If symptoms persist, see a doctor—you may have dysentery. It's extremely important to stay well hydrated if you've got either food poisoning or diarrhea.

DISEASE
Dysentery

Dysentery is a health risk for foreigners traveling in Honduras and other underdeveloped countries. The disease, which results from fecal-oral contamination, comes in two strains: bacillary (bacterial) and amoebic (parasitic). Bacillary dysentery hits like a sledgehammer, with a sudden onset of vomiting, severe diarrhea, and fever. It is easily treated with antibiotics.

Amoebic dysentery, caused by an infestation of amoebas, takes longer to develop and is also more difficult to get rid of. The most effective cure is a weeklong course of Flagyl, a very strong drug that wipes out all intestinal fauna. During and after a course of Flagyl, it's important to eat easily digestible food until the body has a chance to rebuild the necessary bacteria used for digestion. Yogurt is helpful. Weak cases of amoebas can sometimes be treated with a half-course of Flagyl or other less traumatic drugs.

Symptoms for either form of dysentery are not unlike those for malaria or dengue fever, so see a doctor and don't try to diagnose yourself. One of the greatest dangers with dysentery is dehydration, so be sure to drink plenty of water if you even suspect dysentery.

Malaria

The *vixa vivax* strain of malaria is present in most lowland regions of Honduras, and it is common on the north and south coasts, the coastal regions of the Mosquitia, and on the Bay Islands. If you're below 1,000 meters, malaria can be present. Thankfully, the Aralen-resistant *P. falciparum* strain has not yet made it north of Colombia.

Symptoms of malaria include high fever, headaches, fatigue, and chills. If these symptoms are present, see a doctor immediately, as medical treatment is effective.

Opinions on how to cope with malaria vary wildly. The most frequent recommendation from doctors is to take 500 milligrams of Aralen (chloroquine phosphate) weekly. Some people react negatively to Aralen, experiencing nausea, rashes, fever, or nightmares. Stop taking the drug if you have these side effects.

In high doses, well above 500 milligrams per week, Aralen has been linked to retina damage and hearing problems. It's not recommended to take the drug longer than six months. If you're on Aralen, continue the course for four weeks after leaving malaria-prone areas. Some travelers, leery of using strong drugs on a regular basis, prefer to carry one powerful dose of Aralen with them to use in case malaria strikes, rather than enough for weekly doses. The problem with this solution is that while chloroquine alone serves as a preventative, *treatment* for malaria should be a combination of chloroquine and primaquine; the latter ensures that malaria doesn't remain dormant in the liver.

Antimalarial drugs are available in many Honduran pharmacies, no prescription required.

Other Diseases

Cholera is not uncommon in Honduras, particularly during the rainy season. The best way to avoid it is to be careful with your food and water, don't eat raw fish, and always wash your hands before eating.

The viral disease **dengue fever** is also a frequent health problem for Hondurans. It is treatable, and rarely fatal. The fever is contracted from the bite of an infected mosquito. Symptoms include fever, headache (especially behind the eyes), muscle and joint aches, skin rash, and swollen lymph glands. Known affectionately as "bone-breaking disease," it'll lay you out flat. Usually, the fever lasts 5–8 days, followed by about a week of the disease. Tylenol can help cut the fever and relieve headaches. Do not take ibuprofen or aspirin, as these can increase the bleeding if it turns out to be hemorrhagic dengue.

Hemorrhagic dengue, which can be fatal, is far less common, but does occur. Symptoms appear similar to classic dengue at first, which makes it essential to seek medical attention immediately for any of the above symptoms. Additional symptoms that may appear include bleeding from the nose or mouth, skin bruising, black stools, excessive thirst, and pale, cool skin. Rush to an emergency room if you have these symptoms, as they require immediate care. Hemorrhagic dengue is fully treatable if medical help is found within the first few days of the illness.

AIDS

After sub-Saharan Africa, the Caribbean Basin has the highest incidence of AIDS infections in the world. More relaxed, easygoing sexual practices and the frequent use of prostitutes by men are two prime causes for the quick spread of the disease.

AIDS is thought to have first arrived in Honduras in 1985; 2008 estimates put the number of HIV-positive at 28,000, although many believe the actual number of cases to be much higher. San Pedro Sula, in particular, has been hit hard by the disease. The government has stepped up publicity campaigns in the past few years and sponsored AIDS campaigns in the prisons, leading to a stabilization (or in some estimates, even a decline) in the rates of HIV.

Many HIV-positive prostitutes continue working, either through ignorance or the need for money. Should you choose to sleep with a stranger or newfound friend anywhere in the country, *use a condom!*

Health Information Sources

For more information on the health situation in Honduras, check the Centers for Disease Control and Prevention (CDC) Health Information for International Travel (tel. 404/332-4565, www.cdc.gov) or the International Association for Medical Assistance to Travelers (736 Center St., Lewiston, NY 14092, tel. 716/754-4883, www.iamat.org).

MEDICAL ATTENTION
Doctors and Hospitals

As might be imagined, the quality of health care in most of Honduras is low. Rural areas are particularly bad off, often with only a small, ill-equipped clinic to cope with several villages, usually staffed by a single doctor. Sometimes out in rural regions, you may happen across foreign medical brigades on temporary missions in Honduras. While their ability to treat chronic diseases is limited, they often provide much-needed, life-changing assistance, ranging from a pair of reading glasses to cleft-palate and club-foot surgeries.

In larger towns and cities, better clinics and hospitals can be found. Steer clear of the state-run clinics, which are inexpensive but also very crowded and can provide poor service. Smaller clinics are sometimes staffed by doctors with training in Mexico or the United States. The three largest cities in the country—Tegucigalpa, San Pedro Sula, and La Ceiba—each have good-quality private hospitals that can handle most ailments.

© AMY E. ROBERTSON

The largest cities have good-quality private hospitals, such as the Honduras Medical Center in Tegucigalpa.

If you require special medical attention on a trip to Honduras, or want a doctor to come along with your group, contact **Emergency Medical Services** (tel. 504/552-2255 or 504/557-0080, www.honduras.com/EMS) in San Pedro Sula on 5 Calle at 11 Avenida NO. Red Cross ambulances can be reached by dialing 195 in most cities; payment is due at time of transport.

Pharmacies

Most basic pharmaceutical drugs are available in Honduras, many without a prescription. Almost all are generic versions manufactured in Mexico and Guatemala. Nevertheless, it's always best to bring an adequate supply of any prescription medication you require, including blood-pressure medicine, insulin, epilepsy drugs, birth-control pills, and asthma medication. Keep in mind that allergies may be triggered by unfamiliar allergens encountered in a new environment.

Pharmacists in Honduras are much less demanding about prescriptions for medication, and in fact frequently prescribe to clients who describe their symptoms. Although this can be convenient, particularly for simple problems, you are also taking a chance. There are drugs available that are not FDA-approved, and for good reason; and both pharmacists and doctors have been known to prescribe combinations of medicine that while fine separately, together are contraindicated. Also, tolerance to antibiotics is a growing problem as a result of over-prescription of powerful antibiotics by pharmacists.

Pharmacies in Honduras normally operate on the *turno* system, in which one local shop stays open all night for emergencies on a rotating basis. Often the *turno* pharmacy of the night is posted on a sign in the downtown square. If not, ask at your hotel, or look for a listing in the local newspaper.

VACCINES

No vaccines are required to enter Honduras, but travelers should be up to date on their rabies, typhoid, measles-mumps-rubella (MMR), tetanus, and yellow-fever shots. A hepatitis vaccine is now on the market, taking the place of the questionable gamma globulin shot. For hepatitis A, getting two shots of Havrix six months apart is now recommended. For hepatitis B, the recommendation is three shots of Engerix over the course of six months. Each course of Engerix shots is good for three years.

BITES AND STINGS
Mosquitoes and Sand Flies

Mosquitoes are found just about everywhere in Honduras and can be particularly bothersome during the rainy season. Everyone has a favorite method for dealing with the bloodsuckers. It's hard to beat a thick coat of DEET, but many travelers are loath to put on such a strong chemical day after day, especially on a long trip. There are many natural repellents available, including in Honduras (look for Cactus Juice on Roatán, or Nuvy's Repelente de Insectos in grocery stores and pharmacies on the mainland). Best of all are loose, long-sleeved shirts and light pants, with socks.

Sand flies, or *jejenes,* can be a plague on the Bay Islands, depending on the season and the wind level. Insect repellent will keep them away, and some swear by Avon Skin-So-Soft lotion, which is sold on the islands. The bites are annoying but will usually stop itching quickly if not scratched. As their name suggests, sand flies live on the sand and can be avoided by swimming, sunning yourself on a dock over the water, or just staying away from the beach. A few spots on the islands are known to be free of the pests, and on Roatán and Utila the government has started spraying some areas with environmentally friendly products to eradicate them. Sand flies are generally not as much of a problem on mainland beaches.

Ticks

First, the good news: Lyme disease is not present in Honduras. However, incredibly itchy little ticks, known locally as *coloradillas,* inhabit pastures in rural areas of Honduras. They normally live off cows and donkeys, but are in no way averse to infesting the flesh of an unsuspecting backpacker who decides to camp in a pasture because it's the only clear land around for the tent. You will likely not see them at all, as the ticks are tiny—practically microscopic. If they get into you, the itching starts a day or two later and is usually concentrated around the ankles and the waist area, though they can spread everywhere if given a chance. The torture doesn't go away for at least a week, and sometimes lingers for several weeks, long after the little buggers are dead. Some topical creams are helpful in alleviating the infestation and itching.

Larger ticks, called *garrapatas,* are found also. The best way to get rid of them is to pull out their heads with tweezers as soon as possible. You can also rub the spot first with a strong alcohol like *aguardiente,* which should make the beastie come out easier. Make sure you get the whole tick out, to avoid infection. Ticks favor warm, moist environments, like armpits, the scalp, and pubic hair.

Chagas' Disease

The chronic Chagas' disease, caused by the parasite *Trypanosoma cruzi,* is transmitted by the bite of certain bloodsucking insects (notably the assassin bug and conenose) found from southern Texas through South America. The disease is estimated to affect 12 million people in the Americas. The bugs prefer to bite while victims are asleep and usually bite the victim's face. While taking in blood, the bugs often deposit feces, which transmits the disease to the victim's bloodstream. Such bug bites are common in Honduras, but before panicking, note that only about 2 percent of those bitten will develop Chagas' disease. Young children are the most susceptible.

After an initial reaction of swollen glands and fever, 1–2 weeks after the bite, the disease goes into remission for anywhere from 5–30 years, with no symptoms apparent. It may, in fact, never reappear, but if it does, the disease causes severe heart problems sometimes leading to death. There is no cure for Chagas' disease.

To avoid Chagas', avoid being bitten. The bugs are most prevalent in rural areas, often living among dead palm fronds or piles of wood. If you are sleeping in a thatched-roof hut and do not have a mosquito net, try to cover your face with a cloth or put on a bug repellent containing DEET. A spray of pyrethrin insecticide will kill the bugs. If staying in an old hotel, check the room carefully for bugs, including under the mattress.

Chagas' is present in all departments of Honduras except the Bay Islands and Gracias a Dios (the Mosquitia). Infestation is minimal in Atlántida, Colón, and Yoro, while it is a particular problem in Intibucá and parts of Olancho.

Snakes, Bees, Scorpions, and Roaches

Honduras has its share of scorpions, wasps, bees (including the aggressive Africanized honey bee), and poisonous snakes. Most of the dangerous snakes live in the tropical forests of the Atlantic coast, particularly in the jungles of the Mosquitia, where pit vipers (including the deadly fer-de-lance) and coral snakes are common dangers.

The fer-de-lance is considered one of the most venomous snakes in the world. Bites are fatal unless the victim receives medical help within a few hours after being bitten. The fer-de-lance is easy to spot by the bright patch of yellow under its throat, a marking that earned it the nickname *barba amarilla* (yellow beard). Other poisonous snakes include the black-, red-, and white-striped *coral,* or coral snake, and the *cascabel,* or rattler.

When hiking in the jungle, wear boots and long pants. Watch where you put your feet, and if possible, let a guide precede you. Be particularly careful around piles of dead wood or stones, which offer shade to snakes during the day. Jungle lore holds that fer-de-lance are most frequently found near water holes and light gaps created by fallen trees.

While roaches are generally harmless, a friend of ours who is a triage doctor at the public hospital in Tegucigalpa reports having to remove roaches from patients' ears on a not-infrequent basis. (If somehow you are unlucky enough to have a roach in your ear, and are far from medical care, know that you must drown the roach in order to remove it safely from the ear.) If you are staying somewhere that you know or believe might have roaches, tuck a tiny wad of tissue into each ear to avoid this problem.

SAFETY
Crime

Street crime is a growing problem in Honduras, although it is still nothing on the level of most U.S. cities, despite recent bad publicity. La Ceiba has taken the honor of the city with the highest murder rate in the country, followed by San Pedro Sula and then Tegucigalpa. A particular problem are the *maras,* young gang members, frequently drugged out, armed, and with no fear of anybody. However, if you are unlucky enough to be confront by a *marero* (or other thug for that matter), what they are interested in is to steal your belongings, and rarely further harass. Give over your possessions without saying a word, and you can usually avoid problems. Your passport or your money is not worth being pistol-whipped (or worse) over.

To avoid problems, simply take the same precautions any sensible traveler takes anywhere. Don't walk around with a lot of money in your pocket or flashy jewelry; keep copies of your passport somewhere safe; don't walk around at night in cities; and avoid seedy areas during the day. On the beach, don't bring a lot of stuff with you, to avoid tempting thieves while you're in the water. And, very importantly, don't walk isolated stretches of beach outside of the towns on the north coast. A tourist police force was created in 2000 that now has units in Tegucigalpa, San Pedro Sula, Tela, La Ceiba, Roatán, Copán Ruinas, and Puerto Cortés, whose members are happy to help out tourists and are great people to talk to if you have any questions or problems.

The most high-profile crimes these days in Honduras are kidnappings, picking off family members of wealthy business people, cattle-ranchers, and coffee-growers, and holding them for ransom. Sometimes the victim is returned unharmed, other times not. Many Hondurans suspect former or even current military and police are involved in many kidnapping rings. To date, travelers are not targets for kidnappers.

For the most part, rural Honduras is remarkably safe. Foreigners can generally wander around at will with little fear. The mountain country in western and southern Honduras, in particular, is exceptionally safe and wonderful for trekking and backpacking.

There are a few exceptions to this, however. First and foremost are certain parts of western and northern Olancho, well known for their gunslingers and highway bandits. The two most important places to avoid are around Dulce Nombre de Culmí, near the edge of the Mosquitia rainforests; and the dirt highway between Gualaco and Tocoa. The roads from Tegucigalpa to Catacamas and from the main highway up to Gualaco are considered perfectly safe, but it is wise to ask for current information before traveling around La Unión and Yoro.

For the U.S. government's opinion on safety and travel issues in Honduras, check the site www.state.gov.

Drugs

Though not a major drug-producing country itself, apart from small-scale marijuana growers supplying the domestic market, Honduras is becoming a favored conduit for South American cocaine on its way north to the United States. The deserted, unpatrolled expanse of the Mosquitia coast is a choice drop-off point for Colombian drug smugglers, as are the Bay Islands. From the Mosquitia, the cocaine is transported overland through Guatemala and Mexico to the United States, while from the Bay Islands, the merchandise usually continues north by boat. But other parts of the country are used also—in September 1999, a helicopter ferried in a shipment of 369 kilograms of cocaine to a village near Yoro. Low-paid police, customs, and military officials are easy targets for corruption, and in recent years many have been arrested for their involvement with drug-trafficking.

The use of both cocaine and marijuana is illegal in Honduras, and the police will happily throw you in jail if they catch you. Drug-consuming travelers may assume they can easily bribe their way out of difficulties, and sometimes this is the case, but not always. As prison terms for drug use are stiff, it hardly seems worth the risk, not to mention it's irresponsible tourism because it adds to the country's already growing drug problem.

Police

Formerly known as Fusep (Fuerzas de Seguridad Pública), Honduras's police force was for many years a division of the armed forces, but in early 1997, it was finally placed under civilian leadership. It is now called the **Policía Preventiva Nacional.** A militaristic command structure remains in place, and the police still act more like a private army than public servants, but the situation seems to be improving slowly. Joint patrols with soldiers in more conflictive neighborhoods of the larger cities are common now, in an effort to combat the gangs and drug dealers.

Police generally receive little formal training and survive on abysmal pay, and many are undeniably corrupt and incompetent. If you are stopped for a traffic infraction or other minor offense, making an offer of a bribe would be a mistake. It's better to go through the proper channels, which often means paying a not very expensive fine. If the topic of a bribe were to arise (which of course does take place, but should not be encouraged), it should always be at the behest of the official, as offering a bribe to a straight police officer could get you further into trouble. This may seem silly to those who have a picturesque view of Honduran law enforcement, but some of the disciplined paramilitary officials at checkpoints on Honduran highways look like they might take a rather dim view of an offer of 50 lempira to look the other way.

If you are the victim of a crime, the police can sometimes be helpful, particularly in smaller towns where it's likely the culprit will be easily found. Police officers are usually happy to explain local laws or help tourists with directions. Of particular help are the tourist police in Tegucigalpa (tel. 504/222-2124), San Pedro Sula (tel. 504/550-3472 or 504/550-0001), Tela (tel. 504/448-0150), La Ceiba (tel. 504/441-6288), Roatán (tel. 504/9982-8542), Copán Ruinas (tel. 504/651-4108), and Puerto Cortés (tel. 504/9859-2822)—although don't hold your breath if you're hoping they might help recover stolen items.

Information and Services

MONEY

The national unit of currency is the lempira, often shortened to "lemp" by English-speaking Hondurans and expatriates. Bills come in denominations of 1, 2, 5, 10, 20, 50, 100, and 500 lempira, while coins are worth 1, 2, 5, 10, 20, and 50 centavos. Coins are worth so little they're more of an annoyance than an asset. A slang word for cash is *pisto.* At the time of writing, the lempira was trading at 19.1 to US$1. A good website for checking the current rate is www.xe.com.

Note: It can often be difficult to change 500 lempira notes, especially in smaller towns, so try to carry lots of smaller bills and change whenever possible. It's also better to avoid beaten up or torn notes, as they can be hard to spend.

EXCHANGE

Travelers to Honduras have the option of financing their trip with U.S. dollars, travelers checks (American Express preferred), expensive wire transfers, Visa or MasterCard cash advances, or through an ATM with various international networks.

Most banks in Honduras are open 8 A.M.–noon and 1:30–4:30 P.M. Monday–Friday, 8 A.M.–noon Saturday.

Banks or Black Market?

Exchanging money at banks is usually not an arduous affair, especially if you have cash. That said, in late 2008 certain banks began to adopt a policy allowing only account holders to exchange dollars. Banco Atlántida is one bank that continued to allow anyone to exchange dollars.

There are also authorized money exchangers (*casas de cambio*) at the airports, on the *peatonal* in downtown Tegucigalpa, and hanging out on 2 Calle SO in San Pedro Sula (although it's wise to only change small amounts with these guys, simply because you don't want to flash a lot of cash around).

In other towns and cities, certain shop owners are often known to change dollars. The rates offered are usually similar to the banks' rates. Transactions are quite open and safe, and not at all shady.

If you need to change lempiras into dollars, the black market changers are the best source. Banks have strict limits on how many dollars they are allowed to sell, and *casas de cambio* offer poor rates.

Travelers Checks

Any traveler on a long trip without means of accessing money on the road should bring travelers checks. However, be aware that travelers' checks are not always easy to change in Honduras outside of cities and tourist areas like the Bay Islands or Copán. If you are planning to travel in rural areas, be sure to change enough to cover your time away from the cities.

American Express is by far the most recognized travelers check—others, such as Thomas Cook or Visa, are more difficult to exchange. On rare occasions, banks may require you to show your original purchase receipt to change checks, so keep it with you.

The American Express agent in Honduras is **Mundirama Travel,** with offices in Tegucigalpa (at Edificio Ciicsa, corner Av. República de Chile and Av. República de Panamá, tel. 504/232-3943 or 504/232-3909, fax 504/232-0072) and in San Pedro Sula (next to the cathedral on 2 Calle SO, tel. 504/550-0490 or 504/550-1193, fax 504/557-9022). AmEx holders can purchase travelers checks with their card at these offices.

Credit Cards and ATMs

Visa and MasterCard are often accepted at the more expensive hotels and restaurants in cities and some large towns, as well as with travel agents, tour groups, and car-rental agencies. American Express is much less commonly accepted, and the Diner's Club or Discovery card even less so. In small towns and villages, credit cards won't get you much more than blank looks.

Visa holders can get cash advances from several banks, including many branches of Banco Atlántida and Banco del Occidente. **BAC Bamer** will also offer advances on a Visa and is the only place to go for those using a MasterCard. In general, the banks don't charge excessive commissions, if at all, but they usually offer a poor exchange rate. Unless you have a debit card link, the advance is then posted to your credit card account, where it begins to compound interest daily, rather than monthly like any normal purchase. So if you plan to use this method, find some way to make payments by phone directly with Visa (if your account is linked to a bank account) or with the help of someone back home immediately after the advance, to avoid wasting money. While both HSBC and Citibank have branches here, the systems are not linked internationally (as per Honduran law), although if you have a HSBC or Citibank account in another country, these may be the places where you are able to get the lowest transaction fees.

A number of **ATMs** now work with international networks. This is, in our experience, by far the easiest and cheapest way to deal with money in Honduras. The exchange rate is always the best available (outside the black market, which isn't much different), and, of course, it's very fast and convenient. Extra charges are not excessive (around US$3), and they're easily offset by taking out US$300 in lempira at a time, if the machine allows. Visa networks are available at the ubiquitous Banco Atlántida, while Plus and Cirrus are common in the bigger towns and cities.

Note: More than one traveler has written in about getting temporarily scammed, apparently by Honduran banks, through ATMs. The travelers used their card, but the machine said it couldn't give money and returned the card. However, they later learned their accounts had been charged the amount of the attempted withdrawal. In the end, the travelers were, through their home bank, able to get the matter dealt with, but not without a lot of hassle. For the record, we've never had a problem, and it appears to have been a couple of isolated instances. Keep an eye on your account anyhow, by Internet if possible, while on the road.

Sending Money

It is possible to receive **MoneyGrams** at Banco Atlántida in Honduras, while Western Union transfers are received at **Banco de Occidente** and at **Western Union** offices. Money can be sent and received at any Western Union representative—to retrieve the money, all you need is the transfer number and a passport. Money is received in lempiras, unless you have a dollar account with the receiving bank. These should only be used in desperation, as they charge exorbitant service fees and offer very poor exchange rates. If you must use them, the service fees are larger for smaller amounts of money—US$12–15 for US$100 sent, but only US$50 for US$1,000 sent.

COMMUNICATIONS AND MEDIA
Postal Service

Regular mail service (Honducor, or *correos*) between Honduras and other countries is, at best, a lengthy process. Street numbers are almost nonexistent in Honduras, even in Tegucigalpa and San Pedro Sula. Addresses are usually given as on "X" Calle between "Y" and "Z" Avenidas, or on "X" Calle next to the church,

etc. Miraculously, mail does get delivered, though expect to wait anywhere from two to four weeks to receive mail or have it reach its destination. Packages of up to two kilograms can be sent regular mail.

Many post offices now have Express Mail Service (EMS), which reliably sends letters and documents of less than 250 grams to the United States in 3–4 days for US$10–15, depending on the destination, or to Europe in 4–5 days for US$20–25.

It's possible to receive mail general delivery in any post office in the country. The letters should be addressed to your name, Lista de Correos, town, department, Honduras. A fee of a couple of lempiras is charged when the mail is collected. Usually, offices will hold letters a couple of months, or longer if you advise them ahead of time to await your arrival.

The best places to receive mail general delivery are in large towns—though mail may get lost in the chaos of *correos* in San Pedro Sula or Tegucigalpa, it may *never* make it out to small towns or villages.

Three of the big international couriers, **UPS, Federal Express,** and **DHL,** all have offices in the largest cities and charge a whopping US$35 or so to send documents to the United States in three days. Several low-priced courier services catering to Hondurans with relatives in the states, like **Urgente Express,** send letters to the United States in about the same amount of time, but for only US$3 or so, and are generally reliable. Within Honduras, packages can be sent quickly and reliably between most towns in one or two days for US$3–7 by **Expreco,** with offices all over the country.

Telephone Service

Hondutel, the notoriously inefficient national telecommunications company, has offices in every town. Efforts to privatize Hondutel have been ongoing for several years, but as of yet with no success.

The best way to place an international call is at an **Internet café.** Just about every Internet café in the country has telephone service now, usually charging around US$0.10 a minute

TELEPHONE INFORMATION

The following numbers can be dialed from any coin or private telephone.

INTERNATIONAL OPERATORS
8000-123 – AT&T
8000-121 – MCI

PUBLIC SERVICE AND EMERGENCY NUMBERS
191 – Long-distance national
192 – Information
195 – Red Cross ambulance
196 – Official time
197 – Long-distance international
198 – Fire department
199 – Police

CALLING FROM ANOTHER COUNTRY
504 – Honduras international area code

to the United States (sometimes more, sometimes less—shop around) or US$0.20 a minute to Europe—a huge discount from making calls with Hondutel or one of the international companies.

Many foreigners who spend some time in Honduras end up getting a **cellular phone,** because land lines are so problematic. You can get a phone for US$25 or less, and prepaid cards in amounts of US$5 or less. Tigo and Digicel are the leading service providers; just stop by any shop carrying their goods. Cell phone rental is available at the airport in Roatán.

Internet

Internet cafés are springing up all over Honduras at an impressive rate, with multiple cafés even in smaller towns, and sometimes even in villages. Rates are usually around US$1 per hour, usually prorated by the minute (although sometimes not, so make sure to check), with the exception of on the Bay Islands where service is more expensive (US$2–3).

Connection speeds vary dramatically but are usually more related to the time of day and system traffic than the quality of the hardware in different cafés.

Media

Newspaper reporting in Honduras is a simplistic affair, with little investigation beyond rewriting press releases, and often not even doing that accurately. Most stories are exceedingly short on hard facts and numbers and long on quoting the empty phrases of politicians. But local papers are nonetheless well worth reading to get a better feeling for the main events and trends of Honduran society. It's good practice for Spanish, too. The five main daily newspapers in Honduras are **La Prensa, La Tribuna, El Periódico, El Heraldo,** and **Tiempo.** All are owned by politicians (*La Tribuna* is owned by ex-president Flores) and tend to favor one or the other of the two main political parties. Some articles can be incredibly slanted. *La Prensa,* which is published in San Pedro, has more of a business angle and comes the closest to balanced coverage of national news. This paper also has 2–3 pages of international news, including some international sports coverage. *El Heraldo,* the main Tegucigalpa paper, also often features several pages of international wire copy.

Newspapers are usually sold on the street in small stands or merely on a designated street corner, and often sell out by midday. A welcome find for foreign travelers is the English-language weekly newspaper, **Honduras This Week.** Unlike many expatriate-oriented newspapers in the Americas, *Honduras This Week* covers issues of importance to the nation and doesn't shy away from touchy topics like corruption and the military. The paper also has useful information for travelers and interesting features. It's sold (or often given away) at higher-priced hotels and tourist-oriented stores. The newspaper has an excellent website at www.hondurasthisweek.com.

One good weekly newsmagazine in Honduras is **Hablemos Claro,** also online at www.hablemosclaro.com.

Eleven television and 176 radio stations operate in Honduras. The president's channel is Channel 8. Cable television is widely available.

WEIGHTS AND MEASURES
Time

Honduras is six hours behind Greenwich mean time and equal to central standard time in the United States. Daylight saving time is not practiced in Honduras.

Electricity

Almost all outlets in the country operate on 110 volts and are designed to fit two parallel flat blades. Sometimes a two-pronged round plug is required. A few outlets are 220 volts, but these are extremely rare. If in doubt, ask first.

Power outages and brownouts are frequent in Honduras, especially in the dry season when the El Cajón dam water level is low.

Measurements

Honduras has adopted a confusing mix of metric and nonmetric measurements. Old colonial *libras* (pounds) are more frequently used than kilograms as a unit of weight. Twenty-five *libras* equal one *arroba,* and four *arrobas* equal one *quintal.* One quintal equals 46 kilograms. Gas is sold by the gallon, but milk by the liter. Distance is measured in kilometers and meters.

Land sizes are often quoted in *varas,* equal to 838 square meters, or *manzanas,* equal to 0.7 hectare.

MAPS AND INFORMATION
Maps

Finding totally accurate road maps of Honduras is, unfortunately, an impossible task. Several decent maps correctly show the main highways but invariably mess up the placement of many rural dirt roads, while some incompetent cartographers go so far as to show main highways through tracts of virgin jungle and forest.

The **Instituto Geográfico Nacional** (IGN, tel. 504/225-0752) publishes a tourist map for US$3 that shows the departments, main roads,

---

PUBLIC HOLIDAYS

- **January 1** – New Year's Day
- **Week leading up to Easter Sunday** – Semana Santa
- **April 14** – Día de las Américas
- **May 1** – Labor Day
- **September 15** – Independence Day
- **October 3** – Morazán's Birthday
- **October 12** – Día de la Raza (Columbus Day)
- **October 21** – Armed Forces Day
- **December 25** – Christmas

---

and some geographic features. It can be purchased at IGN's main office in Comayagüela at the Secretaría de Transporte (SECOPT) on 15 Calle one block east of 1 Avenida.

IGN also publishes a complete set of 1:50,000 topographical maps, several sheets of 1:250,000 topographical maps, geological, hydrographic, mineral, and official-boundary maps. The best map of the country available is IGN's large official map, which shows the latest border settlement with El Salvador. It costs US$11, but it may be out of stock.

If you need maps of Honduras before going to the country, it is possible to send the IGN money and they can send the maps to you, preferably by DHL or UPS. The office staff is friendly, competent, and knowledgeable, but you need to speak Spanish and know which maps you're looking for before calling.

It's usually easier to get IGN topographical maps through **Omni Resources** (tel. 336/227-8300 or 800/742-2677, www.omnimap.com/catalog/int/honduras.htm) in the United States for US$10–12 per sheet. Their stock of 1:50,000 topos is about as good as the IGN's—about half of the series is available.

Tourist Information

The **Instituto Hondureño de Turismo** (Honduran Tourism Institute, www.letsgo honduras.com) is not geared to the casual traveler. Instead, a growing number of municipalities, awakened to the potential revenue tourism can generate, now have their own tourist offices to help promote their regions. Worth contacting if you need information are those in La Ceiba, Santa Rosa de Copán, Gracias, and Comayagua. Others are springing up all the time, even in more obscure towns.

The English-language weekly newspaper **Honduras This Week** (www.honduras thisweek.com) is a good source of general news and cultural information on the country, as well as specific travel hints.

The quarterly, free magazine **Honduras Tips** (www.hondurastips.honduras.com), sponsored by the Honduran Tourism Institute, has hotel, restaurant, and travel information on some of the more popular tourist destinations, such as Copán, the north coast, and the Bay Islands. It can be found at many travel agencies and better hotels.

RESOURCES

Glossary

aduana customs

agencias aduaneras customs agencies

aguardiente the favored Honduran poor-quality booze

aguas calientes, aguas termales hot or thermal waters, hot springs

alcalde mayor

alfarda an inclined plane of decorative stonework, an example of which can be seen at the Mayan ruins of El Puente

almuerzo lunch

anafre refried bean dip

artesanías handicrafts

atol a warm beverage, usually made of cornmeal

ayudante helper; specifically a young man who helps the driver of a bus by seating passengers and collecting fares

baleada a popular Honduran snack, made with a flour tortilla filled with beans, crumbly cheese, cream, and sometimes other ingredients, then grilled lightly

balneario swimming hole or pool

bando a spicy fish stew popular on the north coast and the Bay Islands

barra river mouth

billar pool, billiards

bistec beef steak

bodega storeroom

busito literally, little bus, frequently used in rural areas

camacha a traditional Pech instrument similar to a maraca

camino real royal road (old Spanish road)

campesino peasant; usually a small-scale farmer

canícula a brief dry spell in August during the middle of the rainy season

canoa canoe; used in the Mosquitia to refer to large canoes, often with a roof, that can accommodate up to some 50 people

cantina a low-priced bar

caoba mahogany, the most prized wood in Honduras

capitalino someone from Tegucigalpa (the capital)

caracol literally, the shellfish conch, but also the nickname given to Bay Islanders by mainland residents

casa cural the administration office of a church

caseta toll building or place where admission is collected; also a guard's booth

cassava a yucca dish made by the north-coast Garífuna

catrachos Hondurans; also a snack food of fried tortilla chips with refried beans and cheese

cayuco canoe

ceibeño someone from La Ceiba

cena dinner

champa a thatch-roofed hut with no walls

chichicaste a stinging shrub found in Honduras

colones Salvadoran currency

comayagüense someone from Comayagua

comedor a simple eatery

comida corriente a set meal, usually the least expensive choice on a restaurant's menu

copaneco someone from Santa Rosa de Copán or Copán Ruinas

córdobas Nicaraguan currency

criollo a term used in colonial times to denote peoples of Spanish blood born in the Americas

cueva cave

curandero a healer using traditional indigenous spiritual techniques and herbal medications

danlidense someone from Danlí

desayuno breakfast

desayuno típico typical breakfast (beans, tortilla, cheese, and plantain)

desvio turnoff, as from a highway onto another road (these are frequently given names in Honduras); also alternative route

dugu a Garífuna dance

dulce de leche milk-based caramel

encomienda the colonial system of allotting Spaniards land and the right to tribute and labor from Indians living there; also a courier package

especial private

feria fair

graciano someone from Gracias

guancascos a Lencan word that means "pact of peace"; the actual guancasco refers to a traditional ceremony in which a statue of the patron saint of one village is brought to visit the patron saint of another town (this happens with a procession and other celebrations that include music and dancing)

guisado stew

hacienda a partially or fully self-sufficient ranch (the department of Olancho is known for its haciendas)

invierno rainy season

jalón word used to ask for a ride, as in hitchhiking

jejenes sand flies

junco a type of palm native to the Santa Bárbara region, used to make baskets, hats, and other crafts

juticalpense someone from Juticalpa

ladino people of mixed Spanish and indigenous blood, comprising most of the population of Honduras

lancha launch; small, motor-powered boat

libra pound (the unit of weight)

licuado a popular drink made by blending sugar and fruit with water, orange juice, or milk

loroco an edible flower produced in Central America, often used as a stuffing for pupusas; its season is May–October

machuca a Garífuna stew made with fish, bananas, and coconut milk

maíz corn

manzana a unit of land measurement equal to 0.7 hectare; also, an apple

maras gangs (a gang member is a marero)

mestizo a person of mixed indigenous and European blood, a term commonly used in the colonial era but less so now

milpa a small patch of farmland on which peasants grow beans, corn, and other vegetables, mainly for their own consumption rather than to sell

mínimo banana

mondongo tripe (intestine) soup

nacatamale a cornmeal food boiled in banana leaves and stuffed with spiced meat and vegetables

nance a small fruit, often sold on the street in bags as a snack

noreste northeast (abbreviated NE)

noroeste northwest (abbreviated NO)

olanchano someone from the department of Olancho

panadería bakery

pan de coco coconut bread, a Garífuna specialty

parque park, usually the downtown square. Unlike many of their Latin American neighbors, Hondurans do not use the word "plaza."

pastelito a favorite Honduran snack consisting of a puff of dough filled with spiced beef and deep fried

patronatos local organizations dedicated to preparing saint's day festivals. In Tegucigalpa and other cities, these groups have evolved into grassroots social organizations.

peatonal pedestrian street

pinchos a shish kebab-style meal with beef or chicken and vegetables served on a skewer

pipante a dugout flat-bottomed canoe propelled by poles, common in the Mosquitia

piropo a flirtatious compliment, the kind given on the street by men when a pretty woman passes by

plátano plantain

plato del día plate of the day, an inexpensive set meal

plato típico the Honduran national dish, which usually includes beef, fried plantain, rice, beans, a chunk of salty cheese, a dash of cream, and lots of tortillas

pulpería a general store, minimart

punta traditional Garífuna music, a modern version of which has become a popular Honduran dance music

pupusa a thick tortilla filled with sausage and/or cheese, more common in El Salvador but also found in Honduras

quebrada gulley

quetzal a beautiful long-tailed bird living in the cloud forests

retablo an altarpiece at a church. Many are gilded and intricately carved.

revueltos scrambled eggs

ron rum

sacbé an elevated Mayan roadway (one is visible at Copán)

salón de billar pool hall

sampedrano a resident of San Pedro Sula

sin baño without bathroom

sopa de caracol conch soup, frequently made with coconut milk

supermercados supermarkets

sureste southeast (abbreviated SE)

suroeste southwest (abbreviated SO)

tajadas fried bananas or plantains, eaten like chips

tapado a fish, yucca, and coconut dish made by the Garífuna (although the *tapado olanchano* has meat and cabbage, and is made by *olanchanos*)

tenpuca a traditional Pech drum

terminal de buses bus terminal

timbre a type of stamp sold at banks for different amounts, sometimes required to renew a tourist card

totopostes like tortilla chips, but larger and unsalted

tramitador someone who helps deal with official paperwork

tranquilo relaxed, sometimes said to another person as an admonition to relax

tránsito the traffic police

tuk-tuk a motorized canoe in the Mosquitia, so called for the noise it makes

túmulos speed bumps

utilian someone from Utila

varas a unit of land measurement equal to 838 square meters

verano dry season

viaje especial a private trip, in a taxi or boat, which will cost more than a normal *colectivo*, or shared, ride

vigilante a guard

villa city

voluntario/voluntaria del Cuerpo de Paz Peace Corps volunteer

wabul a traditional Miskito Indian drink made from bananas and coconut

yancunú a Garifuna dance about war, which men perform wearing masks of women's faces; the dance commemorates a battle that took place on Roatán during the 17th century

yoreño someone from Yoro

zancudos mosquitoes

zarpe international permit for a boat

ZIP abbreviation for *zona industrial de procesamiento para exportaciones*, a free-trade industrial park (there are several scattered across Honduras)

zona viva a district of a town or city known for its nightlife

Spanish Phrasebook

PRONUNCIATION GUIDE

Spanish pronunciation is much more regular than that of English, but there are still occasional variations.

Consonants

c before a, o, or u, like c in "cat"; before e or i, like s

d like d in "dog," except between vowels; then like th in "that"

g before e or i, like ch in Scottish "loch"; elsewhere like g in "get"

h always silent

j like h in "hotel," but stronger

ll like y in "yellow"

ñ like ni in "onion"

r always pronounced as strong r

rr trilled r

v similar to b in "boy" (not as English v)

y similar to in English, but with a slight j sound; when standing alone, it's pronounced like the e in "me"

z like s in "same"

b, f, k, l, m, n, p, q, s, t, w, x   as in English

Vowels

a as in "father," but shorter

e as in "hen"

i as in "machine"

o as in "phone"

u usually as in "rule"; when it follows a q, the u is silent; when it follows an h or g, it's pronounced like w except when it comes between g and e or i, in which case it's also silent (unless it has an umlaut, ü, when it's again pronounced as English w)

Stress

Native English speakers frequently make errors of pronunciation by ignoring stress. All Spanish vowels – a, e, i, o, and u – may carry accents that determine which syllable of a word gets emphasis. Often, stress seems unnatural to nonnative speakers – the surname Chávez, for instance, is stressed on the first syllable – but failure to observe this rule may mean that native speakers will not understand you.

USEFUL WORDS AND PHRASES

Most Spanish-speaking people consider formalities important. When approaching someone for information or any other reason, do not forget the appropriate salutation – good morning, good evening, etc. Standing alone, the greeting *hola* (hello) may sound brusque.

Hello. *Hola.*

Good morning. *Buenos días.*

Good afternoon. *Buenas tardes.*

Good evening. *Buenas noches.*

How are you? *¿Cómo está?*

Fine. *Muy bien.*

And you? *¿Y usted?*

So-so. *Más o menos.*

Thank you. *Gracias.*

Thank you very much. *Muchas gracias.*

You're very kind. *Muy amable.*

You're welcome. *De nada* (literally, "It's nothing").

yes *sí*

no *no*

I don't know. *No sé.*

It's fine; okay. *Está bien.*

Good; okay. *Bueno.*

please *por favor*

Pleased to meet you. *Mucho gusto.*

Excuse me (physical) *Perdóneme.*

Excuse me (speech) *Discúlpeme.*

I'm sorry. *Lo siento.*

Goodbye. *Adios.*

See you later. *Hasta luego* (literally, "until later").

more *más*

less *menos*

better *mejor*

much, a lot *mucho*

a little *un poco*

large *grande*

small *pequeño, chico*

quick, fast *rápido*

slowly *despacio*
bad *malo*
difficult *difícil*
easy *fácil*
He/She/It is gone (as in "She left," "He's gone"). *Ya se fue.*
I don't speak Spanish well. *No hablo bien el español.*
I don't understand. *No entiendo.*
How do you say…in Spanish? *¿Cómo se dice…en español?*
Do you understand English? *¿Entiende el inglés?*
Is English spoken here? (Does anyone here speak English?) *¿Se habla inglés aquí?*

TERMS OF ADDRESS

When in doubt, use the formal *usted* (you) as a form of address. If you wish to dispense with formality and feel that the desire is mutual, you can say, *"Me puedes tutear"* ("you can call me 'tú'").

I *yo*
you (formal) *usted*
you (familiar) *tú*
he/him *él*
she/her *ella*
we/us *nosotros*
you (plural) *ustedes*
they/them (all males or mixed gender) *ellos*
they/them (all females) *ellas*
Mr., sir *señor*
Mrs., madam *señora*
Miss, young lady *señorita*
wife *esposa*
husband *marido* or *esposo*
friend *amigo* (male), *amiga* (female)
sweetheart *novio* (male), *novia* (female)
son, daughter *hijo, hija*
brother, sister *hermano, hermana*
father, mother *padre, madre*
grandfather, grandmother *abuelo, abuela*

Special Note: *Vos*

In Honduras, as well as in several other Central and South American countries, the pronoun "*tú*" is not frequently heard, and it sounds to locals (especially out in the countryside) like a sophisticated affectation. More commonly used, and rarely taught to Westerners in their Spanish classes, is *vos*.

Essentially, *vos* is used in the same instances as *tú*; that is, between two people who have a certain degree of casual familiarity or friendliness, in place of the more formal *usted*. The *vos* form is derived from *vosotros*, the second person plural (you all) still used in Spain. However, *vosotros* is not used in Latin America, even in places where *vos* is common.

For all tenses other than the present indicative, present subjunctive, and command forms, the *vos* form of the verb is exactly the same as *tú*. Hence: *tú anduviste/vos anduviste* (past tense), *tú andabas/vos andabas* (past imperfect), *tú andarás/vos andarás* (future), *tú andarías/vos andarías* (conditional).

In the present indicative, the conjugation is the same as with *tú*, but the last syllable is stressed with an accent. The exception is with -ir verbs, in which the final i is retained, instead of changing to an e. Hence: *tú andas/vos andás, tú comes/vos comés, tú escribes/vos escribís.*

In the present subjunctive, the same construction is followed as with the normal subjunctive, except the *vos* "á" accent is retained. Hence: *tú andes/vos andés, tú comas/vos comás, tú escribas/vos escribás.*

In radical changing verbs like *tener, poder,* or *dormir*, the *vos* form does not change from vowel to dipthong (*tienes, puedes, duermes*) in the present subjunctive form. Hence: *vos tengás, vos podás, vos durmás.*

Vos commands are formed by simply dropping the final "r" on the infinitive and adding an accent over the last vowel. Hence: *vos andá, vos comé, vos escribí.* When using object pronouns with *vos*, *te* is still used. Hence: *Yo te lo escribí a vos.*

One common irregular *vos* form is *sos*, for *ser* (to be). Also, because the conjugation would be bizarre, the verb *ir* is not used in the *vos* form. Instead, use *andar: vos andás.*

GETTING AROUND
Where is...? ¿Dónde está...?
How far is it to...? ¿A cuánto está...?
from...to ... de...a...
highway la carretera
road el camino
street la calle
block la cuadra
kilometer kilómetro
north norte
south sur
west oeste; poniente
east este; oriente
straight ahead al derecho; adelante
to the right a la derecha
to the left a la izquierda

ACCOMMODATIONS
Is there a room available? ¿Hay una habitación disponible?
May I (we) see it? ¿Puedo (podemos) verla?
What is the rate? ¿Cuál es el precio?
Is that your best rate? ¿Es su mejor precio?
Is there something cheaper? ¿Hay algo más económico?
single room una sencilla
double room una doble
room for a couple matrimonial
key llave
with private bath con baño
with shared bath con baño general; con baño compartido
hot water agua caliente
cold water agua fría (when Hondurans refer to agua normal, they mean it's not heated)
shower ducha
electric shower ducha eléctrica
towel toalla
soap jabón
toilet paper papel higiénico
air-conditioning aire acondicionado
fan ventilador
blanket cobija; colcha
sheets sábanas

PUBLIC TRANSPORT
bus stop la parada
bus terminal terminal de buses

airport el aeropuerto
launch lancha
dock muelle
I want a ticket to ... Quiero un pasaje a...
I want to get off at ... Quiero bajar en...
Here, please. Aquí, por favor.
Where is this bus going? ¿Adónde va este autobús?
round-trip ida y vuelta
What do I owe? ¿Cuánto le debo?

FOOD
glass taza
fork tenedor
knife cuchillo
spoon cuchara
napkin servilleta
soft drink fresco; refresco
coffee café
cream crema
tea té
sugar azúcar
drinking water agua pura, agua potable
bottled carbonated water agua mineral (con gas)
bottled uncarbonated water agua sin gas
beer cerveza
wine vino
milk leche
juice jugo
eggs huevos
bread pan
watermelon sandía
banana banano, guineo, mínimo
plantain plátano
apple manzana
orange naranja
meat (without) carne (sin)
beef carne de res
chicken pollo; gallina
fish pescado
shellfish mariscos
shrimp camarones
lobster langosta
fried frito
roasted asado
barbecued a la parrilla
grilled a la plancha

breakfast desayuno
lunch almuerzo
dinner (often eaten in late afternoon) comida
dinner, or a late-night snack cena
menu la carta, el menú
the check, or bill la cuenta

MAKING PURCHASES

I need . . . Necesito...
I want . . . Deseo... or Quiero...
I would like...(more polite) Quisiera...
How much does it cost? ¿Cuánto cuesta?
What's the exchange rate? ¿Cuál es el tipo de cambio?
May I see...? ¿Puedo ver...?
this one ésta/éste
expensive caro
cheap barato
cheaper más barato
too much demasiado

HEALTH

Help me please. Ayúdeme por favor.
I am ill. Estoy enfermo.
pain dolor
fever fiebre
stomachache dolor de estómago
vomiting vomitando
diarrhea diarrea
drugstore farmacia
medicine medicina
pill, tablet pastilla
birth control pills pastillas anticonceptivas
condom condón, preservativo

NUMBERS

0 cero
1 uno (masculine)
1 una (feminine)
2 dos
3 tres
4 cuatro
5 cinco
6 seis
7 siete
8 ocho
9 nueve
10 diez
11 once
12 doce
13 trece
14 catorce
15 quince
16 dieciseis
17 diecisiete
18 dieciocho
19 diecinueve
20 veinte
21 veintiuno
30 treinta
40 cuarenta
50 cincuenta
60 sesenta
70 setenta
80 ochenta
90 noventa
100 cien
101 ciento y uno
200 doscientos
1,000 mil
10,000 diez mil
1,000,000 un millón

DAYS OF THE WEEK

Sunday domingo
Monday lunes
Tuesday martes
Wednesday miércoles
Thursday jueves
Friday viernes
Saturday sábado

TIME

Latin Americans mostly use the 12-hour clock, but in some instances – usually associated with plane or bus schedules – they may use the 24-hour military clock. Under the 24-hour clock, for example, las nueve de la noche (9 P.M.) would be las 21 horas (2100 hours).
What time is it? ¿Qué hora es?
It's one o'clock Es la una.
It's two o'clock Son las dos.
At two o'clock A las dos.
It's ten to three Son tres menos diez.
It's ten past three Son tres y diez.

It's three fifteen Son las tres y cuarto.
It's two forty five Son tres menos cuarto.
It's two thirty Son las dos y media.
It's six A.M. Son las seis de la mañana.
It's six P.M. Son las seis de la tarde.
It's ten P.M. Son las diez de la noche.
today hoy
tomorrow mañana

morning la mañana
tomorrow morning mañana por la mañana
yesterday ayer
week la semana
month mes
year año
last night anoche
the next day el día siguiente

Suggested Reading

GENERAL

Alvarado, Elvia. *Don't Be Afraid, Gringo: A Honduran Woman Speaks from the Heart.* New York: Harper and Row, 1989. An excellent and often unsettling account of life as a poor peasant woman in rural Honduras.

Joe, Barbara E. *Triumph & Hope: Golden Years with the Peace Corps in Honduras.* BookSurge Publishing, 2008. A recounting of the author's experience as a Peace Corps volunteer in Honduras in the 1960s.

Nazario, Sonia. *Enrique's Journey.* New York: Random House, 2006. *Los Angeles Times* reporter Sonia Nazario recreates the true story of Enrique's harrowing journey from Honduras to the United States as a teenager, in an effort to reunite with his mother who left for the United States when he was only five.

Pine, Adrienne. *Working Hard, Drinking Hard: On Violence and Survival in Honduras.* Berkeley: University of California Press, 2008. As crime rates rise across Honduras, the publication of this analysis on the roots of violence in Honduras is particularly timely.

Yuscarán, Guillermo. *Gringos in Honduras: The Good, the Bad, and the Ugly.* Tegucigalpa, Honduras: Nuevo Sol Publications, 1995. Otherwise known as William Lewis, Yuscarán has written several volumes of short stories about his adopted country, as well as two interesting short histories, one on foreigners

who have lived in Honduras and the second about Honduras's best-known painter.

HISTORY
Culture and Ethnicity

Chapman, Anne MacKaye. *Masters of Animals: Oral Traditions of the Tolupán Indians, Honduras.* Philadelphia: Routeledge, 1992. Although dated, anthropologist and filmmaker Chapman has written what is certainly the most comprehensive book on Tolupán legends and beliefs, based on her studies of the Tolupán during 1955–1960 and 1964–1965.

Fash, William L. *Scribes, Warriors, and Kings: The City of Copán and the Ancient Maya.* rev. sub. ed. New York: Thames & Hudson, 2001. While the text is geared toward other archaeologists, the book is full of excellent photos and is packed with information about the dynasty of Copán.

González, Nancie L. *Sojourners of the Caribbean: Ethnogenesis and Ethnohistory of the Garífuna.* Urbana: University of Illinois Press, 1988. An academic examination of how the Garífuna came to Central America's Atlantic coast and of the Garífuna culture.

Ramos, Karen D. *Por Cuentas, Aquí en Choluteca; Por Cuentas, Aquí en El Corpus;* and *Por Cuentas, Aquí en Nacaome.* Tegucigalpa: Secretaría de Cultura y las Artes, 1996. Three volumes of oral legends from southern Honduras.

Colonial Era

Chamberlain, R. S. *The Conquest and Coloniza-tion of Honduras, 1502–1550.* Washington, D.C.: Carnegie Institute, 1957. Although dated, Chamberlain's book remains the only detailed, practically day-by-day account of Honduras's conquest.

Floyd, T. S. *The Anglo-Spanish Struggle for Mosquitia.* Albuquerque: University of New Mexico Press, 1967. The book focuses on the centuries-long battle for the Caribbean coast between the English and the Spanish, a little-studied aspect of Central American colonial history.

Newson, Linda. *The Cost of Conquest: Indian Decline Under Spanish Rule in Honduras.* Boulder, Colorado: Westview Press, 1986. Rather than trace the specific course of events in colonial Honduras, Newson relates the broad panorama of Honduras before, during, and after colonization to assess its impact on the region's indigenous populations.

The Banana Companies and Banana War

Acker, Alison. *Honduras: The Making of a Banana Republic.* Boston: South End Press, 1988. Acker's account of Honduran history is somewhat cursory, but the slim volume makes good reading.

Amaya Amador, Ramón. *Prisión Verde.* 3rd ed. Tegucigalpa, Honduras: Editorial Baktun, 1983. Although technically a novel, Amaya's famed (in Latin America) work provides an excellent though chilling account of life in a banana plantation from the point of view of a Honduran worker (in Spanish).

Langley, Lester, and Thomas Schoonover. *The Banana Men: American Mercenaries and Entrepreneurs in Central America, 1880–1930.* Lexington: University of Kentucky Press, 1995. Although the first chapter is numbingly theoretical, the rest of the book is a fascinating account of the wild characters involved in creating and running the Central American

banana empires. Special attention is paid to Lee Christmas, a man who deserves a full-length feature film to do his story justice.

Soluri, John. *Banana Cultures: Agriculture, Consumption, and Environmental Change in Honduras and the United States.* Austin: University of Texas Press, 2006. A look at the dramatic impact the banana and its production have had on Honduras.

The Soccer War

The two books below provide solid information on the economic trends and population pressures that contributed to the so-called Soccer War of 1969.

Anderson, Thomas. *The War of the Dispossessed: Honduras and El Salvador, 1969.* Lincoln: University of Nebraska Press, 1981.

Durham, William H. *Scarcity and Survival in Central America: Ecological Origins of the Soccer War.* Stanford, California: Stanford University Press, 1979.

Honduras and the Central American Crisis

LaFeber, Walter. *Inevitable Revolutions.* New York: W.W. Norton, 1983. Not specifically about Honduras, LaFeber's classic work brilliantly traces the development of U.S. foreign policy in Central America and the revolutionary fermenting of the 1970s and 1980s.

Schulz, Donald E., and Deborah Sundloff Schulz. *The United States, Honduras, and the Crisis in Central America.* Boulder, Colorado: Westview Press, 1994. Possibly the best book of Honduran history written in English, the Schulzes' book minutely traces the course of the country in the 1980s, with special emphasis on relations with the United States and the Contras. For anyone interested in understanding Honduras during that time and today as well, this extremely well written, balanced, and occasionally very funny book is a must-read.

LITERATURE AND TRAVELOGUES
19th-Century Travelers

For some reason, Honduras seemed to attract foreign travelers with literary proclivities during the 19th century. Of the four books listed below, Stephens's is by far the most famous. Wells, a mining engineer sent to prospect in Honduras, wrote a lively account with a wealth of detailed observations, particularly regarding Olancho.

Cecil, Charles. *Honduras: A Land of Great Depth.* New York: Rand McNally, 1890.

Soltera, Maria. *A Lady's Ride Across Honduras.* Gainesville: University of Florida Press, 1964.

Stephens, J. L. *Incidents of Travel in Central America, Chiapas, and Yucatán.* New York: Dover, 1969, two volumes. Originally published by Harper and Brothers, New York, 1841.

Wells, William. *Explorations and Adventures in Honduras.* New York: Harper, 1857.

Fiction

Henry, O. *Cabbages and Kings.* New York: Doubleday, Page and Co., 1904. Famed short-story writer O. Henry (the pen name of William Sydney Porter) spent some time in Puerto Cortés and Trujillo around the turn of the 20th century while on the run from U.S. authorities, who were pursuing him on charges of embezzlement. With the material gathered during his stay, he wrote this collection of stories.

Quesada, Roberto. *The Big Banana.* Houston: Arte Publico Press, 1999. *Bananero* Eduardo Lin heads to New York to make it big, the Big Banana in the Big Apple. By one of Honduras's most popular authors.

Theroux, Paul. *The Mosquito Coast.* New York: Avon, 1982. This novel, along with the movie version starring Harrison Ford, has probably done more to put the Mosquitia region

of northeastern Honduras on the map than anything else. Unfortunately, the site was apparently chosen by Theroux to represent the lowest state of humanity, and he shows little appreciation for anything Honduran.

Yuscarán, Guillermo. *Blue Pariah.* Tegucigalpa, Honduras: Nuevo Sol Publications. William Lewis, now known by his adopted name, Guillermo Yuscarán, lives in Honduras, where he paints and writes short stories and novels. A born storyteller, Yuscarán has published several fiction and nonfiction books on Honduras, including *Blue Pariah, Conociendo a la Gente Garífuna, Points of Light, Beyond Honduras, Northcoast Honduras,* and *La Luz Hondureña.* These can be found in several bookstores and more expensive hotels in Tegucigalpa, San Pedro Sula, Copán, the Bay Islands, and the north-coast beach towns.

RECREATION AND TRAVEL

Collins, Sharon. *Diving and Snorkeling Guide to Roatán and Honduras' Bay Islands.* 2nd ed. Houston: Pisces Books, 1997. Informs those interested in exploring the underwater world surrounding Roatán, Utila, Guanaja, and the Cayos Cochinos about depth and visibility, required expertise, bottom terrain, currents, marine life, and safety.

Fiallos, Maria. *Roatan: Relocation & Investment Guide.* Roatán, Honduras: Maria Fiallos, 2008. A must-buy for anyone considering moving to Roatán, with information on Utila, Guanaja, and La Ceiba as well. (Information is kept current with updates on the website www.roatanguide.com.)

Garoutte, Cindy. *Diving the Bay Islands.* Locust Valley, New York: AquaQuest Publications, 1994. If you can't find this book in stores, call U.S. tel. 516/759-0476 or 800/933-8989. Garoutte's book is obviously the product of much time spent diving in the islands. It provides an excellent overview to diving on all the main islands and is accompanied by some spectacular photos and useful dive-site locator maps.

Kelly, Joyce. *An Archeological Guide to Northern Central America: Belize, Guatemala, Honduras, and El Salvador.* Norman: University of Oklahoma Press, 1996. Detailed site information for 38 archaeological sites and 25 museums throughout Central America, complete with photos.

NATURAL HISTORY

Gollin, James D. *Adventures in Nature: Honduras.* 2nd ed. Emeryville, California: Avalon Travel Publishing, 2001. An overview of protected areas in Honduras, combining nuts-and-bolts travel practicalities with environmental information.

Forests

Carr, Archie. *High Jungles and Low.* Gainesville: University of Florida Press, 1953. Well-known biologist Archie Carr spent several years in Honduras, most of it at the Escuela Agrícola Panamericana in the Valle de Zamorano. His account of this time combines plant and animal biology, particularly regarding the cloud forest and the tropical rainforest, with anecdotes and stories about local people. This well-written volume, obviously a labor of love, clearly shows the author's affection for Honduras and its people. Carr also wrote "Animal Habitats in Honduras," one of the best English-language essays on the subject, which appeared in *The Bulletin of the American Museum of Natural History,* 1950, volume 96.

Forsyth, Adrian, and Ken Miyata. *Tropical Nature: Life and Death in the Rain Forests of Central and South America.* New York: Charles Scribner's Sons, 1984. Not specifically about Honduras, this book is nonetheless a good anecdotal overview of the workings of the rainforest ecosystem found in the Mosquitia, written for the general reader.

Kricher, John, and Mark Plotkin. *A Neotropical Companion: An Introduction to the Animals, Plant, and Ecosystems of the New World Tropics.* Princeton, New Jersey: Princeton University Press, 1997. Another good general study for nonspecialists, more thorough and less anecdotal than *Tropical Nature.*

Reef

DeLoach, Ned, and Paul Humann. *Reef Fish Identification: Florida, Caribbean, Bahamas.* 3rd ed. Jacksonville, Florida: New World Publishing, 2002. This picture-packed three-volume set is without a doubt the best available on Caribbean reef life.

Birds

Alderfer, Jonathan, and Jon L. Dunn. *National Geographic Field Guide to the Birds of North America.* 5th ed. National Geographic, 2006. Although it is titled for North America, this is a useful guide for identifying the birds of Honduras, with 4,000 full-color illustrations of more than 960 species.

Bonta, Mark. *Seven Names for the Bellbird: Conservation Geography in Honduras.* College Station: Texas A&M University Press, 2003. This is a different kind of bird book, a narrative of "conservation geography"—the study of human beings and their landscapes—that weaves descriptions of Honduran birds and local traditions of bird appreciation with an analysis of how to ensure locals participate in and take ownership of conservation efforts.

Bonta, Mark, and David Anderson. *Birding Honduras: A Checklist and Guide.* New York: Ecoarte, 2002. This is the only guide specifically to Honduran birds. More information about the guide and birding in Honduras can be found at the authors' website, www.birdinghonduras.com.

Van Perlo, Ber. *Birds of Mexico and Central America.* Princeton, New Jersey: Princeton University Press, 2006. While birders criticize the tiny drawings, the plus is that more than 1,500 species are packed into this relatively small volume.

FOR KIDS

Bramann, Arlette N. *The Maya: Activities and Crafts from a Mysterious Land.* San Francisco: Jossey-Bass, 2003. Ideas for hands-on learning include making a macaw headdress or mixing up a chocolate-chile drink. Ages 6–10.

Harris, Nathaniel. *National Geographic Investigates: Ancient Maya: Archaeology Unlocks the Secrets of the Maya's Past.* Des Moines, Iowa: National Geographic Children's Books, 2008. This slim volume has a good balance of text and photos providing an excellent overview on Mayan culture from Mexico to Honduras. Ages 8–12.

Trueman, Terry. *Hurricane: A Novel.* New York: HarperCollins, 2008. A fictional account of a 13-year-old boy's survival of 1998's devastating Hurricane Mitch. Ages 10–14.

Internet Resources

A number of websites about Honduras have sprung up in recent years, many created by Hondurans living in other countries. As with just about any topic, the Internet can be an invaluable tool for learning about current conditions in Honduras and contacting other people interested in the country (as well, of course, a source of wild misinformation). Here are just a few suggestions to get you started—links from these sites will open up a world of information on Honduras to the web surfer.

GENERAL INFORMATION
www.honduras.com
A general clearinghouse, with plenty of its own information as well as links to many other sites.

www.angelfire.com/ca5/mas/datos/ datos.html
Essentially a book online, with extensive information about Honduras, in Spanish only.

www.travel.state.gov
http://honduras.usembassy.gov
For U.S.-government-produced information on Honduras.

www.hondurasthisweek.com
Contains an excellent archive of the weekly English newspaper *Honduras This Week.*

www.laprensahn.com
www.hablemosclaro.com
If your Spanish is up for it, the daily newspaper *La Prensa* and the weekly magazine *Hablemos Claro* both have good websites.

www.hondurastips.honduras.com
The online version of Honduras's bilingual travel guide, *Honduras Tips.* Not always up to date, but generally useful.

http://groups.yahoo.com/group/ honduras_living
This Yahoo group is made up of people living in or planning to move to Honduras and is chock-full of helpful practical tips as well as hotel recommendations.

NGOS AND VOLUNTEERING IN HONDURAS
www.volunteerhonduras.com
Has links to dozens of opportunities to work with NGOs and social projects in Honduras, as well as homestays with families accustomed to hosting foreigners.

www.idealist.org
An international volunteer website with many links in Honduras.

www.projecthonduras.com
Offers a wealth of socially oriented information, with many links to national and

international social organizations working in Honduras.

DESTINATION-SPECIFIC SITES

Bay Islands
www.bayislands.com

Comayagua
www.comayagua.com

Copán Ruinas
www.copanruinas.org

Gracias and the Lencan Highlands
www.colosuca.com

Parque Nacional Pico Bonito
www.en.picobonito.org

Río Cangrejal
www.cangrejal.com

Roatán
www.roatanet.com

Santa Bárbara
www.santabarbara.gob.hn

Santa Rosa de Copán
www.visitesantarosadecopan.org

Swan Islands
www.islasdelcisne.com

Tegucigalpa
www.capital450.hn

Tela
www.tela-honduras.com

Utila
www.aboututila.com

ECONOMIC AND SOCIAL STATISTICS AND INFORMATION

Banco Central de Honduras
www.bch.hn

Inter-American Development Bank
www.iadb.org

Comisión Económica para América Latina y el Caribe
www.eclac.org

MISCELLANEOUS

www.honduras.net/foods
Recipes (some in English, some in Spanish) of typical Honduran foods.

www.birdsofhonduras.com
Lots of information about species, locations, and tours for birding, by one of Honduras's expert birders, Robert Gallardo.

Index

List of Maps

Acknowledgments

First and foremost I want to thank my family, Luca, Matteo and Francesca Renda, for all their support, for holding down the fort when I travel, and for keeping me company on so many of the journeys. I would like to thank everyone at Avalon Travel that contributed to this project, in particular Grace Fujimoto, Kathryn Ettinger, Kathryn Osgood, and Albert Angulo. I would also like to thank this book's original author, Chris Humphrey, for his support with this update. The more I researched, the more impressed I became with Chris's understanding of the country I now call home.

I am indebted to many, many people who helped make this edition possible, and am particularly grateful for the local knowledge so generously shared by: Howard and Angela Rosenzwieg, and Geert Van Vaeck in Copán Ruinas; Josué Avila, Samuel Muñoz, Lizeth Perdomo, Marco Aurelio Rodriguez, and Kate Weber in Gracias; Sharon Jones in Guanaja; Manuel Vilchez, and Yeny Arelys Moreno in Juticalpa; Elmor Wood and Reyes Wood in the Mosquitia; Sarah West in Nueva Ocotepeque; Steve Hasz, and Mark Havey in Roatán; Marta Garomar, and Javier Terceros in San Marcos de Colón; Steve Smith and his crew (John, Kees, Norbert) in San Pedro Sula; Kate Suchomel in Santa Rosa de Copán; Jim Bowers in Trujillo; Owen O'Neil and Thelma Bodden in Utila; and Carlos Rodríguez in Yuscarán. Your help was indispensable.

I would also like to thank many others who gave their tips, insights and advice, including Van Alston, Jimmy Andino, Tanya Barnett, Carissa Cooper, Max Elvir, Sofia and Henrik Franklin, Roland Gassman, Bruce Hartnett, Carlos Melgar, Frony Miedema, Danielle Mosse, Matt Mulka, Bruce at the Driftwood Café in Utila, and Kelsy in Omoa/Nueva Ocotepeque.

Many spectacular photos grace the pages of this guidebook, and I am grateful to the following photographers for the use of their beautiful images: Greykelin Martinez, Franklin Ramirez, Marcus Sabini, and Juan Velasquez of the Guaruma youth organization; Fuad Azzad, Laura Helena Bermudez, Guillermo Cobos, Mike Jones, Jozef Maerien, Javier Maradiaga Melara, Andrea Renda, Luca Renda, Sarah Steinberg, Kate Suchomel, and Peter Svanberg.

My thanks also go out to the travel buddies who accompanied me from time to time on my explorations, waiting patiently while I popped into every hotel in town to check prices and rooms: Kris Angerthal; Argelia Castro; Juan Antonio Diaz; Jackie Greene; and Elizabeth Morrison.

Lastly, a special thank you to those who helped watch over my little ones when I was traveling or busy writing: Daysi Flores, Sofia Franklin, Carolina Villareal, and Isbela Perdomo; and to my parents for their ever-present support.

www.moon.com

DESTINATIONS | ACTIVITIES | BLOGS | MAPS | BOOKS

MOON.COM is all new, and ready to help plan your next trip! Filled with fresh trip ideas and strategies, author interviews, informative blogs, a detailed map library, and descriptions of all the Moon guidebooks, Moon.com is all you need to get out and explore the world—or even places in your own backyard. As always, when you travel with Moon, expect an experience that is uncommon and truly unique.

MAP SYMBOLS

▦ Expressway	◖ Highlight	✗ Airfield	⌁ Golf Course
Primary Road	○ City/Town	✈ Airport	P Parking Area
Secondary Road	◉ State Capital	▲ Mountain	▰ Archaeological Site
Unpaved Road	⊛ National Capital	✛ Unique Natural Feature	▯ Church
Trail	★ Point of Interest		
Ferry	• Accommodation	⌇ Waterfall	⛽ Gas Station
Railroad	▼ Restaurant/Bar	▲ Park	◠ Glacier
Pedestrian Walkway	■ Other Location	⬛ Trailhead	Mangrove
Stairs	△ Campground	�skiing Skiing Area	Reef
			Swamp

CONVERSION TABLES

°C = (°F - 32) / 1.8
°F = (°C x 1.8) + 32
1 inch = 2.54 centimeters (cm)
1 foot = 0.304 meters (m)
1 yard = 0.914 meters
1 mile = 1.6093 kilometers (km)
1 km = 0.6214 miles
1 fathom = 1.8288 m
1 chain = 20.1168 m
1 furlong = 201.168 m
1 acre = 0.4047 hectares
1 sq km = 100 hectares
1 sq mile = 2.59 square km
1 ounce = 28.35 grams
1 pound = 0.4536 kilograms
1 short ton = 0.90718 metric ton
1 short ton = 2,000 pounds
1 long ton = 1.016 metric tons
1 long ton = 2,240 pounds
1 metric ton = 1,000 kilograms
1 quart = 0.94635 liters
1 US gallon = 3.7854 liters
1 Imperial gallon = 4.5459 liters
1 nautical mile = 1.852 km

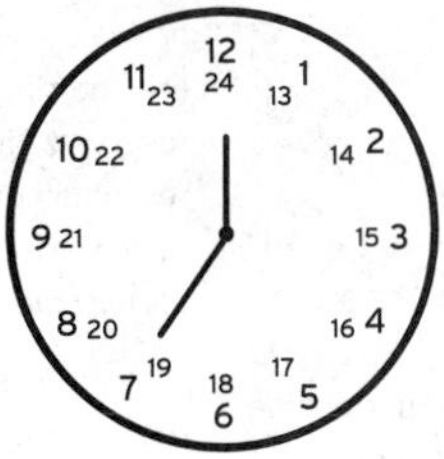

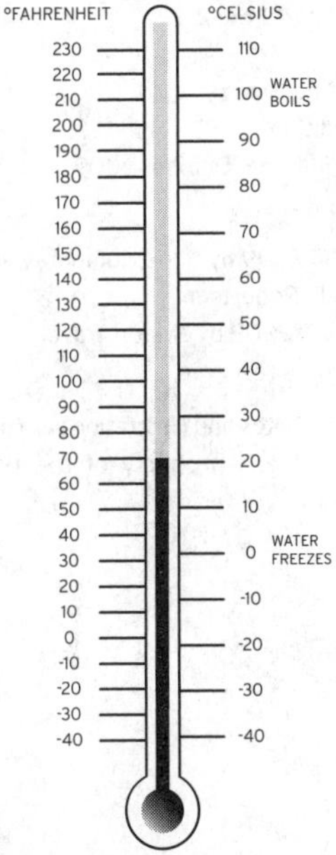

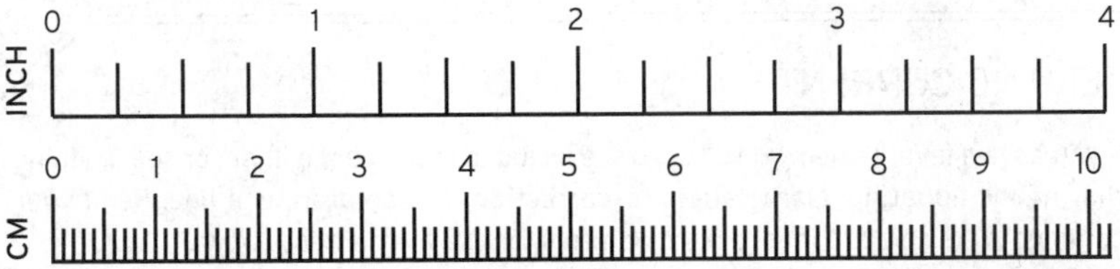

MOON HONDURAS & THE BAY ISLANDS
Avalon Travel
a member of the Perseus Books Group
1700 Fourth Street
Berkeley, CA 94710, USA
www.moon.com

Editor and Series Manager: Kathryn Ettinger
Copy Editor: Deana Shields
Graphics Coordinator: Kathryn Osgood
Production Coordinator: Darren Alessi
Cover Designer: Kathryn Osgood
Map Editor: Albert Angulo
Cartographers: Chris Markiewicz, Kat Bennett
Indexer: Greg Jewett

ISBN: 978-1-59880-222-1
ISSN: 1948-6472

Printing History
1st Edition – 1997
5th Edition – October 2009
5 4 3 2 1

Text © 2009 by Chris Humphrey and
Amy E. Robertson.
Maps © 2009 by Avalon Travel.
All rights reserved.

Front cover photo: keel-billed toucan, Honduras
© Stuart Westmorland/getty
Title page photo: © Greykelin Martinez, guaruma.org
Interior color photos: Page 4 © Peter Svanberg;
page 5 (left) © Fuad Azzad, (middle) © Mike Jones -
Guanaja, (right) © Amy E. Robertson; page 6 (inset)
© Franklin Ramirez, guaruma.org, (bottom) © Andrea
Renda; page 7 (top left) © Amy E. Robertson, (top
right) © Javier Maradiaga Melara, (bottom) ©
Peter Svanberg; page 8 © Amy E. Robertson; page
9 © Fuad Azzad; pages 10, 11 © Amy E. Robertson;
page 12 © Mike Jones - Guanaja; page 13 © Amy E.
Robertson; pages 14-17 © Amy E. Robertson; page 18
(top) © Jozef Maerien, (bottom) © Amy E. Robertson;
page 19 © Amy E. Robertson; page 20 © Guillermo
Cobos; page 21 © Mike Jones; pages 22-24 © Amy
E. Robertson

Printed in Canada by Friesens Corp.

KEEPING CURRENT

If you have a favorite gem you'd like to see included in the next edition, or see anything
that needs updating, clarification, or correction, please drop us a line. Send your
comments via email to feedback@moon.com, or use the address above.